BYZANTINE AND RENAISSANCE PHILOSOPHY

PETER ADAMSON

BYZANTINE AND RENAISSANCE PHILOSOPHY

a history of philosophy without any gaps

volume 6

OXFORD
UNIVERSITY PRESS

OXFORD
UNIVERSITY PRESS

Great Clarendon Street, Oxford, OX2 6DP,
United Kingdom

Oxford University Press is a department of the University of Oxford.
It furthers the University's objective of excellence in research, scholarship,
and education by publishing worldwide. Oxford is a registered trade mark of
Oxford University Press in the UK and in certain other countries

First Edition published in 2022

Impression: 2

Published in the United States of America by Oxford University Press
198 Madison Avenue, New York, NY 10016, United States of America

British Library Cataloguing in Publication Data
Data available

Library of Congress Control Number: 2021941852

ISBN 978–0–19–285641–8

DOI: 10.1093/oso/9780192856418.001.0001

Printed and bound in Great Britain by
Clays Ltd, Elcograf S.p.A.

For Judy and Fred

CONTENTS

PREFACE

It's always nice when you're forced to do something, and then discover that you should have done it anyway. That's more or less what happened with this book. Having covered two traditions of medieval thought in previous installments of the series, those of the Islamic world and Latin Christendom, there was Byzantium still to tackle. I am giving Byzantine philosophy (much) more coverage than you might have expected: many general histories of philosophy cover it fleetingly, or not at all. Nonetheless, I knew it would not give me enough material for a volume comparable in size to others in the series. So just for pragmatic reasons, it seemed unavoidable to combine it with the next topic, philosophy in the Italian Renaissance. Happily, it turns out that this makes a huge amount of sense in intellectual terms, to an extent that I myself did not fully appreciate when I first embarked on this part of the project.

Any overview of either culture will inform you about the links between Byzantium and Renaissance Italy, explaining how an influx of manuscripts and scholars from the Greek East helped to trigger Italian humanism. But treating the two philosophical traditions together in one volume, as I will do here—and as no other book has ever done, as far as I know—reveals a much stronger degree of continuity. There is a single story of humanist achievement that stretches from early Byzantine collectors like Photius (or even from late antiquity, if one thinks of figures like the commentator Simplicius) all the way to the late fifteenth century, when Ficino rendered Plato's dialogues into Latin, and early printed editions made Greek texts available as never before. Nor did the influence travel in just one direction, given that Latin scholasticism also influenced Byzantine thought (see Chapter 19). When we divide up the history of philosophy, we tend to overestimate the relevance of language barriers. In this case it is easy to assume that there must have been a sharp divide between philosophy written in the Greek East and the Latin West. But in fact there was extensive overlap between the values, interests, and preoccupations of Byzantine and Renaissance philosophers, just as there was between the concerns of late ancient thinkers who wrote in Greek and philosophers who wrote in Syriac and Arabic.

One way that I've tried to bring this out is by exploring certain issues in both contexts, for example gender (Chapters 12, 29–30), economic theory (Chapters 13, 43), mathematics (Chapters 17, 48), rhetoric (Chapters 9, 24–5), and history writing (Chapters 10, 41). Some of the same sources will also come up in both halves of the book. This applies to Aristotle and Plato, of course, but also Averroes (Chapters 20, 46), Plotinus and Proclus (Chapters 6–7, 31–3), and the ancient commentators on Aristotle (Chapters 11, 44–7). To understand both traditions, we will also need to familiarize ourselves with the changing technology for the preservation and transmission of texts (Chapters 14, 45).

All of which is not to minimize the distinctive nature of Byzantine philosophy, on the one hand, and Italian Renaissance philosophy, on the other. Several factors combine to give Byzantium its special character. If pressed, I would name above all: the centrality of Constantinople as a seat of "Roman" power (however diminished); continuity of language and textual transmission from ancient Greek culture; the concerns of Orthodox Christianity; and the direct challenge posed by neighboring polities, especially those that were in Muslim hands. Thanks to these features of Byzantine society, we'll be seeing monarchial political theories in Byzantium (Chapter 8) that contrast starkly with the republicanism of medieval and Renaissance Italy (Chapters 38–40). Iconoclasm and Hesychasm are unique to Byzantium, both of them much discussed by historians but routinely underestimated in terms of their philosophical interest (Chapters 3, 18). Then there is the fact that Greek Christianity in the Near East went beyond the borders of the Byzantine empire, and also existed in the lands of Islam (Chapters 2, 16). As for the Renaissance, I need not belabor its singularity as a transformative period in the history of European thought. But, aside from the epochal contributions of figures like Bruni, Ficino, and Machiavelli, I might note that Italian philosophy in the sixteenth century will already give us a foretaste of what is to come in the seventeenth, thanks to the empiricist anti-Aristotelianism of Telesio and of course the revolutionary ideas of Bruno and Galileo (Chapters 51, 53–4). I have stretched past the chronological boundary of 1600 to include some of these figures, especially Campanella, whose works were well paired with Telesio in natural philosophy, and with earlier utopian treatises written in Italy (Chapter 42).

This would be a good moment to admit that the title of this volume is both misleadingly narrow and misleadingly broad. Narrow, in that it speaks of "Byzantine" philosophy. In fact, as just mentioned, we will venture outside the confines of Byzantium and the Orthodox tradition, to consider Near Eastern Christian thought more broadly. Also, I will not end the story with the fall of Constantinople, but give you a quick survey of philosophy in Eastern Greek culture all the way down to the twentieth century (Chapter 21). As for "Renaissance" philosophy, that term arguably promises more than I will be offering, in this book at least. As I've already noted a few times, the second part of this volume is only going to deal with the *Italian* Renaissance. In the fifteenth and sixteenth centuries, Germany, the Netherlands, France, and the British Isles produced philologists to match anyone Italy had to offer, like Erasmus and Isaac Casaubon. In the same period, the Protestant Reformation was unfolding, with its untold significance for European history including the history of philosophy. This then provoked a religious and cultural backlash in southern Europe, sometimes called the "Counter-Reformation," though not all historians like this term. That was the context for, among other things, exciting developments in scholasticism in the Iberian peninsula. In fact, the story of philosophy in these centuries outside Italy is so rich and diverse that it is going to need a book of its own.

More accurate, then, would have been to call this volume "Philosophy in Byzantium, Near Eastern Christianity, and the Italian Renaissance," while the title of a further planned volume should be something like "Philosophy in the Northern Renaissance, the Reformation, and the Counter-Reformation." But faced with a choice between snappy book titles and strictly accurate ones, I have to admit that I found the choice pretty easy, and am thus using the labels "Byzantine and Renaissance Philosophy" and "Philosophy in the Reformation." More difficult was the decision of where to place certain figures who cross the Italian/non-Italian divide. Two prominent cases are Nicholas of Cusa, who was from Germany but spent time in Italy and was strongly influenced by the humanist climate there, and Christine de Pizan, who conversely was from Italy but lived and wrote in France. I have postponed Nicholas until the next book, in hopes of enriching my portrayal of German philosophical culture in the fifteenth century, while Christine is covered here, since her works resonate so well with those of the female Italian humanists (Chapters 28–30).

A related problem is that, occasionally, developments outside Italy had a major impact on philosophers of the Italian Renaissance. That applies especially to the printing press, whose impact on all European thought was immense. In Italy this technology arrived in 1465. While I will touch on its impact here (especially in Chapter 45), a fuller discussion of print culture is reserved for the volume on the Reformation, since this invention played such an important role in the dissemination of ideas from Luther, Calvin, and other reformers. Texts written elsewhere in Europe will occasionally enter our story too, notably with the case of Thomas More's *Utopia* (Chapter 42). Finally, it almost goes without saying that the astronomical theories of Copernicus made an impression on Italian scientists, especially

Galileo (Chapter 54). This gives us another foretaste of the seventeenth century, when I'll often find it necessary to refer to the influence exercised by thinkers who haven't yet been properly covered in the book series, because of the way that texts and ideas passed from one part of Europe to another. But since the seventeenth century is two volumes away still (assuming I even get that far), let's not worry about that yet. We have plenty to keep us busy, starting with the question of why the Roman empire didn't fall until 1453.

ACKNOWLEDGMENTS

Like other volumes of this series, this book has benefited at every stage of its development from expert advice. This began with input from several colleagues on my initial list of topics to cover, and ended with extremely helpful feedback on the final manuscript from Michele Trizio, Cecilia Muratori, and Melina Vogiatzi. For suggestions, corrections, and encouragement, I would like to thank both of them as well as Lela Alexidze, Charles Burnett, Börje Bydén, Thony Christie, Brian Copenhaver, Sabrina Ebbersmeyer, Christophe Erismann, Guido Giglioni, Dag Nikolaus Hasse, Judith Herrin, Katerina Ierodiakonou, Giorgi Kapriev, George Karamanolis, Jill Kraye, David Lines, Andrew Louth, Dominic O'Meara, Robert Pasnau, Oliver Primavesi, Denis Robichaud, Ingrid Rowland, Quentin Skinner, Okihito Utamura, and Dimitris Vasilakis. Many of these scholars also kindly agreed to be interviewed for the podcast series, and I highly recommend listening to those episodes as a supplement to reading this book.

I am also grateful to Peter Momtchiloff from Oxford University Press for his support of the book series, and Konrad Boeschenstein for preparing the index. The podcast series for the relevant episodes was supported by Jim Black, Julian Rimmer, and Bethany Somma.

I could not keep pursuing this series without the love, patience, and support I receive from my family: my wife Ursula, my daughters Sophia and Johanna, my brother Glenn, and my parents Joyce and David. The book is dedicated to two of my biggest fans (and the feeling is mutual): my Aunt Judy and Uncle Fred.

DATES

d. = date of death
fl. = flourished

Philosophers and other authors		*Selected historical events*	
Bardaiṣān	d. 222		
Ephrem of Edessa	d. 373	Council of Nicaea	325
		Constantinople founded	330
		Council of Chalcedon	431
Philoxenus of Mabbug	d. 523	Reign of Justinian I	527–65
Sergius of Resh'aynā	d. 536	Code of Justinian issued	529
Paul the Persian	fl. mid-6th cent.		
Agapetus	6th cent.		
David the Invincible	6th cent.		
Maximus the Confessor	d. 662	Arabs triumph at Battle of Yarmuk	636
Severus Sebōkht	d. 666/7		
Athanasius of Balad	d. 686		
Jacob of Edessa	d. 708		
George of the Arabs	d. 724	Seige of Constantinople	717–18
John of Damascus	d. 749	Iconoclasm begins	726
		First restoration of icons	787
		Charlemagne crowned emperor	800
Timothy I	d. 823	Iconoclasm resumes	815
Theodore Abū Qurra	d. *c.*820		
Theodore the Studite	d. 826		
Patriarch Nikephoros I	d. 828		
Abū Rā'iṭa	d. *c.*835	End of iconoclasm	843
Leo the Mathematician	d. after 869	Macedonian dynasty	867–1028
Photius	d. *c.*893		
Arethas	d. 932		

Symeon the New Theologian	d. 1022	Reign of Constantine IX Monomachos	1042–55
Ibn al-Faḍl al-Anṭākī	fl. 1050s		
Attaleiates	d. *c.*1080	Battle of Mantzikert	1071
Michael Psellos	d. after 1081	Reign of Alexios I Komnenos	1081–1118
John Italos	d. 1082	First crusade arrives at Constantinople	1096
Symeon Seth	d. after 1112		
Eustratios	d. *c.*1120		
Michael of Ephesus	d. 1129		
Anne Komnene	d. *c.*1153		
Nicholas of Methone	d. 1160s		
Theodore Prodromos	d. *c.*1170		
John Petritsi	fl. second half 12th cent.		
John Tzetzes	d. 1180		
Eustathios	d. *c.*1195	Pisa becomes self-governing commune	1195
Niketas Choniates	d. 1217	Constantinople sacked in Fourth Crusade	1204
Theodore II Laskaris	d. 1258	Palaiologan Dynasty begins	1259
Nikephoros Blemmydes	d. *c.*1269	Constantinople retaken by Byzantines	1261
George Akropilites	d. 1282		
Bar Hebraeus	d. 1286		
Manuel Moschopoulos	fl. *c.*1300		
Maximos Planoudes	d. 1305		
George Pachymeres	d. *c.*1310	Rule of Visconti begins in Milan	1311
Nikephoros Choumnos	d. 1327		
Joseph Rhakendytes	d. 1330		
Theodore Metochites	d. 1332	Hesychasm controversy begins	1335
Theodore Palaiologos	d. 1338		
Barlaam of Calabria	d. 1348	Black Death comes to Italy	1348
Gregory Palamas	d. 1359		
Nikephoros Gregoras	d. 1361		
Prochoros Kydones	d. 1369/70	Ciompi Revolt in Florence	1378
Demetrios Kydones	d. 1397/98	Great Schism of papacy	1378–1414
		Founding of Medici bank	1397
Coluccio Salutati	d. 1406	Florence conquers Pisa	1406
Manuel Chrysoloras	d. 1415		

Blasius of Parma	d. 1416		
Christine de Pizan	d. *c.*1430		
Cosma Raimondi	d. 1436		
Niccolò Niccoli	d. 1437	Council of Florence and Ferrara	1437–9
Leonardo Bruni	d. 1444	Cosimo de' Medici exiled, then returns	1433–4
Bernardino da Siena	d. 1444	Invention of printing press	*c.*1440
Vittorino da Feltre	d. 1446		
George Gemistos Plethon	d. 1454	Fall of Constantinople to Ottomans	1453
		Peace of Lodi between Milan, Florence	1454
Lorenzo Valla	d. 1457		
Poggio Bracciolini	d. 1459		
Guarino Guarini Veronese	d. 1460		
Nicholas of Cusa	d. 1464	Death of Cosimo de' Medici	1464
Enea Silvio Piccolomini	d. 1464		
Isotta Nogarola	d. 1466		
Benedetto Cotrugli	d. 1469		
Basil Bessarion	d. 1472		
George Gennadios Scholarios	d. 1472		
Leon Battista Alberti	d. 1472		
George Trapezuntius	d. 1473		
Theodore Gaza	d. 1475		
Donato Acciaiuoli	d. 1478	Pazzi Conspiracy	1478
Francesco Filelfo	d. 1481		
John Argyropoulos	d. 1487	Ficino publishes translation of Plato	1484
		Pico's *Oration* and *900 Theses*	1486
Elijah del Medigo	d. 1492–3		
Angelo Poliziano	d. 1494	France invades Italy, expulsion of Medici	1494
Giovanni Pico della Mirandola	d. 1494	Aldine printed edition of Aristotle	1495–8
Gentile de' Becchi	d. 1497		
Cristoforo Landino	d. 1498		
Pomponio Leto	d. 1498		
Girolamo Savanarola	d. 1498		

Marsilio Ficino	d. 1499		
Laura Cereta	d. 1499		
Nicoletto Vernia	d. 1499		
Alamanno Rinuccini	d. 1499		
Giovanni Pontano	d. 1503	Occupation of Naples by Spain	1503
Alessandro Achillini	d. 1512	Medici power returns to Florence	1512
Aldus Manutius	d. 1515	First Jewish ghetto in Venice	1516
		Luther begins the Reformation	1517
Marcello Adriani	d. 1521		
Judah Abravanel (Leone Hebreo)	d. after 1521		
Pietro Pomponazzi	d. 1524		
Nicolò Leoniceno	d. 1524		
Niccolò Machiavelli	d. 1527	Sack of Rome	1527
Baldassare Castiglione	d. 1529		
Berengario da Carpi	d. 1530	Fall of Florentine republic	1530
Luca Prassicio	d. 1533		
Gianfrancesco Pico della Mirandola	d. 1533		
Francesco Guicciardini	d. 1540	Founding of Jesuits	1540
		Beginning of Roman Inquisition	1542
Agostino Nifo	d. *c.*1546	Council of Trent	1545–63
Pietro Bembo	d. 1547		
Agostino Steuco	d. 1549		
Giannozzo Manetti	d. 1549		
Girolamo Fracastoro	d. 1553		
Tullia d'Aragona	d. 1556		
Cassandra Fedele	d. 1558		
Bernardo Segni	d. 1558	Pauline Index of prohibited books	1559
Andreas Vesalius	d. 1564		
		Tridentine Index of prohibited books	1564
Anton Francesco Doni	d. 1574	Turks defeated at Battle of Lepanto	1571
Girolamo Cardano	d. 1576		
Alessandro Piccolomini	d. 1579		
Benardino Telesio	d. 1588		

Jacopo Zabarella	d. 1589		
Moderata Fonte	d. 1592		
Francesco Patrizi	d. 1597	Edict of Nantes	1598
Giordano Bruno	d. 1600		
Francesco Piccolomini	d. 1607		
Giambattista della Porta	d. 1615		
Giulio Vanini	d. 1619		
Hieronymus Fabricius	d. 1619		
Lodovico Zuccolo	d. 1630		
Cesare Cremonini	d. 1631	Condemnation of Galileo	1632
Tommaso Campanella	d. 1639		
Archangela Tarabotti	d. 1652		
Lucrezia Marinella	d. 1653		

MAPS

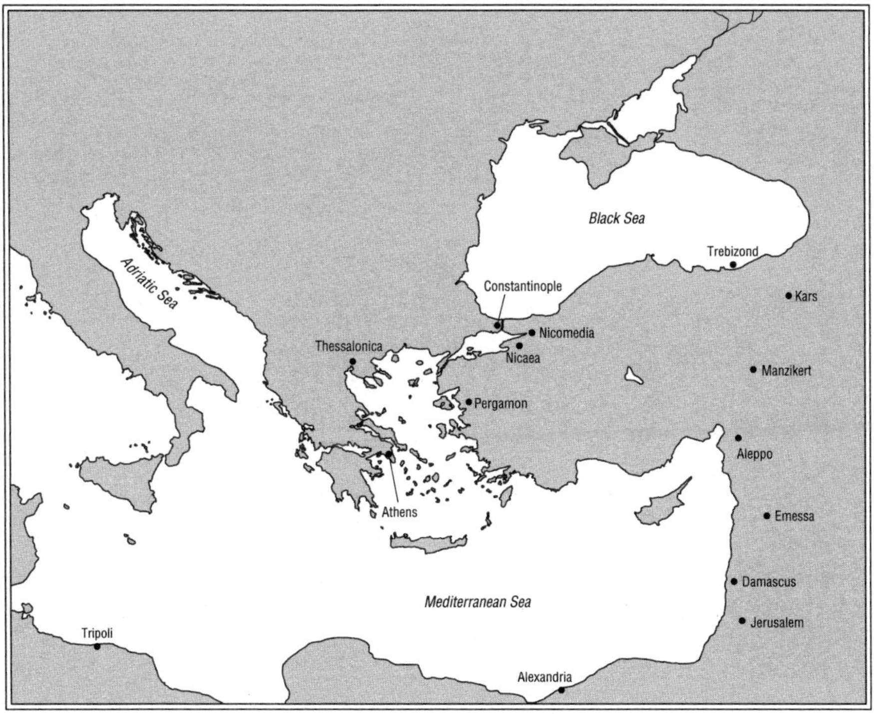

Map of Cities in the Eastern Mediterranean

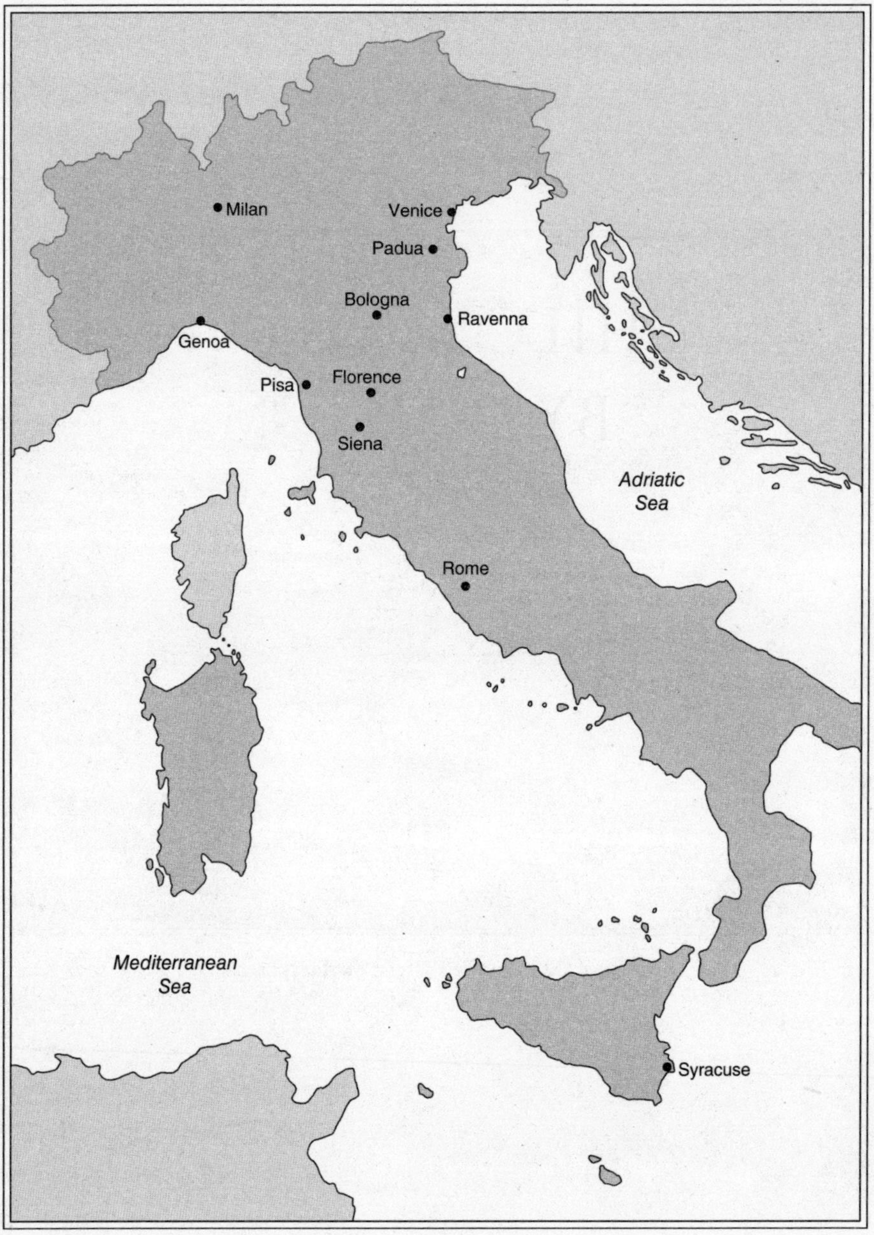

Map of Italian Cities

PART I

PHILOSOPHY IN BYZANTIUM

1

THE EMPIRE STRIKES BACK INTRODUCTION TO BYZANTINE PHILOSOPHY

There almost was no Byzantine philosophy. In fact, there was almost no Byzantine empire, at least not in the sense we usually think of it. If the capital city of Constantinople had fallen to a year-long siege laid by Arab forces from 717 to 718, then we would not bother to speak of "Byzantium" at all but just say that the Eastern Roman empire collapsed somewhat later than the Western empire. And we might well be saying it in Arabic. If it hadn't been for the Byzantines holding the line against the armies of Islam, those armies would have made their way into Europe. Probably they would have brought their religion and language into central Europe and perhaps as far as the English Channel and the North Sea, just as they brought it to northern Africa, Spain, and central Asia. That this alternate history did not occur was thanks above all to the fortifications of Constantinople, built generations earlier at the behest of Emperor Theodosius. They surely rank as one of history's most successful building projects and would be finalists in a "most important ever walls" competition, alongside the Great Wall of China, Hadrian's Wall, the Berlin Wall, and an album by Pink Floyd.

The Theodosian Walls would be needed many times, because the Byzantines were surrounded by enemies and not infrequently riven by internal conflict. Here's a quick overview of historical developments starting in the seventh century or so.[1] It was at this time that the Byzantines were confronted with the rise of Islam, a challenge that caught them unprepared—it didn't help that in the sixth century they'd been weakened by wars of attrition with the Persians and outbreaks of the plague. Following a catastrophic loss at the Battle of the River Yarmuk in 636, the Christians lost the symbolically crucial city of Jerusalem and then vast swathes of territory in Anatolia and the agricultural heartland of Egypt. To make matters worse, there was pressure from the other direction in the form of the Bulgar tribes in Thrace. This sort of thing would continue to be a problem, as Byzantine emperors had to cope with threats on two fronts, the armies of Islam to the south and east and various "barbarian" tribes like the Bulgars, Magyars, Pechenegs, and Rus to the north and west; not to mention forces from Western Christianity such as the Franks and Normans.

The losses of the seventh century ushered in a period often called the "dark ages" of Byzantium. It's not a time that will be featuring much in this book, because of the lack of surviving texts. Much as with the seventh and eighth centuries in the Latin West, philosophical activity was evidently sparse in the Greek East. The empire had lost Alexandria, home of so much intellectual endeavor in late antiquity, and other cities where philosophy was pursued, like Gaza. By seizing these urban centers, the Arabs administered a kind of lobotomy to Greek Christendom. Of course there was still Constantinople, which will be the home for most of the developments we'll be considering under the heading of Byzantine philosophy. But even there, the political upheaval of this early period did not provide an ideal context for scholarship.

Some of the upheaval was occasioned by that most famous response to military defeat: iconoclasm. For a full century the Byzantine elite were consumed by the question of whether it was acceptable to venerate icons of Christ and the saints. The iconoclasts said no. They believed that this was an idolatrous practice for which the empire was being punished. Leo III, the same emperor who had successfully faced down the siege in 718, began the removal of icons in 730, and his policy was carried on with enthusiasm by Constantine V. After decades of iconoclasm, the empress Irene reintroduced the icons, only for them to be banned again from 815 to 843. As we'll be seeing, philosophical justifications were offered by both iconoclasts and their opponents, the iconophiles. For now we might just note that one outcome of the dispute was the destruction of many texts, because when the iconophiles prevailed they destroyed the works of the iconoclasts. So this is another reason for the relative silence of the historical record leading up to the ninth century.

That century is a more important one for us,[2] in part because it was at this time that we see changes in book production, making it a landmark era for the dissemination of philosophy and other sciences. Again, we'll be getting into this in detail later. But to make a long story short, ninth-century scribes began using a more efficient script and, gradually, the new technology of paper, which had come from China via the Islamic world. Around the same time, the Byzantines were able to recover significantly in political and military terms. Thanks in part to the breathing space afforded by Islamic infighting, especially the disintegration of the Abbasid state in the tenth century, the empire struck back between the years 800 and 1000. It took control of Bulgaria, re-extended its territory towards the west as far as the River Danube, and recovered some of what had been lost to the Muslim armies. By the middle of the eleventh century, the empire included southern Italy, the islands of Crete and Cyprus, mainland Greece, Macedonia, and the region around the Black Sea including all of Anatolia, plus a foothold in what we would call the "middle east" with the city of Antioch. This isn't to say that the rulers had a firm grip on all those territories. There was always the danger of raids if not outright warfare across the borders. In many regions within direct Byzantine control that control was actually rather nominal, and some of the areas you'll see marked on maps as part of the "Byzantine empire" were really buffer states ruled by independent Christian allies, like the Serbs and Armenians.

Still, if we generalize and ignore the many individual losses and victories experienced from the ninth to mid-twelfth centuries, we can say that this was the most politically successful period for Byzantium, and hence the time that will get the lion's share of our attention. In the late twelfth century, though, things started to go wrong. Political infighting at Constantinople was compounded by territorial losses, for instance of Thessalonike at the hands of the Normans. Then disaster truly struck. The farcical fourth crusade brought a Latin Christian army to the gates of Constantinople in 1204. After a dispute over money, the crusaders managed to get into the great city and ruthlessly sack it, a shocking tragedy in which a Christian army destroyed the greatest of Christian cities. As the historian Judith Herrin has pointed out, some of the negative connotations still evoked by the word "Byzantine"—absurd bureaucratic complexity and a soft, luxurious lifestyle—go back to Western attempts to justify the sack of Constantinople after the fact.[3]

As with the wars of our own times in places like Iraq and Syria, the obvious violence was accompanied by a more quiet cultural destruction. There was massive loss of artworks, some spirited back to Latin Christendom, like the four bronze statues of horses that were brought to Venice and used to decorate the church of San Marco. The sack of 1204 was also a tremendous blow to the history of philosophy. It was here, and not in the eventual fall of Constantinople to the Ottomans, that we lost the many texts that were known to earlier Byzantine scholars but are no longer preserved today.[4] On the political front, the fall of the city ushered in a long period of relative weakness for Byzantium.[5] After retrenching to Nicaea, the Eastern Greek Christians managed to retake Constantinople from the Latin Christians in 1261. A new dynasty, the Palaiologoi, would rule there for the better part of two centuries. Then came May 29, 1453, when the Ottomans did what their Muslim predecessors had failed to do in 718: get past those walls and finally put an end to the Roman empire.

That it was still a *Roman* empire is something worth bearing in mind, as we approach this third tradition of medieval philosophy alongside those in the Islamic world and in Latin Christendom. We tend to think of the Western medievals as the heirs of the Romans, in part precisely because they used Latin. But Greek had always been the dominant language in the Eastern realms under Roman domination, so the inhabitants of those places would have seen no break with antiquity on that score. Nor was there any break in religious terms. Christianity had already become the religion of the empire in late antiquity. As for the idea of a Roman empire not centered in Rome, that too was a development that came well before the fall of the West, never mind the rise of Islam. Even the Muslims called the Eastern Greek Christians the "Romans": a rare point of agreement between the two sides, since the Greek Christians too thought of themselves as Romans. So in this volume we are really just circling back to where we left things in late antiquity with the Cappadocians and Maximus the Confessor, and carrying on the story of "Roman" philosophy written in Greek.[6]

Suppose, though, that there had been no Byzantine empire, and thus no Byzantine philosophy. What would we be missing? For starters, pretty much all of ancient philosophy. I will be making a case for the idea that historians of philosophy should be interested in Byzantium in its own right, and not only because its scholars preserved older texts for posterity. But it's hard to deny that our greatest debt to them lies here. Without the scribes of Constantinople, nearly all ancient Greek literature would be lost, with the sole exception of a few papyrus texts like those found in Egypt or encased within volcanic ash at Herculaneum. We have the original works of Plato and Aristotle, for instance, only thanks to Greek manuscripts of their works that were dispersed across Europe after the fourth crusade. Without such manuscripts our access to Aristotle would be almost only through medieval Arabic translations. Which would actually be convenient for those of us who are of European descent, since as already noted, if it wasn't for the Byzantines we might be speaking Arabic anyway.

Of course, if all the Byzantines had done was to make copies of older Greek philosophical works, I could pass over them briefly. But they did more: they engaged with the ideas of both pagan and Christian antiquity, carrying on the late ancient practice of writing commentaries, especially on Aristotle. This is something that unifies the three medieval traditions. In tenth-century Baghdad and twelfth-century Spain, in thirteenth- and fourteenth-century Paris and Oxford, and throughout Byzantine history, philosophers busied themselves with the careful exegesis of Aristotle's works—the difference being that unlike such commentators as al-Fārābī, Averroes, Aquinas, or Buridan, the Byzantine commentators could read him in the original Greek instead of having to use Arabic or Latin translations. We will see, especially with the group of scholars associated with the princess Anna Komnene in the first half of the twelfth century, that there was even a completist ambition to comment on all the Aristotelian works that had not yet received this treatment in late antiquity. Nor was Aristotle the only non-Christian thinker who was admired by the Byzantines. Also in the twelfth century, a heated dispute broke out between proponents and critics of Proclus, one of the most enthusiastically pagan philosophers of antiquity. Later on, in the fifteenth century, there was another debate about the relative merits of Plato and Aristotle, with George Gemistos Plethon asserting the superiority of Platonic philosophy and Bessarion coming to Aristotle's defense.

It may seem surprising that the Eastern Christians were so concerned with the preservation, exposition, and evaluation of these pagan thinkers. But it fits into a wider tendency of the Byzantines to cherish classical culture. They recognized the value of writings that pre-dated Christianity, in part on aesthetic grounds. As in late antiquity and Latin Christendom, education had at its center the three linguistic arts of the "trivium"—grammar, rhetoric, and dialectic or logic—which were supplemented with the four mathematical arts of the "quadrivium." Youngsters, at least those elite enough to receive such an education, were schooled in Homer and other classical authors, just like students learning Greek today. Late ancient authors such as Galen, the great doctor of the second century AD, had already venerated Attic Greek as a particularly exalted form of the language, and the Byzantines followed suit. A good illustration would be the philological annotations that were added to the plays of the Athenian poet Aristophanes. These were intended to help readers understand and appreciate the archaic language, much like the footnotes that guide the modern-day reader through an edition of Shakespeare. The Byzantines also preserved the works of classical historians, and imitated their example by producing a number of histories about their own times. The just-mentioned Anna Komnene was one such historian, as was Michael Psellos, one of the thinkers who raised eyebrows with his embrace of pagan Neoplatonism.

But of course, the leading preoccupation of Byzantine intellectuals was not pagan philosophy or history. It was the Christian faith. As in the books this series has devoted to the Islamic world and medieval Latin Christendom, we'll be seeing that philosophically intriguing ideas were often put forward in the context of theological movements and writings. A notable example is the Hesychast movement associated with the fourteenth-century theologian Gregory Palamas. According to Hesychasm, humans cannot grasp God directly but only through His *energeiai*, or "activities." You might recognize the term *energeia* from Aristotelian philosophy, and indeed Palamas' teaching reaches back to Aristotle by way of the late ancient Cappadocian fathers, who took up the tools of classical philosophy to explain our epistemic access to God (or lack thereof) as well as the divine Trinity.

Of course, it's a contentious question whether theological doctrines like this should be counted as "philosophy." For a spirited argument against this idea, one can turn to a chapter in the recently published *Cambridge Intellectual History of Byzantium*.[7] Its authors Dimitri Gutas and Niketas Siniossoglou would object to the first sentence of this chapter, when I said that there almost was no Byzantine philosophy—because they would strike the "almost." To quote their exact words: "the Byzantines had no philosophy (or very little of it, in the margins)." For them, the attempts of recent scholars to integrate Byzantium into our histories of philosophy are a case of "political correctness." Their point is that we should not just grant every culture the compliment of having managed to produce philosophy, and that the Byzantines in particular do not pass the test. These Christian intellectuals were, with a handful of exceptions, so committed to the superiority of revelation over human reason that they could see pagan learning only as a "dangerous antagonist." As a result, though some attention was paid to classical philosophy, this was an "ancillary scholarly pursuit" alongside the exposition of religious orthodoxy. They complain that "classroom philosophy" was not allowed to "freely compete with doctrinal, clerical, and ascetic tradition," and that the scholars of Byzantium "do not show signs of entertaining the possibility that the Hellenic metaphysical, cosmological, and moral outlook might be *more true* than Orthodox doctrine" (my emphasis). Here they seem to catch themselves realizing that this is implausibly demanding, and concede in parentheses that it would be enough if philosophy was at least conceived as offering "different solutions," as a kind of independent alternative to Christianity.

Of course, even that is raising a pretty high bar for the Byzantines to clear. For Gutas and Siniossoglou, a given thinker only counts as a philosopher if he or she pursues rational argument wherever it leads, without being constrained by religious dogma. While that might strike you as eminently reasonable, a moment's reflection shows that it would have some very surprising consequences for our study of the history of philosophy. It would imply that there was also no philosophy at all in Latin medieval Europe, or, to borrow their phrase, only "philosophy in the margins." It would be found, if at all, then only in the works of confirmed members of the university arts faculties like John Buridan. Just consider Anselm, Aquinas, Scotus, or Ockham. They may have been among the greatest philosophical minds in history, yet none were "philosophers" according to this exclusivist definition. Nor by the way was the aforementioned Proclus, who was just as devoted to paganism as Aquinas or your average Byzantine thinker was to Christianity.

What about the Islamic world, where intellectuals were in explicit competition with the Byzantines, and often presented themselves as the true heirs of Hellenic wisdom? As it happens, Gutas is a leading expert in this area. He could point to a small number of outright rationalists like al-Fārābī, Avicenna, and Averroes, and identify them as the true philosophers of the medieval age. For they were prepared to see human reason as independent from and even in some ways superior to religion. But the fact is that, in Islamic culture and even within the intellectual elite, they were the ones who were "marginal." Philosophy and rational argumentation in the Islamic world, as in Latin Christendom and Byzantium, was mostly used to buttress and expound the teachings of one or another Abrahamic religion. This is what we find in such diverse thinkers as the Muslim al-Kindī, the Christian Ibn ʿAdī, and the Jewish Maimonides, all of them expert readers of Aristotle and deeply committed to the idea that Aristotelian philosophy could be interwoven with sensitive exposition of revealed texts and religious doctrine.[8]

Gutas and Siniossoglou make an important and valid point in noting that pagan thought was greeted with more unease than enthusiasm among Byzantine churchmen. Yet some theologians would have rejected, or just been puzzled by, the idea that philosophy means using reason independently of faith. Gutas and Siniossoglou themselves quote the early medieval thinker John of Damascus defining philosophy in the following way: it is "love of wisdom, and true wisdom is God; therefore the love of God, this is the true philosophy." So in approaching this tradition we do need to recognize that the Hellenic philosophical heritage was much debated, and occasionally outright condemned, by Byzantine theologians; but we don't want to miss out on the philosophically fruitful ideas that were put forward even by the harshest critics of that heritage.

If that is our goal, it seems to me unhelpful to focus on the question of which thinkers should and should not be classified as "philosophers." After all, the job of the historian of philosophy is not to police the textual traditions of earlier times, discarding any thinkers who might be tainted by theological, mystical, or other ideological concerns. Rather, we should look for and study texts that address perennial philosophical questions, for instance about knowledge, being, human nature, and ethics. The Byzantines did this when commenting on Aristotle, but they also did it in explicitly religious contexts, when arguing about the nature of God, the sense in which God is accessible to the human mind, the virtues of the monastic life, and so on. Thus I'll deliberately be taking what Gutas and Siniossoglou would call a "relativist" approach. That is, I will discuss whatever strikes me as philosophically interesting, or rather anything I think will strike you, the reader, as philosophically interesting, rather than restricting my attention to works that would have been seen at the time as falling under the literary genre of "philosophy."

There's another, more distinctive sense in which the following chapters will cast a broad net. Usually the phrase "Byzantine philosophy" is applied only to the intellectual output of the Greek intellectuals of the empire, who as I've said were mostly in Constantinople. But in fact, quite a lot of philosophy was going on elsewhere and in languages other than Greek. I just mentioned John of Damascus, who did write in Greek but lived in the Islamic world, as his name indicates. There was philosophy written in Syriac and Armenian, some of it in that familiar genre of commentary on Aristotle. And there was philosophy in Georgian, notably with the twelfth-century philosopher John Petritsi. In fact, it would be strictly speaking more accurate to say that the first half of this book covers "philosophy in Eastern medieval Christianity." We'll kick things off in that spirit by turning first to the reception of Aristotelianism in Syriac and Armenian.

2

ON THE EASTERN FRONT
PHILOSOPHY IN SYRIAC AND ARMENIAN

Let's say you wanted to read every pre-modern translation and commentary on Aristotle. How many languages would you need to learn? Well, obviously Greek. There are dozens of late ancient commentaries on Aristotle beginning in the second century AD if not earlier, with the work of Aspasius and Alexander of Aphrodisias. The Greek commentary tradition arguably peaked with the school of Alexandria in the fifth century, though as we'll be seeing the Byzantines too contributed numerous commentaries on his works. Then there's Latin. Already Boethius drew on the exegetical productions of Alexandria in his commentaries on Aristotle's logic. Later came the rich medieval tradition in Latin, featuring such authors as Aquinas and Buridan, which carried on into the Renaissance. You'll definitely need Arabic, too. There are extant commentaries on Aristotle from the tenth-century "Baghdad school," a mostly Christian group who also included the famous Muslim philosopher al-Fārābī. The greatest of all medieval commentators on Aristotle was the Muslim Averroes, who lived in twelfth-century Spain. He did write in Arabic, but a number of his commentaries are preserved only in Latin or Hebrew, plus there are Hebrew supercommentaries on his explanations of Aristotle. So you'll certainly need a sound grasp of Hebrew as well.

Surely that should do it? No, actually. You need to learn at least two more languages, Syriac and Armenian. In late antiquity and the early medieval period, there were translations of Aristotle into these languages, focusing especially on logic, and introductions and commentaries to this material were also produced in Syriac and Armenian. And that's just Aristotle! Things get more daunting still if we broaden our remit to the reception of Greek philosophy as a whole. Then we must include Georgian, the language used by the twelfth-century Neoplatonist John Petritsi to write a commentary on Proclus; he also translated works by Aristotle into Georgian, though these versions are lost. We can add at least one more, the Ethiopian language Ge'ez. Consider the story of a philosopher named

Secundus.[1] It tells of how he unintentionally brings about the suicide of his mother, takes a vow of silence out of remorse, and is then challenged to share his wisdom by a powerful king. After refusing to speak despite the king's threatening him with death, Secundus agrees to write down a series of aphoristic remarks encapsulating his philosophical insights. Now, this text was originally Greek, and was translated into Latin and Arabic, but also into Ge'ez, Armenian, and Syriac. Secundus is all but forgotten today, but was an inspiration to an ascetically minded and monastic readership across Eastern Christendom. Hence we find the seventh-century spiritual author Isaac of Nineveh praising the discipline of the philosophers, with the remark that one of them "had so mastered the will of the body that he did not deviate from his vow of silence, even under threat of the sword."[2]

What we learn from such cases is that the textual transmission of Greek philosophy was not just, as many people suppose, a simple handover of Aristotelianism and Platonism into Latin. Nor was it only, as you might have supposed on the basis of this book series so far, a matter of Greek ideas being transmitted to both the Islamic world and Latin Christendom. In fact it was a nearly global phenomenon, in which Greek literature including philosophy was rendered into local languages on the east coast of Africa and around the Black Sea, in Spain, Syria, and Iraq, with the Arabic translations produced in those realms making their influence felt as far as central Asia, and eventually in India and China too. Obviously that whole story is not on our agenda just at the moment. I want to look at just one underappreciated corner of the reception of Greek thought: the Eastern Christian communities that used Syriac and Armenian as their languages of scholarship.

In addition to the obvious interest of discovering the breadth and depth of Hellenic philosophy's penetration into these cultures, our topic boasts some of my favorite scholarly names. Actually medieval translators in general have more than their share of fabulous names. One memorable sobriquet belonged to a translator of Aristotle and Averroes into Latin, Hermann the German. The Syriac tradition meets that challenge with Paul the Persian and raises the stakes with Philoxenus of Mabbūg, who sounds like he should be pursuing Frodo and Samwise across Mordor. Literally unbeatable, though, is the Greek and Armenian translator and commentator "David the Invincible (Dawitʿ Anałtʿ)."[3] These splendidly titled scholars were only a few among those who labored to bring Aristotle and other works of Greek science into the languages of Eastern Christianity, alongside theological literature beginning, of course, with the Bible. While some of them did study in Constantinople, they directed their energies towards fellow intellectuals in Syria and Armenia.

These learned men were usually clerics or monks who did not accept the Chalcedonian form of Christianity that became orthodox at Constantinople. The difference of agreement had to do with the nature, or natures, of Christ. According to the Chalcedonians, he had two natures, divine and human, united in a single person—they used the technical Greek word *hypostasis* to express this unity. Many Syrian Christians, by contrast, belonged to the Church of the East, called "Nestorian" by its opponents. This group emphasized the two natures and rejected the idea of a hypostatic union. Another group, the Monophysites—they called themselves "Jacobites" after the sixth-century bishop of Edessa who was, rather boringly, just named Jacob—accepted a single nature that fused humanity and divinity. The Armenian church was and still is Monophysite. Indeed, it's worth emphasizing that these late ancient rifts within Christianity are not yet healed. The most surprising example is that by the fourth century there was an outpost established by the Church of the East in India, and it too survives down to the present day.[4]

It was within this Christian context that Syriac and Armenian emerged as written languages. Syriac was the dialect of Aramaic spoken around Edessa, so a Semitic language like Arabic and Hebrew, not an Indo-European one like Greek. Already in late antiquity it distinguished itself from other forms of Aramaic and came to be a literary language, used by Jews to translate the Old Testament and then by Christians to translate a wide range of religious material starting in the fifth century.[5] The texts rendered into Syriac included Greek church fathers like the Cappadocians and Pseudo-Dionysius, who drew extensively on pagan philosophical ideas. At first the translations tended to be rather loose, but in the seventh and eighth centuries the scholars developed a highly literal, even overly exact style which they used to render Aristotle and other philosophical works into this language of Eastern Christian culture; and this just during the period labeled as the "dark age" of Christian literature in Greek.[6]

If we're looking for the first philosopher to use Syriac, we might settle on Bardaiṣān, who died in the easily remembered year AD 222. His *Book of the Laws of Countries* was influenced by Platonism, and he debated the topic of fate with a rival Christian sect. Like the Jewish philosopher Philo of Alexandria, who had lived a couple of centuries earlier, Bardaiṣān saw resonances between Plato's dialogue on cosmology, the *Timaeus*, and the biblical creation story.[7] When we reflect that important pagan Neoplatonists of late antiquity also came from Syria, we realize that the roots of Hellenism and philosophy were planted deeply in this eastern soil. (Here I'm thinking of Iamblichus and also Porphyry, author of an introduction to Aristotle's logic that would become standard reading in Syriac and Armenian, just like in Arabic and Latin.) Another example would come several centuries later, with

Sergius of Reshʿaynā. He too was interested in cosmology and worked on logic as well, for instance by commenting on Aristotle's *Categories*. Sergius evidently studied at the school of Ammonius in Alexandria and reproduced the ideas of these Neoplatonizing Aristotelians in his own commentaries. Thus his undertaking can be compared to that of Boethius in the West, especially since like Boethius he had the unfulfilled ambition to cover the entirety of Aristotle's logic with his translating and commenting activity.[8]

But the most significant group of Aristotelians who worked in Syriac was that gathered around the monastery at Qenneshre. In the seventh century, the logician and mathematician Severus Sebōkht taught several other men who would form something of a small-scale translation movement.[9] These included Athanasius of Balad, Jacob of Edessa, and—here comes another enjoyable name—George of the Arabs, who wrote translations with his own introductions and commentaries to three works from Aristotle's logical corpus. So this group was a forerunner of the translation circles that would emerge in the ninth century with the support of the ʿAbbāsid caliphs, the ones led by the philosopher al-Kindī and the medical expert Ḥunayn ibn Isḥāq. I discussed their output in the volume on philosophy in the Islamic world, and made brief mention there of the fact that Ḥunayn's circle often translated from Greek into Syriac and then from Syriac into Arabic.[10] The apparently unnecessary middle step of rendering the target text into Syriac in fact made perfect sense, given that there was a long-standing tradition of using Syriac to translate Greek science.[11] Once the material had been brought into this Semitic language, getting it into another one (namely Arabic) was perhaps seen as relatively straightforward.

All of which is not to say that every Syriac author was an enthusiastic Hellenist. The fourth-century poet Ephrem of Edessa despised pagan philosophy, remarking, "Happy is the man who has not tasted of the venom of the Greeks." Broadly speaking, though, Greek was the language of educated culture and was valued as such. An amusing story from the turn of the sixth century tells of a mother pleased by her son's pale complexion, which she assumes is due to his long study of the liberal arts that formed the Hellenic educational curriculum. She is horrified to discover that actually he has been memorizing the psalms, and in Syriac! The more religiously minded tended to value Greek too, even for religious purposes. Thus the aforementioned Philoxenus of Mabbūg remarked on the difficulty of doing Christian theology in Syriac, because it "is not accustomed to use the precise terms that are in currency with the Greeks."[12]

Much of what I have just said about the Syrian context was mirrored in Armenia.[13] Here, too, we have a language that comes into literary use during late antiquity, with the script for Armenian emerging at about AD 400. The purpose of this was, in the first instance, Christian missionary work: a figure called Maštocʿ translated part of the Bible and dispatched students to convert the people, while some members of his circle went abroad to learn Greek or Syriac.[14] In a telling story from about 600, a man named Anania of Širac tells of his struggles to find a teacher of mathematics in Armenia. He finally locates one in Trebizond, a well-traveled man who had been in Alexandria, Rome, Athens, and Constantinople. When Anania returns home, he grumbles about his countrymen, who lack all interest in such educational pursuits. But in fact the Armenian translation movement was already under way by this point. For the sake of studying the liberal arts, there was an early Armenian translation of a grammar written by a man with yet another pleasing moniker, Dionysius Thrax. This was followed by Aristotle's logic, commentaries on his works by Iamblichus, and the writings of Pseudo-Dionysius, in addition to many religious and theological texts.[15] As with Syriac the translations were often overly literal, to the point of being essentially incomprehensible to the untutored reader. It has been commented that they are really just written in "Greek, with Armenian words."

The most remarkable figure here, and not just for his comic-book-ready title, was David the Invincible, who was something like an Armenian version of Boethius and Sergius of Reshʿaynā. Like Sergius, he studied in Alexandria, in David's case with Olympiodorus, one of the very last pagan teachers of antiquity. David's commentaries on Aristotle's logic are extant in both Greek and Armenian. We are told that he wrote them in Greek but then translated them himself for the benefit of his fellow Armenians. His interests went beyond Aristotle; he apparently translated Platonic dialogues into Armenian too.[16] But it is his logical works that give him a claim to what fame he still has. One of today's leading scholars of Aristotelian logic, Jonathan Barnes, commented that David's exposition of Porphyry's introduction to logic is "one of the two best commentaries written on that much commented work."[17] David does not advertise his Christianity while commenting on the pagan logical corpus, perhaps a sign of his training in a school where Christians were collaborating closely with pagans, both sides striving to keep the peace for the sake of their joint intellectual endeavors.[18]

To what extent are David's commentaries, and those of the Syriac scholars, valuable contributions to the history of Aristotelianism? To be honest, you should not read them for their entertainment value, though David does at one point prove that irrational animals do not grasp universal concepts on the basis that a rooster remains calm when it sees the farmer slaughtering the other chickens, which proves that the rooster doesn't know it is a member of the same species.[19] But what they otherwise lack in laughs, they make up in terms of philological importance. The Armenian and Syriac translations are very early, usually earlier than any manuscripts we have for the Greek version. This means we can use them to help reconstruct the original Greek text, since earlier texts lack errors that inevitably crept in during the process of copying out books by hand. (We'll get back to this issue in Chapter 14.) There are also a few ancient texts that are lost in Greek and preserved only in Syriac, for example a treatise on meteorology by Aristotle's student Theophrastus.

Beyond that there is the philosophical interest of the commentaries. As with commentaries in Greek, these are works of exegesis intended for use by students, so they are not full of advanced, innovative ideas. Yet they carry on traditions of thinking about logic that we know from late antiquity, and that will be passed on to the Arabic and Latin spheres. Thus David argues in detail for the long-standing Peripatetic view that logic is not really a part of philosophy, but only its instrument. This indeed is why Aristotle's logical works were called the *Organon*, meaning "tool." It's a point on which Aristotelians like Alexander of Aphrodisias had insisted back in the second century, when this was a good way of marking their opposition to the Stoics, who did think that logic is a part of philosophy, on a par with ethics and physics. Or to take another example, it seems that Paul the Persian's logical writings continue a trend away from formalization in logic, and towards a more metaphysical reading.[20] What I mean by this is that for Paul, when a scientific demonstration yields its conclusion, the conclusion is necessarily true because of the natures of the things the demonstration is about, not because the argument's form is necessarily valid. Thus if we argue "giraffes are ungulates, ungulates walk on tip-toe, therefore giraffes walk on tip-toe," that result is a necessary truth and its necessity resides in the immutable nature of giraffes, not just in the unimpeachable structure of the proof.

The reason that logic was a primary interest of Syriac and Armenian scholars is that it had already had this status at Alexandria. You began your study of philosophy with logic, the necessary instrument for everything that came after, which meant that students had more need for commentaries and translations of logical works than for exegetical help with natural philosophy or metaphysics. But logic was only the beginning, and we do see the intellectuals of these traditions pursuing other interests. Sergius translated a treatise on cosmology and works of medicine, while Severus Sebōkht, the influential teacher at Qenneshre, had particular expertise in astronomy and other areas of mathematics. There are also examples of history writing, for example with the *History of Armenia* written by Moses of Khoren, notable for its lack of theological framing: his purpose is to tell us what happened, not to display God's providence at work in the world.[21]

Still, there's no denying that theological interests did motivate much of what these translators and commentators were doing. As I've said several times, there was extensive effort to translate Christian theological literature, and even the attention paid to logic had a theological dimension. Severus' pupils thought that logic was just as much an instrument of theology as of philosophy. In Armenia one churchman remarked that the devising of a script for Armenian was in part so valuable because one would otherwise need knowledge of Greek and Syriac to resist the seduction of old pagan traditions.[22] A point I made in the previous chapter, that in Byzantium philosophy itself was defined in a theologically colored way, applies in these other Eastern Christian cultures too. Plato had prepared the way for this by saying in his dialogue the *Theaetetus* that philosophy is the attempt to achieve "likeness to God, insofar as is possible for humans." This appears repeatedly in Armenian and Syriac texts as one popular definition of philosophy.[23]

A fine example of the interpenetration of philosophical and theological concerns is provided by George of the Arabs.[24] In his Syriac works on logic, he is not content merely to quote that Platonic definition. He explains how likeness to God is achieved, using a whole series of metaphors that have to do with vision and light. The intellect is the "eye" of the soul and it is by seeing the light of truth that we fulfill our calling as images of the divine. God Himself is a light, with which the light of our souls can mingle when they approach Him. They do this by "polishing the mirror of intellect" through virtue, something that even some pagans managed to do. The path is full of danger, since reason is bound to go astray when it is not guided rightly by the will. Still, when things do go wrong it is the evil will that should be blamed, not reason itself. Thus, George implores his reader, "let no man find fault with philosophy, but with those who make use of it wrongly!"

3

DON'T PICTURE THIS
ICONOCLASM

There is a nice, though presumably apocryphal, anecdote told about Picasso. A man asks him, "Why don't you paint people the way they really look?" The artist asks what he means and the man opens his wallet and produces a photo. "Like this picture of my wife," he says. "She's remarkably small," says Picasso. "And surprisingly flat!" The story draws our attention to the fact that an image of something is never exactly like the thing it represents. If you say that a painting is a "good likeness" of your mother, you don't mean that it resembles her in the way that an identical twin would, or a clone in a science fiction film. The picture might be blurry or in black and white, as well as small and flat, yet still seem to capture your mother—even to *be* your mother, in some sense. Thus if someone sees the picture on your wall and says "who's that?" you would just say "that's my mother." Pictures of people also elicit the same emotions that the people themselves would, provoking such responses as kissing the photograph of one's mother or using a picture of one's enemy for target practice at a shooting range. Yet of course we know that the picture is not genuinely the same as the person. You wouldn't be arrested for attempted murder for shooting at your enemy's picture, and you don't expect your mom's photo to kiss you back.

Here we have one of the central questions of the branch of philosophy known as aesthetics: how exactly do representations relate to the things they depict? In a dramatic example of the way that theological debates can bear on central philosophical themes, it turns out that one of the most interesting pre-modern engagements with this question emerged in Byzantium in the course of the notorious controversy over the veneration of icons. The Byzantines put the point by asking how an image relates to its archetype, for instance a painted icon of a saint and the saint who is shown in the painting. To make a long story short, the "iconoclasts"—literally "breakers of icons"—argued that it is wrong to venerate an image unless the archetype is genuinely present in that image. The supporters of icons, called "iconophiles" or "iconodules," held that the likeness between an image and its archetype does license taking certain attitudes towards the image that we might fittingly take towards the archetype, and that veneration is one such attitude.

Now for the not-so-short version of the story. Iconoclasm is usually reckoned to have begun during the reign of Emperor Leo III, who is said to have removed an icon of Christ from a palace gate in 726. Modern scholars have, however, cast doubt on his role, instead giving his son Constantine V the credit, or blame, for making iconoclasm into a serious official policy.[1] He called together a church council in 754 which set down this policy, and writings ascribed to Constantine himself make the case against venerating images. There is a popular conception to the effect that Leo and Constantine were here imitating restrictions on pictorial art that we find in Islamic culture, but there is little or no evidence for that idea.[2] If Islam played a role, it was by subjecting the Byzantine empire to a series of military defeats. Clearly God was angry with the Greek Christians, and the question was: why? The iconoclasts' answer was that the increasingly popular use of imagery in churches and private settings amounted to idolatry.

Actually this concern emerged long before the eighth century. Back in the fourth century, the theologian Epiphanius of Salamis had already associated paintings with idolatrous practices, remarking, "when images are put up the customs of the pagans do the rest."[3] Slightly earlier, a Christian hagiography had its hero remark to someone who venerated an image of John the Evangelist, "why, I see you are still living as a pagan!"[4] Yet the use of icons was well established by the time of the Arab conquests. The church father John Chrysostom had one, and in the sixth century Hypatius of Ephesus defended their use among common believers. Christians had to respond when Jews accused them of idolatry, pointing to a passage in the Book of Exodus that reads, "thou shalt not make any graven image, or any likeness of anything" (20:4). An interesting document for this interreligious controversy is a dialogue written by Leontius of Neapolis in the 630s. Arguing against a hypothetical Jewish opponent, he contends that a picture can serve to prompt memory of the thing depicted, just as a cross can direct our thoughts to Christ. In such cases the material image itself is not being worshiped. To the contrary, the material object has little or no worth in its own right. As Leontius says, "as long as the two planks of the cross are bound together, I venerate the figure for the sake of Christ, but after they are separated from each other, I throw them away and burn them."[5]

A first premonition of outright iconoclasm came in a council of 691–2. It accepted the religious use of pictorial representation but introduced certain restrictions, for instance that Christ should be shown as a human and not symbolized as a lamb. The iconoclasm of the middle of the eighth century was far more radical, and called for using the cross alone as a symbol of Christ. No longer would it be acceptable to depict him or the saints with material likenesses. As an iconoclast poem put the point, "the Lord does not tolerate that Christ be depicted as a form voiceless and bereft of breath in earthly matter."[6] But popular conceptions are again misleading here. When you think of iconoclasm, you probably imagine soldiers or monks rampaging through churches and private homes, defacing or burning every image they could find, in a violent anticipation of the destruction of images that would later be seen in Protestant Europe. In fact, though, the practical effects of iconoclasm were rather limited.

For one thing, the movement was mostly limited to Constantinople, and even there icons continued to hang in churches. Later iconoclasts would offer a compromise that the images could just be put higher up to prevent people from venerating them. What we're dealing with here is not a social struggle with fighting in the streets, but a political and theological controversy among the elite,[7] with several changes of policy over the course of the century. Under the empress Irene, iconoclasm was reversed in a council held in 787. The emperor Leo V, who wanted to associate himself with the military successes of the iconoclast Constantine V, reintroduced the policy. Then another female ruler, Theodora, restored veneration of images for good in 843. In the end, iconoclasm was an entirely counterproductive policy. Like most programs of censorship, it merely intensified attachment to the banned artworks, something you can still confirm today by walking into any Orthodox church, where you'll find icons hanging on every wall.

For us, of course, the question is not so much the practical effects during and after iconoclasm as the intellectual rationale offered for and against the policy. Constantine and other proponents of iconoclasm, like John the Grammarian, echoed the complaints made by the Jewish opponent in the dialogue by Leontius. For them icons were nothing but idols, and venerating them meant worshiping creatures instead of the divine. The iconoclasts' distaste for what they called the "carnality" of physical images is reminiscent of attitudes familiar from late antique Platonism. Particularly striking is a story told about the great Neoplatonist thinker Plotinus. When asked to sit for a portrait, Plotinus refused, arguing that his body was a mere image of his true self. Why would he want a painted image of this image?[8] But the Neoplatonists were simultaneously potential allies for the iconophiles. As pagans, they too wanted to make use of religious art, like statues of the gods. The pagan emperor Julian the Apostate had written in defense of this practice, saying, "our fathers established images and altars . . . not that we may regard such things as gods, but that we may worship the gods through them."[9] At a theoretical level, the ritualistic use of images and symbols known by pagans as "theurgy" was already Christianized in late antiquity by Pseudo-Dionysius. He focused not on artworks, but on the sacraments and the use of everyday language for God. Much as the pagans said when defending theurgy, Dionysius argued that it is through earthly means that we imperfect humans can access the divine.[10]

So iconophiles, just as much as iconoclasts, could draw on earlier sources for inspiration. The most important authors to write in favor of venerating images were John of Damascus, Theodore the Studite, and the patriarch Nikephoros.[11] Since they were on the winning side, we have a much better sense of their arguments than we do regarding the iconoclast side of the story. Indeed, we usually know the arguments of the iconoclasts only because the iconophiles quoted them for the sake of refutation. For the iconophiles, the first thing to be clarified was that they were not "worshiping" painted images. Rather, as the iconophile council of 787 stated, the icons are objects of "veneration" (*latreia*, not *proskynesis*). Furthermore, when we do venerate an image we are doing so because of a relation (*skhesis*) of likeness between the image and its archetype. Here strict fidelity is not important. It doesn't matter whether an icon really shows a saint just the way he or she looked, or even whether the painter of the icon was highly skilled. Simply by offering some degree of likeness, pictures represent their archetypes in a way that a symbol like the cross would not.

Here we come back to the question of what, exactly, representational likeness consists in. The iconoclast position was a stark one: a real image should involve the actual presence of the archetype. Thus the best, and indeed only, case of an adequate "image" of Christ is the eucharist, where his body is genuinely present. The iconoclasts put this in explicitly philosophical language by saying that the "essence (*ousia*)" of the archetype should be in the image. In the case of a painting, the essence is simply absent. Thus John the Grammarian argued on behalf of the iconoclasts that a visual representation of a man cannot convey his deeds or character, the way that a verbal description of him might do. In light of this, the artwork is just a "waste of time."[12] The iconophiles, by contrast, denied that an image needs to share in the essence of the archetype. That would be more like the case of the identical twin or clone I mentioned earlier.

We can understand this point better by alluding to the philosophical debate over universals, and in particular the treatment of the issue we find in John of Damascus (on whom more in the next chapter). For him, the nature or "essence" of humanity is fully present in every human, with each individual human being a so-called *hypostasis* of that essence—here we might translate *hypostasis* as "instantiation." Clearly this is not what is going on in the case of a visual representation. The photo of your mother is not an individual human, which is why it doesn't kiss you back or tell you to clean your room. How then does the image capture the archetype, if not by including the archetype's essence? Here the iconophiles gave several answers. John of Damascus considered that the "activities (*energeiai*)" of the archetype may manifest themselves in the image. Though John would not appreciate the analogy, this sounds a bit like the pagan idea of theurgy, since there too the spiritual effects of a higher cause could show themselves in a material thing. Another idea was that the image "participates" in the archetype, much as Platonists thought that an individual thing participates in a transcendent Form, like giraffes in the Form of Giraffe or just actions in the Form of Justice.

But perhaps the most fruitful and persuasive idea offered by the iconophiles was that the image and archetype share a *name*. Here they could look back to a passage from the beginning of Aristotle's *Categories*, which would have been well known to all Byzantine intellectuals since this was a basic textbook for training in logic. Aristotle wanted to illustrate the concept of homonyms; that is, two things with different natures but the same name. His example, startling in its relevance for the debate over icons, is that a real man and a figure in a painted picture are both called "animal," in Greek *zoon* (*Categories* 1a). Now, Aristotle probably meant by this that in ancient Greek, the word *zoon* did mean "living thing," that is "animal," but also meant "painted image," presumably because living things were such common subjects for painting. But the passage could easily be taken to mean that Plotinus the man and a painting of Plotinus (made in secret, since he refused to sit for it) both share the name "Plotinus," even though the man and the painting are distinct things with different natures. And this is exactly what the iconophiles wanted to say. Thus, though Theodore the Studite disavowed the use of technical Aristotelian logic in his iconophile writings, both he and Nikephoros helped themselves to the Aristotelian idea that image and archetype are homonyms.[13] Nikephoros added that this is one reason the icon is a more powerful representation of its archetype than a mere symbol, like the cross. Again, you might say of a photo of your mother, "that's mom," whereas you wouldn't do that with something that merely reminds you of her, like her favorite necklace.

Here one can imagine the iconoclasts responding that, if we want *names*, then we should just do as they had already been urging and limit ourselves to linguistic representations of Christ and the saints. A written account would provide more detail and pose no danger of worshiping (or if the iconophiles insist, "venerating") base material things. Some iconophiles effectively refused to admit this distinction. For instance, Theodore Abū Qurra, a follower of John of Damascus who wrote in Arabic to defend the use of images against criticisms from Muslims, said that words are just another kind of icon. After all, Aristotle has taught us that sounds represent ideas the way that a painting represents its subject.[14] For other iconophiles, visual representations do offer something that verbal accounts cannot. Nikephoros offered a detailed explanation of the difference. Both writing and painting are forms of representation (*graphe*), but images lead the mind directly to what is depicted. Words, by contrast, require a greater degree of interpretation and for this reason are often the occasion for disagreement and dispute.[15] Of course, Nikephoros did not mean that written accounts are useless, since that would undermine the importance of the Gospels as a representation of Christ. Still, the painting relates to its archetype more intimately than any verbal description can ever do.

So far we've been discussing the problem of icons in general terms, considering the debate as it would apply to any venerated image, as of a saint. But there were special problems that arose with the depiction of Christ in particular—and here it is worth recalling that the first image removed by the iconoclasts was indeed one of Christ. In his rationale for iconoclasm, the emperor Constantine argued that painting an icon of Jesus is not just idolatry, but also has problematic implications concerning Christology. After all, it is obviously impossible to depict Christ's divine nature in a painting. The icon would show only his human nature, and thus divide the two natures that were joined in his single *hypostasis*, according to the orthodox Chalcedonian formula. Alternatively, the painter might suppose that he is managing to depict the divine nature in the act of showing Christ's human form, but that would show that the painter is "confusing" the two natures, divine and human. Either way, to paint an icon of Jesus is to fall into heresy. Then too, in the incarnation, Christ was meant to take on and redeem human nature in general, something that cannot be shown by painting his individual human body.

To this line of argument, the iconophiles responded that it was Constantine and the other iconoclasts who failed to understand the implications of Christology for artistic representation. It is precisely because Christ was incarnated that we can, in this one case, represent a divine person in an image. Here it was important to insist that Christ remained incarnated, retaining his body even after his crucifixion and resurrection. The iconoclasts, with their Platonist scorn for the material, were thinking like Manicheans or other dualists who despised the physical realm, not realizing that it has been redeemed and even exalted when Christ took on human flesh and retained it forever.[16] This is why he can be "circumscribed" in the limited form of an image, something Constantine considered impossible for a being whose divinity makes him infinite and thus "uncircumscribable." As for the point that Christ redeemed all of human nature, which cannot be shown in a painting of one individual, the iconophiles again refer us to the standard view on universals. Of course, human nature is something general or common, but it can exist only in individuals. We never have access to essences or natures except by encountering them in concrete, material things. So the only way for us to understand the redemption of human nature is to consider that nature as it appears in one particular case, namely in Christ's incarnated form, which is precisely what is shown in the icon.

Famously, history is written by the victors, and that tends to go for the history of philosophy too. Given that our evidence is largely from the iconophile camp, and that the iconoclasts are tainted by the lurid accusations thrown at them in iconophile histories—burning the hands of icon painters, tormenting and humiliating monks who refused to take down their icons, and so on—it is always going to be hard to avoid sympathizing with the iconophiles. But I tend to think that philosophically speaking, the iconophiles had the better of this debate anyway. It seems just false that a genuine image of something needs to share the essence of that thing. That central question of aesthetics—what does the representation share with its archetype?—needs to be answered in terms of likeness or even partial identity, precisely as the iconophiles suggested.

Less clear, to me anyway, is whether the iconophiles were right to think that "veneration" is an appropriate attitude to take towards an image. As we saw at the outset, in some cases it seems natural to treat pictures as an extension of the people they depict, but in other cases it does not. You might kiss a picture of your mom, but you wouldn't buy it a Mother's Day present. Here too, though, I tend to think that the iconophile position fits tolerably well with our intuitions. Indeed, kissing icons is one of the forms of veneration that became standard practice in Orthodox Christianity. Then again, in less technical and less philosophically inspired iconophile literature we sometimes get the sense that icons were seen as more than just pictures. We hear, for instance, of Muslim invaders stabbing the icon of a saint, which then began to flow with real blood. As one scholar has remarked apropos of this example, "as soon as we leave the rarefied atmosphere of learned theological treatises, the properties of the sacred portrait so carefully distinguished by Byzantine churchmen collapse."[17]

4

BEHIND ENEMY LINES JOHN OF DAMASCUS

The first thing that comes to mind when you hear the word "Byzantine" is probably exaggerated and unnecessary complexity, in honor of the Eastern empire's formidable and intricate bureaucracy. The second thing to come to mind might be the concept of "orthodoxy," in honor of the empire's equally formidable and intricate theological tradition. The term comes from the Greek words *orthos* and *doxa*, meaning "correct belief," and of course it features in the title of the Greek Orthodox Church. The doctrines of that church emerged from late antiquity and the early Byzantine period, a time of fierce debate as to which religious beliefs are, in fact, correct. To be an orthodox Christian obviously involved rejecting paganism and the two other Abrahamic faiths: Judaism, which was seen as superseded by the incarnation and the Gospels, and Islam, which was seen more unfavorably still as an outright heresy. Orthodoxy also meant rejecting certain teachings that had been adopted by other Eastern Christian communities during centuries of controversy over the Trinity and the nature, or indeed natures, of Christ.

No one text, church council, or theologian was solely responsible for establishing the theology of the Orthodox Church. But a few key figures were particularly important in that process, among whom we must count John of Damascus. He would eventually be honored as a theological authority alongside the late ancient church fathers whose ideas animate his own writings, like the Cappadocians, Pseudo-Dionysius, and Maximus the Confessor. John's influence was fundamentally due to his having been on the correct side of all the religious debates of his day, or at least, the side of these debates that would eventually be acknowledged as correct in the Orthodox tradition. He catalogued and rebuked the various sorts of heretical belief that lay outside what he saw as the true faith, including Islam. He was a stalwart defender of Chalcedonian Christianity and a fierce advocate of the veneration of icons, this at a time when the emperor in Constantinople was promulgating iconoclasm.

It may seem strange that this champion of Eastern Orthodoxy should have lived outside the borders of the Byzantine empire. Actually, though, this makes perfect sense. Living as he did in the Umayyad empire in the first half of the eighth century, John could not take the dominance of his version of Christianity for granted.[1] As his name indicates, he was born in Damascus, to a Greek-speaking Christian family of well-placed administrators who managed to flourish despite the transition to Islamic rule. In the Syria of his day and in Palestine, where he would become a monk, John lived among a religiously diverse population with plenty of opportunity for debate between Christian and Jew, between Christian and Muslim, and between Chalcedonians like himself and other Christian groups. In addition to the groups I've already mentioned, namely the Church of the East and the Monophysites, there were also the Monothelites. They adopted a compromise position according to which divinity and humanity come together in Christ's single will. Hence their name, which comes from the Greek words *mono* and *thelesis*, meaning "one" and "will."

John wrote polemics against all these groups, maintaining the line established at the Council of Chalcedon in 451 and already defended by Maximus. This meant distinguishing two natures in Christ, while seeking to safeguard his unity with reference to the single existing person in which these natures resided. Following the same line of thought, John also rejected another compromise formula which would acknowledge Christ's two natures but ascribe to him a single activity or *energeia*. Aristotle had already used this word to refer to "actuality" as opposed to "potentiality." So it's a concept familiar from ancient philosophy and the other medieval traditions. But *energeia* is being used in a somewhat more specific way here, to refer to the activity that proceeds from a given nature, the way heat comes from fire. This is the basis of John's objection to the Monothelites. If Christ had two natures, He cannot have had only one "activity," because every nature generates an activity of its own. Similarly, John's response to the Nestorians and Monophysites turns on the Greek technical term *hypostasis*, which can be found in late ancient texts but with a somewhat different connotation. Christ has two natures but is still a single, unified being, because he is only one "*hypostasis*." Roughly this just means that he was a single existent; we'll see more exactly what it means a couple of paragraphs below.

If you're tempted to ask what any of this has to do with philosophy, a perusal of John's masterwork the *Fountain of Knowledge* (*Pege Gnoseos*) might help answer your question.[2] It's a massive text with three parts, the first of which is called *Philosophical Chapters*.[3] This section is a kind of textbook which gathers together definitions and explanations of basic terms and concepts, drawn from both Christian authorities and also pagan authors, whom he calls the "outside (*exo*)" philosophers. Sometimes John contrasts the teachings of the pagans and the Christian fathers (as at §31, 48). But for the most part the *Philosophical Chapters* read like an elementary introduction to logic and other philosophical basics that could have been handed to pagan students by a pagan professor in late ancient Alexandria. This textbook is supposed to prepare the reader for tackling the remaining two parts of the work, called *On the Orthodox Faith* and *On Heresies*.

John's fame and importance rest above all on the second part of the *Fountain*. *On the Orthodox Faith* was translated into Latin and became a major source for the scholastics; you'll see it cited on many pages of Aquinas' *Summa theologiae*, for example. It was also rendered into Old Slavonic and Arabic, enabling it to become a mainstay of Christian theology across much of the globe. It offers what its title promises, a comprehensive explanation and defense of the religious doctrines that John accepted as orthodox, and would indeed become accepted as orthodox by the Greek church in due course. Now, this is most certainly a work of theology, but it is not for nothing that John has prepared the way with a survey of basic philosophical concepts. He is convinced that we can rely on natural human reasoning, albeit that he grounds this assumption in the further assumption that reason was given to us by God.[4] Thus Christian truth, for him, must include all the deliverances of successful philosophical reasoning. Furthermore, to explain and establish his theological teachings he often needs first to clarify how he sees various philosophical issues.

This is well illustrated by the "correct beliefs" about Christ expounded in *On the Orthodox Faith*. Since he is here trying to explain the special case where divinity is somehow united to humanity, John has to tell us what humanity is in the cases that are not so special. Yet again he deploys a standard bit of terminology familiar from earlier Greek philosophy, namely *physis* or "nature" (this is where we get the word "physics"; that is, the study of nature). For John, a "nature" is the same thing as the "essence" or "being" of something (its *ousia*).[5] Thus the nature of a giraffe is just what makes giraffes to be the sort of thing they are. In itself a nature like this is not an individual thing, because it is shared among all the beings that have the same nature. The essence of giraffe belongs to all giraffes, and furthermore, we can grasp this nature in our minds as a general or universal concept (*On the Orthodox Faith*, §3.11). By contrast, an individual giraffe, like Hiawatha, comes about when the giraffe nature exists concretely, and when this happens we can speak of *hypostasis*. So now we can explain more clearly what John means by this term: a *hypostasis* is the instantiation of a nature or essence in one particular individual.

He uses this idea to account for the Trinity, where we have only one divine nature that is instantiated in three persons, each of which is its own *hypostasis*. He also uses it to account for the incarnation. Christ is only one *hypostasis* but with two natures, both divine and human, thus ratifying the Chalcedonian formula. Now, this might sound pretty strange. How can a single individual exemplify two natures, especially two such different natures, one created and one uncreated? This would be as if Hiawatha were somehow simultaneously a giraffe and a lion, which would at least mean she wouldn't have to venture far to find dinner, but seems metaphysically absurd. John's response would be that the difference between the two natures in Christ is precisely why they cannot coalesce to become one single nature, as the Monophysites held (§3.3). In general, it is possible for things with various natures to come together and "mix," as when the elements fuse to form a complex body.[6] But in that sort of case, the two natures being mixed together are lost: fire and water are taken up into the compound body and are no longer present as elements. By contrast, if Jesus was indeed both fully human and fully God, as Christianity requires, then he must have had two natures that were preserved and not lost by being commingled.

We do have some hope of understanding how this is possible, because there is another case of two natures remaining unmixed in one single *hypostasis*, namely the case of an ordinary human. Each of us has both a soul and a body, and these two "parts" retain their different natures (§3.16), as we can see from the fact that souls are able to outlive the body. Another case John is fond of mentioning is a burning hot sword, where the nature of fire occurs together with the nature of iron. He compares the soul's presence in body to the fire's presence in the sword (§1.13) and points out that both the fire and iron retain separate activities, the fire burning and the iron cutting (§3.15). A problem here, about which John seems surprisingly relaxed, is that it now sounds as if Christ actually had *three* natures, namely His divine nature and then the two natures that make up any human, corresponding to body and soul. It seems this problem would be solved by saying that the natures of body and soul are not, so to speak, on the same level as the divine and human natures. They are rather sub-natures that form parts of the human nature.

Another philosophically interesting dimension of John's discussion of humanity, his philosophical anthropology if you will, comes with his polemic against Monothelitism. In an attempt to mollify those who wanted to be more protective of Christ's unity, it had been proposed that Christ had only one will. And why not? Indeed, what would it even mean for a single *hypostasis* or person to have multiple wills? Then it would seem I could will to do something while also willing not to do it, leading to a stalemate: choosing to see the giraffe enclosure at the zoo even while choosing to see the lions instead. But again following Maximus on this point, John argues that will is like activity. It is tied inextricably to nature, so that if there are two natures there are two wills. Normal humans do not have two wills, since our power for willing has to do only with our souls and not our bodies. In fact, it has to do with our power of rationality, which expresses itself in deliberative choice, a manifestation of self-control that is impossible for non-human animals.[7] Christ had such a will also, but his situation was radically different from that of a normal human, because he had access to divine omniscience. Thus neither God nor Christ as incarnated actually has to "deliberate" between alternatives: He simply chooses what is good. Given this, there is no possibility that the divine and human wills in Christ would come into conflict (§2.22, 3.14). The same goes for his activity. What looks to us to be a single action can in fact be a manifestation of both divine and human nature, something especially clear in a miracle like walking on water, which required both a human body for walking and a divine nature for doing something that is naturally impossible.

The nuance and sophistication of John's response to his Christian opponents is not, in truth, matched by his attack on Islam. Several documents directed against the Muslim faith come down to us under his name, including the final chapter of *On Heresies* and—probably not in fact by John but close to his thought in spirit[8]—a dialogue between a Christian and a "Saracen" or Muslim, which seems to be designed to equip Christian readers with arguments to use in real-life debate.[9] A somewhat later Christian author who also lived in the Islamic world, Theodore Abū Qurra, took up John's polemic and offered further arguments against what was then a new religion posing an existential threat to Christianity.[10] That explains the note of alarm detectable in both authors. John begins his chapter on Islam in *On Heresies* by describing this rival faith as the "harbinger of the Antichrist" (74), while Theodore compares it to a virulent disease (86).

But these writings are not hysterical jeremiads, or at least, not only that. They also address a deep question that arises in times and places where multiple religions compete for adherents: on what basis are we to choose between them? Nowadays we call this the problem of religious pluralism, and both John and Theodore are well aware of it. Alongside more *ad hominem* arguments, for instance aspersions cast on the character of the Prophet, they offer proofs that might convince a neutral referee between the claims of Islam and Christianity. Prominent among these are the miracles performed by Moses and by Christ, which were seen by many witnesses. The same cannot be said for the Prophet Muhammad, our authors claim, and John shows some knowledge of the Quranic texts by alluding here to the Muslims' own emphasis on the legal importance of witnesses (76). Theodore adds the interesting point that, without such independent proof, religion is simply a matter of thoughtlessly adopting the beliefs of one's parents (94).

John and Theodore formulated these arguments while living among their adversaries, behind enemy lines, so to speak. But it's worth remembering that John might have found the Christian Byzantine empire no more congenial than the Umayyad realm at this time, because of his defense of the icons. He was condemned by the emperor Constantine V in the year 754 for this position, and it's said that the emperor referred to him as *manzeros*, Hebrew for "bastard," cleverly playing on John's Arabic name Manṣūr.[11] It's presumably for this reason that John's works started to be influential among Byzantine readers only a century or so after his death, once the icons had been brought back into Orthodox practice and worship. He deals with the issue in *On the Orthodox Faith* and also in three shorter treatises, which gather authoritative testimonies and arguments in favor of venerating the icons.[12]

This material also reveals something of how Christians in this period saw the Jews.[13] As we saw the iconoclasts built their case in part on passages in the Hebrew Bible condemning the making of idols. John states that these restrictions were appropriate for the Jews, who were indeed at risk of "sliding into idolatry" (§8). But things have changed with the incarnation, which licenses the use of physical images to represent the divine (§16). While we should not actually *worship* the images of Christ and the saints, it is appropriate to show them reverence. More generally, we can see created things as images of God. The icons are simply a central instance of the way that spiritual things can manifest themselves in the physical sphere. Thus we might say that a rose, a flower, and its fragrance are an image of the Trinity (§11). In this sense, the icons are not so much signs and symbols of what they represent, as revelations of these things in the world.[14]

That example with the rose is a telling one. Like John's comparison of Christ to a fiery sword, it shows that he thinks the careful consideration of natural things can give us insight into the supernatural. We may find it unsettling that he moves so seamlessly from discussing what seem to be philosophical issues, like the relation between nature and its individual instantiation, to religious questions like the incarnation or Trinity. But in John's works there is no disentangling the two. Perhaps there is no more eloquent testimony to this than one of the numerous definitions of philosophy offered in his *Philosophical Chapters*, in fact one that I already mentioned in Chapter 1. Noting that etymologically, the word "philosophy" means "love of wisdom," John infers that philosophy can be understood as the love of Wisdom itself, namely God (§3).

Those definitions of philosophy illustrate another feature of John's writings that may unsettle us: he didn't invent any of them. Like the *Philosophical Chapters* as a whole, in fact like most of the *Fountain of Wisdom* as a whole, they are a patchwork of material drawn from other sources. In the case of John's treatises in defense of the icons, we see him doing little more than offering quotations from a variety of authoritative sources, sometimes with commentary but sometimes without. John's influence as a theologian was, to put it mildly, not owing to his originality. To the contrary, he was above all useful because of his command of many sources, which he wove together into powerful works that are often little more than compilations. And John was not the only one. Some of the most frequently copied and consulted works of Byzantine philosophy were not so much written as gathered.

5

COLLECTORS' ITEMS
PHOTIUS AND BYZANTINE COMPILATIONS

Like Rodney Dangerfield, obsessive collectors get no respect. The word "trainspotter," which refers to a railway enthusiast, is in British English synonymous with "loser," and there is indeed something slightly tragic about someone who spends all their free time looking for things the rest of us find pointless. We've all shaped our faces into a frozen smile and uttered a forced "wow" when being shown, say, a neighbor's collection of Star Wars figurines or a cousin's treasure trove of memorabilia from the career of Donny and Marie Osmond. At such moments, I remind myself that I too am prone to the collector's impulse. I refer not to my complete edition of Buster Keaton's silent films, for which I make no apologies, but to my embarrassingly large collection of books about ancient and medieval philosophy. The roots of addiction were planted early in my own career, when a young man who was considering studying philosophy looked around my office and said, "So I guess you're new here?" When I asked how he knew this, he said, "Because you hardly have any books." That was about twenty years ago. Nowadays, a visitor might reasonably conclude that I am preparing for a cataclysm in which all of Western civilization is destroyed, with the lucky exception of my office, so that future historians will be able to reconstruct the early history of philosophy using nothing but my private library. What they will make of my knee-high, plastic, dancing James Brown doll, I hesitate to guess.

In my defense, I would point out that collectors of the distant past achieved more or less exactly what I just described. We owe much of our knowledge about antiquity to obsessive collectors whose efforts defied civilizational collapse, preserving precious texts and information like Noah saving the animals aboard his ark. Pride of place, at least as concerns the history of classical philosophy, must go to Simplicius. A Platonist living in the sixth century, he feared that the rise of Christianity would make it even more difficult to get access to ancient pagan literature that was already hard to find. So he packed his commentaries on Aristotle with extensive reports about, and quotations from, Presocratic philosophers and other thinkers.[1] We should also be grateful to the Byzantine scribes who copied out those massive commentaries, and to other scholars of Byzantium who usually get no respect: those whose literary output consisted of compilations and summaries of earlier texts. While not the most innovative of thinkers, they produced works that survived through the collapse of their own society, and that transmit otherwise lost parts of the history of philosophy.

We've just seen with John of Damascus that in Eastern Greek culture, philosophical writing often meant compilation rather than original composition. His *Philosophical Chapters* gathered together all the logical materials one needed to master in order to do Christian theology. Though unprecedented in ambition and influence, the approach of John's book was, like its contents, nothing new. From the so-called "dark age" of the early Byzantine period, around the seventh century or so, we have several logical compilations with a similar pedagogical purpose. John himself drew on such summaries, while the authors of the earlier textbooks in turn looked back to the late antique school of Alexandria, where the aforementioned Simplicius studied.

Though these compilations occasionally show some originality in their arrangement of the materials, their purpose was simply to present the basics of Aristotelian logic, much as was being done in Syriac and Armenian at about the same time. Thus Mossman Rouché, who studied and edited several of these treatises, has remarked, "Perhaps 'philosophical activity' is too generous a term to bestow upon works of so little effort and originality."[2] Yet their mere existence demonstrates the importance of logic to Byzantine intellectuals. They found it unproblematic to take over at least this part of the Hellenic intellectual inheritance, because it seemed to them neutral with respect to the divide between pagans and Christians. As Rouché puts it in his study of another logical compilation from the ninth century, "in so far as logic was a tool of philosophy and not a doctrine, its use by the Christian apologist was encouraged. As its application was inexorable and its utility common to all, often only the meaning of its terminology was open to dispute."[3]

Of course, thanks to the scribes of Constantinople, we have the original treatises of Aristotle devoted to logic and for that matter a wealth of late ancient commentary on those treatises. So if these early compendia were lost, it would deprive us of little more than the insight that an interest in logic did persist through the dark ages. The same cannot be said for the numerous texts known as "scholia," a technical term that refers to comments written in the margins of manuscripts. We don't usually place much value upon marginalia, but these scholia were seen as important in Byzantine culture, enough so that scribes would routinely copy out scholia found in a manuscript along with the main text. Scholia seem first to have come into fashion because readers had difficulty understanding works of antique literature, such as the plays by Aristophanes and other classical authors whom they took to be the ultimate representatives of good Greek style.[4] Marginal notes would explain the meaning of words that were no longer in use, or make observations about grammar, much as students of English literature nowadays need footnotes to help them navigate their way through a text of Chaucer. In due course scholia were used for other purposes too. Sometimes they preserve parts of otherwise lost philosophical commentaries, or make pertinent observations about the life of the author of the work being copied.

Such information could also be set down in an independent book rather than in the form of scholia. The most impressive and important example is the so-called *Suda*, a staggeringly huge text from the tenth century with entries on individual Greek terms and personages, explaining each entry by pulling together information from earlier sources. Many of those sources were themselves derivative, so that this Byzantine encyclopedia has been called a "compilation of compilations."[5] The *Suda* wouldn't make for good bedtime reading—it's really a reference work, whose modern edition runs to five volumes—but it is an invaluable resource for scholars of classical antiquity.[6] The entries can also provide a revealing window into the minds of Byzantine intellectuals of this period. Consider its definition of the word "philosophy." It first draws on a historian named George the Monk, to tell us that "philosophy is correctness in ethics, along with belief in true knowledge about being."[7] The *Suda* then abbreviates George the Monk's complaint about the philosophical failures of Jews and Greeks, before adding a division of philosophy into ethics, physics, and theology, which is drawn from John Philoponus. So this little passage, despite being entirely unoriginal in its contents, reflects a moderate view according to which Christian truth is the full culmination of philosophical reflection. Such reflection, however, does involve philosophical disciplines apart from theology, including natural philosophy, which is understood as an inquiry into bodily things and their forms.

Probably no Byzantine expected to become famous for writing scholia, but the man who came closest was Arethas, who lived from the ninth into the tenth century. We still have volumes that belonged to his library, the full version of which would have put mine to shame. The surviving eight books include Euclid, Plato, and Aristotle, and feature notes written in Arethas' own handwriting. We even know how much he paid for these books. The Euclid cost him 14 pieces of gold, and Plato 21. For comparison, employment in the famously vast Byzantine civil service paid a starting salary of about 72 gold pieces annually. So you can see that even a modest library back then would have cost a small fortune.[8] Arethas' expensive taste was also a controversial one. In a letter written in 903 he confesses to having been "an ardent lover of Aristotle and a warm inquirer of his works."[9] In the end, though, he has decided that the call of Aristotelian philosophy is like that of the Sirens luring ships to their doom in Homer's *Odyssey*—tellingly, Arethas alludes to classical Greek literature even as he disowns Hellenic philosophy. It's been speculated that his enthusiasm cooled after he was accused of impiety in the year 900, with the charge sheet perhaps including an undue attachment to pagan ideas.

Arethas came by his fondness for philosophy the same way Aristotle did: he got it from his teacher. This was Photius, the prize exhibit in our assembly of Byzantine collectors. He can take a good deal of credit for inspiring a revival of interest in Greek literature, science, and philosophy that has been termed the "ninth-century Renaissance." (In case you're keeping track, that makes three medieval "Renaissances" that came along well before the one we'll consider in the second half of this book. Along with ninth-century Byzantium, the term has been applied to Islamic culture in the tenth century and Latin Christendom in the twelfth.[10]) And as long as we're handing out titles, we can mention that Photius has been called the "inventor of the book review."[11] This in honor of his writing of a work called the *Bibliotheca* or *Library*, which collects 280 entries covering no fewer than 386 texts, a number of which are known only or primarily thanks to the summaries offered here by Photius.

Unlike most of the figures we'll be covering in the history of Byzantine philosophy, Photius played a significant part in actual Byzantine history.[12] Thanks to his reputation as a man of learning, he was tapped for the role of patriarch, despite being a layman. A breakneck round of ordinations saw him being made subdeacon, deacon, priest, and then patriarch in time for Christmas of the year 858 (this sort of fast-track ordination was then forbidden in a council of 861, to avoid a repeat of the unseemly procedure). Not everyone saw him as the ideal stocking stuffer. The previous patriarch Ignatius had supporters who still considered him to be the rightful holder of the post, and the confrontation between the two sides ran on for years. The already heated debate got even hotter when the Roman pope Nicholas I asserted the right to adjudicate in the affair, which was not welcomed in Constantinople. Lamenting all the while that he would much rather be spending time with all those books, Photius found himself deposed and exiled, then restored as patriarch in 877, only to be removed yet again in 886. He died while in exile in 893.

For our purposes it isn't necessary to get into the details of his checkered career as a churchman, whose complexity I feel almost obligated to describe as "Byzantine." I do, however, want to mention his role in the famous rift between the Western and

Eastern churches known as the *filioque* controversy.[13] *Filioque* is Latin for "and the son." The debate concerned the acceptability of saying that the Holy Spirit proceeds from the Father *and the Son*, not only the Father. When it came to Photius' attention that some Western Christians were including this in their recitation of the creed, he was unsparing in his critique. His diatribe against the *filioque* clause nicely illustrates the point I've been making, that logical and other philosophical ideas could be pressed into the service of theological dogmatics.[14] For Photius, the capacity to generate other Persons of the Trinity is the characteristic "property" that distinguishes the Father, so it cannot belong to the Son as well. He speaks of this in quasi-political terms as the "monarchy" of the Father, and complains that the *filioque* would instead introduce a "duarchy"; that is, rule by two rather than one. Then too, if the Spirit has two causes, it would have to be a composite thing made up of parts introduced by its different sources. Yet we know that the divine Persons are utterly simple.

Photius certainly knew whereof he spoke, because his *Bibliotheca* is nothing if not a composite drawn from many sources.[15] As he explains in a brief preface, the work was written for his brother in anticipation of a diplomatic mission to the Islamic world, which must have been in either 845 or 855.[16] Here's what Photius says: "when we were chosen by the members of the embassy and by imperial appointment to go on an embassy to the Assyrians, you asked us to write down for you summaries of those books that had been read when you were not present, my dearest brother Tarasius, so that you might have some consolation for the separation that you bear unwillingly, and also the knowledge, even if somewhat impressionistic and rather general (*diatupotiken kai koinoteran*), of those books that you have not read in our hearing." The point of this, then, is that Photius and his brother have been taking part in a kind of literary salon at which texts were apparently read aloud to the group, which makes sense if you think again about the expense and scarcity of handwritten books. But now Photius is going away on a lengthy trip, so he is going to give his brother consolation and edification with a wealth of information about the books he, Photius, has read.

Impressive is not only the fact that Photius has read the hundreds of works discussed in the *Bibliotheca* but also that he is recounting their contents from memory, or so he claims.[17] He will not arrange the works thematically but jumble together disparate genres and topics, for the sake of a more entertaining overall product. In this, and in some of his wording here in the preface, Photius looks back to a female scholar of the Roman empire, Pamphila of Epidaurus. She likewise mixed together heterogeneous materials in her writing on history, and is a good example of how Photius preserves information about otherwise lost figures. Since she was a historian, the example also illustrates that Photius' collection is not devoted only to philosophy. Indeed, our favorite discipline plays a pretty minor role in the work, which covers a wide range of genres including history, literature, and of course Christian theology, though it should be noted that a good half of the works covered are secular.[18]

Probably the assortment of topics is not so much a reflection of Photius' tastes as what he has been able to get his hands on and commit to memory.[19] Yet the selection does seem to betray certain of his intellectual interests. These would include medicine, as well as the relevance of philosophy for doctors. Photius discusses Galen's work *On the Sects* (§164), and rightly notes that it is really a treatise on scientific methodology, one that to his mind is required reading before embarking on medical studies.[20] Another philosophical issue that clearly caught Photius' imagination was free will. Probably his most valuable contribution to our knowledge of ancient philosophy is his summary of an otherwise lost work on the subject of providence by Hierocles of Alexandria, a Platonist of the early fifth century AD.[21]

Photius devotes two sections of the *Bibliotheca* to this treatise (§214 and §251). He explains that in it, Hierocles wanted to "treat providence while bringing the thought of Plato and Aristotle into sympathy,"[22] a project he was taking over from Ammonius, head of the school of philosophers in late ancient Alexandria. Following this perceptive remark, Photius goes on to explain that Hierocles attacked rival conceptions about providence: the skeptical view of the Epicureans and the determinism of Stoics and astrologers. Hierocles' champions were (of course) Plato and also such ostentatiously pagan authorities as Orpheus and the Chaldean Oracles. According to the true, Platonic theory, providence flows forth from the highest god through the heavenly world, and then manifests itself in the earthly realm as "fate." Within this system, humans retain their freedom. For it is in response to free actions that we receive just reward or punishment at the hands of fate. As Photius emphasizes, Hierocles was able to establish this only by taking recourse to a belief in reincarnation: our fate in this life was "chosen" by us in our actions in a past life.

This teaching is evidently problematic from a Christian point of view. Photius has clearly noticed this fact, as he writes that Hierocles, "starting from strange notions, puts forward incoherent reasonings . . . without it entering his mind on what grounds the doctrine of providence could truly be defended."[23] But that hasn't stopped him from offering a detailed report of Hierocles' ideas, which is otherwise largely free of editorial remarks on Photius' part. He even goes so far as to wrap up the first of the reports on Hierocles by praising his clear and unflashy writing style as "appropriate to the task of a philosopher." Photius' approach is similar in recounting the ideas of that hero of Hellenic philosophy, Pythagoras (§249). Here one could easily have the impression that one is reading a pagan Neoplatonist explaining his own intellectual lineage, perhaps because it's exactly that sort of text that Photius is drawing on. We are told that Plato and Aristotle were the ninth and tenth successors in a line of teachers stretching back to Pythagoras himself, and then treated to an exposition of supposedly Pythagorean doctrine that touches on topics ranging from the creation of all things out of the cosmic mathematic principles of monad and dyad, to theories of color, the soul, and wind. Photius also takes time in this section to defend Aristotle from the charge that he denied the immortality of the soul.

As these examples suggest, the *Bibliotheca* is the work of a scholar of Hellenism who was a devout Christian, but who didn't let his religious convictions stop him from telling us whatever he knew about ancient culture. Usually he simply ignores the question of why all this material would be useful for a Byzantine intellectual to know. But there is at least one interesting exception. In a section devoted to the Pyrrhonian skeptic Aenesidemus (§212)—which again is valuable testimony, since his works are lost—Photius clearly explains the distinctive nature of this form of skepticism. Whereas the so-called "Academic" skeptics asserted the impossibility of achieving knowledge, the Pyrrhonists made no definite assertions at all, about knowledge or anything else.[24] Having explained all this, Photius adds, "it is clear that [Aenesidemus] makes no contribution to philosophical doctrine . . . but for students of dialectic the book is not without its uses, provided that its arguments do not impose upon unstable intellects and its subtlety does not affect the judgment." Perhaps we could extrapolate from this to an attitude about philosophy as a whole, or even Hellenic culture more generally: enjoy it and make use of it, but do so carefully.

6

CONSUL OF THE PHILOSOPHERS MICHAEL PSELLOS

When Socrates proposes in Plato's *Republic* that philosophers would be the best rulers for the ideal city, he recognizes that the suggestion may seem ridiculous. As well he might. If you've spent as much time around philosophers as I have, you'll know that often their organizational talent barely extends to wearing matching socks. No wonder then that, even if Plato's authoritative status meant that philosophers in antiquity and the middle ages continued to envision perfect rulers as philosopher kings, real-life philosophers often found themselves outside the halls of power. In Latin medieval Christian culture, they were far more often monks or university masters than courtiers. Monasticism was also an important context for philosophical thought in Byzantium, as we'll be seeing. Yet there were major intellectual figures who had significant access to the imperial court. We just met one of them, Photius; another was Michael Psellos, arguably the outstanding author of the whole tradition of Byzantine philosophy.

He earned this status in part by writing about non-philosophical topics. His most frequently consulted work is surely the *Chronographia*, a portrait of numerous emperors that has made him a key source for the study of Byzantine history in the eleventh century. As Psellos emphasizes, he is providing first-hand testimony, having known personally many of the protagonists of his history.[1] He came into court circles having achieved a reputation for learning, thanks to the encouragement he received from his mother Theodota, who made sure he was closely acquainted with such classics as Homer's *Iliad*. He served emperors as a scribe and as a judge, and in 1047 was then honored by Emperor Constantine IX Monomachos as "consul (*hypatos*) of the philosophers," a title that aptly combines the political with Psellos' main intellectual interest. But in Byzantium no one stayed in favor forever, and Psellos would duly find himself packed off to a monastery, which is when he took the name "Michael." He endured the ascetic life there for only a year. A contemporary poem satirizes his inability to commit himself to chastity by comparing him to the famously lustful god Zeus, in what has been seen as a dig at his fascination for pagan learning.[2]

That commitment to pagan thought is evident from his multifaceted literary output, which has been preserved for us in astounding abundance: almost 1,800 manuscripts of his works survive today.[3] Along with the *Chronographia*, they include many letters, rhetorical showpieces like funeral orations, theological treatises, and philosophical writings. Among the latter we have a commentary on a logical text by Aristotle (*On Interpretation*), and a work that gathers together philosophical wisdom from many sources to answer a range of questions, often known by the Latin title *De omnifaria doctrina* (in Greek *Didaskalia pantodapê*). From this we can see that Psellos was to some extent continuing trends in the previous intellectual life of Byzantium. The presentation of philosophical nuggets in *De omnifaria doctrina* has an obvious forerunner in the work of John of Damascus, Photius, and other compilers. One can easily imagine the bibliophile Photius saying, as Psellos did to his patron Constantine Monomachos, "I came into the world for books and am in constant conversation with them."[4] Likewise, his choice to comment on Aristotle's logic fits with widespread interest in that field of philosophical endeavor going right back to late antiquity.

Indeed, Psellos' efforts were often directed towards what the Latin Christians called the *trivium*; that is, the arts of grammar, rhetoric, and dialectic or logic. This was not in a university setting. Nothing quite like the universities of Latin Christendom existed in Constantinople, though palace schools were established there. This was done already in the ninth century by the caesar Bardas, with Leo the Mathematician being given a chair for philosophy.[5] Psellos, though, seems to have taught grammar and rhetoric on an informal and independent basis, and compared the resulting group to a chorus with its leader.[6] This was not atypical. Psellos boasted that he was "a lone philosopher in an age without philosophy," but we know from his own letters that he had teachers as well as students, and we know too of other intellectuals in his day with an interest in such disciplines as logic and rhetoric.[7] Those letters of Psellos also reveal that the relations between teachers and students were politically significant. We find him offering his disciples patronage, recommending them to other aristocrats, and in general warming to the role of head boy in an old boys' network.

All this—including the reluctant entrance into the monastic life—might make Psellos sound like a Byzantine version of Peter Abelard, who worked in France only a few generations later. But unlike Abelard, Psellos reserved his greatest admiration for pagan Neoplatonists, not Aristotle and the logical tradition. In an often cited passage from his *Chronographia* (6.38), he gives us a brief intellectual autobiography:

> I came to Plotinus, Porphyry and Iamblichus, after which I progressed to the most admirable Proclus, as if arriving in a great haven, where I sought all science and accuracy of thoughts. After this, intending to ascend to first philosophy and to be initiated to pure science, I took up first the knowledge of incorporeals in what is called mathematics, which have an intermediate rank between the nature that concerns bodies and the thought that is free of relation to bodies.[8]

Actually, that threefold classification of sciences into physics, mathematics, and metaphysics or first philosophy, with the three disciplines corresponding to three types of being, does go back ultimately to Aristotle (*Metaphysics* 1026a13–19). But it's still clear from the passage that Psellos is most enthusiastic about Platonism. Strikingly it is Proclus who receives particular praise—Psellos elsewhere calls him second only to Plato—despite Proclus' flagrant paganism, something not nearly so prominent in some other late ancient Platonists like Plotinus.

Here we come to a crucial question, or even *the* crucial question, about Psellos' philosophy. What was his attitude towards non-Christian Hellenic culture generally, and towards the pagan elements of ancient philosophy in particular? It is not easy to give an answer, in part because it is hard to know which parts of Psellos' vast corpus of writings record his considered, personal views. Sometimes, as when he responds to a request for a philosophical treatment of the soul, he quite openly says that he is simply going to collect the views of other authors.[9] Even in this sort of case, though, his choice of material may seem to imply approval. Indeed, it has been said that Psellos "quotes what he agrees with and tends to leave under silence statements with which he disagrees."[10] Others think that a philosophical compilation like *De omnifaria doctrina* is unreliable as a guide to his true convictions, and thus point us towards his theological writings.[11] The most radical view has been put forth by Anthony Kaldellis, who wrote a study of the *Chronographia* arguing that Psellos cloaked his true, essentially anti-Christian, sentiments in all his writings, betraying them only with hints and indirect allusions. But this interpretation is difficult to square with Psellos' writings on theology, and Kaldellis is often forced to resort to the expedient of insisting that Psellos means the exact opposite of what he says.[12]

In fact, it seems clear that Psellos was both a sincere Christian theologian and a devotee of classical learning who was fascinated by pagan philosophy. His solution to this tension was to present Hellenic materials in a positive light, while also distancing himself from them. We see this in a letter he wrote to his colleague John Xiphilinos, who was given a chair of rhetoric the same year that Psellos was honored as "consul of the philosophers"; Psellos would later write a funeral oration for him. In the letter, Psellos takes umbrage at Xiphilinos' calling him a "follower of

Plato." On the one hand, Psellos is glad to style himself as a "Platonic philosopher," but he rejects the implication that he is thereby departing from orthodox religious belief. Allegory can be a useful tool for finding the truth in Hellenic sources, and Psellos takes this approach to the *Iliad* and *Odyssey* (just as the Neoplatonists had done before him). When Homer speaks of Zeus and the other gods, we should take this to refer to the one God of Christianity surrounded by the angels, while Troy's seizing of the beautiful Helen symbolizes foolish attachment to the things of this world.[13]

Psellos says that it would obviously be "madness" to expect anyone to abandon Christianity in favor of pagan wisdom, yet the Christian should nonetheless "take cognizance (*eidesin echete*)" of Hellenic thinkers "and if they somehow stand a chance of helping you towards the truth, then make use of them."[14] Confirmation of this can be found in Psellos' commentary on the *Chaldean Oracles*. Of unknown authorship, this late ancient body of writings was seen by Neoplatonists as a work of divine inspiration. Its paganism could hardly be denied, and Psellos makes no effort to do so in his commentary, which draws on a lost commentary to the work by Proclus. Instead, Psellos presents the pagan teachings one by one and remarks on the compatibility of each with the Christian truth.[15] He is not afraid to label certain ideas in the *Oracles* and even in Proclus as "ridiculous," for example the originally Platonic notion that the whole universe has a single soul.[16] He is also forthright in his rejection of astrology and beliefs in the efficacy of magical items like amulets, though he is clearly interested in the occult aspects of pagan culture and writes a work about demons that will be read avidly by Marsilio Ficino (see Chapter 52 below).

Conversely, Psellos is not afraid to trumpet agreement between Christianity and paganism when he can find it. He remarks that Plato was not far off the truth and "in an alien guise mystically discourses on our theology." In a discussion of the possibility of receiving a revelation from God, he points out that pagans had similar ideas: "do you see how the strongest part of the Greeks agree with us, despite disagreeing on the words? For what we name Holy Spirit, they call 'intellect as a whole' and 'intellect from outside'."[17] That last phrase, "intellect from outside (*nous thurathen*)," is a favorite philosophical borrowing of Psellos'. He takes it from Aristotle's zoological works (*On the Generation of Animals* 736b28–9), where it is remarked that intellect comes into the animal "from outside," and that "it alone is divine" because intellectual reasoning involves no physical process. For Psellos this is an anticipation of the Christian idea that God, and in particular the Holy Spirit, can bestow knowledge on humans.

This sort of help is needed, because God is in Himself inaccessible to the human mind. He appears to us only through His workings in the world and most perfectly in the "gifts of the Spirit." Around the time Psellos was writing, monastic writers like Symeon the New Theologian and his student Niketas Stethatos were urging that extreme asceticism was the best way to receive such gifts.[18] The path to God lay through wailing, gnashing of teeth, mortification of the flesh, and other activities that don't sound like much fun. Now, Psellos actually owned some monasteries. Yet he was little impressed by many of the supposedly holy men of his day, seeing them as hypocrites.[19] He was also unsparing in his criticism of emperors who lavished money on the church, seeing this too as hypocrisy: true piety lies within and is not demonstrated by spending projects. And as events at court would force him to discover, the monastic life was not for Psellos. In a letter to a friend he wrote, "I am a human being, a soul bound to a body. Therefore I take pleasure in both ideas and sensations. If someone places his soul above the body, he is both happy and blessed, but I would be content even if I lived half for the body." And in another letter, to a judge: "I am partly divine while living in a body. So I do not like to be completely earthbound nor am I convinced by those who compel us to soar beyond nature."[20] He then adds that his favorite proverb is "avoid extremes." His attitude towards Christian asceticism, then, is not unlike his attitude towards pagan philosophy: admiring, but also taking critical distance.

To put the point in the terms of ancient ethics, Psellos' more rigorous contemporaries urged their fellow Christians to achieve the state of *apatheia*; that is, freedom from all bodily passion and desire. Psellos was content with the more modest goal of moderating the passions (*metriopatheia*). This brings us full circle to the question of what it means for a philosopher to be involved in political life. For Psellos "political" virtue lies in the middle between a bodily life devoted to pleasure and a "divine" life that separates the soul from body as much as possible, and consists in pure contemplation.[21] Such contemplation can never reach true fulfillment in this life since, as just mentioned, God is ungraspable. This teaching is one that Psellos could find in both the Greek fathers and in Neoplatonists like Proclus, who put the First Principle beyond the world of intellect. Psellos thus imagines a supra-rational state in which the mind "drinks from the river in silence," an allusion to the tale of Christ's suffering.[22]

Despite such enthusiastic, even mystical, remarks, in his own life Psellos was content with mere political virtue. His approach to ethics was a realistic one, committed to virtue and aspiring to divinity, yet in the end not demanding too much. This is well illustrated by his attitude towards the monk Elias, who features in a number of Psellos' letters. Psellos expected this man to be a paragon of self-restraint, and was taken aback when Elias turned out to be a fun-loving chap with a good line in amusing anecdotes about brothels.[23] Psellos cannot help enjoying his company and after Elias' death, he expresses the hope that this entertainingly naughty monk may find a place in the afterlife between heaven and hell. Psellos applies a similarly forgiving standard to the rulers of his day. Thus Basil II, the earliest emperor covered in the *Chronographia*, is revealed as an admirable character even though he was corrupted by exposure to the pressures of political life, and Constantine Monomachos is praised for his personality even though he wasn't a very successful emperor. In general, Psellos seems to have thought that it is unreasonable to expect an emperor to be both exemplary in virtue and effective in political rule. He did not set unreasonably high standards for himself, and was happy to extend a tolerant attitude towards others. Unfortunately, as we're about to see, the emperors did not always return the favor.

7

HOOKED ON CLASSICS ITALOS AND THE DEBATE OVER PAGAN LEARNING

Suppose you meet someone at a party who recommends a new restaurant that has just opened in your neighborhood. You make a mental note to go there next time you get a chance. As your chat continues, this same party guest begins to argue that the 1969 moon landing was faked by the government. In addition to excusing yourself to go freshen your drink, you would probably also tear up that mental note about the restaurant. This might be a mistake, given that partisans of wacky conspiracy theories are probably able to appreciate good food just as well as the rest of us. Yet it's almost irresistible to downgrade the value of testimony in this way. We want to take advice from people who are reliable, and when someone makes a dramatic lapse in judgment, we are apt to dismiss that person's other beliefs.

Which raises the question: why would the Byzantines have been interested in anything that pagan philosophers had to say? As deeply committed Christians, they were convinced that Plato, Aristotle, and other Hellenic thinkers were wrong about the most important beliefs of all. They failed to understand the true nature of God and knew nothing of the salvation offered by Christ. So why treat them as philosophical authorities, having their works laboriously copied out by hand and made the subject of extensive study and commentary? Why not start from scratch, or rather, consult only the late ancient church fathers whose works offered an acceptably Christian basis for doing philosophy and theology?

The same dilemma confronted thinkers of Latin Christendom, and to some extent the solutions devised there were also echoed in Byzantium. One strategy was to compartmentalize: Aristotle may not have understood God properly, but he was reliable on logic and natural philosophy. This would be rather like discovering that the moon landing conspiracy theorist happens to be a respected food critic, which would encourage you to take that advice about the restaurant seriously after all. Another strategy was to give the Hellenic thinkers credit for achieving everything, or almost everything, that can be achieved with natural powers of reasoning. Being deprived of revelation, they were hardly at fault for being ignorant of Christ or the Trinity. Occasionally pagans were even credited with having discerned something of God's Trinitarian nature using nothing but their natural wit. In an anticipation of the twelfth-century School of Chartres, Michael Psellos proposed that Plato's *Timaeus* gestures at a threefold divine source of all things.[1]

There were also special reasons for the Byzantines to be open to pagan literature. A great premium was placed on stylistically excellent Greek such as could be found in Plato's dialogues. This is certainly a big part of the explanation for the choice to preserve and transmit Greek philosophy and other literature, but it obviously implies no attachment to the ideas found in the texts. Indeed, one modern-day scholar has rather grumpily remarked that this was "an age of uncreative erudition, sterile good taste," when "form was more important than content."[2] Yet there was another factor at play. The works of those church fathers explicitly instructed a Christian readership to make use of the so-called "outside" philosophy. Particularly important here were the three theologians we call the Cappadocians: the two brothers Basil of Caesarea and Gregory of Nyssa, along with Gregory of Nazianzus.[3] In one representative passage Basil wrote that it is good to start one's studies with pagan material, because "our eyes must first get used to seeing the brilliance of the sun when it is reflected on the water and then look at the real light." Even if the Hellenic material is false this will do no harm, since the Christian truth will look all the better alongside it.[4] In a work of advice for Christian youth, Basil encouraged them to approach pagan literature the way that bees gather nectar: "they do not come to all the flowers indiscriminately, nor do they try to carry away whatever they happen upon, rather they take only what is serviceable for their work, and leave the rest alone."[5]

As this suggests, the Greek fathers were not recommending the indiscriminate use of non-Christian authors. To the contrary, they warned that the application of logic to the exalted matters of theology can lead astray, and they accused some of their opponents of falling into just this trap. Their stance was, then, a version of the compartmentalization strategy already mentioned. Pagan material is helpful for certain topics, but always to be used with caution and while having in mind the superiority of Christian truth.[6] In applying this strategy to Aristotle, especially his logic and natural philosophy, the fathers were in a way echoing the approach of late ancient pagan Neoplatonists. They had likewise seen Aristotle's works as a good introduction to philosophy, something for students to read before graduating to higher truths—though for them, the higher truths were to be found in the works of Plato rather than the Bible.

The church fathers could also be moved to harsh criticism of even the greatestpagan thinkers. Gregory of Nazianzus wrote in one passage, "strike against . . . Aristotle's uncharitable providence, his artificiality, his perishable arguments about the soul and the humanity of his doctrines!"[7] This is just the flip side of the compartmentalization strategy. Where Aristotle strayed into matters beyond his ken, he was unreliable, even pernicious, and Gregory was not afraid to say so. All of which left the Byzantines to perform a delicate balancing act, as they sought to apply Hellenic philosophy in support of Christian theology, while making sure never to endorse philosophy where it might come into conflict with that theology. Each intellectual had to decide where to draw this line, in full knowledge that they might live to regret drawing the line in the wrong place.

We already found (Chapter 5) that the bibliophile and scholiast Arethas, a student of Photius, was charged with impious teachings in the year 900, and that this may have had something to do with his literary tastes. But the most notorious case of persecution against philosophy in Byzantium involved John Italos, who was put on trial in 1082. He was forced publicly to denounce his own teachings, or at least certain teachings that he had supposedly adopted. We can read the list of anathematized positions in the *Synodikon*, an authoritative document setting out orthodox belief. This anathema was in fact the first addition to the *Synodikon* made since the defeat of iconoclasm.[8] The list makes explicit mention of the pagan tradition and its excessive use, referring to "those who offer courses on Hellenic subjects and do not teach these subjects solely for the sake of education, but follow the vain opinions of the Hellenes and believe in them as being true, and thus, considering them to be correct, induce others to follow them."[9]

The document also sets out specific doctrines that were found objectionable: "anathema upon those who of their own accord invent an account of our creation along with other myths, who accept the Platonic Forms as true, who say that matter possesses independent substance and is shaped by the Forms, who openly question the power of the Creator to bring all things from non-existence to existence."[10] Alongside these characteristically philosophical points, Italos was also deemed to have fallen into a range of heresies on theological matters, including Arianism and Sabellianism.[11] The accusations thrown at him were almost absurd in their inconsistency. He supposedly went too far by saying that icons should be worshiped, and not only venerated, yet he was also denounced as an iconoclast. In a letter that has come down to us, Italos unsurprisingly complains that his words were twisted to create a false impression of unorthodoxy. In due course the ban on him was apparently lifted. His name was lastingly associated with an undue attachment to Hellenic culture, though, as we can see from a legendary anecdote about his death, which has Italos leaping suicidally from a cliff while shouting "Receive me, Poseidon!"[12]

Who then was John Italos, to cause so much fuss? As his name indicates, he was an Italian, who came to Constantinople as a young man and became a student of Michael Psellos. One of the more informative texts about Italos is an encomium written about him by Psellos, who saw Italos as his intellectual son and Italos' own students as his intellectual grandchildren. Psellos admits that Italos, who after all was a non-native user of Greek, was no great stylist, but he made up for that with his acute mind. To quote from Psellos, "for the inattentive listener his discourse is distasteful—it merely consists of syllogistic theses . . . He does not entice with style nor does he attract with sweetness, but he conquers and subdues his listener with the content of his arguments."[13] And he was indeed an argumentative character, who would get into heated debates with Psellos' other students. A less favorable report about Italos is found in the *Alexiad* of Anna Komnene. She complains about his awkward Greek and equally awkward temperament, but even she grudgingly admits that he was outstanding in logic.

It's no wonder that Anna is unfriendly towards Italos, because it was her father Alexios Komnenos who was emperor when Italos was put on trial. Much speculation has been devoted to the motivations behind this act of persecution.[14] One factor may have been Italos' origins, since at this time there was a Norman invasion from Italy threatening the Byzantine position.[15] Italos was also sufficiently prominent that it was worth making an example of him. Both Italos and Psellos addressed some of their works to members of the powerful Doukas family, including the recent emperor Michael VII. Another factor may have been that the new emperor Alexios was a military man bent on humbling the civil aristocracy, the class to which men like Psellos and Italos belonged. In light of such factors scholars tend to agree that this was a show trial with largely political motivations, and that the charges had little or no basis in Italos' genuine teachings. Certainly this imperial intervention in the intellectual affairs of the capital does not seem to have been intended to promote any one approach to pagan philosophy. As Michele Trizio has written, the charge sheet was "directed more towards a set of generic philosophical standpoints . . . than towards undermining one school of ancient philosophy, such as Neoplatonism, in favor of another."[16]

Indeed, when we turn to Italos' actual writings we find that he was pretty far from being a radical Aristotelian, Platonist, or supporter of potentially heretical views. Regarding some of his productions, the worst you can say is that they are entirely derivative. A preserved commentary by Italos on parts of Aristotle's *Topics* proves to be made up of nearly verbatim quotations from a much earlier commentary by

Alexander of Aphrodisias.[17] Rather more interesting are the short treatises he wrote for patrons and students on a variety of philosophical topics. In one treatise Italos takes up the problem of universals, a mainstay of philosophical reflection in Byzantium just as in late antiquity and Latin Christendom. His remarks here make an interesting contrast to those of Photius, who in a short treatise of his own was critical of Aristotle's treatment of universals.[18]

Photius complained that in the *Categories* Aristotle recognizes universals as a kind of "substance," which is, however, "secondary" in comparison to the concrete, particular substances we encounter in everyday life. Thus the species *giraffe* is, for Aristotle, a second-class substance, whereas the particular giraffe Hiawatha is a sterling example of a primary substance. Photius objects that on this Aristotelian view two very different sorts of thing—universals and particulars—are being jammed together into a single class of entity, both dignified with the title of "substance." Besides, Aristotle himself recognizes that something is either a substance or not; substantiality does not admit of degrees. So how can Aristotle speak of substances that are more and less primary? Instead, Photius argues, we should adopt the understanding of substance we find in the Cappadocian fathers. According to their terminology, which often features in discussions of Christology, "substance (*ousia*)" is the same as "nature (*physis*)." It should be identified with the species kind that belongs to each particular thing, for instance *giraffe* or *human*.

In comparison to Photius, Italos is much more inclined to follow the lead of pagan Greek philosophy. Taking up a classificatory scheme found in late ancient commentaries on Aristotle, Italos recognizes three kinds of universal or common natures, namely those "before the many," "in the many," and "after the many." The universals "before the many" are paradigms in the mind of God, the models used in divine creation. The universals "after the many" are human ideas. We form them in our own minds by abstracting a general notion from our encounters with many particular instances of a given kind. As for the natures that are "in the many," Italos says that these are actually particular and individual (*merika, atoma*). By this he probably means that outside God's mind and human minds, there is no such thing as *giraffe* apart from individual giraffes, the actual ones that lope across the savannah and nibble leaves off trees.

While none of this is radically new, it does show Italos' familiarity with the late ancient tradition and his willingness to adopt a broadly Neoplatonic metaphysics. Particularly significant is his insistence on universals that are divine ideas. Ultimately it is these paradigms that the philosopher wishes to know, and in knowing them we can ourselves become divine.[19] Italos also applied a Neoplatonic approach when discussing classical Greek literature. We have comments from him on some lines from Homer's *Odyssey* which speak of two "gates" through which our dreams pass, one of horn and one of ivory.[20] For Italos this refers to the way that our dreams have their origin in either the intelligible or the sensory realm, with our imaginative powers in the middle receiving messages from both sides. He rejects a different reading that glosses the passage in terms of diet—that is, the way that the foods we eat affect the dreams we have—deeming this interpretation "low class (*demodes*)."

But we should not leap to the assumption that Italos' accusers had a point after all, that he (and possibly Psellos) were happy to follow the Neoplatonists wherever they might lead. He was forthright in rejecting standard Platonic doctrines such as the existence of the World Soul, an animating principle that makes the entire cosmos into a single organism. And in some of his treatises, he surveys pagan philosophical views on a given topic expressly for the purpose of rejecting those views. Two good examples are short treatises by Italos on matter and on nature.[21] They argue that, going by classical literature, we might easily conclude that neither matter nor nature can exist, because the pagan discussions of both topics are rife with contradictions. Echoing what we just saw in Photius, Italos says that we should prefer the patristic view of nature as "that which embraces the individuals (*to ton atomon periektikon*)." This is the "nature" that is common to many things, like *giraffe* or *human*.

As for matter, Italos attacks an idea found in Plotinus that was very influential in Latin Christendom, thanks to its adoption by Augustine. According to this account, matter is the source of evil or even identical with evil. Italos thinks that another Neoplatonist, namely Proclus, was right to criticize this theory. After all, matter is part of the divine creation, so it cannot be intrinsically evil; rather it should turn back towards or "revert upon" its source, and strive for goodness. On the other hand, Italos isn't happy with Proclus' theory of matter either. For Proclus matter is simple, because it underlies all form and differentiation. Yet he also thinks that matter is furthest away from the One that is the source of all things, so it should be not simple, but multiple and differentiated to the highest degree. In his treatise on matter, Italos' objectives seem to be entirely critical. He is content to set up a dialectical refutation of the Hellenic theories, hardly what we'd expect from a man who was anathematized for blindly following "the vain opinions of the Hellenes."

If we ask ourselves why Italos singled out this topic of matter for special attention, we may suspect that it had something to do with his rejection of another notorious thesis of pagan philosophy: that the world has always existed and will continue to exist for ever. Italos denied this, in part on the grounds that in an everlasting world there could never be a resurrection of bodies, since the available matter would always be in use.[22] His stance on the eternity question fits well with his rejection of real universals outside the mind, too. Italos considers and rejects an argument according to which universals are indestructible, so there must always be a universe in which they are instantiated. His answer is simply that real things are always particular. So there are no permanent universals or forms out there at all, never mind permanent universals that demand a permanent universe to house them.

These treatises by Italos hardly represent a sustained attempt to set out a personal philosophy or system, or even to take a stance one way or another on the validity of pagan thought. But they do suggest that he was not a particularly radical thinker. His keen interest in pagan literature and philosophy was tempered at least by prudent caution, and to all appearances by a sincere conviction that the doctrines of Aristotle and the Platonists needed to be corrected in light of Christian belief. Of course, he was not as severe with the pagans as some of his contemporaries, for instance Niketas Stethatos, who wrote that all right thinking is guided by the Holy Spirit and who polemicized against those who "teach matters different from what the divinely inspired Fathers teach."[23] Then too Italos was identifiable as something like a "professional" philosopher, a man who devoted his energies to the exposition and teaching of the Hellenic legacy rather than to, say, the Bible. This may help to explain why he was politically vulnerable. But he was hardly alone in pursuing philosophy as an intellectual speciality. As we'll be seeing (Chapter 11), his harsh critic Anna Komnene was herself deeply involved in the promotion of that same Hellenic legacy, and she supported a group of scholars who produced commentaries on Aristotle. The fact that John Italos in particular was anathematized may show simply that he occupied the right place intellectually speaking, but at the wrong time politically speaking.

8

PURPLE PROSE
BYZANTINE POLITICAL PHILOSOPHY

Maybe you've seen an old sketch from the American TV show *Saturday Night Live*, in which customers to a diner are rudely made to understand that they can't have anything other than a cheeseburger and Pepsi. Given that the skit is set in a Greek diner, I have always assumed it was meant as a satire of political life in the Byzantine empire. There the menu of options was similarly limited to one choice: absolute rule by a single man, or occasionally woman. For this reason scholars have made rather discouraging remarks along the following lines: "Byzantium did not produce any *original* political theory, nor did it trouble itself to discuss *rival* theories and the nature of the Empire"; "perhaps the most striking feature of middle Byzantine political culture is the paucity of political theory: the dearth of treatises on government and of philosophical discussions about the ideal constitution and the function of the state."[1] As in that Greek diner, there was only one possible order, namely untrammeled imperial power.

And this despite the fact that Byzantine intellectuals were well aware of other ways of structuring society. A standard class assignment for students of rhetoric was to write an essay about the relative merits of the three classically recognized "constitutions," namely monarchy, aristocracy, and democracy.[2] Monarchy was the preferred option, on the grounds that a single authority is needed to ensure a stable and harmonious state. Another kind of authority encouraged this way of thinking: the intellectual authority of Plato, whose *Republic* was an influential text. The elite of Constantinople warmed to his vision of a completely just society ruled by philosopher kings and queens, and accepted his critique of the other constitutions as defective.

This ideology of the single, wise, virtuous ruler is evident from a number of sources, including the showpiece speeches written in praise of various emperors as a display of rhetorical brilliance leavened with judicious flattery. Already among the pagans of late antiquity, rhetorician-philosophers like Themistius had pushed the idea further than Plato had done. In one speech he compared the *basileus* or emperor to Zeus, arguing that the virtuous ruler on earth exercises a sovereignty like that of the father of the Gods. Eusebius echoed the theme in his speech in praise of Constantine the Great, the ruler responsible for the Christianizing of the empire. As one scholar has written, this became the basis for a political theory that "went almost unchallenged in its essentials for over 1000 years."[3]

Moving past late antiquity into the early Byzantine period, we have a pair of interesting texts on political philosophy written under Justinian I. Both fall into the genre called "mirrors for princes," works aimed at rulers giving advice on how best to carry out the duties of their office. The Byzantines will produce several more texts along these lines and later on in this book we'll discuss famous examples from Renaissance Europe, notably Machiavelli's *The Prince*. One of the two texts from the time of Justinian is an anonymous work *On Political Science*, known only from a single manuscript and Photius' summary of the work. The other is an influential and widely diffused treatise by a deacon named Agapetus.[4] His "mirror" was even translated into English in 1564 in a version dedicated to Mary, queen of Scots.

In these writings the influence of Plato's *Republic* and other philosophical sources is palpable. Agapetus is not content to commend Justinian for his godlike virtue, but praises him as a philosopher king, writing, "in philosophizing you were deemed worthy of kingship, and in being king you have not left philosophy. For the love of wisdom makes philosophy, and the beginning of wisdom is the fear of God, which you cherish throughout in your heart."[5] Notice here the Christianizing of the very idea of philosophy, something we've seen already in John of Damascus. As for the anonymous author, he too shows knowledge of Plato and the ideal of the philosopher king, but also Aristotle and even Cicero's Latin political treatise, likewise titled the *Republic*.

This author does seem to be critical of some of the more radical ideas in Plato's original *Republic*, such as the common sharing of children among members of the elite guardian class. But Dominic O'Meara has argued that this may simply be because the anonymous author sees it as an arrangement that could be adopted only in an ideal society, not in real life.[6] That would be similar to the way such proposals were handled by the pagan Neoplatonist Proclus. Our anonymous political theorist also betrays a Neoplatonic mindset when he describes kingly authority flowing down through the ranks of society, the way that divine providence emanates through the cosmos. This idea appears frequently in Byzantine literature on the emperor, especially in the form of a metaphor that compares him to a sun shining benevolently on all his citizens. The metaphor was made concrete in a court ceremony called the *prokypsis*, in which the emperor would emerge onto a lighted stage like the rising sun.[7] In the same vein, a treatise written under Constantine VII

Porphyrogennetos compared the imperial court itself to the cosmos, because of its harmonious and hierarchical arrangement.[8]

What exactly were the virtues possessed by the ideal emperor? In theory, all of them, since he was meant to be an image of God's goodness. But particular emphasis was laid upon the four cardinal virtues identified in Plato's *Republic*, namely courage, temperance, wisdom, and above all justice. Also distinctive of the emperor was a trait called *philanthropia*, which has a somewhat more capacious meaning than our cognate term "philanthropy," as the Greek term just means "love of humankind." So, even though *philanthropia* did show itself as material generosity shown by the emperor to his subjects, which is close to "philanthropy" in our sense, it could also include such things as merciful restraint in punishing the guilty. Such idealistic sentiments run right through Byzantine history and were still being expressed in a work on the emperor written in the thirteenth century by Nikephoros Blemmydes.

Some few authors inclined more towards hard-nosed realism. I mentioned earlier that in his work of imperial portraiture, the *Chronographia*, Michael Psellos seems to recognize that a successful emperor will sometimes have to be less than virtuous. This is clear from his occasional remarks on the role of emotion in good governance.[9] He certainly believes that emperors can fail when they are too vulnerable to emotion and desire; for him Constantine VIII was a good illustration. Yet Psellos also says that anger, when justified, can be useful and praiseworthy, something clear from his description of yet another Constantine (in Byzantium there's always another Constantine), namely Constantine IX Monomachos. Mirrors for princes also recognize that rulers may have to get their hands dirty, morally speaking, and accordingly take up the question whether an emperor has to do penance for his official actions.[10] Rather than answering, as one might have expected, that a good emperor is virtuous and therefore has nothing to repent, a distinction is made between the emperor as a private person and as a public official. This would make it possible for him to, say, impose the death sentence on someone who deserves it, while keeping a clean conscience as an individual Christian, despite the commandment not to kill.[11]

Of course, it's hardly a shock that works written for the emperor himself would offer the emperor absolution for his own morally dubious actions. But mirrors for princes and speeches of praise also sought to influence the emperors and bring them to a more merciful and ethical style of rule. As Dimiter Angelov has written, "The personal concerns and agendas of the orators . . . were supposed to remain hidden below the glittering surface of laudatory discourse,"[12] but these authors and speechmakers certainly had their own axes to grind. Emphasizing the emperor's generosity and advising leniency in taxation makes quite a bit of sense when you yourself might be in line for gifts at court, or a visit from the tax collector. At a less self-interested level, praise for righteous rulership could go hand in hand with warnings against wicked rulership.

Another of the running themes in Byzantine political writing is therefore the contrast between the good ruler and the tyrant.[13] A true king rules for the good of his subjects rather than his own good. To use an analogy found in the first book of Plato's *Republic* and repeated in the anonymous treatise from the time of Justinian, the ruler is like a shepherd whose occupation requires him to look to the good of his flock. Just as there is an art of shepherding for achieving that end, so the goal of "political science" is to help the citizens of the state to flourish. Again this is fairly predictable, and again it can still be found much later in authors like Blemmydes. But we may not have expected to hear from Theophylact, a student of Michael Psellos, that tyrants differ from true kings in that they seize power by force rather than assuming their office through the consent of the people.[14] Didn't men don the purple robes of the emperor precisely by seizing power, or by inheriting the throne from family members who had done so? Yes, but even usurpers usually made a show of having the people acclaim their support, so that popular consent was in principle included within imperial ideology.

Another way to conceptualize tyranny was as defiance of the laws, or just arbitrary changing of the laws. Here we come to a question that was rather unresolved among the Byzantines themselves. On the one hand the emperor was seen as a "living law," a formulation that appears in the corpus of laws compiled under Justinian. On the other hand, in those same documents we find the rule, "let the general laws apply to the emperor." In keeping with the latter idea intellectuals sometimes encouraged, if not demanded, that emperors govern within the law. Photius is an example.[15] In an introduction to a law code he wrote during the reign of Basil I, he stresses that kings should obey legal guidelines and also allow a degree of autonomy to the patriarch of Constantinople. Yet it was also seen as a right of the emperor to promulgate laws. Indeed, this is part of what distinguished imperial power from other forms of power. Then too, departing from the letter of the law could be praiseworthy. Remember what we said about "philanthropy": a benevolent emperor might refrain from imposing a justly deserved penalty. That too would be "breaking the law," albeit in a way no one would describe as tyranny.

All this concerns standing laws laid down by previous emperors or inherited from antiquity. But there was another source of hypothetical constraint in the form of what Aristotle called "natural" justice. A commentary written on Aristotle's *Politics* by Michael of Ephesus contrasts natural to artificial, or "political," justice and follows Aristotle in saying that what is naturally just applies to all humans at all times and places.[16] This is fairly close to the Latin medieval concept of "natural law," and is inspired by the same passages in Aristotle. A typical example of an artificial, or non-natural, law would be that the British drive on the left while in most countries you drive on the right. Michael gives the far less typical example that incestuous sexual relationships are not—I repeat, *not*—against nature. His rationale here may be that the first generation of humans after Adam and Eve would necessarily have propagated through incest between brother and sister, and this could hardly have been against God's plan. Michael holds that what is truly just by nature is recognized as such by everyone, which undermines the moral relativism he associates with "sophists." To the objection that some people do in fact violate what is supposedly just by nature, which shows that not everyone values justice, he gives the question-begging response that such people don't count because they are wicked. Their judgment is skewed, like sick people who don't find naturally sweet-tasting things to be sweet.

I mentioned the patriarch of Constantinople just now, but should say a bit more about the relationship between the emperor and religious life. Medieval Latin Christendom was beset by a long-running antagonism between the church and the secular powers.[17] The Byzantines sought, not always successfully, to avoid that kind of tension. The emperor was crowned by the patriarch and smooth collaboration between the two was seen as essential to the health of the empire. Already Eusebius credited Constantine with uniting secular and religious authority in his single person, and this combination was seen as a distinctive feature of the emperor's office in later Byzantine history. So his influence extended over religious affairs to no small extent, with the decisions of church councils ratified by the emperor and rulers such as Justinian getting deeply involved in the making and enforcing of orthodoxy. Iconoclasm, and the subsequent restoration of the icons, displayed the potential for imperial interference in Christian ritual and belief. Remember that some of the most revealing iconoclast documents to survive today were originally published in the name of the emperor Constantine V. Yet that same controversy shows us that political power could not constrain religious conscience. A man like John of Damascus was hardly going to give up the icons just because the emperor told him to. He even wrote that as a matter of principle, he could not be "persuaded that the church is governed by imperial edicts."[18]

As John of Damascus' own life story shows, the emperor never had effective authority over all Christendom, however unwelcome that fact may have been at Constantinople. For starters, there were the lands that had belonged to the Western Roman empire in antiquity. Despite a long-standing foothold in southern Italy, these largely fell outside the control of the emperor. Then there were those places and communities that were under his nominal control, but in practice had their own local rulers. These rulers were not, in the normal course of affairs, allowed to style themselves as *basileus*. Nor, as already mentioned, could they promulgate laws. The carefully chosen wording of diplomatic documents emphasizes the supremacy of Constantinople over client peoples like the Russians, Hungarians, and Petchenegs.[19] Yet local rulers had an annoying habit of acting as if they were something other than inferior, provincial lieutenants. Just as the Byzantines were more than a little disquieted when Charlemagne provocatively began to style himself emperor in 812, it was a blow to the dignity of the court of Constantinople when Symeon, the ruler of Bulgaria, got himself proclaimed "emperor" of his people in 913.

Yet a third position was occupied by Eastern Christians who did not recognize the so-called "orthodox" teachings established at the council of Chalcedon. An interesting book by Philip Wood investigates the political dimension of a culture we've already examined, namely Syrian Christianity.[20] One work from this milieu written in the sixth century tells the story of the Roman emperor Julian, who temporarily restored paganism as the official state religion. Since Julian is obviously a villain from the Christian point of view, the story forms a kind of reverse of the texts written in praise of the virtue and piety of Byzantine emperors—like a funhouse mirror for princes. Julian's lust and impiety are brought into sharp relief by descriptions of contemporary Christian saints and his pious successor Jovian, who pointedly refuses to accept the imperial crown until he is acclaimed by good Christians. Other works from Syria, especially hagiographies (tales about the lives of saints), praise the holy and ascetic leaders of the Miaphysite community and show how God's displeasure with Chalcedonian Christianity has manifested in natural disasters like plagues. That by the way is another typical feature of Byzantine political ideology. Epidemics, earthquakes, and also military failures were routinely understood as signs that God was withdrawing His support for an emperor, which could encourage usurpers to make a bid for power.

Speaking of disasters, let's conclude this chapter with a few remarks about how political thought developed after the catastrophic fall of Constantinople to the crusaders in 1204.[21] Imperial ideology and ritual survived to some extent in the smaller states that were spun off from the fallen capital, especially the court at Nicaea. Eastern rule then resumed at Constantinople after the capital was retaken by the Palaiologan dynasty in 1261. The sorts of political writing I've been discussing continued to be produced for the Nicaean and Palaiologan courts, right down to the last Byzantine emperor who was called (of course) Constantine XI Palaiologos. The intellectual John Argyropoulos wrote an oration in his honor, falling into the genre of mirrors for princes.

But it wasn't purely business as usual. A particularly interesting author in this period was Theodore II Laskaris, himself a ruler. He reigned in Nicaea from 1254 to 1258 and wrote treatises expressing his personal political philosophy.[22] He was critical of the way that Byzantine political life was dominated by family connections, something that had become especially prevalent during the earlier Komnenoi dynasty. For Theodore, the imperial elite and indeed society as a whole should be held together by friendship (*philia*), not kinship. Here he was drawing on Aristotle's *Nicomachean Ethics*, which identified three ways that friendship can arise: two people might be friendly to one another because they enjoy each other's company; or because they find each other useful; or in the best case, out of admiration for one another's character. Aristotle also thought that a perfect friendship presupposed equality between the two friends. Theodore ignored that bit, in order to propose that the emperor is the ultimate friend. Of course, no one is more useful or a more reliable source of pleasure, given the resources at his disposal. And we already know that any emperor worthy of the title has a virtuous and admirable character. For Laskaris it is virtue and not aristocratic blood that makes someone truly noble and fit to rule.

As the Byzantines steadily lost power and territory in this later period, other theorists proposed alternatives for shoring up imperial legitimacy and stability. Writing around 1300, Manuel Moschopoulos put forward a sophisticated theory of political development according to which political institutions emerge from a chaotic state of nature, through a kind of contract between the people and the ruler. That sounds like a breathtaking anticipation of Thomas Hobbes, but it is not entirely original with Moschopoulos, since it is another idea one can find in Plato's *Republic*. More innovative was Moschopoulos' point that a monarchy based only on this contract will always be unstable, because of infighting among the subjects. The citizens must be brought into harmony, and the only power that can establish true harmony is the authority of God, which no one can hope to escape. So the most binding political arrangement is loyalty to the emperor secured through a sacred oath sworn before God.

Yet another noteworthy text from this period was written by a member of the royal family, Theodore Palaiologos, not to be confused with the aforementioned Theodore II Laskaris. The Greek version of this treatise is lost, and in fact we know it only through a medieval French translation of a Latin version. Not exactly the ideal way to access Theodore's ideas. Having lived as a young man in Italy, he was apparently impressed by the way that rulers there took advice from a council of advisors; in the French translation this is actually called a *parlement*. So in this work, called *On the Rule of the Prince*, Theodore argues that good governance requires the monarch to be open to such advice. He criticizes certain Byzantine rulers, including the Palaiologan emperor Andronikos II, for failing to pay attention to their counselors.

In the final analysis, then, Byzantine political theorists were like restaurant patrons who happily accept cheeseburgers as the only item on the menu, but tactfully suggest that the cook should make sure the burgers are well done and have only the best toppings. Monarchial rule was indeed taken as a fact of life and as the best form of constitution. But emperors were constantly reminded that this form of rule could succeed only through divine favor, personal virtue, and a generous, friendly, and open-minded attitude from the emperor towards his subjects, or at least his elite advisors. Also, being named Constantine wouldn't hurt.

9

THE ELEMENTS OF STYLE RHETORIC IN BYZANTIUM

When was the last time you had to speak in public? Plenty of people find it a stressful experience, hence the popular advice that you should soothe your nerves by imagining that the audience are clad in nothing but underwear. I've never really understood that, myself. I don't know how I'd react if I walked into a lecture hall and found a hundred people waiting for me in their underwear, but I doubt it would be to relax and think, "Okay, I got this." More helpful, to my mind, would be a set of rules you could follow, a list of foolproof techniques for winning over any audience, no matter how large. Apparently the Byzantines agreed. They set great store by manuals of rhetorical instruction that had been written in antiquity by now largely forgotten authors, such as Hermogenes and Dionysius of Halicarnassus. These works were part of the Byzantine educational curriculum, so their terminology and conceptual tools were familiar to a wide swath of the Byzantine elite. The men who wrote those speeches of praise in honor of various emperors could have told you, evoking the classificatory schemes found in Hermogenes, what type of address they were giving, what style they were adopting in any given passage, and which rules lay behind the eloquence of every single sentence.

This presupposed a lot of training, and from an early age. Students began with "grammar," where one first of all learned basic literacy and then moved on to the study of classical texts.[1] Students would read about thirty lines of Homer's *Iliad* each day, this monument of pagan Greek literature having retained its centrality even in a medieval Christian culture. Michael Psellos claims that as a boy, he was made to memorize the entire epic and be prepared to explain every turn of phrase, as well as the overall structure of the work. Next the young scholars would move on to other antique authors, like Sophocles and Aristophanes. As we already know, the dialogues of Plato were also admired as models of good Greek. Ideas gleaned from the rhetorical textbooks found their way into the teaching of all these texts. Marginal comments or "scholia" made in Byzantine manuscripts of Homer explain what sort of rhetoric is being deployed by characters in the poem, highlighting the features of each speech that make it particularly appropriate for its context. They are also compared to the works of ancient rhetoricians like Demosthenes or Isocrates.

For the most part it was stylistic perfection that concerned the Byzantine teachers and students. That concern was embodied by new textbooks on "figures and tropes," in which it was explained why apparent flaws or solecisms found in literary classics are in fact acceptable.[2] We might think of how English-speaking kids are at first taught not to leave prepositions hanging, and to not under any circumstances split an infinitive, though in due course they will learn that such departures from the norm can be rhetorically effective. Alongside an obsession with the niceties of composition and grammar, though, we do also find recognition of the political and moral dimension of rhetoric. A recent study of scholia on Homer points out that they "commend the use of rhetoric as a tool for correct political behavior and civic concord."[3] Even attempts to define rhetoric gesture towards its role in political life. An attempted definition of rhetoric as an art of persuasion on all topics was deemed too general, because rhetoric is really about persuasion in specifically *political* contexts. In this respect rhetoric is unlike dialectic, an art of argumentation that really does apply to any subject matter whatsoever.[4]

Here we are brought back to a central confrontation of classical philosophy, between the ancient sophists and their greatest critic, Plato.[5] Plato was appalled by the fact that sophists like Gorgias did indeed boast of their ability to induce any belief on any topic in any audience. Against the seductions of sophistry, Plato championed the discipline of dialectic, the only route to certain knowledge rather than mere persuasion. Rhetoric, he argued in the dialogue named after Gorgias, is no true art or science but a mere "knack" for pleasing an audience, something he compares to making delicious pastries rather than nourishing, medically balanced meals. Yet, like an almond croissant, the charms of rhetoric were hard for the ancients to resist. In the third century AD, the so-called "Second Sophistic" saw a resurgence of rhetorical artistry, and rhetoric survived as a standard part of the liberal arts curriculum in both Latin and Greek Christianity.

These tensions are visible in a body of texts well known to the Byzantines: the writings of the three Cappadocian Fathers. A friend of Gregory of Nyssa once accused him of choosing rhetoric over Christian piety. When he responded by asking, "was I not a Christian while practicing rhetoric?" he received the answer, "not to the extent that befits you."[6] Gregory himself tells us that his brother Basil had to be dissuaded from a commitment to rhetoric by their saintly philosopher sister Macrina, and Gregory also contrasts Macrina's ascetic "philosophy" to worldly rhetoric in his hagiographical biography of her.[7] And we've already seen how Gregory's brother Basil advised the Christian youth to enjoy the delights of classical pagan writing selectively, like bees gathering nectar. Readers of the Cappadocians thus got a rather mixed message, especially given that their writings were themselves outstanding achievements of Greek style. Gregory of Nazianzus in particular was held up as both a great theologian and a great, perhaps even the greatest, rhetorician of the Greek language.

In the early Byzantine period, pious fears about rhetoric seem to have weighed more heavily than the enticements of eloquence. Between Procopius in the sixth century and the tenth century, we find no author styling himself as a "rhetorician."[8] Better to engage in "philosophy" according to the definition of that term we found in John of Damascus: the love of wisdom, meaning ultimately the love of God. But things changed in the eleventh century, when Psellos and other authors like John Doxapatres initiated something we might fairly call a "Third Sophistic."[9] By the first half of the twelfth century it is possible to find Michael Italikos (not to be confused with John Italos) blaming Plato for his unjustified attack on the art of eloquence, and saying that he finds philosophy "quite lacking in comparison to rhetoric."[10] Several generations earlier, John Sikeliotes had written a commentary on the rhetoric of Hermogenes, and in it explained the importance of mastering rhetorical improvisation. We never know when we may be called upon to give an oration, he says, so we must hone our technique and have pre-prepared bits of speech memorized, lest we "bring shame on the reputation we bear from being called rhetors and philosophers." Indeed, Sikeliotes adds, without his proficiency in rhetoric he would be "unworthy to bear the name and fame of philosophy."[11]

For the notion that philosophy and rhetoric are ideal partners rather than rivals, and for the use of rhetoric as a path to fame and reputation, we must return to Michael Psellos.[12] He occasionally shows signs that rhetoric is a less exalted pursuit than philosophy, just as he recognizes that the concerns of the soul trump those of the body. But, much as he is content to live "only half for the body" (as we saw in Chapter 6), Psellos cannot help but devote himself to both eloquence and wisdom. He proclaims that he mixes in his soul, "as if in a mixing bowl," both philosophy and rhetoric, and writes to a student in praise of this combined ambition (160):

> Just as philosophical concepts are inaccessible to rhetors, so too rhetorical twists and subtleties are, as it were, unapproachable to philosophers. I wanted you to come to know both abilities well so that philosophical meaning would be dressed in rhetorical diction and your form of discourse would be beautiful in its entirety, with respect to both visible and intelligible beauty.

But there were practical, as well as aesthetic, benefits to be had from mastering rhetoric. In the competitive world of eleventh-century Constantinople, brilliant speechmaking could be a crucial tool for advancement and a way of defeating rivals. As Stratis Papaioannou has put it in his book on Psellos' use of rhetoric, "his mastery of discourse was the main asset that he brought to the struggle for preferment."[13]

In his *Chronographia,* Psellos gives us a vivid sense of just how powerful, and politically profitable, the effects could be. In the midst of what Papaioannou calls a "disturbingly self-confident praise of his own rhetorical nature,"[14] Psellos speaks of the enthusiasm his rhetoric provoked in Constantine IX Monomachos. Upon hearing these speeches, the emperor was "like a man possessed" and nearly moved to shower kisses on Psellos. For an ironic confirmation of the way Psellos presents himself here, we can look to a twelfth-century satirical work called the *Timarion.*[15] It pokes fun at both Psellos and his student John Italos, both of whom are imagined attempting to take seats alongside the great figures of Hellenic philosophy. The treatment of the unfortunate Italos is particularly harsh, though amusing. The philosophers roughly reject his advances (Diogenes the Cynic even bites him), and Italos stumbles away crying out, "o syllogism, o sophism, where are you now that I need you?" Psellos, by contrast, is treated politely by the ancient philosophers but not actually offered a seat. He winds up sitting among so-called "rhetorician sophists," a collection of figures from the Second Sophistic.

Actually, though, it is not these late ancient "sophists" who draw most admiration from the real Psellos. Among pagan authors, he follows the Neoplatonists in extolling the style of Plato in particular. But his all-time favorite is the aforementioned Gregory Nazianzus. As Psellos puts it, Gregory is for Christian readers what the orator Demosthenes is "for the opposing side, that is, the pagans" (112). Gregory combines the best features of Demosthenes and other Hellenic authors like Plato, managing to bring together what seem to be contrary qualities like brevity and expansiveness, solemnity and beauty, or the political and the philosophical (136, 143), so that his language represents "the ultimate summit of excellence in seriousness as well as charming Graces" (106). Or as Psellos says in a longer passage (114):

> Gregory's discourse is not an aggregate of foreign and disparate elements. Rather, it is both uniform in nature, like the rose rising from the womb of the earth along with its natural color, and also multiform, if one were able to divide the color (as if it were some kind of mixture) into different tones and shades.

The idea that rhetorical speech should be varied, multiform, or many-colored (*poikilon*) in fact runs throughout Psellos' descriptions of well-executed rhetoric. Its effect upon Psellos is not unlike Psellos' own effect on his emperor patron. Wandering in the "rose garden" of Gregory's words, Psellos says, "I adore my ravisher and cover him with kisses" (127).

It is no accident that Psellos turns to this sort of erotic language when he wants to describe the effects of eloquence. Where other Christian authors—including Gregory himself, actually—sought to justify beautiful language by arguing that it can turn us towards higher ends, Psellos is unafraid to say that pleasant speech is wonderful in part because it brings pleasure.[16] Nor is he embarrassed by the thing that so bothered Plato, the power of rhetoric to persuade an audience to believe in falsehoods, or at best to believe in truths but for the wrong reason. To the contrary, Psellos admires the myths of the ancients because the compelling falsehoods of their fictional tales are such a powerful way of conveying deeper truths.[17] On the other hand, he does think that in a political context the best speech is the one that marshals persuasive speech for the sake of truth. In his *Chronographia* he writes:

> The pride [of rhetoric] is not persuasive falsehood merely, or speaking on both sides of an issue . . . it blossoms with philosophical thoughts and finely spoken turns of phrase, and its audience is willingly drawn in by both . . . Its greatness is to be neither confusing nor unclear but to fit itself to the circumstances and the facts.[18]

Of course, Psellos would say that Gregory, as a perfect wordsmith, uses rhetoric like this too. It's telling that he singles out Gregory on this basis, and not just on the grounds he is a Christian theologian, whereas the other great authors were pagans. Of course, Gregory wins on substance, but he could also carry the day on style alone.

It's pretty obvious that Gregory did not reach these heights simply by reading rule books like the ones written by Hermogenes. His rhetoric is true artistry, not a kind of paint-by-numbers. To use analogies Psellos is fond of, crafting language is like sculpting a statue or finishing a gemstone. No one can simply tell you how to write so well, and in fact Psellos himself cannot understand how Gregory managed it. This is a matter that lies beyond rational explanation (134). Ultimately, the best comparison for Gregory is not any other ancient author but a divine creator like the craftsman god of Plato's *Timaeus* (136). Here we should recall the idea that various, opposed elements should be blended into a single harmonious speech, since it is of course precisely this sort of assembly of disparate elements that a god must achieve in fashioning the cosmos. With his exaltation of godlike, genius authors, his admiration for the beauty of language as such, and his analysis of the features that make for perfect eloquence, Psellos is obviously going far beyond the rather dry and technical conception of rhetoric we find in the textbooks and their commentaries. He seems to be articulating a conception of rhetoric that is closer to what we might call "literature."[19]

At this point, there's a question that may be nagging at you: what about Aristotle? He wrote a treatise called the *Rhetoric*, after all; did it play no role in the discussions of the topic offered by Psellos and others? It was certainly available to the Byzantines, but does not seem to have been much read until around the turn of the twelfth century. This was no doubt in part because Hermogenes and other authors of rhetorical textbooks were perceived to have covered the subject adequately. Also, Aristotle is not always an easy or pleasant read.[20] Psellos contrasts the difficulty of reading him with the wonderful clarity of Gregory Nazianzus, and adds that Aristotle was making himself hard to understand on purpose (146).

In due course Aristotle would find readers who were ready for the challenge. The circle of scholars gathered together by Anna Komnene for the purpose of producing commentaries on the Aristotelian corpus produced not one, but two surviving commentaries on the *Rhetoric* (and we have fragments of a further commentary and a paraphrase summary).[21] We can't be sure why, but one reason must have been the simple fact that they had no late ancient commentaries on this work, as they did for many other Aristotelian treatises. For these commentators, one anonymous and the other identified as Stephanus Skylitzes, Aristotle's *Rhetoric* is one of his works on logic. This may seem strange, but it is an idea that goes back to late antiquity. The idea was that, after treatises setting out the elements of logical proof, and then in the *Prior* and *Posterior Analytics* articulating a theory of syllogisms in general and demonstrative proofs in particular, Aristotle wanted to say something about proofs that are defective in various ways.

The treatise that most obviously pursues this task is the *Sophistical Refutations*, which analyzes the kind of bad arguments deliberately used by those paradox-mongers the sophists. (And since we're interested in language at the moment, can I just point out that there are very few things that have mongers? Just cheese, fish, and paradoxes, which coincidentally would all have been on offer at a dinner hosted by Michael Psellos and John Italos.) Alongside sophistical arguments, Aristotle supposedly saw rhetorical speeches, dialectical arguments, and even tragedies as inferior ways to prove a point, hence his treatises *Rhetoric*, *Topics*, and *Poetics*. This is a rather unpersuasive attempt at systematizing Aristotle's writings, but it must be agreed that at least the *Topics* and *Rhetoric* do seem to have a relation to his more properly logical works. Whenever they can, the Byzantine commentators stress this feature of the *Rhetoric*, contrasting the merely persuasive discourse of the orator to the perhaps less persuasive, but in reality far more decisive, proofs offered by the philosopher who is proficient in the techniques of demonstration. It's a very different idea of rhetoric than we find in Psellos, who could be said to pursue a more classically "Platonic" project in which philosophy is combined with literature. This won't be the last time in our survey of Byzantine thought that we'll be contrasting Aristotelians and Platonists.

10

PAST MASTERS BYZANTINE HISTORIOGRAPHY

Regrets? I've had a few. And not too few to mention. I might start with that unnecessary second helping at dinner last night, and finish with every article of clothing I wore between the years 1977 and 1989. Frankly, this book series is also an inexhaustible source of potential regret. Many of the puns I've made, some of the puns I almost made and thought better of (well, that actually hasn't happened but it might at some point), and of course things I didn't cover but really should have covered, given the "without any gaps" mantra. At the top of this list would be Herodotus and Thucydides, towering intellectuals of ancient Greece whose approach to writing history could and really should have been part of the story of classical philosophy told in the first volume of the series. Their work has directly or indirectly influenced all later European historians, including historians of philosophy like me. I'm not going to fill that gap retrospectively here. But I am going to look at a few of the Byzantine historians who read Herodotus and Thucydides and carried on their legacy.

History writing is among Byzantium's greatest cultural achievements, and perhaps the genre of medieval Greek literature that is best studied in modern scholarship. Beginning in late antiquity, a series of intellectuals compiled and summarized the works of earlier historians, sometimes adding material of their own. The tradition goes down to the fall of Constantinople to the Ottomans and beyond, with Chalkokondyles, a student of the philosopher Plethon, writing a chronicle in the 1480s. Two central figures in the history of philosophy in Byzantium are actually better known as historians. There was of course Michael Psellos, whose Neoplatonic eyewitness historical treatise the *Chronographia* we've already had occasion to discuss. And there was Anna Komnene, sponsor of a philosophical circle and author of the *Alexiad*, a historical account of the reign of her father Alexios I Komnene.[1] We might also mention the later George Pachymeres, who worked on completing his teacher's treatise on Byzantine history, and also wrote about science and Aristotelian philosophy.

As with the shirts I wore growing up in the late 1970s, the pattern is too striking to be a coincidence. I have two explanations to offer—one that's rather speculative and one that's pretty obvious. The speculation is that history, like philosophy, offered independent-minded authors an opportunity for being creative and original. If you are writing on a previously unchronicled period of history you are positively required to break new ground, and this was the case with a number of Byzantine historians. They might first draw on, summarize, or simply repeat earlier histories but then add further material to take their story up to the recent past. This is what we have in the case of the *Epitome of Histories* by an author named Zonaras. Despite its title it is an enormous work, longer than any previous surviving historiographical treatise.[2] Contributing to the genre of "world histories" already devised in antiquity, Zonaras started his *Epitome* at the creation of the world and went all the way to the year 1118. For almost all of this he drew on earlier histories, in the process preserving much that would otherwise now be lost. But he did write his own account of the recent emperor Alexios Komnene, one far more critical than that of Alexios' daughter Anna.

Anna, by contrast, was no compiler. She tells us that in producing the *Alexiad* she drew on her own memories, court documents, and interviews conducted with eyewitnesses (especially for military engagements, which as a woman she could not have experienced first hand). The approach of Psellos was similar, in that he relied on his own personal impressions to present the series of imperial political portraits that makes up his *Chronographia*. In between Psellos and Anna Komnene there was Attaleiates, whose *History* was completed in 1079 and dedicated to the emperor Nikephoros III.[3] These were the three great historians of the middle Byzantine age, notable for an opinionated and personal style which has been called "subjective and individual."[4] We should probably give special credit to Psellos for inspiring the writing of history in this mode, because Attaleiates and Anna Komnene were both aware of his work. Anna drew on him extensively, citing Psellos in her *Alexiad* more often than she cited the Bible!

Another text that appears in her history more often than the Bible is Homer's *Iliad*.[5] Which brings me to the second, more obvious explanation for the link between philosophy and history. Both genres of writing were deeply engaged with the classical tradition by way of the study of rhetoric.[6] The practice of gathering together earlier historical materials may already have reminded you of those philosophical compilations by scholars like John of Damascus and Photius. Some histories, rather than repeating or condensing the work of earlier authors, transpose material from older histories to describe recent events, as when Thucydides' famous account of the plague in Athens was recycled (more than once) to describe epidemics in Constantinople.[7] Even when our historians are not regurgitating or repurposing classical sources, they take great pains to write like their much-admired antique forebears. This includes even the use of grammatical constructions that had fallen out of use in normal Byzantine Greek, for example the special "dual" ending used for talking about exactly two things. My favorite remark on this Byzantine habit comes from Warren Treadgold, who reports that Anna Komnene "quotes a popular jingle praising Alexius' ingenuity, but she carefully translates it into literary Greek in case an ancient Athenian should return from the dead to read it."[8]

Of course, one of the most profound effects of studying history, and for that matter the history of philosophy, is that it allows you to step out of your own time and inhabit a past worldview. The Byzantines' enthusiasm for classical culture put them in an excellent position to enjoy this benefit. A spectacular example is provided by several so-called "novels" written in the twelfth century, like Eustathios Makrembolites' *Hysmine and Hysminias* and Theodore Prodromos' *Rhodanthe and Dosikles*, which in some passages imitates Plato.[9] These novels are set in the archaic past, and the authors seem to revel in the pagan setting, Christian religious disapproval set aside for this fictional context. Something similar happens in the works of certain historians, whose study of the distant past has given them an appreciation for other, older ways of organizing society.

When discussing Byzantine political philosophy I said that the absolute monarchy embodied in imperial rule was uniformly taken as the ideal constitutional form. But we also saw that emperors liked to claim the support of the people, like the institutions of Rome before the transition to imperial rule. More generally, republican Rome could still cast a spell upon many Byzantines, something we see reflected in the historical chronicles.[10] Already in classical imperial Rome, many aristocrats pined for the days before monarchial rule—as well you might if you were in the senatorial class, since back then senators had had real power. This sentiment was still being expressed at the twilight of antiquity, as we can see from the bitter reflections of a historian named Zosimus, who lived in the sixth century. As a pagan, Zosimus blamed Christianity for the final decline of the Roman empire, but he thought things had already been going downhill before the Christians took over. For him the rot set in with the abandonment of republicanism under Augustus. With the new imperial system, the Romans effectively "threw dice for the hopes of all men through the risk of entrusting such a great empire to the energy and power of one man."[11]

In medieval Byzantium positive comments about the republic can be found in Psellos, and even Anna Komnene compares her emperor father to heroes of the republican period. But the most interesting case is Michael Attaleiates, who accords the people of Constantinople a significant and legitimate role to play in political life.[12] Whereas most Byzantine historians would describe popular uprisings strictly in terms of mob violence, Attaleiates recounts in rather approving terms how the people of Constantinople deposed the emperor Michael V in 1042. In another display of his remarkably detached perspective, Attaleiates is able to admire the moral character of non-Christians, even enemies of the empire.[13] In the eleventh century, a formidable threat to Byzantium had emerged in the shape of the Seljuk Turks, who were sometimes referred to anachronistically by our historians with classical names like "Persians," "Scythians," and even "Huns." Attaleiates commends their sultan for having a natural tendency to love his enemies, as Christians are commanded to do on religious grounds. Looking further back, he even argues that faithful devotion to *pagan* religion was key to the success of the Romans. Of course, it is best to be a devoted Christian, but in practical terms a committed pagan may outdo a half-hearted or hypocritical Christian. God sometimes gives the pagans victory because they do better at honoring justice than the Christians do.

Yet it would be a mistake to suppose that religious beliefs play no role in the Byzantine histories. The otherwise exceptional Attaleiates proves the rule. In his rather positive description of the way the people overthrew Michael V, he remarks that they were an "instrument of divine justice." Byzantine chroniclers were in general confident that the study of history reveals the workings of God's plan. Again, it's a tendency that can be traced back to antiquity. Alongside the classical histories and the "world histories" of the kind recreated by Zonaras, another model was provided by religiously oriented works like that written by the fourth-century bishop Eusebius. His *Ecclesiastical History* focused on the story of Christianity from the Apostles through to late antiquity, and the triumph of the new faith over paganism. This was not history as just one thing after another. Rather, world events were understood as the stages in God's plan for humankind.

Eusebius still respected the ground rules of traditional historical writing to some extent, as we can see from the fact that he never associates miracles with Constantine the Great, the first Christian emperor, in his *Ecclesiastical History*, despite speaking of such miracles in a separate *Life of Constantine*.[14] But once we get to the Byzantine historians, we frequently find miracles being invoked to explain military victories, while wonders and natural disasters are taken as having portentous and divinely intended meaning. An interesting case is found in the *History* of Attaleiates, with his account of an earthquake that struck in 1063.[15] He mentions a naturalistic theory of earthquakes endorsed by some philosophers, namely the building up of wind under the ground as the result of underground waterways. He allows that there may be something to this explanation, but insists that in this case the calamity was sent by divine providence "to restrain and control human urges," "not utterly to destroy humankind but turn it to a better path" (for more on earthquakes, see Chapter 45).

As we saw with Photius' report on a treatise about divine providence by the Neoplatonist Hierocles, Byzantine thinkers were fascinated by the tension between human freedom and God's ordaining of all things. This theme too appears in the historical chronicles. Back in the sixth century, an author named Theophylact approached the topic from both a philosophical and historiographical perspective. In addition to writing a historical treatise with an explicitly religious approach, he produced a dialogue on the question whether God predetermines how long each of us will live.[16] Theophylact tries to take a middle course, affirming that God does foreknow all that will happen including human actions, but insisting that God knows we will perform our actions freely.

Attaleiates' approach to the question is not unlike his attitude towards earthquakes: he is open to both natural and divine modes of explanation. He follows Psellos in emphasizing the moral character of individual rulers to explain their success or failure. Indeed, we just saw him doing that with the Seljuk sultan. Yet he is also happy to credit providence with giving victory to the Byzantines against their enemies.[17] Anna Komnene frequently mentions how God's benevolent protection helped her father. At one point she even asserts that divine power inspired his horse to leap to safety during a battle—characteristically, the very same sentence shows her classicizing sensibility, as she compares this horse to the winged Pegasus.[18] Her pious respect for providence apparently ran in the family, given that according to her, Alexios himself unfailingly credited his own successes to God's will.[19]

Was such faith in heavenly governance shaken when earthly governance failed altogether? To answer this question we can turn to the later historian Niketas Choniates, who reflected on the fall of Constantinople to the crusaders in 1204.[20] Like many of our historians, he inserted fictional speeches into his chronicle, this technique itself being another imitation of the ancient historians, and of course another sign that in Byzantium history writing was closely related to rhetoric. Niketas devises such a speech for his own former self, a despairing monologue he supposedly uttered upon seeing the fall of Constantinople. And what is it that especially prompts him to this lament? A true antiquarian, he dwells especially on the destruction of the capital's classical monuments.[21] Though Niketas had the misfortune to live through extraordinary times, he was in some respects a typical Byzantine historian. Like his predecessors, he saw himself as participating in an unbroken "chain" of scholars who built on each other's chronicles to tell the continuous story of the world. He was also highly classicizing, using a style so ornate that it prompted one medieval reader to scrawl a complaint about it in the margin of a manuscript of Niketas' work.[22] His explanation of the 1204 sack of Constantinople was also typical in its assumption that this disaster was a sign of

God's anger, brought on by human failure. He traces the decline back to Anna's family, the Komnenoi, and their foolish foreign policy. The recent emperor Alexios III, who reigned until 1203, drew Niketas' ire for having put the empire in such a weak condition that it was ripe for the despoiling it received at the hands of the Western Franks (who of course get an archaic nickname: Niketas calls them "Celts").

In one telling passage, Niketas both invokes providence and makes clear that it is possible for humans to act freely, indeed against God's will. It's also a remarkable passage for its general condemnation of Byzantine emperors. Niketas writes that these rulers "generally make war against Providence and are insolent to the Divinity, eviscerating and slaughtering like sacrificial animals every good man from the masses, simply so that they may be able to squander and dissipate the public goods by themselves in tranquility as their own ancestral inheritance, to treat free men like slaves."[23] Such outright criticism was nothing new. I've already mentioned that back in the twelfth century, Zonaras provided a far more critical assessment of Alexios I than we find in Anna Komnene's *Alexiad*. For Zonaras, Alexios was too focused on lining the pockets of his friends and family and not sufficiently attentive to the needs of the rest of his subjects—meaning, of course, other aristocrats who were not fortunate enough to be in the emperor's inner circle. As Zonaras put it, Alexios did not act like an ideal household manager (*oikonomos*) but like a master of slaves (*oikodespotes*). You might remember that about a century later, Theodore II Laskaris was still making this complaint about Alexios and his successors.

This kind of opinionated history writing was not to everyone's taste. Another middle Byzantine historian, John Skylitzes, complained in the introduction to his wholly derivative *Synopsis of Histories* that other historians were insufficiently "accurate."[24] Rather than just telling us the facts, they grind various axes, being either favorable or critical or just writing to please the sitting ruler. Comparing these wildly diverging accounts the reader is "plunged into dizziness and confusion." We've seen that Anna Komnene's history seems designed to give her father Alexios good press. She anticipated this complaint, arguing that it was perfectly possible for her to be fond of both her father and the truth.[25] But in another passage, she shows that she's aware of the conflict between writing a personal account and setting down a neutral historical record. Coming to tell of her father's death she writes, "my grief compels me to utter a lament over him; the law [or 'custom': *nomos*] of history, however, restrains me." As we'll see in the next chapter, such concerns were particularly pressing for Anna, a historian who was also, against the expectations of her readers, a woman.

11

QUEEN OF THE SCIENCES
ANNA KOMNENE AND HER CIRCLE

When I imagine the ideal workplace, I picture a group of industrious, committed collaborators engaged in an enterprise they deeply value, so much so that they would have been willing to do the same work for free. They willingly put in long hours, paying close attention to the smallest details. And the boss is a woman. This utopian scenario remains a rarity, yet it was realized almost a millennium ago in Byzantium. The happy workers were philosophers who devoted themselves to studying and completing the late ancient tradition of commentary on Aristotle. Their patron was Anna Komnene, a princess who had withdrawn from political life. After the death of her beloved father Alexios and the accession to the throne of her brother John, Anna dedicated herself to a life of scholarship. As we've just seen, she herself composed the *Alexiad*, an epic portrayal of Alexios' political and military exploits. She also gathered together a group of scholars who produced commentaries on Aristotle, especially texts that had not yet received commentaries earlier in the Greek tradition. They included Eustratios of Nicaea, who is praised in Anna's *Alexiad* (14.8) as learned in both scripture and pagan philosophy and rhetoric, and also Michael of Ephesus, the most accomplished Byzantine commentator on Aristotle. He did indeed work long hours, to the point that he ruined his eyesight reading by candlelight.

We owe that last detail to a funeral oration dedicated to Anna Komnene by another member of her circle named George Tornikes.[1] Speaking in praise of her devotion to learning, he tells us that Anna was following the example of her father with her support of scholarship, and that a goal of her circle was the production of exegetical works on so far uncommented treatises of Aristotle. Confirmation of this is provided by one of those commentaries. In the prologue to his commentary on the sixth book of Aristotle's *Nicomachean Ethics*, the aforementioned Eustratios alludes to a patron who is evidently Anna. Furthermore, Anna herself tells us of her acquaintance with pagan philosophy. When she announces herself as author of the *Alexiad* she says modestly that she is "not without some acquaintance with literature, having devoted the most earnest study to the Greek language, and being not un-practiced in rhetoric and having read thoroughly the treatises of Aristotle and the dialogues of Plato" (*Alexiad*, Preface). The *Alexiad* occasionally refers to Aristotle by name and also quotes him without naming him. I mentioned an example in the last chapter, where she said that as a historian, truth is even dearer to her than devotion to her father, so that she is willing to criticize him where appropriate (14.7). This is an evocation of Aristotle, who justified his refutation of Plato's theory about the Form of the Good, on the grounds that truth takes precedence over friendship (*Nicomachean Ethics* 1.6).

Of course, the *Alexiad* is a work of history, not philosophy, and it has been argued that Anna Komnene's grasp of Aristotle was in fact rather superficial.[2] Unfortunately we have no work from her on a specifically philosophical topic, which would have helped us to test this proposition. In his oration in her honor, Tornikes actually praises Anna for writing nothing apart from the *Alexiad*, since this shows her lack of unseemly ambition. But he also assures us that she was enthralled by pagan learning from an early age. Her parents did not approve of the study of such material, especially by girls, who are more easily corrupted than boys. But, like someone arming themselves against a possible ambush, Anna fortified her soul against the potentially insidious aspects of pagan thought. Tornikes describes her young infatuation with learning by switching from this masculinizing, military metaphor to an explicitly feminine one: "like a maiden who takes a furtive glance at her bridegroom through some chink, she had furtive meetings with her beloved grammar." Her wide reading, combined with critical distance, is also clear from a passage in the *Alexiad* itself, which touches on the topic of astrology. In what may be an implicit critique of her nephew Manuel, an emperor who was enthusiastic about astrology, Anna mentions that she acquired some knowledge of this art herself but only in order to refute its pretensions (6.7).[3]

Of course, we might be reluctant to take the word of Anna herself and her propagandist Tornikes as to her scholarly credentials. But the historian Zonaras, who was no great admirer of the Komnenos family, said that Anna "was engrossed by books and learned men, and spoke with them not superficially."[4] Besides, the *Alexiad* itself is ample evidence for Anna's intellectual attainments. It suggests a cultural, and also political, motive for her support of such scholarship as commentating on Aristotle. She championed Hellenic culture as a marker of Byzantium's superiority over the rival populations that surrounded them, whether Muslim or Western Christian.[5] For Anna, these were all "barbarians" lacking the sort of refinement displayed in fine Greek rhetoric or a mastery of Aristotelian logic. If Hellenic literature was a jewel in the crown of Byzantine supremacy, then it shone most brightly on the crowns of Anna's own family. As we've seen, she was at pains to stress her father's support for scholarship, and she praised her late husband Nikephoros Bryennios as both a great warrior and a fine scholar. Another member of Anna's circle, Theodore Prodromos, likewise spoke of Nikephoros' expertise in both philosophy and poetry.[6]

This brings us to a fundamental question concerning the *Alexiad*: did Anna Komnene really write it? No one doubts that she authored the text as we now have it, but it has been alleged that the work was mostly composed by Nikephoros before he died, with Anna just editing her husband's manuscript and adding a few personal touches.[7] A central reason for this suspicion is that the *Alexiad* is much concerned with military matters. Nikephoros was indeed an army man who could have drawn on his personal experiences in describing the battles fought under Alexios, whereas Anna, as a woman, would have been both physically and culturally removed from the scenes of battle. Furthermore, Anna herself tells us that she used a work by her husband in writing the *Alexiad*. But she also remarks that it was "half-finished and hastily put together" when he died (*Alexiad*, Preface). Furthermore, as already mentioned, she explains how she was able to assemble such a compelling account of Alexios' military exploits. She could draw on her own memories of discussions at court, and got further material by interviewing men who were present at various battles. Nor need we see the *Alexiad*'s focus on military affairs as a sign of male authorship. In fact, it fits squarely with Anna's classicizing interests, since the *Alexiad* is (as its title suggests) a kind of rewriting of Homer's war epic the *Iliad*, with her father in the lead role.[8]

Anna herself would probably not be surprised that later interpreters doubted her authorship in this way. As has been argued in a study of the *Alexiad* by Leonora Neville, Anna was well aware that readers might be disconcerted by a woman—even one "born in the purple"—daring to compose such an ambitious historical treatise. She carefully manipulates her own authorial persona, both disarming her potentially hostile audience and, more boldly, making various claims to authority. She tries to win them over by adopting what Neville calls "an exaggeratedly feminine persona of extreme emotionalism," especially in passages where she laments such events as the death of Alexios.[9] Her claim to be merely completing her husband's work might actually be another way of forestalling objections to her authorship. Yet she also boldly asserts her reliability as an author, for instance by underscoring her ability to suppress those same emotions of grief in order to carry on writing. A similar function is played by her claim to have conducted interviews and used court documents in writing the *Alexiad*, and by her assertion of scholarly prowess in fields as varied as philosophy, rhetoric, medicine, and astrology. Anna was a woman undertaking a project that would have been expected from a man, and she wrote her book accordingly. Neville explains her authorial strategies in the following terms: "Anna's repeated practice of breaking out of the proper boundaries of history, breaking out of a masculinized historian's voice, to speak and participate in the discourses her culture marked as feminized, only to point out and apologize for her transgression, focuses attention both on her essentially female nature, and her ability to transcend that nature."[10]

A strange feature of Byzantine misogyny, though one familiar from ancient Roman misogyny, is that men deemed women too weak and feeble-minded to do things like, say, writing epic historical works, while also fearing that power-hungry, scheming women could triumph over men in political affairs. It can feel like every highly placed woman of Rome was accused of poisoning a near relative. Similarly, Anna has gone down in history as a sinister conspirator who sought to put herself and her husband on the throne at the expense of her brother John. It was only when she failed to become a real queen that she settled for being a queen of the sciences. As evidence for this, modern scholars have pointed to the fact that John doesn't get great press in the *Alexiad*. Notably, he is absent from her description of the family gathered around the dying Alexios, because John has run off to the palace to take power. But we certainly find no outright character assassination directed towards him. In fact, we have to wait for Niketas Choniates, writing several decades after her death, for any hint in Byzantine sources that she schemed to seize power. A revisionist reading offered by admirers of Anna has sought to absolve her of any such underhandedness. But an alternative feminist interpretation of Anna's story could emphasize her supposed political ambition rather than denying it, seeing her attempted power grab as continuous with her confident self-presentation in the *Alexiad*.[11]

It's ironic that Anna Komnene's ethical character should be a matter of such debate, because she was responsible for a revival of interest in that greatest of works on this very topic: Aristotle's *Nicomachean Ethics*. Surprisingly it received no full commentary in antiquity, so it must have been high on the list of treatises to be dealt with in the completist project of her circle. The resulting commentary is perhaps the best illustration of their group enterprise, with different books of the *Ethics* assigned to different scholars. Michael of Ephesus and Eustratios both commented on some parts, while other books were handled by scholia and commentary by authors who remain anonymous. A partial commentary by the antique author Aspasius was also included in the manuscript tradition that has come down to us. This illustrates the fact that the circle drew on earlier exegetical material when they could. Michael of Ephesus' commentaries on the *Ethics* and on other Aristotelian treatises often integrated previous scholia, while also adding new material by Michael himself.[12]

As this suggests, Anna's circle was not merely completing the work of late antique philosophers, but also carrying on their intellectual agenda. This has been shown in studies of Eustratios' *Ethics* commentary, which have drawn attention to his use of Neoplatonic materials.[13] Eustratios is quite open about this, at one point begging the reader's indulgence for introducing so many apparent digressions into his commentary as he draws on authors who lived long after Aristotle. He has a particular taste for Proclus, who influences his idea that ultimate wisdom (*sophia*) is the grasp of the highest principles (*archikotera*), and that when we grasp these principles our limited human intellect is participating in an eternal, perfectly good intellect that permanently grasps all intelligible forms.

This doesn't sound very Aristotelian, and Eustratios knew it. One particularly interesting section of his commentary deals with a chapter where Aristotle refutes Plato's idea that there is a single Form of the Good, which makes other things good when they participate in it.[14] (This is in fact the chapter that occasioned Aristotle's comment that truth is to be honored even more than friendship.) Eustratios' first move in defending Plato is to turn him into a Neoplatonist. This version of Plato thinks that the Good is a first principle that produces all other things necessarily by its very nature, not by will, and that the other Forms are ideas in the mind of the divine craftsman. Faced with Aristotle's argument that things are "good" in many different ways, which cannot all be brought under one single idea, Eustratios replies that to the contrary, the arrangement of better and worse goods requires some greatest Good that provides a measure for them all. Other things receive goodness from it to a greater or lesser extent, simply because of their varying capacities to acquire perfection.

In this and other passages Eustratios develops the idea of paradigmatic Forms that serve as causes for the things that participate in them. He agrees with what he takes to be Aristotle's position that "universals" have no genuine reality, if we understand by "universal" a general concept that we abstract from the things we encounter. Thus elsewhere, in the theological context of discussing the natures of Christ, he notes that we do not worship Jesus' humanity because humanity as a general, universal notion is nothing at all. Nonetheless, Eustratios departs from Aristotle by positing Platonic Forms, which can also be called "universal (*katholou*)" in a different sense, meaning simply that they are each a single "whole (*holon*)" that stands over the many corresponding participants. The character of the Form—humanity, for instance—also exists immanently in various individuals, in this case the many humans. Using Neoplatonic terminology Eustratios calls the immanent form a whole "in the parts," whereas the paradigm in the divine mind is a whole "before the parts."

Eustratios concludes this defense of Plato with the caveat that he is not necessarily endorsing the theory of Forms himself, since opponents of that theory would no doubt find other ways to argue against it. But it is hard to avoid the suspicion that in approaching his task of commenting on Aristotle, Eustratios is a committed Platonist. This is not terribly surprising since he was a second-generation disciple of Michael Psellos, having studied under John Italos. Eustratios had disowned Italos by signing a letter rejecting his master's doctrines, which helps to explain how Anna Komnene (who was no admirer of Italos) could have accepted Eustratios into her circle of intimates. Eustratios was well placed during the reign of Alexios, but ran into trouble during a theological controversy and was ultimately, like Italos before him, put on trial for supposedly heretical views. One of the accusations against him has Eustratios claiming that in the Gospels, Christ gave arguments in an Aristotelian fashion (*sullogizetai aristotelikos*). While one scholar has commented that this "is more entertaining than philosophically significant,"[15] it is clear that Eustratios did put his philosophical skills to work in theological contexts. For instance he wrote a treatise defending the doctrine of Christ's two natures on the basis of "logical, physical, and theological arguments."

Eustratios' fellow commentator Michael offers something of a contrast. For one thing we know much less about his life: even the fact that he was from Ephesus is clear only from his reference to Heraclitus of Ephesus as a compatriot. More significantly, he was less Platonist and more Aristotelian. This is clear from his contribution to the group commentary on the *Ethics*. He displays familiarity with Neoplatonism but tends to take distance from Platonic views on such matters as the highest Good and the paradigmatic Forms.[16] Then too, Michael commented on a greater range of Aristotelian texts than any contemporary author. Aside from his work on the *Ethics*, he dealt with part of the *Metaphysics*, a collection of Aristotle's short psychological treatises (the so-called *Parva naturalia*), and, most remarkably, the works on animals. Like Albert the Great in the Latin sphere (but about a century earlier), Michael thus revived the study of Aristotle's zoology after this aspect of his scientific achievement had been almost completely ignored since Aristotle's own day.

The zoological commentaries provide us with a concrete example of Michael's willingness to favor Aristotelianism over Platonism. He apparently accepts Aristotle's theory that the father's seed is the sole source of form for the offspring.[17] To this he contrasts what he thinks is Plato's view on generation, which will sound rather strange to readers who know the dialogues better than Michael seems to. He thinks that Plato is a two-seed theorist, in other words that both father and mother are involved in shaping the embryo, and that the seed derives from the various organs of the parents. Thus the parents' heads provide little models for the head of the child, the parental feet indirectly generate the child's feet, and so on. Aristotle does describe a theory like this but does not identify its author; apparently Michael assumed Aristotle was talking about Plato. Michael rejects the "Platonic" theory, assuming instead that there are formative principles (*logoi*) in the paternal seed that actively cause the form of the gestating child. And in another sign of his fidelity to Aristotle, he holds that the heart and not the brain is the central organ of governance for the animal, a notion that had been abandoned by most philosophers after Galen's proof of the importance of the brain in the second century AD. This despite Michael's evident knowledge of medical theory, which emerges at various points in his writing.

The commentaries just discussed are not the only ones to derive from Anna Komnene's circle; you may remember the two devoted to Aristotle's *Rhetoric*, mentioned in Chapter 9. Nor were they the only ones written in Byzantium.[18] We have alluded to earlier commentaries on Aristotle by Michael Psellos and John Italos, and there were later commentators too. They included Leo Magentios, who some generations after Anna's circle made use of the commentaries produced by that circle. This shows that the Byzantine commentary tradition, despite being built upon late ancient exegesis, was continuous in its own right. Leo dealt with the full range of Aristotle's logical works; later still George Pachymeres commented on several treatises including the *Ethics*. We should also not forget the importance of epitomes and scholia devoted to the Aristotelian treatises, which were produced pretty well throughout Byzantine history. Some of this material would help readers of Latin to make their way through Aristotle. Eustratios is a good example, since his commentary on the *Ethics* was received among the Western scholastics. So there's a lot of material here, and modern-day scholars have not yet explored it fully. It used to be thought that the commentaries of late antiquity were dull, arid monuments of pedantry, but now a thriving branch of research is devoted to them. Perhaps a similar reappraisal is in store for Anna's collaborators, and the other Byzantine scholars who carried on the labors of ancient exegetes like Alexander of Aphrodisias, Philoponus, and Simplicius.

12

WISER THAN MEN GENDER IN BYZANTIUM

Anna Komnene was unique. No other Byzantine woman wrote a work with the scale and intellectual ambition of the *Alexiad*, and no other Byzantine woman played such a significant role in the interpretation of pagan philosophical literature. Yet Anna was also one example of a familiar type: the aristocratic woman close to, or at the center of, the circles of political power in Constantinople. The historical chronicles we've been discussing are full of information about royal women like Irene, Theodora, Zoe, and Eudokia, to the point where whole books have been devoted to the subject of Byzantine empresses.[1] Such historical reports can be combined with hagiographical accounts of holy women, with writings in which male Byzantine authors talk about women from their own families, and information about the life and reading habits of nuns in female monasteries. As a result there is plenty of material for learning about the situation of women in this culture, and the extent to which they could aspire to intellectual pursuits.

Anna's own writings are already revealing in this respect. We already know about her early efforts to gain an education, and the way she carefully curated her persona as a female author. Occasionally she refers to this quite explicitly. In one passage of her *Alexiad* she shies away from detailing a heretical movement, writing: "'modesty prevents me', as the beautiful Sappho says somewhere, for though a historian, I am also a woman . . . and the talk of the vulgar had better be passed over in silence" (15.9). Of course, it is entirely in character for her to quote, and tacitly compare herself to, a classical pagan author like Sappho. Similarly, Tornikes' oration in Anna's honor calls her "wiser than men" and compares her to the female Pythagorean sage Theano and the late ancient mathematician and pagan martyr Hypatia. Anna herself already compared her own mother to Theano in the *Alexiad*. She tells a famous anecdote about Theano, who was complimented on her shapely forearm and said, "yes, but it is not for the public." Anna then adds that her mother was so modest that she did not like showing her eyes either, or allowing anyone but intimates to hear her voice (12.3). As this passage illustrates, women were encouraged to be private and retiring individuals. Pale skin was admired in women but not in men. The latter should be out proving themselves on military campaign, whereas elite women should stay indoors and allow their servants to run all the errands, emerging from seclusion only for events like religious ceremonies.[2] When they did venture into public, upper-class women seem to have worn veils, which may be what Anna means when she says that her mother kept her eyes hidden away. A full veil could be worn as a show of piety, though a scarf framing the face was probably more common.[3]

Given this cultural context, it is remarkable that women did manage to hold political power, and unsurprising that men often grumbled about their doing so. The most famous case is the empress Irene,[4] who in 780 ascended to the throne as regent to her young son who was called, with grim inevitability, Constantine. Coins from the period depict her alongside her son but the image of family harmony was misleading. As Constantine grew older he pushed her aside but was then forced to share power with her again. Ultimately, and notoriously, she had him blinded in order to secure rule for herself. This may have encouraged the Western ruler Charlemagne to take the provocative step of adopting the title "emperor" for himself, the rationale being that, with a woman sitting on the throne in Constantinople, it was effectively vacant.

It's interesting to see how historians deal with such female rulers. The chronicler Theophanes accuses Irene of being seduced by wicked advisors into grasping after power, and says in this context that she was "deceived like a woman." Yet the same Theophanes admits that when Irene was ultimately deposed in favor of her finance minister, the social climber Nikephoros, the people of the city were angry and bewildered that God "had permitted a woman who had suffered like a martyr on behalf of the true faith to be ousted by a swineherd." Similarly mixed feelings were provoked by the sisters Zoe and Theodora. Michael Psellos admitted the legitimacy of their rule as offspring of a male emperor, but also voiced some disquiet at the spectacle of women ruling the empire, commenting that the "women's quarters were transformed into an imperial council chamber."[5]

It is of course these affluent women of the ruling and literary class who are best represented in our written sources.[6] You won't get any sense of the life of an Anatolian peasant woman from reading Anna Komnene or Psellos. Nor are texts produced in a monastic context liable to be informative. The famous monastery at Mount Athos not only stopped women from visiting the peninsula on which it was located, but kept only male animals so that the monks need not "defile their eyes with the sight of anything female."[7] Then too most women of the empire, and most men for that matter, would have been illiterate.[8] The ability to read had to be acquired from tutors, at an expense that would have been unaffordable for most, or in a religious context, particularly among those cloistered in religious institutions. Even in the latter case there was a distinction between "church" nuns and "laboring" nuns, with the former having an upper-class background and instructing their illiterate sisters.

The usual reading list was thoroughly Christian. A story about one of the most popular female saints, Thecla, has her miraculously granting literacy to another woman so that she can read the Bible. Even a royal woman like the twelfth-century "literary patroness" Irene Sevastokratorissa—perhaps the figure most comparable to Anna Komnene—was warned by male advisors not to concern herself with the potentially corrupting literature of the pagans.[9] Here we should recall the story of young Anna's taking precautions against the potential "ambush" laid by non-Christian texts. We should also make mention of one other famous female author from the Byzantine period, the poet and musical composer Cassia, widely admired for her religious hymns.[10] A nice anecdote has her standing up against misogyny: when a man remarked to her that evils came to humankind through a woman, namely Eve, she retorted that "it was through another woman that better things began," namely Mary.[11]

We can get more light on female literacy from a study by Claudia Rapp, who looked at how women used manuscripts in Byzantine history.[12] She confirms that female readers were often nuns, and that they were often reading hagiographies, that is, the life stories of saints. This genre of literature, which goes back to late antiquity, offered moral instruction to both men and women, or perhaps we should say "boys and girls" because this kind of text was often read by, or read out to, young readers. The saints were to be admired and imitated, and stories about miracles enlivened the tales. As we might expect, women readers were steered especially towards lives of female saints. There they could find both bad news and good news. True, they had been born with an inferior gender, but this did not prevent them from becoming moral exemplars. One hagiography explains that the good works of women are in fact more impressive than those of men, "for they have the lot of a weaker nature and yet they were not hindered by this at all to climb up to the summit of virtue, but they made the female [element] male through a virile mind and accomplished the same and even more than the men."[13]

It would be worth focusing on one female saint in particular, because of her importance in the history of philosophy: Macrina the Younger, sister of the Cappadocian church fathers Gregory of Nyssa and Basil of Caesarea. We know her especially from two works by her brother Gregory: his biography of her and a remarkable work called *On Soul and Resurrection*. Here Macrina is depicted on her death bed in dialogue with Gregory himself, calmly providing him with philosophical arguments for the immortality of the soul.[14] The setting is of course intended to remind us of Plato's *Phaedo*, with Macrina replacing Socrates as the philosopher facing bodily death and proving that it is not true death, even as intimates are giving in to their grief. This is highlighted by a passage at the beginning of the dialogue, in which Macrina is described as "reining in" Gregory's emotions like a skilled charioteer so that the two of them can have a rational discussion about the nature of the soul.

It goes almost without saying that this is an inversion of stereotypical gender roles. In an infamous passage at the start of the *Phaedo*, Plato describes how Socrates sent away his lamenting wife Xanthippe, so that he could spend his final moments in philosophical discourse with his male friends (60a). At the end of the dialogue, Socrates chastises these same friends for acting like women as they weep over his imminent demise (117d–e). Thanks in part to these passages, a typical way to present someone as a consummate philosopher was to show them unmoved in the face of their own death, or the death of family members. Just as typical was the assumption that women were, by nature, all but incapable of such self-restraint. We can see this from a number of surviving letters of consolation written in the Byzantine period.[15] Our bibliophile friend Photius wrote one of them to his brother, on the occasion of the death of his niece. He admits that he himself is distraught but encourages his brother "not to give way to lamentation, for men must set a good example to women . . . [and] not act like women." Similarly, his friend Nikolaos Mystikos wrote to the emperor Romanos I Lekapenos, when his wife Theodora died in 922. He offered the consoling thought that it was better that she should die than the emperor himself, since as a woman she would have been less equipped to deal with the grief.

By having his sister Macrina adopt the role of a perfectly rational philosopher, Gregory was therefore offering the most striking of role models to his readers, both male and female. We might assume that he was showing how even a woman could act in a properly masculine fashion. Certainly Byzantine women were sometimes praised for acting like men. A classic case would be so-called "transvestite nuns" like the third-century saint Eugenia, who disguised herself as a man to enter a monastery. A thirteenth-century account of her life has her say, "not wishing to be a woman but to preserve an immaculate virginity, I have steadfastly acted as a man . . . I have acted the part of a man by behaving with manliness, by boldly embracing the chastity which is alone in Christ."[16] But I think that Gregory was trying to say something slightly different by presenting his sister in this fashion. In the dialogue Macrina argues that the soul must be immortal because it is an image of God, and it is most of all an image of Him when it engages in pure reasoning. Furthermore God, as Gregory affirms in other works, has no gender. So by subduing her emotions and living in accordance with nothing but reason, Macrina was not necessarily acting like a man. Rather she was acting like God, and thus transcending gender altogether.[17] This was part of a philosophical project of attaining likeness to God insofar as is possible for humans, a goal named by Plato in one of his dialogues and embraced by Macrina in this Christian rewriting of the *Phaedo*.

These ideas, and in fact this very dialogue by Gregory of Nyssa, would have been on the mind of Michael Psellos when he wrote a rhetorical showpiece called *Encomium for his Mother*.[18] It was praised in magnificent terms by the twelfth-century scholar Gregory of Corinth, who judged it one of the four best speeches ever written. In the speech, Psellos describes his mother Theodote's extraordinary virtue and piety. He tells of how she valued scholarship, studying in secret as a young woman (3b) as Anna Komnene would later do, and then seeing to it that Psellos himself received the finest education possible (5c–d). Her character is praised in much the same terms that Psellos uses to praise good rhetoric. We saw him admiring the way that Gregory Nazianzus was able to combine contrary qualities in his writings. Likewise, Theodote's nobility consisted in her combining apparently opposite personality traits: she was both contemplative and given to action (4a), both humble and authoritative (7a), both gentle and stern in moral judgment (8c).

Psellos does have his culture's assumptions about the weakness of women, and so praises his mother by saying that she "knew nothing feminine, except what was decreed by nature; in all other respects she was strong and manly in soul" (7b). Psellos himself was different. In another of his writings, he spoke of himself as "female by nature," in the context of admitting how emotionally he reacted to the birth of his grandson.[19] None of that for his mother. Psellos describes how she greeted the death of Psellos' sister by "expounding at great length to [Psellos' father] about the passage to the better life" (16b), which looks to be an obvious reminiscence of Macrina. Theodote was also valiant in her war against the desires and demands of the body, eating so little that she became "like a shadow on a wooden board" and seemed almost dead (17c). Alluding to a famous remark about Plotinus, Psellos says that his mother seemed to be "ashamed of being in a body" (17b) and that she resisted the attempts of her family to get her to see to the needs of her body. On one occasion, she was almost persuaded to eat a fine meal but then gave it away to a destitute woman (22b). Psellos seems to have mixed feelings about his mother's asceticism, which he calls her "philosophy" (22a). He is unable to follow her example, and admits modestly that his "devotion to philosophy is limited to its cloak" (26a), though he goes on at the end of the encomium to describe his own philosophical inquiries. Here we have an unusually explicit contrast between the two meanings of "philosophy" in Byzantine culture. His mother was a "philosopher" because of her pious, ascetic way of life, whereas Psellos is a "philosopher" because of his book-learning and expertise in pagan intellectual literature.

Though Psellos would no doubt like to have the last word on this subject, we can't conclude a discussion of gender in Byzantium without saying something on the much-discussed topic of eunuchs.[20] You'll probably be aware that eunuchs were present at court and as servants in aristocratic society more generally. Eunuchs played a vital social role because they could serve and protect noble women with no danger of seducing, or at least impregnating, them. Also, since they could not have offspring they were considered unthreatening in political terms, effectively unable to seize power for themselves. Yet eunuchs could rise to great eminence. Some were generals or powerful officials, like Basil Lekapenos, son of an emperor and successful as a military leader.

Much of what we have observed regarding Byzantine attitudes towards women reappears, in exaggerated form, in remarks about eunuchs. They were thought to be given to greed and to bodily desires, desires they might be physically unable to satisfy. Often they were associated with homosexuality, a common assumption being that eunuchs enjoyed being the passive partner in male–male sex. Yet they were also resented for being quite literally "cut off" from other kinds of sexual activity, because they had achieved the virtue of chastity on the cheap. For this reason some churchmen condemned the practice of deliberately turning youngsters into eunuchs surgically, or even worse, castrating men who were past the age of puberty. Eunuchs who arose "naturally," through accident or disease, were more likely to be accepted. Sometimes presentations of their sexless condition were strikingly positive, as in texts where they are compared to or confused with angels. Yet even as they became a fixed part of the Byzantine ruling elite, or perhaps precisely for this reason, eunuchs were by and large subject to abuse and critique. A brutal aphorism from the twelfth century advised, "If you have a eunuch, kill him; if you haven't, buy one and kill him."[21]

Such hostility could be explained by a fascinating proposal, made by Kathryn Ringrose, to the effect that eunuchs constituted a "third gender." Despite being biologically male—that is, men in respect of their "sex"—they were perceived as occupying an ambiguous cultural middle ground between the male and female genders. Thus we find them being called "androgynous," "womanish," or "artificial women." As Ringrose writes, this "made their contemporaries uneasy because they were seen to move too readily between the worlds of men and women, between earthly sensuality and heavenly spirituality, between imperial presence and ordinary space, and between the church and the secular world."[22] Such uneasiness provoked abuse, but also at least one text which speaks out boldly in defense of eunuchs. It was written by Theophylact of Ohrid, who cunningly compared the condition of the eunuch to that of the monk. With their vows of chastity, monks were also refusing to employ their sexual organs in the way nature intended. Castration was simply a more radical step in the same direction, like cutting down an unwanted tree. Theophylact admitted that some eunuchs are wicked, devious, and debauched, but then again plenty of non-eunuchs are too, and moral judgment should concern the individual, not the group. One might argue that with this line of argument, Theophylact was merely asking his contemporaries to apply to eunuchs the sort of perspective normally taken on women. While inferior as a class to physically intact, or "bearded," men, on an individual basis they are frequently worthy of great admiration.

13

JUST MEASURES
LAW, MONEY, AND WAR IN BYZANTIUM

"The welfare of the state springs from two sources: weapons and laws." With these words, the sixth-century emperor Justinian put before his people the fruits of a remarkable undertaking. At his behest, a team of jurists led by the indefatigable Tribonian had gathered together centuries' worth of Roman law. The result was a legal codification in three parts, the *Digest, Codex,* and *Institutes,* followed later by so-called *Novels*; that is, new laws devised in Justinian's own reign. We've looked already at other works that were basically compilations or presentations of earlier material, like Photius' *Library* or the *Suda,* and hopefully we've learned to take such works of scholarship seriously. But none of them can match Justinian's legal corpus for influence. Written in Latin, it became the crucial source for Western medieval law when it was taken up by the jurists of twelfth-century Italy.[1] And it was crucial in the East too, effectively supplanting previous Roman law and setting down rules that would be invoked in courtrooms throughout Byzantine history.

This is exactly what Justinian had in mind. Any laws that failed to make it into his codification were rendered obsolete, effectively repealed by omission. This made his law code the point of reference for future generations of lawyers and judges. That had its downsides. We're talking here about a massive body of technical writing, and it was written in Latin, which was not the working language of the Eastern empire. No wonder then that future emperors commissioned further legal works in Greek: under the iconoclast Isaurian dynasty a selection of laws entitled the *Ecloga,* and under the Macedonian dynasty in the ninth century, a work called the *Eisagoge* or *Introduction* whose composition apparently involved the aforementioned Photius. Around 900 the emperor Leo VI, known as "Leo the Wise," issued his own laws. And there are many other examples of smaller-scale legislation being handed down by Byzantine emperors.

We should be struck, if not surprised, by the fact that all this lawmaking was done in the name of individual emperors. As we've seen (Chapter 8), it was a uniquely imperial prerogative to hand down new laws, a powerful expression of the emperor's supreme authority. Even if he was mostly in the business of reorganizing and reissuing earlier Roman juristic material, Justinian gave these old laws new force when they were uttered "through his mouth." This seems to have been a fundamentally secular project, but later emperors increasingly presented their legislating authority as an instrument of God's justice.[2] Law in general is a gift from God to humankind, which leads us to happiness by laying down guidelines for justice. It's in keeping with this that, as we also observed, the emperors were increasingly encouraged to see themselves as falling under the law rather than dispensing justice from a position above the laws, as Justinian had done. In the legal *Introduction*, Photius made this point by describing the emperor as one of no fewer than three fundamental sources of authority in the Christian community, the other two being the patriarch and the law itself. Quite likely he intended this as a political image of the Trinity.

We normally assume that judges need to follow precedent, but also that new laws overturn old laws. In theory this was also the case in Byzantium. In practice, though, the Justinianic corpus had such weighty authority that it was difficult to resist. We can see this from the legal writings promulgated under Leo the Wise, which are ambitious in tone and rhetoric but actually rather modest as an attempt to revise the existing law.[3] He sought to borrow some of the glamor of the legal productions that had put the "just" in Justinian, even going so far as to imitate him by putting out a collection called the *Basilica* (i.e. "imperial" laws), containing a *Digest*, *Codex*, and *Novels*. But this was not nearly so radical a project as its model. Leo reorganized but mostly retained the old laws, albeit now in Greek. One interesting idea we do find here, though, comes in Leo's statement that he is in many cases elevating custom to the status of law (*eis nomou prostaxin kai timen*). In other words, certain practices that have become widespread should be given a legal basis so that they can be properly enforced. Conversely, such customs as Leo thinks are not so wise will be overturned by depriving them of such enforcement.

All of this may give an impression of a rather conservative, even stagnant, legal worldview on the part of the Byzantines.[4] Which may not be such a bad thing. One man's stagnation is another's reassuring stability, and already in antiquity authors such as Plato (in his *Statesman*) had emphasized the importance of adhering to the laws laid down by earlier, wiser, legislators. Emperors who dared to innovate in matters of law were duly criticized in historical chronicles for ruling by arbitrary fiat rather than in accordance with the laws. This criticism was directed at Constantine X by the historian Attaleiates, for instance.[5] But we also need to remember that individual judges and rulers had considerable discretion in applying the laws, and that lawyers could exercise great ingenuity in their arguments.

As a contrast to the more rigorist attitude expressed by Attaleiates, we might mention Michael Psellos. Law was one of the many subjects he studied and taught, though its practical dimension seems to have bored him. He speaks rather dismissively in the *Encomium to his Mother* (§30c) about the way that practitioners of legal theory, which he calls "the science of the Italians," wind up dealing with tiresome cases where people have been gored by bulls or bitten by dogs. Elsewhere he praises emperors precisely for using good judgment instead of applying the laws, and writes letters appealing to correspondents to follow the incitements of friendship rather than legal niceties. When he himself writes in a legal context, as in an accusation directed against a patriarch on behalf of the emperor Isaac Komnenos, he mostly uses the tricks of a different trade, namely rhetoric.[6] This gives us an insight into how philosophers might think about the courtroom. Aristotle's *Rhetoric*, whose study would soon be revived thanks to Anna Komnene, investigates how the rhetorical art can be used in legal speechmaking, and despite Psellos' more formal legal training it is this approach that he carries on in his polemical writings.

So far I've been talking about laws rather generally; what were the laws actually about? The quick answer is that Justinian's laws were about everything: criminality, business, family relationships, and even religion. In the Latin West a contrast was made between canon and civil law, canon law applying to ecclesiastical affairs and civil law to the secular realm. That contrast existed in Byzantium too, but in both Christian cultures the line was a rather blurry one. The oldest works of canon law pre-date Justinian and remind us that Eastern Christianity is about more than what happened in Constantinople.[7] One very early collection from about AD 500 is in Syriac. But as with civil law, it was the codification of Justinian that laid down a platform for subsequent legal writing. His *Codex* in particular has much to say about church affairs: laying down sanctions for heretics, rules for monastic life, and so on. Shortly thereafter, though, the two kinds of law became more independent, because the determinations of church councils were recognized as a further basis for canon law. Thus we later have famous councils with rulings on matters like iconoclasm. There would be many attempts to disentangle the political and legal spheres of the church and secular state, for instance in a synod of 1115 which forbade clergy to hold state offices. But the religious standing of the emperor, and the fact that the patriarch of Constantinople lacked fully independent authority, meant that in Byzantium the separation between church and state was less marked than in Latin Christendom.

On the secular side, one of the primary functions of Byzantine law was to regulate economic affairs.[8] There were rules about legal contracts, inheritance, and ownership of everything from land to slaves (slavery was, unfortunately, accepted as legitimate by the church). The legal machinery of the empire was also directly concerned with finances, insofar as the royal treasury and its tax collectors kept track of who owned what, and also because confiscated property and fines flowed into the coffers of the emperor. In one letter, Psellos is frank enough to recommend someone for the post of judge on the grounds that he will help increase state revenue![9] Much as we've just seen with canon law, on the economic front there were parallels to the Latin West but also differences. The biggest contrast was the centralized authority of Constantinople, which was lacking in the West. The emperor's dominance over the economy was buttressed by the practice of demanding taxes in money rather than payment in kind like foodstuffs, meaning that the proceeds could more easily find their way to the capital rather than being exploited locally.[10]

Indeed, imperial hegemony was inextricably linked to the physical coins minted in the emperors' (and occasionally empresses') names. Today's historians learn about political dynamics on the basis of the portraits stamped onto the coins—you may recall how Irene had her image depicted alongside that of her son when she was his regent. Even the physical form of the coin can be informative. A nice example is the gold *miliaresion* issued under the Isaurian dynasty, which was modeled on the *dirham* of the then dominant Islamic empire. The power and geographical spread of the Byzantine realm meant that its coins served, in the words of one modern-day scholar, as the "dollar of the Middle Ages."[11] But there was a constant threat of debasement, that is, reduction in the amount of precious metal in the coins, and people of the time were well aware of this. Michael of Ephesus realized that coins themselves are a kind of commodity that can fluctuate in value, and some historical chroniclers complained about emperors who introduced relatively valueless currency. As one measure to help them avoid debasing the money, emperors legislated against the export of precious metals from the empire. And there are other signs that rulers were alive to the threat of trade imbalances, as when the Nicaean court established after the crusaders' sack of Constantinople tried to shore up its precarious position by forbidding the enjoyment of imported luxury items.

As these examples suggest, the Byzantines tended to assume that economics is a "zero-sum game," in which resources can only be redistributed, without the overall wealth of society being increased or decreased, except when wealth is exported to or seized from a rival power.[12] This assumption manifested in an abiding concern with the relations between rich and poor. No less an authority than the Bible stated, "the poor you will always have with you" (Matthew 26:11), and though the rich and powerful were encouraged to show generosity to the poor rather than exploiting them, there was no thought of trying to lift all of the poor to a more prosperous state. One famous case was a new law ("Novel") introduced in the year 934 by the emperor Romanos I Lekapenos. It attempted to prevent the rich from increasing their holdings by buying up land from poorer tenants. This initiative was, to put it mildly, not entirely successful. Indeed, scholars have often spoken of a Byzantine version of medieval feudalism in which the poor became tenants on vast estates.[13] That is potentially misleading, in that the tenants seem to have retained a greater degree of freedom than in the feudal states of Western Europe, and also because, as we've already said, political and legal authority was more centralized in the East. In the Byzantine context we do not find local lords exercising their own brand of justice in feudal courts.

From a philosophical point of view, a particularly important feature of Romanos' legislation from 934 is that it defined an illegally unfair sale as one in which the land was purchased at less than half its true value. In itself this was nothing revolutionary. The half-price rule went back to the Roman laws gathered together by Justinian. But the new law was unusually bold in its protection of the seller, dictating that in such a case the buyer would simply forfeit ownership with no restitution. The rationale underlying the law is also intriguing, as it seems to presuppose that a given parcel of land does have an objective, absolute value, instead of assuming that its value is just determined by whatever it can fetch on the market at a given time. That same assumption may lie behind the way that the Byzantines taxed land: not on the basis of the agricultural yield in any given year, but simply in light of the land's permanent features of size and quality. More generally, attempts to fix just or maximum prices for a range of goods go back to the Roman emperor Diocletian at the dawn of the fourth century. As any economist would predict, though, the attempts of the authorities to hold prices at a maximum level were constantly undermined by activities on the ground that were closer to a free market.[14] The historian Attaleiates noticed this phenomenon: he describes Michael VII's attempts to fix grain prices, supplanting a previous situation where buyers were able to go from one grain dealer to another looking for the best deal. Attaleiates also astutely noticed that when the price of a fundamental commodity like grain goes up, it drives up other prices and also wages.[15]

There's one other area of economic activity that you might expect to be restricted in Byzantine culture: lending with interest, or usury. This was a matter of intense concern for Latin Christians, routinely condemned by Western theologians (as we'll see in Chapter 43).[16] But the situation was more relaxed in the East. The civil law allowed usury with certain restrictions, and canon lawyers respected this ruling. Still, a number of religious writers did inveigh against the greed of rapacious moneylenders; Gregory Palamas would call usury the "child of vipers."[17] The most interesting text on this is by a thinker from fourteenth-century Thessalonike named Nicholas Kavasilas. He was a staunch defender of property rights—without the ability to acquire property, he argued, no one would have a motive to work—but an equally staunch critic of usury. He wrote a polemic against it that is particularly worth reading for the opposing arguments he considers and refutes, mounted in *defense* of usury. One argument is that lending with interest is acceptable because the borrower enters into the contract willingly. Like some Western medieval critics of usury, Kavasilas replies that economic need is effectively forcing the borrower to accept whatever terms are available, so that it is not truly voluntary. He also considers the point that if the civil law allows usury, it is surely not evil. Here the response is that maximum limits are placed on interest rates. This shows that the lawmakers have taken a critical attitude towards the moneylenders and, ideally, would prefer that we not engage in this sort of business at all.

A more general moral concern with poverty is of course frequent in religious literature of the period. But perhaps no Byzantine text captures the issue so well as the *Dialogue Between Rich and Poor*, written by Alexios Makrembolites at Constantinople in 1343, hence in a time of upheaval as the empire was in its final decline.[18] Makrembolites is obviously on the side of the poor, who are shown accusing the rich of selfishness and of failing to help their needy fellow humans. So greedy are the rich that if they could, they would appropriate the sun for themselves and prevent the poor from enjoying its rays. The rich should instead imitate God in His infinite generosity. Indeed, the whole purpose of wealth is nothing other than aid of the less fortunate. All this is heartfelt but not particularly groundbreaking. Much as with Kavasilas' treatise on usury, this dialogue may be more interesting for the counterarguments brought forward by the rich. They defend themselves on the grounds that there is no obligation to help those who have performed no service, and that it is simply "in the nature of things" that the poor suffer. Besides, the rich point out, they have their own problems, with the government coming to tax them and meddling in their affairs. (Sounds familiar, doesn't it?)

Let's now move on to one final topic that follows naturally from the spectacle of the rich ignoring the needs of the poor: warfare. Actually there was no class warfare in Byzantium, nothing like the Peasants' Revolt. But there were plenty of other wars, and plenty of writing about the topic including theological discussions of the moral status of soldiers, and military manuals on the best strategies to use in battle. Again there are parallels to the medieval West,[19] with the difference that, according to some scholars, the Byzantines were far less belligerent than the Latin Christians and also compared to contemporary Muslims.[20] They launched no crusades, no jihad, but largely fought wars of defense or to reclaim lost territory. In one military text, the *Taktika*, written under Leo the Wise, we even find the statement that war can be justified only as defense of territory from an invading enemy. Yet the Byzantines were obviously not pacifists, and their usual avoidance of aggressive warfare was probably more a matter of judicious caution and military weakness than moral principle.

One other factor to consider, though, is that the Byzantines may have lacked an ideology of religious warfare such as we see in the two medieval cultures that surrounded them on either side. Did they have the notion of a "holy war"? The answer is not a simple one. The idea of war as holy, or encouraged by God, did not sit well with the Christian commandment not to kill, and already in antiquity Greek church fathers had critical things to say about the life of soldiering. Origen advised Christians to struggle towards faith, not with the sword, and an influential passage in St Basil suggested that soldiers were so morally tarnished by their deeds that they should refrain from taking communion for three years after killing in battle. Yet religious regalia and rituals were frequently adopted by the military. Icons might be placed on city walls or gates during a siege as an additional protective measure. The army was encouraged to fast before battle in hopes of securing God's favor. And prayers were a standard part of imperial triumphs celebrating victory in the field.

Christianity was, then, involved in warfare just as in every other aspect of life in Byzantium. But acknowledging this is not the same as speaking of holy war.[21] God, Christ, the Virgin, and the saints were regularly invoked in conflicts with the infidel, but also in internal conflicts between Christian armies. Thus we have, to give only one famous example, the emperor Basil II riding off to do battle with Bardas Phokas holding an icon of Mary. Furthermore, Byzantine intellectuals were dismissive of some aspects of the ideology of holy war known to them from other cultures, such as the Muslims' belief that fallen warriors would go directly to heaven, and the idea that crusaders would have their sins remitted. For them it was a nonsense to suppose that you could free yourself from the stain of sin by going to war. If anything, fighting would expose you to further evils, even if the evil in question was a necessary one.

14

MADE BY HAND
BYZANTINE MANUSCRIPTS

Walk into any decent bookshop in the English-speaking world, and you'll find Plato's dialogues on the shelves. Maybe even a collection of all his dialogues, which takes up more than one and a half thousand pages, even if you exclude the works that were not really written by Plato but only transmitted under his name. Strictly speaking, of course, Plato didn't write the rest of the book either, for the simple reason that he didn't know English. Happily, you can also get Plato in ancient Greek, for instance in the "Oxford Classical Texts" series where it takes up five volumes. But here's the thing: Plato didn't write those Greek texts either, at least not exactly. Most readers, even most professional historians of philosophy, don't give this much thought, and proceed as if the printed version was ordered straight from Plato's Academy. In fact, though, the modern edition is simply scholars' best guess at what he may originally have written.

You'll be relieved to learn that the texts of Plato's dialogues are actually relatively secure. But like all other ancient works, they are moving targets and will never be fully established beyond all doubt. The individual words and sentences in that edition have in some cases been a matter of intense philological debate. Nor are modern editors hiding this fact. At the bottom of each page, they've supplied a dense collection of footnotes bristling with Latin abbreviations and bits of Greek, which are alternative versions, called "variants," of what Plato may have written. To understand what lies behind those footnotes is to appreciate more fully the astounding fact that we are able to read Plato at all, never mind one and a half thousand pages worth of him, a good two and a half millennia after he lived. It means tracing the long and hazardous journey those writings traveled, surviving more or less intact as empires rose and fell, as Attic Greek fell into disuse as a language of everyday speech, and as philosophical tastes changed. That journey went straight through Byzantium. Without the efforts of Byzantine scholars and scribes we would not be able to read Plato today; ancient philosophy, indeed ancient literature as a whole, would barely exist anymore.

To see why, let's go back to the beginning of the journey, and talk about how writing would have been set down and preserved in Plato's day.[1] There were several options. Many inscriptions in stone survive from antiquity, including at least one philosophical text: a statement of Epicurean doctrine by the Roman-era philosopher Diogenes of Oinoanda. There are also shards of clay pottery with writing on them. Such a shard is called an *ostrakon* and there was a legal procedure in Athens where political figures could be exiled, or "ostracized," by writing their names on such shards, and some of these survive. But you aren't going to write Plato's *Republic* as a stone inscription or on bits of pottery. For that, the first stage would probably have been inscribing the text onto wax tablets. Hence an ancient report tells us that Plato's final work, the *Laws*, had just been recorded in wax when he died.[2]

Longer term, though, texts would be set down on papyrus. This is made from the leaves of a plant that grows especially in Egypt. It came in various grades of quality, with the poorest grade even being used as packing material. Typically it would be fashioned into a long scroll which would be gradually unrolled while reading; the text had to be re-rolled after use. The text would be arranged in columns, written entirely in what we might think of as capital letters and without punctuation:

JUSTIMAGINEREAD
INGPLATOSWHOLE
REPUBLICLIKETHIS

Learning to read was thus, in large part, learning to see where one word or sentence stopped and another began. Furthermore, there were none of the accents and diacritical marks you'll see on Greek in modern editions, which were invented later. These don't make reading significantly easier but do sometimes resolve possible ambiguities, such as the one exploited in a clever remark of Heraclitus, "the bow: its name is life, its work is death." The point of this is that the Greek word ΒΙΟΣ can be accented in two different ways, one of which means "bow (βιός)," the other "life (βίος)."

By the time we get to Byzantium all of this will be different, apart from the fact that all documents will still have to be written out by hand, this being the meaning of the word "manuscript." The first major change is the introduction of "parchment," a word that derives from the name of the Greek city Pergamon, where it was supposedly invented. Parchment is leather that has been carefully treated to make it as smooth and light in color as possible. If you look closely at some texts written on parchment, you can tell what they are made of, because the surface where the hide was will be lighter in color than the inner side. Parchment came into use already around 200 BC but did not immediately displace the use of papyrus. Once it did become the dominant material for writing, it clung on tenaciously, even after the introduction of paper. In the Palaiologan period we still find, for example, the scholar Planudes asking a correspondent to send him some of this scarce material, and then complaining that the donkey hide parchment he received was useless.[3] Even into the Renaissance, parchment was used for particularly elegant or important book production. Among the Byzantines, court documents were occasionally made from parchment that was dyed an imperial purple.

As for paper, its introduction was the most important change in the technology of writing between the invention of the alphabet and of the printing press. Paper is typically made from used fibrous material like linen or hemp; it can readily be made from used rags. The technology came into the Islamic world from China in the seventh century and was taken up in Byzantium in the ninth. In both cases, paper's arrival was followed about a century later by an explosion of intellectual activity. This is not a coincidence. Without paper, we would not have had al-Kindī and the massive Greek–Arabic translation movement in the Islamic world, or Photius and Psellos in the Byzantine world. Since it was scholars like them who led the effort to study and preserve ancient Greek literature, you can thank the Chinese inventors of paper for the fact that you can still read Plato.

The reason paper made such a difference is that it is much cheaper than parchment, and much more durable and readily available than papyrus. Actually, papyrus had already been in short supply once its main source, Egypt, fell under the sway of Islam. In the late seventh century a Muslim ruler there even placed an interdict on the export of papyrus. This encouraged the use of parchment in the Christian world, despite its costliness. We can see how valuable parchment was from the fact that, sometimes, the ink would be removed from it to create a more or less clean writing surface on which a new text could be set down. This is called a "palimpsest," from a Greek word meaning "scraped off" (*palimpsestos*). Otherwise lost works have been discovered in the undertext of palimpsest manuscripts. A sensational example is a work by Archimedes that was found on parchment written underneath a religious work from Byzantium, and was rendered readable through the use of X-rays and other technology. In the philosophy world, there was recently similar excitement at the discovery in a palimpsest of an unknown commentary on Aristotle's *Categories*.[4]

There were two other big changes between classical antiquity and the Byzantine period. Unlike Plato, Michael Psellos would not have had to work his way through a scroll while reading.[5] By his time, the standard format was the "codex," which is basically like a modern book, with pages made from folded paper or parchment, bound between covers. The codex begins to appear in about the third century AD, especially with legal texts, having evolved from the practice of tying together leaves of parchment to make a sort of notebook. Codices begin to outnumber scrolls at about AD 400, but do not displace them fully until the seventh century or so. A couple of centuries later, the scribes introduce a second innovation. They begin writing in so-called "minuscule" text, which you can roughly think of as lowercase letters, instead of the old "majuscule," uppercase letters. But the use of majuscule for more formal texts persists for a good while. Our oldest surviving minuscule text is from the year 835, but still in the eleventh century majuscule is found in liturgical manuscripts. Paper comes in about a century after scribes started writing everything in the new minuscule script.

All this might lead us to expect that a pagan work like a treatise by Aristotle would have initially existed on papyrus scrolls written in majuscule, one or more of which would be copied in the same script into a papyrus codex, then into a parchment codex, then into a minuscule version also in parchment, before finally being copied in the sort of format that usually survives to us, a paper codex with minuscule script. While this is the right sequence in technological terms, a given work might not have existed in every form I've just listed. In particular, during the so-called "dark ages" of Byzantium few pagan works were copied. Once interest in them reawakened, the scribes would have had to use texts in long outmoded formats as models. Thus a ninth-century paper minuscule copy might be based directly on majuscule parchment from the sixth century. So it's a good thing that parchment is such a durable material.

Books were copied and kept in a number of different contexts. The first thing that leaps to mind would be major institutions like the famous library at Alexandria. It was important not only because of the sheer quantity of literature it held, but also because scholars working there produced the editions that usually lie behind later Byzantine copies. Generally speaking, when modern-day philologists try to establish the text of a classical author like Homer or Plato, they are really seeking to get as close as possible to the Alexandrian edition of late antiquity; it simply isn't possible to go back further than that.[6] In Byzantium, monasteries were less important centers of text production than in the Latin West, with a more significant role played by royal and patriarchal libraries. But we should not underestimate the role of smaller schools and private libraries. Institutions such as the ancient libraries at Alexandria and Pergamon, or the collection of books we assume existed at a philosophical institute set up by the Byzantine caesar Bardas, were threatened by mass destruction in times of political upheaval, whereas a private library might survive. The very preciousness of books also exposed them to threat. We've already seen how parchment was reused in palimpsests, and books might also be sold off to raise funds. A twelfth-century archbishop of Byzantium complained about illiterate monks who did this: "just because you have no trace of culture, must you empty the library of the books that transmit it?"[7]

The upshot is that, as Richard Goulet has observed, ancient philosophy is not really *preserved* down to the present day, but rather *transmitted*.[8] We have almost no physical texts by philosophers from the classical period, with a few exceptions like that Epicurean inscription in stone or the private collection of rolls owned by another Epicurean, Philodemus, which were preserved thanks to a volcanic eruption. Texts wore out, were discarded or lost in fires. Already in late antiquity scholars were conscious of this. Simplicius copied out quotations from Presocratic philosophy when commenting on Aristotle because he knew that readers might not otherwise have access to these texts. Themistius, writing in the fourth century on the occasion of the founding of an imperial library, mentioned that some authors, like the early Stoics, were already in danger of becoming unavailable. Texts were often lost in times of transition for book technology. When codices replaced rolls, and minuscule script replaced majuscule, the priorities of the scholars of the time dictated what would be copied into the new format and survive through the change.

As a result, the surviving corpus of ancient philosophy is basically what a Neoplatonically inclined Byzantine scholar like Psellos would think worth preserving. So we have thousands of pages of commentaries on Aristotle and the entire output of Plato and Plotinus, but not a single work by those early Stoics who Themistius was already fretting over. The same goes for other fields of ancient literature. We have more than 230 manuscripts of Aristophanes, because Byzantine philologists valued him as an exemplar of fine Attic Greek, while the single Greek author for whom the most text survives is Galen, because his writings formed the basis for the study of medicine. The quantity of surviving manuscripts for any given author is a fairly reliable indicator of how interested the Byzantines and Renaissance humanists found that author, and also of whether the author was used in teaching contexts. Thus we have a good 260 manuscripts containing Platonic dialogues, but more than a thousand for Aristotle.[9] Within Aristotle's corpus, the individual works are also very unequally represented in the manuscripts. There exist many copies of his logical treatises because they were regularly used in the classroom, but comparatively few for works like the *Poetics*. Even among the logical writings the manuscripts for the introductory works *Categories* and *On Interpretation* greatly outnumber, for instance, the *Sophistical Refutations*.[10]

With the exception of one fragment from that work, all of our manuscripts for Aristotle's philosophical treatises are in various minuscule scripts. Given that minuscule started to be used in the ninth century, this means that our textual evidence for Aristotle begins about one and a half millennia after his death. So it's hardly a surprise that many of his books are lost—we know this because we have ancient lists of his works, with our surviving corpus representing only a fraction of what is listed—and his surviving works are not what would have been read by his students at the Lyceum. Almost all Aristotle goes back to an edition of his works produced in the Roman period by the scholar Andronicus.[11] Some treatises by Aristotle, notably the *Metaphysics*, were only compiled as single works at this editorial stage. But the target of a modern editor of Aristotle is not really even Andronicus' edition. It is, rather, the lost copies in majuscule script that were the basis for the surviving Byzantine manuscripts that are in minuscule. Even if we have a large number of manuscripts for a given work, they will often all go back to one single copy in majuscule. That copy was transliterated into minuscule in, say, the ninth century, and then discarded. All further copies, which could number in the dozens or hundreds, would thus go back to the initial transcription.

If you're asking yourself, "who cares?" then you haven't thought about the challenge of copying out an entire book by hand. This was of course tiresome work, as shown by the prayers that scribes often insert at the end of a copy, giving thanks that their labor is completed. But more to the point, it is effectively impossible to copy out a text of any length without errors. Even if you were copying from a modern printed text with spaces between letters and punctuation, you'd make mistakes. But imagine copying from a handwritten text like those papyrus rolls or ancient codices, with columns of unbroken majuscule. Certain kinds of slip happen quite often. The scribe might skip a line, or miss out a phrase because the phrase that follows begins with the same letters: glancing back and forth between his source copy and his new copy, he jumps from one line or phrase to the next. Or one letter may be misread as another, especially if the letters look similar, as do the Greek letters A and Λ (*lambda*) in majuscule script.

Another problem is that manuscripts often have notes in the margin, as we've seen with our previous mentions of such scholia. This was routine practice and anticipated in manuscript production. Scribes routinely left wide margins so that they themselves, or their successors, could make notes. Some manuscripts even leave gaps in the main text, for instance in a historical chronicle, so that an uncertain date can be filled in later. Or notes might be made between the lines of the text, for instance by writing a correction above a word or phrase. All of this apparatus might or might not be retained in a later copy. Sometimes the marginal glosses might be retained and integrated into the original text. If you're now trying to produce an edition of that original text, you want to eliminate such extraneous material that has crept in. On the other hand, scholia can also be very helpful: the scribes often compared manuscripts and noted down alternative readings from copies that are now lost. This is valuable information for scholars who are now trying to establish the text.

Which takes us back to those footnotes in a modern-day edition of Plato or Aristotle. The notes record the different versions in the Greek text found in various manuscripts—not all of the variants, but only those the modern editor deems significant. As I said, in the main text above those notes, you're seeing the decision of that editor about which variants to accept, or in some cases Greek that has been hypothesized by the editor as an improvement on what we find in the manuscripts. How does one go about doing this? Let's take as an example a short work by Aristotle called *On the Motion of Animals*, which was recently re-edited by Oliver Primavesi.[12] This is a case where all existing copies do indeed go back to a unique manuscript that was written in majuscule. We know this because there are some mistakes in the Greek found in all copies; this means they must all derive from one single copy with those mistakes in it.

This gives us an insight into a more general point, one that is key to the task of editing Greek manuscripts. In the first instance, you look not for correct Greek, but for *errors*. Imagine you have four manuscripts, numbered 1 through 4. If manuscripts 1 and 2 share the same mistake, whereas copies 3 and 4 preserve a correct reading, then you know that 1 and 2 must be copies of the same manuscript (or perhaps 2 is a copy of 1, or vice versa), while 3 and 4 are based on some other manuscript that was free of this error. On this principle, it's possible to arrange all the existing manuscripts in a branching diagram that shows which were copied from which; this diagram is called a *stemma codicum*. Primavesi's new edition of *On the Motion of Animals* was needed because of a major revision he realized was needed in the *stemma*. A comparatively late manuscript from the fifteenth century turned out to have correct readings that were not found in any other copies. Previous editors had focused on earlier textual witnesses that could take them back to a version from the tenth century. This seems to make sense: all else being equal, an older manuscript should get you closer to the original. But as philologists like to say, because philologists enjoy speaking in Latin, *recentiores non deteriores*: "the more recent are not necessarily worse." In this case, a manuscript that is a good 500 years newer than others contained readings that helped Primavesi to get a more accurate text. His edition has 120 changes over earlier ones, and that in a text of only a few pages. Remarkably, many of the improved readings match the medieval Latin translation by Thomas Aquinas' colleague William of Moerbeke, who evidently had access to the same line of transmission exploited by Primavesi.

It's worth bearing in mind that with this meticulous labor, the modern textual editor is simply doing what ancient, medieval, and Renaissance scholars already did in their own time. They too compared manuscripts to eliminate errors. Thus late antique and Byzantine commentators on Aristotle sometimes record variants found in other texts. The fact that they were so conscientious actually complicates the business of figuring out which manuscripts are copied from which. The medieval editors might look at additional manuscripts to fix errors in the one they are copying. When modern scholars do this it's just good scholarship; when older ones do it, it's rudely called "contamination" between lines of textual transmission. Then too, like modern editors the Byzantine scribes might correct the text on their own initiative, so that it will make more sense. Hence another principle followed by philologists, which of course goes by a Latin name: *lectio difficilior*, or "more difficult reading." This means that if you have two variants, one of which is somehow stranger though still grammatically possible (like a very unusual word), while the other is familiar and straightforward, you should suspect that the easier version could actually be a scribe's conscious or unconscious correction, and thus consider adopting the "more difficult" variant.

It should now be clear that we owe a lot to the Byzantine philologists. One of their greatest legacies is the so-called "philosophical collection,"[13] a group of seventeen manuscripts on philosophical and scientific topics that go back to a multi-volume edition produced in Constantinople. It was probably compiled from material gathered by Platonist philosophers in late ancient Alexandria and Athens, maybe for use at the aforementioned institute established by Bardas.[14] The "philosophical collection" is a treasure trove, which includes among other things Plato's dialogues; works by Neoplatonists like Proclus, Simplicius, and Philoponus; and treatises of Middle Platonists and by Aristotle and his followers. From the handwriting we can tell that it was copied out by no fewer than eight different scribes who worked closely together.

The manuscripts from the collection are now scattered across a number of European libraries, which is typical. For these and other philosophical texts to survive, it was of course necessary not only that the Byzantine scribes copied them out, but that those Byzantine copies themselves survived. Some Greek manuscripts are still to be found in Istanbul—the Ottomans knew Greek manuscripts were valuable and did not just destroy them. But mostly, Greek literature exists today because it was spirited away from Constantinople to the Latin West after the capital fell to the crusaders in 1204, or copied by Western scholars who took advantage of the situation to visit Constantinople and make copies of the manuscripts there. One fairly immediate result was the sudden rediscovery of Aristotle's works by the scholastics, whose far-reaching consequences for medieval philosophy we've explored in a previous volume.[15] In that context, a surge of interest in classical pagan thought provoked significant opposition, in an unwitting echo of events that had already occurred in the East. As it turns out, the enthusiasm for Platonism embodied in the manuscripts of the "philosophical collection" was not shared by everyone.

15

GEORGIA ON MY MIND PETRITSI AND THE PROCLUS REVIVAL

Those who reject philosophy are doomed to engage in it. If you tell a philosopher that philosophy is a waste of time and can't possibly prove anything, the philosopher will brighten up and say, "What an interesting philosophical claim that is! What's your argument for it?" Hence the fate of the numerous figures in the medieval age who attacked philosophy, and who for their pains have become the object of intense study by historians of philosophy. As I observed in another volume of this series, when covering Ibn Taymiyya, this is in large part because the critic's arguments are themselves inevitably philosophical.[1] Disputation over the art of logic drew Ibn Taymiyya into detailed analysis of theories of proof and knowledge going back to Avicenna. Avicenna was the obvious target for any polemic against philosophy in the Islamic world, already identified by al-Ghazālī as such within a few generations of his death. Similarly, in Latin Christendom anti-philosophers like Manegold of Lautenbach attacked Plato in the early period, when he was the dominant figure. Once Aristotle became central to the university curriculum in the thirteenth century, he and his followers were in the firing line, as we can see with the condemnations issued at Paris in the 1270s.

So who would a Byzantine critic of philosophy take as their antagonist? You might expect it to be Aristotle in this case too, given all those commentaries that scholars were devoting to his treatises. But remember that the Byzantines knew ancient Greek literature much better than did those who were dependent on Arabic or Latin. They could read everything we can today, and more. And whatever the bishop of Paris may have thought, there were ancient philosophers who were far more problematic from a Christian point of view than Aristotle. None more so than Proclus. Working in the fifth century AD, he resisted the rise of Christianity with a vigorous defense of paganism.[2] His lengthy commentaries on Plato were written from an explicitly religious point of view, and allude frequently to the traditional pantheon of gods. A more popular, and in some ways more provocative, text was his *Elements of Theology*. As the title indicates, it was inspired by the axiomatic method of Euclid, and presents Neoplatonism as a deductive system. This rational reconstruction of paganism is all the more powerful for not mentioning the pagan gods by name. They instead appear as principles of unity, or "henads," surrounding the highest One which is the principle of all things, and as abstract intellects whose existence and nature is established through Proclus' ironclad argumentation.

As a result, signaling an interest in Proclus was an eloquent way for a Byzantine intellectual to display open-minded appreciation for pagan Hellenic culture. And no Byzantine intellectual was more eloquent than Michael Psellos. We saw that his *Chronographia* singles out Proclus as Psellos' most valued philosophical authority. Elsewhere Psellos draws on the *Elements of Theology* in various works of philosophical compilation, though not always without criticism. He even dismisses some of what he finds in Proclus as obviously absurd, and compares the study of pagan authors including Proclus to familiarizing oneself with not just medicines but also poisons, "in order to become healthy with the former and to avoid the latter, without embracing extraneous doctrines as if they were ours."[3] Nevertheless Psellos draws on Proclus when expounding Christian theological doctrine, and even speaks without criticism of the "henads" that stand in for pagan deities in Proclus' *Elements.*

A safer way to make use of Proclus would have been to deal with him indirectly, through Pseudo-Dionysius, an anonymous Christian author of late antiquity who lived after Proclus and borrowed his ideas. As in Latin Christendom, in Byzantium this author was taken to be an authority of the biblical era, Saint Dionysius. So his works already repackaged Platonism in irreproachably Christian form. But rather than discarding Proclus in favor of Pseudo-Dionysius, Psellos actually says that Proclus—who he wrongly assumes wrote later than Dionysius—made the latter's teaching "more precise." This is in sharp contrast to what we find in the Latin West with Thomas Aquinas. His commentary on a version of Proclus' *Elements* called the *Book of Causes* misses no chance to show how Dionysius' teaching is superior to that of Proclus, representative of the pagan "Platonists."[4]

How typical was Psellos' affection for Proclus? It's hard to say. Psellos' student Italos and Italos' student Eustratios both make use of his ideas, and an author named Isaac Sebastokrator revised treatises by Proclus to make them more Christian.[5] But the best evidence for a "Proclus renaissance" is provided by authors who complain about his popularity.[6] These include George Tornikes, whose encomium of Anna Komnene makes a point of saying that unlike some, she much preferred Dionysius to Proclus. Then there was Nicholas of Methone. Writing around the middle of the twelfth century, Nicholas was the author of several theological works and a lengthy, blow-by-blow refutation of Proclus' *Elements*.[7] In a prologue to this frontal assault on the ultimate systematic presentation of paganism, he suggests that he is motivated by Proclus' popularity among his own contemporaries. But it's conceivable that he is really thinking of Proclus' enthusiastic reception back in the eleventh century, in the works of Psellos and Italos. The same goes for Tornikes' remarks about Anna's resistance to Proclus' siren song.

Rather than Christianizing Proclus, as Pseudo-Dionysius and Isaac Sebastokrator had done, Nicholas of Methone correctly sees the *Elements* as a philosophical rationale for polytheism. He finds something to criticize in nearly every one of its many propositions, which he compares to bricks built into a new Tower of Babel. So despite the official title of the refutation, which calls it an "unfolding (*anaptuxis*)" of the *Elements*,[8] this is not a commentary in the style of the circle around Anna Komnene. Actually Nicholas does take pains to understand Proclus and at one point even hypothesizes a correction to the manuscript he is reading (§28). But he only wants to get Proclus right so that he can then show that Proclus is wrong. In place of Proclus' austere first principle, a pure unity that necessarily gives rise to a complex hierarchy of immaterial principles, Nicholas defends a Christian understanding of God as a freely creating cause who directly brings all other things into being. His approach is unmistakably theological. He piously insists that his doctrine is based entirely on the scriptures, since there can be no other source for human knowledge of God (§114). On this basis he complains of Proclus' temerity in attempting to lift the gaze of his mind beyond even his own intelligible principles to the first principle itself (§121).

Yet Nicholas cannot avoid doing some philosophy. Actually, he doesn't even want to. Like other Byzantine thinkers he values the title "philosopher" and thinks that the pagans failed to live up to it (§195). He also realizes that he needs to do more than point out the inconsistency of Proclus with Christianity. He has to show that the axiomatic project of the *Elements* is a failure. After all, if Christianity is in conflict with indisputable demonstrations offered by a pagan, then that's bad news for Christianity, not for paganism. So Nicholas attempts to defeat Proclus on his own ground, identifying his opponent's logical failings (§8) and imprecise terminology. Nicholas' defense of a freely creating, Trinitarian God emerges in part from an internal critique of Proclus' philosophical theology. The Neoplatonic One is meant to be an all-powerful source of everything, so why would it need the henads as supplementary causes? Either God can create everything, in which case the henads are superfluous, or He cannot, in which case He lacks the perfection and majesty Proclus pretends to ascribe to Him (§133, 156). Furthermore, we must envision a God that has some kind of internal activity, or "motion," since otherwise we will have an inert principle that cannot initiate anything on its own. Hence the need for divine will (§76), and more fundamentally for the dynamic interrelations of the Trinity. For this idea he cites a much-quoted line from the Greek church father Gregory Nazianzus: "from the start the monad moved toward a dyad until halting at the triad" (§1).[9]

It is not only the henads that Nicholas wants to eliminate. Proclus postulated a number of principles, like Being, Limit, Unlimited, and Intellect, which were meant to explain the various features of the things that come after them. This was a kind of theological, hierarchical reworking of Plato's theory of Forms. Nicholas argues that such general features of things are not existent in their own right. Here he is appealing to what had become the standard view of universals within Aristotelianism, according to which general concepts are just that, concepts in the mind rather than objectively existing things (§14, 60, 60, 108, and 161; §102 and 159 for the rejection of Limit and Unlimited). When we speak of something that in itself has being, this has nothing to do with a Platonist principle called "Being," but just means that some created things are substances as opposed to accidental properties (§40–5). With scarcely concealed delight, he also quotes Aristotle (who was himself quoting Homer) in support of monotheism: "the rule of many is not good; let there be one ruler" (§21).

This elimination strategy is one way that Nicholas chops Proclus' hierarchy down to size. Another is to identify Proclus' various principles with aspects, or names, of God Himself. He is even willing to accept the term "henad" as a way of referring to the divine, so long as we remember that there is only one such deity and that this henad, or unity, is also three Persons (§116, 135). Likewise, if we do accept a principle called "Being" that is the source of all being, then this is just to be identified with God Himself. The same goes for Intellect, Life, and so on: just many names for one God (§139). Thus the various sources of determination for reality, which for Proclus were spread across numerous levels, are concentrated in one creating principle. In light of this, it's ironic (not to say unfair) that Nicholas also charges Proclus with being too confident in his ability to describe God.[10] Nicholas throws in his lot with Dionysius, who he assumes was Proclus' source for the occasional good ideas that are mixed in with the prideful errors strewn throughout the *Elements* (§122). Following Dionysius, Nicholas believes that God is beyond our mental grasp and beyond our language, but with that qualification he still allows himself to transfer positive attributes from created things to Him (§7).

In short, then, Nicholas of Methone saw Proclus as a dangerous figure, one who might lead Christians into error and who could in fact be associated with a number of real heresies (§32).[11] But it's worth emphasizing again that Nicholas was not rejecting philosophy as a whole, or suggesting that philosophy is incompatible with Christian belief. To the contrary, he thought Proclus had failed on his own terms, and Nicholas claimed superiority in argument as well as faith. What we have here then is a conflict between two thinkers who were both using philosophy to establish the truth of their respective religions. But there was another strategy for dealing with this pagan thinker. Other Byzantines saw Proclus more positively, as a resource for expounding Christianity in a philosophical idiom. This was evidently the view of Pseudo-Dionysius, of Psellos, and of one other figure we need to discuss: Ioane Petritsi.

Like James Brown and the world's best peaches, Petritsi hailed from Georgia, though in his case we're dealing with the Georgia located between the Black Sea and Caspian Sea. Petritsi was in fact the leading figure of medieval philosophy written in Georgian. Among other works, he produced a surviving translation and commentary for Proclus' *Elements of Theology*. Unfortunately Petritsi's chronology, like a Georgia peach, is a little fuzzy. One intriguing hypothesis is that he was actually a student of John Italos, who we know wrote a letter to a Georgian scholar; some assume that this must have been Petritsi. But linguistic studies of Petritsi's writings have suggested that he may have worked in the second half of the twelfth century, which would be too late for him to have studied with Italos, who died in the 1080s.[12] Either way it seems clear that Petritsi studied in Constantinople and shared the Neoplatonic proclivities of Psellos, Italos, and whoever else was annoying Nicholas of Methone by admiring Proclus. He was expert on Greek philosophy in general and Proclus in particular. For Petritsi, Proclus was the greatest of the pagan philosophers, because of his masterful unfolding of ideas that were expressed less clearly in Plato's dialogues.

Petritsi's commentary thus makes a perfect contrast to that of Nicholas.[13] Where Nicholas had tirelessly attacked Proclus' polytheism, Petritsi mostly sticks to exposition of the Neoplatonic system, and avoids the question of whether that system may be in conflict with Christianity. When he does address the issue, he is outspoken in his defense of Proclus. Rather implausibly, he simply rejects the charge that Proclus was, strictly speaking, a polytheist (§12). The series of principles that descend from the highest One do not share the lofty status of the true God, even if Proclus calls them "gods (*theoi*)," and the word "divine" is applied to such things as the heavenly bodies simply to mark their relative superiority to other creatures.[14] Though he criticizes Aristotelian philosophers for failing to recognize God as a creating cause (§11), Petritsi does not go as far as Nicholas would want in asserting that all things are made to exist through a gratuitous and free act on God's part. Instead, he is happy to retain the Neoplatonic idea that the first principle "emanates" its effects. These flow forth from it like light from a source or water from a spring. Still it would be wrong to speak of God as "necessarily" causing things to exist, since God is in fact transcendent above necessity.[15] In general Petritsi would agree with Nicholas, and for that matter Proclus, that God is exalted beyond His effects. Some of these effects are "eternal" in the sense of being timeless, but God or the One is placed even higher than that, too exalted even to be called "eternal" (§51).

How can Petritsi, as a good Christian who believes in the Trinity, accept Proclus' account of a first principle that is utterly without multiplicity? By finding Trinitarian patterns in Proclus' own thought. In both the commentary and especially in an epilogue he added at the end, he suggests that the Trinitarian Persons can be associated with features of Proclus' system, with the Son or *logos* being identified either with the principle called "Limit" or with the first Intellect that descends from the One. At one point in the commentary (§24) he speaks of a series of three "ones" in Proclus, and just in case we didn't get the point, a gloss in the margin of the manuscript says that this is to be understood as the Trinity.[16] Petritsi goes so far as to trace this pagan intuition of the Trinity back to Plato himself.[17]

Apart from the epilogue, though, it does not seem that Petritsi's primary goal is to establish the harmony between pagan Neoplatonism and Christian orthodoxy. As I've said, the commentary itself mostly skirts that issue, with Petritsi apparently seeing exegesis of Proclus as a worthwhile end in itself. He seems more worried by the difficulty of expressing Greek ideas in Georgian language. He admits the difficulty of rendering Greek terms like *dianoia*, or "discursive thinking,"[18] introduces a passage from Plato in Greek before then translating it into Georgian, and even refers to the etymology of Greek words (§50). With his head full of pagan material and the Bible, he describes the soul's sojourn in the physical realm both in terms of an image from Plato's *Phaedrus*, in which the soul must regain its wings to return to a heavenly abode, and with an image from the Book of Genesis (3:21), comparing the human body to the animal skins donned by Adam and Eve (§209).[19]

Petritsi has no real peer in the Georgian philosophical tradition, even if he has been convincingly located within a more general cultural flowering made possible by the reign of the Georgian king David "the Builder" around the turn of the twelfth century. We can, however, find analogies in other language groups among the Christians of the East. An obvious comparison would be to David the Invincible, who back in the sixth century translated Aristotelian logical treatises into Armenian. (See Chapter 2. On this point, it's worth noting that Petritsi's version of Proclus became the basis for an Armenian translation made in the thirteenth century.[20]) And as you'll remember, Georgian and Armenian were not the only languages for doing philosophy. Christian philosophers wrote in Arabic, and also in Syriac. We have not yet explored this phenomenon fully. To do so we'll need to look once again beyond the confines of the Byzantine empire, as we did when discussing John of Damascus, giving us an opportunity to resume the question of intellectual exchange between Christians and Muslims.

16

PEOPLE OF THE SOUTH
BYZANTIUM AND ISLAM

If you're looking for an argument, I have two places to suggest you go. First, any room containing an analytic philosopher. Analytic philosophers love arguing so much that, not content with arguing for a living, they go out for drinks with one another after work to argue in their free time, and then go home, where they get into arguments with their loved ones about whether they are too argumentative. Second, if you can find a way to get there, the medieval Near East. Starting in late antiquity, the goddess of history devoted all of her efforts to producing the ideal conditions for disagreement. After breaking the Roman empire in half so that Latin Christians could come into conflict with Greek Christians, she also oversaw sectarian disputes between Christians in the Eastern realms: the Chalcedonians, the Miaphysites, and the Church of the East (as we've seen, these groups are sometimes referred to respectively as Melkites, Jacobites, and Nestorians). But she was just getting warmed up. The rise of Islam cut the size of the Byzantine empire in half, as Syria and Egypt were lost, and gave Christians a whole new set of opponents.

That rivalry was often pursued the good old-fashioned way, namely with hideous violence. The history of Byzantium is in no small part the history of warfare with Muslim powers: the Umayyad and ʿAbbāsid caliphates, the Fāṭimids, the Seljuks, then, finally and fatally, the Ottomans. In many periods annual raids were a fact of life for anyone living in striking distance of the border. Emperors could secure legitimacy by defeating the Muslims on the field of battle, or lose it by being defeated. The same was true on the other side. Caliphs and other Muslim rulers tested their armies against those of the Christians and attempted numerous times to fulfill a promise supposedly made by the Prophet: "The first among my people who conquer the city of the Caesar," that is, Constantinople, "will have his sins forgiven."[1]

Yet the relationship between the two faiths involved more than military conflict. To see this, we need look no further than the actions of these same emperors and caliphs. They wanted to be seen as religious leaders, not just as warlords. On the back foot after the Arab invasions, Byzantine emperors presented themselves as being victorious in faith, if not in war, as leaders of a process of reform and renewal that would win back God's favor.[2] Throughout the history of the empire emperors also sought to overawe and humble Muslim visitors with the glory of their court at Constantinople, and they sent emissaries who could display the best that Greek scholarship had to offer. We saw that in the middle of the ninth century, Photius was chosen for such a diplomatic mission; a somewhat earlier example was John the Grammarian, a scholar dispatched to Baghdad in 829. Emperors were also known to send documents instructing their opposite numbers in the errors of Islam. We have a letter supposedly written by the iconoclast emperor Leo III to the reigning caliph, one of the earliest Christian refutations of Islam.[3] The correspondence went both ways. In the ninth century the famed ʿAbbāsid caliph Hārūn al-Rashīd had a letter sent to Constantinople, penned by a scholar named Muḥammad ibn al-Layth. It explains the superiority of Islam to Christianity and then suggests that the emperor either come to his senses and convert, or agree to pay the tax owed by Christians to their Muslim overlords.[4]

Many if not most religious refutations, though, were not aimed at members of the rival faith. Instead they were, almost literally, preaching to the choir. In the middle of the ninth century Niketas of Byzantium wrote an attack on the Quran condemning it as untruthful, inconsistent, and idolatrous.[5] Far from being a true revelation founding a new religion devoted to the one God, this book leads to worship of the devil. Niketas' goal was obviously to strengthen the confidence of his co-religionists, not to win over potential converts, even if the treatise is remarkable for showing some knowledge of the Quran, which was at least partially available to him in Greek translation.[6] Other diatribes against Islam include one written by a fourteenth-century emperor, John VI Kantakouzenos,[7] and several pages from Eustratios' commentary on Aristotle's *Ethics*.[8] This rare allusion to Islam in a strictly philosophical work is no more polite than what we find in Niketas. It describes Muhammad, without naming him, as a false prophet who engaged in adultery. Eustratios depicts Muslims in general as hedonists who are under the impression that it is good to give full reign to the base functions of the body rather than giving primacy to reason. This polemic draws on Proclus, giving us another example of enthusiasm for this pagan Neoplatonist. Evidently Eustratios thought far more highly of Proclus than of the Prophet of Islam, whom he compares to the notoriously debauched Persian king Sardanapalus.

Of course, it was easy to be rude about Islam when you were sitting safely in Constantinople. Encounters between Christian and Muslim scholars in the Islamic world tended to be more polite. Most of the surviving works of interreligious disputation actually come from there, not from the Byzantine empire. This stands to reason, because of the large Christian population in places like Syria and Egypt.

The Arab conquests occurred with breathtaking speed, but the spread of Islam was a much slower process. In part this is because the Muslim rulers had a concrete disincentive to promote conversion. All non-Muslims were made to pay a special tax, the *jizya*, a policy already mentioned in the Quran (9:29), so as more people converted, tax revenues would decrease. Furthermore the Quran instructed, "Let there be no compulsion in religion" (2:256), and commanded Muslims to be courteous when disputing with the so-called "people of the Book" (29:46); that is, groups like Jews and Christians who were in possession of their own revelatory texts. The Old Testament prophets are recognized in Islam, and Jesus is also held to be a genuine prophet. Verses in the Quran do, however, deny that Christ was the son of God, critically remarking that the Christians "exaggerate" in their religion (4:171). The revelation also rejects the fundamental Christian belief that God is a Trinity, insisting that God is one (4:171, 5:73, 6:22–3, 16:18).

So we see that the goddess of history, for all her mischief, is capable of subtlety. Christians living in Muslim territory were free to pursue their religion, even if they suffered from that extra tax and certain other measures, for instance the requirement to wear distinctive clothes. Christians could pursue philosophy and the sciences, too. Indeed it was Christian scholars living under Islam who did most of the work translating Aristotle and other philosophers into Arabic.[9] None of those translators was more highly placed than Timothy I, an East Syrian patriarch who died in 823. At the behest of the Muslim caliph al-Mahdī, Timothy translated Aristotle's *Topics*, a handbook of dialectic. It's been speculated that this was chosen as an early text to render into Arabic precisely because of its usefulness in interreligious debate.[10] Al-Mahdī evidently had a personal interest in such debate. He personally challenged Timothy to defend the cogency of Christianity at the royal court.

We have a record of the debate between the two men, written by Timothy in Syriac and also extant in Arabic translation.[11] It was probably written to give other Christians guidance, showing them how one should answer the frequently asked questions of Muslim opponents. Yet it is far less disrespectful of the Islamic point of view than what we just found in authors from the Greek-speaking realm, like Niketas and Eustratios. The caliph is shown to be an acute and clever opponent, and Timothy does not denigrate Islam (of course, it would have been foolish of him to do so, given the setting). In this respect, and in the issues covered, Timothy's account sets the tone for later works of disputation. Much attention is paid to the cogency of the Trinitarian teaching, with Timothy offering several analogies that reappear in other Christian texts: God the Father gives rise to the Son like the sun emanating its rays, or like the soul giving forth speech (5–6, 10, 14, 22–3, 80, etc.). Al-Mahdī challenges this by pointing out that speech disappears as it is uttered, whereas the divine Son is meant to be eternal (16), but Timothy points out that the meaning of a speech remains in the soul of the one who is speaking (25).

This is one of many passages in the disputation that touch on philosophical issues, in this case philosophy of language. Another example comes when al-Mahdī demands to know whether God willed the crucifixion to happen, or willed the sins of Adam and of the fallen angel Satan (48–9). Here we have a particularly challenging instance of the problem of evil. The caliph is asking whether God does not merely allow evils to occur, but actually *wants* them to happen so that His divine plan may be fulfilled. To this Timothy replies that evils are freely committed, but God uses them to good ends, as the caliph himself might take advantage of a burnt down house to build something new (51–2). Yet Timothy admits the limitations of his, or any human's, ability to explain Christian doctrine fully. God is ultimately unknowable and the metaphors he uses to explain such things as the Trinity remain just that: metaphors (22, 82).

Timothy's response to Islam is very different from what we found in John of Damascus, who lived only a couple of generations earlier.[12] Where John presented Islam as one of many heresies, an unacceptable divergence from Christian belief, Timothy sees it more as a misstep on the road from Judaism to Christianity. He goes so far as to cite a passage from the Quran that could be read as supporting the Trinity, and al-Mahdī returns the favor by mentioning passages in the Bible that foretell the coming of the Prophet. But in the long run, this debate was not going to be fought over scriptural exegesis, if only because neither group accepted the legitimacy of the other's revelatory text. Of course, Christians rejected the Quran, while Muslims claimed that the New Testament distorted Jesus' true teachings and argued that the biblical text had been corrupted (back then, people were well aware of the difficulties of accurately transmitting handwritten documents).

The weapon of choice for interreligious dispute was, instead, rational argument. Muslims were confident that they could show Christianity to be incoherent, given its commitment to a God who is both one and three, both divine and human. Not long after Timothy, we have Muslim authors like al-Qāsim ibn Ibrāhīm and Abū ʿĪsā al-Warrāq, who composed diatribes against the irrationality of Christian belief.[13] These are well-informed texts. They mention those Christian metaphors for the Trinity, like comparing God to the sun; are able to quote from the Gospels; and display an understanding of the differences between the various Christian sects. A favorite Muslim argument is that there is no way to describe God as a Trinity without running into self-contradiction. The Son would have to be both created and uncreated, and God would have to be both one and many. This provides us with a context for understanding the emphasis on God's unity found in the contemporaneous philosopher al-Kindī, who actually wrote a short treatise against the Trinity in much the same spirit, explicitly deploying the tools of Aristotelian logic.[14] The treatise provoked a counter-refutation from Yaḥyā Ibn ʿAdī, who was a leading member of the so-called "Baghdad school" of Christian Aristotelian philosophers in the tenth century.

They represent an early peak for philosophical activity among Christians in the Islamic world, and provide us with a reminder that serious interest in philosophy was compatible with serious interest in theology. The last member of the Baghdad school, Ibn al-Ṭayyib, devoted himself to both Aristotle and his own faith, writing logical commentaries and a massive commentary on the Bible. As for Ibn ʿAdī, he wrote not only that response to al-Kindī but several more treatises in defense of the Trinity. The Christian founder of the school, Abū Bishr Mattā, was humiliated in a public debate with a Muslim linguist who argued for the superiority of Arabic grammar to Greek logic. This was among other things a proxy debate, interreligious disputation transposed to the context of an argument about language, as is clear from the fact that the grammarian mocks Abū Bishr for his belief in the Trinity.

Which brings us to the question: what is the difference between medieval Christians and myotonic or "fainting" goats? (For several minutes of good fun, look them up online.) Answer: the Christians were not going to take this aggression lying down. The tradition of apologetic writing inaugurated by Patriarch Timothy would continue throughout the classical period of Islam and beyond.[15] An example from about the same time as Timothy is provided by Abū Rāʾiṭa, a Miaphysite theologian from the Iraqi city of Tikrit.[16] He proposes to defend his own religion on rational grounds, presupposing that his opponents the Muslims, whom he calls the "people of the south" (165), ought to be reasonable enough to accept valid demonstrations (171). To explain the Trinity he offers analogies like those given by Timothy—the unity of the Persons is like the mingled light of three lamps (105)—but likewise admits that such analogies can never be really adequate (185). He also deploys the tools of Greek logic, suggesting that the one God relates to the three Persons as a species relates to its individuals. Three fainting goats will, despite sharing a species, differ in specifying characteristics, like the pattern on their fur or how loud an alarming sound needs to be before they topple over. In much the same way, the Persons are distinguished by "properties (*khawāṣṣa*)" yet agree in being divine (187). The species functions here as the "substance" (*jawhar*, rendering Greek *ousia*), a line of thought we already found in John of Damascus.

Usually, when people think at all of Christian philosophy in the medieval Middle East, they imagine the sort of figures I have discussed so far: translators and the members of the Baghdad school. But this is to forget two remarkable cultural developments that occurred somewhat later. First, a blossoming of scholarship in the city of Antioch. It temporarily fell under Byzantine control beginning in the year 969, creating the conditions for a further transmission of knowledge across linguistic lines.[17] Works were translated from Greek into Arabic, Georgian, and Armenian, and the productions of Antioch were later used by Coptic Christians in Egypt and rendered into Ethiopic. One figure worth mentioning here is ʿAbdallāh ibn al-Faḍl al-Anṭākī. Alongside his works as a translator, al-Anṭākī wrote another defense of the Trinity, echoing the way that Abū Rāʾiṭa used Aristotelian logic. Again, the Persons are described as individuals with distinguishing properties, and the Godhead itself can be understood as a kind of "universal." That might surprise a faithful Aristotelian, since Aristotle tends to see universals as in some sense "less real" than individuals (he calls them "secondary substances" in his *Categories*, whereas individuals are "primary substances"), and the Christians obviously don't want to say that God is less real than the Persons. Al-Anṭākī is presumably following a more Platonist line of thought, according to which universals are indeed fully real, more genuine cases of being than their individual participants.[18]

A second cultural development unfolds from the eleventh to fourteenth centuries or so. It has been called the "Syriac renaissance."[19] This too is often overlooked. Philosophy in Syriac is typically considered (again, when it is considered at all) as a minor transitional phase between the more celebrated philosophical literature written in Greek and Arabic. But if you were going to name the most significant philosopher to write in Syriac, you might plausibly choose a relatively late author whose name was Gregory Abū l-Faraj bar ʿEbroyo; you'll be glad to know he's usually known in English by the more memorable name Bar Hebraeus.[20] He was a well-traveled man, who spent time in Aleppo, Baghdad, and most importantly Marāgha, site of a famous observatory erected by the newly arrived Mongol regime. Here Bar Hebraeus would have come into contact with the circle gathered around the Avicennan philosopher and astronomer Naṣīr al-Dīn al-Ṭūsī.

As a result, Bar Hebraeus was able to draw extensively on philosophical works by Muslims, which he gathered together in encyclopedic treatises of his own written in Syriac. Note that this was in the middle of the thirteenth century, so not long after some of these same works were being received by Christians in Latin over in Western Europe. Particularly important for Bar Hebraeus, just as for the Latin schoolmen, was Avicenna. In his most important work, called *The Cream of Wisdom*, Bar Hebraeus follows the model of the *Healing*, Avicenna's masterpiece, though he uses many other authors too. Especially for topics like ethics and politics where Avicenna was less central, he drew on other authors like al-Ṭūsī.[21] Bar Hebraeus freely admitted the need to make use of Muslim scholarship. As he ruefully admitted, "we, from whom [the Muslims] have acquired wisdom through translators, all of whom were Syrians, find ourselves compelled to ask for wisdom from them."[22]

This brings us to another way that philosophical learning was important for interreligious rivalry: such expertise was recognized as a sign of cultural superiority. Back in the ninth century, the polymath al-Jāḥiẓ acidly remarked that "the Christians and the Byzantines (*Rūm*) have neither science, nor expository literature, nor vision, and their names should be erased from the registers of the philosophers and the sages."[23] On the other side of the border, there was understandably not much willingness to concede that the Muslims were outdoing the Greek Christians in mastery of Greek science. But occasionally we find acknowledgment of the achievements being made in the Islamic world. Symeon Seth, who died in the early twelfth century, pointed out that much could be learned from consulting the literature of the Muslims, Persians, and Indians.[24] Symeon translated texts from Arabic into Greek, adding to our sense that in this period pretty much every language of scholarship was being translated into pretty much every other language. He himself was an expert on astronomy and medicine, and followed his own advice when it came to learning from the Muslims. He was unusual in his linguistic expertise and openness to Islamic learning; but as we'll see next, less so in his ambition to cultivate an interest in science.

17

DO THE MATH
SCIENCE IN THE PALAIOLOGAN RENAISSANCE

Next time you're helping a child with math homework and get the inevitable question, "When am I ever going to need to know any of this stuff?," I suggest you tell the story of Leo the Philosopher, also known as Leo the Mathematician. He was a ninth-century Byzantine scholar whose student was captured by Muslim forces and then dazzled his captors with the learning he had received from Leo.[1] So impressed were the Muslims that the caliph wrote to offer Leo a position at court, but he was outbid by the emperor. Leo wound up staying in Constantinople, enjoying a healthy salary. It's a particularly impressive story given the high standard of sciences in the Islamic world at that time and the fact that, as we've seen, Muslims were usually very disparaging about the state of Byzantine learning.

The feeling was, for the most part, mutual. Very few Byzantines were alive to the intellectual achievement of their contemporaries in the Islamic world. We just met an exception, Symeon Seth.[2] He went so far as to borrow from Muslim medical authors while criticizing the greatest of the Greek physicians, Galen. Symeon translated works by the ninth-century Persian philosopher and doctor al-Rāzī, who had had the temerity to assemble a list of errors in Galenic works which he candidly titled *Doubts About Galen*. Symeon followed suit, mentioning places where Galen seemed to contradict himself and preferring the authority of Aristotle. More generally, the Byzantines carried on the tradition of Greek medicine, though it seems they did less to improve on Galenic medicine than their counterparts in the Islamic world. Like the Muslims they did have hospitals, pharmacists, and surgeons. We even hear of an operation to separate conjoined twins which was a partial success, in that one twin survived it and lived on for a few more days.

A more profound engagement with science from the Islamic world can be found with the disciplines of astronomy and astrology. Symeon Seth is again relevant here, because he is mentioned in Anna Komnene's *Alexiad* as one of the numerous astrologers present at her father's court (§6.7). Already in the eleventh century we see astronomical calculations being done on the basis of Arabic material. But the most remarkable such case comes later, with George Choniades. He studied in the Persian city of Tabrīz in the late thirteenth century, and translated astronomical works from Persian into Greek. There was sufficient enthusiasm for this sort of material that in the following century, a theologian was moved to condemn it and one emperor banned the prediction of eclipses because they were thought to be omens of political upheaval. This made for quite a change from the days of an earlier emperor, Manuel I Komnenos, whose embrace of astrology was heavily criticized by later authors. He even wrote a treatise in defense of the discipline, insisting that astrology should not be confused with the sinful practice of magic.

It's significant that when Anna mentions Symeon Seth and his intellectual interests, she calls him a *mathematikos*. That may seem a strange way to refer to an astrologer, but in a Byzantine context it made perfect sense. Like the Latin Christians with their *quadrivium*, the Greeks recognized four mathematical sciences (*mathematike tetraktus*), namely arithmetic, geometry, spherics or astronomy, and harmonics or the study of music. The pursuit of these sciences might be used as a rough indicator of whether Byzantine society was flourishing in any given period, something else you might mention to homework-shy kids. (If this distracts them into a discussion of Byzantine history, there's nothing wrong with that.) By this measure Byzantium in the thirteenth and fourteenth centuries was doing rather well. That may sound surprising, given the radically reduced territory of the empire in this late period and the cataclysmic sack of Constantinople by the crusaders in 1204. But after that disaster there was some scientific activity around the court in exile at Nicaea. And once the capital was retaken from the Latins in the year 1261, we find a remarkable resurgence of scholarship over several generations under the Palaiologan dynasty.

The scholars in question thought of themselves as reviving disciplines that had been ignored for generations, and modern-day scholars have agreed, to the point that they speak of a "Palaiologan Renaissance."[3] And yes, we've heard this before. It seems that the learned men of Constantinople were constantly congratulating themselves for a revival of learning, and we were only just speaking of a "Syriac Renaissance." But to quote Börje Bydén, who has done fundamental studies of the scientific output of this period, even though in Byzantium renaissance "is a hackneyed idea, it normally contains a germ of truth."[4] Scholars of the time complain of difficulty finding books and teachers, and though that may be in part an attempt to claim originality for themselves it's clear that the waning political fortunes of the empire really did lead to poor conditions for intellectual activity in previous generations.

The good news is that this is the last renaissance I'll be mentioning before I get to the real thing. In fact, you could say that in a sense we have now finally arrived at the real thing. We'll be seeing in the next chapters how the work of late Byzantine scholars anticipated, and then inspired, the blossoming of humanism in Renaissance Italy. That's most obvious with figures like Gemistos Plethon, who actually traveled to Italy in the fifteenth century (Chapter 20). But it applies already to authors of the Nicaean and Palaiologan periods, who engaged in many of the activities characteristic of Italian humanism: editing Greek texts, writing commentaries, and of course mastering a wide range of disciplines, as befits true "renaissance men."

Consider Nikephoros Blemmydes, who survived the sack of Constantinople as a child and was trained at Prousa and Nicaea. Though he was offered a post at the Nicaean court he decided instead to join the church, where he rose to a high rank. He was tutor to Theodore II Laskaris, whom you might remember from our look at Byzantine political philosophy (Chapter 8). Blemmydes has even been given credit for inspiring Laskaris to try to become a kind of "philosopher emperor."[5] In an account of his own life, Blemmydes tells us of traveling extensively as he tried to track down manuscripts. He saw precious books at the monastery of Mount Athos that could not be found elsewhere. Among his own works are an *Introductory Epitome* on logic and natural philosophy. It draws on Aristotle, of course, and also on commentaries by figures like the late ancient Platonist Simplicius.[6]

Alongside Theodore Laskaris, another of Blemmydes' students was George Akropolites, who brings us back to Constantinople. He was the first head of an imperial school reestablished at the capital under the Palaiologan emperor Michael VIII. He features in an incident that has been taken as emblematic of the way that these scholars were restoring science after an age of ignorance. While still at the court of Nicaea, Akropolites was asked to explain why eclipses happen and gave a (correct) answer that he had learned from Blemmydes. This was greeted with mockery by another scholar who was present, and by the empress herself! Another author of the time was kinder, praising Akropolites as the equal of Aristotle in logic and natural philosophy, and of Plato in theology and Attic Greek.[7]

Perhaps he was their equal as a teacher, too, because one of his students was among the most outstanding of these men we might call "Byzantine humanists." This was Maximos Planoudes, who was highly placed under Andronikos II; we still have a letter he wrote to this emperor and speeches he gave at court. Planoudes copied and edited Greek works on an impressive range of subjects, from Plato's dialogues to Plutarch's *Moralia*, from Ptolemy's treatise on geography to the *Arithmetic* of Diophantos, on which he also wrote a commentary. He even copied from Marcus Aurelius' *Meditations*. Actually I just said that the Byzantine humanists were "men" but we know that at least one woman shared Planoudes' scholarly interests: Theodora, the emperor's niece, also collected books, copied a work by Simplicius, and wrote to Planoudes asking that he correct her copy of a work on harmonics.[8] With Planoudes we are in the happy situation of having manuscripts that actually belonged to him, something that will become more and more common as we move forward into the Italian Renaissance and philosophy in early modern Europe. This is exciting, because we'll be able to know exactly what various philosophers were reading; sometimes we even have the notes they made on these texts. Modern-day researchers can reconstruct entire scholarly libraries, even hold in their hands the very copies of the books used by these long-dead philosophers.

But let's not get ahead of ourselves. I still need to mention the scholar who is perhaps most central for present purposes, one who also flourished during the reign of Andronikos II. In fact he was even this emperor's chief minister. His name was Theodore Metochites. Like Blemmydes he wrote epitomes or paraphrases of works by Aristotle, for this purpose drawing on earlier commentators like Michael of Ephesus. But Metochites was by no means a slavish follower of Aristotle. To the contrary, he found Aristotle's criticisms of his own teacher Plato distasteful, and thought that in these passages Aristotle was being needlessly contentious and competitive, since in fact the two great philosophers agreed about pretty well everything. Two paragraphs back, I mentioned that when George Akropolites was compared to Aristotle, this was in recognition of his prowess in logic and natural philosophy. The same sentiment can be found in Metochites, for example in a poem he addressed to Nikephoros Gregoras, encouraging him to the study of philosophy in general and, in the case of Aristotle, "his works on logic and physics" in particular.[9] For Metochites Aristotle was authoritative for the rather introductory subject of logic and the study of crude material things, but not a specialist in the more refined discipline of mathematics.

Metochites had philosophical reasons for this preference. In the preface to a work on astronomy, he expresses the classically Platonic attitude that physical things are subject to inevitable change and variation, unlike the secure and immutable truths of mathematics. In light of this, he rates the natural sciences rather low in epistemic terms. They can provide no certainty, unlike the mathematical arts, and also theology thanks to the certitude that comes with faith.[10] Here we have yet another anticipation of Renaissance Italy, where the rediscovery of the Hellenistic philosophical schools will have a huge impact. Metochites shows a remarkable awareness of the Skeptical school of the Hellenistic period. He sees the Skeptics as fundamentally agreeing with his own Platonic stance on the unknowability of a world that is in constant flux. For him, then, Skepticism amounts to a negative claim, namely that the human mind cannot achieve knowledge of things. Metochites does not seem to adopt the more subtle approach of the "Pyrrhonist" skeptic who simply suspends judgment about everything (including the question whether knowledge is possible: this allows the Pyrrhonist to avoid the apparent contradiction of claiming to know that they can't know anything). This despite the fact that the work of the great exponent of Pyrrhonism, Sextus Empiricus, was being copied at about this same period in the late thirteenth century.[11]

By an irony of history, or just because these Byzantines weren't very creative when it came to naming their kids (who, you can bet, did their math homework without complaining), Metochites' greatest rival and his most accomplished student were both named Nikephoros. The rival was Nikephoros Choumnos, another minister under Andronikos II.[12] Things between them started politely enough, with Choumnos seeking Metochites' judgment on works he had written about topics in natural philosophy. But when Choumnos wrote a diatribe about poor writing style and Metochites understood himself to be the target, their relationship soured; they sniped at each other over topics such as astronomy and the correct exegesis of Plato and Aristotle. As one scholar has remarked of this unedifying spectacle, "one observes with mixed wonder and distaste that a contest for supreme political power between two leading imperial ministers should produce this offshoot of scholastic controversy."[13]

Metochites had a more favorable reception from his student Nikephoros Gregoras, who called his teacher a "living library (*bibliotheke empsychos*)" and said that the souls of Homer, Plato, Ptolemy, and Plutarch were united in Metochites. Gregoras inherited his master's scientific interests. He proposed a calendrical reform that anticipated by some two and a half centuries the changes that would be made to produce the Gregorian calendar in the West. He also seems to have shared Metochites' philosophical posture, as we can see from a dialogue Gregoras wrote called the *Florentius*.[14] Here he echoes Metochites by charging Aristotle with disrespect towards Plato. He shows independence of mind, though, when it comes to specific doctrines of Aristotelian natural philosophy. Some of those doctrines were, of course, routinely rejected in Byzantine culture, obvious examples being Aristotle's claim that the soul cannot survive bodily death and his view that things are always made from pre-existing matter, which would rule out God's power to create from nothing.[15] But Gregoras and other Palaiologan thinkers also make such un-Aristotelian moves as accepting the existence of void, both outside and inside the cosmos; rejecting Aristotle's account of how vision works; and denying that the heavens are made of a fifth element distinct from those we find in the earthly realm.

The nature of the elements was in fact much debated at this time. One point of contention was Nikephoros Choumnos' arresting claim that air is wetter, or more moist, than water.[16] His namesake Nikephoros Gregoras found this incredible, and it certainly seems that he has the better side of the argument: surely water is as moist as anything could be? But we should step back and ask ourselves why Choumnos would have adopted such an outlandish position. It was first a matter of conceptual tidiness. Choumnos wanted to take each of Aristotle's basic qualities, namely heat, cold, wetness, and dryness, to be the dominant feature of one of the four elements. Clearly fire is the element that is primarily hot, and earth primarily dry. Since air is not cold at all, in the Aristotelian scheme, but rather both hot and wet, that leaves only water to be primarily cold. So by process of elimination, it is apparently air that is primarily wet.

Perhaps then we should just give up on assigning the four qualities to the four elements, however tidy it would be. But there is a more profound rationale underlying Choumnos' view, which is that moisture is not really what you might suppose it to be. The wet or moist is not necessarily what soaks, or what quenches thirst. Rather it is most fundamentally that which is *fluid*, just as the dry is that which is solid. (In keeping with this Choumnos holds that both fire and earth, the two dry elements, are solid.) And air is indeed more "fluid" than water: it is more easily moved and even less apt to retain a shape than water. So we gain a useful insight from what may seem to be a rather technical scholastic debate. It calls our attention to the fact that Aristotelian elemental theory was more like modern chemistry than you might suppose. The qualities and elements it invoked were not just the everyday things we experience, like clods of earth, flickering flames, or the sopping wetness of a sponge. They were, instead, theoretical postulates that underlie and explain such phenomena. You will never encounter pure fire or pure earth, only bodies that are mixed out of pure elements, and the properties those pure elements possess may, as Choumnos realized, be defined in quite abstract terms.

If this debate shows how intricately the Palaiologan scholars engaged with Aristotelian natural philosophy, their devotion to the mathematical sciences shows them adopting a fundamentally Platonic outlook. Plato had, after all, said in more than one dialogue that astronomy or mathematics is a step towards higher philosophy, one that must be studied and mastered before attaining true wisdom (*Republic* 529a, *Timaeus* 47a–b). In keeping with this, Michael Psellos described mathematics as a rung on the ladder of disciplines he ascended, culminating in metaphysics. In the same spirit Nikephoros Gregoras states that the mathematical art of astronomy is a "ladder adjacent to theology." Lest we miss the Platonist overtones, he adds that its study helps us to separate the soul's concerns from the corrupting pleasures of the body.[17]

It is easy to miss the broader theological motives and context of works that look like more or less faithful repetition of Aristotelian physics or other ancient Greek scientific works. But these were deeply pious scholars and their pursuit of science cannot be disentangled from that piety. This emerges at the end of a commentary on Aristotle's *Physics* by yet another Byzantine humanist of this period, George Pachymeres.[18] The commentary is rounded off with a poem in ecstatic praise of Aristotle, who, says Pachymeres, understood "what pagans did not teach." But hang on a second, wasn't Aristotle a pagan? Of course, but Pachymeres thinks that Aristotle has outdone the *other* pagans with his account of a first cause of all motion, a theory that shows him glimpsing the nature of the Christian God. Pachymeres, by the way, is another scholar whose own books still survive. We have copies of Platonic dialogues and works by Proclus in his handwriting, and also the autograph of Pachymeres' own commentary on the *Physics*, only one of numerous Aristotelian works to get this treatment from his pen. He also wrote a work on the mathematical arts of the *Quadrivium*, one of two surviving Byzantine texts that cover these sciences in their entirety (the other is anonymous).

With their revival of philosophy and science the Nicaean and Palaiologan authors show us the remarkable endurance of Byzantine intellectual culture. The fortune of their own works confirms the same point. The writings of these men were read in Renaissance Italy, whose culture they did so much to presage and to facilitate. Their writings were also recycled and recopied in the later Greek tradition, with Pachymeres' compilatory work (the *Philosophia*) being used in further compilations,[19] and manuscripts of Blemmydes still being made as late as the nineteenth century! But we're not ready to look ahead that far just yet. More immediately we need to consider a dispute in which theological concerns were far more evident. This famous set piece of late Byzantine culture will involve one of the figures we've just met, namely Nikephoros Gregoras. But its main character, and Gregoras' main opponent, was a dominant personality of the time and indeed of the whole history of Byzantine theology.

18

THROUGH HIS WORKS YOU SHALL KNOW HIM PALAMAS AND HESYCHASM

If you have come to this book after reading the previous volume in the series, devoted to medieval philosophy, you may have been struck by several differences. There have been fewer Marx Brothers references, and more rulers named Constantine, albeit—like a good pasta sauce—with some Basil thrown in for good measure. Also, religious institutions have played a far less dominant role. Our account of Latin medieval philosophy included extensive discussion of mendicant orders and monastic contexts. In Byzantium too we've met our share of churchmen, such as the monk John of Damascus, the bishop Nicholas of Methone, and the Syrian patriarch Timothy. But many of our protagonists have been men and women of the secular world. An exception who proved the rule was Michael Psellos, whose brief stint as a monk convinced him that he preferred the life of the courtier and scholar.

In fact, though, monastic traditions were of tremendous importance in Byzantine culture, and not only as centers of spirituality. Some of those manuscripts we discussed were made or stored at monasteries. They were also institutions of political and economic importance. Their status under imperial tax law was a matter of heated dispute, and it was common for aristocrats to become patrons of monasteries. Psellos is again an example, as is a figure we met last time, Theodore Metochites, whose refurbishment of a monastery at Chora included the sponsoring of mosaics that survive to the present day and are a highlight of extant Byzantine art.[1] But of course monasteries were not just places where the rich could simultaneously display both wealth and piety. They were above all dedicated to ascetic religious devotion, following advice laid down by the Cappadocian father Basil of Caesarea and subsequently by Theodore the Studite.

This earlier Theodore was abbot of one of the most important monastic institutions of the empire, the monastery of Stoudios, founded in the fifth century and located in Constantinople. It was admired for its role in opposing iconoclasm and seems to have played a key role in the introduction of the minuscule script we spoke about as one of the main advances in Byzantine writing technology. The Stoudion was home to other famous names too, such as Symeon the New Theologian, a contemporary of Psellos and like him an aristocrat who entered monastic life as a refuge from politics.[2] Actually, a hagiography of Symeon makes him sound more like Harry Potter than Michael Psellos, firstly because of the supernatural feats ascribed to Symeon, such as miraculous acts of healing, and secondly because at the monastery he slept in a small cupboard under the stairs.

Unlike Harry Potter, though, Symeon had a good relationship with "He who must not be named." Under the influence of theologians like Pseudo-Dionysius and Gregory Nazianzus, Symeon was convinced of the utter transcendence of God above human language and thought.[3] He therefore called God the "Unattainable." Insofar as a connection to God could be attained nonetheless, it would certainly not be by the study of pagan philosophy. When a theologian quizzed Symeon on matters of doctrine, he scornfully replied that the Holy Spirit is sent "not to rhetoricians, not to philosophers, not to those who have studied Hellenistic writings . . . but to the pure in heart and body, who speak and even more live simply."[4] For Symeon rigorous asceticism was a path towards a mystical vision of God. He described that experience as a light filling all the space around the mystic, with the mystic himself seeming to become one with the light.

In retrospect it is hard to read about Symeon without seeing him as the forerunner of a later thinker, a man who lived two centuries later and who occupies an even more prominent role in the history of Byzantine theology. This was Gregory Palamas. He was associated with another famous monastery, located on the peninsula of Mount Athos, and his name is all but synonymous with the approach to monastic practice called Hesychasm.[5] This word comes from the Greek *hesychia*, meaning "silence" or "restfulness," a term that had been used in a spiritual context since the fourth century. It refers to the monk's quiet devotion in the form of unceasing prayer, a practice that involved bodily disciplines like breath control and fasting in order to aid mental concentration. Palamas was a powerful defender of this life against its detractors, something that ironically meant that his own career would be anything but peaceful.

Instead he was at the center of the Hesychast controversy,[6] a debate that went on for years, with the fortunes of its protagonists rising and falling with the star of their supporters among the political elite. To do what J. K. Rowling could not manage with her Harry Potter novels, and keep a long story short, everything began in 1335 when a Greek-speaking Italian, Barlaam of Calabria, was asked to refute theological errors held by the Latin Christians. Part of his strategy was to argue that the Latin scholastic theologians were inappropriately striving to establish syllogistic proofs concerning the nature of God, as if the divine could be captured with the tools of Aristotelian logic. Barlaam denied that this was possible, holding instead that God is too transcendent to be grasped by humans with the certainty that is required in Aristotelian science.[7] Palamas agreed with Barlaam that God cannot be grasped by human reason, but argued that God could be grasped with certainty nonetheless, through faith. He added, in a rather Platonist vein, that the physical world is subject to constant change whereas God is eternal and immutable. So if we expect certain knowledge to concern what is forever true, as Aristotle himself says, then this sort of knowledge in fact applies especially to God, not to created things.

Barlaam tried to defuse the situation by claiming that it was effectively a terminological misunderstanding. One might achieve "demonstration" or "certainty" about God in some loose sense, but not the technical sense described by Aristotle. But there was no denying that he and Palamas had a serious disagreement on one other point. For Barlaam human reason and philosophy may be incapable of discerning the divine nature, but they are still the best tools we have for understanding God and His creation. Palamas, by contrast, believed in the possibility of a mystical vision in which God appears to the believer as a brilliant illumination. Monks like Symeon the New Theologian had enjoyed such visions and so had the disciples who, according to the Bible (Matthew 17:1–2) saw Christ appear to them on Mount Tabor, clothed in light. Of course, Barlaam accepted the reality of such experiences, but said they were created by God. For Palamas, though, the light was God Himself.

Well, sort of. We've now come to the key move in Palamas' defense of Hesychasm, his contrast between what is in Greek called the *ousia* and *energeiai* of God, that is, His essence and His "activities" (often translated in secondary literature with "energies," since the English is close to the original Greek, but this to my mind privileges etymology over understanding). The distinction goes way back in the Christian theological tradition.[8] It was used by Maximus Confessor, who argued that since there were two natures in Christ, divine and human, Christ must be capable of "activities" that express His two natures. For instance walking is a human activity but His divinity makes it possible for Him to walk on water.[9] The Cappadocian fathers too distinguished nature or essence from activity.

This can easily look like a purely theological point, so it's worth taking a moment to explain why it is of general philosophical interest. The Cappadocians applied the point to all things, not only God. They held that the essence even of an insect is ultimately inaccessible to us, never mind the essence of God. Since in this life, at least, our understanding is based entirely on sense-perception, we can never hope to know true natures, but we access those natures indirectly through their external manifestations. All of this sounds much more skeptical than what we might find in

Aristotle, but it has at least a family resemblance to ideas put forward by pagan Platonists. In particular, Plotinus had distinguished between the internal and external "activity (*energeia*)" of things, giving the everyday example of fire which naturally gives off heat and light as outer manifestations of an inner essence.[10] Christian thinkers took note of this distinction, and also took note of the forbiddingly ambitious standards that pagan thinkers had laid down for true philosophical understanding. You only understand the essences (or "inner activities") of things if you grasp unchanging, necessary, universal truths about them. Beginning with Plato, philosophers had been expressing doubt that mere sense experience would be enough to reach such a lofty ambition. Yet it is clearly possible to experience the *effects* that naturally arise from essences. Harry Potter has no clue what the essence of an owl is; not even Hermione can figure that out. But it's easy to observe the activities that flow from the owl's nature, such as flying or delivering the mail.

Now we can return to that claim that Palamas was making, but only sort of, namely that when Jesus' disciples or a monk behold a divine light, they are beholding God.[11] If we want to speak strictly we should say that they are not beholding God's essence or nature, but experiencing the activity or "energy" that makes manifest that essence or nature (*Triads*, §§2.3.8, 3.2.8). One should not be misled by this, however, into thinking that the mystic fails to behold God after all. Just consider that when you stretch out your hand to feel the warmth of a fire, you are really experiencing the fire. Just so, the mystic who encounters God's light is experiencing God through His activity. This is how it is possible to "participate" in or "unify" with God (*Chapters*, §§75, 78). Furthermore, God's activity is not created, as Barlaam claimed, but itself divine (*Chapters*, §72). God remains unnamable and incomprehensible in His essence (*Chapters*, §144), yet the union or participation of a mystical vision allows us to go beyond the purely negative approach of theologians who allow us only to say what God is *not* (*Triads*, §§1.3.4, 2.3.35). It is a higher way of grasping God born of practice and known only through experience.

This shows how wrong Barlaam was to extol the admittedly limited achievements of rational philosophy as the highest that can be attained by humankind. Palamas would agree with the somewhat earlier author John Tzetzes who wrote, "The kind of philosophy which is puffed up with arguments is false, the philosophy of real monks is the real kind. The latter is preparation for death and killing of the flesh and knowledge of the true and real beings, assimilation to God, as far as possible for humans, and love of wisdom and of God."[12] But notice that in the midst of this remark Tzetzes quotes Plato, who was the first to speak of "assimilation to God, as far as is possible" (*Theaetetus*, 176b). Similarly, we've just seen Palamas drawing on the pagan philosophical tradition in differentiating activities from essence, even if his immediate references are Greek theologians like Maximus and Gregory Nazianzus. In any case, Palamas is not out to denigrate natural reason.[13] Though he is highly critical of pagan philosophers, this is not because they used reason but because they *misused* it, leading them to embrace such erroneous doctrines as Plato's belief that the whole cosmos has a single "World Soul" (*Chapters*, §3, *Triads*, §1.1.18).

Palamas won the first round of the Hesychasm controversy when Barlaam was condemned in 1341. But the debate was far from over. This story has already had its fair share of Gregories, and Hesychasm was now criticized from a different direction by another one: Gregory Akindynos. He believed that Palamas was putting forward innovative doctrines and misinterpreting authoritative texts. Worst of all, by crediting the visionary with a true participation in God, Palamas was suggesting that the visionary can himself become divine. Palamas was vindicated again in 1347, only to be attacked anew by a figure we met in the last chapter, Nikephoros Gregoras. Both Akindynos and Gregoras believed that applying the distinction between essence and activity to God would have the consequence of splitting the divine realm into two. Or actually, since there are many activities, Palamas was dividing the divine into many more than two: there would be God's essence, and then His various activities or energies.[14]

This was the most difficult challenge for Palamas to meet, and in fact modern-day exegetes have not always agreed about how he meant to do so. In part he goes on the offensive by pointing out the dire consequences of rejecting the Hesychast theory. Given that various fathers of the church insisted on the ineffable transcendence of God's very essence, denying the reality of activities "around" the essence would mean cutting us off from God entirely. Also it cannot be the case that everything but God's essence is created, as His opponents claim, because then God's activity of creation would need to be created, which leads to a regress (*Chapters*, §73). The plurality of activities does not imply splitting up the unity of God. To the contrary, it proves that God's many activities must indeed be distinguished from His essence, since if they were not then God's essence would be subject to plurality (*Chapters*, §§99–100).

This is all clear and pretty convincing, but when he comes to defend his own view, Palamas' arguments are not so easy to follow, or for that matter to swallow. He is emphatic that the activities are "inseparable" from the essence, yet not "identical" with it. But when he tries to explain how this can be he tends to say such things as that God is "indivisibly divided and united divisibly" (*Chapters*, §81). It's hard to imagine his opponents were much impressed by this sort of thing, and as I say, more recent readers have been unsure what to make of it too. One school of thought holds that the distinction between essence and activity is merely conceptual, just a contrast we introduce in order to understand God better. But it seems more likely that he takes the distinction to be a real one, made between two things that are very intimately connected.[15]

Or rather, we should resist the urge to think of the activities as further "things" that might or might not be distinct from God.[16] We might instead understand them as what God *does*, and things that He does freely. This would be a significant difference from the original, Neoplatonic idea of an "activity" as a natural expression of an inner nature. After all, fire does not choose to radiate heat, and neither does Plotinus' first principle, the One, "decide" to emanate the rest of the cosmic hierarchy as if it might have refrained from doing so. For Palamas, by contrast, God does choose to manifest Himself to the prayerful monk as a brilliant light (*Triads*, §3.1.26). The visionary mystic is thus allowed to participate in God by freely offered grace (*Chapters*, §§69, 93).[17] To this extent it must be said that Palamas' theory is unmistakably a Christian one, a kind of metaphysical variation on the theme that God freely offered Himself as a sacrifice to redeem humankind.

This applies also to his celebration of the practical and even physical side of monastic practice. Intellectually minded opponents like Barlaam and Gregoras could not accept the idea that God might be received by the mystic in a physical way, not even if the physical phenomenon in question was light. This could be at most a symbol of divinity, not the real thing (*Triads*, §3.1.11). For Barlaam especially, the body was something to be fled for the sake of intellectual contemplation. But Palamas was thinking less Neoplatonically than him, and more Christologically. What could be more true to the idea of the incarnation than supposing that God comes to us when He sees fit, by making Himself manifest in the bodily realm?

An irony of this whole debate is that when Barlaam originally complained about those Latin scholastics, who believed that they could "syllogize" about God, he was saying something that should have been quite congenial to Palamas. Barlaam was trying to be faithful to the idea, so strong in Greek authorities like Pseudo-Dionysius, that if God can be grasped it can be only by a kind of "unknowing."[18] Being much less well acquainted with Latin literature than Barlaam, Palamas was slow to appreciate the force of this response to scholasticism, and quick to leap to the defense of monastic approaches to God.[19] Barlaam was an unusual figure in the degree of his openness to Western Christian culture. He abandoned Constantinople after his condemnation to join the papal court at Avignon, where he encountered Petrarch and offered him lessons in Greek. As meetings between East and West go, that's a pretty stunning one. But this was a period of many such encounters, of theological disputes between Latin and Greek Christianity, and of attempts to unite the two spheres that had been so divided.

19

UNITED WE FALL LATIN PHILOSOPHY IN BYZANTIUM

When I covered Latin medieval philosophy in this book series, perhaps I was a little bit unkind to Thomas Aquinas. Though I did give him extensive coverage, one of the main points of that coverage was to shift him away from center stage, to emphasize that he was only one of several important thinkers of high scholasticism, and one who was in some ways out of step with his contemporaries. I pointed out that other philosophers of the thirteenth century, such as Albert the Great, Henry of Ghent, and Duns Scotus, had a greater impact in the following century than Aquinas did. If you're an admirer of Aquinas who is still nursing a grudge about this, then you'll be glad to know that in this chapter I won't be doubting Thomas or his influence. To the contrary, I will be pointing to a largely unknown aspect of his legacy: the Greek translation and Byzantine reception of his works.

Usually we think of philosophy as moving from Greek to Latin, not the other way around. That process began with Cicero and Boethius in antiquity, was pushed forward by medieval translators like Eriugena and William of Moerbeke, and culminated with the scholars of the Renaissance we'll be meeting in the second part of this book, men like Marsilio Ficino with his translation of Platonic works. To think of Aquinas and other philosophers being translated from Latin into Greek, just as the Renaissance was about to begin in the West and in the final years of the Eastern empire, seems like history getting things backwards. But the Latin–Greek translations can also be seen as the culmination of a long series of encounters between West and East, encounters that had been going on throughout the whole Byzantine period.[1]

For the most part this is a story of political and religious interaction and rivalry. The two realms began to drift apart in about the fifth century, if not earlier, as the sole languages of church and state became Latin in the West and Greek in the East. There were frequent diplomatic contacts between the Carolingian West and the court at Byzantium, though, and in the tenth century a strong connection was made when the Byzantine princess Theophano married the Western emperor Otto II. This was among the highpoints of influence from the East upon the West, noticeable in artworks and the design of coinage. But there were many other examples of cultural exchange. Michael Psellos mentions having Westerners among his students (calling them "Celts"), while monastic life in the West was influenced by Eastern models, and Western romance literature was known and imitated in Greek. There are even Byzantine retellings of the story of King Arthur and his court.

Yet theological concerns constantly prevented true unity between Latin and Greek Christendom. A famous turning point was the so-called "Photian schism," named after the scholar and patriarch Photius and involving the aforementioned *filioque* controversy (see Chapter 5).[2] While the *filioque* clause would remain a key point of contention, there were to be other disagreements. The Latins were not comfortable with the Eastern devotion to icons that emerged out of the defeat of iconoclasm. Conversely, the Byzantines rejected the Latins' use of unleavened bread in the eucharist, because it was too reminiscent of Jewish practice at Passover, and because for them the presence of air in leavened bread symbolized the second, divine nature of Christ. They also objected to the idea of Purgatory as an unacceptable innovation, meaning that if Dante had been from Constantinople his *Divine Comedy* would have been one-third shorter.

The one thing Byzantine theologians enjoyed more than putting forth their own ideas was showing that the ideas of others are absurd. We've seen this in debates that pitted Greek theologians against one another and in texts written against Islam. They also wrote critically of the Latin church. One example, which because of my own allegiances as a sports fan has my favorite title from all of Byzantine literature, is the *Sacred Arsenal*.[3] It is not a prescient appreciation of London's greatest soccer team, but a lengthy theological treatise written in the 1170s by a scholar connected to the court of the Komnenoi named Andronikos Kammateros. The *Sacred Arsenal* is divided into two parts, the first attacking the Latin Christians, while the second is a collection of more than 1,000 proof texts and more than 200 arguments or "syllogisms" intended to establish the Greek position. Similar works were written on the other side, too. To take one notable case, Anselm of Canterbury (of "ontological argument" fame) composed a treatise *Against the Errors of the Greeks* in the context of a council held at Bari in 1098.

Religious harmony was a goal worth striving for. The political elite were keen to close the rift so as to present a united front against the threat of Islam. A repeated dynamic was that the members of this elite would reach agreement with the other side, only for the wider church membership to reject the deal. Thus a council at Lyons held in 1274, in celebration of the union of the two churches, was met with horror back in Constantinople: people shouted at the delegates, "You have become

Franks!"[4] Almost two centuries later a series of meetings was held in Florence, which in 1452 issued in a compromise on the *filioque* problem; but it would be rejected by an Eastern synod a few decades later.

Now, 1452 was the year before the fall of Constantinople to the Ottomans. What, you may be wondering, were the Byzantines playing at? At this point the Eastern empire's chances of survival were about the same as those of a snowball receiving vigorous back rubs in a Finnish sauna, yet the brightest minds of Constantinople were devoting their energies to disputing the niceties of Trinitarian doctrine. But actually this makes perfect sense. It was just the latest example of the Byzantines offering concessions to the West in hope of military assistance. Yet this was hope triumphing over experience. Emperor John V Palaiologos had gone so far as to accept the Catholic faith and abase himself at St Peter's in Rome, only to be forced to accept vassalage from the Ottomans. Nonetheless, the desperate military situation of the empire gives us a context for understanding the way that intellectuals, especially those who favored a union between the churches, became interested in the works of Western scholars.

Which brings us finally to the promised topic of the impact of Latin philosophy in the East. As I commented earlier, we've been getting the impression that philosophy was passing from every language used around the Mediterranean into every other language. The Latin–Greek translations complete that picture.[5] They were not on the scale of the translation movements that rendered Greek philosophy into Arabic, or Arabic and Greek philosophy into Latin, but they did have a significant impact on the final generations of thinkers who lived in the Byzantine empire. One of the translators was Maximos Planoudes (mentioned in Chapter 17): he produced Greek versions of works by Augustine, Boethius, and Anselm of Canterbury.[6] Of these his translation of Augustine's *On the Trinity* was particularly significant, and a surprising choice given that Augustine had helped to inspire the adoption of the *filioque* clause by theologians in the Latin West. Yet no less a Byzantine theologian than Gregory Palamas drew on this work by Augustine, taking over his idea that there are Trinitarian structures within the life of the human soul that mirror the inner dynamic of the three divine Persons.[7] It has also been suggested that Augustine may lie behind a passage in a work of uncertain origin that refutes absolute skepticism on the grounds that no one can doubt that he himself is "living, thinking, remembering, willing, and considering."[8] This argument, also found in Augustine, is famous for anticipating Descartes's anti-skeptical argument, "I think, therefore I am." So it is especially intriguing to see that an anonymous Byzantine author was struck by Augustine's idea.

The Latin Christian philosopher who made the biggest splash in Byzantium was Thomas Aquinas.[9] An astonishing number of his works were rendered into Greek, including both the *Summa contra gentiles* and *Summa theologiae* as well as commentaries on Aristotle and a variety of other treatises. This was mostly the work of three men: two brothers, named Demetrios and Prochoros Kydones, and then George Gennadios Scholarios. Let's leave Gennadios Scholarios aside for now, since we'll have an opportunity to discuss him in the next chapter, and focus on the Kydones brothers.[10] With them we return to the Hesychast controversy. As we just saw, the spark for that intellectual battle was lit by an encounter with Latin scholasticism, as Palamas reacted to Barlaam of Calabria's complaint that the schoolmen of the West ought not to be applying the tools of syllogistic reasoning to God. Palamas' view that God is known through his "activities" was approved by the Byzantine church in the mid-fourteenth century, which opened another divide with the West and also provoked dissent within Eastern Christianity. Like Palamas, Prochoros Kydones was a monk at Mount Athos, but he was a committed enemy of Hesychasm. He was expelled from the monastery there and in 1368 condemned as a heretic for his opposition to Palamite theology. This drew his more moderate brother Demetrios into the fray, as he began to write on behalf of Prochoros.

As Marcus Plested has remarked in a monograph on the Eastern reception of Aquinas, Prochoros was the better theologian of the two but much the worse diplomat.[11] In refuting the Hesychasts' views the two brothers were able to draw on extensive knowledge of Aquinas. Demetrios Kydones had acquired this knowledge by, quite literally, doing his homework. Some years previously Demetrios had been a court official and found that the interpreters tasked with translating for visitors from the Latin West were not up to the task. By this period the Dominican order had been sending representatives to Byzantium for some time. They had already sent missionaries to convert Orthodox Christians to the Catholic point of view in the early thirteenth century, and it was a Dominican who wrote the first critique of the "Greek" theology that could be read in the Greek language.[12] So it was to a Dominican friar that Demetrios turned to acquire facility with Latin, and this instructor set him the task of working on texts by Thomas Aquinas. It's advice that remains valid, by the way: Aquinas' Latin is fairly straightforward, and I would recommend him to anyone who is starting to read medieval Latin philosophy in the original.

In any case, Demetrios Kydones was very much taken with Aquinas and moved on to translating his works. In doing so he displayed the philological care that distinguished so many Byzantine forerunners of Renaissance humanism. He consulted the original texts of Aristotle used by Aquinas while making his Greek translations from Aquinas' Latin, and he sought to collate multiple manuscripts to avoid errors, though he complained that these were difficult to track down.[13]

Demetrios and his brother Prochoros used Aquinas against their theological opponents. Pivotal to the theory of Palamas and the Hesychasts was a contrast between God's activities or actualities (*energeiai*) and His essence; we can know the former, but not the latter. By contrast, Aquinas had drawn on Aristotle to argue that God is, in His essence, already being itself (*esse ipsum*), in other words pure actuality.[14] The Kydones brothers accepted this equation between actuality and essence, thus eliminating the key contrast of Palamas' philosophical theology. They also put to use Aquinas' famous theory of analogy, by arguing that the light shown to Christ's apostles and in mystical visions is not divine, as Palamas insisted, but symbolizes him only analogically.

By being so open to the Latin Christian sphere, which according to Demetrios formed a single "people (*demos*)" with the Eastern Christians, the brothers departed from the long-standing Byzantine habit of sneering at the Catholics and the very language that they wrote in. It was sometimes claimed that the lamentable introduction of the *filioque* clause was occasioned by the inflexibility of Latin, and naturally such events as the 1204 sack of Constantinople by the crusaders did not improve the reputation of the West. Indeed, Barlaam of Calabria once pointed out to representatives of the pope that poor treatment of the East by the West did more to undermine church unity than genuine disagreements in doctrine.[15] But by the time of the Hesychast controversy, the Orthodox were starting to appreciate the subtlety and rigor of Latin scholasticism. Demetrios openly stated that the intellectual standard among the Greeks was well below that of the Latin West and even suggested that Latin is more precise than Greek, not less.[16]

The Hesychasts too found much to admire in Aquinas.[17] Take, for instance, the emperor John VI Kantakuzene, who was a supporter of Palamite thought both before and after he stepped down from his office to become a monk. He could have made the obvious move of criticizing the Kydones brothers for indulging in the logical games of Latin scholasticism. But, despite snidely remarking that Aquinas "breathes syllogisms rather than air," he did not make this the hallmark of his defense of Hesychasm. To the contrary, he made free use of Aquinas' ideas. For on his view the problem was not to use syllogisms in theology, but to use them badly, as did Prochoros in setting forth his heretical views. Another Palamite, Theophanes of Nicaea, even used typical phrases from Aquinas in his own writings, for instance by introducing counterarguments with the phrase "to which I answer that...," Aquinas' Latin *respondeo dicendum* transformed into the Greek *pros de ta toiauta rheteon*.

It's worth emphasizing this point, because it warns us not to assume that mystically inclined thinkers like the Palamites, or devout Byzantine theologians more generally, were uniformly opposed to the use of rational argumentation in matters of religion. Admittedly, some did see this as both a hallmark and weakness of Latin scholasticism. Again we may recall Barlaam initiating the Hesychast controversy by making precisely this complaint. Other thinkers of the late Byzantine period can be found saying things like "Aristotle and his philosophy have nothing in common with the truths revealed by Christ."[18] But remember too that the *Sacred Arsenal* produced hundreds of "syllogisms" in support of the Greek theological position. The Palamites followed suit by using Aquinas and other Western thinkers against themselves, as they defended Hesychasm and charged the Western position on the *filioque* with being irrational and inconsistent. Even those who were more firmly opposed to Latin scholasticism were willing to meet it on its own argumentative ground. An author named Kallistos Angelikoudes wrote a massive refutation of Aquinas' *Summa contra gentiles*, showing its flaws point by point in something like the way Nicholas of Methone had attacked Proclus—an appropriate comparison since Kallistos' main problem with Aquinas is that he was overly dependent on pagan philosophy.[19]

The use of Aquinas in the Hesychast controversy is the most eye-catching and well-researched case of influence from the Latin West on philosophy in the Greek East. But such influence can be found elsewhere, even when it comes to topics that had been under discussion for a very long time. A nice example is the problem of the so-called "term of life."[20] Back in the seventh century, several authors had raised the question whether God predetermines how long a person will live. This is of course just a specific version of a question asked in all the medieval traditions, as to whether God foreknows, and thus decides in advance, everything that happens down here on earth. The more specific idea that each of us has a predefined term of life is also found in Islamic texts. One author, Anastasios of Sinai, even made a point that would more famously appear a few centuries later in the Muslim theologian al-Ghazālī: that if God decides how long a person will live, sinners could complain that He did not arrange for them to die before they committed their more grievous misdeeds.

Among early Greek Christian authors it was generally agreed that God at least knows beforehand how long each human will live, in keeping with a remark made by the Cappadocian father Basil of Caesarea: "death comes to those whose term of life is completed." Anastasios admitted this, while cautioning that human free will is not impeded by God's foreknowledge. More than half a millennium later, this conclusion was known to Nikephoros Blemmydes. Yet Blemmydes went against Anastasios, and a number of intervening figures including the just-mentioned Nicholas of Methone, by arguing that "there is no limit set for each person's life, nor has death been predetermined for each person by God." One study has suggested that Blemmydes was moved to this new conclusion by contact with Dominican friars who visited Constantinople and who held a similar view to the one accepted by Anastasios: God foreknows, but does not cause or predetermine, the length of life. Blemmydes therefore describes the view as an unacceptable novelty rather than an age-old solution, and rejects it as a bit of Latin sophistry.

Empires tend to die with more fanfare than individual humans. The more observant residents of Constantinople could tell, in the years leading up to 1453, that whether divided from the Latin West or united to it, the Greek East was about to see its own term of life come to an end. One scholar presciently remarked that even if the world was not about to end, as he deemed likely, at least the Byzantine nation was enjoying its final days.[21] This was Gennadios Scholarios, the third Latin–Greek translator I mentioned earlier and, as it happens, the author of no fewer than five treatises on the question of the term of life that show the influence of Thomas Aquinas.[22] But Scholarios is known best, not for his translations or his considera-tion of this question of divine foreknowledge, but for a dispute over the relative merits of Plato and Aristotle. His opponent in this dispute can be described as the last great philosopher of Byzantium, and simultaneously, as one of the first philo-sophers of the Italian Renaissance.

20

PLATONIC LOVE GEMISTOS PLETHON

In the popular imagination, the middle ages were a time of unremitting repression. The threat of persecution and book burnings ensured that intellectuals would stay well within the bounds of accepted orthodoxy, which is why medieval philosophers were rather uncreative and tradition-bound in comparison to the innovative thinkers of the Enlightenment. This cliché is basically wrong, though it contains a grain of truth. Of the three medieval philosophical traditions we've covered in this book series, it is least applicable to the Islamic world. There, political persecution of philosophy was almost unheard of, in part because there was no obvious institutional framework for enforcing religious orthodoxy. Things were rather different in the Latin West, where we do see reprimand or imprisonment of philosophers including Peter Abelard and Roger Bacon. Worse was the fate of Marguerite Porete, who not only saw her writings destroyed but was ultimately executed for heresy.[1] For the most part, though, philosophers were not punished for heresy, for the excellent reason that they were not heretics. Another popular conception has it that any philosopher worthy of the name should challenge the beliefs of their society. But in fact the vast majority of philosophers, in the middle ages and still today, argue in support of widely held beliefs, seeking to clarify and explore the consequences of commonly accepted doctrines rather than trying to undermine them.

All this applies to Byzantium too. As we've seen, there was plenty of creative and sophisticated philosophical reflection that stayed well within the bounds of religious acceptability. This is exactly what we should expect: devout Christian cultures produce philosophers who are devout Christians. This is so true that the most notorious exception to the rule, the anathematized John Italos, probably wasn't really an exception. As he himself protested, his devotion to pagan philosophy did not really lead him to adopt genuinely unorthodox teachings, which is why his accusers had to defame him by ascribing to him a variety of (mutually incompatible) doctrines that he didn't in fact hold. But now, as we reach the end of our examination of Byzantine philosophy, we have finally arrived at a figure who can plausibly be described as "unorthodox" in every sense of that word. His name was

George Gemistos, and he called himself "Plethon." That name is probably a pun—"Gemistos" and "Plethon" mean roughly the same thing, "abundant" or "full"—but it was also a tribute to the similarly named philosopher whom Plethon most admired, Plato (in Greek *Platon*). Plethon loved Plato so much that he wrote an attack on Aristotle for his departures from Platonic teachings, and then went even further by embracing full-blown paganism... maybe.

The idea that Plethon was a convinced pagan goes back to the immediate reception of his writings, and especially to his great rival Gennadios Scholarios.[2] These two men lived at the twilight of Byzantium: Plethon died in either 1452, just before the fall of Constantinople, or more likely 1454, one year afterwards.[3] Scholarios lived for some time thereafter and even served as patriarch under Ottoman rule, using his authority to have one of Plethon's books banned and burnt in 1460. The work in question, the *Book of Laws*, nonetheless partially survives. By one calculation we still have almost half of it,[4] in part thanks to excerpts preserved by Scholarios himself when he was explaining why he was forced to take this draconian measure. On the basis of this material we can see that Plethon presented a lengthy and complex metaphysical doctrine along broadly Neoplatonic lines and full of references to pagan gods: the highest God he called "Zeus," with lower divinities named "Poseidon," "Hera," and so on.[5]

That sound you hear is Nicholas of Methone turning over in his grave. He would have seen Plethon as the predictable and lamentable outcome of the revival of interest in pagan Neoplatonism back in the eleventh and twelfth centuries, and especially the pernicious influence of Proclus. Indeed, Scholarios charged that Plethon took many of his ideas from Proclus.[6] But Plethon himself claimed to find inspiration in a long line of sages going back to Zoroaster, the Indian brahmans, the Magi, and Greek thinkers ranging from Parmenides and Plato to late ancient philosophers like Plutarch, Plotinus, Porphyry, and just for the sake of variety one whose name didn't begin with a P, Iamblichus. So in his *Laws*, tellingly named after Plato's work of the same name, Plethon presented himself as resurrecting a set of ancient doctrines.

Were these ideas intended to replace Christianity? The most explicit evidence for that interpretation comes not from Scholarios, but from another Greek scholar, George Trapezuntius. He met Plethon at the council of Ferrara and Florence, which as we saw attempted to forge a union between the churches of West and East. As you'll know if you have ever attended an academic conference, all the interesting stuff happens during the coffee breaks. Similarly, here Plethon and George fell to talking during a lull in the proceedings. Supposedly Plethon predicted that before long, a single religion would unite Latin Europe, the Greek East, and indeed the whole world. It would be neither Christianity nor Islam, but a faith that "does not differ from paganism."[7] Pretty shocking stuff, especially given the setting; it would be like attending a Star Wars convention and mentioning your devotion to Star Trek. But there is some room for skepticism here, since George Trapezuntius was perhaps the only man even more polemically opposed to Plethon than Scholarios was. In addition to which we must ask, what was Plethon doing at a top-level summit of Christian theologians, if he was actually a convinced pagan?

The answer is in part that Plethon was getting to know local scholars, and in so doing, singlehandedly inspiring the Italian Renaissance. Well, that's a bit of an exaggeration, but Plethon can in fact be credited with helping to trigger a resurgence of interest in Greek philosophy.[8] Among others, he met and taught Leonardo Bruni and (maybe) Cosimo de' Medici. No less a witness than Marsilio Ficino seems to name the latter encounter as a key moment in the history of Renaissance Platonism. He suggests that it was Plethon who inspired de' Medici to sponsor a so-called "Platonic Academy" in Florence, though as we'll see later this may be a metaphorical way of describing a less dramatic turn of events (see Chapter 31). But Plethon was not just using the summit as an opportunity for intellectual tourism. Though some modern-day scholars assume that he couldn't have cared less about the differences between Latin and Greek theology, he is said to have remarked that the theological debate was a matter of life and death, and he wrote on the subject as well. More generally, the writings that he made public in his lifetime give no explicit signs of sympathy for paganism. Despite its prodigious length the *Laws* was apparently intended only for a more intimate readership or even private use. We might compare this to the way that in early modern Europe, especially daring treatises like David Hume's *Dialogues on Natural Religion* were published only posthumously.

If Plethon did have an intimate circle of readers in mind, who would they have been? A long-standing hypothesis is that he was at the center of a group of similarly minded thinkers in the Peloponnesian city of Mistra, located near ancient Sparta. Plethon moved there in 1409. In his time Mistra was an almost independent city ruled by so-called "despots"; I say "almost" independent because the rulers were relatives of the imperial family, the Palaiologans. Plethon had cordial relations with them. Setting himself up as Mistra Know it All, he wrote missives to the rulers of the city offering advice on political affairs, and even declared himself willing to help implement the measures he was proposing. Plethon would no doubt appreciate it if you noticed the parallel to Plato arriving in Syracuse and attempting to advise the rulers there.

His specific proposals also echo those made by Plato in the *Republic* and *Laws*.[9] Plethon envisions an ideal society with three classes, so-called "helots" who labor in agriculture and animal husbandry, the middle merchant class, and the rulers at the top. Like so many other Byzantine political theorists, he praised monarchy as the most perfect political system: just as a boat needs a captain and an army a general, the state needs a single figure at its head. At the back of Plethon's mind here may be the notorious rebellion that had occurred in Thessalonika in the previous century, when the so-called "Zealots" overthrew the local imperial representative and achieved autonomous popular rule. In Plethon's ideal scenario, Mistra would represent a different kind of city-state, run from the top down by a wise despot who listens to a philosopher-advisor, a role Plethon was graciously willing to play. The military posture of the state was to be strengthened by abolishing the use of mercenaries and instead having a dedicated soldier citizenry, who should be supported by taxes raised from the laboring class. Again one may think of Plato here and the class of warrior "guardians" in his *Republic*, though Plethon probably also took inspiration from reports about ancient Sparta.[10]

Some readers have also detected in Plethon's proposals a remarkable endorsement of Greek nationalism, something that had played no real role in the ideology of the multi-ethnic Byzantine empire. Emphasizing that the Peloponnese had been governed by "Hellenes" since antiquity, Plethon believes that the people of Mistra could find solidarity by seeing themselves as representative of a Greek *genos*, or "race." Equally remarkable are Plethon's recommendations concerning land redistribution. In a slap at the way aristocratic magnates had gathered property to themselves across the empire, he insists that land should be held in accordance with use: if you farm it, you own it. Thanks to such proposals Plethon has been hailed as anticipating modern utopian ideals, and it would fit well with this that his political theory is relatively secular. Christian ideology is strikingly absent, and his religious prescriptions go more along the lines of recommending a rather generic and rational theism: the ruler is to ensure that people believe in one, all-ruling god, who exercises providence over all things.

Here we have a link to the teachings of Plethon's openly pagan *Book of Laws*. In the one section of this work that did circulate publicly, Plethon again discusses the providence exercised by this God.[11] As we've just seen with the controversy over the "term of life," a belief in God's oversight of the world could threaten to tip over into determinism, the view that all things that occur do so necessarily. Plethon doesn't just tip over into determinism, though, he leaps enthusiastically. He assumes that nothing can occur without a cause, and that true causes guarantee their effects. After all, a cause that didn't guarantee its effect would still leave something to be explained, namely why the effect arises from the cause when it might not have done so, with the result that we would need to seek a further cause. Ultimately all causes go back to the highest God Zeus, who stands at the top of every explanatory chain. For Plethon, as for the ancient Stoics—clearly an influence on him here—human freedom does not consist in uncaused or indeterministic action, but in aligning one's will with that of God. This argument in favor of inevitable fate resonates with a discussion found in Plethon's *On Aristotle's Departures from Plato*.[12] It charges Aristotle with contradicting himself on many issues, including the question of fate. Aristotle understood that causes should necessarily give rise to their effects, says Plethon, yet was unwilling to accept the deterministic consequences of this fact.

As its title suggests, the main goal of Plethon's *Departures* is to itemize points where Aristotle failed to adhere to his master's doctrines. Plethon is particularly vexed by Aristotle's arguments against Plato's theory of Forms, which he finds unconvincing and, worse, would make it impossible to explain God's production of the world. As we know from his *Book of Laws*, Plethon believes that the highest God gives rise to other gods that transcend the physical universe: these are pure intellects, and can be identified with the world of Platonic Forms. They in turn produce the heavenly realm, with the stars and planets also being understood as divine. All of these things, the gods and the heavens, are eternal. It's only in the world down here below the heavens that we find things that are subject to generation and destruction.

The references to multiple gods and the determinism of Plethon's system hardly sound compatible with Christianity as any medieval Byzantine would have understood it. Yet Plethon complains that it is Aristotle, not Plato, who is unacceptable from a Christian point of view. Plato shows how God is genuinely a creator of the universe, whereas Aristotle is content to make his divine principle a cause of nothing more than heavenly motion. Aristotle's admirers weren't about to concede this point, though. In a lengthy response to Plethon's treatise, Scholarios rose to Aristotle's defense, devoting particular attention to the question of whether Aristotle's god can be understood as a creator, like the God of the Abrahamic religions. He affirmed that this is indeed the right way to understand Aristotle, because in causing motion the Aristotelian god becomes a genuine "maker (*poietes*)" of the cosmos. By contrast Plato depicted god as a mere "craftsman (*demiourgos*)" who fashions the universe from pre-existing matter.

This unconvincing interpretation has a surprisingly good pedigree. One of the last important pagan commentators on Aristotle, Ammonius, who was the head of the Neoplatonist school at Alexandria, also thought the Aristotelian god must cause the existence of the heavens if it causes them to move.[13] But Plethon is having none of this. He thinks that, if there is truly a source of *being* for things, then we have to accept an account like Plato's theory of Forms, which postulates a paradigm of

Being participated by all other beings. Plethon therefore criticizes Aristotle for his famous claim that "being is said in many ways." No, argues Plethon: being is a unified, univocal concept, because all created being is rooted in the divine, which is nothing other than Being itself. With this Plethon moves decisively away from the negative theology that has characterized so much of Byzantine thought. The contrast is especially strong with contemporary followers of Gregory Palamas, who taught that God is in Himself unknowable, never grasped in His essence but only in His activities or "energies." Plethon is having none of this either. Like other opponents of Hesychasm he thinks it is absurd to distinguish God into two aspects, essence and activity.

This at least is one thing all interpreters of Plethon can agree about: he really didn't like the Hesychasts. In his political writings he makes withering remarks about the pointless wastefulness of monasteries, which of course were the institutional base for Hesychasm. As a result, Plethon occupies a rather anomalous place in late Byzantine philosophy. This period is often framed as a clash between men like Scholarios and the Kydones brothers, Aristotelians who were enamored of Latin scholasticism, and the Hesychast, Palamite faction whose views would ultimately prevail in the East. Actually, we already know that this is an oversimplification: some of the Palamites also drew on the Latin scholastics, especially Thomas Aquinas. But Plethon's position should give us further pause, since he was deeply unimpressed by both the scholastics in the West *and* the Hesychasts in the East.

In fact, it was the reception of Latin scholasticism in Greek that seems to have triggered Plethon's attack on Aristotle. He explains the Westerners' excessive admiration for Aristotle by saying that they have followed the lead of Averroes, the Muslim commentator who was so avidly used by scholastics as a guide to understanding Aristotle's works. Scholarios by contrast was a translator and avid reader of Aquinas. So in leaping to the defense of Aristotle, he was also speaking up on behalf of the Latins, and of authors from the Islamic world like Avicenna and Averroes, known to Scholarios primarily through Aquinas.[14] He was much less impressed by the Italian humanists with whom Plethon consorted, remarking in his *Defense of Aristotle* that they "know as much about philosophy as [Plethon] knows about dancing." Above all Scholarios was convinced of Aristotle's compatibility with Christianity: his occasional lapses may be forgiven in light of his lack of access to revelation. For this reason, he took Plethon's criticism of Aristotle to be further evidence of Plethon's pagan leanings. Since Aristotle was in fact easy to harmonize with Christian teaching, Plethon's denunciation of Aristotle could only be taken as an implicit rejection of the faith.[15]

Scholarios' accusations came backed with an explanation of how Plethon was led astray.[16] It was supposedly through an encounter with a Jewish philosopher named Elissaeus, and for good measure the malign influence of demons, that Plethon was exposed to the teachings of Zoroaster and inducted into secret pagan doctrines. Scholarios adds that Plethon tried to conceal his heretical beliefs, though you have to say that if this is true Plethon wasn't very good at keeping secrets. Not only did he write the *Book of Laws* with its references to the Hellenic pantheon of gods, but he also wrote a commentary on that classic text of pagan religion, the *Chaldean Oracles*, drawing on the earlier commentary by Michael Psellos. As with Psellos, this commentatorial activity can be given a more innocent explanation. It may simply express fascination with ancient Platonist literature, which would also explain why Plethon did extensive editorial work on Plato's dialogues.

It is still debated whether Plethon should be understood in this second way, as a particularly adventurous exponent of Byzantine humanism who nonetheless retained his Christian belief, or instead as a secret pagan in line with the accusations made by Scholarios and George Trapezuntius. Two recent books on Plethon make a case for these two very different options.[17] For Niketas Siniossoglou, he was a "radical Platonist" who merely "posed as a Christian" and who anticipated modern European philosophy with his secularist utopianism. Vojěch Hladký instead assumes that the *Book of Laws* was simply a kind of literary experiment, an "exercise book" in which the names of pagan gods were assigned to the principles of a Neoplatonic metaphysics just for the sake of practical convenience. For Hladký, Plethon did not abandon Christianity, as we can see from his engagement with debates over the correct understanding of the Trinity.

My own hunch lies somewhere between these two approaches, though it is perhaps closer to that of Hladký. As both he and Siniossoglou stress, Plethon was a firm believer in the power of human reason. He assumed that we are able to grasp all of reality, including God Himself. This suggests that we do not really need a revelation, whether pagan or Christian, to give us access to truths that would otherwise have remained hidden. For many of his contemporaries this would already be tantamount to heresy. But it need not imply a total abandonment of Christian belief. Like other medieval rationalists, such as Averroes (a comparison Plethon would not have appreciated, of course), Plethon may have supposed that religions convey the same truths discovered by philosophy, but in a different register. Perhaps he assumed that ancient pagan religion and Christianity were both more or less adequate representations of one and the same metaphysical system, the very system discovered in Platonist philosophy. This would explain why he blamed Aristotle for failing to envision God as a creator, as does

Christianity, and also why he thought it was worth defending the Orthodox position on the Trinity. For him, to speak of Zeus fathering Poseidon and Hera, or of the Father generating the Son and the Holy Spirit, would have been alternative descriptions of the same thing.[18] It's also worth noting that Plethon does not seem to have engaged in actual pagan ritual practice. This suggests that he embraced paganism only as a symbolic discourse, just an alternative way to express a fundamentally rational theology.

It may seem that Scholarios prevailed in his clash with Plethon: he outlived his opponent, occupied the powerful position of patriarch several times, and had the satisfaction of seeing Plethon's book consumed in flames. But arguably, it was Plethon who had the last laugh. His impact on Ficino and other Platonists of the Italian Renaissance makes him a key figure in European thought. Plethon was among the first to grasp an important insight, made possible by the humanist project that spanned from Constantinople to Florence, by way of Mistra: deep knowledge of ancient literature revealed the diversity of classical philosophy. This opened the possibility of saying that pagan literature is valuable as a whole, but that some pagans are better than others. For Plethon and his Renaissance heirs, it was Plato and his followers, not Aristotle and his commentators, who produced the best that philosophy has to offer.

21

ISTANBUL (NOT CONSTANTINOPLE) THE LATER ORTHODOX TRADITION

Say what you will about Byzantine philosophy, but at least it has a nice clear endpoint. It's rarely a simple matter to demarcate chronological periods in the history of philosophy. In the next part of this book we'll be considering the "Italian Renaissance" and considering this to run from about 1400 to 1600, even though the lines between medieval, Renaissance, and early modern philosophy are as fuzzy as kittens emerging from a tumble dryer. In this first part of the book and earlier installments of the series, we've seen how late ancient philosophy merged fairly seamlessly with medieval philosophy in different languages, with the texts and preoccupations of pagan and Christian thinkers alike being passed on to the Latin, Islamic, and Greek Byzantine spheres. As a result you'll see figures like John Philoponus or the Cappadocian fathers being classified as late ancient thinkers or as Byzantine thinkers, depending on which scholar is doing the classifying. By contrast, we can even name a specific day when the curtain fell on Byzantine philosophy: May 29, 1453, when the Ottomans breached the walls of Constantinople and finally ended the Roman empire.

On the other hand, the Ottomans had no interest in exterminating Greek Orthodox Christianity, and their arrival did not make it wholly impossible for Greek speakers to engage in scholarship. If we again think more broadly of philosophy in Eastern Christian cultures rather than restricting our attention only to "Byzantium," we can actually see the fall of the capital as a beginning rather than an end. A new phase of Greek scholarship sees Orthodox theologians and philosophers living under Islamic rule, much as their counterparts in the Syrian church had been doing for centuries. Think not of Plethon, who died just about the time that Byzantium ended, but of his enemy Scholarios. Once Constantinople got the works, he carried on his business with the Turks.

It wasn't business as usual, of course. Instead of a Christian emperor there was now an Ottoman sultan, Mehmet II "the Conqueror," who personally installed

Scholarios as the first patriarch after the fall in 1454. The two apparently had a cordial relationship, being on good enough terms to engage in respectful debate over the differences between their two faiths. Continuing the tradition of apologetic writing we've explored in previous chapters, Scholarios even wrote a summary of the Orthodox faith for Mehmet, which was translated into Turkish. A member of Scholarios' circle, the historian Kritobulos of Imbros, commented that the sultan valued his patriarch's wisdom and virtue. Kritobulos' historical chronicle also shows that the former Byzantines were quick to adapt to the new political situation.[1] While still identifying strongly with the Greeks (which he, like Plethon, calls his *genos*), he portrayed Mehmet as a new Alexander the Great, taking inspiration from the ancient historians Thucydides and Arrian in his descriptions of the taking of the city and the first years of Ottoman rule. Another member of Scholarios' circle by the name of Amiroutzes, nicknamed "the philosopher," translated the works of Ptolemy into Arabic, a version still extant today in a manuscript that is held in Istanbul.[2]

So the end of Byzantium wasn't the end of the world. This would have come as a surprise to many, including Scholarios, who thought the apocalypse was nigh as the Ottomans were closing in. Christians had been making this sort of prediction for a long, long time. Already early Latin church fathers had linked the prospective fall of Rome to the end times, with Lactantius prophesying that "if the capital of the world does fall . . . then without doubt the end of mankind and of the whole world will come."[3] After the rise of the new Rome and Islam, Christians kept confidently predicting that history would end, with either the fall of Constantinople and arrival of the Antichrist or, as predicted in an influential apocalyptic text written in Syriac in the seventh century (by Pseudo-Methodius), the final defeat of Islam at the hands of a Christian emperor. Eschatological expectations were especially high around the year 1000, a millennium after the birth and then crucifixion of Christ. When the world failed to end with either a bang or a whimper, the prophecies didn't go away. They just got more vague about the dating.

After 1453 history yet again continued along in its stubborn way, as did the Christians' perception of their own situation, which was surprisingly unchanged by the Ottoman conquest. Scholars had been complaining for some time about the parlous state of the Orthodox, with Dimitrios Kydones writing in 1387 that the empire was only a faded image (*kamon eidolon*) of itself; you may recall him lamenting that Latin scholastics had become the intellectual superiors of the Greeks. Naturally this sort of bleak self-assessment continued under the Ottomans. A letter written in 1575 remarked that since losing the empire, the Orthodox had lost wisdom too, and that having been forced to associate with the barbarian Turks, the Greeks had themselves become barbaric.[4]

I take this example from a remarkable book written by the German historian Gerhard Podskalsky, called *Griechische Theologie in der Zeit der Türkenherrschaft*. It is packed with information about dozens of scholars who worked between the time of Scholarios and the early nineteenth century, which is when Greece achieved independence from the Ottoman empire. Though Podskalsky's focus is on theology and not philosophy, he shows that philosophical texts were still being read across the Orthodox world throughout the centuries of Ottoman rule. Schools and monasteries provided centers of learning in many places, most prominently Constantinople and Mount Athos. Many scholars also trained in the Latin West, especially in Italy, where there were large Greek speaking communities in Venice and Padua.

Because of this constant interaction with the West, an abiding concern of Orthodox theologians remained the question of church unity. What had been a two-way debate between the Roman Catholic and Greek Orthodox churches now became a three-way affair, as the Protestants joined the fray. So alongside the familiar disputes aired at events like the council of Florence not long before the fall, there were now controversies over such topics as the Protestant idea of basing religious belief on scripture alone (*sola scriptura*); that is, understanding biblical passages as the only authoritative source of doctrine, without appeals to reason or church tradition. This was one of the issues at stake in an exchange of letters between theologians in Tübingen and the Orthodox patriarch Jeremiah II from 1573 until 1581.[5] Perhaps the most remarkable development along these lines was the work of another patriarch, Kyrillos Lukaris. He was favorably impressed by Protestant ideas and adopted a view on free will and predestination that was clearly inspired by Calvinism. The reward for his broad-mindedness was arrest and death, in 1638.[6]

Patriarch Lukaris was not the only man to be seduced by the siren song of the West. One might also name Leon Allatios, a humanist from Chios who traveled to Italy and received a doctorate in philosophy and theology at Rome in 1610. He was a unionist who argued that the differences between the two churches were merely apparent. Greeks ventured beyond Italy, too. Especially widely traveled was Metrophanes Kirtopulos, who in the early seventeenth century went as far as Oxford and Cambridge, and visited many cities in Germany and Switzerland, before finally becoming patriarch of Alexandria. In the same century George Koressios, a nobleman from Constantinople, studied and taught medicine and philosophy in Padua before going to practice medicine in Chios. His writings make reference to a range of medieval scholastic authors, showing his command of the Latin theological tradition. As Western philosophy developed, its leading lights were reflected in Greek literature, as in the writings of Methodios Anthrakites from Epeiros, who lived well into the eighteenth century. He too went to Italy and was exposed to ideas of the

Enlightenment. His interest in figures like Malebranche, whose works he translated into Greek, led him to being accused of "innovation." If Orthodox scholars must take an interest in philosophy, his critics felt, they should stick to good old Aristotle.[7]

Speaking of Aristotle—as we so often are—the rest of this book will show that his works did not fall wholly out of fashion in the Renaissance. To the contrary, he continued to be a vital source for philosophical reflection well into early modernity. And the same is true for the Greek-speaking world. Any number of the figures mentioned by Podskalsky wrote textbooks or commentaries on Aristotle, especially his logic, which remained an important preparation for the study of theology. Particularly notable for their engagement with the Hellenic philosophical legacy were Theophilos Korydaleus and Athanasius Rhetor, who died in 1646 and 1663 respectively.[8] Taking an attitude like that of the Arts Masters at the university of Paris or the Averroists of Padua, Korydaleus sought to make room for the study of Aristotle by observing a strict separation of philosophy and theology. Much like them, he devoted great energy to expounding Aristotelian thought and covered himself with quick disclaimers, as at the end of a commentary on *On Generation and Corruption*: "if any of these doctrines contradicts sacred revelation, we must of course reject them."[9] Korydaleus' commentaries on Aristotle would become the standard works for philosophical education down to the end of the eighteenth century. His contemporary Athanasius had more Platonic tastes. While he too commented on Aristotle, he also produced an introductory work for Plato's *Sophist* and a commentary on Plato's *Parmenides*, which draws extensively on Proclus. Here we glimpse the possible afterlife of the Platonist enthusiasms of men like Psellos, Petritsi, and Plethon. Athanasius went so far as to name a flagrantly pagan Neoplatonist, the "great Iamblichus," as his greatest inspiration.[10]

An interest in classical literature persisted through the early modern period. One outstanding name here was Adamantios Korais, a humanist born in Smyrna in 1743.[11] As an editor of a series of modern Greek translations of classical texts, Korais was just as devoted to ancient Hellenic language and thought as the Byzantine humanists who had come centuries before. Yet he was also influenced by the ideas of the Enlightenment. He took inspiration from figures such as Voltaire and Rousseau, and from the French Revolution, as he promoted the cause of Greek nationalism. In old age he even made contact with Thomas Jefferson to seek support for the independence of his own country from Turkish dominion. We can see the impact of the Enlightenment on Greek culture also with figures like Athanasios Psalidas, who lived in Russia and Vienna before returning to his original home in Yannina.[12] There he taught the ideas of Locke and Kant and wrote works that bear the imprint of Hume, for instance in a skeptical discussion of causality.

This passing mention of Russia may inspire you to wonder what was going on in other Eastern Christian communities during this period. Plenty, as it turns out.[13] If you want to get from Byzantium to the concerns of modern-day Orthodox Christianity, you have to go through Russia and Eastern Europe. At the center of this story is Hesychasm. The Russian Hesychast tradition goes back at least to the turn of the sixteenth century, and to a monk named Nil Sorskii.[14] Originally from Moscow, he studied at Palamas' home monastery at Mount Athos. His emphasis was less on the metaphysical issues for which Palamas is best known, and more on questions of practice. Thus his major writing is a treatise on how to resist the temptation of distracting thoughts and worldly pleasures. Nil Sorskii was also important for his embrace of monastic poverty, a bone of contention in Orthodox religious life just as it had been in the Latin medieval West.[15] Around the same time, Hesychasm was central to the thought of Neagoe Basarab, a ruler of Wallachia in modern-day Romania who wrote a work of political advice for his son. He combined the deep piety of this aspect of the Orthodox tradition with an impressively wide selection of cultural inspirations: in the work he mentions figures ranging from Aristotle to the Buddha.

One reason the Russian sphere would be important for later Orthodox thought is that it has often been the context for the preservation and dissemination of Greek literature. Among the figures who took a hand in the transfer of knowledge into Russian culture was, in the sixteenth century, Michael Trivoles, also known as "Maksim Grek." He's yet another man who went to study in Italy, where he assisted at the workshop of the great humanist Aldus Manutius, a pioneer in the printing of philosophical works (see Chapter 45). Maksim wasn't necessarily impressed by what he found in the West, though. He wrote against the Latins and railed against the way that scholasticism had diverged from the true path of faith. In 1518 he went to Russia where he helped transmit texts into the Slavic language. Another name worth mentioning would be that of the Croatian scholar Jurij Križanič, active in the middle of the seventeenth century. He compiled information on Latin theology, the better to refute it, and translated from Greek directly into Russian.

One advantage of Russia, as compared to Constantinople, was the opportunity to print texts. Printing in the former capital was shut down by the Ottomans in 1628, whereas around the same time printing houses were churning out books in Moscow and Kiev.[16] Moving closer to the present day, Russians really took center stage in the story of Orthodox thought around the nineteenth century. An early milestone was the 1782 publication of a book called the *Philokalia*, meaning *Anthology*.[17] The Greek version was printed in Venice in that year, but the *Philokalia* became especially influential once it was translated into Slavonic. A compilation of Hesychast literature, the *Philokalia* promises to help the reader purify the mind through spiritual practices. Following on from this the nineteenth century saw an explosion of philological work on, and translation of, Greek patristic literature in Russia.

This laid the groundwork for re-engagement, re-interpretation, and re-appropriation of aspects of the Byzantine legacy—especially the Greek fathers and the Hesychasts—over the last century or so. Several of the key contributors to this process were Russian or Eastern European, and as pious Orthodox Christians had difficulties with the communist governments of the Soviet Union and its allies. One tragic case is that of Pavel Florensky who was from Azerbaijan, and studied in Tblisi in Georgia. He was arrested in 1933 and executed in 1937 at the time of Stalin's purges. Like many recent Orthodox philosophers, Florensky borrowed from Western philosophy even as he grounded his ideas in Greek Christian thought. For instance, he adopted Immanuel Kant's idea of an "antinomy of reason," a case where rational argument seems to point in opposite directions, and applied it to the case of the Trinity. It seems a paradox, or even a contradiction, to say with the Orthodox tradition that God is one substance but three Persons. Actually, though, this just shows that God outstrips the capacity of human reason to understand Him.

And good thing too, because if reason always pointed unequivocally towards a single conclusion, then we would in a sense be constrained to follow it. The fact that rational argument does not always have the last word opens a space for human freedom. Florensky quoted of all people Augustine, so often blamed by the Orthodox for the failings of the Western church, to make his point: "no one believes except voluntarily."[18] In another case Florensky took inspiration from the Byzantine veneration of icons to develop an original aesthetic theory. He criticized what he saw as an ineffective tradition of Western European art since the Renaissance, on the grounds that linear perspective simply tries to render literally the appearance of whatever the artist depicts (for the philosophical significance of perspective, see also Chapter 48). For Florensky, icons were preferable because of their symbolic nature. An icon is successful precisely because the painting is *not* made from life, but is a visual means of the saint in heaven showing himself or herself in the earthly realm.[19]

Several other scholars avoided Florensky's fate by emigrating, especially to Paris, which became the scene for a concentration of Orthodox thinkers after the Russian Revolution. These included scholars who were inspired in part by Western medieval texts, like Myrrha Lot-Borodine, who was an expert on medieval French romances, and Vladimir Lossky, who published on Meister Eckhart. Lossky's *Mystical Theology of the Eastern Church*, published in 1944, is a classic of twentieth-century Orthodox philosophy. It takes as its central theme the "apophatic" current that comes down to Lossky from Pseudo-Dionysius and other Greek fathers: the conviction that God is ineffable and ungraspable for the human mind. Not unlike Florensky arguing that the antinomies of reason open a space for freedom in human belief, Lossky wrote that "apophaticism, so far from being a limitation, enables us to transcend all concepts, every sphere of philosophical speculation."[20] He also connected apophaticism to existentialism. By avoiding an abstract and intellectual approach to God, the apophatic attitude allows the believer to be open to a "direct intuition" of God as a person rather than an idea. That critique of intellectualism in philosophical theology is not atypical of modern Orthodox philosophy.

Another Russian émigré who found refuge in Paris, George Florovsky (not to be confused with the aforementioned Pavel Florensky), was critical of the way that Orthodox thought since the fall of Constantinople had so often been influenced by Western ideas. Calling this a "pseudomorphosis" and a "Babylonian captivity," Florovsky too emphasized the importance of approaching God as a "person" rather than through the sort of arid concepts devised in Latin scholasticism. He was, obviously, not undertaking a merely philological or antiquarian engagement with the Byzantine tradition. As Florovsky himself put it, "one must be steeped in the inspiration of the patristic flame and not simply be a gardener pottering around amongst ancient texts."[21]

Which brings us to our final stop on this whirlwind tour of the later Orthodox tradition: Christos Yannaras, who was born in 1935 and has been a prominent public intellectual over the recent decades in Greece.[22] Though Yannaras too is critical of the Western tradition, he is not entirely averse to engagement with its texts. In fact, one of the main touchstones for his own philosophy has been Martin Heidegger, a twentieth-century German philosopher whose ideas I am not going to try to summarize here. But I will mention that Heidegger was critical of a tradition of what he called "onto-theology" in European thought, which makes God one being among others rather than the source of all being. Picking up on this idea, Yannaras agrees that, if we think of God as just a particularly outstanding, maximal, or perfect being we approach him in the wrong way. Instead, as Lossky had suggested, we should adopt an apophatic theology in recognition of the limits of our own reasoning.

This is part of what it means to approach God as a person. Trying to grasp God with philosophical concepts is fruitless. In light of which, Yannaras observed, within a Western context Nietzsche had been right to claim that God was dead! But if we think of God as a person, as in the Eastern tradition, He remains alive for us. For persons, in their irreducible particularity, cannot be captured by abstract notions. Here we come back to Hesychasm and the ideas of Palamas, especially his pivotal distinction between essence and activity (*energeia*). Just as we know God only through His outward activities, so we can know any person only through his or her activities, not in his or her essence. This means that our relationships with other people are inevitably just that: relational. As Yannaras put it, "the person is known as existential otherness through the 'rational' otherness of the relations it constitutes."[23]

Yannaras thus takes love or *eros*, not intellectual understanding, as the model of interaction between human and human, or human and God. For him this has far-reaching consequences in ethics and politics. He thinks that the West is trapped within a political framework built around the idea of individuals, which are just iterations of a type, namely human nature. You and I are just two examples of humans, and our political status—for instance, our claim to certain rights—is based on nothing more than being members of that class. Yannaras finds in the Eastern Orthodox tradition, and especially its idea of the Trinitarian persons, resources for an alternative grounding of political life. By thinking of one another as persons rather than individuals, we see each other not as iterations but as inevitably other and unknowable, yet approachable through freely performed activities. Through these activities we should forge relations with one another, relations that constitute a community.

With Yannaras we have brought this story to the present day—admittedly a story told with many gaps, for a change. It's noteworthy that unlike many other European philosophers, Yannaras takes his inspiration from texts written in the medieval period. The continuity of Greek Orthodox culture after the fall of Constantinople is one reason I wanted to include this chapter before forging on in strictly chronological terms to look at the Italian Renaissance. Also, I wanted to avoid doing to the Greek Christians what historians of philosophy so often do to thinkers of the Islamic world. It's all too typical to ignore everything that happened in that culture after 1200 or so, the time when Arabic philosophy was translated into Latin, as if the value of philosophy written in other cultures can only ever be a matter of its contribution to Western European thought. Similarly, Byzantine philosophy leads so naturally into the Italian Renaissance that it would have been easy to end our consideration of Greek Orthodoxy with figures like Plethon who had an impact in Italy. But as we've just seen, many generations of scholars in what had been the Byzantine empire continued to do what Byzantine intellectuals had done: read and comment on Aristotle and Neoplatonism, and develop philosophical ideas within a theological context.

This is not necessarily to say that the level of learning after 1453 matched the highpoints of Byzantine learning. Besides, as we've also just seen, the Orthodox thinkers have often lived in what had been Latin Christendom, or taken ideas from

Western contemporaries, whether this was Patriarch Kyrillos Lukaris taking a few leaves from Calvinism, or Psalidas reacting to Enlightenment philosophy, or Yannaras with his use of Heidegger. This story is even harder to disentangle from that of the rest of European thought than the earlier story of Byzantium was. Still, like later Islamic thought, this is clearly a sorely underestimated and under-researched part of the history of philosophy. Taking myself as an example, I'm supposedly an expert on Greek philosophy. But in all honesty, before I read up to write this chapter I had never heard of Theophilos Korydaleus, even though his works were standard reading for centuries among Greek speakers who still took an interest in Aristotle.

And I see one more parallel to Islamic philosophy. In that case, attention was first drawn to post-classical texts by modern scholars who took inspiration from a single thinker who came late in the tradition. With Islam this was the philosopher Mullā Ṣadrā, who lived in seventeenth-century Iran.[24] In the Orthodox tradition it was Palamas, who becomes a key for Yannaras and others to unlock the true meaning of Eastern Christian thought. In both cases we might celebrate the impulse to pay attention to previously underappreciated texts and ideas, while also noting that it is reductive to see a whole tradition through the lens of one figure, valuing what came earlier primarily insofar as it led up to a single, pivotal philosopher. In reality the story of Byzantine philosophy is not just the story of how we got to Palamas, or the story of a philosophy whose value lies in its difference from the West. Nor for that matter is it just the story of how Aristotle and the Neoplatonists were received in a Christian culture. It is a complex and multifaceted tradition, whose most fascinating philosophical ideas are often found in unexpected places, such as the debate over icons or historical chronicles. It is, in short, a story that more than merits inclusion in any general history of philosophy, with or without gaps.

PART II

THE ITALIAN RENAISSANCE

22

OLD NEWS
THE ITALIAN RENAISSANCE

If you want to be reborn, the first thing you need to do is die in the first place. In Latin Christendom, ancient civilization and culture met their doom around the time the Western Roman empire itself passed away at the end of the fifth century AD. This ushered in the so-called "dark ages," the first part of a longer period we still call the "middle ages"—"middle" because the medievals had the misfortune to live between the time of the Romans and time of the Renaissance. We usually picture a sudden falling away from a high plateau of culture, followed by a trough of about one thousand years, with a sudden ascent to previous heights in the fifteenth and sixteenth centuries. Ancient culture was reborn, and modernity and the Enlightenment were right around the corner.

It's this way of thinking that leads people to skip over almost half the history of philosophy in their reading and teaching, vaulting from antiquity straight to the seventeenth century, with perhaps a brief stop at someone like Aquinas in the middle. I don't need to labor the point that this book series aims to show how much gets missed when we ignore medieval philosophy in the Islamic world, Latin Christendom, and Byzantium. But I might dwell for a moment on a different point, namely that the dismissive attitude towards the "middle ages" itself has a history. It was born at the same time that ancient culture was supposedly being reborn, in the Renaissance. Ancient literature, including philosophy, was rediscovered and re-evaluated. It was out with the crabbed, overly technical, and reliably barbarous Latin of the schoolmen, in with the elegant Latin of Cicero. Unreadable translations of Aristotle were old news, and the very latest thing was something even older, as Greek texts were studied in the original.

But was this really new? There had already been a major recovery of Greek thought during the late twelfth and thirteenth centuries, thanks to scholars who gained access to the manuscripts of Constantinople.[1] Way back in the first half of the twelfth century James of Venice traveled there and translated Aristotle into Latin. His example was followed in the thirteenth century by men like Robert Grosseteste, who produced a Latin version of Aristotle's *Ethics*, and William of Moerbeke, who strove to produce a complete Latin Aristotle. In a parallel development, Arabic philosophical works were also rendered into Latin, providing invaluable guidance to the works of Aristotle and into the bargain the innovative and influential ideas of figures like Avicenna. So if you must picture the history of philosophical culture as a kind of elevation chart, you should at least think of it as a high plateau plunging to a low level, then thrusting up again around 1200, with a further jump during the Renaissance that brings things back to the heights of late antiquity. But the real story is more complicated still. As already noted, the term "renaissance" has been bestowed upon the Carolingian period—when John Scotus Eriugena grappled with the works of Greek fathers in the original—on the twelfth century, when figures like John of Salisbury were already cherishing Cicero, and on the revivals of ancient wisdom that were a regular feature of Byzantine culture.

So why is it that when we see the word "renaissance," we think first and foremost of the fifteenth and sixteenth centuries, which we take to mark a decisive shift away from the medieval period? Did these centuries have a better public relations team, or something? Yes, actually: we call them the humanists. It was they, and not Enlightenment figures like Descartes and Hume, who first complained about tedious scholastic philosophy and sought to replace it with a new philosophical paradigm. This new way of doing philosophy would be modeled on antiquity, as the pursuit of linguistic refinement led to a revival of Greek Platonism and Latin rhetoric. Though the humanist endeavor was indeed anticipated in medieval times, it was also bound up with other changes going on at this time, changes that went well beyond the world of philosophy. It was a time of upheaval in economics and politics, of developments in family life, the sciences, and awareness of the world beyond Europe. Perhaps most famous is the change in the visual arts.

If you were growing up in fifteenth-century Italy, you could have experienced this cultural transformation in your early education.[2] Already back in the fourteenth century, cities like Genoa, Turin, and Venice began organizing communal education by appointing teachers of Latin. The offspring of wealthier families might instead be taught at home. A standard curriculum would include mathematical training with the abacus and gaining literacy, in at least the vernacular, often in Latin as well. Even girls, especially from the nobility, could acquire a high proficiency in Latin, something encouraged by the humanist Leonardo Bruni, who emphasized the power of classical literature to instill virtue in both men and women. For boys, the study of classics was a route to effective citizenship. As another humanist educator, Pier Paolo Vergerio, put it, "for those with noble minds and those who must involve themselves in public affairs and the community, it is useful to study history and moral philosophy."[3] Just such study was put to use by the greatest political mind of the era. Niccolò Machiavelli could never have written *The Prince* or his historical works without his initial formation. In his case it began at age 7 with attendance at a school of Latin grammar, followed by mathematics to the age of 12, and then reading of the classics with a communal master.

Such details give us an insight into the way that the rise of humanism reflected changes in Italian political life. Rather ironically, the fourteenth century had seen both a precipitous decline in population as a result of the plague, and the political ascendancy of the so-called *popolo*, literally meaning "the people." The term refers to a middle class whose wealth and social influence peaked with the establishment of republican governments around Italy. Humanism was in part an expression of the *popolo*, often highly literate merchants and lawyers and who looked back to Roman history for a model of republican institutions.[4] This is one reason you might have an association in your mind between humanist thought and republicanism (see further Chapter 38). Yet, when elite families emerged to dominate some city governments in the fifteenth century, they continued to celebrate and support humanist scholarship. The most famous example would be the Medici of Florence. Cosimo de' Medici, in particular, was patron to the Platonist thinker Marsilio Ficino and endowed an important library at San Marco.

Humanism was not only, not even primarily, a philosophical movement. The intellectual ideal of the period, as still remembered today in our phrase "Renaissance man," was the scholar who mastered a forbiddingly wide range of disciplines. Take for instance Fabio Paolini, who lived at the end of our period, dying in 1605.[5] He took degrees in both philosophy and medicine in Padua, and went on to teach both Latin and Greek literature. He wrote commentaries on Cicero, Avicenna, and Hippocrates, treatises on medicine and about the nature of humanism itself, and even a translation of Aesop's fables. Much as we saw with the humanists of Byzantium, for instance Maximos Planoudes and other scholars of the so-called "Palaiologan renaissance," the humanists of the Italian Renaissance were interested in philosophy simply because it formed a part of ancient literature. Carrying on the values of the Byzantine humanists, these Italian scholars devoted themselves to the collection and preservation of Greek manuscripts.

Most eye-catching here are the texts that were rediscovered and read for the first time since antiquity (see Chapter 27).[6] A famous case occurred in 1417 when the humanist Poggio Bracciolini found a manuscript of the Latin poem *On the Nature of Things*, written by Lucretius, an Epicurean philosopher of the Roman Republic. Lucretius was only one of numerous Greek thinkers to attract newfound attention. Sextus Empiricus, the most significant ancient Skeptic, had not been totally lost in the medieval period. But he became a much more important source in the Renaissance, cited by such figures as Angelo Poliziano and Gianfrancesco Pico della Mirandola. The most important single text for disseminating knowledge of the Hellenistic schools was *Lives of the Philosophers*, originally written by Diogenes Laertius in the third century AD. Alongside summaries of the teachings of many ancient thinkers and, it must be said, a lot of rather dubious biographical material, this work contained such gems as two short works by Epicurus himself, which Diogenes had inserted into his report of Epicurus' life and teachings. A Latin version of the *Lives* was made at the behest of Cosimo de' Medici, and it enjoyed wide diffusion in manuscripts before appearing in a first printed edition in 1472. As a result of these and other findings, Renaissance readers were in an unprecedented position. In all three medieval cultures, the legacy of antique philosophy had largely been Aristotelianism laced with Platonism. Only in the fifteenth century did ancient philosophy re-emerge in full, with Skepticism, Epicureanism, and Stoicism given their proper due.

Yet the humanists also made great strides in understanding Aristotelianism and Platonism, and these traditions remained dominant. We tend to think of Italian humanists as abandoning Aristotle for Plato, and this is not entirely unjustified. The father of Italian humanism, Petrarch, complained in the fourteenth century of scholastic contemporaries who "worship Aristotle, whom they don't understand, and accuse me for not bending my knee before him."[7] But notice his suggestion that it would be better to understand Aristotle properly, unlike the schoolmen. This presupposed a deeper engagement with his Greek texts, a project pursued from early in the fifteenth century with improved Latin translations by Roberto Rossi and Leonardo Bruni. Over the next two centuries there would be nearly 300 translations of Aristotle into Latin, produced by about 70 translators.[8] That's not to mention renditions of his works in various European vernacular languages. Meanwhile, the original Greek of Aristotle was finding new readers. Almost half our surviving manuscripts for Aristotle date from the fifteenth and sixteenth centuries, and the history of printing him in Greek goes back to the five-volume edition produced by Aldus Manutius and his team at the end of the fifteenth century (see Chapter 45). We also find humanists lecturing on the Aristotelian corpus, as did Angelo Poliziano in Florence and Niccolò Leonico Tomeo in Padua.

Yet we should not underestimate the continuing vitality of the scholastic approach to Aristotle. Medieval commentators were widely read, and given early printings. For instance, there were printed editions of Aquinas' commentaries on Aristotle, and in the middle of the sixteenth century Tommaso Giunta printed Averroes' commentaries in Venice, along with the works of Aristotle on which Averroes had been commenting. Giunta did this as a corrective to the humanists' enthusiasm for Greek sources, which led them to neglect the riches of the Arabic tradition.[9] As we'll be seeing, Averroes was a significant source for Renaissance Aristotelians, and also a significant source of controversy, just as he had been back in the thirteenth century when Aquinas was attacking members in the arts faculty at Paris for their excessive devotion to "the Commentator" and his doctrines.

If the story of Aristotelianism in the Renaissance is fairly continuous with medieval tradition, the revival of Platonism was really something new—at least in the Latin Christian sphere. True, Plato had inspired philosophers throughout the middle ages, his influence peaking in the twelfth century with the so-called "school of Chartres." But for the most part Plato was known only through a partial translation of his cosmological dialogue the *Timaeus*. Now in the Renaissance, the whole collection of his dialogues makes a dramatic entry onto the stage of philosophy, bringing the knowledge of his works to the same level as had been possible in Constantinople. This was thanks especially to Ficino, whose complete Latin translation of Plato appeared in 1484, but his efforts had been anticipated by earlier scholars such as Leonardo Bruni and George Trapezuntius. Meanwhile Ficino and others also made a close study of late ancient Platonists, including Plotinus and Proclus. Now Platonism could finally compete with Aristotelianism on more or less equal footing, in a contest that carried on from the debates we've found in Byzantium.

The upshot of all this is that a remarkably diverse array of sources could attract the attention of Italian Renaissance thinkers. It was a time when, depending on your literary taste, your educational background, and your city, you might cherish Cicero, Plato, or Averroes above all other thinkers. If you were a humanist, you would place highest value on the thinkers who wrote the best Latin; and beyond that, those who seemed to contribute the most in the sphere of ethics. The humanists borrowed from Hellenistic texts the assumption that all philosophy worthy of the name should help us to live better lives. Already Petrarch had gone so far as to say, "it is better to will the good than know the truth." Furthermore, there were powerful links between ethics and political philosophy in this period. We will find humanists like Bruni contending that a certain kind of virtue fits well with the institutions of republican city-states, a notion taken up and transformed out of all recognition by the (in)famous Machiavelli (see Chapters 38–40).

Speaking of institutions, the contrast between humanism and scholasticism has in part to do with institutional contexts. In Florence, for instance, there was no university, which allowed the new humanist paradigm to flourish in the absence of competition. The existence of philosophy outside universities was, in itself, nothing new. A handful of intriguing and well-known medieval thinkers also wrote beyond the university setting, such as Petrarch and Dante. But in the Renaissance this will become increasingly common, if not the norm. Similarly, medieval philosophy was enriched by the contribution of numerous thinkers who, as women, were excluded from the world of the schoolmen. That too will continue into the Renaissance (see Chapters 28–30). Still, we should not underestimate the importance of universities in the formation of Renaissance Italian philosophy. The curricular emphases of these institutions meant that some cities were strongly associated with certain disciplines, as with the pursuit of medicine at Bologna, or with a certain approach to philosophy. Alongside Florence with its importance for the history of Platonism, the best example is Padua, where university professors were known for pursuing Aristotelian and even Averroist philosophy. As usual, there are caveats to be issued, since it is not as if there was one set of "Paduan" doctrines shared by all the scholars who worked there. But there is no denying that this city played host to an impressive array of Aristotelian thinkers, who will be covered especially in Chapters 46–7.

An abiding interest of the Paduan schoolmen was science, and especially scientific methodology. I will follow their lead by exploring the scientific achievement of the Renaissance, with particular focus on medicine and the mathematical disciplines (Chapters 48–9), without ignoring "pseudo-" or occult sciences like magic (Chapter 52). Among the social sciences, our look at political philosophy will be complemented by an exploration of economics and the writing of history, something else we've seen foreshadowed in Byzantium (Chapters 41 and 43). Indeed, as I've already flagged numerous times and as will become especially clear in the next chapter, we are not really taking up a whole new topic in this second part of the book. Rather, we are carrying on a story that leads naturally from Byzantium into Renaissance Italy.

23

GREEKS BEARING GIFTS BYZANTINE SCHOLARS IN ITALY

It speaks well of philosophy that we have managed to get so far into this history of the subject without mentioning a single fistfight. Philosophers get into arguments, but usually without coming to blows. I will confess to wondering what might happen if they did. The biographical compilation written in antiquity by Diogenes Laertius provides rich material for the imagination here. He informs us that Plato studied wrestling and that the very name "Plato," meaning "broad," may have referred to his muscular build; by contrast Aristotle is described as having slim legs and the affected dress of a courtier. Diogenes leaves little doubt that if these two got into a fight, then there would be only one outcome. To paraphrase the jock character played by Emilio Estevez in the classic 1985 teen comedy *The Breakfast Club*, there would be two hits: Plato hitting Aristotle, and Aristotle hitting the floor.

Sadly, but if we're honest also rather entertainingly, the peaceable record of philosophers is now going to end. Two of the greatest humanists of the fifteenth century, Poggio Bracciolini and George Trapezuntius, had a quarrel which escalated to the point that Poggio attacked George and tried to gouge out his eyes. George retaliated with a punch and went for a knife, chasing Poggio into a hasty retreat. Later George would complain to the pope that Poggio hired a hit man to take revenge.[1] Not an edifying spectacle, especially from two men who devoted their lives to the edification of their contemporaries. Yet the event was entirely characteristic of the backbiting and rivalry that raged between humanist scholars. In fact the hostility with Poggio is not even the most famous clash between George and another humanist. Better known, and more interesting in philosophical terms, was the conflict between George Trapezuntius and Bessarion.

This despite the fact that George and Bessarion had a good deal in common. Both of them hailed from the Greek East. Ironically Bessarion was actually from Trebizond, whereas George was from Crete (he is "Trapezuntius" to indicate that his grandfather was from there). Both moved to Italy and converted to Catholicism, in Bessarion's case after he was persuaded of the Latins' theological views at the council of Ferrara and Florence. He was elevated to the rank of cardinal and would only narrowly miss out on being elected pope later in his career. Native Greek speakers who mastered Latin, George and Bessarion became ambassadors of Hellenic literature to the Italian scholarly world. Both supported the cause of unity between the Western and Eastern churches, with Bessarion arguing that the hopes of Christianity lay especially with the Western church once the East fell to the Turks.[2] The two men even died at about the same time, Bessarion in 1472 and George in that same year, or possibly the following year.

It's worth emphasizing that these two scholars came to Italy well before the fall of Constantinople, with George arriving already in 1416 and Bessarion attending the aforementioned council (along with George) in 1437. This was hardly atypical. Before the influx of Greeks to the Latin West after the Ottomans took the capital, scholars had already been leaving for generations, during the long decline of the Byzantine empire.[3] So there were a significant number of Greeks in Italy throughout the fifteenth century, especially in certain cities: Bessarion called Venice "almost another Byzantium." This helps to explain how so many Italian humanists learned Greek. George Trapezuntius taught Greek to his later sparring partner Poggio, and had stints teaching in Venice and Florence before moving to Rome. Another important teacher of Greek was Manuel Chrysoloras, who led an Eastern embassy to Venice already in 1390 and returned to Italy six years later. He wrote a grammatical textbook for Greek modeled on medieval books of Latin grammar, and taught a generation of early Renaissance humanists. Leonardo Bruni was one of them, who explained his choice to study with Chrysoloras: "for seven hundred years now, no one in Italy has been able to read Greek, and yet we admit that it is from the Greeks that we get all our systems of knowledge."[4] Others were inspired to travel east themselves, as did Guarino Veronese. He accompanied Chrysoloras on a return trip to Constantinople, and then later became a teacher in his own right, working in various cities including Florence.

In addition to such personal connections, the transplanted Eastern scholars had a major role to play in the translation and interpretation of Greek philosophy, science, and patristic literature. Such was their influence that one humanist remarked, after the fall of Constantinople, that in Italy many people had "gone Greek" as if they'd been educated in Athens.[5] The Greek scholars imported the values of Byzantine humanism, with its exaltation of good style and commitment to philological exactitude. Then they transposed these values to the Latin language. Bessarion is famous as the "most Greek of the Latins and most Latin of the Greeks," praise supposedly bestowed upon him by Lorenzo Valla. But in fact George Trapezuntius was the superior Latinist. It would seem that Bessarion had to get the help of his secretary Niccolò Perotti to pursue his rivalry with George without being embarrassed by his inferior grasp of the language.[6] George, by contrast, boasted that he learned Latin so well that he could dictate to two scribes on different topics at the same time, and that he might be mistaken for a native speaker from the time of Cicero.[7]

We've seen how Byzantine scholars as far back as Psellos esteemed the Attic Greek of authors like Aristophanes and Plato. Similarly, George and other humanists in Italy held up Cicero's language as the standard against which Latin should be judged. In an influential work on rhetoric, George referred constantly to Cicero, whom he called "the best of rhetoricians (*summus orator*)," for examples to illustrate the general rules of the art. He was disdainful of the medieval tradition of writing on rhetoric, seeing it as unsystematic and inadequate. He took his cue instead from Greek works on the subject, especially by Hermogenes, a theorist of rhetoric from the second century AD who wrote in Greek. George also translated the *Rhetoric* of Aristotle, but rejected Aristotle's approach to the subject, which encouraged the orator to focus on the emotional and psychological states of the audience. Following Hermogenes, George instead laid out general rules of style for achieving certain effects.

John Monfasani, the foremost modern-day scholar of the Greek humanists in Italy, has hypothesized that it was George's love of rhetoric that turned him into a critic of Plato.[8] This was evidently quite a change of heart, given that George had translated the dialogue *Parmenides*, at the behest of Nicholas of Cusa no less, and also Plato's *Laws*. Upon translating this dialogue in 1451 he said how pleased he was to discover that the constitution of Venice seemed to echo the proposals made by Plato. But, perhaps taking umbrage at the attacks on rhetoric in Platonic dialogues like the *Gorgias*, George turned against Plato and wrote a work called *Comparison of the Philosophers Plato and Aristotle*. It was round two of the fight between adherents of Plato and of Aristotle.

As you'll remember, the first round pitted Plethon against Scholarios, the former chastising Aristotle for rejecting his teacher's doctrines, and the latter coming to Aristotle's defense (Chapter 20). Where Plethon struck out at Aristotle's rejection of Platonic forms and divine creation of the universe, George prefers to hit below the belt, by accusing Plato of sexual depravity. He points to the erotic elements of the dialogues themselves and also to Diogenes Laertius' report that Plato took male lovers. The polemic against Plato provides George with a welcome opportunity to take a swipe at Plethon. George was one of the more hostile witnesses called for the prosecution when we considered the question of Plethon's paganism. It was he who, rather implausibly, accused Plethon of openly revealing his pagan sympathies at the council of Florence and Ferrara. From his point of view, this was only to be expected given Plethon's philosophical tastes. Trading on a standard bit of anti-Muslim polemic, George comments that the Prophet Muhammad had been a "second Plato" seeking to corrupt the sexual morality, with Plethon coming along as a third.[9]

Alongside such accusations, George does mention more substantive philosophical failings in Plato. Having translated Plato's *Laws*, he is well placed to critique the Platonic political theory.[10] In a remarkable section of his diatribe, he attacks the elitist and xenophobic elements of that theory. He is appalled by provisions in the *Laws* that prevented aliens from settling permanently in the ideal city. George reflects explicitly on his own life story here, remarking that it would be unjust to exile him from his new Italian homeland just because he hails from Crete. He praises the ancient Romans and, remarkably, the Ottomans of his own day for their cosmopolitanism, their willingness to integrate citizens of different ethnic groups and backgrounds into a single state. Furthermore, George rails against the way Plato calls for a strict division of the classes, something we also know from the *Republic*. How will the citizens ever be united in bonds of friendship if one class is permanently and significantly disadvantaged, and why would the upper class ever look on their inferiors with anything but disdain? Not a bad question even today.

But most extraordinary is George's point that Plato, or his philosopher-rulers, have no business prescribing to all citizens how they should spend their lives. Who is Plato to say that a humble laborer may not aspire to gain wealth and standing in his community? George's argument may reflect the greater social mobility of Renaissance Italy, and resonates with ideas we'll consider later under the heading of "civic humanism" (Chapter 38). But he sometimes sounds remarkably like the modern-day philosophy student who, having grown up in a Western liberal democracy, is confronted with the totalitarian paternalism of the *Republic*. Consider the following lines: "Isn't man free? . . . Don't you see that judgments differ, that pains and pleasures differ? Perfectly honorable things which I find pleasant you snatch away from me and substitute things you find pleasant."[11]

The gauntlet had been thrown down, and Plato was in need of a champion. Stepping into the Platonic corner to fight this rematch of the Byzantine debate, we have Cardinal Bessarion.[12] Against the accusation that Plato and his works were sexually depraved, Bessarion retorted that if this were true, the Greek fathers of the church would hardly have admired Plato as they did. The fault is with George, who is evidently unable to get his mind out of the gutter. He fails to realize that the erotic themes in the dialogues have nothing to do with physical lust, which Bessarion calls "earthly love," but concern a more exalted "divine love."[13]

Just as George had devoted himself to studying and translating Plato before attacking him, so Bessarion was an accomplished Aristotelian by the time he came to defend Plato. He produced a Latin version of the *Metaphysics*, perhaps the most difficult treatise in the Aristotelian corpus, if not the entirety of ancient philosophy. And as an admirer of Latin scholasticism, he was one of those Byzantine scholars who avidly read texts by Western Aristotelians like Aquinas, right from the earliest stages of his career.[14] In another direct link to the Byzantine controversy over Plato and Aristotle, Bessarion had been educated at Mistra under none other than Plethon, to whom he referred as his "father and guide." In a letter written to Plethon's sons, Bessarion went further still, hinting that his master was the reincarnation of Plato and calling him most honored man in Greece.[15] Yet he distanced himself from Plethon's anti-Aristotelianism, while also rejecting George's anti-Platonism. Bessarion wasn't really spoiling for a fight, but trying to make peace. His aim was to demonstrate the agreement between the two authors, and their suitability for use by Christian thinkers.

Here's an example. Plethon had complained about a passage in the *Physics* (199b26–9) where Aristotle said that, whereas a craftsman may deliberate (*boulesthai*) in using his art, the art itself does not do so.[16] A carpenter needs to make careful plans to build a ship, but if the art of carpentry were in the wood instead of in the carpenter's mind, the wood would just turn itself into a ship the way that natural things like trees grow to maturity on their own. Against this Plethon asserted that nature involves a guiding intelligence no less than carpentry does, because it is an expression of higher, intellectual causes. Rather than rebutting this bit of obvious Platonism, Bessarion tries to make Aristotle agree with it. He reminds his reader that Aristotle did believe in God, a prime mover ultimately responsible for all change in the universe. So Aristotle too acknowledged that there is a divine intellect providentially guiding nature. Yet Aristotle was still right to say that nature does not "deliberate" because the kind of intelligence involved in providence and its natural results is different from the kind of hesitant, uncertain deliberation we humans perform when we are, say, building a ship.

Another man who sought to defend Aristotle by establishing his harmony with Plato was Theodore Gaza. He too was a Greek scholar who made his way to Italy, after being called to Rome from Constantinople to work for the pope as a translator. Like George Trapezuntius and Bessarion, who became his patron and close associate, Theodore Gaza distinguished himself as a translator from Greek into Latin. He produced a widely used version of Aristotle's zoological writings, which would go on to be reproduced in early modern printings. Actually he did more than just translate. Convinced that the Greek texts at his disposal were faulty, he re-edited and even re-ordered them before translating them, making some organizational changes that have still been followed in modern editions of Aristotle. Alongside this bold and influential philological work, Theodore wrote on philosophical questions, though not always very convincingly. The aforementioned expert on the field, John Monfasani, has called him "learned and serious, but startlingly trivial."[17]

A good test case for this judgment is a brief work on the topic of fate.[18] Like his ally Bessarion, Theodore is reluctant to admit that Plato and Aristotle were in serious disagreement. Again prompted by a supposed divergence of Aristotle from Plato mentioned by Plethon, Theodore takes up the question of free human action. In a famous section of the *Nicomachean Ethics*, Aristotle distinguished between the voluntary and the involuntary. He proposed that a voluntary action is one that is neither compelled nor done in ignorance; it is a sign of voluntariness that the person who performs the action does not later regret the action or its consequences. This theory makes it possible to do bad things voluntarily. Indeed, part of Aristotle's purpose was to decide when it makes sense to blame someone for their bad deeds: if they did it without compulsion and not in ignorance, then they did it voluntarily and are thus blameworthy. By contrast Plato—or rather the character of Socrates in various Platonic dialogues—held that no one *ever* does bad things voluntarily. After all, isn't the fact that someone willingly does something evidence enough that they take it to be a good thing to do?

By way of resolution, Theodore points out that Aristotle too says that all actions aim at some good outcome or other. So he would agree with Plato that when we act badly, we are ignorant in a way, in that we have failed to understand the best course of action. Yet we are not ignorant in a more basic sense, because we know the facts concerning what we are doing. If you get into a boxing match with your mother and break her nose, you've done something bad. But it makes a difference whether you did this because you are ignorant of the fact that it is wrong to break your own mother's nose, or because you don't realize that this person you're hitting is your mother, because she's wearing one of those padded helmets. Moral ignorance is no excuse; ignorance of the facts might be.

The clash between Bessarion and George Trapezuntius was the mother of all battles involving Greek émigré scholars in Italy, but it certainly wasn't the only one. Never mind dog eat dog, this was humanist eat humanist. In addition to the aforementioned fisticuffs between George and Poggio, there was the time that Theodore Gaza stood up at a lecture given by George Trapezuntius and berated him for making philosophical errors. George also tangled with Lorenzo Valla, the two arguing whether ancient Greek generals were superior to their Roman counterparts.[19] Then there was the spat between George and Guarino Veronese, that student of Chrysoloras who traveled to Constantinople. Guarino was considered a fine Latin stylist by most, but not by George. In his work on rhetoric he provocatively rewrote a speech by Guarino, showing how it could be improved by making it sound more like Cicero. As if this weren't bad enough, he added some insulting comments on Guarino's style: no one with any taste could bear to hear it. The two patched it up, at least in theory, at that same church council in Ferrara (with all the scandals erupting and being calmed down, it's amazing the participants had any time to debate the Trinity). And there were still other quarrels, like a critique of George's commentarial work on Cicero by Giorgio Merula, a student of yet another Greek scholar named John Argyropoulos.[20]

To be fair, a lot of these events seem to be traceable to George's character. An arrogant man who was well aware of his own talent, he provoked his colleagues so routinely that you have to think any ignorance involved was moral, and not only concerning the facts of the case. Yet it was entirely possible for humanists to savage one another without George's involvement. In another case, a mistake made by Bessarion was noticed by the same Argyropoulos, provoking Theodore Gaza to write a rather unconvincing treatise in Bessarion's defense.[21] When they weren't going so far as to sharpen their swords, the humanists were sharpening their pens, the better to take jabs at one another in the status-conscious and competitive atmosphere of Renaissance Italy, when a scholar's present reputation was as precious as facility with the languages of the past.[22]

24

REPUBLIC OF LETTERS
ITALIAN HUMANISM

At the risk of sounding like a crotchety old fogey, I'd like to complain that no one writes letters anymore. When was the last time you got one? Not an email, I mean, but something on paper in a stamped envelope, preferably handwritten. A friend of mine who is a historian of the American Civil War once pointed out to me that experts on his chosen speciality have many nineteenth-century letters to draw on in their research, whereas future historians of our present day may well curse the fact that our correspondence took the form of ephemeral data, long deleted or trapped in no longer readable storage devices. Historians of philosophy too can learn a lot from letters. Beginning in antiquity, they were often written with a view to wider publication, not only for the private reading of one recipient. Thus the letter, or "epistle," has long been a popular form for writing philosophy, used by Plato, Seneca, Peter Abelard and Heloise, al-Kindī, and John Locke, to name only a few.

Around the turn of the fifteenth century, the master of the letter was Coluccio Salutati.[1] He studied epistolary techniques, called in Latin *ars dictaminis*, at the university of Bologna, where he obtained his degree in 1350 before becoming chancellor of Florence in 1375. As the Florentines contended with the papacy and rival cities such as Milan, Salutati's elegant letters were the most powerful weapon in a war of words. Thus the Milanese duke Gian Galeazzo Visconti remarked that "one letter of Salutati's was worth a troop of horses." Not that Salutati's audience would necessarily have been capable of understanding his high-flown Latin.[2] But his rhetoric did honor to his city and lent dignity to any diplomatic occasion.

Salutati's style was not only about being stylish. Alongside state business he devoted himself to carrying on the tradition of Italian humanism. I say "carrying on," rather than "beginning" that tradition, because as Salutati himself would have been the first to point out, Italian humanism took inspiration from an earlier Florentine: Petrarch.[3] In the middle of the fourteenth century Petrarch already embodied the values and activities taken up by Salutati and his followers. Actually, modern-day scholars have pointed to still earlier anticipations.[4] The tradition of Italian *dictatores*, masters of rhetorical letter-writing, stretched back as far as the twelfth century. One can name such figures as Albertino Mussato, a Paduan scholar who wrote plays inspired by Seneca and history based on Livy. But for Salutati it was Petrarch who could be credited with "initiating" (*excitare*) the humanist movement, which had its symbolic birth on Easter Sunday 1341, when Petrarch was crowned with laurels by a Roman senator.

Salutati was not a student or close colleague of Petrarch, though he was in touch with him at one point (by letter, of course). For him Petrarch was, to use a word that will make any Roman senator nervous, one of a triumvirate of Florentine authors worthy of veneration, along with Dante and Boccaccio. Their exalted status is at the heart of a founding document of fifteenth-century humanism, the *Dialogue* written by one of Salutati's protégés, Leonardo Bruni.[5] Bruni was one of several younger scholars who were inspired and promoted by Salutati. The group also included Poggio Bracciolini, whom we just met coming to blows with George Trapezuntius, as well as Niccolò Niccoli. Members of the group studied Latin with Giovanni Malpaghini, who had been Petrarch's assistant,[6] and Greek with the Byzantine scholar Manuel Chrysoloras. It was Salutati who invited Chrysoloras to Florence as a teacher.

Bruni's *Dialogue* is, among other things, a testament to the cockiness that young men may adopt once you give them this level of education. Salutati himself initiates the discussion, as Bruni shows him exhorting the circle to engage in disputation and not only bookish research (64–6). This is met with a speech by Niccoli, who complains that there is little prospect of refined debate given the parlous state of education in Italy at this time. Thanks to a lack of both books and refinement, the intellectual level of the time cannot measure up to what we see in the works of a man like Cicero. The situation is, as Niccoli puts it, nothing short of a "shipwreck of learning" (68). When it's put to him that he is being too pessimistic, given the achievements of the aforementioned heroes of literature in Florence, Niccoli responds with an irreverent speech attacking Dante, Petrarch, and Boccaccio as failing to match the high standards set in antiquity. This is a surprising, even shocking, line of argument. But in a second part of the work Niccoli reveals that he was only trying to provoke Salutati to defend these three role models (77–9). When he does not rise to the bait, Niccoli agrees to give a second speech answering his own criticisms.

What is going on here? Well, for starters, the *Dialogue* is an ironic and playful work. How seriously should we take Niccoli's supposedly devastating complaint that in the *Divine Comedy*, Dante describes Cato as an old man, when we all know he died before turning fifty? No more or less seriously than the answer, which is that the white beard sported by Cato is just a symbol for virtue befitting an older sage (73, 80). Yet the standing of Dante and the others is no trivial matter. Around the same time the *Dialogue* was written, Salutati had a falling out with Poggio when the younger man brashly insulted Petrarch's knowledge of Latin; needless to say, they exchanged letters over the matter. There was also a good deal of civic pride at stake. These three authors were heroes of Florentine culture, and insulting them was accordingly an affront to the city. But this is only the beginning of the political import of Bruni's *Dialogue*.[7] Another of Niccoli's complaints is that Dante quite literally reserved a special place in hell for the murderers of Julius Caesar, Brutus, and Cassius. Natural enough for Dante, whose political philosophy envisioned a single monarch ruling over the whole world.[8] But it hardly seems an attitude that good Florentine republicans should endorse. This too was a point of contention in other humanist writings. Salutati himself wrote a work called *On the Tyrant* in which he tried to explain why Dante had meted out this punishment to Caesar's killers. His argument was that Caesar actually ruled with a popular mandate, so Dante was right to condemn Brutus and Cassius.[9]

The humanists' devotion to republican government, rule of the "people" and not a tyrant or a group of oligarchs, gave them another reason to admire Cicero. Not only did he write fabulous Latin, but he was a martyr to the cause of the Roman republic. Later we'll be discussing an encomium to the city of Florence written by Leonardo Bruni (see Chapter 38), which begins by extolling the well-balanced structure of the city's government, preserving as it does both justice and liberty.[10] Salutati's group was delighted when some historical research proved that Florence had not been founded by Caesar, as often supposed, but already existed in the time of the republic. Having said that, humanist literary tastes did not require republican political leanings. Humanism was practiced in cities that lacked republican institutions, like Venice.[11] Even in Florence, the rhetoric of liberty masked the fact that power was exercised by a relatively small group of citizens. Scholars have pointed out that between the years 1282 and 1532, only about two dozen families held the reins of the government.[12] Then again, one might make similar observations about Rome in the generations leading up to Julius Caesar. The humanists were never better students of Cicero than when they followed his lead by squinting hard enough to make an oligarchy look like a genuine republic. It's also important to bear in mind that, whatever the political appeal of Cicero, the main attraction was indeed that fabulous Latin. Tellingly, Bruni compares the perfect constitution of Florence to a well-formed sentence, as if he can think of no higher praise.

Perhaps you have friends who are "language purists," always telling you off for using "who" when you should say "whom" and "which" when you should say "that." Well, I can practically guarantee that these friends have nothing on Coluccio Salutati. This was a man who could get seriously upset about people using the second-person plural pronoun *vos* as a polite form of address, because the ancients consistently used the second-person singular *tu*. (We don't have this grammatical feature in English, unless you count "y'all," but it's the same as the difference between *vosotros* and *tu* in Spanish, or *ihr* and *du* in German.) Salutati believed in using Latin correctly, and believed that the standard of correctness was set by ancient authors like Cicero. The humanists are famous for decrying the repugnant Latin and neologisms of the medievals, and this is certainly true. It's a point made by Niccoli's opening speech in Bruni's *Dialogue*, and Salutati is unsparing in his scorn for the crass style of medievals like Abelard. Even John of Salisbury, another twelfth-century philosopher whom[13] many see as a forerunner of the humanists, gets low marks. But Salutati believed the rot had set in earlier, with the inelegant writing style of late ancient authors like Martianus Capella.

It would be easy to accuse the humanists of snobbery here, of indulging in pedantry and self-satisfied display of an education available only to the elite. But for the humanists, the pursuit of rhetorical skill was not just about showing off. It led to higher aims. Salutati advised that eloquence should be paired with wisdom, and that a well-turned sentence could turn souls to virtue: "Let the things you write produce something in your readers which not only charms them, but does them good."[14] I've already mentioned in passing that Leonardo Bruni was in favor of teaching the classics to women. It's worth mentioning the context where he said that, namely a letter to an admittedly quite aristocratic woman, Lady Battista Malatesta of Montefeltro.[15] After the usual lament about the poor state of learning, which is "so far decayed that it is regarded as positively miraculous to meet a learned man, let alone a woman," he assigns her an ambitious reading list of Greek and Latin classics. He concedes that women have no opportunity to use rhetoric in public speeches, but still believes that women should study eloquent literature for the sake of moral improvement.

With all this fetishization of antique literature, you could be forgiven for assuming that the humanists disdained the use of vernacular languages. But while they did exalt Latin and Greek above their mother tongue, they also preferred good Italian to bad Latin. How else could they have so admired the Florentine poets Dante, Petrarch, and Boccaccio, all of whom wrote at least sometimes in the vernacular? Thus Salutati remarked that "whatever is well spoken is eloquent," while his fellow humanist Benedetto Accolti said, "To me it is not important whether one speaks in Latin or the mother tongue, provided that he speaks with gravity, ornament, and abundance."[16] The humanists were well aware that Italian and other vernaculars were derived from Latin, and wondered about the way these new languages had evolved. Lorenzo Valla, for example, noted that Spanish had introduced definite and indefinite articles, but dropped the declension of nouns.

Still less clear was the relation of Latin to the vernacular of classical times. When Cicero delivered the speeches that left the humanists in such rapture, would the average Roman even have been able to understand him? Or would they have been like the nobles presented with speeches and letters of Salutati, pleased and flattered, but secretly uncomprehending? The question became a point of dispute between Bruni and yet another humanist, Flavio Biondo.[17] Biondo wrote to Bruni asking whether the ancients really spoke the language studied in the grammatical education that was, depending on your perspective, either inflicted on or enjoyed by the Italian youth. To put it bluntly: did Romans actually speak Latin? Bruni found the very notion preposterous. How could proper Latin, with all its grammatical complexity, have been spoken by every man on the street?

In fact, never mind the men. Immediately losing the feminist credentials he won for that encouraging letter he sent to Lady Battista, Bruni asks whether we can really imagine that "nursemaids and little women" could have mastered the language of Cicero. Here Bruni is arguably projecting the situation of his own day back onto antiquity, unable to conceive that this language of refinement and literature, now used only in rather artificial contexts, had ever been anyone's mother tongue.[18] He also shows himself prey to a common misunderstanding, namely that some languages are more inherently complex than others, to the point that they are not even serviceable for everyday use. After all, every language has its own difficulties, things that will trip up those of us who try to learn them as adults; yet every language can effortlessly be mastered by children if given even half a chance. Some years later, Poggio Bracciolini made this very point, adding that plenty of adults still manage to learn Latin for use at the papal court.[19]

It seems then that for Poggio, Roman children and peasants had better Latin than Petrarch did. Salutati and Bruni evidently disagreed about the case of Petrarch. But as we've seen, the humanists were united in their low opinion of most other medieval authors, especially the scholastics. Bruni summed up the attitude after rapturously quoting a passage of Virgil's *Aeneid*: "When we read these lines, what philosopher do we not despise?"[20] Yet none other than Salutati tempered the critique of medieval scholasticism by reminding his audience, and perhaps himself, that the schoolmen were after all Christians. In this respect they must be reckoned superior to even the most eloquent pagan author. Indeed, Salutati argued that even the "most poorly educated person" in his own time was better than Cicero, Plato, or Aristotle.[21] The goal was therefore to make the best use of pagan literature, but while staying within a Christian moral and theological framework. For guidance the humanists could look to that treatise by the Greek father Basil of Caesarea, which gave advice to young readers of classical, non-Christian texts (see Chapter 4). It's no coincidence that Bruni translated the work soon after learning Greek from Chrysoloras.[22]

What Bruni and the other humanists really couldn't abide, though, was incompetent medieval scholarship devoted to these same classical texts. Hence their ambitious undertaking to produce new, more acceptable translations of works that had already been available in Latin for some time. "More acceptable," of course, meant more Ciceronian. Bruni translated the *Nicomachean Ethics* of Aristotle (his choice of text again showing the moral emphasis of the humanist endeavor) in a bid to replace the version executed by Robert Grosseteste in the thirteenth century. Some readers felt that the gain in elegance was matched by a loss in precision. Alonzo of Burgos, a Jewish convert to Christianity, argued that Grosseteste had often captured Aristotle's point better than Bruni. For instance, the Greek word for "pleasure," *hedone*, was rendered into Latin as *delectatio* in the older medieval version, but by Bruni as *voluptas*. Alonzo felt that Grosseteste's version was preferable since it sounds more general, and could apply to intellectual as well as bodily pleasure.[23] We've already seen enough of the humanists to predict what happened next. Bruni penned a furious reply, pointing out that Alonzo was in no position to assess his translation, since he didn't even know Greek. And of course he reiterated that any acceptable Latin version must adhere to proper classical usage.

Again, proper usage was defined above all by Cicero. For all the variety of opinion and different emphases we've found in this tour of the early Italian humanists, you can hold on to that one point: they really, really liked Cicero. In fact, if we go back to Bruni's *Dialogue*, we can observe that it is closely based on Cicero's own philosophical dialogues. The very structure chosen by Bruni, a speech followed by a counter-speech, is Ciceronian and evokes the ancient rhetorical skill of speaking on both sides of an issue.[24] One particularly witty display of this ability was already put on in the year 1386 when Cino Rinuccini produced orations praising, and then attacking, rhetoric itself. There is a danger lurking here, one that should have been evident from reading Cicero himself and would have become even more obvious as Plato's dialogues came back into circulation, with their searching critique of the sophists. If you can argue persuasively on both sides of any issue, then won't the result be skepticism? That would have been just fine with Cicero, who declared his allegiance to the Academic skeptical school. But would it have been fine with the humanists? One could hold out the hope that, as Poggio put it, "by discussing an issue from both sides, truth usually emerges."[25] But Salutati sounds more faithful to Cicero when he writes, "Every truth grasped by reason can be made doubtful by a contrary reason."[26] It won't be the last time we see ideas from Hellenistic philosophy making a disconcerting appearance in the Italian Renaissance.

25

LITERARY CRITICISM
LORENZO VALLA

As I observed in the volume on medieval philosophy, the scholastic philosophy of that period and the analytic philosophy of today have much in common: the proliferation of distinctions, the delight in logic and linguistic analysis, the technical vocabulary that shuts out the uninitiated. And something else, namely the criticisms these features tend to provoke. Already in the thirteenth and fourteenth centuries you can find sentiments that are routinely echoed by contemporary observers frustrated by the professional philosophy scene. All this logic-chopping and distinction-mongering is mere obfuscation. Philosophers should keep it simple and speak in a way that everyone can understand. Why aren't they telling us how to live, instead of retreating into arcane, hermetic disputes? Now, I'm no fan of needless technicality. But I tend to think that these critics are impatient with scholastic and analytic philosophy because they are, indeed, impatient. Any philosophical problem worth thinking about (including the ones about how to live) will lead you into complex and difficult territory once you do start to think about it. Fans of the simple answers often just haven't reflected hard enough about what these answers might imply, and what might be said in favor of rival answers.

We need to decide whether this applies to the Italian humanists. When they denounced the methods used by the medieval schoolmen and by the scholastics still active in their own day, was that a well-informed and philosophically serious rejection? Or were they the Renaissance equivalent of people who haven't studied philosophy going on social media to complain that professional philosophy is a waste of time? To answer this question, we can do no better than to turn to the works of Lorenzo Valla. In addition to being one of the most prolific and brilliant of the Italian humanists, he was also especially vocal in his disparagement of scholasticism and Aristotelian philosophy more generally. Above all, he had the intellectual integrity and, it must be said, boundless self-confidence necessary to fight the schoolmen on their own ground, clashing with them on topics like dialectic, the soul, and the metaphysics of free will, alongside his contributions to more typically humanist subjects such as ethics and philology. He even wrote an encomium of that leading scholastic Thomas Aquinas, a document that shows it's entirely possible to damn someone with extravagant, instead of faint, praise.

But it's with the philology that we should begin, since it is for his achievements in this area that Valla is best known. He already made a splash in 1428, at the tender age of 21, when he circulated a now lost work to other humanists in Rome, including Poggio Bracciolini and Antonio Loschi. Here he argued for the merits of the ancient rhetorician Quintilian over the much-admired Cicero.[1] Struck more by Valla's uppity ambition than his precocious learning, Poggio and Loschi advised against taking him on at the papal court. Valla was a man who knew how to hold a grudge, so this led to long-standing mutual hostility. Of Valla's widely used textbook *On the Elegance of the Latin Language (Elegantiae linguae Latinae)*,[2] Poggio remarked that it should instead have been called *On the Ignorance of the Latin Language*. In fact it was only one of numerous works displaying Valla's profound knowledge of Greek and Latin. Other examples include his rather provocative set of notes to the New Testament,[3] also attacked by Poggio, translations of Thucydides and Herodotus, and most famously his attack on the *Donation of Constantine*, in which Valla gave the world its most entertaining and readable discussion of textual authentication.[4]

As Valla would be delighted to know, the *Donation* is now universally thought to be a forgery. Probably dating from the eighth century, it pretends to be a letter from the emperor Constantine to Pope Sylvester giving the papacy rule over Rome and the Western empire. Because of course Roman emperors are famous for voluntarily giving up control over huge swaths of their own territory. Valla of course points out the implausibility of this (11–17), but by no means does he stop there. Indeed he pulls out all the stops, deploying every weapon in his formidable arsenal of rhetoric and philology. He puts imaginary speeches in the mouths of those who would have denounced such an imperial gift: the protests that Constantine's own children would have made, the complaints that would have been made by the people of Rome whose freedom was being curtailed, and, most tellingly, what Pope Sylvester himself would or at least should have said to such an offer (21–43). Namely that his dominion is purely spiritual, and that the mission of the church would be undermined by acquiring so much temporal power. The papacy ought to be in the business of *evangelium*, not *imperium*: spreading God's word, not extending its political authority.[5]

Next, and perhaps most persuasively, Valla points out many details of the text that prove it could not have been written back in the fourth century. It includes words Constantine would not have used, like "satrap" (67), displays lamentable historical ignorance (103–5), and uses Latin "like a barbarian" (87). In sum, says Valla in what may be the worst insult he can imagine, the forger who produced the

Donation had "no talent and no literary taste" (79). This approach is liable to strike us as remarkably modern. Instead of focusing on the question of whether the *Donation* is authoritative in institutional terms, as his contemporaries might have done, Valla concentrates on such issues as historical, psychological, and above all linguistic plausibility.[6] In other words, he brings forward the sort of evidence that a textual historian of today might use to verify or deny the authenticity of a text.

Valla himself said that he had "written nothing more rhetorical." Aptly so, given that his penchant for sarcastic invective, high-flown Latin speechifying, and refined stylistic judgment are here on full display. He would also have seen the work as rhetorical because it showed him speaking truth to power. Right at the start, Valla says that the true orator has a responsibility to stand up for his opinions: being able to "speak well" means being willing to "speak out" (5). In the present case, he may have had ulterior motives for doing so. Valla was attached to the court of Alfonso of Aragon, who had a tense relationship with the sitting pope Eugenius IV. But whatever the occasion or political context, Valla was consistent in stating his views with all candor. He suffered for his frankness, and for his habit of making enemies. He was put on trial for heresy in 1444, an event that seems to have ended the most prolific period of his writing career, though he would later receive positions at the papal court.

Another show of irreverence came when Valla was asked to deliver one of the speeches at a celebration of Thomas Aquinas, the most ill-conceived invitation since the Romans said to the Goths, "Sure, come on in!" Despite his notorious disdain for scholastic philosophy, Valla is actually generous in his praise of Thomas.[7] He even finds a few nice words to say about Aquinas' writing, which as I've pointed out before is nice and clear but hardly conforms to Valla's standards of good Latin. However, as Valla puts it in the biggest understatement since the Goths told the Romans they might be staying for a while, "it is not my way to remain silent." Many of the inquiries pursued by scholastic theologians are pointless: "what they call metaphysics," and also the theory of the modes of signification. Valla makes clear his preference for the ancient church fathers, and his distaste for the newfangled, spurious Latin terminology devised by the schoolmen, which is of course scattered throughout Aquinas' works.

In the preface to a short dialogue he devoted to the problem of free will, Valla is still less diplomatic.[8] The topic at hand may be a philosophical one, but he makes no bones about his opposition to what passes for philosophy in his culture. Indeed it shows a "poor opinion of our religion" to "think it needs the protection of philosophy." If anything philosophy has more often been a source of dissension and heresy. This preface gets across a point that is in danger of being overlooked when we think of Valla just as a defender of good Latin and champion of classical rhetoric over scholastic philosophy. He saw his project as a deeply Christian one, a defense of the faith against those who, like the pope wielding secular authority, stray from the simpler path of spiritual truth. Even if some of his works were well received, it clearly galled him that contemporary humanists and churchmen failed to appreciate his efforts properly. As Christopher Celenza has quipped, "Valla saw himself as a unique, singular reformer and as—it is no exaggeration to say it—a man of destiny. No one else saw him that way, of course."[9]

But the aspects of Valla's writing that annoyed his colleagues are precisely those that may appeal to us. Coming from the medievals with their relentless and complex Aristotelianism, it can be downright refreshing to see Valla call Aristotle "stupid" and see him make fun of Boethius, or refer to the legal scholars of Bologna and theologians of Paris as the "Goths and the Gauls." Valla makes up his own mind, and, as he admits in the context of writing about ethics, finds himself "disagreeing with everybody (*ab omnibus dissentire*)." Alongside the entertaining invective and admirable independence of mind, Valla will appeal to those who think philosophy should stick to common sense, which for him is embodied above all in language use. Usually he means the usage of classical Latin as established by the best ancient authors. But he's capable of saying, for example, that listening to housewives might give us more insight into an issue than listening to philosophers, because housewives use language in practical contexts whereas the philosophers simply play around with it. Or, as he puts it elsewhere, "Quibbling about everything, philosophers are the first to distort the very nature of words."

Valla makes both remarks in his most philosophically rewarding work, which I'll just call the *Dialectical Disputations*—he produced several, revised versions of it, changing the Latin title as he went.[10] This ambitious treatise is Valla's attempt to beat the scholastics at their own game. In particular he contests their views on logical matters; but medieval logic tended to touch on issues within metaphysics and even natural philosophy. Thus the *Disputations* becomes a wide-ranging attempt to undermine the foundations of Aristotelian philosophy. For an alternative basis, Valla turns to Quintilian, whom he quotes at length and uses as a chief source for his own approach to logic and philosophy as a whole.

One eye-catching feature of this approach is Valla's reduction of the categories. Aristotle and his followers classified all predicated terms into ten types: substance, quality, quantity, relation, time, place, and so on. Valla thinks he can make do with only three: substance, quality, and action (§I.13). This reflects his method of looking to linguistic usage for a guide. To oversimplify a bit, his three categories correspond to nouns, adjectives, and verbs. Of course, Valla is not the first to wonder whether ten categories is too many. Already in antiquity there were attempts to reduce the list, and just a century before him, the nominalist William of Ockham had taken his razor to Aristotle's scheme, yielding just two categories, substance and quality. But Valla is no follower of Ockham. He has no stake in a nominalist or anti-realist revision of category theory, and instead assumes that language is a guide to what is in fact out there in the world.[11]

Another, more obviously metaphysical question tackled by Valla concerns the so-called "transcendentals" recognized in medieval scholasticism. These were features that cut across the division between categories: they included being, goodness, truth, unity. All predicates, it was claimed, manifest these transcendental properties, for the good reason that every way that anything might be derives ultimately from God. As pure being, goodness, truth, and unity, God bestows these features on everything He makes. But Valla thinks he can make do with less. There is only one transcendental, namely "thing (*res*)," and to speak of goodness, unity, and so on is really only another way of talking about "things" (§I.2). Again, he takes his cue from language, observing that the medievals allowed themselves to indulge in typical barbarisms in setting out their theory, like speaking of each thing as an *ens*, or "that which is," or as an "entity (*entitas*)" (§I.2, I.4). If a normal speaker of Latin really wanted to express this idea, he would instead just say *res quae est*, "thing that is." This example, incidentally, shows that Valla is nothing if not consistent in his carping about scholastic verbiage. He also complains about the word *ens*, along with such artificial terms as "entity (*entitas*)" and "quiddity (*quidditas*)," in the supposed encomium of Thomas Aquinas.[12] And he can hardly believe the contortions that the Aristotelians get into when trying to explain how beings are at first potential, and then caused to emerge into actuality. "Will we say that 'this wood is a box in act?' Has anyone ever talked that way? Who would not laugh at anyone talking that way?" (§I.16.)

This is only the beginning of Valla's list of complaints. He doesn't buy the Aristotelian idea that virtue is a habit, or settled disposition of character, because someone can on a single occasion display spectacular virtue or, for that matter, vice (§1.10).[13] You can permanently become an adulterer or murderer thanks to a single evil act. It's a bit like losing your virginity, and need have nothing to do with permanent habits. Or what about the soul (§I.9)?[14] Aristotle tries to convince us that the human soul is compounded of a rational part and two irrational parts, with the latter respectively possessing the capacities we share with animals and plants. But this undermines the unity of our soul, underestimates non-human animals, and overestimates plants. Plants have no souls at all, since all they do is grow. After all, our hair grows (well, mine doesn't but maybe yours does), and no one thinks that hair has its own soul. Animals, by contrast, have souls just like ours because, as Valla's beloved Quintilian observed, they have "thought and understanding to a certain extent." They even have the power of will, as we can see by considering such cases as the horse that decides which path it should take. Valla takes the opportunity here to show off his Greek skills. He observes that, when the ancients called animals *aloga*, meaning "things with no *logos*," they did not mean that animals have no reason, or cannot think, but only that they cannot speak—because *logos* means both "reason" and "speech."

Usually, though, it's his Latin that Valla wants to show off, and exploit in his demolition of scholastic theories. He has good fun with the artificial regimentation of Latin employed by the schoolmen, as with their arbitrary and ignorant rules about how to negate sentences (§II.3), or their strange idea that "not just" might mean something other than "unjust" (§II.12). When it comes to the "modal" notions that modify propositions by stating that they are possible, necessary, or impossible, he thinks the scholastics were in a sense being profligate—because you can actually get by just with "possible" and "impossible"—and in a sense too restrictive, since there are many other such modifiers possible in good Latin, like "easy," "usual," or "certain" (§II.19). He ventures into the most technical parts of logic, wielding not so much Ockham's razor as a machete of mockery. Why should the schoolmen insist on arranging syllogistic arguments in certain arbitrary ways? This is just a matter of convention, like the way that Italians use a knife to slice away from themselves, and the Spanish towards themselves (§III.2). Then too, some of their inferences seem to him plainly invalid. Their acceptance of the third syllogistic figure moves him to call them a "nation of lunatics" (§III.8).

This is all good fun, but is it philosophically convincing? To be honest, the answer is often no. Sticking for a moment with logic, he at one point scoffs at the use of variable letters to clarify logical form—for instance saying "All A is B, all B is C, therefore all A is C"—as mere obfuscation. Simple though it is, this device is in fact one of Aristotle's most brilliant and useful contributions to logic. Indeed it has some claim to be the single most important breakthrough in the entire history of the discipline, since it allows us to isolate and consider logical form in itself, rather than giving possibly distracting concrete examples of argumentation. Yet Valla compares it to showing a prospective bride to a suitor in the dark, in hopes he won't notice how ugly she is (§III.9). In other cases he falls into the trap I mentioned earlier, of criticizing without thinking hard enough about what he is criticizing. His discussion of time and place offers supposed "insights" that Aristotelian philosophers had thought of, and dealt with, many times over.

In still other cases, he simply reproduces scholastic solutions to philosophical problems without giving them credit for it. That short dialogue on free will I mentioned, for instance, simply restates the common fourteenth-century position that God can foreknow an event without causing that event to happen or rendering it impossible that it *not* happen.[15] As far as I can see, the only halfway original point brought forward by Valla is that someone who had foreknowledge could cause additional problems by explicitly *predicting* what will happen to the person involved. It's fine for God to know I will eat eggs for breakfast tomorrow, but if He tells me I shall do so, then I would paradoxically be in a position to render His foreknowledge false, just out of spite.

Perhaps the greatest irony is that for all his anti-Aristotelian rhetoric, Valla is in many ways close to Aristotle in approach and philosophical temperament. Consider again the dispute over the categories. Aristotle too thought we should divide up the categories by considering language use. Had Valla been more generous, he might have admitted that he was following Aristotle's strategy, but updating the account in the light of better grammatical theory. One specialist on Renaissance rhetorical theories, Peter Mack, has written that Valla was "too disrespectful to Aristotle to succeed as an Aristotelian, and too dependent on him to succeed in presenting a wholly different solution."[16] I think that gets him about right, though we should add that Valla was not only a critic. His impertinence towards Aristotle is matched by his deep respect for Latin classical authors, especially Quintilian, whose works are quite literally unimprovable (§II.20). Valla should thus be credited with conceiving an ambitious positive project as well as a negative, critical one. With the resources of authoritative texts other than Aristotle, he wanted to build something new, something we might call a properly humanist logic and metaphysics.

26

DIFFICULT TO BE GOOD HUMANIST ETHICS

As I suggested at the beginning of the last chapter, if you think philosophers should devote themselves to discovering how to live the good life, you're liable to be disappointed by any encounter with today's professional philosophers. Many philosophers specialize in topics like epistemology or metaphysics, and would be more likely to associate the phrase "meaning of life" with a Monty Python film than with their day job. True, most philosophy departments do have at least one expert on moral philosophy, but I once knew a philosopher who said he offered courses on ethics because "those who can't do, teach." I myself am skeptical as to whether the study of moral philosophy will turn you into a moral person. It might just make you realize how challenging the demands of morality really are. As Poggio Bracciolini remarked in a letter he wrote in 1425, "According to the ancient Greeks, it is difficult to be good."[1] Yet he and his fellow humanists held out hope that those same ancient Greeks could help them do just that. On these grounds the humanists often saw ethics as superior to other philosophical disciplines. Leonardo Bruni said that those who ignore it in favor of natural philosophy are "minding somebody else's business and neglecting their own."

Bruni made this remark in an *Introduction (Isagogue)* he wrote to moral philosophy. It takes the form of a dialogue Bruni supposedly had with a friend.[2] The work is meant to encourage its reader to take up philosophy as a means of self-improvement, a way of dispelling the "fog" that conceals from us the true good we all naturally desire (267). But what is this true good? The options laid out by Bruni are those already considered by his role model Cicero, and there aren't many of them. Either you follow the advice of Stoics and Aristotelians by pursuing virtue, or you throw in your lot with Epicureans and other hedonists by taking pleasure to be the good. This is painting with a pretty broad brush, befitting the introductory nature of the work and also Bruni's admitted aim of showing the fundamental agreement between the Greek ethical schools. For him the Epicureans are not that different from the champions of virtue, since they wind up saying that a life marked by temperance and other virtues is the most pleasant (273). So they too endorse a moral way of life; they simply give a different, hedonist rationale for it.

As for Aristotelianism and Stoicism, Bruni sees the main difference between them as being that, for the Stoics, virtue alone is enough, so that good people remain happy no matter what misfortunes, poverty, or tortures befall them. This, says Bruni, is a "stout and manly creed," but hard to believe (272). Probably Aristotle is right that the best life requires "external goods" like health, wealth, friends, and family. Aristotle is also right to say that virtue always lies in the mean between two extremes, like courage which is the middle course between cowardice and rashness. When it comes to the emotions, Aristotle is again vindicated by Bruni. The Stoics taught that we should work to restrain our emotional reactions, even (or perhaps especially) when we are severely provoked. But Bruni thinks the Aristotelians are right that it would be inhuman and even irrational not to feel anger when, say, a slave beats your father or rapes your daughter (277). Our goal should be to let reason rule over the emotions, rather than extirpating them, which means the higher part of the soul dominating the lower (280). That, along with a sufficient supply of those external goods, constitutes happiness.

Bruni's synthetic approach may remind us of the way that late ancient authors, or more recently Bessarion in his debate with George Trapezuntius, tried to establish harmony between ancient authorities. But where Bessarion tended to read Platonism into Aristotle, Bruni achieves his synthesis by making all the other schools agree with Aristotle and framing their disagreements with his teachings as relatively trivial. His partiality is no doubt connected to the fact that he translated Aristotle's *Nicomachean Ethics*. Bruni's version had to compete with the old medieval translation and the new one of John Argyropolous, and as we've seen, it attracted criticism. But it is extant in nearly 250 manuscripts, and some fifteenth-century commentators on the *Ethics*, like Niccolò Tignosi, preferred Bruni's rendering to its rivals.[3] This despite the fact that Bruni was really just offering what one scholar has called a "mere revision" of the medieval translation by Robert Grosseteste, "dressed in elegant Latin."[4]

As this already begins to suggest, rumors of the death of Aristotelian ethics during the Renaissance are greatly exaggerated. The revival of Platonist and Hellenistic ideas is more eye-catching, because it is such a contrast to the medieval scholastic tradition. But scholastic ethics continued to thrive during the Renaissance, both in Italy and elsewhere. The schoolmen matched the humanists' stress on moral philosophy by adding this subject to the curriculum of studies at several Italian universities during this period.[5] For them Aristotle was of course the primary authority, for ethics just as for other branches of philosophy. The teaching of the *Nicomachean Ethics* called for new commentaries. A significant one appeared in 1478, authored by Donato Acciaiuoli, who should be congratulated for having no fewer than five consecutive vowels in his name. He was apparently following closely the lectures given by his teacher Argyropolous, the aforementioned translator of the *Ethics*. A later commentator named Bernardo Segni in fact gave them joint credit for the commentary, and lavished praise on them for their distillation of earlier scholastic commentaries, like those by Thomas Aquinas and the Byzantine philosopher Eustratios.[6]

Segni himself is also an interesting figure for the reception of Aristotle, since he chose to do a translation and commentary for the *Nicomachean Ethics* in Italian rather than Latin, published in 1550. And there were other sixteenth-century scholars who worked to usher Aristotle's *Ethics* into the vernacular. The year 1583 saw the appearance of Francesco Piccolomini's massive treatise based on Aristotle's writings about ethics and politics, the *Universal Philosophy of Morals*.[7] It was in Latin, but Piccolomini also produced a compendium of ethics in Italian, written for Christina, duchess of Tuscany. By sheer coincidence, it has lots of nice things to say about the Medici clan. A bit of judicious sycophancy was not the only way that philosophers calibrated their approach for their intended audience. Both Acciaiuoli and Segni carefully rationed the dosage of technical scholastic methodology so as not to overwhelm a vernacular readership. Thus Segni's commentary occasionally shows how you can set out Aristotle's ethical teaching in syllogistic form, but only by way of example, to show it is possible. Likewise Piccolomini structured his Latin treatise as a series of scholastic "questions," but dropped this style of organization for the compendium in Italian.[8]

Of course, not all humanists were so keen on Aristotle. I'm not sure what the opposite of "keen" is in English, never mind Ciceronian Latin, but one man who could have told me was Lorenzo Valla. We saw how his *Dialectical Disputations* took issue with the notion that virtue is a settled habit, as opposed to something that can be displayed or lost on a single occasion. That's only one of the irreverent points Valla makes about ethics.[9] Against Aristotle, he argues that virtue is not really a mean between two extremes. Rather there is one virtue per extreme. Thus courage is opposed to cowardice, but not to rashness, whose opposite is merely caution. And against just about everyone, Valla argues that there are not four central or "cardinal" virtues, namely prudence, justice, fortitude, and temperance. Just as he reduced Aristotle's ten categories to a tidy list of three, he thinks that all virtues can be reduced to the single virtue of fortitude. This is the will's determination to pursue what is good, instead of being swayed by counterproductive emotions. Prudence is actually not a virtue at all, but simply the knowledge of good and evil. One becomes morally praiseworthy or blameworthy only once the will is involved, once we choose whether to pursue the ends that prudence has identified as good.

Thus far it may seem that Valla's objections to traditional ethics are rather superficial; as a humanist would say, that he is disputing about names rather than the things themselves. But the originality of his moral theory emerges more fully when we turn to another work of Valla's, which like the *Disputations* went through several revisions and bore different titles, including *On Pleasure* and *On the Good*.[10] Valla imitates Cicero by writing it in the form of a dialogue, in which two spokesmen argue in favor of Stoicism and Epicureanism. Then in a final section, a third, Christian spokesman offers what is presumably Valla's own considered view. Valla is far from endorsing Bruni's thesis that the various ethical teachings of the Greeks boil down to the same thing. He draws a sharp contrast between Epicurean hedonism and the Stoics' valorization of virtue (*honestas*). Surprisingly, Valla prefers the Epicurean view.

He allows the Stoic spokesman to cut a rather unappealing figure, whose signature attitude is pessimism. Valla's Stoic sees human nature as all but inevitably prone to sin and evil indulgence in pleasures. This might be thought to point to a Christian truth: it would be the doctrine of original sin that explains why people are so bad.[11] But it rather seems that the far more optimistic Epicurean theory is meant to emerge as the more attractive option. The spokesman for this view rejects as implausible the Stoic claim that human nature is intrinsically bad. To the contrary, it is nature that provides us with both our desire for pleasure and with pleasure itself, which is the true good. So far, so appealing. But as the Epicurean goes on, the typical Renaissance reader would probably start to frown with disagreement. Such paradigm cases of good action as sacrificing oneself for one's city are condemned as foolish, since death cuts off access to pleasure. On the other hand, such actions do not constitute an exception to the Epicurean claim that people are always motivated by pleasure and pain. Patriotic self-sacrifice, or suicide committed for other reasons, can be explained on hedonistic grounds. Someone who kills themselves to avoid shame, for instance, may just be seeking to escape from the suffering brought on by social disapproval.[12]

When we reach the speech of the third spokesman, we learn that the Stoic and the Epicurean are both mistaken, because they have failed to grasp the Christian truth that we will live on after death. Still the Epicureans are closer to being right than the Stoics. A Christian hedonist can look ahead to an everlasting, and exceedingly pleasant, reward in heaven.[13] Virtue is not, as the Stoic has claimed, valuable in itself. It is only a means towards attaining this blessed state. Yet for the same reasons, the traditional Epicurean is wrong when he advises us to pursue the pleasures of this world, especially bodily pleasures. Even in this life, these are as nothing compared to the pleasures of the soul. The highest pleasures of all, though, await us once we are freed from our earthly existence, when we will receive perfect bodies and all the higher pleasures the soul could possibly desire.

This fusion of Christianity and Epicureanism is not unique to Valla. A short letter written in 1428 by his fellow humanist Francesco Filelfo expresses similar sentiments.[14] If you're in the business of pursuing pleasure, it makes all the difference what kind of pleasure you seek, and the pleasures of the mind are those that are "true and Christian." So Filelfo dismisses those who accuse Epicurus of "lascivious" devotion to the delights of the body. Putting this letter together with Valla's rehabilitation of pleasure and Bruni's claim that Epicureans too pursue virtue, we can see that this hedonistic Hellenistic school had a surprisingly positive reception among the humanists.

So the Lorenzo Valla who wrote *On the Good* can be seen to agree with contemporaries like Filelfo. Does he also agree with himself; that is, with the Lorenzo Valla who wrote the *Dialectical Disputations*? Not entirely. Consider again the virtue of fortitude. We saw that it was central in the *Disputations*, but when it appears in the Epicurean's speech in *On the Good*, it does so only to be criticized on hedonist grounds. When you measure everything in terms of pleasure, it's a losing game to endure great suffering for the sake of honor and glory, especially if you might get killed in the process. But the Valla of the *Disputations*, the Valla who puts fortitude at the center of a life that is happy insofar as it is virtuous, does find allies among his humanist contemporaries, including Poggio Bracciolini. He wrote a moral dialogue of his own called *On Nobility*, which argues along Stoic lines that true nobility consists in virtue, rather than an aristocratic lineage.[15] In a related work, *On the Unhappiness of the Prince*, Poggio complains that most political leaders are vicious people. He encourages his readers to avoid political life, and goes so far as to suggest that a noble family background may even be ethically counterproductive, since the highborn are typically enmeshed in political intrigues and the upheavals of court life.[16]

This brings us back to the question of "external goods," with Poggio firmly adopting the Stoic view that they are a matter of indifference, so that we should focus on struggling against our own vices rather than on acquiring wealth or political influence. The same note is struck in the work of another humanist, Enea Silvio Piccolomini, not to be confused with the aforementioned Francesco Piccolomini. Enea Silvio was bishop of Triest and of Siena, and then reigned as Pope Pius II from 1458 to 1464. So he knew something about political life, and put this knowledge to good use in his *On the Misery of Courtiers*.[17] It begins by stating bluntly that "those who serve kings are fools" (24) and goes on to explain that court life makes it nearly impossible to be virtuous, because the courtier has so little freedom to choose his own actions. As the best philosophers tell us, happiness lies in virtue, so it is folly to seek happiness through proximity to power (28–30). Even if the hedonist doctrines of the Epicureans were true, political engagement would still be a bad idea, because life at court is far from pleasant (56). Enea Silvio is obviously drawing on a wealth of personal experience here, as when he points out that being a courtier turns out to be surprisingly boring, because you have to spend so much time waiting around for the ruler (78).

The fact that Poggio and Enea Silvio both devoted works to critiquing political or courtly life reminds us that this was the life that many humanists led. They often wrote their works while in the service of princes or popes. For them, the ancient ethical school to follow was going to be the one that gave the best advice for surviving life at court with one's dignity, and ideally one's happiness, intact. For those who committed themselves to such a life, Aristotle seemed to be the best guide. He gave them good reason to be proud of their intellectual attainments at the end of the *Ethics*, when he stated that philosophical contemplation is the best life of all. And in the rest of the work he showed that one could manifest virtue by pursuing a life of civic engagement, seeking to amass enough wealth to display munificent generosity, and forging alliances through family and friends.

One author who adopted this ideal of a virtuous, politically engaged life was Giovanni Pontano, a student of George Trapezuntius who died in 1503 after an eventful career as a diplomat at the royal court in Naples.[18] Pontano shows Stoic leanings in a work entitled *On Fortitude*, which praises those who bear up under the suffering inflicted on them by fortune. Rebuking the sentiments expressed by Valla's Epicurean spokesman, who disdained political heroism as more painful than pleasant, Pontano thinks it makes good sense to seek out difficulties in life. Only those who face tribulations can conquer them, thus displaying fortitude and valor. This sounds closer to Valla's Stoic spokesman, but Pontano fails Bruni's test for true Stoicism, in that he embraces the importance of external goods. The best and most happy man is one who has physical strength, good looks, and at least a degree of wealth. As this suggests, Pontano's primary allegiance in moral philosophy is to Aristotle, who offered a theoretical basis for Pontano's own idealized self-conception as a virtuous man of political action.

Finally, I must say something about the *Book of the Courtier*, written by Baldassare Castiglione in 1528, and my personal choice as the most entertaining ethical treatise produced by an Italian humanist (Lorenzo Valla, please forgive me).[19] It is a dialogue set at the court of Urbino, featuring a number of real historical figures from among the nobility, both male and female. They want to find a diversion to pass the time and, in the process, impress one another and the papal envoys who are watching.

After considering several games they might play, they hit upon the idea of attempting to describe the perfect courtier. He will need skills ranging from the art of warfare to music and mastery of the literary arts. He should also be witty, which gives Castiglione the chance to record a number of jokes and humorous anecdotes to illustrate how good wit functions. Some of these have not dated well, but others are legitimately funny. Have you heard the one about the prince who needs to find something to do with a huge pile of excavated earth after a building project? His advisor suggests, "Dig a hole and bury it." When the prince asks, "But what about the dirt from the new hole?" the advisor replies, "Just make the hole twice as big."

For Castiglione wit is serious business, because it is one of the attributes the courtier will need in order to guide his prince. If he is lucky enough to have a virtuous master, things will be easy: he need only tell the truth. More likely the prince will fall short of moral perfection, which puts the courtier in a more difficult position. He should avoid being a flatterer, but will need to be able to soften hard truths with wit and charm. More ambitiously still, the courtier should seek to instill virtue in the prince, being a moral educator as well as a practical advisor. In this he is a mirror of his prince, because the virtuous prince too should make those around him good. The best prince is like a straight edge that rectifies other things when placed against them, so he is a "ruler" in every sense of the term, as Castiglione's witty courtier might observe (if he spoke English). If all goes well, then, there should be plenty of virtue to go around. But, as one character cynically remarks, if the prince is to have only good people as his subjects, the population will be pretty small. Sadly, as Poggio had noted, good princes are likewise the exception and not the rule. We cannot rule out that the good courtier may have to abandon, or even overthrow, a sufficiently wicked prince.[20]

In setting forth this account of the best courtier, Castiglione's characters make the most tasteful possible display of their learning. One passage alludes to Aristotle's point that virtue is not instilled by nature, even giving his example that stones cannot be habituated to go upwards when dropped. Another refers obliquely to the Stoic idea that virtue alone is valuable, with other apparent "goods" like health or wealth having true value only when they are used virtuously. There are even debates about fine points of philosophy, such as whether our reason is overwhelmed by our passions when we make bad choices, or whether this just shows that our rational beliefs about the good are not secure enough. Great philosophers of antiquity appear by name, too, notably when it is pointed out that there is no conflict between being a philosopher and being a courtier. Plato, after all, served the rulers of Syracuse and Aristotle tutored Alexander the Great.

One philosopher Castiglione could not have mentioned in this context is Epicurus. He and his followers were famous for their political disengagement, for choosing to enjoy a quiet life in their communal garden rather than pursuing the false pleasures of power, honor, and glory. We've just seen that for some Renaissance thinkers, like Pontano, this was a flaw in the Epicurean ethical program. In fact, the only humanist we've found developing an original ethical theory based on Epicurus' hedonism was the idiosyncratic Lorenzo Valla, and even he needed to bring in Christian ideas of the afterlife and resurrection in order to identify pleasure with the highest good. Given its hedonistic ethics and also its atomist cosmology that puts the formation of the world down to chance instead of divine agency, it may seem unlikely that Epicureanism would find further admirers or interpreters in the Italian Renaissance. But as Epicurean physics taught, even unlikely events are bound to occur eventually.

27

CHANCE ENCOUNTERS REVIVING HELLENISTIC PHILOSOPHY

Dip into any introduction to Renaissance philosophy, and you'll quickly find a reference to Poggio Bracciolini's rediscovery of *On the Nature of Things*, an ancient Latin poem by the Epicurean philosopher Lucretius. This book is no exception: I mentioned this event in Chapter 22. But what exactly did it mean to "rediscover" an ancient Latin text? Nowadays tracking down a book usually involves little more than entering its title into Google (other internet search engines are available). You'd probably be annoyed even at having to click through to the second page of search results. In the fifteenth century the process was a bit more taxing. It was more like today's record collectors who sort through bins of dusty vintage vinyl, or perhaps even gold prospectors in pioneer-era California. Finding lost works required willingness and opportunity to travel long distances. It called for patience and a connoisseur's eye. These were all assets that belonged to Poggio.

The famous discovery happened in 1417 in Germany, probably at a Benedictine abbey in Fulda.[1] Poggio had come so far north because he was in attendance at the council of Constance in 1415 as secretary to Pope John XXIII. Things didn't go so well for the pope, who was deposed after fleeing the council, but Poggio's book collection fared much better. In addition to finding the Lucretius, he had the triumph of tracking down a copy of Quintilian's work on rhetoric at St Gall. In one of the more than 500 surviving letters written by Poggio, he explains that this priceless text was lying in a jumble of moldering books, in a "sort of foul and gloomy dungeon at the bottom of one of the towers" (195).[2] Like a modern-day vinyl enthusiast hoping to locate the rare first pressing of a 1960s Beatles album in the bargain bin at a record store, the humanists hunted for treasures that most people considered to be old junk. Parchment manuscripts were often scraped clean of their ink, destroying old texts just to have new blank writing material.

To make new discoveries of old books the humanists usually had to leave Italy, since the collections there were pretty well explored. Poggio spent some years in

England but reported bitterly that the libraries there were useless; in other words, full of medieval works and not ancient ones (46, 48, 55). But in France and Germany, especially in monasteries and other religious institutions, you could find long unread texts listed in library catalogues, or just have a lucky chance encounter looking through discarded manuscripts, as at St Gall. The humanists had no scruples about bringing antiquities home to Italy. Poggio himself talks enthusiastically in another letter about having marble busts sent from Greece for his house: he quivers with excitement at the prospect of installing the head of Minerva in his library (166–7). But as I can tell you from personal experience, German librarians tend to be strict. So when he found Lucretius, Poggio was not able to abscond with the manuscript. Instead he had his scribe copy it out, and sent this transcription to his friend and colleague Niccolò Niccoli, who made a second copy that still survives today.

This whole story should remind us of what we learned about Byzantine manuscripts. As in medieval Constantinople, in early fifteenth-century Italy books were unique, handmade objects. The arrival of printing was still decades away, and making a single copy of a sizeable work could take many weeks. These scholars would have killed to have access to a Xerox machine (other office copiers are available). So humanists like Niccoli and Poggio had to be craftsmen as well as intellectuals. These two men were involved in developing a new, clearer style of handwriting based on the minuscule lettering of early medieval manuscripts from the Carolingian period. They worried about pens and ink, about paper and parchment. Indeed requests for parchment and comments about its quality are a constant refrain in Poggio's correspondence (91–3, 100, 105, 118, 153).

Because books were so valuable, you had to be careful what you did with them. Another running theme in Poggio's letters is the trading of manuscripts between humanists. He wrote to Niccoli asking to borrow a text so he can have his scribe make a copy, or do it himself (89). The book will be sent straight back, promise! And Poggio was a lender as well as a borrower. He complained of books that were not returned (114), such as that copy of Lucretius, which Niccoli held on to for a full twelve years, to Poggio's mounting frustration. "Your tomb will be finished sooner than your books will be copied," he complained to his friend (154, cf. 92, 160). So bent were these men on getting books into their libraries that you wonder whether this was an end in itself. Were the humanists like the vinyl collector whose records just gather dust on a shelf, unlistened?

No, they did read them as well as collecting them. In her study of annotations found in surviving Renaissance manuscripts and early printings of Lucretius, Ada Palmer has shown that these were working texts.[3] Scholars made lines or dots next to passages that particularly struck them, revealing the interests they brought to the text, and added comments in the margins. As Palmer explains, the annotations are most often philological in nature: notes about Latin vocabulary, indications of names of noteworthy ancient people and places, and so on. One scholar, Pomponio Leto, made extensive notes throughout his copy, which were so useful that they were taken over in subsequent copies made from his manuscript. While many of these are also of a philological nature, they also reveal something about Leto's reaction to the philosophical content. Next to a passage arguing that the soul is not immortal, he cautioned the reader with an annotation that said "non-Christian teaching (*opinio non christiana*)."[4]

Here we come to the crux of the matter. That copy of Lucretius unearthed by Poggio was worth its weight in gold, but also explosive like dynamite. Thanks to Cicero, the humanists were already well acquainted with Epicurean ethics. As we've just seen, Lorenzo Valla found it relatively unproblematic to integrate these doctrines into those of the Christian faith. If a blessed afterlife is the most pleasant of all prospects, then Epicurus' hedonism pointed in the right direction. In the words of Jill Kraye, this amounted to "wrenching an Epicurean doctrine from its pagan context and using it to reinterpret Christian theology."[5] Yet the same point was made in a letter written by another humanist, Cosma Raimondi.[6] He admits that the Epicurean obsession with pleasure may seem "effeminate," but praises the school for valorizing the natural urge to pursue pleasure and beauty. Epicurus is not, after all, recommending the "pleasure of animals" but a more sophisticated approach that locates the most pleasant life in a moderate lifestyle. This understanding of Epicureanism can also be found in the letters of Poggio, as when he invites Niccoli to dine at his house but warns that the fare on offer will be "Epicurean" in the truest sense of the term: nothing but "water and mush" (127, cf. 97).

The discovery of Lucretius' poem brought home to its readers that Epicureanism involved more than pursuing pleasure while avoiding fun. It argues at length that the soul dies with the body, the point flagged in that annotation by Pomponio Leto. Lucretius also presents a detailed theory of atomism. This by itself was perhaps not so shocking, as some medieval scholastics had flirted with atomist physics.[7] But he also contends that our universe emerges through brute physical necessity through the random entanglement of atoms. These are chance encounters that no pious Christian could accept, since the Epicurean cosmology involved denying divine providence. Epicurus and Lucretius did accept the existence of gods, but thought that they pay no attention to our lives, which is actually a good thing because it means we don't need to fear them.

Now, it's not as if all this had been completely unknown before Poggio went to Germany. Since antiquity the word "Epicurean" had been a near synonym for "atheist," and more recently within Italian culture, Dante had put the Epicureans in hell for their teaching on the soul. But now that Lucretius had been added to the list of classical texts admired for their outstanding Latin, the humanists were confronted as never before by the problematic nature of Epicurean thought. An annotation found in one early printed copy suggested that readers of Lucretius should simply accept the true parts and reject the falsehoods.[8] For some, this meant rejecting all of it. A good example is Marsilio Ficino, who studied Lucretius as a young man while learning about Cicero from Cristoforo Landino.[9] Ficino even wrote a "short commentary (*commentariolum*)" on the poem, but when he became a convinced Platonist he destroyed this juvenile text. He turned against the poet he had admired, refuting Lucretius on the issues of the soul's immortality and divine providence. A more tolerant approach was taken by Ficino's fellow student Bartolomeo Scala, who wrote a letter in 1458 summarizing Lucretius' doctrines. Scala continued to draw on these doctrines later in life, for instance in a dialogue about the wisdom of marriage in which the positive case is put by a character with Epicurean leanings.

One of the things that attracted Scala to Epicureanism was its emphasis on the role of chance. Though this might fly in the face of Christian teachings about providence, it made good sense of the political instability experienced by humanists in Florence, especially towards the end of the fifteenth century when the French invaded Italy and the Medici lost their grip on power. In the wake of these events, the theme of chance and fortune was emphasized in the work of Marcello Adriani, one of the Renaissance philosophers who engaged most closely with Epicureanism.[10] He admired this philosophy for its promise to help us retain happiness even in times of misfortune and political upheaval, and more generally for its aim of freeing us from disturbance and fear. This was thematized in a lecture by Adriani called *Nil admirare*, meaning *Wonder at Nothing*. We fear what we do not understand, and Lucretius can help us to dispel our fears by explaining natural phenomena and teaching us not to live in terror of divine wrath.

Though he was atypical in his enthusiasm for Epicurean thought, Adriani was very much typical in his concern with the question of human autonomy in a world apparently governed by chance. Here the most obvious example is Niccolò Machiavelli. We still have a copy of Lucretius with annotations in Machiavelli's hand, which show that he was especially interested in the atomic theory and the fact that the randomness of atomic motion explains why humans have free will.[11] Prefiguring a central theme from his famous work *The Prince*, Machiavelli wrote a poem on the topic of fortune, and, in a marginal note added to another of his early works, described how the successful man copes with chance. "Each man must do what his mind prompts him to—and do it with daring, then try his luck, and when fortune slackens off, regain the initiative by trying a different way."[12]

Epicureanism was not the only Hellenistic philosophical school offering advice for coping with chance. Some Renaissance humanists were attracted by the uncompromising view of the Stoics, that good fortune and bad fortune are both matters of indifference, since only virtue truly matters. Poggio was one of them. He wrote a whole work about the vagaries of fortune, in which he used an image that he may have borrowed from Lucretius, but to make a Stoic point. He advised cultivating an attitude of Stoic detachment, looking upon the miseries of this world as a kind of theatrical performance that cannot affect our happiness.[13] On the other hand he also made a point worthy of Machiavelli, that chance may be seized and exploited by men of action. This explains the success of figures like Alexander the Great who, as we might say, boldly "trusted his luck" and was rewarded for doing so.[14] But what to do when fortune does not favor us? Poggio thought the Stoics had the right answer. In one of his letters, he nicely summarized their idea that, whereas all other things are subject to the influence and control of others, "virtue is our own" (32). So it should be our paramount, if not sole, concern.

These issues were also of great interest to Leon Battista Alberti, a humanist who is famous among other things for his treatise *On Painting*, which we'll be discussing later (Chapter 48). In other works, especially a series of so-called *Dinner Pieces* (*Intercenales*), charming literary productions that often touch on philosophical issues, Alberti dramatized the confrontation of virtue and fortune.[15] One of them describes a personification of Virtue being accosted by Fortune, stripped, beaten, and left to complain of her rough treatment. Mercury regretfully informs her that Fortune cannot be controlled, not even by him and the other gods. So Virtue will just have to hide herself, "naked and despised," until Fortune smiles on her again (20–2). Another piece imagines a philosopher visiting the underworld and learning how souls are set to navigate the "river of life." Those who have the smoothest sailing are the virtuous, who enjoy the support of the gods. But even they can be dashed on the rocks (25). Alberti advises clinging to the "planks" that are the liberal arts, which offer the best stability in the rough waters of life. Others were less optimistic that knowledge and virtue can shield us from the slings and arrows of outrageous fortune. The pioneering humanist Salutati, for instance, was at first impressed by Stoicism but then found its "cold-hearted" advice to be of little comfort when he was faced with the death of his son. The same experience came to another humanist, Giannozzo Manetti. When his own son died he rebuffed consolatory remarks inspired by Seneca, instead voicing his agreement with the Aristotelians, who teach that moderate grief is appropriate.[16]

Then there was a third major Hellenistic school, one that offered good reason to think knowledge will forever remain out of reach, in both ethical and theoretical matters: Skepticism. One humanist who was influenced by the Skeptics was Francesco Guicciardini, a historian and statesman who was a friend of Machiavelli (see Chapter 41).[17] He tended to think that philosophy, especially metaphysics, was an all but fruitless pursuit, since men are bound to remain "in the dark" about such things. In practical affairs, a knack for dealing with each situation as it arises—which Guicciardini calls "discretion (*discrezione*)"—is far more useful than all the general precepts laid down in ethical treatises. But ultimately the insane may prosper while the wise suffer, depending on the whims of fortune.

This was an unusually bleak view for the time, though not without parallel. As with Epicureanism, the humanists had some awareness of Skepticism thanks to Cicero, who alongside his various presentations of Hellenistic philosophy gave his own allegiance to the so-called "Academic" Skeptical tradition. But Renaissance thinkers tended not to emphasize this aspect of Cicero's thought, probably because they found it disconcerting and difficult to reconcile with Christianity.[18] Cicero's major work on Skepticism, the *Academica*, was not among the humanists' favorite texts by this most admired of Latin authors. When they did engage with it, they usually did so in order to fend off its critique of non-skeptical, or "dogmatic," philosophy.[19] Mario Nizolio and Giulio Castellani, both working in the second half of the sixteenth century, repudiated Cicero's stance, suggesting that dogmatic thinkers like Aristotle could withstand skeptical attack if their systems were properly appreciated. Castellani was downright annoyed by Cicero's presentation of the dogmatic approach to philosophy, because he thought it stacked the deck in the skeptic's favor by presenting that approach too weakly.

Much as Cicero's portrayal of Epicureanism was complemented by the discovery of Lucretius, so renewed access to long unread ancient works allowed the humanists to go beyond his presentation of Skepticism. Through the biographies of Diogenes Laertius, Renaissance readers learned about the teachings of the first Skeptic, Pyrrho. More important still was the recovery of Sextus Empiricus, whose writings were brought to Italy from Constantinople by Francesco Filelfo. Cardinal Bessarion also owned a manuscript of Sextus, in fact a better one than Filelfo's, which had what he called "windows" in it, meaning gaps in the text. If the humanists had taken Sextus really seriously, he might have caused even more disquiet than Lucretius did. Sextus' "Pyrrhonian" Skepticism provides the tools to undermine all beliefs, leaving the proficient user of these tools in a state of suspended judgment. But for the most part, the humanists were not inclined to turn Sextus' arguments against other philosophical schools, to say nothing of the teachings of the church. They had good reason to be wary of the Skeptics, since they could read in the Greek patristic author Gregory Nazianzus that this movement was a kind of disease that threatened to infect the church. The result is that, as one scholar of skepticism in the period has put it, "the fifteenth century witnessed a revival not of sceptical philosophy but rather of sceptical texts."[20] A good example would be Angelo Poliziano, who engaged with Sextus but only at the level of philology and as a doxographical source, an approach that he also took with Lucretius.[21]

To see true appreciation of ancient Skepticism, we're going to have to wait for figures beyond Italian humanism, with the most famous example of its influence being the works of the French sixteenth-century philosopher Montaigne. But within the present context, there is one figure we should highlight, namely Gianfrancesco Pico della Mirandola. He was the nephew of a more famous philosopher, named Giovanni Pico della Mirandola, who is going to come into focus later on (Chapter 35). Nephew Gianfrancesco was a member of the intellectual circle around the religious crusader Girolamo Savonarola. As we'll see later, this remarkable figure was at the heart of political developments in Florence at the close of the fifteenth century (Chapter 37). You'd think this would have kept Savonarola too busy to concern himself with the humanist project of recovering and translating Greek texts. But he took an interest in the work of Sextus Empiricus, because he realized its potential as a weapon for undermining the pretensions of rationalist philosophy.

Though a Latin translation envisioned by Savonarola did not come to fruition, Sextus' ideas were put to use by Gianfrancesco, who echoed Savoranola's agenda when explaining his own motivation: "the skeptics can be helpful in fending off the arrogance of the philosophers and in displaying the superiority of the Christian faith . . . The principles of our faith are not derived from human beings, but from God himself . . . through the light of faith as well as through wonders and miracles, against which no one can argue."[22] From our modern-day vantage point, this attitude may seem stunningly cavalier. What, we might think, could be less immune to skeptical worry than unargued religious faith? But Gianfrancesco assumed that the methods of Skepticism laid out by Sextus—relentless demands for justification, arguing on both sides of every issue, identifying disagreements between the philosophical schools—were designed for undermining merely *human* claims to knowledge. These were methods of earthly philosophy, fit for use against other earthly philosophers like Epicureans, Stoics, and Peripatetics. The supernatural truths of Christianity would remain serenely untouched by such methods, and would thus be the only doctrine left standing after the demolition of all the philosophies devised by human nature.

28

WE BUILT THIS CITY CHRISTINE DE PIZAN

Towards the end of the installment of this series that dealt with medieval philosophy, we first met Christine de Pizan. It's fitting that she should appear in both that volume and this one, since she could hardly be more suitable to represent the transition from one age to the other, and to undermine any notion that that transition was a sudden cultural shift as opposed to a gradual evolution. Her lifetime went from the fourteenth to the fifteenth century; geographically and in self-identity, she spanned Italian and French culture; she drew on medieval ideas even while foreshadowing such paradigmatically Renaissance figures as Machiavelli. Like other female authors of the middle ages, she wrote in the vernacular and not in Latin. Unlike those other authors, she was not a beguine, a nun, or an anchorite, but an independent, secular intellectual. Her writings ranged widely, including poetry, moral advice, political works, an influential treatise on chivalry and conduct in war, and attempts to defend the honor of the female gender.[1]

That multifaceted career was made possible by aristocratic beginnings. She called herself Christine "de Pizan" in honor of her father Tommaso, who hailed from the Italian town Pizzano. At the nearby university of Bologna, Tommaso served as professor of astrology, until he was summoned by the French king Charles V when Christine was only 4 years old. It was in this setting that Christine grew up, absorbing the cultivated and urbane values of Charles's court, which boasted a massive library and supported the translation of Aristotle and other classical authors into French. Unfortunately for Christine, this auspicious beginning was followed by a series of personal and political disasters. Within the decade spanning from 1380 to 1390, the king, Christine's father, and her husband all died, setting off turmoil in France and in Christine's financial affairs. Her experiences in a series of lawsuits gave her cause to complain bitterly later on about lawyers and their treatment of women. But she was able to keep moving in aristocratic circles, associating herself with a series of patrons, for whom she wrote many of her works.

In the meantime, French political life was as unsettled as the bar tab at a misers' convention. The successor of the admirable Charles V was at first too young to rule, and then proved to suffer from mental illness, leading to a struggle by other contenders who wanted to hold the reins of power. Christine reacted to this situation in her writings, pleading for an end to infighting amongst the French nobility. The very titles of some of her works are telling: *Lamentation on the Evils of Civil War*, written in 1410, and the *Book of Peace*, written from 1412 to 1414.[2] She is often working within the genre of writing known as "mirrors for princes." Christine herself uses this metaphor, speaking of her *Book of the Body Politic* as a mirror in which a prince or other noble reader may see himself, the better to eliminate his vices.[3] She is here drawing on a tradition that goes back to antiquity, by way of such medieval authors as John of Salisbury and Giles of Rome. A core assumption of these works is that the state can flourish only when it is led by a virtuous ruler, and Christine certainly shares this assumption. Her *Book of Peace*, for example, is addressed to the grandson of Charles V. She holds up Charles as a paragon of seven virtues that any ruler must possess, namely prudence—the excellence in practical reasoning from which all the other virtues arise—followed by justice, magnanimity, fortitude, clemency, generosity, and truthfulness.

Of course, we should all strive to possess these virtues. But they are especially incumbent upon the ruler, who is held to a higher moral standard than other people because the welfare of the entire community depends on his character. In an age when some Italian cities were experimenting with republican forms of government, and despite her own experiences of a chaotic and violent France ill served by the principle of inherited monarchy, Christine continues to assume that the best rule is exercised by a single man. She is also a great believer in breeding. God may have created all humans equal, but those of a noble lineage have acquired better traits through their ancestry, just as some animals display a finer pedigree. Rather than questioning such elitist assumptions, she presupposes them as she tries to persuade her noble reader to strive for virtue. "It is not enough to be descended from good, noble, and valiant people," she writes, "if one is not like them oneself in goodness and conduct."[4] Yet Christine is not envisioning an autocracy guided by nothing but the autocrat's own integrity. She frequently warns that the ruler must take advice from reliable advisors, who should themselves be of good character. Vicious advisors can do just as much harm as vicious rulers if they manipulate the ruler for their own ends, usually by playing on whatever moral weaknesses they can find in the ruler.

Often, thinks Christine, war is the dire result of such wicked advice. Her constant refrain is that the ruler must ponder the havoc unleashed by war, and never be overly confident of his chances in a prospective battle. Military engagements are decided in large part by fortune, after all, and fortune is more powerful than even the stronger monarch. This is not to say that Christine is a thoroughgoing pacifist.

Echoing medieval ideas about just war,[5] she states that war may be rightly waged only in order to uphold justice, punish injustice, or recover land or other goods that have been stolen. However, she adds something new by connecting the theme of war to the importance of good advice. What makes a war just, in Christine's view, is not just the cause over which it is fought, but the procedure through which it is declared. A ruler should pay careful heed to his council and only begin a war after giving the enemy a chance to justify himself.[6]

In her pleas for peace, Christine lays special emphasis on the potentially damaging consequences for the ruler himself. This fits with an overall characteristic of her political writings, namely their appeal to the self-interest of her noble readers. For example she explains that the wealthy should treat poorer citizens well, simply because otherwise the underclass may rise up in revolt. Perhaps because of the political context, in these works she tends to emphasize practical, not theological virtues, encouraging that the ruler engage in action rather than prayer.[7] She warns occasionally that vice will be punished by God, but more commonly that it will be punished by events, and she defines her goal in the *Book of Peace* as helping a young noble to improve himself in respect of "soul, body, and reputation."[8] This hard-headed, if not cynical, approach seems a departure from the writings of the earlier medievals, and even an anticipation of what we will find in Machiavelli.[9] Her use of classical sources, ranging from Aristotle to Ovid, Seneca, Cicero, and Boethius, likewise seems to foreshadow the more elaborate classicism of Machiavelli.

One cannot help but be (pleasantly) surprised that a woman of this time period was in a position to write such innovative, and learned, works. Her contemporaries were a bit taken aback too. When it suited her rhetorical purpose, Christine was happy to pose as inferior and inadequate owing to her gender. Even in the debate she initiated over the anti-woman diatribes of the *Romance of the Rose*, where her whole point was to stand up for the honor of the female sex, she refers to herself as a "woman of untrained intellect and uncomplicated sensibility."[10] But a story found in another work called the *Vision* (*L'Avision*) sounds more convincing as a representation of the real Christine: "one day, a man criticized my desire for knowledge, saying that it was inappropriate for a woman to be learned, as it was so rare, to which I replied that it was even less fitting for a man to be ignorant, as it was so common" (*Vision*, 118).[11]

That's probably my favorite single passage in all of Christine's writings, but I'm biased, because it comes from her most obviously philosophical work. The *Vision* is a contribution to another genre familiar from the middle ages, in which the author recounts an allegorical dream. It has its ancient roots in Plato and Cicero, with medieval examples including Langland's *Piers Plowman* and the aforementioned

Romance of the Rose. The thematic unity and purpose of Christine's *Vision* is at least as difficult to pin down as with either of those poems. Thankfully it begins with a helpful introduction by Christine explaining the meaning of some of the symbolic characters and imagery. The body of the work opens with a section on the history of France, followed by a survey of ancient philosophical ideas, and then a kind of autobiography of Christine herself. To some extent the point of this is pretty obvious: Christine is describing the way that "Fortune" has its unpredictable way with earthly affairs. Her own life story in the final section mirrors the roller coaster of prosperity, warfare, and deprivation depicted in the first part on French history, and in the middle, the exposition of ancient philosophical theories conveys the equally haphazard attempts of philosophers to discern the truth.

That part of the *Vision* is also, of course, a demonstration of Christine's own learning. Her deft summary of Presocratic views, which are then dismissed as "bizarre" and critiqued from an Aristotelian point of view (74), is the fruit of her encounter with scholastic philosophy, here presented as a journey through the halls of the university at Paris (in this case the allegory is not too hard to decode). She tells of how she encountered a personification of our favorite subject, Lady Philosophy. In another moment of false modesty, she writes, "I knelt while thanking her to fill my lap with treasure, but since they were too heavy for my weak and feminine body, I carried away very little by the measure of my great desire, not so little, however, that I would exchange it for any other treasure or wealth" (105–6).

Of course, the appearance of Lady Philosophy is an allusion to Boethius. His *Consolation of Philosophy* inspired a number of medieval authors to write dialogues featuring a female personification of Philosophy, Nature, or some other abstract concept educating a character who stands in for the author. This is typical of Christine's *Vision*, which refers self-consciously to a wide range of earlier writers. Even the first sentence is an obvious echo of the opening line from Dante's *Divine Comedy*. But Boethius is particularly central, because Christine took inspiration from him to write her own consolation in the third part of the book. After a lengthy autobiographical lament, which is a source for some of the information I mentioned earlier—such as her legal battles and her father's interest in astrology—Lady Philosophy gives her some tough love. She chastises Christine by arguing that her sufferings stem from a misperception of what is truly valuable. In part happiness can be attained just by looking on the bright side, as illustrated most strikingly by the suggestion that her husband's early death had a silver lining, namely that it gave Christine more time for her learned studies (129). Most important is to abandon desire for earthly riches, pleasures, and other goods, focusing instead on God as the true and perfect good.

That's pretty typical advice that you might get from any number of medieval and Renaissance authors, even if it takes on a special resonance for us, since it situates Christine within the wider debate that keeps coming up, as to whether "external goods" like family and health have any true value. More distinctive of Christine is the way this advice is subtly woven into an extended meditation on epistemology. Let's turn back to the second section, the part about the history of philosophy. There, Christine is discoursing with another allegorical personification, whose identity is revealed only at the end of the section: Dame Opinion, who is responsible for the various convictions we all come to hold. Philosophical theories are only one example. Opinion also claims credit for inspiring religious beliefs, as well as political aspirations and plans. In fact she complains that Christine has elsewhere been too impressed by the power of Fortune when it is she, Opinion, who is most often the true driving force behind historical events.

It is, according to Christine, in the nature of opinion that it lacks certainty (63). This is not to say that opinions must be false, or counterproductive. Dame Opinion is pleased to take responsibility for the beginning of philosophy itself, when thinkers first had the curiosity to try to understand the world in general terms (61–2). Rather, opinions are what modern-day epistemologists would usually call "mere beliefs," that is, beliefs that may be true or false, but need something further (like justification) to rise to the level of true knowledge. Furthermore, for Christine opinion is always inspired by the functioning of the imagination. I would take all this to prepare the way for the autobiographical lament, and correction by Lady Philosophy, found in the final part of the work. Christine's unhappy assessment of her own life story is itself a mere, and mistaken, "opinion" that derives from her imagination and its faulty conception of the good (see 124, 131). This is a kind of psychological malady that Lady Philosophy must treat, borrowing a medical analogy for philosophical advice that was already used by Boethius (107). In the same way, God Himself acts as a kind of doctor for the soul, administering the bitter medicine of our trials and tribulations, that we may emerge from them confirmed in virtue (124, 126).

In the year 1405, the same year that saw the composition of the *Vision*, Christine produced what is probably her most famous and celebrated work, the *City of Ladies*.[12] It begins with Christine picking up a now obscure book and finding it full of misogynistic sentiments (§1.1.1), the same sort of sentiments she had earlier found in the *Romance of the Rose*. Somewhat unpersuasively, given her strident defense of womanly virtue in her earlier critique of the *Romance* (reprised here at §1.2.2), Christine claims that this book led her to despair at the weakness of women. In the face of so many esteemed authors who have written diatribes against the moral and intellectual failings of women, how can Christine avoid lamenting that she herself was born female? It seems to her a mistake on the part of God to create women, if they are indeed "monstrosities in nature." Christine cries out to Him, asking why He could not have been kinder to her by creating her as a man (§1.1.1–2).

At this point, an early fifteenth-century reader would feel they know what to expect. A philosophically minded author, sitting alone and in despair? Sounds like Boethius at the beginning of his *Consolation of Philosophy*, lamenting his fate as he awaits his execution. So our reader might expect to turn the page and see a female personification turning up to offer consolation, like Lady Philosophy in Boethius. A pretty good guess, but not quite right. Christine outdoes Boethius by having no fewer than three personifications appear to her: Reason, Justice, and Rectitude. Reason speaks first to defend the honor of womankind. In a clear allusion to Christine's favorite writing genre, Reason holds a mirror in her hand, and promises to help Christine achieve self-knowledge (§1.3.2). In particular, she will come to have the knowledge of female virtue.

All this serves as a preliminary to the central metaphor of the text. The three ladies will help to build a city for women, one stronger even than the kingdom of the Amazons in antiquity (§1.4.3). Here we may see a more subtle dig at Jean de Meun's *Romance of the Rose*. Not only did he too personify Reason as a character in his poem, but his *Romance* depicts how a male Lover batters his way through a fortification to ravish his beloved. Christine's city will be able to withstand such assaults. Before its foundations are laid, the ground must be cleared: Reason critiques the male authorities who have spoken so unkindly of women. Perhaps in some cases, they had good intentions and only sought to steer men towards sexual virtue and away from passionate love (§1.8.3). It's a noteworthy admission, since this is what the defenders of the *Romance of the Rose* said Jean de Meun was seeking to do. But Reason adds that this is really no excuse, since it is wrong to depict admirable things as wicked, like someone complaining about fire because it burns things, forgetting how useful it can be. Christine turns the screw by having Reason add that men often complain about female vice because they themselves are vicious, or because age has made them impotent and bitter (§1.8.5).

Now it's time to build the city itself. She has the three ladies describe the deeds and qualities of a wide range of virtuous heroines. Those named by Reason exemplify intellectual merit and are drawn from pagan antiquity. She stresses that women have been "great philosophers" (§1.11.1), and made novel discoveries that advanced the cause of human knowledge. One example is Minerva, whose many insights concerning mathematics, writing, weaving, and other endeavors convinced the Greeks that she was in fact a goddess (§1.34.1). Women have also been successful political rulers, even if they often had the chance to do so only because their husbands died, leaving them to rule as widow queens. Similarly, if their achievements in science have been lesser, this is simply because women are typically not educated as men are. If girls were sent to school like boys, they would show an equal aptitude for science (§1.27.1). This is a remarkable anticipation of later pleas for the education of women, something we associate more with modern figures like Mary Wollstonecraft.

Christine chooses to have pagan figures praised by Reason because they show what women have achieved through natural gifts, outside the context of Christian religion. But Christine reminds us that the Virgin Mary "opened the door to Paradise" for all of us (§2.30.1), and other female saints and martyrs feature later in the speech of Rectitude. Thus Christine can claim to have both reason and faith on her side. Not content to defend women, she also takes time to excoriate the viciousness found among men, including Roman emperors like Claudius and Nero (§§2.47.3–48.1). In fact, misogyny itself is an unnatural vice, for we see in nature that all other male animals love the females of their species (§1.8.9). Above all, men have no monopoly on virtue. To the contrary, women's bodily weakness is compensated by their moral character, something Christine compares to the way that Aristotle is said to have been profoundly ugly, something compensated by his brilliance (§1.14.1). On the basis of her historical examples, Christine takes herself to have shown that the virtue of women is unassailable, to the point that it can form the substance of an invincible, imaginary city (§3.19.1). This city is built to last, and last it will, so long as her women readers are inspired to be virtuous themselves (§3.19.6).

29

MORE RARE THAN THE PHOENIX ITALIAN WOMEN HUMANISTS

I know I was just complaining about how people don't write letters anymore. But at the risk of sounding difficult to please, I have to say that when people did write letters they often weren't very interesting. College students wrote to mom and dad, but just as an excuse to ask for money, and don't get me started on the literary merits of the average love letter. The letters of Italian humanists are another case in point. Elegant though they are, they tend to follow predictable motifs. There's the epistle of consolation, sharing in the grief of losing a loved one before saying it's time to pull oneself together.[1] There's the letter in which the recipient's eloquence is extravagantly praised, and the answer to such a letter, where the done thing is to respond with even more extravagant false modesty. Closely related is the plea for patronage, a showpiece of verbal dexterity in which fulsome praise of some rich person is used to entice that rich person to pay for more of the same. Most characteristically, there is the letter that is not about much of anything, apart from the fact that one is writing a letter. It begins by apologizing for not writing sooner and goes on to apologize again for having to be brief, before closing with the admonition that the recipient should reply as soon as possible. Renaissance rhetoric is at its purest when it uses beautiful, well-balanced, Ciceronian sentences to say nothing.

The epistolary art was so prized by the humanists, and so central to their project of refined self-representation, that it became standard for them to publish volumes of collected correspondence. Petrarch had already done so, and his example was followed by such figures as Salutati, Poggio, Bruni, and Filelfo. Remarkably, the Italian Renaissance also saw the publication of collections of letters by women. No less remarkable is the fact that these letters tend, for the most part, to read just like letters written by male humanists. Well-educated aristocratic women showed that they too could use high-flown Latin to appeal for patronage, offer consolation, and get through a whole letter without saying anything. Here we have a development such as we have hardly, if ever, seen before in the history of European philosophy: women writing on equal terms with men.[2] Since the humanists prized eloquence and linguistic facility above all else, women who excelled in rhetoric were able to participate in humanist discourse, in a way that no medieval women had ever been able to participate in scholastic discourse. Writing letters was an obvious opportunity for them to do so, because the substance of a humanist letter was its style. In fact the letters are not really about *nothing*, they are about writing itself. This most self-conscious of literary forms was the perfect vehicle for women authors who were self-consciously laying claim to social terrain dominated by men.

We already know that humanists were, with some exceptions and restrictions, in favor of offering their brand of education to girls and women. Remember Leonardo Bruni recommending a curriculum of classical education to a female correspondent. The result was that a significant number of women in fifteenth- and sixteenth-century Italy learned, and even mastered, Latin and Greek. An early example was Maddalena Scrovegni, praised for her learning in an encomium by Antonio Loschi. Later examples would include Olimpia Fulvia Morata, who died in the middle of the sixteenth century and wrote extensively in Latin and Greek, and Tarquinia Molza, who lived well into the seventeenth century and translated Plato's *Charmides* and parts of his *Crito* into Italian. Here I'm going to focus especially on three other female humanists of Italy. In chronological order they are Isotta Nogarola, who died in 1466; Laura Cereta, who died young at the close of the fifteenth century in 1499; and finally Cassandra Fedele, who lived until an advanced age and died in 1558.[3] We have collections of letters for all three of them, as well as some independent works like Nogarola's dialogue on the sin of Adam and Eve, which I'll be looking at in the next chapter.

To attain the high level of education displayed in their letters, all three women had to be lucky in finding teachers. Nogarola was taught by a student of the great humanist Guarino Veronese, while Cereta speaks of a nun who instructed her, and frequently emphasizes her evening "vigils" studying by candlelight. At one point she even criticizes those who "waste their nights sleeping" (*Cereta*, 55). These women were not merely allowed to learn Latin, they were enthusiastically celebrated for doing so. Here was a chance for men to show off their own Latin by bestowing lavish, if somewhat condescending, praise, and they did not hesitate to do so. Cassandra Fedele especially was widely admired, the admiration unfailingly linked to wonderment that a young lady could display such gifts. The humanist Angelo Poliziano waxed enthusiastically about this girl who preferred to "stitch with a pen rather than a needle, and rather cover papyrus with ink than her skin with white powder" (*Fedele*, 90). Both he and Cassandra's relative Balthassare Fedele compared her to women of antiquity famous for their eloquence, like Aspasia and Sappho. Balthassare added that she was "more rare than the phoenix," combining as she did proper female virtue with the intellectual abilities more usually associated with men (39). Others praised her as a "unique glory and jewel of the female sex," as having "surpassed her sex," and as proving that "a manly mind can be born in a person of the female sex" (65, 128, 110).

One might wonder whether all these admiring men were laying it on a bit thick, even by the standards of humanist encomium. The leading scholar of women humanists in Italy, Margaret King, has remarked that Fedele's works were actually quite typical, even "mediocre," in comparison to the productions of her contemporaries. "One is forced to conclude," says King, that Fedele "was praised beyond her merits."[4] It reminds me of the compliments I sometimes get, living in Munich as an American who can speak German more or less competently: my managing it at all is so unusual that it hardly matters what I say. (Germans who speak English, by contrast, are taken entirely for granted.) In the case of Fedele, the welcome she received was in part politically motivated. Lodovico Maria Sforza spoke of her as an "ornament for the greatness of [Venice's] empire" (*Fedele*, 54), as if she were the human equivalent of a stylish humanist epistle: praised to the skies as culturally significant, but only as a showpiece.

In the previous century Isotta Nogarola—whom King rates much higher—had ironically been somewhat less celebrated. But one correspondent did write of being incredulous when told of her attainments: "since I knew that men rarely receive such praise, I found it very difficult to concede that a woman might" (*Nogarola*, 65). Even her great friend and confidant Lodovico Foscarini applauded Nogarola in terms that put her squarely in her place: "in Isotta, whom none surpass in virtue, that sex greatly pleases, which is otherwise burdened by the frailty of lesser women" (136). This sort of thing left Laura Cereta unimpressed. She denied that she was unique, insisting that many women had achieved a comparable degree of cultivation, among them Nogarola and Fedele, both of whom she mentions by name (*Cereta*, 78). In her view, men who saw her as extraordinary were simply underestimating the capabilities of women (75, 176). Cereta was under no illusions about the dynamics of power that usually kept women from competing fairly with men despite their gifts. An aphoristic remark found in one letter to a male correspondent sums it up well: "yours is the authority, ours the inborn ability (*ingenium*)" (79).

She sought to compete with men nonetheless, just as did Nogarola and Fedele before her. All three of them displayed an open desire for literary renown. After Nogarola's death she was given the honor of a eulogy by the humanist scholar Giovanni Mario Filelfo (son of the previously mentioned Francesco Filelfo), who noted with approval that she "gave herself to the pursuit of fame and glory in all her efforts" (*Nogarola*, 17). During her life she had come to learn that dealings with male scholars could both enhance, and tarnish, a reputation. When praised by her teacher's teacher Guarino Veronese, she wrote one of those letters of thanks for praise, saying that through his admiration she had "achieved immortality and need no longer be anxious about the public's opinion and estimation of me" (51). But when another letter she sent him was ignored, this brought scorn and mockery down upon her. Naturally she wrote again to complain. At the second time of asking Veronese responded supportively, but also chastised her: "up to now I believed and trusted that your soul was manly, and that brave and unvanquished you could face all adversities. But now you seem so humbled, so abject, and so truly a woman, that you demonstrate none of the estimable qualities that I thought you possessed."[5]

Cassandra Fedele was equally concerned with her own reputation, and saw her own quest for glory in terms Veronese might have recognized: as a kind of transcending of gender boundaries. She wrote, "at the beginning of my labors, when I had abandoned feminine concerns and turned to those pursuits that pertain not only to honor during this brief life but to the enjoyment of God's majesty, I considered that I would find immortal praise among men. And so my goal has been to exercise my virile, burning, and incredible—though not improper, I hope—desire for the study of the liberal arts so my name will be praised and celebrated by excellent men" (*Fedele*, 44, cf. 159). And elsewhere, more succinctly, "It is a very sweet victory indeed to outstrip men of eloquence" (71). As for Laura Cereta, she too sought to win acclaim for her literary skills early in her career, at one point expressing the hope that she would be a second "Laura" to achieve immortality, the first being Petrarch's beloved (*Cereta*, 49). Like Nogarola, she suffered from a degree of envious criticism, especially in response to an early satirical work, a funeral eulogy in honor of a donkey, which she admitted was written out of a "desire for fame" (39). But as she matured Cereta came to see notoriety as a hollow pursuit. We should study the liberal arts to become virtuous, not to win praise (149).

Indeed, all three of our protagonists faced questions about their ultimate goals after establishing a humanist pedigree. Learned women were forced to choose between family life and the life of the mind. A vivid example is provided by Isotta Nogarola and her sister Ginevra. Whereas Ginevra's literary activities stopped as soon as she was married, Isotta was able to continue her studies, but only by swearing herself to lifelong chastity and residing with a male relative.[6] In keeping with this pious and ascetic lifestyle, she started to focus more on religious literature like the church fathers, whose influence shows itself increasingly in her writing. Cassandra Fedele too was well aware of the problem, and admitted to facing a choice between scholarship and marriage. And so it proved. After marrying in 1499, she produced little in the way of a literary legacy in the last half-century and more of her life.[7] On this score Laura Cereta is the exception that proves the rule, because she did marry, but her husband died soon thereafter. We saw how Christine de Pizan, faced with the same situation, consoled herself with the thought that this would at least give her an opportunity for continued scholarship. Cereta was less cheerful, remarking in several letters that the death of her husband had deprived her of the desire for learning: she is still awake at night, but to grieve, not to study (*Cereta*, 95, 101). Yet as we can see from the fact that these letters exist, she likewise took advantage of her widowed status to keep writing.

Writing about what? Well, if humanists more generally tended to write letters about writing letters, then women humanists tended to write letters about writing as women. Just as their male correspondents always praise them as *female* humanists and not just humanists, so the female humanists themselves allude to their sex on a regular basis. In many cases they seem to accept a subordinate status. The letters of all three authors are littered with passages where they admit to being an "unlearned" or "insignificant" girl, excuse themselves for their "girlish letters," lament their mere "womanly ability," and so on. Fedele liked to refer to herself as a "bold little woman," constantly apologizing for troubling her correspondents by sending what were in fact carefully crafted literary productions. But then false modesty was typical of humanist letters in general, so perhaps we should not take all this too seriously. Occasionally, one of the authors does seem sincerely to regret being female. Nogarola, when complaining of the abuse she received after being ignored by Veronese, wrote, "since I often ponder what the worth of women is, it occurs to me to bemoan my fate since I was born female and women are ridiculed by men in both word and deed" (*Nogarola*, 53). But even here the blame falls more upon envious men, a theme she sounds elsewhere when complaining about men "who consider learning and women a plague and public nuisance" (38). Fedele met with the same sort of envy, but optimistically said that she could rise above it, thereby following the example of both Christ and the philosophers (*Fedele*, 51–2).

Which brings us neatly on to the question you've probably been waiting for: did these female humanists also follow the example of some male humanists by engaging with philosophy? We've already seen plenty of evidence that, in the Italian Renaissance, the study of eloquence was a kind of gateway drug to the intoxications of pagan philosophical thought. Our women humanists fit this picture. The scholar Lauro Quirini advised Nogarola to build on her humanist studies by delving into Aristotelianism, the works of the scholastics, and even the writings of thinkers from the Islamic world like Avicenna, al-Ghazālī, and Averroes (*Nogarola*, 107–13). Cassandra Fedele said herself that she had "dared to set sail on the vast sea of philosophy" (*Fedele*, 145) and spoke of her labors studying through the night, "wholly fixated on studies in the Peripatetic philosophers" (76–7, cf. 148).

She was praised for her resulting philosophical facility by no less a judge than Angelo Poliziano, who thought she could compare favorably with Giovanni Pico della Mirandola (91).

Unfortunately, we don't see too much direct evidence of that facility in the letters. Fedele does make a joke about Aristotelian logic at one point (75), and refers in passing to philosophical issues, like whether rhetoric can overwhelm free will with its persuasive power (72). She's also acquainted with a range of ancient philosophical figures, whom she tends to interpret with what we might call a spirit of generosity. Thus she presents the Presocratic philosopher Empedocles in unduly optimistic terms, with his principle of Love as a force that binds the universe together (138); she omits to mention that he posited a second principle, Strife, that tears it apart. Similarly, Epicureanism appears in a form made suitable for use by Christians, as Fedele manages to make Epicurus a spokesman for the notion that we should not seek happiness in this life (45). Laura Cereta too presents an expurgated version of this particular Hellenistic school. She takes Epicurus' chief teaching to be a rejection of the passing pleasures of this life (*Cereta*, 120), and even admires him for teaching that happiness comes from virtue *rather than* pleasure (132). That sound you hear is the hedonist Epicurus rolling over in his grave, or at least it would be if Epicureans thought it possible to survive death.

While Cereta earns no marks here as a historian of philosophy, she scores points as a philosopher in her own right. She has ascribed to Epicurus the idea that the pleasures of this life are transient, and thus ultimately empty. As she puts it in the same passage, bodily pleasures "grow old" but we want goods that are permanent. This ethical principle is of course a familiar one, and does go back to antiquity, albeit more to the Platonists than to the Epicureans. But it also relates to an abiding concern more distinctive of Cereta, which runs throughout her letter-writing career: the question of the attitude we should take towards time and change. In fact, her views on this question themselves change over time. In earlier letters, she is very much concerned with the best use of time, which she sees as a kind of scarce resource.[8] Hence the aforementioned advice not to fritter away your valuable time at night by sleeping; hence too complaints she makes about her limited time for study given domestic chores (*Cereta*, 24, 31). Time is, as she puts it, "not something that belongs to us," but passes relentlessly along with the motion of the sun (51). So in this phase of Cereta's career, we can see her as exemplifying a more general tendency in the Renaissance and early modern Europe to think of time as a resource or commodity, one that can be squandered or used wisely (see also 81, and for this theme also below, Chapter 48). In her view, the best use of time is the study of the liberal arts and philosophy.

However, as Cereta's thought develops she comes to have a different, even a negative, view towards time. This seems to go hand in hand with her abandonment of the pursuit of glory, and with her experience of grief after the death of her husband. Like pleasure, she comes to see glory as a merely worldly good that has no lasting value, and thus no real value at all. To concern oneself with this world is to make one's well-being depend on that which is undependable and unpredictable, since such things are ruled by fortune, or rather by random chance; here she refers to her husband's passing as a personal example (156–7). So, as she puts it, "I abandoned my plan to seek fame through human letters, lest my mind, bereft, unhappy, and unaware of the future, should seek happiness through diligence" (112). Life is not after all a valuable resource to be used wisely, but a brief vigil waiting for one's own death (132, 190). Having given up on pleasure, glory, and all the other things that can be bought with time well spent, Cereta instead undertakes to focus on the eternity of God. His providential law is worth valuing, because it remains the same through all the unpredictable ups and downs of earthly life (75, 140). Cereta summons her rhetorical gifts in the service of Christian philosophy: "Not I but God should be the object of my soul's desire, since I am subject to death . . . Since this mortal life of ours will live on after death, I have renounced—for it is holier to do so—that glory, transitory and slipping, which being full of the contrariness of earthly beings, separates us from the true religion of pious faith" (105).

30

ALL ABOUT EVE THE DEFENSE OF WOMEN

Of course, sometimes humanists did use their rhetorical skill to write showpiece letters that had substance as well as style. We've seen examples already: dialogues about ethics, treatises on the shortcomings of scholastic philosophy, meditations on the history of the Latin language itself. Another conventional topic within humanist literature was the virtue of women, or lack thereof. Actually, this genre of writing already existed in the medieval age. Way back in the twelfth century, Peter Abelard had spoken up for the virtue and honor of women. This could be a rhetorical exercise, as is shown by the still earlier case of Marbod of Rennes, who wrote two poems on the issue, one attacking women and one praising them. Among earlier authors, the most influential for authors of the Italian Renaissance was probably Boccaccio, thanks to his work *On Famous Women*, written in 1361. He helped inspire such works as *In Praise of Women* by Bartolomeo Goggio;[1] Christine de Pizan's *City of Ladies* also mentions Boccaccio explicitly (e.g. §1.28.1, §1.37.1).

When you look through catalogues of virtuous women you see why it was a genre that would appeal to Renaissance humanists. They could display their learning by recounting anecdotes about figures from the ancient world and religious history. Under the latter heading one of the most frequent names that arises is an African one, Nicaula, also known as the Queen of Sheba.[2] Occasionally authors also took pride in the excellence of more recent ladies from the Italian aristocracy, all the better if they were the author's own family members. A related genre that offered some of the same attractions was the treatise on family life. This too had ancient roots, as a number of classical authors had written on what they called "economics"; that is, household management. Economics in this sense was a topic closely associated with women since, as Aristotle had made clear in his *Ethics* and *Politics*, running the household is the proper task of the wife. So it is that we see reflections on gender in a work like Francesco Barbaro's *On Marriage* (*De re uxoria*).[3]

This is a treatise about women that is unapologetically written for men, indeed for rich men (§1.6), and above all for one man in particular, Lorenzo de' Medici. Barbaro advises Lorenzo on the criteria to be used in selecting a wife, as well as the duties and appropriate comportment of the wife after marriage. Along the way he invokes a wide range of classical authors and historical figures, and occasionally alludes to the more recent past including, naturally, a preeminent member of the Barbaro clan (§1.1). But despite his tales of praiseworthy women, Barbaro is far from a feminist. To the contrary, he unwittingly shows us what women of the period were up against. For Barbaro, women are quite literally put on earth to love and serve men, and to bear their children. Their comparative physical weakness is proof that Aristotle was right to say their place is in the home, though Barbaro congratulates himself for being more moderate in his views than the ancient sophist Gorgias, who thought they should never be seen in public at all (§2.3). Still Barbaro warns that when they do go out, just enough to display their virtue, they should mostly remain silent (§2.4). Let them show their good character by gesture and posture.

In an echo of the ethical debates we've seen in other authors, Barbaro again takes what he would see as a middle path by accepting the importance of "external goods" while putting chief emphasis on virtue. Thus it is a prospective wife's character that should concern a husband, but on the other hand beauty complements virtue well, and nobility and wealth don't hurt (§1.3–5). It's an attitude summed up nicely in the remark of one Jacopo Morosini, who wrote of how grateful he was for his excellent wife, "because of her admirable conduct, and also for all the cash."[4] Still, Barbaro says it would be absurd to take a wife just for her money, something he revealingly compares to picking out a helmet for its gold trim, or a book for its decoration. It's hard to imagine examples more obviously chosen for a wealthy, male readership.

The virtue of one's wife is not its own reward. Her character is important because she needs to be able to run the household well. In this designated sphere, the wife has significant authority. Though she should of course obey her husband in all things (§2.1), everyone else should obey *her*. She is to deal with the servants and oversee the household with strict vigilance (§2.8), something Barbaro illustrates with the Platonic comparisons of the good statesman and pilot of a ship (§1.1). In sum, Barbaro's treatise makes it clear why female humanists saw a stark choice between family life and intellectual endeavor. In fact his own daughters faced that choice, since they were given a good education. Ironically enough, this self-professed expert on marriage had children who opted to avoid wedlock by entering the convent.[5]

His book also nicely illustrates the way humanists included ancient philosophical lore right along with other classical sources, like works of history and epic poetry. It was especially Aristotle who inspired the default view of women among male authors, such as we find it in Barbaro and others who wrote on the topic of female virtue. On the Aristotelian view women can indeed be good, even outstandingly good. Still, since women are inferior to men, their virtue should be exercised in the household and not in the public sphere of political life. In the *Politics* Aristotle justified this attitude with the remark that women are defective in respect of their rational capacities. Barbaro and other humanists did emphasize the importance of love and friendship in marriage, but would have done so while recalling Aristotle's claim that there can be no perfect friendship between man and woman because of their inequality. Then too, Aristotle's works on animals can be read as saying that the birth of a female human or animal is a kind of failure, with only the male members of each species representing natural perfection.

But this was, of course, a period during which the works of Plato were becoming better known, making him a second authority to rival Aristotle. And Plato had some very un-Aristotelian things to say about women.[6] He was certainly capable of crude misogyny himself, as at the end of the *Timaeus* where bad men are said to be reincarnated as women. But his most famous treatment of the topic, and the one most frequently cited by Renaissance authors, comes in the *Republic* when he argues that the most talented women can do philosophy, should be involved in warfare, and ought to participate in ruling of the best city. So this was an obvious classical source for authors who sought to defend women against misogyny. A perfect example comes in a text I've mentioned previously, Balthassare Castiglione's *Book of the Courtier*.[7] Its third part is devoted to a debate between two characters, a misogynist and an anti-misogynist. The anti-misogynist gets Plato about right by saying that he was "no great friend of women" yet still allowed them to participate in warfare and politics (273). When the misogynist presents the Aristotelian view that women are naturally defective, like blind people or trees that bear no fruit, he is refuted on the grounds that nature needs women for the sake of reproduction, so their birth can hardly be a matter of accidental misfiring (277).

While Castiglione includes a spirited defense of women in his dialogue, it is hard to see the text as unambiguously feminist. The most philosophically sophisticated of the characters remarks at the end of the debate that both protagonists have exaggerated (350), suggesting that Castiglione himself adheres to the supposedly "moderate" view that women are often good, yet still less worthy than men. The perfect court lady, who is the mirror image of the ideal male courtier presented in the rest of the work, has the carefully constrained role we would predict. She should run her household well and be modest and charming (267). For a bolder defense of women, we need to turn to authors who were, well, women.[8]

We met one of them already in the last chapter: Isotta Nogarola. I saved her most remarkable work for now, because it deals with the virtues of men and women. Or rather about the vices of one particular man and one particular woman, as this is a dialogue devoted to the sinfulness of Adam and Eve. It's another well-worn topic. Misogynists right back through the middle ages had delighted in blaming Eve for the sinful choice that first corrupted human nature. The usual response from anti-misogynists, which we actually find in Castiglione (282), is that if sin was introduced through Eve it was repaired through another woman, Mary, through whom Christ was given to us. Nogarola has a different approach. Her two main characters are Isotta, that is, the author herself, and her great friend Lodovico Foscarini.[9] This is a humanist dialogue, and a rather intimate one at that, offering testimony to one of Nogarola's most important personal relationships. Yet it also recalls a scholastic disputed question, which takes its departure from Saint Augustine's claim that Adam and Eve "sinned unequally according to their sexes, but equally in pride." The real Nogarola and Foscarini might in fact have debated the question in an open forum. I like to imagine Francesco Barbaro sitting at the back, frowning at this public display of feminine intelligence.

At first glance, Nogarola's way of defending Eve might warm the heart of the coldest misogynist. Her character takes the line that Eve's weakness as a woman—her inferior intellect and temperamental inconstancy—helps explain her sinful choice (146). As a man Adam had no such excuse. So, just as we should blame a nobleman more than a peasant for committing the same infraction, or an adult more than a child, so we should condemn Adam more than Eve. Ironically, Foscarini is thus put in the position of having to refute sexist assumptions about womanly frailty in order to blame Eve as he wants to. Though he doesn't go so far as to argue that Eve was *equal* to Adam, he thinks that her more modest natural gifts were adequate to make her fully culpable. "Just as teeth were given to wild beasts, horns to oxen, feathers to birds for their survival, to the woman mental capacity was given sufficient for the preservation and pursuit of the health of her soul" (156).

Yet there is a more radical line of thought pursued by the character of Isotta in the dialogue, namely that Eve acted out of a natural desire for knowledge of good and evil (153). This comes dangerously close to excusing her sin completely, though of course Nogarola doesn't explicitly suggest that conclusion. The same justification of Eve appears in another dialogue about women, written in Italian by Modesta Pozzo de' Zorzi in 1592, on the eve of her death during childbirth. Taking the pen name of Moderata Fonte, she wrote a number of poems, a chivalric romance, and this remarkable work called *The Worth of Women*.[10] Unlike Nogarola's dialogue, this one would pass the modern-day "Bechdel test" (are women depicted talking to one another, about something besides a man?). In fact, we get a large cast of characters, all of them female, explicitly reveling in their freedom as they sit together in a garden with no one to monitor their discussion (45). In fact, one of them says

(53) that this is the best thing about the garden: no men! That comment sets the tone for the work, as some of the characters enthusiastically praise women and complain about men, who are seen as largely vicious and useless, so that one would be well advised not to marry them (48, 240). When women do marry it debases them, because of their husbands' natural inferiority (91).

But this is the sixteenth century. Don't Fonte's characters have to admit that women are subject to men, who are their superiors? No, except in the sense that we are all "subject" to natural disasters. Men are in fact "given to [women] by God as a spiritual trial" (59). While it is true that there are worthy men, they are the exception. Though one can find accounts of great men in historical chronicles, excellent men are mentioned precisely because they are so rare (88). Among the female sex it is conversely wickedness that is unusual, and vicious women typically get that way by being corrupted by the men in their families (72). Here Fonte is implicitly critiquing the genre of "famous women" established by Boccaccio. It is ridiculous to list cases of female virtue as if this were exceptional, when what is really exceptional is female vice (95). In the face of all this, other characters in the dialogue do put the case in favor of men and marriage. But it's pretty clear that Fonte's sympathies lie with the critics, who are more eloquent, wittier, and also more learned. Indeed the second part of the work is given over to disquisitions on natural philosophy by these characters, meaning that almost half the work consists of digressions from its main topic.

More relentless in its focus, and bolder still in its argument, is the most powerful treatise in defense of women written in our period: *On the Nobility and Excellence of Women, and the Defects and Vices of Men*, composed by Lucrezia Marinella at the close of the sixteenth century.[11] This is a straightforward essay, not a dialogue, though it responds to a separate misogynist work by Giuseppe Passi, called *The Defects of Women*. In her lengthy rebuttal Marinella adeptly turns her opponents' arguments against them. Confronted with insulting etymologies of words having to do with women, Marinella offers positive derivations instead. The Italian for lady, *donna*, comes from *domina*, "female lord," while *femina* relates to *fetu*, "fetus." Marinella points to a similar connection in Plato's dialogue about etymology, the *Cratylus* (46, 49). Throughout antiquity and the middle ages, it had been argued that women are inferior to men because of their physical constitution, their bodies lacking the heat that makes men so vigorous. Marinella would have known such arguments quite well, since her father was a doctor who had written on gynecology. She flips them on their head, arguing that in fact men are excessively hot, which is why they are so unreliable (77).[12] As she puts it, "women are cooler than men and thus nobler, and if a man performs excellent deeds it is because his nature is similar to a woman's, possessing temperate but not excessive heat" (131). Even the fact that men are physically stronger than women, which Barbaro took to show that women ought to stay in the home, in fact shows that women are superior, being more delicate and gentle. After all, blacksmiths are not nobler than kings and men of science (131).

Marinella takes the same approach of appropriating her enemy's weapons when it comes to her greatest foe, which is not really Passi, but Aristotle. More than any of the authors considered so far, she highlights the conflict between Plato and Aristotle on the subject of women, making her work another contribution to the running dispute over the authority of these two figures. Marinella's sympathies lie squarely with Plato, and not only for his recommendations about female political participation. She also thinks (speaking of participation) that the Platonist theory of Forms supports her case. Women are the more beautiful sex, and thereby instantiate Forms that are more perfect (53). "Compared to women all men are ugly," she says. "They would not be loved by women were it not for our courteous and benign natures" (63). In the course of this innovative application of Platonist metaphysics to the battle of the sexes, Marinella cites a range of authorities including Plotinus, Ficino, and more unexpectedly Petrarch, who had compared his beloved Laura to an ideal of perfection (54). Women perform a valuable service for men, because their physical beauty is like a step on a ladder that leads to the divine realm of Forms, as described by Plato in his *Symposium*.

As for Aristotle, he was "a fearful, tyrannical man" where Plato was "truly great and just" (79). Like other misogynist authors, Aristotle suffered from envy, anger, and even intellectual limitations, having no rational basis for his views (120, 149). Again this reverses a standard trope used against women. For Marinella it is actually men who are prey to their emotions and shaky reasoning. She knows Aristotle well enough to use his ideas in her own cause, too. She sounds like a scholastic logician when she chastises Passi for illegitimately drawing a *universal* conclusion about female wickedness from a few *particular* examples (127). She points out that in Aristotelian science, women cannot really be naturally defective since they are actually more numerous than men, and nature doesn't fail more often than it succeeds (68, cf. 135). She accepts Aristotle's definitions of the virtues, the better to show that women more commonly satisfy these definitions (115). While Marinella thus displays philosophical learning, she also reflects on the way women are mostly excluded from this arena, something that by the way is well illustrated by the life story of Moderata Fonte, who had to get her brother to repeat his lessons to her after coming home from school. Marinella suspects that this sort of unfair treatment is, again, caused by envy and fear of female superiority: "man does not permit woman to apply herself to such studies, fearing, with reason, that she will surpass him in them" (140).

This is stirring stuff, and perhaps more committed in its polemic than what we find in Fonte's *Worth of Women*. Admittedly, Fonte's characters do make strident remarks on behalf of women. In fact one of them says almost the same thing we just found in Marinella: "we have just as much right to speak about [scientific] subjects as they have, and if we were educated properly as girls, we'd outstrip men's performance in any science or art you care to name" (238). But by depicting her more feminist characters in conversation with other women who are relatively restrained in their views, Fonte leaves her own position less than explicit. Perhaps she is, like Castiglione, less radical than her most radical characters? Moreover, she seems to have a rather ironic attitude towards the whole debate, indeed the whole genre of writing about women's vices and virtues. I already mentioned her undercutting of the catalogues of outstanding female virtue. A similar effect is created when the discussions of scientific matters included in the second part of the dialogue are routinely interrupted by a character named Leonora. She wants to get back to complaining about men (151, 161, 174, 180, 204). At first this seems like a mere running gag, or perhaps a jocular anticipation of what the frustrated reader may be thinking. But it may be a more serious indication of Fonte's own frustrations with the putative topic of her treatise. Why should she have to write about women and their conflict with men, just because she is a woman? As one character says in justification of the scientific digressions, "It's good for us to learn about these things, so we can look after ourselves, without needing help from men" (181).

31

I'D LIKE TO THANK THE ACADEMY
FLORENTINE PLATONISM

When I was younger, by which I mean, before I did the research to write this chapter, I used to think that the ideal life was the one enjoyed by Marsilio Ficino. Admittedly, living in the fifteenth century as he did, he would have lacked access to indoor plumbing, modern dentistry, and almond croissants (the consumption of which makes the need for dentistry all the more urgent). But apart from that he had it made. His patron Lorenzo de' Medici gave him a country house in Careggi, just north of Florence. In this pleasant Tuscan setting he could while away the hours reading and translating Plato and the works of the Neoplatonists with his friends and students who, we are told, formed something like a new "academy." Now I am older and wiser, and realize that Ficino's situation may have been less enviable. He was as often out of favor with Lorenzo as in favor. And it turns out that like reports of Mark Twain's death, the stories of the Florentine "Academy" are greatly exaggerated. Above all, proximity to power in Renaissance Florence was actually pretty dangerous, as shown by the events of April 26, 1478. Encouraged by the pope, the Pazzi family conspired to murder Lorenzo, trying to stab him to death while he was attending church.[1] Lorenzo was wounded, but made a narrow escape and lived to offer patronage another day.

Indeed, this event incidentally highlights the close connections of the Medici to the humanists they sponsored. One of the movement's greatest exponents, Angelo Poliziano, was standing right near Lorenzo during the assassination attempt, while Poggio Bracciolini's son Jacopo was among the conspirators. Along with their patronage of artists like Donatello, Fra Angelico, and Botticelli, the Medici's sponsoring of humanist scholarship continues to burnish their reputation to the present day. It is thanks to the Medici that we associate Renaissance philosophy more with Florence than with any other city. More specifically, Florence is indelibly linked to the history of Platonism. But why did Cosimo and Lorenzo de' Medici support the intellectual activity of Ficino and other Platonist scholars? Was their interest in philosophy and humanist book culture a disinterested, purely intellectual enterprise, or did a political motive lurk in the background?

To answer this question we need to look briefly at the way that the Medici exerted control over their city. Their period of dominance began in 1434 after Cosimo returned triumphantly from political exile. The preceding decades had been difficult ones for the Florentines. The plague had struck seven times since its first arrival in 1350, and wars against Naples and Milan were a drain on the city's resources, both human and financial. Yet Florence remained prosperous, thanks to its silk industry and skilled craftsmen. No one enjoyed the fruits of that prosperity more than the Medici, who parlayed fabulous wealth built up through banking into a network of clients and allies. At no point did Cosimo, his son Piero (who was head of the family for only a few years), or his grandson Lorenzo hold an official position of monarchial rule in the city. They did not need to, because the theoretically republican political system of Florence was in fact subject to their control. The Medici pretended not to be autocrats, as when Cosimo wrote to the pope to plead that as a mere private citizen he could not pledge Florence's support for a crusade on behalf of Constantinople against the Turks. But in fact he was "king in everything but name," as remarked by that unsentimental observer of political life, Enea Silvio Piccolomini (discussed above in Chapter 26).

The Medici displayed their wealth, while cementing their claim to legitimacy, through their patronage of art, architectural monuments, and classical learning. Though they didn't come right out and say so, it's pretty obvious why they might have found Plato in particular to be a congenial classical authority.[2] In his *Republic* and *Laws*—which, perhaps not coincidentally, was the first Platonic dialogue translated for Lorenzo by Ficino—Plato prescribed a top-down political structure in which wise rulers devised the best policies for the unity and prosperity of a city-state. Harking back to Plato and to George Gemistos Plethon's political theories, which were themselves inspired by the *Republic*, the humanists praised the Medici as philosopher-rulers, if not philosopher-kings, eminent in their virtue and wisdom as well as their power. Already Leonardo Bruni made this connection when he translated the Platonic *Letters* into Latin and wrote to Cosimo to urge that he heed the advice given in them. Ficino, for one, thought the message had gotten through. He wrote, "Plato showed me the concept of the virtues but once; Cosimo put them into practice every day." And Poliziano, in the preface of his translation of Plato's *Charmides*, said to Lorenzo, "you alone of the whole universe of men both rule the republic wisely and recall philosophy home from long exile."[3]

None of which is to say that Florence had a monopoly on humanism, or on the study of Plato. Francesco Filelfo, another translator of Plato, was a staunch opponent of the Medici and wound up as a courtier in Milan. That city competed with Florence for philosophical laurels, which is why the Duke Giangaleazzo Visconti enticed the Greek scholar Chrysoloras to move to Milan from Florence. With the help of Uberto Decembrio, Chrysoloras produced a Latin version of Plato's *Republic* that was supposedly requested by the duke himself, and was hailed as a confirmation of the perfection of the Milanese constitution.[4] Decembrio's son, Pier Candido, was also a distinguished humanist who continued the study of Plato in Milan, producing a new version of the *Republic* and defending this text from charges of immorality, leveled because of its teachings on such subjects as the common sharing of sexual partners amongst the ruling guardian class.

But there's no gainsaying Florence's position as the main center of Platonic studies, if only because this was the city of Marsilio Ficino. His complete Latin version of the dialogues appeared in 1484, followed by commentaries on the most important dialogues in 1496. He also translated other Platonist authors, notably Plotinus, and produced a major treatise of his own called the *Platonic Theology*. Effectively Ficino was a one-man revival of late ancient Platonism. Still, he should not be given sole credit for the blossoming of this tradition in Florence. Apart from Bruni, we can recall the name of the Byzantine émigré John Argyropoulos, who lectured on Greek at the university of Florence beginning in 1458.[5] His teaching activity has been linked to the fact that, as Ficino himself put it, "the spirit of Plato flew to Italy" from Byzantium. This is certainly what Donato Acciaiuoli thought. Acciaiuoli, whom we've already met as the author of a commentary on Aristotle's *Ethics* that drew on Argyropoulos, said of him, "he has diligently opened up Plato's beliefs . . . to the great wonder of those who hear him lecture." But modern-day scholars don't agree about the depth of Argyropoulos' interest in or commitment to Platonism. He may have been more interested in presenting a more systematic approach to Aristotle.[6] Another candidate for inspiring the interest in Platonism is Cristoforo Landino, who began as a lecturer at the university of Florence at the same time as Argyropoulos. His speciality was actually rhetoric and poetry, but he discovered Platonic themes hidden in the poetry of authors from Homer to Dante. It's been remarked that he "lectured on philosophers as if they were poets and on poets as if they were philosophers."[7]

This brings us to a key question about the study of Plato at Florence. Was the approach that humanists took to the dialogues, and later works of Platonist philosophy, really all that philosophical? Or was it more a matter of rhetoric and literary appreciation? Certainly Plato's Greek was considered a paradigm of good style, as it had already been in Byzantium. Here it is usual, and to some extent helpful, to contrast Ficino to Poliziano, whose name by the way is sometimes anglicized as "Politian" (his real name was actually Angelo Ambrogini, with the name "Poliziano" alluding to his hometown of Montepulciano). This contrast should not be overdrawn. Ficino was certainly an expert philologist and frequently made textual and terminological observations on the dialogues he translated, while Poliziano certainly had philosophical interests. But it would nonetheless be fair to say that Platonist philosophy was Ficino's true calling, whereas philology was the core activity of Poliziano.

Poliziano said as much himself. Already before him Landino had explicitly distanced himself from the title of "philosopher" in his inaugural lecture, saying, "when I have so much difficulty protecting my own territory, would I dare launch a reckless assault on another's?"[8] Similarly, in a witty and entertaining treatise entitled *Lamia*, Poliziano says that he would certainly not be ashamed to call himself "philosopher" (§6), but admits that it is not a name he really merits.[9] For him it was Plato who best explained the nature of the true philosopher, a figure who thinks of death constantly and relentlessly pursues virtue. Poliziano modestly allows, "I have only barely come in contact with those disciplines that mark the philosopher's competence, and I am just about as far as can be from those morals and virtues" (§28). But this is, to use a term that has somehow crept into the English language while I wasn't looking, a case of "humble-bragging." Poliziano disclaims the status of "philosopher" so that he can claim a status he cherishes more, that of the scholar and philologist, or as he puts it in Latin, *grammaticus*.

His use of this word is apt to mislead, as it makes Poliziano sound like a mere school teacher.[10] He refers to the late ancient Christian commentator John Philoponus as an illustrious predecessor, since Philoponus was nicknamed "the grammarian." But this is rather ironic, because Philoponus' bitter enemy Simplicius had applied that label to him precisely in order to sneer at his lack of philosophical expertise. For Simplicius being a "grammarian" really did just mean teaching children their letters. For Poliziano, it is a much more exalted occupation, one that calls for expertise on philosophical texts and much more besides. A *grammaticus* should work with texts of *all* kinds. The true philologist is the scholar who, in the words of modern-day interpreter Christopher Celenza, has "the breadth of vision suitable to confront human intellectual activity in all of its variety."[11]

Poliziano's *Lamia* is a defense of this approach from certain unnamed critics, colleagues at the university of Florence. Hence the title: he compares these critics to the bloodsucking sorceress called a *lamia*, mentioned by ancient authors like Ovid. Poliziano's backbiting rivals are contemptuous of him because they think him incompetent to teach philosophy, as he has been doing at the university.[12] Poliziano's response is that his comprehensive mastery of antiquity includes an understanding of the texts he's been lecturing on. As he says, "I am an interpreter of Aristotle, not a philosopher" (§69). While he professes to admire those who do earn the title of "philosopher," it's clear why he might want to distance himself from that title. As he understands it, philosophers are not scholars immersed in texts, but rather otherworldly figures. Evoking a portrait of the philosophical life drawn by Socrates in Plato's *Theaetetus*, Poliziano speaks of the philosopher as being at a loss when it comes to the practicalities of everyday life. In particular, he is politically adrift. He doesn't know how to get to the forum and doesn't even know where the Senate meets (§52).

There's more irony here, since some contemporaries saw Poliziano himself as an out-of-touch pedant. Between him and Bartolomeo Scala, who rose to the powerful office of chancellor in Florence, there raged one of those feuds that have become one of the more familiar and, if we're honest, entertaining features of Italian humanism. Scala mocked Poliziano for his concern with such trivia as whether the first vowel in the name "Virgil" should be an *i* or an *e* (Poliziano defends "Vergil"[13]). The practically and politically minded Scala much preferred the work of earlier humanists like Salutati and Poggio.[14] And there's no denying that Poliziano was a master of philological minutiae, and also a book-lover. Quite literally, according to an admiring biography of him written in the late fifteenth century, which describes him waking up in the middle of the night and stroking the volumes on his shelves "like a wife and a girlfriend."[15]

Unlike the earlier Salutati and Poggio, he entered the field of philology when it was already highly developed, and was churning out learned commentaries on classical texts where any originality the commentator might have was typically drowned in a sea of detailed textual remarks. As Anthony Grafton has put it in a study of Poliziano, in such texts "waves of notes printed in minute type break on all sides of a small island of text," that is, the passage being commented upon.[16] Poliziano broke with this tradition by collecting his "miscellaneous" learned remarks so as to highlight his own perspicacity as a textual critic. My favorite of the details he brought to light is, inevitably, his point that the ancient Latin word *camelopardis* is the same in meaning as the fifteenth-century *girafa*, a loan-word from Arabic. That, by the way, is not the only giraffe that lopes into our story: one contemporary witness records that Lorenzo de' Medici received one as a gift from the "Sultan of Babylon."

Like that remarkable livestock shipment, bettering the achievements of the earlier humanists was going to be a tall order. Poliziano managed it nonetheless, by adopting a new, more historically grounded approach to philology. Whereas some measured all Latin prose against the standard set by Cicero, he realized that individual authors have their own styles and that good style also changes over time. For this reason he was not that impressed by the theory of literary aesthetics he found in Aristotle. Whereas Aristotle believed that all good drama should conform to certain universal rules, Poliziano was more interested in the distinctive goals pursued by each poet.[17] And his approach yielded other insights that are still applied by philologists. In particular Poliziano realized that if one manuscript can be shown to have been copied from another, then the copy adds no additional information. The same goes for historical narratives. In both cases, only *independent* evidence should be taken into account. Or, as Poliziano put it, "the testimonies of the ancients should not so much be counted up, as weighed."[18]

If Poliziano was Florence's greatest philosophically minded philologist, then Ficino was its greatest philologically minded philosopher. From early on in his career he was distancing himself from a "rhetorical" approach and adopting a "philosophical" one. As a young man he wrote to a friend, "let us speak in the manner of philosophers, despising everywhere words (*verba*) and bringing forth weighty utterances (*sententiae*)."[19] Perhaps taking a cue from Socrates in Platonic dialogues like the *Gorgias* and *Protagoras*, in which sophists are mocked for offering long speeches aiming at persuasion rather than straightforward statements aiming at truth, Ficino complained that "philology" too often meant speaking at undue, superfluous length. One reason he admired the Neoplatonist Plotinus, to whose works he devoted so much effort, was that Plotinus instead used a compressed, "extremely brief" style.[20] Which is certainly an accurate assessment. What of Plato himself, whose works are far more readable than those of Plotinus? Well, the dialogues adopt a more complex approach to philosophical discourse, in which Plato's own views are rarely put forth. In only a few dialogues, like the *Laws*, does Ficino think this happens. Usually Plato's characters represent multiple points of view, and express theories that may be only probable, being "like the truth (*verisimilia*)" rather than necessarily the truth itself.[21]

We'll look more at Ficino's work on Plato in the next chapter. For now, let's return to the context that made that work possible. Did Cosimo really arrange for the foundation of a new "Academy" in the suburbs of Florence, where Ficino could immerse himself in Platonic scholarship? In a word, no. At least that is the conclusion persuasively established by James Hankins, who in a pair of articles published back in the early 1990s poured cold water on the story of the Florentine "Academy."[22] For one thing, as Hankins nicely put it, "it is highly improbable that the aged Cosimo would have entrusted a dreamy, twenty-nine-year-old medical school dropout with a major cultural initiative." For another thing, not a single contemporary source apart from Ficino speaks of such an institution, and this despite the fact that humanists were falling over themselves to praise Cosimo for his support of humanist culture. When Poliziano and others do praise the Medici, what they especially highlight is their extravagance in paying for those luxury items that kept the humanists awake at night: books.[23]

It is this, according to Hankins, that lies behind a famous passage in which Ficino seems to say that Cosimo, having been inspired by an encounter with Gemistos Plethon, was moved to set up a so-called "Academy." As we know Plethon did attend the ecumenical church council at Florence; it was in fact a major diplomatic coup for the Medici that they got the council to be held in their city. But it seems most likely that Ficino is metaphorically explaining that Cosimo acquired a copy of Plato's dialogues based on a manuscript brought to Italy by Plethon. When Ficino goes on to say that Cosimo "conceived deep in his mind a kind of Academy" and charged Ficino himself with bringing that project to its fruition, the word "Academy" is another metaphor, referring to a Latin version of Plato's writings. Likewise, when Ficino alludes in various places to his colleagues as "academics" he seems to mean, not members of an institution based in his house at Careggi, but simply fellow humanists and students, to whom he offered private instruction in the urban setting of Florence itself.

So that's somewhat disappointing, but it should not detract from our excitement at Ficino's achievement. Even if he did consult previous translations for some dialogues, it was a staggering feat to render all of Plato, plus a wide swathe of Neoplatonism, from Greek into Latin. The right reaction is the one displayed by Giovanni Pico della Mirandola. Ficino tells us himself that Pico came to Florence at Cosimo de' Medici's behest, and arrived on the *very day* that Ficino's Plato edition was published. The two celebrated this historic literary event, and then Pico advised Ficino to get to work on Plotinus. In due course Pico too would become an intimate of the Medici. He was in attendance at the deathbed of Lorenzo, who showed his zeal for patronage to the last, supposedly remarking to Pico, "I only wish I could put off the time of my death to the day when I should have completed your library."[24]

32

FOOTNOTES TO PLATO MARSILIO FICINO

When I discussed Plato in the first book of this series, I mentioned Alfred North Whitehead's famous remark that "the European philosophical tradition consists of a series of footnotes to Plato." I can just about go along with that, with the proviso that a good footnote, like an empty pepper mill, is nothing to sneeze at. Back when I was a grad student, I found myself in the library one day and realized that I was scanning through an article more or less ignoring the main text, and reading only the footnotes. This, I thought, must be some kind of milestone in my scholarly formation, for better or worse. While making our way through the history of philosophy, we've seen time and again that glosses, commentaries, and other exegetical labors have played a central role in the history of philosophy, inside and outside the European tradition. So I mean it as the highest of compliments when I say that no one has written greater footnotes to Plato than Marsilio Ficino.

Well, not footnotes exactly, but full-blown commentaries, which Ficino produced in addition to his full Latin translation of Plato's dialogues. As we've just seen, Ficino tells us himself that this prodigious feat of scholarship was done at the behest of the Medici. He even read from his translations of Plato to Cosimo de' Medici while the latter lay on his deathbed. That was in 1464, the year after Cosimo's gift to Ficino of that villa on the outskirts of Florence. Heady stuff for a scholar who was still in his early thirties. Originally, he planned to become a doctor like his father before him, and Ficino never entirely lost his interest in medicine. Indeed, no less an authority than Paracelsus wrote in 1527 that just as Avicenna was the greatest of the "Arab" doctors, so Ficino was the greatest among the Italians.[1] But Platonism was always his central scholarly interest, from the moment he received the Plato manuscript from Cosimo, to the completion of his Latin version of the dialogues in 1468, to his translation of and commentary on Plotinus in 1492, and finally the appearance of his commentaries on Plato in 1496. The timing was good: he was among the first intellectuals whose works could be read across Europe in printed editions. His own complete works and his Latin Plato would both be printed numerous times in the coming centuries.

Ficino was also a devout Christian, who was ordained a priest in 1473 and became a canon of Florence cathedral in 1487. He saw, or claimed to see, no conflict between his devotion to the faith and his devotion to pagan Platonist texts.[2] To the contrary, he believed that Platonism was part of God's plan for humankind. In a work called *On the Christian Religion*, he argued that late ancient Platonists, pagan though they may have been, were actually influenced by Christian ideas in their interpretation of Plato. But not all Ficino's readers were persuaded of the coherence of these two traditions. Michael Allen, a leading scholar of Ficino's thought, has written that Ficino "spent his whole Neoplatonizing life on the very borders of heterodoxy."[3] He came closest to stepping over the borders when he wrote a work about the arts of extending one's lifespan. The *Three Books on Life*, which we'll discuss later (Chapter 52), got him in trouble with the church authorities because of its talk of magic and astrology. But he was acquitted by the pope in 1490. He died in 1499, at the age of 66, which is not particularly impressive as proof of skill in increasing longevity, but would probably have pleased Ficino no end for numerological reasons.

Indeed, his commentaries on Plato, deeply influenced as they are by late ancient authors, explore Pythagorean numerology, demonology, magic, and astrology as well as a wide range of philosophical themes, taken from Plato's metaphysics, epistemology, ethics, and psychology. Actually, let's not put it that way. It would be better to emphasize that Ficino saw no divide between the Pythagorean and "occult" side of Platonism and the philosophical questions that occupy the attention of most Plato scholars today. He had good reason for this attitude. When discussing demonology, he could point to Socrates' famous "divine sign" which warned him away from ill-omened actions, and he could find numerology in dialogues like Plato's *Timaeus*. In fact he saw Plato as the last of six great sages—the number six being, of course, particularly significant—on a list that also included Zoroaster, Hermes, Orpheus, Aglaophemus (no, me neither), and of course Pythagoras himself. Again we may raise our eyebrows at this ostentatiously non-Christian roster of authorities. But Ficino was at pains to connect his heroes to religion where he could, as when he argued that the wise men who attended upon Christ's birth were disciples of Zoroaster.

Among Ficino's many numerological indulgences, none is more prominent than his fivefold analysis of God and the created universe. He is here drawing on the third-century Neoplatonist Plotinus, who had set forth a hierarchical vision in which a perfectly simple first principle, the One, emanated a universal Intellect, followed by Soul and then finally the material world in which we find ourselves. Ficino's scheme is very similar, but more precise about the exact number of levels, namely five: God,

Angel, Soul, quality, and matter. The great modern-day scholar of Renaissance thought Paul Oskar Kristeller believed that Ficino went out of his way to modify Plotinus so as to put Soul right in the middle of the hierarchy.[4] This would emphasize Soul's function of mediating between the intelligible and sensible realms. Subsequently, though, the aforementioned Michael Allen discovered that Ficino was actually led to his fivefold scheme by reading late ancient commentaries on Plato's *Parmenides*. These commentaries link a succession of five arguments in that dialogue to the layers of a fivefold version of the Neoplatonic hierarchy, and Ficino simply followed suit.

Nonetheless, as Allen would readily admit, it was indeed vitally important to Ficino that Soul occupied the middle place in his scheme. Soul is "nature's center, the mean of everything in the universe . . . the knot and bond of the world." This remark is found in his *magnum opus*, a sprawling work in eighteen books that takes up no fewer than six volumes in a modern edition and translation.[5] It is called the *Platonic Theology*, a title that tellingly enough echoes that of a major work by Proclus. Where Proclus' *Platonic Theology* was a systematic attempt to show how pagan religious beliefs could be connected to Plato's dialogues, Ficino's is mostly focused on a single philosophical claim: the rational human soul is immortal. Reading through it, you might be convinced that Ficino himself must have been immortal in order to find time to devise so many arguments for this conclusion. He also finds time to lay out his fivefold scheme, talk about God's nature, and refute the views of Epicureans and Averroists, two groups that attract his particular enmity.

Though the Neoplatonic basis of Ficino's cosmic vision is evident, closer inspection reveals that he is also drawing on scholastic philosophers, especially Thomas Aquinas. From this tradition he takes, for instance, the theory of transcendentals: that goodness, unity, truth, beauty, and so on are all coextensive and appear in God in their purest form (§2.1). He also makes use of such conceptual items as the distinction between essence and existence, originally devised by Avicenna but also fundamental to Aquinas' metaphysics, and the pairing of intellect and will which had played such a central role in scholastic psychological theories. When push comes to shove, though, he usually goes with the ancient Platonists. For instance he interprets humankind's status as an "image of God" in strictly Platonic terms—we participate in His goodness, unity, and so on—rather than stressing, as medieval scholastics did, that the gift of grace is required to be a true image of God.[6]

We can observe something similar with his handling of angels, which are at the level occupied by Intellect in Plotinus.[7] Ficino has some trouble drawing this equivalence. The Neoplatonic Intellect is a single mind that eternally grasps the Platonic Forms. By contrast, of course, Christian theology recognized many angels, and when it recognized intelligible Forms at all usually made them thoughts in God's own mind. One idea, which we see in the medieval tradition as early as the ninth-century Platonist thinker Eriugena, would be to equate the Forms with the second Person of the divine Trinity. Ficino sometimes speaks this way too. But he is also attracted by the idea that God transcends intellectual life completely, which he sees as the unanimous teaching of the whole ancient Platonist tradition. That would leave angels to be the only pure minds, each of them playing a role analogous to Plotinus' single universal Intellect. Ficino's theory of angels is thus a heavily Neoplatonic updating of what we find in, say, Aquinas. But they no longer play the role of serving as "messengers" between God and the created world, which was really the main function of angels in most medieval theories about them.[8]

That dynamic, intermediary role is instead played by the human soul. It reaches down to the body, giving it life, but also reaches up to the divine, at its best even attaining something like the intellectual understanding of an angel. Like Plotinus, Ficino exhorts the soul to turn away from the body and its concerns. We achieve knowledge not so much by studying the natural world as by learning to avoid its distractions. Some philosophers, more materialist in outlook, would deny this. These would especially include the Epicureans. As we saw in Chapter 27, early on in his career Ficino was enamored of Lucretius and Epicurus, but he turned against them. In the *Platonic Theology* they appear only as opponents to be refuted, who can offer no "cogent argument" for their physicalist view of human nature. Against their down-to-earth, empiricist theory of knowledge, Ficino argues that the soul has many functions it performs without sensation (§9.5). Alongside arguments, he offers picturesque images: the materialist is like a child looking down a well, and thinking that he is the reflection he sees at the bottom (§6.2).

The intermediate position of Soul exemplifies a favorite type of argument found throughout the *Platonic Theology*. It's a line of thought taken especially from Proclus, who in turn got it from Iamblichus, who in turn was inspired by the mathematical musings of Pythagoreanism. It's appropriate that the argument came to Ficino through a chain of authorities, since it has to do precisely with the continuity of the metaphysical chain that holds the whole universe together. A basic assumption of late Neoplatonism was that, between any two extreme terms, there must be a mean term. In arithmetic this would be something like 4 as a mean between 2 and 6. In metaphysics, it demands that two dissimilar kinds of being have, in between them, another kind of being that is similar to both. We need to have an intermediary between God and Soul, because God is unchanging unity while Soul is changing plurality. (Because there are many souls, and they change by entertaining first one thought, then another.) Angels mediate between the two, since they are unchanging like God, but plural like Soul (§1.6).

The same style of reasoning can be used to establish the need for Soul (§3.1). Angels, as just mentioned, are unchanging. They never alter in their nature, nor in their activity, but just permanently engage in thought, like Plotinus' universal Intellect or for that matter the divine celestial movers recognized in Aristotle's cosmology. They are thus above Soul, which, again, does change as it thinks about one thing and then another. But Soul is also like the angels, in that it does not change in its very nature or essence. So it is a mean term between angelic nature and "quality," which is subject to change in both respects. Here we might think of the way that qualities such as heat or color become more or less intense, and disappear altogether. As a bonus, this gives Ficino one of his many arguments for Soul's immortality. It cannot be destroyed, since its immunity to destruction is precisely what makes it superior to quality, and a suitable intermediary between quality and angels. Indeed, as already mentioned Soul is the ultimate mean, the intermediary that binds together the whole universe.

Almost everything Ficino says about Soul can be related to its function as a mean term. Take for instance its relationship to body, which is just matter that has qualitative properties like color and heat. For starters, we know that the soul can't be in the body like quality is (§3.2), dispersed through the body's parts as color is spread across a surface. Instead the soul is fully present in the whole body. Yet precisely by being in a body, it is unlike an angel. So again, it plays a role halfway between the roles of angel and quality. Or consider the fact that your soul can make your body move. The reason your soul can do this is that it too is moving or changing. As we saw, this is what makes it inferior to an angel, which can cause motion too, but not by moving. The soul passes its immaterial motion on to the material body (§1.5), an idea that can be found in dialogues of Plato like the *Phaedrus,* which establishes the need for Soul as a self-moving principle that causes other motions.

Here we might turn briefly from the *Platonic Theology* to Ficino's commentary on the *Phaedrus*.[9] This dialogue features a famous image of the soul as a charioteer steering two horses, a white horse representing reason and a black one representing imagination and lower nature (at least this is Ficino's interpretation). Ficino does not see the black horse as bad, exactly, since he thinks that desire and imagination can be put to good use to orient ourselves towards God. But he follows Plato's mythic narrative by exhorting us to pull the soul upwards into the heavens, until it partakes of the unchanging, perfect intellectual contemplation enjoyed by angels. This, by the way, is something you won't find real horses doing. Beasts have no rational soul, so they lack many of the features that make Soul similar to angelic nature. For this reason animals will enjoy no afterlife. The functions of our own souls that we share with animals, like sensation and bodily desire, will likewise die along with our bodies (*Platonic Theology*, §5.13).

The human soul is, then, special in its ability to survive death. But what about birth? Plato and his late ancient followers were very clear that our souls have existed already before we came into our bodies. This was problematic from a Christian point of view. Still worse, Ficino could find the Pythagoreans and Plato saying that our souls were previously in other bodies, even the bodies of animals, and that if we live badly, we will be reborn the next time as beasts. This must have been rather embarrassing for Ficino, but to his credit he does not try to hide the Platonic teaching. He mentions the theory of reincarnation but dismisses it as merely "poetical" and not "philosophical," a kind of metaphor in which life in an animal body represents living *as if* one were a beast (§17.3). As for existence before birth, Ficino rejects this outright. If souls found themselves in a state of complete freedom they would never be willing to enter into bodies in the first place (§18.3). He has to walk a tightrope here, insisting that the soul's nature means it can never *stop* existing, even though it did *start* existing. His idea is that Soul can, so to speak, keep itself existing "under its own steam." Its capacity for self-motion is a sign of this, and as a pure form it has no potentiality for being destroyed or, for that matter, generated out of matter (§5.1). Yet Soul is not self-*causing*. Though it is not "generated" it is indeed "created," meaning that it acquires existence from some other source, namely God.[10]

You might notice that I keep going back and forth here between talking about "Soul" and "souls," leaving some unclarity as to whether I am talking about a single principle that is part of a cosmic hierarchy, or many life-giving principles that belong to individual humans. That's a habit Ficino has himself, but he came by it honestly, since Plotinus does the same thing. One option would be to identify the single, universal Soul with the animating principle of the physical cosmos, the famous "World Soul" introduced by Plato in the *Timaeus*. While Ficino is happy to accept this doctrine (e.g. at §4.1), he firmly rejects what may look at first like a similar idea, which is that there is a single *mind* shared by all humans. This, of course, is the theory of Averroes that caused so much trouble when it was received in thirteenth-century Paris, where Aquinas launched an attack on arts masters he labeled as "Averroists."[11] As we'll be seeing in detail, the Averroist theory of mind was still being debated in Renaissance Italy (Chapter 46). This explains why Ficino is so keen to criticize it, even though he also sometimes cites Averroes with approval. He devotes an entire book of the *Platonic Theology* to refuting the claim that all humans share a single mind, dutifully explaining the theory and its justification before burying it under a barrage of counterarguments and objections. He is less concerned than Aquinas had been to show that Averroes had misinterpreted Aristotle. Instead he argues on abstract philosophical grounds that there can be no universal potential intellect that receives ideas from a single actual intellect, as Averroes supposed, because mind cannot be pure potency (§15.11).

One reason Averroes thought there could be only one intellect is that intellect has no matter, and matter is needed to distinguish one thing from another. The fact that you and I are two humans is not due to the universal nature of human, which we share, but the difference between the two parcels of matter that make up our bodies. This line of thought had been difficult for Aquinas to rebut, since he too thought that matter (and more generally, potentiality) is what makes things individuals. But Ficino waves it away dismissively: God can simply create individual minds as distinct from one another (§15.12). Relatedly, Averroes supposed that intellect is just the same as whatever it thinks about. As there is only one set of universal forms, there can be only one intellect. To this Ficino replies that the human mind is not actually grasping intelligible Forms in themselves. As a good Neoplatonist he would locate the Forms higher in the system, above rational souls. What the souls get is only a kind of representation or image of the true Forms. Yet again, Ficino here exploits Soul's intermediate status, since he can say that forms in the human soul are in the middle between the transcendent intelligible Forms posited by Plato, and the immanent forms found in matter.

Ficino's forthright rejection of the Averroist theory of mind may suggest that, like George Gemistos Plethon before him, his enthusiasm for Platonism led him into antipathy towards Aristotelianism. But, actually, he does not follow Plethon's harsh criticisms of Aristotle; if anything, he is critical of Plethon himself, as we can see from a few notes he made in a text containing Plethon's works.[12] Though Ficino was willing to stand up for Plato when Aristotle criticized him explicitly, he was not out to emphasize the differences between the two great authorities. On the matter of the soul, for instance, he distanced Aristotle from Averroes by claiming that for Aristotle, the individual rational soul does survive the death of the body, something ruled out by the absurd theory of a single mind put forward by Averroes.[13] That's typical of Ficino, who had no real stake in attacking Aristotle and reserved his ire for contemporaries in Italy whose enthusiasm for Averroes led them into heretical falsehoods.

Which brings us back to the question of Ficino's own orthodoxy. We already saw that he was accused of heresy, but cleared of all charges by the papacy, and he even wound up shaping church doctrine when his arguments encouraged the adoption of the soul's immortality as official dogma in 1513. Of course, Ficino was dead by then, but if the soul really is immortal, he still had a chance to be pleased by the decision. Even in life he believed, or spoke as if he believed, that Platonism could lend support to Christian faith. The anecdote of his reading Plato to the dying Cosimo illustrates the point well. Ficino claims that his patron died straightaway, as if impatient to go to the blessed afterlife affirmed by Plato. In his summary of Plato's *Phaedo*, the dialogue that depicts the last hours and courageous death of Socrates, Ficino remarked that "Socrates' life is a kind of image of the Christian life or its shadow."[14]

Of course, he was well aware of the pagan content in some of his favorite sources, like Iamblichus and Proclus. But he did his best to rationalize these features of the texts, fulfilling his promise in the prologue of the *Platonic Theology* to set forth Platonist arguments insofar as they agree with true religion. Confronted with Proclus' particularly baroque version of the Neoplatonic system, designed to make room for the many pagan deities within the hierarchy, Ficino managed a feat of reverse-engineering, assimilating the pagan gods to his own simpler hierarchy. "Uranus," "Saturn," and "Juno" are just names for God, Angel, and Soul, while other gods are mere aspects of these principles, with Venus for example simply being the beauty of the World Soul's mind.[15] He was expert in finding ways to discover agreement between the Platonists and his faith. The *Platonic Theology* ends with two books on the subject of the bodily resurrection, which certainly looks like a specifically Christian doctrine that would be in tension with Platonism. But Ficino noted that Platonists believed that liberated souls go to the heavenly realm and take on celestial or "aetherial" bodies, a philosophical thesis tantamount to the Christian view that souls will receive perfect, risen bodies from God. It's an appropriate move for Ficino to make, given that his life's mission was nothing less than the resurrection of Platonic philosophy.

33

TRUE ROMANCE
THEORIES OF LOVE

If love had a color, what color would it be? Green, obviously. As in Al Green, the singer whose slinky, seductive, and soulful tributes to this emotion include "I'm Still in Love With You," "Love and Happiness," and the imaginatively titled "L-O-V-E (Love)." I myself would love to know how many people alive today were conceived while Al Green's music was playing in the background. Or am I making a basic mistake here, confusing love with lust? Marsilio Ficino would say so. If you asked Ficino what color love is, he would probably say "white," referring not to Maurice White, whose band Earth, Wind & Fire produced more than its share of slinky soul, but to the snowy white of purity and chastity. Ficino would approve of our using the phrase "Platonic love" for affection that does not involve sex. Indeed, he can take a good deal of the credit for associating this idea with Plato. He made a case that this author of several, often rather sexually suggestive, dialogues about the erotic life was actually encouraging us to turn away from the body, to abandon physical beauty for the sake of higher beauties and ultimately the beauty of God Himself.

Like Cardinal Bessarion before him, Ficino was concerned to rebut charges brought by critics of Plato including George Trapezuntius (see Chapter 23). Drawing on scurrilous details from ancient biographies of Plato and the erotic dialogues themselves, George had condemned Plato as a depraved lover of boys. Ficino's case for the defense began with his translations, as when he rendered the Greek word *paiderastein*, meaning "to love boys," with a less explicit Latin verb.[1] A bit of massaging in the process of translation could turn talk of erotic attraction into talk of fond friendship. But the purification of Plato was carried out especially in Ficino's commentaries. In his summary of the *Republic*, he dismisses as a harmless joke the suggestion that the best guardians of the ideal city will be rewarded by being allowed to kiss their most beautiful fellow citizens.

The highpoint of this bowdlerizing project comes in Ficino's *De amore* (*On Love*), the commentary he devoted to Plato's *Symposium*.[2] It does not take the form one would normally expect from an exegetical work. Plato's dialogue is set at a drinking party where a succession of speakers take it in turn to discuss the nature of love.

Ficino's commentary imitates this format, being written as a kind of meta-dialogue which purports to describe a restaging of the symposium held in Careggi in 1468. At this gathering, each speech in Plato's dialogue is explained by a member of Ficino's circle. Particularly prominent is Giovanni Cavalcanti, the guest of honor and exegete for several of the speeches. This could hardly be more appropriate, since Giovanni was a descendant of Guido Cavalcanti, the thirteenth century's answer to Al Green. This earlier Cavalcanti's famous poem about love, *Donna me prega*, helped invent the "sweet new style" of Italian literature.

In broad outline, the teaching of Ficino's commentary on the *Symposium* is familiar to us from his *Platonic Theology*. It assumes a metaphysical hierarchy in which an angelic world of Mind emanates forth from God, followed by the realm of souls and then the physical cosmos. Plotinus dedicated a brief treatise to the *Symposium*, which clearly informs Ficino's interpretation. Both take an allegorical approach, especially to the more mythological aspects of the dialogue. A good illustration is Ficino's handling of the famous speech given by Plato to the comic poet Aristophanes, explained here by none other than Cristoforo Landino. Again he is an apt choice for this task, since as we saw (Chapter 31) Landino was known for his philosophical readings of literary works. In the speech of Aristophanes, we are told that humans began as eight-limbed, ball-shaped creatures that were split in half by the gods. Humans as we know them are thus each half of a full organism. Erotic desire may be explained as a longing to be made whole once again. There were originally male–male, female–female, and male–female pairings, which explains what we would nowadays call sexual orientation. But Ficino has Landino suppress this frankly sexual aspect of the speech, claiming instead that the masculine, androgynous, and feminine natures represent three virtues that have gendered connotations: courage is manly, temperance womanly, and justice the balance of both (§4.5).

Not that Ficino wants to eliminate all talk of desire. To the contrary, towards the beginning of the commentary he has defined love as a desire for the beautiful (§1.4). So it turns out that explaining love requires explaining beauty; the erotic is closely connected to the aesthetic. His definition of beauty is a bit of a mouthful, but worth looking at in detail. It is "a certain vital and spiritual charm (*gratiam quandam vivacem et spiritalem*) first infused in Angel by the illuminating light of God, thence in the souls of men, the shapes of bodies, and sounds; through reason, sight, and hearing it moves our souls and delights them; in delighting them, it carries them away, and in so doing, inflames them with burning love" (§5.6). Let's start with the end of this definition, and its suggestion that love is a kind of frenzy or inflammation. Ficino—who, let's remember, was the son of a doctor and interested in medicine—adheres to the traditional notion that in some cases love is an illness.[3] The so-called "love sickness" would literally enter the bloodstream of a victim struck, or we might say "infected," by visual contact with a beautiful love object (§7.3). Since this is really just an imbalance of humors in the body, like many other sicknesses, it can be cured with physical remedies like purging the blood (§7.11). For once this literally medieval remedy would probably be quite effective. I reckon that a good round of bloodletting should calm down even the most ardent of lovers.

The idea that the erotic impulse is a kind of derangement has wider significance. Ficino counts it among several types of madness, which also include the inspiration that takes over prophets and poets.[4] When love manifests as desire for physical beauty, it is the most common and crude form of madness. Notice that in Ficino's definition of beauty, he says that even this lower kind of desire is relatively chaste. Beauty can be appreciated only by sight, hearing, and thought, powers that have more to do with the soul and less to do with the body. As for the pleasures of touch, these relate to lust, not love (§1.4, 5.2). "The lust to touch the body," he says, "is not a part of love, nor is it the desire of the lover, but rather a kind of wantonness and the derangement of a servile man" (§2.9). Forget making babies: Ficino wants us to strive for a different kind of conception. Namely the more exalted and transcendent type of erotic "madness," which means being transported by suitably exalted and transcendent beauty. This would be the intelligible beauty of the angelic realm or, even better, the beauty of God Himself.

As we saw when talking about Ficino's *Platonic Theology*, he embraced the medieval doctrine of the transcendentals, according to which being, goodness, truth, oneness, and beauty all correlate with one another. Accordingly, here in his commentary on the *Symposium* Ficino calls beauty the "blossom of goodness" (§5.1). Whatever is good is beautiful, and the more goodness something has the more beautiful it will be. Thus God is the highest of all beauties, desired by Mind or Angel as it turns back towards its principle and origin. Likewise, when soul strives to unite with Mind, it is urged on by its desire for intelligible beauty. Love also explains order and unity in the physical cosmos, employing celestial motion to govern the world of the elements (§3.2). So like Maurice White, Marsilio Ficino uses soul and love to keep Earth, Wind & Fire together. It's also true to what we find in Plotinus, though there are subtle differences. Ficino's remarks on actual sex may be the literary equivalent of a cold shower, but Ficino is warmer than Plotinus had been towards the phenomenon of physical beauty. He thinks it is a natural accompaniment of virtue in the soul, with inner beauty showing itself outwardly.[5]

All this sounds like it would in turn warm the heart of any Renaissance Platonist. So it's a surprise to see Ficino's commentary being harshly criticized by his younger colleague Giovanni Pico della Mirandola, in a commentary of his own.[6] Not on

Plato's *Symposium*, though its influence looms large in Pico's presentation. The occasion is instead a poem by another member of the Florentine Platonist circle, Girolamo Benivieni. Benivieni wove ideas from Ficino into his verses, which were a kind of philosophical updating of the aforementioned *Donna me prega*. Pico responds by setting out his own views about love, emphasizing how these differ from Ficino's. He also criticizes Ficino for failing to observe correct philosophical method. Showing off the scholastic training he received in Paris, Pico insists on the need to define one's terms at the outset of any such discussion, and charges Ficino with blundering at this early stage (§2.1). Love should in fact be defined as desire to possess what is, or merely seems to be, beautiful.

With a stroke, Pico has undermined Ficino's case for eliminating lust and sexuality from discussions of love. Even if physical attractiveness is not truly good or beautiful, its merely *seeming* beautiful is enough to spark genuinely erotic desire. Accordingly, Pico argues that even irrational animals can experience love, which causes them to mate (§3.2). Still, he would agree with Ficino that higher love, which he calls "heavenly" as opposed to "earthly," is directed towards the intelligible beauty we behold in acts of contemplation. I use the word "behold" here advisedly. In another departure from Ficino, Pico insists that beauty is perceived only by sight, not hearing (§2.9). It is analogous to harmony, an attribute of the sort of music we call "beautiful." But really beauty and harmony are different. Beauty is whatever gives delight to vision, whether this vision is that of the bodily eyes or the eye of the mind. And by the way, the beauty that is perceived by either kind of vision is not, as Ficino suggested, an effect or "blossom" produced by all goodness. It is just one of many ways for a thing to be good. Or, as Pico puts it in the scholastic terms he tends to favor, beauty is a species belonging to the genus of goodness (§2.3).

The Platonic circle's interest in these rather abstract questions of love resonates in the work of a follower of Ficino's named Francesco Cattani da Diacceto.[7] They were close enough that Ficino bequeathed a valuable manuscript of Platonic works to Cattani, who wrote a paraphrase commentary on the *Symposium* and independent treatises on beauty and love. In these writings Cattani did his best to smooth over the differences between Ficino and Pico, but where this could not be done he sided with Ficino. More famous are the echoes of the whole debate in more popular, often vernacular, literature. Here a key figure is Pietro Bembo, who wrote an entertaining dialogue about love called *Gli Asolani* (the title just means "the people from Asolo," a town north of Venice).[8] This was a great success, printed initially in 1505 and then dozens of times over the following century, in the original Italian and in French and Spanish translations. It depicts a group of aristocrats meeting over several days in a garden to debate the value of love. The group is of mixed gender, presided over by the queen of Cyprus, Caterina Cornaro, and featuring several other women, though the main speakers are three men who present contrasting ideas about love.

Bembo knows whereof he speaks here, since he engaged in several amorous affairs, one with the celebrated beauty Lucrezia Borgia. His own experience of bitter rejection and unrequited passion is palpable in the speech given by the first main character, Perottino, who emphasizes the suffering caused by love. In fact, he goes so far as to say that *all* of life's griefs result from love (22). Any pleasure taken in the brief attentions of a beloved woman will be more than outweighed by the exquisite pain of rejection later on (54). This speech recalls the laments that were a stock feature of medieval courtly love literature. But Bembo juxtaposes Perottino's bitter pessimism with something more up-to-date, as two further speakers offer more optimistic views of love that recall what we have just found in the Florentine Platonists. Next up is a character called Gismondo, who argues that all love worthy of the term is in fact good (100, 114). How could it be otherwise, since love is natural, and everything natural is good? Gismondo agrees with Ficino that love has to do only with sight, hearing, and reason, not the other faculties of soul (124–5, 158), and that love can be a spur to virtue. Then the tone is raised even further. The last speaker, Lavinello, relates an encounter he has had with a pious hermit. Evoking the most transcendent aspects of Ficino's theory, this character of the hermit rejects the value of all earthly love. It is irrational to desire anything that will change and pass away, so we should direct our love only to God (182).

As with other Renaissance dialogues we've considered, it is not easy to extract Bembo's own position from this work. The diversity of views is, surely, part of the point. A less nuanced version of Pietro Bembo appears in Castiglione's *Book of the Courtier*.[9] This much longer dialogue, which I've already mentioned several times, features Bembo as a character discoursing on the topic of love. The fictional Bembo most resembles the second speaker of *Gli Asolani*, as he speaks very much in favor of love, including erotic love for women. The background of Ficino's ideas is evident here too, though as one modern interpreter has put it, Castiglione's version of Bembo is "interested in philosophy only as a source of literary and conversational conceits" and is concerned especially with "the lowest rung of the ladder of love, where he engages in sensual love in its 'excusable' courtly form."[10]

For this Bembo in Castiglione's dialogue, love is a "longing to possess beauty" (410), which we initially encounter not through touch but through the sight of lovely bodies. Like Ficino, Bembo understands physical beauty to be the outward sign of a virtuous soul (417), just as the beauty we see elsewhere in the cosmos is the manifestation of the good order given by God to the universe. Only "idiotic" people who are content to remain at the level of beasts are satisfied with bodies, though. His speech echoes a famous passage in Plato's *Symposium*, in which the female philosopher Diotima describes moving one's gaze from individual beautiful bodies step by step, up to the Form of Beauty itself, an itinerary sometimes called the "ladder of love." Carried away on a flight of rhetoric, the character of Bembo waxes enthusiastic about the ascent to the beauty of the intellectual realm (428–30), until he is brought crashing back to earth by a tug on his sleeve and teasing comment from one of the female characters. Evidently, Castiglione thinks it is worth including the Platonic tradition of erotic philosophy in his *Book of the Courtier*, but he also pokes fun at it. In a typical move, he furthermore pits Bembo against a more hedonistic character who thinks it is absurd to talk of possessing beauty without pursuing attractive bodies, and who identifies the climax of the erotic life as begetting children with a beautiful woman (423).

So far, women have featured in this story only as beautiful love objects, apart from the relatively minor characters who populate the dialogues written by Bembo and Castiglione. But that changes with one final work I want to discuss, the *Dialogue on the Infinity of Love* published in 1547 by Tullia d'Aragona.[11] Like Pietro Bembo, d'Aragona enjoyed the honor of being both the author of such a dialogue and a character in one, as she was the model for one of the speakers in Sperone Speroni's *Dialogue on Love*, from 1535. There she is presented as a down-to-earth critic of the kind of spiritual approach to love espoused by Ficino, Pico, and Bembo. This no doubt seemed a natural bit of typecasting to Speroni, because d'Aragona was a renowned courtesan. But in her own *Dialogue*, she distances herself from what she calls "vulgar" love, echoing those more high-minded predecessors by associating sexuality with animals and true, "honest" love with rationality (90).

On the other hand, d'Aragona is not just reiterating Ficino's Platonist position. Her dialogue is different from the ones I've been discussing, not least in that it really is a dialogue, not just a series of speeches. Our two characters are Tullia d'Aragona herself and Benedetto Varchi, a prominent intellectual and philosopher of mid-sixteenth-century Florence. The two tease and flirt as they debate with one another, both exploring and embodying the idea of honest love as a refined and rational, but still pleasant pursuit. Thus at one stage, d'Aragona agrees to concede a point made by Varchi but only "out of love" for him (66), and there is much lighthearted jousting about points of logic and grammar as the two try to clarify the thesis that has been proposed for debate. The *Dialogue* is at once a gentle parody of the scholastic "disputed question," and a response to the Platonist treatments of love.

As for the question being disputed, this also distinguishes Tullia d'Aragona's treatise from other works on love. Though she does, like Ficino, exonerate Socrates and Plato from pederasty, insisting that their sole interest was inducing virtue in young men (96), this *Dialogue* is not in any sense a commentary on the *Symposium*. Rather, the characters of d'Aragona and Varchi seek to answer the question "whether it is possible to love within limits?" Again showing a gently satirical approach to scholasticism, Varchi gets downright obsessed with the wording of the question, for instance by pressing d'Aragona to admit that the noun "love" and verb "to love" mean the same thing, despite their different linguistic functions, because they refer to a single essence (60–1, 67). This distantly recalls ideas found in medieval speculative grammar.[12] Once the terms have been clarified, Varchi absurdly declares that he has thereby already answered the question, forcing d'Aragona to point out that he has done no such thing (71). Yet it does not seem that d'Aragona is entirely dismissive of scholastic philosophy, because the ultimate solution to the dialogue's central question turns on a distinction beloved of the schoolmen, originally drawn by Aristotle. Love is boundless, but not *actually* infinite. Its infinity is "potential," in that the lover's desire for the beloved can never end, is never satisfied (84). She compares this to the way that numbers can be counted up without end, or time can pass indefinitely, but without ever reaching an actually infinite number, or actually infinitely long period of time.

As Tullia d'Aragona says openly in her own *Dialogue*, she has taken inspiration from yet another work on the erotic, the *Dialogues of Love* written by Judah Abravanel, also known as Leone Ebreo. D'Aragona prefers him to other authors who had tackled the topic, including Ficino (91–2). This despite the fact that, as she also notes, he was Jewish: she has the character of Varchi say he is willing to "excuse" this though not "approve" of it. This openness towards Jewish intellectuals is something she shared with another of the protagonists of this chapter, Pico della Mirandola. And she was not alone. Like *Gli Asolani*, Ebreo's *Dialogues* were very popular, seeing about twenty-five editions in the sixteenth century. This is just one particularly striking instance of the way that Jewish philosophers, despite their position as outsiders to the Christian culture of the Italian Renaissance, managed to contribute to that culture.

34

AS FAR AS EAST FROM WEST JEWISH PHILOSOPHY IN RENAISSANCE ITALY

Never underestimate the ability of philosophers to be puzzled by things that don't, at first glance, seem particularly puzzling. Take the question of desire. What could be a more familiar, everyday phenomenon? I don't know about you, but I desire things all the time: almond croissants, books about philosophy, and, well, not much else comes to mind really. Still, it seems obvious even to me what desire is. A rough working definition might be something like, "wanting something you don't have." That sounds plausible, and comes with the backing of no less an authority than Plato. In his *Symposium*, he has Socrates tell of how his instructor in matters of love, Diotima, taught him that *eros*, passionate love or desire, is constantly "in need" because it involves striving after something beautiful that one lacks (203d). Thus the gods have no love or desire for wisdom, because they are already wise. The true lover of wisdom—the philosopher—is someone who knows that wisdom is precious, but has not managed to attain it yet. Plausible or not, though, this way of thinking about desire faces some difficulties. Don't I still "desire" an almond croissant even once I have it? Don't people stay in love when they're married? (Sometimes.) To the Renaissance mind, Diotima's remark about the gods not experiencing love could also seem problematic. Christians are fond of saying that, to the contrary, God loves us and all His creation. But surely that is not a manifestation of lack or need on His part?

Nowadays philosophers don't spend that much time being puzzled by love, or at least, not as part of their job they don't. But as we've just seen, ancient and Renaissance Platonists were fascinated by it, with everyone from Plotinus to Ficino writing treatises on the topic. Among these authors, the one who offers the most interesting reflections on our particular puzzle is Leone Ebreo. In his three *Dialogues on Love*, two characters named "Philo" and "Sophia" (see what he did there?) are depicted working through a number of problems about love.[1] How does it relate to desire more generally? What role does love play in human life and the universe?

What is its origin? Throughout their conversations, the two keep returning to this question of whether love implies neediness.

Ebreo makes the nice point that, even if desire is concerned with what is lacking, it doesn't aim at what has no being at all, because to desire something you must at least consider it as having *possible* being (32). One idea might be to distinguish love from this sort of desire for things one could, but does not, possess. Think again of wisdom. The wise person loves it, but already has it and so doesn't need to desire it. This would also be a difference between more exalted and permanent goods like virtue and wisdom, and on the other hand earthly goods. The former can be attained and then possessed indefinitely, without change. The latter perish as they are enjoyed, or if they don't, then their goodness seems to vanish as desire is satisfied (42, 65). Think of how I have to consume that almond croissant in order to satisfy my hunger for it, and how if it is too big, I will have no desire for the part that's too much for me to eat (for me, an admittedly hypothetical scenario).

Upon further reflection, the characters decide that love might be a special kind of desire that is directed towards those higher goods and not carnal satisfactions (202, 327). Even if you already have what you love, you also want to *keep* having it into the future. The mere fact of being subject to the passage of time means that, in a sense, you even lack what you already possess. You can never have what you really want, which is to possess what you love forever (206). What about spiritual beings, who might seem to be able to achieve this? Can they experience love and desire too? Yes. Souls and angels strive towards ever greater union with and understanding of God, and since God is infinite this desire will never be completely satisfied (51, 154, 161). As for God Himself, of course He never experiences lack or deficiency in Himself. But He wants perfection for the things He creates. Since there is, to put it mildly, always room for improvement in the created world there will always be something for Him to desire. This is what we mean when we say that God loves His creation (208, 226).

One brilliant feature of Leone Ebreo's *Dialogues*, and no doubt one reason they were so popular, is that they dramatize the topic of erotic desire as well as thematizing it. The male character Philo is usually the one advancing arguments and theories, which are criticized and resisted by the female character Sophia. She also resists his more literal advances. Especially at the end of the dialogues, we get passages in which Philo pleads with Sophia to give in to his love for her, using the full humanist arsenal of rhetoric and philosophy to talk her into having an affair with him. In each case she rebuffs his entreaties. As she complains at one point, "what I want from you is the theory of love, and what you want from me is its practice" (196). This feature of the text makes it more entertaining while also allowing Ebreo to contrast two approaches to love. Whereas Sophia tends to argue that true love is for intellectual and eternal goods, Philo insists that bodily pleasure has a place in the best life and can be an expression of true love.[2] Like Pietro Bembo before him, Ebreo exploits the dialogue form to juxtapose contrasting ideas about love and, indirectly, human nature. Are we ultimately just intellectual souls, as classical Neoplatonism and Ficino would have it? Or should our theory of love pay due regard to our complex nature as embodied beings?

Ebreo's fusion of literary panache and philosophical content is still winning him admiration down to the present day. One scholar has gone so far as to say, "a Neoplatonist in his soul, and a humanist in his style, Leone succeeded in making philosophical ideas understandable, a task at which Ficino had failed entirely."[3] But there was something else he added to the humanist tradition of Platonist reflection on love: the perspective of a different religious faith. The "Ebreo" part of his adopted Italian name signifies that he was a "Hebrew"; that is, Jewish. As for his original name, it was Judah Abravanel. That sound you hear is the second shoe dropping, as we finally meet the son of Isaac Abravanel, who was covered way back in the third volume of this book series.[4] As a gentle reminder: Judah's father Isaac hailed from Portugal and Spain, and worked for the Christian king and queen Ferdinand and Isabella. He moved to Italy with his family after the expulsion of Jews from Spain in 1492, which is how Judah, a.k.a. Leone Ebreo, wound up in Naples working as a doctor. He would subsequently live in Genoa, Naples again, then Venice, and possibly Rome, where his *Dialogues* were published in 1535, only after his death.

This life story is not atypical. As Robert Bonfil wrote in his history of Italian Judaism in this period, "Jews settled where they were given permission to settle and where life was not rendered unbearable by Christian hostility."[5] Often they came to Italy to escape persecution, as with the aforementioned exile from Spain and an earlier expulsion from France in 1394, or to escape pogroms launched against them in Germany. Once in Italy, they faced further persecution. Numerous cities banned Jews entirely, with Florence for example accepting them only in 1427. Those cities that did allow them hardly put out the welcome wagon. Jews might be forced to wear identifying insignia, like yellow patches of fabric or colored hats, and subjected to enforced teaching intended to bring about their conversion. Pope Paul IV, whose policies were particularly malignant, said that "the Church tolerates the Jews in order that they may bear witness to the truth of the Christian faith."[6] But beginning with Venice in 1516, Italian cities started designating certain areas as ghettos for the Jewish community, implicitly shifting from a policy of conversion to one of segregation.

The social pressure brought to bear by the majority culture could affect even wealthy Jews, and make itself felt in their intellectual pursuits. To see this we can cheat a little bit by going past the usual chronological range covered in this volume, and considering Sara Copia Sulam.[7] She was born in the Venice ghetto in 1590, but to a prosperous family who had her well educated in subjects including philosophy and theology. She would go on to host an intellectual salon at her home, frequented by other philosophers like Leone Modena and her tutor Numidio Paluzzi. As with the female humanists discussed earlier (Chapter 29), we have extensive correspondence from her and sent to her, often from Christian men trying to cajole her into converting. This is also the subtext for the most philosophical exchange involving Sulam. A Christian named Baldassare Bonifaccio, who was a regular at her salon and also archdeacon of Treviso, sent her a letter describing how humans lost their immortality through original sin (271). The point, of course, was to encourage her to become a Christian, so as to cleanse herself of the stain of this sin.

It was with some consternation that Bonifaccio instead received a set of philosophical musings from Sulam, in which she pointed out that material bodies are intrinsically subject to corruption, and so cannot be made eternal through the influence of a soul, no matter how sinless. The question of immortality must concern particular human essences, since otherwise we would be eternal only at the level of species and not as individuals (275–6). The human species would, as Sulam says with an evident allusion to a famous saying of Heraclitus, be like a river, which remains the same river even though it is always made up of different waters. Bonifaccio should have been pleased to receive this sophisticated philosophical reply. He claimed to have no objection to being instructed by a woman in such matters, since "in intellects there is no distinction of sexes" (283). Nonetheless, he reacted by denouncing Sulam for putting the soul's indestructability in question. He confronted her with proofs of immortality drawn from the Jewish Bible and Plato (286), a pretty formidable combination. In response Sulam protested that she was far from denying this thesis, since immortality is affirmed by Jews just as much as Christians (317). She simply wanted to have a good philosophical rationale for her already firm belief. But, she complained, Bonifaccio was too busy hectoring her about her religion to provide that.

This debate shows how difficult it was for Christian and Jewish intellectuals to exchange ideas in the Renaissance. Yet, just as had happened earlier in the Islamic world, we see Jewish authors in Italy adopting the concerns and ideas of the wider intellectual culture, while also exploring problems and traditions unique to their faith. For an example we can return to Leone Ebreo. His dialogues are written in the Italian vernacular, though some wonder whether this is a translation from an original Hebrew version.[8] And in terms of content, he is powerfully influenced by Christian thinkers like Ficino and Pico. On the other hand, the way he responds to this influence displays his different religious commitments. He has the characters in his *Dialogues* affirm that God loves Himself, as well as His creation, and admit that this self-love involves three elements: the lover, the beloved, and the love itself, all of which are identical with God. But where Christian authors saw this as a way to understand the holy Trinity, Ebreo cautions us that God only *seems* to be threefold, because of "the inferiority and impotency of the intellect" (244). Far from being an exposition of Trinitarian doctrine, this looks more like an explanation of how the Christians were confused into putting forth that doctrine.

Nor was humanist Platonism the only Christian philosophical tradition co-opted by Jews. There was also scholastic Aristotelianism. That style of philosophy does not really show itself in Ebreo's *Dialogues*, though a poetic lament he wrote over his son, who was taken from him and forcibly converted, seems to boast of his ability to outdo the schoolmen: "I visited their schools of learning and there were none who could engage with me. I vanquished all who rose in argument against me, and forced my opponents to surrender, putting them to shame... I have a soul which is higher and more splendid than the souls of my worthless contemporaries."[9] Italian Jews recognized the advantages of scholastic education. The rabbis produced voluminous legal scholarship reminiscent of what the jurists of the universities were churning out, and even the design of rabbinical diplomas was similar to that used by the Christian schools.[10] The ambition, only partially successful in the face of Christian obstruction and repression, was to set up a parallel system of legal and spiritual authority, with rabbis as community leaders.

The most intense engagement with scholasticism came with thinkers who carried on the long-standing tradition of Jews reading Aristotle and his greatest medieval commentator, Averroes. After Averroes' works were rendered into Hebrew they were avidly read by Jewish philosophers of the thirteenth and fourteenth centuries like Ibn Falaquera and Gersonides, who went so far as to write commentaries on Averroes' commentaries.[11] Now fifteenth-century Italy offered a new context for Jewish Aristotelianism. The central figure here was Elijah Del Medigo, who originally hailed from Crete and came to northern Italy in 1480. Before returning to Crete ten years later, he would write treatises inspired by or commenting on Averroes' philosophy, and also translate Averroes from the Hebrew versions into Latin. Del Medigo thus contributed to the upsurge of interest in Averroes towards the end of the fifteenth century that we associate especially with Padua (see further Chapter 46).[12]

Averroes was an author who posed particular challenges for reconciling philosophical teaching with religious orthodoxy. Alongside his clear affirmation of the eternity of the world, Averroes' most problematic teaching had to do with the human mind. His *Long Commentary on the De anima* reaches the surprising conclusion that all of humanity shares only one mind. We've already seen Ficino pouring scorn on this doctrine. Del Medigo treats it much more respectfully, seeing clearly how difficult it is to explain the diversity of minds within an Aristotelian framework. It was usually held that substances are differentiated from one another by the matter from which they are made, but human minds are immaterial. So what distinguishes them? Del Medigo was aware of contemporaries who followed Aquinas in making the human rational soul a form that can survive as an individual, even in the absence of matter, but he found that account rationally untenable. This despite his admission that such a view would fit better with Jewish belief, saying, "the Torah might encourage one to believe and accept this view, but scientific investigation does not."[13]

That remark fits well with a work by Del Medigo, written in Hebrew, called *Examination of Religion* (*Beḥinat ha-dat*).[14] It tackles head on the question of how philosophy relates to revealed religion, taking its cue from the rationalism of Maimonides and also Averroes' *Decisive Treatise*. Like Averroes, Del Medigo believes that philosophical investigation is encouraged and even required for those capable of it, as it increases one's understanding of God and the world He has made. But he also thinks that there are some truths found in scripture that human reason cannot discover. This attitude is more reminiscent of those Parisian arts masters of the thirteenth century described as "Latin Averroists." Averroes himself thought that philosophy establishes the same truths as religion, but on the basis of rational demonstration. For the arts masters and now for Del Medigo, by contrast, scripture goes beyond the scope of reason and, in some sense, trumps it. As an expert scholar of Aristotle's and Averroes' philosophy, Del Medigo is willing and able to expound their arguments, but that doesn't mean he needs to agree with them in the end. So in one treatise, after explaining Averroes' rationale for the unicity of the intellect, he says, "let none of my co-religionists think that the opinion which I firmly believe is this one. For my belief is truly the belief of the Jews."[15]

Ironically, one reason Del Medigo opposed Averroes on this point is that it reminded him *too much* of something he could find in the Jewish tradition. The influx of Jews from the Iberian peninsula brought the mystical tradition known as Kabbalah to Italian soil. As a hard-nosed rationalist, Del Medigo might be expected to find Kabbalah distasteful, but he instead argued that in its original form it was in accordance with Averroist teaching, even if it had been corrupted by more recent Kabbalistic authors who introduced Neoplatonic elements into the tradition.[16] A more hostile attitude was adopted by Leone di Vitale, commonly known by his honorific Messer ("Master") Leon. He was a well-rounded Renaissance thinker, who on the one hand commented on Averroes, drawing here on Christian scholastic authors like Walter Burley and Paul of Venice, and on the other hand produced a compendium of rhetoric using heroes of the humanist pantheon like Quintilian and Cicero. His succulently titled *Book of the Honeycomb's Flow* aims to demonstrate the rhetorical excellence of the Bible. But his versatile mind had no place for Kabbalah. He forbade other Jews to study Kabbalistic authors, who, he said, "grope forward through the darkness of their misunderstanding of the purposes of the founders of their doctrine, which, as far as I can see, is definitely in partial accord with the doctrine of the Platonists."[17]

In the meantime, the mystics were also pondering their own standing relative to the philosophers, and declaring themselves the winners. One Kabbalist from Tuscany, by the name of Elijah Ḥayyim Genazzano, attacked a range of rationalists including Gersonides and Isaac Abravanel, the aforementioned father of Leone Ebreo.[18] For Elijah the Jewish revelation is beyond rational knowledge, though he does not claim that it actually shows the deliverances of reason to be false. The fundamental "roots" of Jewish belief, such as God's oneness and incorporeality, are affirmed in common by reason and religion, and as he puts it, "the Torah will not come to cancel the intellect."[19] Still, Elijah is confident that the revelation is best understood through the methods of Kabbalah. Its symbolic and mystical system, centering on the ten letters or *sefirot* that stand for God's relationship to the created universe, provides far greater insight than philosophy. As Elijah says, the two approaches are "as far apart as east from west."

While fulminating against Isaac Abravanel, Elijah failed to notice that Isaac Abravanel and other western (that is, Spanish) Jews had already found ways to fuse Kabbalistic and rationalist methods. From works like the *Zohar*, which presents itself as a work of late ancient Judaism but was in fact composed in thirteenth-century Spain, many Jewish intellectuals in Italy took over the habits of "speculative Kabbalah."[20] An early and influential figure here was Menahem Recanati, already active in the thirteenth century. His *Commentary on the Torah*, strongly influenced by the Spanish tradition of Kabbalah, was translated into Latin and diffused widely in Italy. This strand of Jewish thought helped itself to philosophical ideas, especially Neoplatonist ones, but kept reason firmly in its place. Thus Recanati commented that philosophers did not have "the wisdom of our Torah, since they did not believe in anything except in matters that they derived by logical demonstration." About 200 years later an Italian rabbi named Isaac Mar Ḥayyim was still sounding the same note when he advised a Jewish banker friend, "you must make Kabbalah the root, and try to make reason conform to it."[21]

One way to resolve the long-running tension between philosophical and Jewish wisdom was to claim that the two are ultimately the same.[22] A diverse range of Renaissance Jews, including the aforementioned Elijah Genazzano and Messer Leon, claimed that philosophy, especially Platonism, was in fact based on older ideas traceable to biblical figures like Moses and Abraham. Legends that already circulated in Hellenistic times had Plato visiting Egypt where he met the prophet Jeremiah. This story helped encourage a syncretic style of philosophy in which Kabbalah, Platonism, and to a lesser extent Aristotelianism could all be gathered together into one harmonious body of doctrine. The most famous exponent of this style was Giovanni Pico della Mirandola. He was a Christian, but his philosophical and scholarly achievements were made possible in part by the Jewish tutors he consulted for knowledge of the Hebrew language and Kabbalistic lore. He also learned from them about Averroes.[23]

In fact, Del Medigo explained that it was Pico who prompted him to explore Averroes' theory of the mind. He told Pico, "just as Averroes explained Aristotle's words fully, I have to explain the words of Averroes, since such wisdom has almost been lost in our day."[24] For Kabbalah, Pico turned to Flavius Mithridates, who produced a massive body of translations for him in about 1486. We hear from Ficino about a debate held at Pico's home involving both Del Medigo and Mithridates. Another advisor was Yohanan Alemanno, who came to Florence in the 1450s and studied medicine and philosophy in Pisa. Alemanno showed Pico how to combine philosophy and Kabbalah. This approach earned him the disapproval of some other Jewish mystics, who complained of his making "kabbalistic matters" conform to "speculation."[25] But for Alemanno all the traditions coincided, showing the way to purify the body, then the soul, finally making it possible to seek union with God through the divine names mentioned in the Bible. Through reflection on these, he wrote, one may enjoy "such divine visions as may be emanated upon pure clear souls who are prepared to receive them."[26] And as we'll see next, Pico seems to have reckoned that his soul was pretty well prepared.

35

THE COUNT OF CONCORD
PICO DELLA MIRANDOLA

The phrase "nominative determinism" sounds like it comes from one of the more technical areas of philosophy. But actually it refers to the supposed phenomenon that your name determines your profession, or your fate more generally. Yes, there really is a meteorologist named Amy Freeze, an acoustic engineer named Ron Rumble, a police commissioner named Danielle Outlaw, and even a Russian track and field athlete who competes in the hurdles named Maria Stepanova. As if that weren't good enough, the internet will be very happy to tell you of another hurdle competition where last place went to the Bulgarian runner Vania Stambolova. People have been chuckling over this sort of thing for a long time. There was the Latin phrase *nomen est omen*: your name is a sign. It's a saying well illustrated by the fact that Pico della Mirandola held the title "Count of Concord," Concordia being a landholding of his family near Pico's home city of Mirandola.

As his contemporaries did not fail to note, this was almost too good to be true, because Pico loved to demonstrate the concord between apparently conflicting authorities. He was heir to both a family fortune and the harmonizing project of predecessors like Cardinal Bessarion, who had distanced himself from his teacher Plethon by arguing for the fundamental agreement between Plato and Aristotle. The traditional way to do this, as we saw with Bessarion, was to present a rather Platonic version of Aristotle. Pico took the opposite tack, arguing that Platonists who departed from Aristotelianism were also departing from the original teachings of Plato. This at least is the line taken in a treatise called *On Being and One*, written at the behest of Pico's friend Poliziano and against the teaching of his other friend Marsilio Ficino.[1]

Aristotle had stated that oneness and being coincide, in the sense that everything that is, has unity. Which seems plausible. After all nothing can *be* something without being *one* thing. But this contradicts a doctrine fundamental to Neoplatonism, that the first principle of unity transcends being. Plotinus equated "being" with the realm of the Platonic Forms. These reside below the One, in the transcendent Intellect which is its first effect. As we know, Ficino adopted Plotinus' system, identifying the One with the Christian God and the Intellect with "Angel." We can find this in

Ficino's great treatise the *Platonic Theology* and also in his commentaries on Plato's dialogues, which followed the late ancient Neoplatonists in asserting that for Plato too, one transcends being. For this one can point to several passages in Plato, like the statement in the *Republic* that the Good is "beyond being in majesty and power" (*Republic*, 508b).

But for Ficino the best evidence was to be found in two other dialogues of Plato, the *Sophist* and *Parmenides*. Pico's *On Being and One* offered a contrary reading of these dialogues, simply denying that anything in the *Sophist* could support an elevation of oneness over being (41), and arguing against the whole Neoplatonic tradition by insisting that the *Parmenides* has no metaphysical teaching at all. Its dense and enigmatic argumentation is not an implicit map for the cosmic hierarchy, as interpreters like Plotinus, Proclus, and Ficino would have thought, but only a kind of dialectical or logical exercise (39). The debate concerns more than Platonic exegesis and the agreement of two great authorities. The Neoplatonic interpretation was welcome to Ficino because it gave him a way to articulate the transcendence of God in philosophical terms. If God is the One, and Intellect or Angel is being, then God is beyond being, transcendent above everything that is. Against this, Pico affirms an understanding of being that recalls the position of Duns Scotus.[2] The realm of being is just everything that exists, or, as Pico nicely puts it, everything that is "outside of nothing" (42). And of course God too exists.

Having said that, Pico admits that God is a very special kind of being. To take account of this he uses terminology familiar from another thirteenth-century scholastic, Thomas Aquinas. We can say that God is *ipsum esse*, or "being itself," reserving the Latin term *ens*, which we might render as "what has being," only for created things. This is like the distinction between whiteness and white things. But of course, to say that God is the paradigmatic case of being hardly warrants the claim that He is *beyond* being, any more than whiteness is beyond white. So Pico affirms another scholastic doctrine inspired by Aristotle, which we have come to know under the name of the theory of "transcendentals": that being correlates with unity and other general properties such as truth and goodness. Ficino, by contrast, thought that all this missed the point of Plato's metaphysics. In 1494, the same year that Pico died at the tender age of 31, Ficino published his commentary on the *Sophist*.[3] Here he restated the Neoplatonic reading and, finding another way to pun on the name "Pico della Mirandola," wished that "that marvelous youth (*mirandus ille iuvenis*)" had been more careful in considering the arguments brought by Ficino before criticizing him, his teacher.

By the standards of the combative and competitive world of Renaissance scholarship, Ficino's reaction to Pico was remarkably mild, as indeed was Pico's disagreement with Ficino over the interpretation of Plato's theory of love (see Chapter 33). Perhaps, as implied by the passage just mentioned, Ficino was inclined to excuse the precocious Pico because of his age. Not everyone was so forbearing with him, though. Back in 1486, this wunderkind of the Italian Renaissance had run into trouble with the church authorities by flaunting his learning, not to mention his wealth, in stunningly provocative fashion. Only 23 at the time, Pico already fancied himself a leading intellectual, having received rigorous training in a variety of fields. He'd learned church law in Bologna, been exposed to hardcore Aristotelianism and the dangerous ideas of Averroes at Padua, and studied scholasticism in Paris. As we just saw, he also sought guidance from Jewish scholars to help him learn Hebrew and study the Kabbalah. All of which had, in Pico's opinion, prepared him to debate all comers at a months-long session of disputations at Rome. He sent invitations across Italy and offered to pay travel expenses for those who were willing to come argue with him.

What would be debated? Why, the ideas of Pico, of course, as set down in a list of 900 propositions or "theses."[4] Though actually, not all the theses are labeled as representing Pico's ideas. Some sections are labeled as setting forth his own, innovative proposals, but many items on the list are propositions ascribed to a variety of earlier authorities with whom Pico may or may not agree. He is true to his title as the "Count of Concord" insofar as he emphasizes the doctrinal harmony between three pairs of intellectual forefathers. Of course, he mentions Plato and Aristotle: "there is no natural or divine question in which [they] do not agree in meaning and substance, although in their words they seem to disagree" (§1.1). Further, he claims he can reconcile divergent teachings of Aquinas and Scotus, and of Avicenna and Averroes. But even these latter pairs are not said to agree on everything, and in fact Pico can be quite critical of authoritative figures. He elsewhere charges Aquinas with contradicting himself, never mind contradicting Scotus.[5] In general he is aware that the medieval scholastics often disagreed with one another. But he believes that, as we go further and further back in history, to the ancients like Plato and Aristotle and beyond them to the Egyptians and Hebrews, we find an ever greater degree of consensus.

So the *900 Theses* need to be read with caution, and not just as a list of things Pico asserts in his own right. Even when he clearly does endorse a given proposition, it is often unclear why he does so. The whole point, after all, is that he is prepared to discuss and where appropriate defend these claims, in the grand tradition of the scholastic disputed question.[6] In some cases we can fill in Pico's intended argument, for instance in the case of the propositions that touch on that same question of oneness and being. One thesis has it that "only God is so fully substance that in no sense is He not substance," and God's paradigmatic being is again explained using the contrast between whiteness and white things (§§2.47, 3.10, 3.23). But the theses range over so much territory, covering everything from the eucharist to the inadequacy of Aristotle's explanation of the saltiness of the sea, that we'd need Pico himself to tell us all that he had in mind.

Which, of course, was the whole idea. Unfortunately, the debate was called off after the pope had a look at the list of propositions.[7] In 1487 Pico was condemned, not for the obvious reason that he was acting like an obnoxious and arrogant rich kid, but on the yet more serious charge of heresy. Of the 900 theses, seven were condemned and six censored. Pico fled to France, but his aristocratic connections shielded him and he eventually made his way back to Italy and enjoyed the protection of the Medici. Characteristically, Pico was far from chastened and wrote a furious defense, or *Apology*. Really he should not have been surprised at the reaction of the papacy, given that some of the *900 Theses* are phrased in a deliberately provocative way. Take, for instance, the proposition, "not everything God wills through His benevolence is effective" (§4.21). It's possible to imagine even Ficino choking on his Tuscan wine while reading that in his villa. But when you read it in context, you realize Pico just wants to make the uncontentious point that, even though God wants all of us to be saved, some of us will be damned nonetheless thanks to our wicked use of free will.

In his *Apology*, Pico first excused himself on the grounds that some theses were merely being proposed for discussion, despite being false in his own opinion. But when it came to the condemned and censored theses, he slipped into a more provocative mode, arguing that at least some of these propositions were so evidently true that denying them was senseless or led to contradiction. A striking example is the proposition, "no one believes that something is true just by willing to believe it (*quia vult sic opinari*)," so that "it does not lie within the free power of humans to believe an article of faith to be true just by wanting to (*quando placet*)" (§4.18). On the face of it this looks like an all-purpose rationale for pardoning heresy. If I can't help whether or not I believe the teachings of the church, how can the church punish me for failing to do so? No surprise then that the church deemed this statement unacceptable, if not itself heretical. But Pico argued that, far from being outrageously controversial, the thesis is simply obvious. Surely we can't just believe whatever we want! Rather our beliefs respond to argument and evidence. In this case, Pico claims, the whole faculty of the university of Paris would be on his side.

An unexpected feature of the inquisition against Pico is that the church seems to have had no problem with the substantial sections of the list devoted to magic and

Kabbalistic teachings. We'll get into Pico's ideas about the "occult sciences" later (Chapter 52). For now it suffices to note that fifteenth-century intellectuals could apparently discuss magic freely as long as the discussion didn't stray into theological territory.[8] As for Kabbalah, this is nothing that should lead Pico into conflict with Christianity, at least in Pico's opinion. One of the more breathtaking theses Pico meant to defend at Rome states that a thorough grasp of the Hebrew language gives one the means to understand the ordering of the sciences and knowledge of all things (§3.55). And in the famous *Oration* he wrote as an introduction to the planned debate, he said that Kabbalah is "the heart of understanding, that is, an ineffable theology of supersubstantial deity, the fountain of wisdom, that is, an exact metaphysics of intelligible angels, and the river of knowledge, that is, a most sure philosophy of natural things" (31).[9] He added that this mystical tradition would, ironically enough, also provide Christians with the means of refuting Judaism. That promise is fulfilled in the *900 Theses*, which has a whole section of propositions showing how Christianity can be confirmed with Kabbalistic arguments.

Here Pico draws on such ideas, familiar from the Kabbalah,[10] as *ein sof*, a name signifying the transcendent infinity of God, and the *sefirot*, "letters" that have both numerical and rich symbolic meaning for the Kabbalist. A study of Pico's sources has shown that he draws on a range of authors for these notions, but above all on Menahem Recanati, whose writings Pico used as a guide to central Kabbalistic texts like the *Zohar*.[11] Pico also deployed his Hebrew learning in a biblical commentary of his own, which is called the *Heptaplus*. It explains the meaning of the passage in Genesis about the seven days of God's creation and rest. Once again, Pico turns the methods he learned from his Jewish teachers against their religion. He contends that the chronology of "ancient Hebrew learning" predicts the appearance of Christ as the Messiah (158–9), and then offers a torturous analysis of the first word of the Book of Genesis, *bereshit*, to extract from it a message about the divine Father and Son (172).[12] In short, "there is no science that assures us more of the divinity of Christ than magic and the Cabala" (*900 Theses*, §9.9).[13]

More fundamentally, Pico's *Heptaplus* is structured in keeping with a system he apparently took from his Kabbalistic sources, though it resonates well with the Platonism he shared with Ficino.[14] This system recognizes three "worlds," namely the sublunary realm where we live, the celestial realm, and then an intelligible world which may be identified with Plotinian Intellect, or Angel, or the *sefirot*. Along with this syncretic metaphysical picture, Pico offers a syncretic interpretation of Genesis, according to which the scripture simultaneously has multiple meanings. A single phrase may refer to all three worlds at once, and also to human nature, with humanity making up a kind of "fourth world." Or the phrase might also signify the interrelation of these four worlds. And so on until we have seven levels of interpretation to match the seven days (80). So to give just one example, the distinction between "heaven and earth" in the Genesis account represents the contrast between matter and form in the sublunary realm, the sun and the moon in the heavenly realm, the parts of the angelic hierarchy in the intelligible realm, soul and body in the human being, and so on. Pico is at pains to emphasize the originality of his approach to the biblical text, even though the concept of multiple valid meanings is far from innovative. That had been a fundamental tool of scriptural exegesis since the ancient church fathers. Still, this particular assignment of hermeneutical layers to levels of a cosmological, metaphysical hierarchy is Pico's invention.

The Kabbalistic elements of Pico's philosophy and theology distinguished him from older peers like Poliziano and Ficino. He knew this himself, as we can see from his own comments about his Hebrew studies, proudly boasting to Ficino of his progress and stating frankly in his commentary on Benivieni's poem about love that it was an interest in Kabbalah that primarily drew him to the study of Hebrew (not, you'll notice, an interest in the Old Testament!).[15] But we should not get so carried away by this aspect of his thought that we overlook his equally deep immersion in the scholastic tradition. We've already seen that schoolmen like Aquinas and Scotus played an important role in the *900 Theses*. It even begins with a warning that Pico has "not imitated the splendor of the Roman language, but the style of speaking of the most celebrated Parisian disputers, since this is used by almost all philosophers of our time."

Which brings us to one last important theme I want to cover from Pico's precocious and far too brief career: his views on the style in which philosophy should be done. For this we should turn to yet another famous document from his pen, a letter written to his colleague Ermolao Barbaro.[16] This humanist gave his colleagues another chance to have some fun with nominative determinism, because they could praise Barbaro's elegant Latin as a bulwark against the "barbarism" of scholastic Latin. When Barbaro himself made a complaint along these lines in a letter to Pico, he provoked an extraordinary response: a letter in which Pico adopted the persona of a "barbarian" scholastic speaking in favor of stylistically poor, but intellectually solid, writing. What could be more philosophical than disregarding the rhetorical quality of a work, and paying heed only to its content? Plato knew this full well, which is why he excluded the poets from his ideal city (398). Pico sounds like Plato critiquing the tricks of the sophists as he argues that eloquence serves only to mislead its hearers (395). Of course, Plato is not really a good representative for the "barbarian" view, since he combined sound doctrine with stylistic excellence. So

Pico draws a contrast between two other thinkers of the past. On the one hand, there is Duns Scotus, admirable for his philosophy but (as anyone who has tried to read him will agree) far from elegant in his mode of presentation. On the other hand, there is Lucretius. His poem is a wonderful example of elegant Latin poetry, yet its teachings are anathema to Pico. The sweet verse disguises the "purest poison" of godless Epicureanism (399).

The delightful irony of Pico's letter is that it is itself a model of polished Latin. This was already noted by Barbaro. He wrote back to Pico, saying, "you kill off those you defend," by demonstrating that eloquence is necessary after all (403). Surely Pico did intentionally set out to write a stylish endorsement of bad style. But still today, readers are not sure how to take that. At the end of his letter, Pico steps out of the persona he has adopted—which, by the way, was itself a standard rhetorical technique—to say that he himself does not necessarily agree with the "barbarian" whose perspective he has just been taking. Given that Pico produced the self-consciously scholastic *900 Theses*, he was clearly open to working within the "barbaric" style, but he also took great pains to learn eloquence in both poetry and prose. His ideal was, apparently, to combine the two as Plato and Cicero had done before him. But he cited Cicero himself for the idea that if forced to choose, one should prefer true teaching over fine words. As he said in another letter, "if a philosopher is eloquent, I am pleased; if he is not, I do not mind. A philosopher has one duty and aim: to unlock the truth. Whether you do so with a wooden or a golden key is of no concern to me."[17]

36

WHAT A PIECE OF WORK IS MAN MANETTI AND PICO ON HUMAN NATURE

In the 1970s, the philosopher Peter Singer brought attention to what he saw as an underappreciated form of prejudice. Just as sexism is discrimination on the basis of gender, and racism discrimination on the basis of race, there is also "speciesism," meaning discrimination against non-human animals on the basis of their species. Singer argued that we should include animals within the bounds of our moral concern. It is not being human that makes the difference, morally speaking, but being "sentient." That is why it is wrong to harm an animal without having a very good reason, whereas it's not wrong to smash a rock: rocks can't feel pain. Singer looked back to his fellow utilitarian, Jeremy Bentham. Already in the 1780s Bentham wrote in favor of benevolence towards animals, saying, "the question is not, Can they *reason*? nor, Can they *talk*? but, Can they *suffer*?" Yet speciesism also has a considerable pedigree, as Singer admitted. "The idea of a distinctive human dignity and worth," he wrote, "has a long history; it can be traced back directly to the Renaissance humanists, for instance to Pico della Mirandola's *Oration on the Dignity of Man*."[1]

That's a lot to put at the door of a speech written by a 24-year-old. But Singer is not alone in seeing Pico's *Oration* as a pivotal work in Renaissance philosophy, even in the history of European thought. It is often hailed as signaling a new conception of human nature and of humanity's place in the world, as expressing what you might call a novel philosophical anthropology. ("Anthropology" being the study of the "human," in Greek *anthropos*.) In this speech Pico gave voice to the idea that humans are radically free and irreducibly individual, each of us blessed by God with the opportunity to choose what meaning to give to our life. Perhaps only Shakespeare is more famous than Pico as a spokesman for individualism in this period of European history. But in Shakespeare the obligation to make meaningful choices, and thus to become the creator of one's own self, can seem more like a burden than a blessing. In the most famous instance the character Hamlet spends almost a whole play failing to choose. His lack of resolution is an unwillingness to trade the indeterminacy of freedom for determined action. For Pico, by contrast, it is the malleability of human nature that makes humans the greatest of all God's creatures, greater even than the angels. We humans can decide, if we have the strength, to be like the angels, and even to be like God Himself.

Given that choice is the central theme of Pico's speech, it's rather ironic that someone else chose the name by which it is known. Nowadays it is always called the *Oration on the Dignity of Man*, but this title was associated with it only after Pico's early death. In 1496, his nephew Gianfrancesco Pico della Mirandola (already discussed in Chapter 27) published it along with other works by Pico. Only in a further edition, which came out in 1504, was the now ubiquitous title applied to it. That title gives no hint of the original purpose of the oration. Pico intended it as a kind of introduction to the debate he hoped to stage for his 900 theses. After the pope called off the event, Pico expanded the speech, apparently in several stages. Among other things he added a defense of this project, which seemed to some yet another act of impertinence from this young upstart.[2]

If the posthumously added title unhelpfully obscures the immediate occasion for the oration, it does illuminate the wider context of Pico's ideas. For the "dignity of humankind" was indeed a theme of Renaissance humanism, and the very same title had been used in a much longer work by an earlier author. This was Giannozzo Manetti. As it happens, Manetti was not provoking a pope, as Pico would later do, but instead being provoked by one. The pope in question was Innocent III, who served as pontiff at the beginning of the thirteenth century. Among his writings was a treatise with the gloomy title *On the Miseries of the Human Condition*. It was to be supplemented by a companion piece on the excellence of human life, but this never appeared, leaving a gap open for more optimistic later writers. A scholar named Bartolomeo Facio attempted to fill that gap, but his offering was fairly brief and is mostly remembered for helping to inspire Manetti's longer response in defense of human life. Completed in 1452 and entitled *On Human Dignity and Excellence*, Manetti's treatise extends over four books and praises the exquisite creation that is the human being, from our cunningly designed bodies to our capacity for reasoning, wisdom, and virtue.[3] From the first page, Manetti shows his humanist credentials, starting with etymological discussion of the Hebrew and Greek words for "human" (§1.1) and moving on to extensive quotation from the classical authors Cicero and Lactantius.

These initial quotations concern the perfection of the human body, which Manetti demonstrates by referring to such things as the protection offered by our hair. Fortunately for people like me who lack such protection, he also observes that the skin around the skull is "a solid and rather attractive covering for the bone and brain" (§1.45). Manetti also draws widely on scholastic ideas, some of which go back to the Islamic world, like the theory of internal senses seated in the brain, which derives from Avicenna (§1.48). Praise of the body, focusing on the usefulness of its parts, was itself a long-standing tradition that went back to Aristotle and Galen. Like Galen, Manetti takes it that humans are superior to animals even in respect of their bodies, without even getting into the intellectual and moral powers that are unique to us (§3.24, 3.47). Our bodily preeminence is owing to the perfect balance of the blood from which we are made, when it is generated out of seed as we gestate in our mothers (§4.29).

Of course, the most valuable part of the human is not the body but the soul. Surprisingly to the modern reader—it might have surprised Marsilio Ficino too—Manetti singles out Aristotle, not Plato, as the leading ancient protagonist of the soul's immortality (§2.10). He concedes that Plato too seems to have taught this doctrine, though in a rather "obscure" way and not with straightforward arguments (§2.6). Immortality makes us different from other animals, as we can see from the natural desire we all feel for eternal happiness. This itself proves that we are indeed immortal, since desires that are natural to a species cannot be without purpose (§2.22). Manetti relies throughout on Aristotle's picture of living beings as always having an orientation towards certain ends or purposes, which their bodies and souls are apt to pursue. Christian sources are brought into play too, mostly just to confirm the ideas that can be gleaned from pagan sources (as at §2.28 and 2.36). But he does think that Christianity has supplanted pagan notions of our ultimate end, which is properly understood to be worship and knowledge of God (§3.54).

So it is as both a humanist and a Christian that Manetti dares to take exception with Pope Innocent's more pessimistic assessment of the human condition. He is much more polite about this than, say, Lorenzo Valla was when discussing the donation of Constantine.[4] But this is still a firm rejection of papal opinion, and for good measure the opinions of pagan authors like Seneca, who consoled those grieving over the death of loved ones by suggesting, effectively, that earthly life is not so great anyway (§4.3). Of course, Manetti acknowledges that there is bodily infirmity, disease, and death, but asserts that these are not inherent to human nature. They result from original sin (§4.20). Besides, there is much pleasure in life, and not only suffering, even in old age when increasing debilitation is offset by certain pleasures (§4.56). Just think how baldness allows us to show off the nice skin on our scalps! Above all, we should not forget that in the future, the blessed among us will be resurrected in perfect bodies, which will be only 30 years old and will not suffer from any of the defects that come with our current, fallen nature (§4.59).

It seems then that Manetti's lengthy, elegant treatise had explored the theme of human dignity pretty thoroughly. But Pico's oration has plenty to add.[5] It is a work of brash confidence, in which the young scholar seems to be generalizing from his own genius and creative originality to assert the power of all humans to create themselves as they see fit. He boasts of the "new philosophy" he plans to defend in the envisioned disputation at Rome (25), even though his project in the *Oration* has clear precedents. Apart from Manetti, whose treatise he may have known, no less a theological authority than Peter Lombard—whose *Sentences* was the fundamental textbook of medieval theology—had already proclaimed the superiority of humans over angels.[6] Another intriguing potential influence on Pico is Yohanan Alemanno, one of the Jewish scholars who taught him the ways of Kabbalah.[7] In his own writings Alemanno had argued that humans have no one fixed nature. Rather they are intermediate beings, "the last of the natural creatures and the first among the intellectual creatures." This is because humans have both a bodily and intellectual aspect. For Alemanno, the point of this was to embrace both aspects by using Kabbalah. Like many a philosopher, he believed that we need to perfect our minds through contemplation, but he also thought that the ritual actions undertaken in Kabbalah lead us closer to God.

This is similar to, but not quite the same as, the point Pico makes in a famous passage towards the beginning of his *Oration*. He agrees with Alemanno that humans are the intermediary or "bond" of God's creation, straddling the material and immaterial worlds (3). Alluding to both Plato's *Timaeus* and the Book of Genesis, Pico explains that, by the time God created humans, He had already made the earth and whatever is upon it, and the heavens with their intellects and eternal souls. Having filled the lower and higher realms in this fashion, in a sense there was nothing else left for God to make. The purpose of creating humans was that there might be someone to "consider the reason for such a work, to love its beauty, and admire its magnificence." Since all the natures had already been created in the earthly and celestial realms, God told humankind (in the person of Adam), "you have neither particular seat or special aspect (*nec certam sedem nec propriam faciem*)." It is open to you, "by your choice (*arbitrio*), in whose hands I have placed you, to fix the limits of nature for yourself" (4–5). It is this that makes us "the most happy of animals" and the one most worthy of wonder.

But, as Hamlet knew, momentous choices bring dangers with them. Since we partake of the lower natures found in beasts and even plants, we can embrace these natures, thus failing to take advantage of our literally God-given opportunity. This is the choice made by hedonists, who indulge the faculties of nutrition and reproduction found also in plants. Similarly, those who love things enjoyed by the senses are acting like non-human animals. In a striking example of Pico's eclectic cultural tastes, he even cites "Muhammad," in other words the Quran, for the idea that those who turn away from the divine law become like beasts. We should instead identify with the higher natures within us, becoming no longer earthly nor even heavenly, but a "light that is even more noble, clothed with human flesh" (6). This means contemplating God, as the highest angels do, and ultimately even achieving union with the divine so as to surpass angelic nature (8).

With all this Pico is clearly responding to the revival of Platonism led by his older friend and colleague Marsilio Ficino.[8] We saw Ficino making the point that the human is the "bond of the world" and a fusion of all other natures. He puts the point nicely in his commentary on the *Timaeus*, the dialogue of Plato also name checked in Pico's *Oration*: "it behooves [the human] to be the animal which would worship those above, being the mean between the animals on high which are immortal in body as in soul, and the animals whose soul and body have fallen. That is, humans are mortal through the body but immortal through the soul." On this point, Ficino and Pico are in good company. Since antiquity and throughout the middle ages, philosophers had been insisting that the human is a "microcosm," which literally means a "small world." You can find this in all medieval cultures, with particularly detailed versions in such thinkers as Hildegard of Bingen and the tenth-century group of philosophers in Iraq who called themselves the "Brethren of Purity."[9] They liked the idea so much that they flipped it around, saying that just as the human is a small cosmos, "the cosmos is a great human."

Yet Pico is not just saying in his *Oration* that humans contain all of creation, and even a spark of divinity, within them, combining the familiar ideas that the human is a microcosm and is created in the image of God. He is adding the crucial further point that we can *choose* which of the many natures given to us is our true identity. This too, I think, was simply a matter of drawing out a long-standing idea found in the Platonic tradition. Especially in Plotinus, whose works Ficino had just made available in Latin, we have the idea that the soul exists "on the horizon" of the physical and intelligible realms.[10] In Plotinus' *Enneads*, no less than in Pico's *Oration*, it is argued that the true nature of the soul resides in a power to identify with one of those two realms.[11] In the treatise that was placed at the head of the *Enneads* by Plotinus' student and editor Porphyry, Plotinus asks who "we" are and answers that "we" are neither an animal body nor an angelic or divine mind. Rather each of "us" is a subject endowed with free choice, through which we are capable of choosing to identify with *either* the body *or* the mind. This is, of course, to take nothing away from the significance or ingenuity of Pico's speech. It is to recognize the nature of his achievement, which was to retrieve an idea from the older Platonic tradition and update it for Pico's Christian, humanist audience.

Similarly, Peter Singer was giving Pico more than his fair share of credit, or blame, when he named him and the other humanists as pioneers of speciesism. The superiority of the human to the beast was a well-worn trope of ancient and medieval philosophy, grounded in the Aristotelian and Stoic conviction that reason is distinctive of humankind. So the humanists were actually being fairly traditional when they encouraged us to turn away from our animal natures. It's advice that appears pervasively in the period. Pico himself wrote, in his commentary on Benivieni's poem about love, that our desire for sexual gratification is something we share in common with beasts, whereas rationally we know that such bodily pleasure is in fact "destructive of beauty."[12] Pietro Bembo and Tullia d'Aragona likewise associated vulgar love with animal passion and "honest love" with reason.[13]

Ficino too sees animals as being, in general, helplessly prey to their desires. He writes in his *Platonic Theology* that our ability to resist temptation is something that distinguishes us from beasts.[14] (For the record, this is not true: experimenters have shown that hungry animals can postpone the enjoyment of food if they have good reason to do so.) Again, it is rationality that makes the supposed difference, which is why Bembo thinks that, just as it is animalistic to be sexually licentious, so one turns one's back on human nature by giving in to skepticism. He writes that skeptics "are mistaken to consider themselves humans rather than animals by birth, for in rejecting the faculty which distinguishes us from animals, they deprive the mind of its purpose and strip their lives of our chief ornament."[15]

Yet the Italian Renaissance also saw challenges to this age-old contrast between rational humans and irrational animals. You might remember Lorenzo Valla mounting such a challenge in his attack on scholasticism, and his lead was followed by a number of later thinkers.[16] Writing in 1603, the anatomist Girolamo Fabrici D'Acquapendente went so far as to suggest that animals are capable of rudimentary language (for more on him see Chapter 49). At about the same time another man of the same given name, Girolamo Giovannini, was even more impressed by the linguistic capacities of beasts. For Giovannini, the only reason we say non-human animals are "irrational" is out of courtesy to the classical definition of humans as "rational animals." Writing around 1530, Sperone Speroni similarly said that since beasts can use language, it is only properly *intellectual* thinking that distinguishes humankind.[17] Another late Renaissance thinker who we'll be coming to in due course (Chapters 42, 51), Tommaso Campanella, thought that animals could perform "syllogisms," as when a dog hunting another animal infers which way to go from the smell of its quarry (he here repeats an example already found in ancient

Stoicism). He also offered the nice example of a dog he had met who lived with a Polish family, and could understand Polish but not Italian.

Such discussions suggest that if anything, this was a period where speciesism was not being invented, but being put in question as rarely before. In one breath, philosophers would encourage us to turn away from our animal nature, then in the next breath, they might emphasize the continuity between animal and human spheres. Not all animals are the same, after all. Some seem barely more advanced than plants, whereas others are apparently capable of thinking, emotion, and imagination; they can do practically everything that we can. Thus Renaissance philosophers envisioned a kind of hierarchy in which the more sophisticated beasts are those that are more like humans. This is recognized in Pico's *Oration*, which sees human nature as containing all that is in animal nature. Elsewhere, in his biblical commentary the *Heptaplus*, he suggests that it is especially the domestic animals that come close to being like humans, because they can learn from training. The same sort of point was made by another philosopher we will be discussing in depth later on (Chapter 46), Agostino Nifo. He wrote that "the human is the canon and measure of all animals: for this reason one animal is more perfect than another, because it resembles more closely man, such as pygmies and apes; and for this reason one animal is of lesser worth than another, because it is far removed from men, such as an oyster or sea sponge."[18] Here Nifo is still thoroughly committed to speciesism, but not because he sees a radical gulf between human and animal. To the contrary, it is because he sees humans as the *best* animal.

37

BONFIRE OF THE VANITIES SAVONAROLA

As the people who have the dubious pleasure of living or working with me can attest, my favorite philosopher is usually whichever one I am currently reading and writing about. Over the last months I have seized on the smallest excuse to wax enthusiastic about Ficino and Pico, or the contributions of women to Italian humanism. But I have to admit that I'm finding it difficult to warm to the protagonist of this chapter, Girolamo Savonarola. Remember the various measures taken to persecute Jews in Renaissance Italy? Savonarola was a devout anti-Semite, and would certainly have supported such policies, except insofar as he found them too lenient. He would surely have disapproved of those women humanists. His remarks on women are typically in the mode of patronizing spiritual guidance offered to the weaker sex, and he was scornful of women who reported having the sort of prophetic visions he claimed for himself. Nonetheless a good number of women rallied to his cause and stuck by it even after his death; ironically they included a number of mystical thinkers.[1] Savonarola reserved special ire for homosexuality, demanding that it be punished with violent death: "I'd like to see you build a nice fire of these sodomites in the piazza, two or three, male and female, because there are also women who practice that damnable vice. I say offer [them as] a sacrifice to God" (156).[2] When Florence was faced by a famine, he told the people they deserved it because they were so sinful. And famously, he oversaw the "bonfire of the vanities," in which the tools of gambling and other frivolous pastimes, women's wigs and clothing, musical instruments, artworks, and books went up in flames. Then again, he did also put an end to the tradition of youngsters throwing rocks at people to celebrate Carnival, which led to several deaths each year (209). Even a stopped clock is right twice a day.

So why am I bothering you with a discussion of this horrible man?[3] Well, he was a central figure in a pivotal period of Florentine history, and his story is bound up with those of leading philosophers. Notably he received both admiration and material support from Pico della Mirandola.[4] Girolamo Benivieni, author of that poem on love that received a commentary from Pico, was also devoted to

Savonarola. Ficino too attended his sermons, in what I imagine to be horrified fascination. Ficino held his tongue until Savonarola had been condemned to death, then offered further, post-mortem condemnation by accusing him of hypocrisy: the preacher's vanity had led him to his own bonfire, on which his corpse was thrown after hanging. All this would provide plenty of reason to at least mention Savonarola. More important though is the fact that, while Savonarola may have had a mean streak, he was no mean thinker. His savage and brilliant sermons and treatises set out ideas that are important for the history of theology, philosophy, and political thought. I'll be focusing in what follows on his theory of knowledge, which involved both criticizing pagan philosophy and justifying his own pretensions to prophetic inspiration, and on his rejection of tyrannical rule and support of a republican government for Florence.

By "tyrannical rule," Savonarola meant what Florence had experienced under the Medici.[5] In sharp contrast to Ficino, who saw Medici rule as exemplifying the dominance of an enlightened elite, just as proposed in Plato's *Republic*, Savonarola initiated a popular movement for moral and religious reform. As prior of the Dominican order at San Marco, he used his bully pulpit to issue prophetic warnings of upheaval and apocalypse. He was disturbed by the wealth and worldliness of the church, and took up the argument in favor of voluntary poverty, a contentious ideal endorsed by the mendicant orders in the medieval period.[6] But his proposals for religious reform went further than that, to the point that Martin Luther would later be struck by the extent to which his own movement had been anticipated by Savonarola. Things came to a head when the French king Charles VIII invaded Italy and Lorenzo de' Medici died, in 1492. His son Piero made military and economic concessions to the French, which so angered patricians of the city that Piero was exiled. Savonarola was sent as an emissary to King Charles and pinned his hopes on this invader, seeing in him the catalyst for the renewal of faith and unity in his city and all of Italy.

Many Florentines were convinced that the apocalyptic predictions Savonarola had been making were coming true. Not least among them was Savonarola himself, who remarked of his prophetic gift, "I was fairly certain; then I was certain; now I am more than certain."[7] The pope was not impressed, seeing in Savonarola a dangerous man in both political and theological terms. He excommunicated the preacher, even as many in Florence still supported him. Savonarola had enemies there too, though, who found their chance after a rather farcical sequence of events in 1498. There was to be a literal trial by fire, in which representatives of his opponents and adherents (but not Savonarola himself) would walk into flames to see who had the support of God. After a heavy rain and squabbling over the ground rules, the event fizzled out before this bonfire was even lit. Amidst the ensuing disappointment and disillusionment, Savonarola was arrested, charged with heresy, tortured into disavowing his prophetic gift, and finally executed.[8] Afterwards it would be made a crime even to own a copy of his books.

He would remain a divisive figure. Two leading historians and intellectuals, Machiavelli and Guicciardini, took opposed views on him. Especially early in his career, Machiavelli tended to agree with Ficino's critical assessment.[9] He also took time in his famous work, *The Prince* (§6), to explain why Savonarola had failed. Characteristically, Machiavelli thought that leadership based on belief needs to be backed up with physical force, which Savonarola did not have at his disposal. Guicciardini by contrast saw him as a worthy man who had supported the popular government against tyrants. And, though he spent much of his career railing against the hypocrisy and turpitude of the pope, there was a serious attempt to have Savonarola recognized as a saint about a century after his death.

Something else that divides opinion is how, exactly, he wished to position himself relative to the intellectual currents we've been discussing.[10] At first glance, the answer seems obvious: he knew just enough philosophy to decide that he really, really didn't like it. It's easy to find quotes in his sermons where he attacks philosophers or pagan literature in general. For instance, speaking from his pulpit, "these days up here no one says anything but 'Plato: that divine man.' I tell you, one should sooner be in the house of the devil." Or, "let Plato be Plato and Aristotle Aristotle, and not Christians, because they are not."[11] He also remarked that any old woman Christian would know more about the most important truths of faith than Plato. It's been observed that some of his remarks "border on pleas for irrationalism."[12] But the diatribes against philosophy obscure a more complicated story. We need to remember that in Florence, philosophy and especially Platonism were politically charged. The Medici had supported Ficino's project of reviving its study, and the ideas of Plato were pressed into the service of Medici ideology. In fact, Savonarola's crusade against philosophy really got going right around 1494, in the wake of Lorenzo's death and Piero's exile, when anti-Medici polemic became central to Savonarola's public persona.[13]

Furthermore, even this superficially anti-elitist reformer needed support from the aristocracy of the city. He received some of that support from the Valori family, which makes sense since Francesco Valori had been one of the patricians who helped push Piero de' Medici out of the city. But the Valori were also on good terms with Ficino. Another member of the family, Filippo, had sponsored his scholarly activities, and Ficino had praised yet another, Niccolò Valori, as a precocious philosophical spirit. So it may be that with his attacks on philosophy in general and on Platonism in particular, Savonarola was venting his hostility to the Medici, while competing with Ficino for patronage.

It must also be said that Savonarola's reputation as an anti-philosopher is hard to square with the things he actually wrote. Once you look past the sarcastic condemnations of pagan thought, you see that he is constantly making use of Aristotelian ideas, often via the intermediary of his fellow Dominican Thomas Aquinas, who looms large as an influence on Savonarola. As a young man, Savonarola had planned on a medical career, and towards this end had studied at the university in Ferrara. So he knew his liberal arts, and continued to work in this vein once becoming a friar in 1475. He taught scholastic texts and even wrote epitomizing textbooks on logic, moral, and natural philosophy. Later on, when he became a fire-breathing moralist and reformer, he sprinkled that learning into his sermons. To take a more or less random example, there is a sermon where he explicitly mentions how Aristotle said that we cannot think without using our imagination (43). This in the eminently Savonarolan context of explaining why we should meditate on death while contemplating images, like a picture of heaven and hell, to remind ourselves to avoid sin. Then there is another sermon where he refers to the same teaching with no mention of Aristotle, as if it's something he thought up himself (27).

Thanks to his education in the secular sciences, he was able to use the intellectuals' weapons against them, as with his attacks on astrology. On this point he was in agreement with Pico, who wrote a treatise against the astrological art, and in disagreement with Ficino, who got in trouble with the pope for his own dabblings in the occult sciences (see Chapter 52). Savonarola deploys his knowledge of Aristotelian thought to argue that astrology is impossible. Either natural philosophy is valid, or not (60). If it is, then astrology is falsified, because in Aristotelianism future events are assumed to be contingent, not predetermined as the astrologers would claim. But if natural philosophy is nonsense, then astrology is nonsense too, because it is built on other Aristotelian principles, which supposedly explain how the heavens influence the earthly realm.

To which you might say, that's a bit rich coming from a guy who claimed to predict the future. But Savonarola would have a good answer for you. The future is not determined by the stars or anything else, which safeguards our free will. Yet God does know what will happen through His divine foreknowledge, so He can miraculously reveal future events to us. Or rather, not to *us*, but to a select few like Savonarola. How can he be so certain that God is talking to Him, or showing him true visions? He's glad you asked, because he has prepared a treatise to answer just this question. In the *Dialogue on Prophetic Truth,* he imagines himself meeting seven characters who represent the gifts of the Holy Spirit—the first initials of their names spell out the Latin word *veritas*, meaning "truth"—and speaking with each one in turn.[14] The dialogue is intended to justify Savonarola's own claims of prophecy. But along the way, Savonarola provides us with more a general theory of how the validity of prophecy can be established.

Again drawing on his scholastic training, he alludes to the Aristotelian claim that our psychological powers cannot be deceived concerning their special objects. Vision always grasps color correctly, even if we sometimes make higher-level mistakes about what we are seeing, as when you look up at the heavens and they don't seem to be moving, or you think that red object in the distance is a bonfire but actually it's a cardinal visiting from Rome to investigate a charge of heresy. Likewise, the intellect grasps the first principles of the sciences directly, and cannot be mistaken about these—hardly a point that would be made by any defender of "irrationalism." Savanarola next claims that the power of prophecy too has a special object, namely a revelatory illumination from God. So someone with this gift need have no doubt in what is shown to him, nor indeed does Savonarola have any hesitation in his own case. As he says, "these things so stand in the light of prophecy that, to one who possesses such a light, they can give rise to no doubt whatsoever."[15] He admits, on the other hand, that the grounds of his conviction would not be available for other people. There are false prophets too, after all. Indeed, Savonarola thought that Muslims were following one, namely Muhammad (though he graciously distances himself from the notion that Muhammad was actually the Antichrist[16]). So everyone else needs to decide on other grounds whether to believe in a self-proclaimed prophet. To justify his own claims, Savonarola makes much of the good effects he has had on public morality in Florence, the accuracy of his predictions, and the sudden improvement of his oratorical skills once the sacred gift was given to him.

Though I'm not necessarily convinced that Savonarola was a prophet, I am impressed with his argument philosophically speaking. He has here drawn a nice distinction between the grounds that we might have for *subjective* certainty, and the grounds that are needed to be certain about what *someone else* has experienced. Take a very different case: a cranky child says she has a stomach ache. Is the child just inventing something to complain about, or is she really in pain? As the child's parent you have to guess, but the child herself knows for sure. In general, as philosophers now put it, we have "privileged access" to our subjective states, the things we are experiencing. If prophecy is like this, then the genuine prophet could indeed have certainty that is unavailable for other people. In one of his sermons, Savonarola makes a similar point about the saints of the church, whose knowledge was not acquired by sensation or rational demonstration, yet was still more certain and firm than the scientific knowledge achieved by philosophers (140). So the saint's knowledge and the philosopher's knowledge have different strengths. The special insight of the blessed confers the highest possible level of subjective certainty, one that may never be matched by the conclusion of a rational argument (there might always be an unnoticed mistake in the proof). But unlike the prophet's private revelatory experiences, scientific knowledge is publicly accessible. Anyone who understands a demonstrative proof can check it and have grounds for belief just as good as those of the scientist who came up with it.

In that passage on the saints, Savonarola also says that these holy persons are drawn to God's light as to their ultimate purpose or "end" (141). This is yet another bit of scholastic lore. Drawing on Aristotle, philosophers like Aquinas had emphasized that God is our final end. Savonarola adds the distinctive twist that it is Christ on the cross to whom we are all drawn, the "intended end of man, which moves everyone as the thing he loves and desires" (5–6). This brings us, by a roundabout route, back to his political theory, because Savonarola unsurprisingly thinks that a political structure is admirable insofar as it imitates God's providential and benevolent rule over all things. That idea is pretty familiar from the medieval period, as is his suggestion that the angelic hierarchy, with its ranks arranged under God, is a perfect society that we should be striving to imitate (155). In his *Treatise on the Government of Florence*, Savonarola duly argues that the most perfect constitution for a city would be a monarchy, with a single wise and benevolent king ruling as a human image of God (179). The perverted mirror image of this constitution is tyranny, where a single power or group rules for its own benefit rather than that of the people. Yes, Medici family, Savonarola is looking at you.

Ficino would be nodding along in agreement so far, since these points can all be found in Plato's *Republic*. Here too, though, there's a twist. While monarchy might be the most perfect form for a state in general, it is not one that is suitable for Florence, in Savonarola's view. The Florentines are, for starters, too intelligent and independent-minded to suffer tyranny, which is why there was always resistance to the Medici (180–1). But for the same reason, they are not apt to take guidance from even a good monarch. Instead, they find it "most natural" to follow their longstanding traditions of republican government. Even if a virtuous monarchy would be a more perfect imitation of divine rule, a "civil regime" can also be justified in theological terms. In effect, God Himself would be the king of Florence, with the pious people of the city as his representatives. As Savonarola writes, "who stands in the place of Christ? Not the Signoria, but the people are the lord."[17] Alongside this religious justification, Savonarola has concrete recommendations for the republic. He stipulates that important offices be distributed by election, smaller ones by random lot, with a council that is big enough to represent the people and avoid being corrupted through bribery. With this final point, we have another reason to see Savonarola as a man of his time. However extraordinary his personality and his role in Florentine life, he was certainly not the only Renaissance thinker who argued in favor of republican government.

38

THE SWEET RESTRAINTS OF LIBERTY
REPUBLICANISM AND CIVIC HUMANISM

As we've seen, Italian Renaissance humanism was a pretty fractious movement, featuring heated debates in writing and physical confrontations in person. There was plenty of character assassination and the occasional attempt at actual assassination. Modern-day research on humanism is, by and large, a more placid affair. In fact, I can't think of a single knife fight involving specialists in the field. But it has not been without controversy, and one of the most prominent of the controversies has concerned the ideas put forward by a German historian of the Renaissance named Hans Baron, who died in 1988. His life's work centered on the idea of "civic humanism (*Bürgerhumanismus*)," which he saw as a new and thrilling development in the history of political thought.[1] He traced this development to the turn of the fifteenth century, when the city of Florence was engaged in an existential struggle with Milan, which was ruled by the Visconti family. Florentine intellectuals began to promote republicanism as the ideal form of political life, presenting liberty as the core value for which Florence was fighting against an enemy city whose system they saw as oligarchic, if not tyrannical.

The heroes of Baron's story are humanists like Coluccio Salutati and, above all, Leonardo Bruni. We have met them as experts in classical learning and rhetoric, but both were chancellors of Florence and emphatic in their endorsement of republican ideals. Thus the term "*civic* humanism." Baron was of course well aware that Petrarch and other Italian intellectuals had anticipated these fifteenth-century figures with their love of antiquity and cultivation of eloquence. But he believed that it was only in response to the conflict with Milan that humanists started to use that eloquence for overtly political ends. He pointed to their new ethic of practical engagement, as found in Salutati's remark that virtuous activity is "holier than idleness," or in Bruni's comment: "learning, literature, eloquence, none of these is equal to glory won in battle." While a Plato or Aristotle might be admirable, a good general is more useful to his city.[2]

With this stress on the political involvement of the humanists, Baron was correcting an earlier scholar of the Renaissance, Jacob Burckhardt. Writing in the nineteenth century, Burckhardt proposed that what was really new in the Renaissance was a stress on the value and freedom of the individual.[3] You can see why he might have said this, if you think back to Pico's so-called *Oration on the Dignity of Man*. But Baron thought otherwise. For him the transition from the medieval period to the Renaissance was above all a matter of new ideas about the community, not about individuals. The freedom cherished by the civic humanists was in fact political and not metaphysical in nature. Thus Baron's key text was not Pico's *Oration*, but another oration given generations earlier by Leonardo Bruni, *In Praise of Florence*. It may have been written in 1404 as a kind of audition for replacing Salutati as chancellor, though the dating is something else scholars disagree about.[4]

It was here that Bruni really put the "civic" in civic humanism. This eulogy to his adopted city touches on its physical beauty and its military prowess, as you might expect. But it also puts great stress on the Florentine political system, which calls for a delicate balance of powers comparable to the perfect tuning of a musical instrument (§4). Furthermore all citizens, even the poorest, are equal before the law and can receive justice. This he sees as a kind of birthright of the city, which according to him was founded by the Romans during their own republican period (§2). In fact, Bruni speaks of Florence the way you might talk about an individual member of the nobility, emphasizing the city's lineage and even ascribing to it various virtues that would be more naturally assigned to a single person, like practical wisdom and generosity (§3). But if this is so, then it is because Florence's constitution facilitates the pursuit of virtue among its citizens. These proposals are renewed and extended in another speech of Bruni's, a funeral oration written in 1427, which praises the Florentine Nanni Strozzi by extolling his city.[5] Bruni again stresses the Roman origins of the city and says that its republican institutions give liberty to individuals and allow them to strive for honor and influence. A "popular" government avoids the danger of monarchy, since kings inevitably pursue their own interests over those of their subjects. Thus "praise of monarchy has something fictitious and shadowy about it," and the only truly "legitimate" constitution is that in which there is real liberty, "in which pursuit of the virtues may flourish without suspicion."[6]

This certainly looks like strong evidence for Baron's account, and there is further confirmation to be found in later humanist writings from Florence. The domination of the city's affairs by the Medici provoked a critique from the republican point of view by Alamanno Rinuccini. His *Dialogue on Liberty*, which appeared in 1479, endorses the equality of citizens and even the right of free speech.[7] For Rinuccini as for Bruni, Florence should aspire to great things, taking confidence from its ancient founding by the Romans. The Florentines should seek power as a republic and "when this has been acquired, we will, as the legitimate sons of the Romans and as imitators of their virtue, maintain it."[8] As we just saw, a generation later the visionary preacher Savonarola would be endorsing a republican form of government as part of his own rhetorical assault on the Medici and their supporters. When Piero de' Medici fled from the city in 1494, the streets rang with the cry "the people, and liberty (*popolo e libertà*)!" The invading French king Charles VIII was welcomed to town with a sign bearing that same word, "liberty," emblazoned upon it.

Looking back on these events, the historian Francesco Guicciardini named 1494 as the end of a forty-year period of tranquility and prosperity in Italy, one that had begun with the peace treaty between Milan and Florence in 1454. But Guicciardini did not lament the effort to establish a genuine republic in Florence in place of the Medici oligarchy. He was one of a number of political thinkers who wondered how to set up a republican government so that it would be long-lasting and stable. Like Savonarola before him, Guicciardini looked to the city of Venice as a role model. Guicciardini thought the key was a legislative body that could mediate between the wealthy aristocrats, the *ottimati*, and the relatively poor mass of the "people," or *popolo*.[9] But he also believed that political leadership should be chosen through election. The masses were not themselves qualified to be leaders. He said of them that they "don't think, don't concentrate, don't see, and understand nothing until things are reduced to the point where they are obvious to everyone."[10] Still, he thought the *popolo* could be trusted to choose those who *are* qualified, who would be drawn from the upper classes. The results would not be perfect. Guicciardini wrote, "I do not mean to deny that the people sometimes votes erroneously, since it cannot always know the quality of every citizen; but I affirm that these errors are incomparably less than those committed in any other way of proceeding."[11] Though no one would mistake Guicciardini for Che Guevara, he was at least still defending republicanism in the sixteenth century, albeit one with a strong balance in favor of the *ottimati*.

Actually, it's rather appropriate that the scholar who introduced the concept of civic humanism was named "Baron," because the republican institutions envisioned by the Italian humanists were always rather oligarchic in nature. It's been calculated that at the beginning of the fifteenth century, as this movement was purportedly being born, only 3,000 of the more than 20,000 male inhabitants of the city were qualified to hold public office.[12] A real government of all the people was never really on the cards; at best it was going to be a government of all the people who mattered. This point has been made in correction of Baron's thesis, for instance by John Najemy.[13] He has argued that the Florentine republic endorsed by the humanists actually represented a victory for the wealthy in their struggle against poorer compatriots who had organized themselves around the city guilds. The highpoint of this movement came in 1378 to 1382, when the guilds achieved dominance in Florence.

Recounting the story of that brief shift in power, supposed man of the people Leonardo Bruni spoke with horror of the way that the "people were eager to plunder the possessions of the rich." The lesson he drew was: "never let political initiative or arms into the hands of the multitude, for once they have had a bite, they cannot be restrained, and they think they can do as they please because there are so many of them."[14] When Bruni came to write a treatise on the topic of the Florentine constitution, he praised the city not for being a pure republic, but as a "mixed" constitution in which stable laws keep the wealthy in check, so that the poor are neither oppressed nor given an opportunity for direct political participation.[15] Bruni was here following the teachings he found in Aristotle's *Politics*, which he knew well, having translated the text himself. Aristotle likewise suggested that the best constitution should be one that minimized the chances of factional dispute, what the Greeks called *stasis*. A mixed constitution was a pragmatic solution for achieving this goal.

So it seems that Bruni and others had a rather oligarchic idea of republicanism. And this is only one of numerous qualifications, or outright refutations, that have been aimed against Baron's thesis. One fundamental objection has been that one could be a "civic humanist," writing about and being involved in politics, without being a convinced republican. We've just seen an example in the later writings of Bruni, where he follows Aristotle rather than a set of ideals inspired by the Roman republic. A similar arc was traveled by Francesco Patrizi (this Patrizi, who was from Siena and died in 1494, is not to be confused with another philosopher named Francesco Patrizi, who was from Cherso and died a century later in 1597; he is discussed below in Chapter 42). He wrote a treatise on republican government but went on to write in the so-called "mirror for princes" genre. In one text he directly raises the question of whether a republican or a monarchical constitution is better. He prefers a republic, but admits that they tend to fall apart thanks to factional disputes. For that matter, monarchies or "principiates" can be good and even represent a more "natural" form of government. Unfortunately the success of such a constitution depends on having a good ruler, and even the good ones tend to be succeeded by inferior ones.[16]

This sort of on-the-one-hand, on-the-other-hand attitude obviously falls far short of being a clarion call for the institution of republican governance all over the globe. As does another tendency we find among republican-leaning authors, like Savonarola and the historian Guicciardini. You might recall that Savonarola actually admitted that monarchy is the best form of government, but argued that it was unsuitable for the Florentines in particular. Likewise, Guicciardini said that one must always take into account the particular needs and traits of a people when determining what sort of institutions it should have, much as a doctor takes into account the temperament of the patient before prescribing treatment.[17] This idea goes back to the medieval period, as with Engelbert of Admont, who already died in 1331. Echoing Aristotle and anticipating Savonarola in a single breath, Engelbert observed that the effects of climate make some people, for instance the Greeks and Italians, suitable for popular rule, while others need a firmer ruling hand.[18]

Indeed, the republicans of Florence seem to have felt that even other Italians needed a firm hand, and sought to provide it themselves. The Romans had an imperialist foreign policy well before their republic became an empire, and the humanists were good enough historians to know it. Following that model, they enthusiastically endorsed wars of conquest and subjugation, and pretended that the cities brought under the sphere of Florentine control were enjoying freedom. Thus Salutati wrote that the subject cities had been freed from their tyrants and were now bound only by the "sweet restraints of liberty."[19] Bruni went so far as to see Florence's inheritance from Rome as a kind of natural right to rule over other cities across the whole world. This looks like hypocrisy: real freedom for Florence, fake freedom for everyone else. But the humanists' point can be understood more sympathetically if we reflect that the value of "liberty" could mean at least two things in this period. First, there was the idea of freedom from unpredictable, tyrannical rule. By instituting a reliable system of laws, the Florentines could claim to be offering that to their subject cities. In fact this is how Salutati spells out what he means by those "sweet restraints": "to be free from arbitrary power and live according to the law," that is, the law as imposed by Florence on its dominions. Second, and in sharp contrast, there was the more positive idea of liberty as self-rule or self-determination.[20] That form of liberty was reserved for the republic of Florence alone.

But it's not only that some humanists were less than fully committed and consistent republicans; it's also that quite a few of them were not republicans at all. We're by now well aware of the close connections between humanism and the Medici, autocrats who gave financial, political, and social support to such figures as Ficino and Pico. Baron gets around this by ignoring the political dimensions of the revival of Platonism. He dismisses this movement since it "exhibits little of the political consciousness of city-state citizens; it is a Platonism rooted primarily in art and religion."[21] But this seems wrong, given the way that Medici rule was explicitly connected to Plato's own writings on politics.[22] A better approach would be to use the term "civic humanism," if we use it at all, for the whole range of efforts to merge the humanist agenda with a political agenda, whether or not the agenda was republican in spirit.[23]

We can complicate this picture still further by noting that the Medici themselves made frequent use of republican language, posing as unusually influential citizens within a government that ensured liberty for all. The point was made even at the level of images, as with a medal produced in the memory of Cosimo de' Medici that pictured him on one side, with the motto "public peace and liberty (*pax libertasque publica*)" on the reverse.[24] It was made at the level of words, too, the words that the humanists could produce so well with their expertise in rhetoric. In a critical review of Baron's thesis and responses to it, James Hankins has proposed that the whole history of republicanism among humanists should be taken as rhetorical. Already Salutati and Bruni, according to Hankins, were "providing a decent covering of populist rhetoric to conceal the growing concentration of power in the hands of a few."[25] Nor were the Florentines the only ones to use liberty as window dressing. In the city of Lucca, that was done almost literally. In the seventeenth century, Thomas Hobbes visited there and saw that the word *libertas* was written in large characters on the turrets of the city, even though people there had no more liberty than the people of Constantinople did.[26] Back in our period Lucca, no less than Florence, already adopted a fairly oligarchic notion of what a republic could be.

But should we really settle for the cynical conclusion that the humanists' enthusiasm for the republican ideal was mere lip service? What about Bruni's forthright declaration in his funeral oration for Nanni Strozzi that a government of the people is the only "legitimate" constitution, since the other options fall prey to the wickedness of flawed men, either the few men of an oligarchy or the one man of a monarchy? Hankins suggests that we may be misled by a false cognate here.[27] The word "legitimate" in Bruni's Latin could mean something more like "real," as opposed to the shadowy and unattainable benefits of kingship. Bruni's point might then be that, although in principle the best kind of constitution is indeed oligarchy or monarchy, in practice it's too hard to find a few good men, or one good man. So we have to settle for a republic.

But here's yet another consideration. Even if the rhetoric used by Bruni and others was a kind of "myth" or "propaganda," the choice of propaganda makes a difference.[28] On this telling, what was distinctively new, even "modern," about the humanists' political writings was not that they were republicans, as Baron thought, but that they found it necessary to *pretend* to be republicans. Why would this have been? Well, that takes us to one final, major correction of Baron's thesis, which is that the sort of rhetoric he noticed in Bruni and others was not in fact all that new.

As several scholars, above all Quentin Skinner, have noted, the history of republican discourse is as old as the history of humanism itself.[29] We saw that that history goes well back into the middle ages, with the so-called *dictatores* honing their skills of eloquence by writing show pieces in increasingly refined Latin. As Skinner showed in a survey of this literature, republican ideals went just as far back in Italian history, in the halls of power and on the page.

As early as 1085, the city of Pisa had a government with rotating consulships to prevent the emergence of autocratic rule. By the end of the twelfth century, the major Italian cities had adopted such a system and also carved out relative independence from the Holy Roman Empire. There was still the problem that the medievals were bound to Roman law, which of course assumed that ultimate power would lie in the hands of an emperor. But the fourteenth-century jurist Bartolus of Saxoferrato said that the theoretical authority of empire was legally irrelevant when the facts on the ground meant that cities were independent of imperial control. At the same time, the cities had to withstand pressure from the papacy. So republicanism developed among these earlier humanists as a kind of third option. Never mind the famous "two swords" of mainstream medieval political thought, which juxtaposed secular imperial rule to the theocratic authority of the pope. The cities would do just fine on their own, as republics. As usual, the thinkers of what we are calling the "Renaissance" were not doing something completely new. Rather, the later humanists used their improved understanding of classical literature to find new justifications and expressions for political ideas that their medieval forebears had already explored. Bruni was right that his ideas echoed those of the past; it's just that the past in question was more recent than he cared to admit.

39

NO MORE MR NICE GUY
MACHIAVELLI

Sometimes it seems as if there is only one political dispute, which simply manifests in many different ways. Should we be bleeding-heart idealists, or hard-nosed realists? The idealist wants us to act nobly and morally in political life; the realist knows that this is wishful thinking and that we should instead do what might actually work. The idealist says seek peace; the realist says arm yourself to the teeth just in case. The idealist says help the poor; the realist says this will only encourage them not to get jobs. The idealist says you should read philosophy, perhaps Plato or John Rawls, and the realist agrees, but says read Machiavelli instead. He may be notorious for his irreverence in matters of religion, but Machiavelli is the patron saint of political realism. His most famous work, entitled *The Prince*, instructs its noble recipient on how best to exercise political power.[1] The advice it contains has won Machiavelli a reputation for realism, indeed for cynicism, for being rather, well, Machiavellian. That word is rarely a compliment. It has a rather sinister connotation, and means someone who is happy to use wicked means to attain his or her ends, which is why Shakespeare refers to him as the "murderous Machiavel."[2]

Is this reputation deserved? We might be skeptical if we think of the way we use phrases like "Platonic love" and "Epicurean pleasures." We've seen the fancy interpretive footwork that Renaissance humanists used to bowdlerize Plato's discussions of sexual love. And as those same humanists understood, Epicurus' commitment to hedonism actually demanded strict moderation rather than gourmet eating, precisely because an abstemious diet is more pleasant in the long run. But *The Prince* provides plenty of ammunition to support the popular conception of Machiavelli's thought. Speaking of ammunition, one example comes when Machiavelli takes up the question of whether it is better to control a foreign territory with a military garrison or by sending some of the ruler's own people to colonize it. He recommends the method of colonization. Whereas the garrison will instigate hostility from the locals, the colony will uproot the locals and take away their land, rendering them powerless in the process, which is exactly what the ruler should be trying to achieve. In one of the cold-hearted aphorisms that make *The Prince* a guilty pleasure to read, Machiavelli observes that people with small grievances are more dangerous than those with large ones: if you hurt someone badly enough, they'll be in no position to secure their revenge.

But understanding *The Prince* properly means more than just quoting the nasty bits. We need to realize that Machiavelli is writing for a very specific purpose, which has to do with his historical context. Machiavelli was born in 1469 and died in 1527, and thus lived through a turbulent time in Italian politics. (Then again, when is Italian politics ever not turbulent?) Of particular relevance for *The Prince* is the rise, fall, and rise of a family that has already played a significant role in our story: the Medici. When the Medici were deposed in the 1490s and the republican government brought in, that government featured the talents of Machiavelli himself. He was put in charge of organizing a local militia, anticipating advice he would later give in *The Prince*, when observing that a homegrown military force is far preferable to the use of paid mercenaries. Unfortunately for Machiavelli, the Medici returned to power in 1512, with predictable consequences for his political career. He was even jailed and tortured after being accused of scheming against the government. *The Prince*, later dedicated to one of the Medici, was his attempt to get into the good graces of the city's new, and old, ruling family.[3]

Later, Machiavelli would be accepted back into the fold. A Medici pope gave approval for a play by Machiavelli to be performed, and a Medici cardinal gave Machiavelli an official task. He was told to help arrange the affairs of some Franciscan convents, and then asked by the cloth guild of Florence to appoint a preacher. I wonder whether the cardinal appreciated that these assignments were deliciously ironic, as well as depressingly trivial. Friends were amused that the notoriously impious Machiavelli was taking on such tasks; one compared it to appointing a well-known homosexual to choose somebody a wife. Machiavelli replied with an aphorism that sums him up pretty well. He said he was in fact a good choice for the job, since "the true way to get to Paradise is to learn the way to Hell, in order to escape it."[4]

While he was in the political wilderness, Machiavelli used his enforced leisure to write the books that have secured his lasting renown. In this respect we might compare him to an author he knew well, namely Cicero, who similarly set down his philosophical writings in the idle hours after his enemy Julius Caesar achieved a dominant position in Rome. Cicero wasn't the only ancient author known to Machiavelli. He once signed a letter referring to himself as "historian, comic author, and tragic author," and would surely have been surprised to learn that his modern reputation would rest more on *The Prince* than his much longer historical works. In addition to tackling a history of Florence, he wrote a set of *Discourses* analyzing Livy's *History of Rome*. These are essential reading for anyone who wants to understand Machiavelli's political thought, because he thought about politics historically. Readers of *The Prince* are liable to be surprised by the extent to which it, too, is a historical work. Pages of it are devoted to ancient history and the recent history of Italy, to the extent that it is sometimes unclear whether Machiavelli is setting out his political ideas to explain historical events (including those of his own time) or whether it is the other way around, and the history is just there to support and illustrate his political ideas. In fact, his project must be understood in both directions. His understanding of human nature informs his work as a historian, and his expertise in history has given him the basis to make sound proposals for good government.

You may be taken aback that I speak of "good government" in discussing Machiavelli. It's usually supposed that his advice in *The Prince* has to do solely with political expedience, and goodness be damned. This is a guidebook for powerful men who want to stay powerful. And certainly *The Prince* seeks to speak truth *to* power, and not just *about* power. It is addressed to Lorenzo di Piero de' Medici; this is not Lorenzo the Magnificent, the patron of Ficino who had already died in 1492, but a less celebrated member of the family who was born in that same year and ascended to rule Florence until his untimely death in 1519. So Machiavelli's treatise is no disinterested meditation on the lessons of history. Rather, it is an instruction manual for the young Lorenzo, an exhortation that he and his family should seek to restore the Italian peninsula to its glories by rescuing it from foreign domination, and at the same time, an advertisement for bringing Machiavelli out of political exile and back into the active political life he understands so well. *The Prince* is thus an example of that age-old genre of political writing, the so-called "mirror for princes" in which a philosopher gives advice to a monarch. (Apart from the example of Christine de Pizan, remember the Byzantine works discussed in Chapter 8.) Because he is indeed writing for a monarch, Machiavelli says explicitly that he will simply ignore other possible ways of arranging political rule. But we'll come back to those other ways.

Actually the advice laid out in *The Prince* is aimed at a specific kind of ruler, the one who holds a so-called "new monarchy."[5] It is much more difficult for a man who has seized power to hold on to it than it would be for a hereditary ruler, like one who has taken over the principate from his father (ch. 2). The "new" ruler's goal is, first and foremost, to maintain his position despite his deficit of legitimacy. He must be bold in action and thought, rather than playing for time or waiting to see what happens as crises arise. After all, at the moment he is in charge, and the future is bound to bring change. He needs to make sure that change doesn't involve his downfall: he must constantly work to stay on top, or be toppled.[6] In the *Discourses*, too, a similarly "Machiavellian" note is struck in remarks about the predicament of new princes. Whereas it is normally a good idea to maintain institutions to promote stability in a state, the new ruler is better advised to remake his city completely: new titles for offices, the rich thrown down, the poor raised up. Such upheaval inevitably leads to suffering, and Machiavelli admits that in ethical terms one would be better off staying out of politics than being "a king who brings such ruin on men" (*Discourses*, §1.26). Moral scruples notwithstanding, the point stands that only this kind of bold measure will keep the new monarch in power.

This sort of advice is not just cynical *realpolitik*, though. Though Machiavelli does recommend that the prince be cruel on occasion, this is always in the service of political continuity, which is the precondition for the flourishing of both the prince himself and of his subjects. And as he says, it is stability not justice that must be the primary concern of the state (§3.41). It's in this sense that we may indeed speak of "good government" within Machiavellian politics. It's precisely in the pursuit of this end that the prince needs to dispense with moral scruples in some cases (*Prince*, ch. 15). For there are times when acting morally would undermine the stability of the state. Consider generosity, for instance. Everyone agrees that it's better to be generous. But the prince has the responsibility of looking after the city's finances. Given the choice between displaying generosity and balancing the books, the prince must choose the latter even if it means that he will seem miserly to his subjects.

The same reasoning underlies some of the most notorious passages in *The Prince*. Machiavelli asks whether it is better for a leader to be feared or loved, and says that it is of course best to be both feared *and* loved. But if only one is possible, then fear is a more reliable way to keep the population in line. This is because people are fickle, and will forget their love when the chips are down (ch. 17). It's vital, though, that the ruler not actually be hated, since this itself will undermine his position. In fact, the ruler should strive to be loved, not for the warm fuzzy feeling but because this is itself a step towards stability. As he says in another ready-made aphorism, "the best fortress is the love of the people" (ch. 20). On the other hand, he's already struck a more cynical note earlier in *The Prince*, when he points out that winning the favor of one's people is not that hard a trick to pull off. Really all they want is not to be oppressed (ch. 9). So there is no excuse for not keeping them content.

Here it's worth noting that when Machiavelli speaks of "the people" he is not talking about the whole population of the city, but about the rank of citizens who fall below the nobility. He even asks which group's approval is more important for the prince. This shows the extent to which Machiavelli is still operating within the parameters of ancient political theory. If we look all the way back to Aristotle's *Politics*, we may recall that he also assumed a deep and ineradicable opposition of interests between the people and the nobles, the many and the privileged few. In the *Discourses*, Machiavelli applies his customary hard-nosed realism to this issue, explaining that the best political system is not one that eradicates the antagonism between the two classes but recognizes and takes advantage of it. The Romans managed this by letting the aristocrats run the state as senators, but also giving the plebians a role by assigning them the tribunate (§1.4; I discuss this further in the next chapter).

Machiavelli does not, then, celebrate wickedness for its own sake. But he does think the prince must learn to be wicked sometimes, in order to deal with the weakness of human nature and the inevitable wickedness of others. A celebrated passage in *The Prince* states that the ideal ruler is able to act like both a fox and a lion. He appears mighty like the lion to intimidate his rivals, but must be crafty like a fox to spy the traps those rivals have laid for him. Machiavelli's pessimism about human nature leads him to depart from previous Renaissance political theorists, who were on the idealist side of the spectrum. Authors like Petrarch had argued optimistically that the statesman who acts virtuously will always reap the best results. Himself drawing on Cicero, Petrarch had also identified glory as the objective of political life, as Machiavelli will do. But for Petrarch this could be attained only through upright action; he wrote that "nothing can be useful that is not at the same time just and honorable."[7] For Petrarch it was absurd to prefer fear to love in one's subjects, as Machiavelli recommends, or to think that stability takes precedence over justice. In fact, the two go hand in hand. Machiavelli thinks that such pious sentiments are quite simply detached from reality. Sometimes a leader must be cruel to achieve his political objectives. In *The Prince* he gives the example of Hannibal, whose ferocity enabled him to hold together a disparate army through great hardships in a long campaign against the Romans (ch. 17).

Yet even the leader who is both a lion and a fox, who knows how to inspire fear through cruelty and also win the people's love, is not guaranteed indefinite success. Machiavelli is inspired by his reading of Lucretius, whose Epicurean philosophy taught that events are not predetermined or even predictable; randomness, and not divine providence, rules the universe (for his marginal notes on Lucretius see above, Chapter 27).[8] This is not to say that events are entirely beyond human control, though. Machiavelli reckons that about half our life is ruled by our own actions, with the other half being controlled by fortune (*Prince*, ch. 25). Again, the successful leaders are those who boldly take initiative, because this is how you can exploit chance events: bad luck cannot be thwarted, but good luck can be assisted (*Discourses*, §2.29). So fortune really does favor the brave, and a mixture of ability and luck is essential (*Prince*, ch. 6). The ones who achieve a lasting reputation for success, though, are usually those who died before their good luck ran out. The twists and turns of fortune, and the inevitable resistance the ruler gets from both the *popolo* and the *ottimati*, mean that it is incredibly difficult for a man to bend the city to his will over many years. As Machiavelli will also observe in the *Discourses* on the basis of Roman history, the most skilled and lucky autocratic ruler is only going to achieve in the short run what a free republican government may be able to achieve in the longer run.

Of course, this fundamental contrast, between republican government and princely rule, is itself inspired by Roman history. The paradigm for the former is the Roman republic, for the latter the dictatorial and then imperial rule exercised by Julius Caesar, Augustus Caesar, and their successors. Having drawn his big picture of politics according to a Roman plan, Machiavelli also cites ancient history to fill in the details. Regarding the aforementioned point that colonies work better than garrisons, he observes that this strategy worked well for the Romans. And after issuing his caution that generosity can undermine the state, he refers to Julius Caesar, and speculates that if Caesar hadn't been assassinated he might well have bankrupted Rome given his lavish spending habits. Greek history is also mentioned, as when Machiavelli explains how Alexander the Great was able to conquer and hold such a huge swath of territory. This incredible feat was possible only because Alexander was taking over lands used to centralized, autocratic rule, simply replacing the Persian Great King with his own royal self (ch. 4). Machiavelli also cautions that these ancient figures achieved glory beyond what may be available in Renaissance Italy. When we take them as our exemplars, we are like archers aiming beyond the reach of our bows, in order to shoot as high as possible (ch. 6).

Machiavelli ends *The Prince* with an almost hysterical description of the parlous state of Italy, as he exhorts his addressee Lorenzo to do something about it. He felt he was living through evil times, something he in part blamed on the church. For him, the papacy was a force that divided Italy and undermined religion because of clerical corruption. This makes him sound like a religious reformer, like Savonarola, but his ideas about the religious life were markedly different from those of that firebrand preacher.[9] Machiavelli did write a treatise with the pious-sounding title *Exhortation to Penitence*. But in it, he advised a robustly active approach to the spiritual life, discouraging mere lament over one's sins, and encouraging a disciplined life of bold action. A good example would be the crusades, which he admired as the expression of a more muscular Christianity.

These points fit with comments he makes about religion in his more famous works, especially the *Discourses*. He worries that Christian faith tends to render believers passive and peaceful. Its valorization of humility and contempt for this world weakens its adherents, and leads them to ignore insults to their honor that they should be avenging (§2.2). He associates the fall of the Roman empire with its Christianization[10] and thinks the Byzantine empire fell because the Ottoman Turks had paired intense religious fervor with military aggression, allowing them to crush the more passive Greek Christians. In the *Discourses* he goes so far as to suggest that Christianity is not the sort of religion that is really conducive to the attainment of glory, even if the founders of religion in general can claim to be the "most famous" of all famous men (§1.10).

In this connection, we may return to Machiavelli's diagnosis of the failure of Savonarola in Florence. As we saw, he thought that as an "unarmed preacher" Savonarola relied exclusively on religious conviction among his followers, and had no military force to pair with that conviction. In the *Discourses*, Machiavelli reiterates the need of both religion and arms (§1.11). He adds some agnostic remarks about Savonarola's prophetic gift, but manages to turn this skepticism into a compliment: the preacher's personality was enough to win him followers, and he needed no miracles. Later he commends Savonarola's "learning, prudence and mental power," before saying that he fell foul of public opinion when they noticed his hypocrisy and ambition (§1.45). At any rate, his hope is that Lorenzo may be the sort of complete leader that Savonarola could not be. In the final chapter of *The Prince* (ch. 26), in which he encourages Lorenzo to liberate all of Italy, Machiavelli casts his prospective patron in the dual role of religious and military leader, a man wielding the two swords of faith and violence.[11] Just as Moses led his people from slavery in Egypt, Lorenzo should bring liberation to Italy and defend its cities from foreign exploitation. If he takes Machiavelli's advice on how to establish himself as a prince, he may succeed in this where others have failed.

40

SENSE OF HUMORS MACHIAVELLI ON REPUBLICANISM

When you teach philosophy for a living, there are certain things you find yourself telling students over and over. Try to write shorter sentences; avoid jargon; work on transitions between paragraphs; maybe this point would be clearer if you illustrated it using a giraffe as an example? One of the most common pieces of advice I give is that students should address a tightly focused question. This is true even in a doctoral thesis. Almost every graduate student I've ever supervised wound up narrowing their project from their original conception. They might start out wanting to look at theories of free will in all of ancient philosophy, and wind up writing about the use of a single Greek term in early Stoicism. This is one reason why people outside the academic world think that specialists are in an ivory tower, arguing over angels dancing on the heads of increasingly small pins, rather than tackling big and urgent questions that face all of humankind. Which is true enough, but also not without good reason. Doing the history of philosophy properly means lavishing exquisite attention on the details of texts and arguments, in order to yield insights that have escaped previous readers. If you're trying to do it all, chances are that you'll wind up doing nothing.

For this reason, I frequently tell students who are writing seminar term papers—so this would be, say, a ten- or fifteen-page essay—that they should try to produce a really good interpretation of *just one sentence* in a philosophical work. In this respect, and maybe some others as well, this book and the others in the series are setting a bad example. I typically range widely over an author's works, discussing big themes and rarely dwelling on the small details and individual passages that are the bread and butter of actual research, the kind of research I do in my day job, as it were. But I thought it might be interesting to write a chapter that follows my own advice, by focusing on just one sentence. I have an especially good opportunity to do that at this juncture, because Machiavelli's aphoristic writing style, subtlety of thought, and legion of interpreters makes him ideal for this sort of treatment.

Having mostly concentrated in the last chapter on his most famous work, *The Prince*, I now want to move on to a longer treatise that he wrote between 1514 and

1518, his *Discourses* on the Roman historian Livy. Naturally enough, Machiavelli has a lot to say here about Roman history, but it is not a historical work strictly speaking. Rather his goal is to draw lessons from Roman history that are applicable to political decision-making in Machiavelli's own day. So, even as they follow and comment on Livy, the *Discourses* are not that far from *The Prince* in approach, and scholars routinely draw on both works in interpreting Machiavelli's political thought. Here is the sentence from the *Discourses* that will occupy our attention in this chapter: "it seems to me they do not consider that in every republic there are two different humors, that of the people and that of the great, and that all the laws made in favor of liberty are born from their disunion, as we easily see to have happened in Rome (*mi pare che e' non considerino come e' sono in ogni republica due umori diversi, quello del popolo e quello de' grandi e come tutte le leggi che si fanno in favore della libertà, nascano dalla disunione loro, come facilmente si può vedere essere seguito in Roma*)" (1.4).[1]

So how should we go about trying to understand this remark? First, we need to look at its immediate context. Issues having to do with the wider context, for instance the general aims of the *Discourses* and the historical setting in which the *Discourses* were written, will come later. Our sentence is part of Machiavelli's defense of the idea that class opposition "kept Rome free," as he puts it (1.4). So when the sentence begins "they do not consider . . . " he means those who deny the useful role played by struggles for dominance within Roman society. And in fact, most of his contemporaries would indeed have disagreed with him on this point. Medieval and Renaissance thinkers were nearly unanimous in assuming that unity of purpose and amity between social groups is politically healthy. Commentators like the younger historian and political thinker Francesco Guicciardini rejected Machiavelli's idea out of hand, saying that even if social tumult led to certain good outcomes, praising it would be "like praising a sick man's disease because of the virtue of the remedy."[2] Even Machiavelli himself, in his treatise *On the Art of War*, says that we should look to the Romans to learn how "to live without factions."[3]

But as our sentence shows, Machiavelli is not in favor of just any rivalry or enmity within the political life of a state. He specifically refers to two groups whose contested relationship is an engine of liberty within the state. This brings us to our next task in understanding the sentence. You should never take yourself fully to understand a remark in a historical work unless you've read it in the original language. In this case the relevant Italian terms are *popolo*, "the people," and *grandi*, which I translated rather literally as "the great." We've already encountered the concept of the *popolo*: this "people" consists, roughly speaking, of the citizens who are not rich and powerful, so smaller merchants and the like. In Renaissance Italy the interests of this group would have been represented above all by the guilds.

For instance, in Florence the ruling legislature, the Signoria, included members put forward by the guilds and then chosen by lot. Not exactly a Roman institution, but that doesn't stop Machiavelli from more or less equating the Italian concept of the *popolo* with the Roman lower class, which was represented by the office of the tribune.

As Machiavelli explains, in the ancient Roman political system the office of the tribunes was introduced precisely to stop the more aristocratic elements from ruling with a free hand (*Discourses*, 1.2). As for the rich, called the *grandi* in our sentence but often referred to as the *ottimati*, in the Roman republic they were of course represented by the Senate. There was also a kind of executive position which rotated between leading men. These were the consuls, who had a significant military role. For Machiavelli the secret of Rome's success, at least until the whole thing fell apart and became an empire controlled from the top by Julius Caesar, Augustus Caesar, and their successors, was precisely a balance between these three political institutions. This was a kind of "mixed government," which in Machiavelli's view is "more solid and more stable, because one keeps watch over the other, if in the same city there are princedom, aristocracy, and popular government" (1.2).

This brings us to a more puzzling term in Machiavelli's statement: he calls the lower and upper classes two "humors (*umori*)" in the city.[4] He thereby draws an analogy between the body politic and a real human body, which was of course seen as having four rather than two humors: phlegm, black bile, yellow bile, and blood. Since antiquity the humors had been considered to be the constituents of the human body and the main determinant of health (see further Chapter 49). When the humors are in balance, the body will function well; when they are imbalanced, disease results. The bodily humors have certain innate tendencies, so that yellow bile for instance is hot and dry, and has a corresponding effect on the temperament of the body as a whole. Machiavelli thinks something of this sort is also true of the two political "humors." It is simply in the nature of the nobles that they want to rule, and in the nature of the people that they want freedom from being ruled (1.5). This is just an inevitable fact about the two classes, and does not vary from one time and place to another. As Machiavelli says, "men are born, live and die, always, with one and the same nature" (1.15).

Machiavelli has a bleak assessment of that nature. He thinks that "all men are evil" and that they "never do anything good except by necessity" (1.3). For this reason, confusion and chaos will indeed result in the city if there is "excessive freedom," which is why you can't have a political structure where the *popolo* are allowed to run things with no constraints by the upper classes. That sort of approach tends to result in the destruction of republican governance, as on the other hand will untrammeled power in the hands of the nobility. In both cases, the dominant class will inevitably turn to a single man to represent their interests, who will become a tyrant. Thus as Machiavelli says later in the first book of the *Discourses*, tyranny comes both from "the too great desire of the people to be free and the too great desire of the nobles to command" (1.40). He's skeptical that either group will establish true liberty, left to its own devices. As he writes in another work devoted to the history of Florence, "the promoters of license, who are the people, and the promoters of slavery, who are the nobles, praise the mere name of liberty, for neither of these classes is willing to be subject either to the laws or to men."[5]

We can press the medical analogy a little bit further. According to the humoral theory all humans have the same basic makeup, but there is variation in temperament from individual to individual. Though he doesn't make a big deal about it, Machiavelli evidently thinks that something similar applies to human societies. Thus, while he lays down general principles of political theory based on long-ago examples drawn from Roman history, and insists that these principles remain valid for the Italy of his own day, he also acknowledges something we might call "national character." The French, for example, are known to be avaricious and treacherous (3.43; of course, this is an insult, even coming from Machiavelli). Here we may once again recall Savonarola's idea that monarchy was in general the best form of constitution but inappropriate for the Florentines. However, Machiavelli does not seem to think that humans vary *that* much. His ideas about the best way to organize political life are, in broad terms, universally applicable, which is precisely why the Florentines can learn lessons from reading Livy's history of Rome (with Machiavelli's help).

Let's go back to our sentence, then, and Machiavelli's claim that the laws that supported Roman liberty were born out of the "disunion (*disunione*)" of the *popolo* and the *grandi*, not from their harmony. Notice that the word "to be born (*nascere*)" once again underscores the naturalism underlying Machiavelli's observation. This is not an isolated case. It exemplifies his habit of comparing political affairs to natural phenomena, sometimes more explicitly as when he says that small cities rarely dominate large ones, "because all our actions imitate nature, it is not possible or natural for a slender stem to bear up a large limb" (2.3). More arresting is what our sentence identifies as the happy outcome of class conflict or "disunion," namely liberty. This confirms what we already know from other passages, namely that Machiavelli considers "liberty" an admirable feature of the Roman system and also a valuable goal for the Florence of his own day. From this we may infer that, in the *Discourses*, he is situating himself in the history of Italian republicanism (see Chapter 38). At first this seems to be a sharp contrast with *The Prince*, which explicitly began by saying it would focus only on the political challenges and solutions relevant to autocratic rule. But we saw that even in *The Prince*, Machiavelli made positive remarks about republics and especially their capacity for long-term stability.[6] Taking both works together, then, the question is not really whether Machiavelli was a republican. It is rather: precisely what form of republic did he want?

This turns out to be a highly contested question. Most readers, on the basis of our sentence and other, similar remarks in the *Discourses*, think that Machiavelli wanted a perfect balance between the optimates and the people, and that the laws and cultural norms of the Romans show how this is possible. This seems right, but raises the further question of what a "perfect balance" would be. Running throughout the history of Renaissance republicanism was the tension between "broad" and "narrow" government (*governo largo* vs *governo stretto*). The former would give more scope to the *popolo*, while the latter would reserve most power for the *grandi*, with just enough influence given to poorer citizens that they would be discouraged from overthrowing the government or causing other disturbances. A concrete example can be taken from Florence, where the nobles would vet candidates for elected office and eliminate anyone who didn't measure up to their expectations, on the basis of such criteria as family lineage.

It seems clear that in the *Discourses*, at least, Machiavelli wants to give the people much more power than that. In contrast to the smoke-filled room of patricians just described, he commends the policy of giving all citizens a chance to raise questions in open debate about the suitability of prospective office holders (3.34). The scholar John McCormack has argued that this exemplifies a thoroughgoingly democratic approach to republican government on Machiavelli's part. McCormack contrasts Machiavelli to Guicciardini, whose name has already come up a few times.[7] As we saw Guicciardini was also a republican, who favored the selection of nobles for political office by means of a free election among the people. Tellingly, he felt the need to justify giving the people even this much say in the political life of the city. But Guicciardini was not trying to maximize popular liberty. To the contrary, one reason he favored the use of elections is that rich people with well-known names have an enormous advantage in them. As we can see from the recent history of the United States, where the presidency has tended to go to men with great wealth, a famous name, or both, elections are not necessarily a bar to oligarchy. That's why Guicciardini liked them.

Machiavelli seems to have wanted a more genuinely democratic form of republicanism. Like Guicciardini he has faith in the decision-making powers of the *popolo*. They sometimes make mistakes, but so do princes, and an unlawful prince is even worse than a deluded populace (1.58). The reason writers on politics and history so often criticize the "people," says Machiavelli, is that you can always get away with doing so, whereas complaining about autocrats is risky business. Machiavelli's relative affection for the *popolo* and distrust of the nobility is easy to explain, given his own experiences. He was without illustrious lineage but was put forward as a talented administrator by Piero Soderini, who was elected in 1502 by the nobles to run Florence. Soderini himself was one of the *grandi* and they assumed he would rule the city in their interests. When he instead showed sympathy to the *popolo* and promoted men like Machiavelli, he was deposed, with predictable results for Machiavelli. (He comments that Soderini, like Savonarola before him, was brought down by envy, 3.30.) The Medici family, whose name was synonymous with oligarchy despite their republican propaganda, returned to rule Florence in 1512. Machiavelli's imprisonment and torture at their hands would have been fresh in his mind when he wrote the *Discourses*. When you consider that this work is actually dedicated to noble readers whose patronage Machiavelli hoped to secure, and that *The Prince* is addressed to a member of the Medici family, you realize that Machiavelli is quite daring in the extent to which he argues for republican government in these writings.

So that provides us some of the wider context for understanding our sentence. Why, though, does he say there that liberty comes from the productive rivalry of both the people *and* the "great"? This seems strange, if his main hope is that more authority will be given to the people. But the optimates have an important role to play too. Apart from the point we've already seen, that uncontrolled popular freedom leads to chaos and eventually tyranny, we need to recognize that the natural tendencies of the nobility are useful to the state. In the same chapter from the *Discourses* from which our sentence is taken, he says that "the aspirations of free peoples are seldom harmful to liberty, because they result either from oppression, or from fear that there is going to be oppression" (1.4). Such a literally "populist" agenda is not going to maximize the potential of the city to achieve "greatness," which Machiavelli takes as an axiomatic goal of political life. To reach that goal, the state needs the drive and ambition of the nobles; no *grandi*, no *grandezza*. The lust of the nobles for power and rulership may be unnerving from a republican point of view, but it is like an engine of outstanding achievement, as the *ottimati* constantly push for opportunities to win fame and fortune for themselves. And in a republic, when the nobles undertake great deeds, the results are ultimately to the credit of all citizens: "what brings greatness to cities is not individual benefits but the pursuit of the common good, and there can be no doubt that it is only in republics that this ideal of the common good is properly recognized" (2.2).

Looking back as always to antiquity, Machiavelli observes that the success of the Roman republic did not consist merely in securing long-term liberty for the people.

It was no quiet democracy, but an all-conquering, militaristic superpower. Indeed, expansion and warfare were key ingredients in the recipe for Roman liberty.[8] Idleness and sustained peace lead to weakness in the state (1.6, 2.25), which is dangerous because there are always neighbors ready to exploit weakness. The power-hungry nobility, who want both wealth and fame, push the republic to engage in what Machiavelli sees as a healthy and vital quest for expansion. Again we can invoke the historical context here. In 1494, Florence lost dominion over the city of Pisa, a traumatic event that played a role in the emergence of the Savonarolan republic. Pisa was not retaken until 1509, with the surrender to the Florentines being countersigned by Machiavelli himself, among others, in his capacity as a military advisor. Back in 1499 he had written, "It is necessary to retake Pisa to maintain our liberty," underlining the intimate relation between domestic freedom and military conquest abroad.[9]

The "people" will be involved in such conquest too. One of Machiavelli's favorite themes is that true military strength lies in the citizenry, another lesson he learned from the Romans. He wants to see the people armed, as in the militia he helped organize for Florence, so that they will always be prepared to defend or prosecute the interests of the city. Professional soldiers or mercenaries tend to undermine the city leadership, something that Machiavelli can easily illustrate given the long record of Roman emperors being overthrown by military coup. Mercenaries are expensive, too, to the point that their salaries may offset any riches gained through the conquests they win (2.19). By contrast, properly motivated citizen soldiers will fight fiercely for their city, winning fame for their highborn generals in the process, and then go back to their occupations once the campaigning season is over. As Machiavelli puts it, the ideal citizens "gladly make war in order to have peace."[10] Nearly constant warfare also provides an outlet for ambitious men to seek fame and booty on the battlefield rather than by staging a takeover of the government (3.16). Here we might think one last time of the comparison to a human body implied by that reference to the "humors" in our sentence. For Machiavelli the healthy body is one involved in vigorous activity. Just so, in political life it is, as he says in *The Prince* (3), "very natural and normal" to wish to make acquisitions (*acquistare*).

To round off our examination of this one sentence, we should broaden out to include one final sort of context: Machiavelli's whole writing career. We've seen that the sentence fits well thematically with the *Discourses* and other works, namely *The Prince* and his dialogue *On the Art of War*. But there is a later treatise I haven't mentioned, namely his *Discourse on the Affairs of Florence*, which was not written until 1520. On one interpretation of this work, it departs from the sentiment expressed in our sentence, according to which productive conflict or "tumult" is the key to a vibrant and long-lasting and well-balanced, republican form of liberty.[11] Machiavelli seems to have had a change of heart, fearing that the lust for "greatness" will tend to undermine the city rather than keep it healthy. Instead, he now proposes a carefully calibrated set of institutions designed to prevent any individual or group from gaining too much dominance. This is more along the lines of the idea of a stable balancing act that we considered and rejected before as a reading of the *Discourses*, on the grounds that the Machiavelli of that work would have found it too inert. If he now in his later career accepts a less dynamic, but more secure, constitution, this may be due to his recognition of a middle class that can mediate between the *popolo* and the *grandi*. He has, you might say, found another sense of "humor."

41

THE TEACHER OF OUR ACTIONS RENAISSANCE HISTORIOGRAPHY

They say that those who do not learn from history are doomed to repeat it. But Machiavelli would say that this gets things backwards. The reason to study history is precisely so that you *can* repeat it, solving new problems with solutions that have worked in the past. As Machiavelli says in his *Discourses* on the Roman historian Livy, "he who wishes to see what is to come should observe what has already happened."[1] In particular, we should look back to antiquity, when the Romans provided examples for anyone who seeks to achieve great things, not least in matters of war. Thus he has his main speaker in a dialogue called *On the Art of War* say, "I shall never depart, in giving examples of anything, from my Romans."[2] Admittedly, history can also instruct us on what *not* to do. This is the sort of lesson we can learn from more recent history, thinks Machiavelli, since so many bad decisions have been made by Italian statesmen in general and by the city of Florence in particular. As my grandfather liked to say, everyone is useful, if only to serve as a bad example.

Machiavelli's disparaging remark about Florence comes at the beginning of the fifth book of his history of the city,[3] which was written in the early 1520s at the behest of a pope who was also a member of the Medici family. The project was not, to put it mildly, a novel one. A series of men who held the office of chancellor in the 1400s had each written a history of Florence, beginning with Leonardo Bruni, followed by Poggio Bracciolini, then Bartolomeo Scala. More generally, historical research had been part of the humanist movement at least since Petrarch, who did fundamental philological work restoring the writings of Livy. The humanists liked to say that history is the "teacher of our actions," precisely because of the wealth of examples it offers for emulation. It was also an important part of the study of rhetoric. Both points are made by a humanist we met some pages back, Isotta Nogarola. She wrote, "Our ancestors called history life's teacher, for knowledge of the past fosters prudence and counsel... History encourages a certain perfection of style, adorned with every splendor, an opulence of words, a power of speaking, a wealth of anecdotes that illumine the oration and make it admirable. What more is there to say? All excellent orators gain their vitality and passion from history."[4] That sentiment would have had the full approval of Leonardo Bruni, who throughout his career devoted much energy to the writing of histories. He certainly thought that history should report accurately on events. As he comments in the preface of his treatise on the war of the Italians against the Goths, "it is the business of history to make a literary record of the times whether they are prosperous or adverse...one must write about whatever happened."[5] But even if "history must follow the truth," as he also says, it is still a form of rhetoric and should involve suitable ornament.[6]

Of course, to write history well one should follow the pattern set by ancient historians, those who wrote in Greek, like Polybius and Thucydides, and those who wrote in Latin, like Julius Caesar, Livy, and Sallust. Among them Livy had a special status. As just mentioned Petrarch worked on this historian back in the fourteenth century, and the Greek émigré George Trapezuntius recommended him highly in his treatise on rhetoric. So Machiavelli was coming late to the party when he devoted his *Discourses* to Livy a couple of generations later. The Renaissance humanists also wrote histories of their own, which might just repeat material from earlier historians, albeit with some adaptation. We know of a debate involving the humanist Giovanni Pontano, over the question whether a new work of history should draw on just one source or combine many sources.[7] Failing to reproduce sources at all wasn't even considered as an option. So when Bruni's fellow historian and critic Flavio Biondo accused him of borrowing too heavily from the ancient historian Procopius in a historical treatise, he wasn't complaining about plagiarism. He was charging Bruni with lazily depending on one author when he should have used several.[8] Another way Bruni imitated his classical models was to include many set-piece speeches drawn from his own imagination, in order to capture the thinking behind various historical decisions. This is a technique he would have learned from, among others, Thucydides, whom Bruni was the first Western humanist to know well.

The cultivation of eloquence was only one reason to read and write history; there was also the cultivation of virtue. The humanist Pier Paolo Vergerio thought it an even better tool for instilling good character than moral philosophy,[9] and Coluccio Salutati agreed, on the grounds that history is livelier than straightforward exhortation.[10] Again, the rationale for seeing history as a "teacher of our actions" was that it could provide us with models to imitate. Thus Lorenzo Valla said that it "teaches by example (*per exempla docet*)," Guarino Veronese that it "inspires man to act virtuously and inflames him to deeds of glory."[11] For Bruni, reading history offers the sort of experience naturally acquired by older people, who have seen more of life than the young, so that it "makes us wiser and more modest."[12] His dual interests in rhetoric and virtue are on show in a *Life of Cicero*, his revision of the biography of this great orator and philosopher written by Plutarch. He is not to be confused with Petrarch: Plutarch lived in the first and second centuries AD, and was himself a philosopher and historian, who wrote a set of paired lives of prominent Greeks and Romans, including Cicero. When Bruni read this he found it insufficiently admiring of this leading humanist role model, which is why he wrote a new biography, as he explained in a preface to the work.[13]

Though Bruni also once commented that "history is one thing, panegyric another," this gives us a hint of the close connection between rhetoric offering praise of someone or something (which is what "panegyric" means) and the kind of rhetoric involved in writing history. Hence those histories of Florence written by the chancellors of the city, which were among other things works of praise. We're told that Bruni boasted of giving Florence "immortality" by writing his history of the city. His successor Poggio echoed that assessment in his funeral oration of Bruni: the work itself deserved "the highest praise from all ages," and secured eternal fame for the city.[14] Bruni's *History* is indeed still admired today, especially for its empirical and source-critical approach to history, which allowed him to unmask earlier legends as being just that, legends. He showed that the city was not really founded by Julius Caesar, as claimed by an earlier historian of Florence named Giovanni Villani.[15] And he poured cold water on another idea of Villani's, namely that the man who revived the city after it declined along with the Western Roman empire was none other than the living revival of that empire, Charlemagne.

But, while we should not discount Bruni's evidence-based approach to history, it should also be noticed that these details from his *History* promoted a political agenda. The interpretation of that agenda has changed over the past decades, along with the interpretive line taken on Bruni more generally. We saw how Hans Baron championed the idea of "civic humanism" in the Italian Renaissance, and made Bruni the leading figure in that movement, a proponent of republicanism and thus an opponent of imperial oppression. Baron read Bruni's *History of Florence* as fitting perfectly into this pattern, arguing that Bruni emphasized the Etruscan roots of Florence, making it a kind of counterpoint to Rome.[16] No wonder then that Bruni sought to distance the history of his city from figures like Julius Caesar and Charlemagne. In stark contrast to the earlier Dante, whose work *On Monarchy* celebrated Roman empire and wished devoutly that all Christendom would be united once again under a single ruler,[17] Bruni was no imperialist. He saw ancient Rome as "draining Italian cities of their strength," like a large tree preventing the smaller ones around it from flourishing. When it came to more recent history, Bruni praised the Florentines for their stand against tyrannical Milan, whose leader Gian Galeazzo Visconti threatened "all free people in Italy."

But as Baron's reading of Bruni has come under criticism, so scholars have begun to see different motives at work in his *History*. We saw that Bruni always had a fair degree of sympathy for oligarchy, and had no trouble making peace with Medici power. Given that he received lucrative tax concessions from the city's government, probably in return for his work on the *History*, it's hardly surprising that it tends to promote the viewpoint of that government and of the nobles who dominated it. The latter part of the work was written under Medici rule, and duly commends members of the family for their civic virtue. Even if these illustrious figures were already dead, it still reflected well on the Medici. As the Bruni scholar Gary Ianziti has written, "Image was all, and history writing was an image-making (or breaking) enterprise . . . The events referred to might have taken place decades earlier. No matter. Reputation hinged on the actions of one's immediate ancestors as much as on those of oneself."[18] Another critic of Bruni, Francesco Filelfo, accused him of turning his *History* into a propaganda piece for the Medici, and though this is an exaggeration, the work certainly shows that Bruni knew who was buttering his bread.

The more ideological aspects of the *History* duly reflect the values of the nobles who dominated the republican government of Bruni's time. He openly endorses those values, writing, "I am moved by what men think good: to extend one's borders, to increase one's power, to extol the splendor and glory of the city, to look after its utility and security."[19] You could hardly summarize better the goals of the *ottimati* as Machiavelli would later understand them. This also explains why, as I mentioned earlier, Bruni was horrified by an earlier episode in Florentine history, the Ciompi revolt, in which the guilds took over the city and installed a truly popular republican government. Bruni had no time for this sort of thing, and was also strongly opposed to the distribution of government offices by random lot, on the grounds that it would cut the link between political leadership and the individual "virtue" cultivated by the nobility.

Bruni's interest in that sort of virtue helps to explain a feature of his history that distinguishes it from earlier chronicles, those written in the middle ages. Where they typically sought to show how God's plan was revealed in history, Bruni placed great stress on individual human agency, and saw this as the driving force behind events. He was followed in this by his fellow humanist, historian, and chancellor Poggio Bracciolini.[20] Poggio's *History of Florence* is a kind of sequel or continuation of Bruni's, much as we saw with the Byzantine historians, who would carry on the story where earlier accounts had left off (Chapter 10). In this case Poggio takes up the history of Florence in 1402 and brings the tale to 1454, the year that peace was agreed with

Milan. Like Bruni, he depicts Florence as the brave protector of Italian liberty against Milanese aggression, and says that this justified their participation in warfare: "how much more just it is, to fight for liberty, and to avoid coming under the domination of others."[21] He also echoes Bruni's support for an oligarchic or "narrow" republic, pointing to the Ciompi revolt as an example of the way that factionalism can bring down republics and also remarking that the "people," or *popolo*, are often too cowardly to support the performance of great deeds by the city.[22]

In light of all this, we can see that with his contrast between the *popolo* and the nobility or *ottimati*, Machiavelli was hardly being innovative. Still, his historical works could not have been written by anyone else. They are stuffed with his characteristic aphorisms, as in this quotable passage from his *Discourses on Livy*: "ancient writers say that men usually worry in bad conditions and get bored in good ones, and that either of these afflictions produces the same results. Whenever men cease fighting through necessity, they go to fighting through ambition... The cause is that nature has made men able to crave everything but unable to attain everything." There are also moments of cynicism to match anything in *The Prince*: "it is enough to ask a man for his weapons without saying: I wish to kill you with them. For when you have the weapons in your hands you can satisfy your desire." And the one-liners routinely offer genuine insight. If only Robespierre had read Machiavelli's *History of Florence* and underlined the sentence, "nobody should start a revolution in a city in the belief that later he can stop it at will or regulate it as he likes."[23]

As we've seen, he uses history to generate, and then illustrate, his own theories about political life. He presents his positive view on republican government by explaining the strengths of the Roman republic, but that view is in the first place inspired by his historical research into the Romans' achievements. So the modern state should imitate the Romans as much as possible. In the preface of his *History of Florence* Machiavelli echoes the claim of our favorite sentence from his *Discourses*, saying that internal dissension can be helpful for the vibrancy of a republic. But to prevent this dissension from turning into factionalism, the city needs to direct its aggression outward. As the *Discourses* put it, "if a republic does not have an enemy outside, it will find one at home."[24] Unfortunately, Florence has mostly failed to live up to the Roman standard, its progress constantly undermined by bad laws and self-interested factionalism.

That failure is an illustration of the general law that opposition "between the people and the nobles, caused by the latter's wish to rule and the former's not to be enthralled, bring about all the evils that spring up in cities."[25] But such evils are not inevitable; as he's argued, Rome was able to deal with this very opposition and even benefit from it. Machiavelli explains that the "people" of Rome had more realistic expectations and desires, being happy to let the nobles get on with conquering and winning glory so long as they were not actively oppressed. In Florence, by contrast, the *popolo* were always trying to constrain the nobles from seeking their natural goals. Like Bruni, Machiavelli likes to invent rhetorical showpiece speeches for his history. One of these is given on behalf of the "people," and is full of cynical hostility towards the nobility. It's fine to attack the *ottimati* and seize their wealth, argues the spokesman: "of conscience we need take no account, for when people fear hunger and prison, as we do, they cannot and should not have any fear of Hell."[26]

As usual, Machiavelli invokes the constancy of human nature to justify his claim that the lessons of Rome will apply just as well to Renaissance Florence. It is because "all people have the same desires and the same traits" that "he who diligently examines past events easily foresees future ones."[27] His assumption that the plebeians of ancient Rome may be readily compared to the *popolo* of fifteenth-century Florence is a good example of this kind of thinking. (By contrast, Bruni sometimes used the term *popolo* in something like the modern sense in which "the people" are the whole body politic.[28]) One of those chancellor historians, Bartolomeo Scala, might have been criticizing Machiavelli in advance when he complained about historians who "want to trace everything back to antiquity and omit with silence much that has been changed or innovated since then."[29]

Machiavelli displays this habit even, or in fact especially, when discussing warfare, which you'd think would have changed quite a lot since the Roman phalanxes were efficiently mowing down barbarians (until they weren't). In his dialogue *On the Art of War* he insists that this is actually a domain of political life that can be modeled on the ancients especially well. Supposedly, such developments as gunpowder weapons make surprisingly little difference: "artillery does not make it impossible to use ancient methods and show ancient vigor."[30] Machiavelli is at his most Machiavellian when discussing this topic. He assumes a zero-sum distribution of power, territory, and wealth between cities and seems to think there are only two relationships possible between states: peaceful enmity and active warfare. Medieval concerns with justice in matters of war seem to be, if you'll pardon the expression, ancient history as Machiavelli states as an obvious fact that war is only ever fought to strengthen oneself and weaken one's opponents.[31]

This attitude would be echoed by Francesco Guicciardini, who as we've seen disagreed with Machiavelli on other points. He wrote a critical commentary on Machiavelli's *Discourses* and a series of his own historical works. Guicciardini makes great use of the rhetorical set-piece, often pairing two speakers who argue on either side of a political issue.[32] Often the speeches concern the wisdom of declaring a war, and it's astonishing how rarely the speeches raise the question of whether a prospective war is or is not justified. Thus a speaker who opposes a war against the papacy doesn't worry about the religious implications, except to note that it could be bad for the city's reputation. Elsewhere, a spokesman urges the citizens of Venice to aim for "noble and high goals" but, again, only for the sake of reputation. All of which is no wonder, since Guicciardini is just as persuaded as Machiavelli that foreign policy is a dog-eat-dog business: any city "must either be powerful enough to oppress others or she must be oppressed by others."[33]

Frequently he has historical figures argue against launching wars on the grounds that it opens one to adverse turns of fortune. Fortune is a theme that runs through all the histories we've looked at, and increasingly so as the generations go on. It is not so much emphasized by Bruni, but Poggio wrote a treatise on the topic and described political rulers as actors performing in what he called the "theater of fortune."[34] As for Machiavelli, fortune is one of his favorite concepts and he offers much advice concerning it, as when he suggests that it's better to starve an enemy army than to attack it, because in open warfare "fortune is much more powerful than ability."[35] He often credits specific political successes to good fortune, seeing this as key to the career of Cosimo de' Medici for example.[36] But as we saw, for Machiavelli fortune determines only half of human events. Wise decisions like those made by the Romans can enable one to master it to some extent: its "malice can be overcome by prudence."[37] Furthermore, he tends to see the vagaries of fortune as a mere ebb and flow in the tide of historical cycles, which have a kind of natural inevitability, such that states always fall away from the peak of their power and perfection.[38]

Guicciardini is if anything even more impressed by the unpredictability of fortune. He writes that "human affairs are as subject to change and fluctuation as the waters of the sea, agitated by the winds." So he is less confident than Machiavelli that one can apply the lessons of history to predict the future: "experience shows that almost always the opposite happens to what men, no matter how wise, expected."[39] Nonetheless a constant refrain of his writings is the trait of "prudence." It helps to restrain emotion in political decision-making, and allows rulers to spot opportunities as they arise.[40] With this Guicciardini applies a lesson of his own taken from antiquity. Aristotle envisioned a virtue of practical wisdom which allowed the wise man to deal effectively with particular situations as they arose. If one has encountered a wide range of problems and challenges, one has far better chances of reacting to new problems successfully. The study of history can provide this at second hand: it offers experiences on which to draw, not models to imitate. But it would be dangerous to take general lessons from history and apply them directly to one's own situation. Those of his own day who, like Machiavelli, urge leaders to follow the example of the ancient Romans are like people claiming "that a donkey can run a race like a horse."[41]

It should be noted that the figures I've discussed in this chapter were far from the only historians of the Italian Renaissance. It was an interest widely shared among humanists, and even members of socially marginal groups were getting in on the act: two sixteenth-century Jewish authors, Elijah Capsali and Joseph ha-Kohen, wrote chronicles of recent European history, and Lucrezia Marinella produced a history of the fourth crusade (for her contribution to the debate over the virtues of women, see above, Chapter 30). But I'd like to end with a remark by another historian named Francesco Vettori, one that might have struck even Machiavelli as overly cynical. Vettori said that all the talk of freedom and liberty is a mere fantasy. "All the republics and principates I know of from history or have seen for myself, were tyrannies," he said. "To speak freely, all governments are tyrannical."[42] It is only in the pages of utopian works by authors like Plato and Thomas More that one could see a population living without tyranny. Which is perhaps why some authors found them so inspiring.

42

THE GOOD PLACE UTOPIAS IN THE ITALIAN RENAISSANCE

If you were given the task of designing a perfect city, what would you put in it? High on my own list of priorities would be plenty of green spaces, pedestrian zones, independent booksellers, coffee shops, and of course cinemas showing silent films and other classic movies. I'd also have statues put up in honor of my favorite philosophers, like Plato, Avicenna, and Christine de Pizan, plus one of my twin brother, in part because he deserves one and in part because people might think it was me. I suppose we should also have a statue of Thomas More, whose 1516 treatise *Utopia* is of course the most famous example of a project like the one I'm describing. Forget fantasy islands: More proposed a whole fantasy society and the ideal educational, political, and economic conditions that would prevail there. It's convenient that I've already decided to have a statue of Plato, since More was in turn looking back to the *Republic*, the original utopia of the European philosophical tradition, which anticipated some of More's radical proposals, such as the common sharing of property.

More's *Utopia* illustrates a point that has so far gone largely unacknowledged in this book. I've been focusing on developments in Italy, implying that Renaissance philosophy began there, with the rest of Europe having to catch up later. This is a traditional way of telling the story, in part on the grounds that the quintessentially Renaissance movement, humanism, was triggered by the presence of Eastern Greek scholars in Italy, and then taken up by northern scholars like Erasmus. But it's not as if Italian intellectuals were immune to influence from the rest of Europe. Two obvious examples are the arrival of the printing press and the Protestant Reformation. The latter provoked the Counter-Reformation (some historians prefer "Catholic Reformation") in southern Europe, providing the context for developments in Italian thought in the sixteenth century. Likewise, Thomas More's *Utopia* was written by an Englishman, but turns out to be an important source for Italian intellectuals in the sixteenth century.[1]

The work may have been brought to Italy by More's friend Antonio Buonvisi. Its initial publication (as *La republica nuovamente ritrovata del governo dell'isola Eutopia*) caused little fanfare but the Italian translation, which appeared in 1548, was a hit. It came with an introduction written by Anton Francesco Doni, which promised the reader, "you will find in this republic, which I present to you, the best customs, good orders, wise regulations, holy teachings, sincere government, and regal men; the cities are well established, as are the offices, justice, and mercy."[2] Doni was inspired to write a short utopian work of his own, with the enticing title *Wise and Crazy World*, a dialogue between two characters named simply "Wise (*Savio*)" and "Crazy (*Pazzo*)."[3] The "wise" character tells his crazy friend about a dream he has had, of a city where the people are "of one mind and all human sufferings are taken away" (23).

It was the opening salvo in a veritable barrage of imaginary polities. Around the same time a work called simply *The Happy City* was published by the polymath Francesco Patrizi da Cherso.[4] (Not to be confused with Ioane Petritsi, whom we covered in Chapter 15, or the other Francesco Patrizi mentioned in Chapter 38.) The works of Doni and Patrizi paved the way for the most famous Italian utopia, *The City of the Sun*, written by Tommaso Campanella in 1602 but first published only in 1623. Two years after that, the *Dialogues* of Lodovico Zuccolo were published, containing a fourth utopian work called *The Republic of Evandria* as well as an attack on the model for all of this literary activity, Thomas More's *Utopia*. According to Zuccolo, More was less than convincing. His ideal society was too much of an idealization, realizable only on the impossible assumption that the citizens of Utopia would all be perfectly virtuous and willing to live in conditions akin to monasticism (137, 150).

Fans of utopian literature might be tempted to respond that, even if the ideal society cannot be realized, it might still serve a useful purpose by giving us something to aim at. But that sentiment had already been anticipated and rejected about a century earlier, by none other than Machiavelli. In his *Prince*, he wrote with his characteristic realism and cynicism, "many have fancied for themselves republics and principalities that have never been seen or known to exist in reality. For there is such a difference between how men live and how they ought to live that he who abandons what is done for what ought to be done learns his destruction rather than his preservation, because any man who under all conditions insists on making it his business to be good will surely be destroyed among so many who are not good."[5] Machiavelli was writing too early to be thinking of More or his Italian imitators, and may instead have had Plato in mind. If so, he was giving Plato too little credit, since the *Republic* is far from optimistic about the prevalence of virtue in real Greek society, and goes out of its way to argue that the ideal city is genuinely possible, if unlikely.

Of course, Machiavelli didn't need to invent utopias, because in his view real life had provided a model to imitate and ideal to strive for, in the shape of the ancient

Roman republic. But the authors of utopian treatises also looked back to antiquity. Patrizi openly admitted that he was taking many of his ideas from Aristotle's *Politics*, albeit with a good deal of creative elaboration (76), while Zuccolo's Evandria is meant to be more realistic than Thomas More's Utopia in part because it has so much in common with Rome. Antonio Donato, translator of several of the utopias, has commented that for Italian humanists Rome was "both imaginary and real."[6] That's an observation you could apply with some justice to Machiavelli and his fellow historians.

Something else Machiavelli didn't need to do, by the way, was look back to antiquity to find examples of people imagining states that don't exist in reality. It might be argued that the tradition of utopias in Renaissance Italy began well before the arrival of Thomas More's work, with works on architecture by authors like Leon Battista Alberti, Antonio Averlino, known as Filarete, and even Leonardo da Vinci.[7] They explained the best way to lay out a city, as well as the ideal construction of individual buildings, with Alberti alluding explicitly to Plato's *Republic* as an inspiration. He and other city planners thought that Plato's strict division between social classes should be reflected in the urban landscape. Thus da Vinci proposed a "two-level" city with the rich literally living above the poor. In this imagined city, the layout would express in physical terms the pervasive dichotomy found in political philosophy of the period, between the *popolo* and the *ottimati*.

Another theme taken over from ancient authors was the ideal shape for a city. Plato mentions that the lost city of Atlantis was circular, and the great architectural writer Vitruvius, a major source for Alberti, suggested that a city should have its streets laid on a radial plan, like the spokes of a wheel.[8] That idea is taken up by Doni in his *Wise and Crazy World*. In such a radial city, it would be almost impossible to get lost, making for a sharp contrast to real Italian city centers, as anyone who has been there will know. Someone standing in the center would be able to see the whole city just by turning around (24), an apparently innocent remark that seems more sinister once you notice that it anticipates Jeremy Bentham's idea of the "panopticon," a jail in which the inmates can be observed at all times from a central viewing position. My ideal city would definitely not work like this, but perhaps my preferences have been formed by my own home town, of which Ralph Waldo Emerson said: "we say the cows laid out Boston. Well, there are worse surveyors."

One of the reasons that Tommaso Campanella's *City of the Sun* is so famous is its remarkable account of the layout and physical appearance of the utopia.[9] It has a series of concentric circular walls, making it almost impossible to take by military force—or so Campanella says, despite the fact that the Ottomans had not so long ago managed to batter their way through the formidable walls at Constantinople. In the City of the Sun, the walls are painted with all the images and information one needs to learn the sciences, including everything from pictures of various animal species to definitions for use in metaphysics and ethics. Education is of vital importance for Campanella, because just like Plato's republic this city is ruled according to the principles of philosophy. The highest ruler is a consummate scientist and intellectual, and has subordinates who oversee the various disciplines which include the liberal arts as well as applied sciences like medicine.

It may seem both unnecessary and overoptimistic that rulers should be deeply learned scholars; one can imagine Machiavelli snorting in derision. But Campanella has the main speaker in his dialogue explain that if his readers find such proposals incredible, that is because of the scientific culture to which they are accustomed, which is corrupted by mere book learning and memorization of the teachings of figures like Aristotle (22–3). As we'll be seeing (Chapter 51), these remarks fit perfectly into Campanella's philosophical agenda. He rejected Aristotelian science in favor of theories inspired by his predecessor Bernardino Telesio. Even the importance of the sun in his utopia is a reflection of those theories: Telesio and Campanella saw heat as a fundamental explanatory principle in their new physics. In the *City of the Sun* Campanella duly explains that the citizens see the sun, the greatest source of heat, as an image of God. That's yet another idea we can trace back to Plato's *Republic*, and its famous analogy between the sun and the Form of the Good (69).[10]

So Campanella's ideas about philosophy, especially natural philosophy, provide us with an obvious context for understanding aspects of his *City of the Sun*. Presumably his political ideas and experiences are also relevant, but it's not so easy to say how. Campanella's life was a difficult one. He was arrested by the Inquisition in 1594 and for a time imprisoned alongside another famous victim of persecution, Giordano Bruno. A further run-in with the authorities came in 1599, when he was accused of conspiring against the Spanish domination of Naples. Arrested for treason, and for good measure heresy, he would endure horrific torture and decades of imprisonment, albeit under conditions which allowed him to compose many treatises including *The City of the Sun*. He was finally released in 1626, and in 1634 he made his way to France, before dying in 1639.

Given this life story, it is surprising that one of his main contributions to political thought, *On the Monarchy of Spain*, argues *in favor* of the universal rule of the Spanish power that subjected him to so much misery. An obvious suspicion is that he may have written it to persuade his jailers that he was on their side after all, but questions about the exact dating of the work make it hard to know for sure.[11] Campanella does seem to have good reasons for supporting an expansion of Spanish dominion, even if he also suggests that this might be the least bad option available.[12] Spain had proved its ability to take on the Ottomans at the pivotal Battle of Lepanto in 1571, whereas the Italian princes were too weak, even collectively, to defend Christian interests against Ottoman aggression.

The aforementioned background of Reformation and Counter-Reformation is also relevant here. Campanella considered Luther to be a harbinger of the Antichrist, so looked to the southern European powers to push back against the tide of Protestantism. Whatever mixed feelings he had about the Spanish, they were at least willing to recognize the spiritual authority of the pope. In this respect Campanella should be distinguished from earlier imperial monarchists like Dante. Where Dante wanted to put all authority in the hands of a secular emperor, Campanella saw unified governance under the Spanish crown as compatible with, indeed justified by, a political alliance with the papacy. All of which allowed him to transfer his support to the French crown as soon as he moved there, and conveniently decided that the Spanish were professing Catholic piety for merely pragmatic, political reasons.[13] That cynical approach to faith is something he associated with Machiavelli, whom he called the "scandal, ruin, scourge, and fire of this century."[14] He wrote a work against Machiavelli's thought, which bears the forthright title *Atheism Defeated*. He was particularly outraged by the Machiavellian advice that rulers should instrumentalize religion as a way of binding together a political community.

Often the most heated polemics are provoked by near agreement, and that may apply here, because Campanella also saw religion as a powerful source of social cohesion. He also offered some fairly "Machiavellian" thoughts on how the Spanish monarchy could exploit division between its enemies, for instance by lending support to the Calvinists in England to sow dissension there. But as we can see from *The City of the Sun*, in his ideal polity religion would not be the tool of the rulers, but their central purpose. His political leaders are scholars and philosophers, but also priests, and his utopia is neither a principate nor a republic, the two forms of governance considered by Machiavelli. It is a full-blown theocracy. Campanella recognizes, indeed insists upon, the novelty of this approach. Because religion has never been truly central in historical governments, he says, "there has never been on this earth a state (*respublica*) wholly without injustice, without sedition, without tyranny."[15]

With this, Campanella can be seen as anticipating and answering a complaint about utopian treatises. The authors of such works seemed to be offering happiness in a perfect city on this earth, rather than in the "city of God" in heaven, as Augustine so memorably put it.[16] But for Campanella the "rational" or "natural" religion observed by the people of his city would already be remarkably like a Christian community. Though they are not actually Christians, they have learned from their travels about other religions and particularly admire the Christian faith. Their customs even involve the confession and absolution of sins, a detail that is perhaps inspired by the rise of confessional culture as part of the Counter-Reformation.[17] It's also relevant to note that his spokesman in the dialogue, who has visited the utopian city and is describing it to an interlocutor, is a Knight of Malta, a religious warrior whose authority as a speaker comes from both his piety and his philosophical learning.[18]

These themes in Campanella's *City of the Sun* find echoes in the other Italian utopias. Patrizi also talks about religion as a natural trait of humans (88), and pretty well all the utopias lay great stress on unity among the citizens. No trace of Machiavelli's productive class tension here. Instead, the city is imagined as a single organism, something we already see in those earlier works on architecture, like a drawing by Francesco di Giorgio that superimposes a human body on the ground plan of a fortified city.[19] For Alberti, this idea of organic unity was paramount in the making of individual buildings. He wrote that these should have "that reasoned harmony of all the parts within a body, so that nothing may be added, taken away, or altered, but for the worse," and that "a building is very like an animal, and that nature must be imitated when we delineate it."[20]

But we see variety between the works when it comes to the groups of people within the utopian community, and how they are meant to form a unity. To an astounding degree, our authors are willing to follow the provocative recommendations of Plato when it comes to gender and sexuality. Campanella, making the cosmos the model for his city and seeing both as an organic unity, remarks that the sun is like a father and the earth a mother, with the universe as a whole like a "large animal."[21] His theory of heat leads him to see women as being, in effect, defective men, who lack vigor because of their lesser heat. Nonetheless he follows Plato as far as he can bear to, agreeing with the stipulations in the *Republic* that all labors are shared by the two sexes, with the caveat that more physically demanding tasks should be carried out by men. He also adopts Plato's policy of eugenics, according to which mates are chosen by a scientific procedure, and says the citizens of this city would find us ridiculous for taking care over the breeding of horses and dogs, but not humans. Even more outrageous is Doni, who (perhaps satirically) proposes a "street of women" in his perfect city where men go for sex, with the resulting children shared in common by the whole community (26).

What about the economic classes, which played such a key role in the historical analyses of Bruni, Machiavelli, and Guicciardini? Of the four authors, Patrizi is the most aristocratic in attitude. He identifies six classes, namely farmers, artisans, merchants, warriors, officials, and priests. Of these the first three are useful workers supporting the elite, with only the latter three groups considered as full citizens. As he puts it, the "city consists of two parts: one that serves and is unhappy; the other part meanwhile rules and is blessed" (90). It's therefore been commented that his "happy city" is "a utopia for philosopher-kings."[22] The more satirical and antic Francesco Doni, by contrast, wants to get rid of class distinctions all together. In his utopia "one person is not richer than another" (25), and wealth is passed around so that everyone has the chance to enjoy it (32). This echoes a comment he makes elsewhere: why should the nobles (*signori*) have so much, and everyone else so little?[23] It's no coincidence that Patrizi was born into a noble family, Doni a poor one. In all the utopias, though, it seems that no one is subject to genuine poverty or enjoys great affluence. Zuccolo says so explicitly, writing that "in Evandria, there is not even a single beggar and there are not excessively wealthy people" (217).

The most interesting reflections concerning economics are once again to be found in Campanella. In particular, he argues explicitly against the practice of slavery.[24] There are no slaves (*schiavi*) in the City of the Sun, because everyone does their share of work. This is in contrast to the Italy of his day: he reckons that only one in six of the people who live in Naples actually do anything useful, and that if the labor was spread out fairly each person would need to work only four hours per day. Elsewhere, in a work on economics, he is less provocative and simply accepts slavery as a fact of life, even giving advice on which peoples are best for which purposes: "you may treat Negroes as you wish for burdensome occupations."[25] Yet he does not have a race-based theory of slavery, or a theory of natural slavery like that of Aristotle. Instead he seems to think the practice is a violation of nature, which is why he bans it from his utopia and elsewhere writes that "every human being is equal to every human being with respect to divine, natural, and civil commutative law."

The economic policies recommended in these utopias are striking, but not stunningly innovative, since they echo the proto-communist ideas of Thomas More and, before him, Plato. Just as work is shared in common, so is wealth, and the citizens may not even have any use for money. In Campanella's city money does exist, but only to trade with foreigners, and the people are said to be "rich because they want nothing, and poor because they possess nothing." Thanks to passages like this he has been hailed as a forerunner of modern-day socialism. His name is even inscribed on a Soviet obelisk. There's a certain irony here, in that the Italian Renaissance is sometimes seen as a kind of crucible for the birth of capitalism. The utopian thinkers dreamt about abolishing private property, even as other writers were coming around to the idea that there might be advantages in a widespread human tendency that was wishfully eliminated from perfect imaginary cities: greed.

43

GREED IS GOOD ECONOMICS IN THE ITALIAN RENAISSANCE

"Economics" is one of those words that has wandered pretty far from its etymological origins, while retaining a connection to those origins. As any Renaissance humanist would be quick to tell you, it comes from the Greek *oikos*, meaning "house." So the ancient works devoted to "economics" dealt with household management, and included discussion of such topics as the relation between man and wife, the raising of children, the ideal location to build one's home, and the treatment of slaves.[1] Economics in something like our modern sense did belong to this discipline too, since the householder's art also involved knowing how to handle money. Economic treatises advised on the sorts of property to invest in, the importance of balancing expenditure and income, and the division of tasks among family members and household staff. Equally important was to encourage an appropriate attitude towards wealth. An early example of the genre, written by Plato's contemporary Xenophon, is a dialogue featuring Socrates. At one point Socrates is made to say that real wealth is having enough to satisfy one's needs; a richer man may be needier than a poorer one, if his desires are excessive, and thus in truth less wealthy.[2]

Xenophon's treatise was one of several ancient works on household management that came into circulation during the Renaissance, in this case because a manuscript was brought to Italy from Byzantium in 1427. A few years before that, Leonardo Bruni translated and commented upon another treatise on economics, which was falsely ascribed to Aristotle. It was only a matter of time before new works were composed in imitation of the ancient ones. One of them was produced by Leon Battista Alberti, whose writings on architecture have been discussed in the previous chapter. He composed a dialogue called *On the Family*, featuring members of the Alberti clan.[3] In keeping with the expectations of this genre, it devotes a lengthy discussion to the householder's relationship with his wife. The *pater familias* should oversee all things, like the spider at the center of a web, but delegate many tasks to the wife, since it is effeminate for a man to concern himself overmuch with this domain (*Fam.* 76–8).

Still, the wife should not be allowed to deal with financial affairs. The account books should be kept away from her, and the husband should never trust her with secrets (*Fam.* 79–80).[4] It's up to him to make the economically significant decisions. Alberti, or rather the lead character in his dialogue, has plenty of advice to give on this score. For instance it is better to hold land than cash, since land can be enjoyed and is a secure investment, whereas money tends to wind up getting spent (*Fam.* 103–5). A similar conception of the male householder can be found in another fifteenth-century work on economics, written by Giovanni Caldiera.[5] He compares the role of the husband to that of God overseeing the universe, or the ruler overseeing a city. Here Caldiera is thinking of the doge in his city of Venice, who was set up as a kind of autocrat over the city in a rather authoritarian, and at the time widely admired, example of the "mixed constitution" that I talked about in Chapter 38.

Paging through these works on household management, it's abundantly clear that the households in question are wealthy ones. Xenophon and other ancient writers thought in the first instance of a large estate in the country, with a sizeable staff living alongside the family. The southern plantations of nineteenth-century America would not be a bad comparison here, especially since slavery was involved in both cases. But in Renaissance Italy, the paradigm of the wealthy man was not necessarily the large landowner. He could be a denizen of the city, who made his money from trading and shrewd investments. This inevitably calls to mind the Medici, a family whose political influence was based on their vast fortune, and whose vast fortune came from banking. Theirs was a European-scale venture, with branches of the Medici bank in such cities as London, Cologne, and Avignon as well as many Italian cities, including Florence of course, but also Rome and even Florence's sometime rival Milan. This enabled them to become the most famous patrons of the Italian Renaissance, who lavished support on intellectuals like Ficino and artists like Michelangelo. Nor were they the only family that was quite literally enriching Florentine culture. There was also, for instance, the Rucellai family, which used its staggering wealth to hire the aforementioned Alberti to design a stunning palazzo that still stands today.

The ancient genre of household management needed to be updated for this new reality: it was time for someone to put the economics into home economics. This someone turned out to be Benedetto Cotrugli, whose 1558 book *On the Art of Trade* combines traditional elements of the genre with advice for the man who wants to be a successful merchant in fifteenth-century Italy.[6] Cotrugli was not himself Italian. He hailed from the Republic of Ragusa, which is modern-day Dubrovnik, but studied philosophy and law in Bologna and lived in a number of Italian cities, especially Naples. And he did write in Italian. A preface to the work explains his decision to write in the vernacular, rather than Latin, to reach a wider audience (*Trade*, 26). Traditional aspects of the treatise include his remarks on family life, for instance that a good relationship with one's wife should involve no violence—unfortunately followed by the advice that if you do find you must beat your wife, you should at least keep it secret to protect your reputation (153–4). This appalling passage notwithstanding, it seems that Cotrugli considers himself to be practically a feminist by the standards of his day. He boasts of his decision to have his own daughters highly educated (155).

The more innovative aspects of the text are those that have to do with what Cotrugli calls *mercatura*, or trading, which he defines as "an art, or rather a discipline, practised between qualified persons, governed by the law and concerned with all things marketable, for the maintenance of the human race, but also in the hope of financial gain" (*Trade*, 31). It is an art learned especially through experience, which to Cotrugli's mind explains why no one has ever tried to lay down its principles in writing before (30). Thanks to his own hands-on knowledge, he is able to give his reader many useful pointers. One of them is particularly noteworthy, at least to those interested in the history of accounting. Cotrugli is the first to describe the practice of "double-entry bookkeeping," where debts and credits are written down separately in two columns—though other documents show that merchants had already been doing this for a century and a half.[7] He also offers practical, even psychologically insightful, tips about buying and selling, as in passages about negotiating favorable prices for one's wares, while being careful not to scare the buyer off (43, 50).

The topic on which Cotrugli has the most to say is ethical character. A successful merchant needs to have a reputation for honesty. Unlike Machiavelli, Cotrugli assumes that this will be achieved by actually being honest (*Trade*, 115). To make money the merchant must be willing to endure hardship, ignoring the needs of the body to make his sale, while rigorously observing moderation even in less pressing circumstances (38, 80). Cotrugli thinks fortunes are built slowly and steadily, not by greedily snatching at every promising opportunity (139). Stability is his watchword. For this sake, he takes a leaf out of Alberti's book by recommending the acquisition of land outside the city. In fact it's better to have *two* villas in the country, one to produce income, the other as a vacation home (144). In the likely event that you're not in a position to take that advice, you might instead benefit from his surprisingly long rant about how moral defects are shown by the way men wear their hats (130).

I have to take my own hat off to Cotrugli for making a long and impassioned case for the proposition that the pursuit of wealth and the pursuit of virtue make for a happy marriage, as happy as the one between the merchant and his demure, ideal wife. He was not alone in this. We've seen several Renaissance humanists agreeing with Aristotle that the so-called "external goods," like health, family, and friends, should be part of the best life. Among those external goods was money. Great wealth makes possible great virtue, especially when it comes to generosity, though one might also think of the financial outlay required for military adventures and the glory they bring. Thus Leonardo Bruni wrote in a letter, "wealth should be striven after for the sake of virtue, as an instrument, so to speak, for bringing virtue into action."[8]

He applied the same idea in the preface to his translation of the pseudo-Aristotelian *Economics*: "as health is the goal of medicine, so riches are the goal of the household. For riches are useful both for ornamenting their owners as well as for helping nature in the struggle for virtue."[9] Money-making and, just as important, money-spending were part of the active, engaged life of practical virtue recommended by Bruni and other figures whom Hans Baron associated with "civic humanism," like Salutati. He anticipated Cotrugli by seeing the honest and energetic merchant as a paradigm of virtue, even calling such men "most blessed" for the service they give to the community. For, without the merchant, "the whole world would be unable to live."[10] A similar note was struck by Christine de Pizan, who said that "it is very good for a country and of great value for a prince and to the common polity when a city has trade and an abundance of merchants."[11]

But there was an obvious problem here. It seems evident that the point of banking and trading is not really to achieve virtue or help the city. The point is to get rich. As even the moralizing Cotrugli said, in that definition of the merchant's art I quoted above, this art is practiced "in the hope of financial gain." Even if economic activity is connected indirectly to virtue and is also "vital to human activity," as he also says (*Trade*, 25), it would be very implausible to say that merchants are motivated only by such high-minded concerns. Cotrugli walks a fine line here, allowing the merchant to make wealth his goal, but condemning the excessive love of wealth that goes by the name of "avarice." Those who "make gold and silver their god," he says, should be ejected from society, or still worse, have liquid gold and silver poured down their throats (127). A similar attitude may be found in Alberti's dialogue about family matters, which says that avarice is something one should wish on one's worst enemy, since it destroys both reputation and happiness (*Fam.* 31). For him the avaricious are not miserly, but rather spendthrift. Alberti does accept the Aristotelian doctrine that external goods, including wealth, are part of the best life (50). But he thinks the secret is to earn enough to live comfortably, while restraining one's outlay to the "necessary" expenses required to keep one's family in honorable condition (72). Actually, unnecessary expenses are allowable too, if they do no harm. Under this heading Alberti naturally mentions "beautiful books." Once a humanist, always a humanist.

Even if profit-seeking was seen as an acceptable motive, there were constraints to observe. Preachers of the time campaigned against the wickedness of avarice, with one of the foremost figures in this crusade being Bernardino of Siena.[12] We have a series of sermons given by Bernardino attacking greed and, especially, the sinfulness of usury and other dishonest financial dealings. These diatribes were part of a long-standing tradition in which schoolmen and clerics laid down moral lines that merchants must not overstep.[13] Bernardino's contributions to this genre did not much impress Poggio Bracciolini. As he explained in a letter to his friend Niccolò Niccoli, he felt that Bernardino and other churchmen had not attacked avarice properly. Poggio thought he could do better, which led him to write a dialogue called simply *On Avarice*.[14]

The work is basically a greed sandwich. It starts and ends with speeches about the evils of lusting after money, but in the middle there is a speech *in favor* of avarice. This startling material is delivered by a fictionalized version of Antonio Loschi, who was a secretary of the papal curia. His aim is to refute the opening diatribe against avarice, which presents itself as an improvement on the preaching offered by men like Bernardino. A third speaker in turn refutes Loschi: this is a theologian from the Greek-speaking East, who says that the defense of greed must have been a sort of rhetorical exercise (*Avar.* 266). Poggio also has Loschi introduce the second speech by alluding to the Academic skeptics who cultivated the skill of arguing on both sides of any issue (256). So on the surface level, it would seem that Poggio is sincere in his desire to warn the reader against avarice, with the middle section in favor of greed included only (and quite literally) for the sake of argument. But given the humanists' love of irony and literary gamesmanship, readers have been unsure how to take this juxtaposition of speeches. The attacks on avarice can be read straight, or instead as a kind of parody, with a pastiche of Bernardino's moralizing disapproval set against a (mock?) vindication of a more realist, or cynical, attitude.[15]

If Poggio really did want to reject avarice, then the work belongs to another genre, one I find even more interesting than treatises on household governance. I like to call it the "philosophical own goal." This happens when authors present arguments for positions they want to reject, only for readers to find these arguments more compelling or intriguing than the position the authors want us to accept. There are plenty of examples. From late antiquity we might think of Simplicius' quoting Philoponus so he can refute him. Modern readers find Philoponus far more interesting, to the extent that there's an English translation that only keeps the Philoponus and jettisons all of Simplicius' replies on behalf of Aristotle. Speaking of whom, one might also mention Bertrand Russell's remark about his *Politics*: "I do not agree with Plato, but if anything could make me do so, it would be Aristotle's arguments against him." The most influential philosophical own goal, though, is probably Descartes's use of absolute skepticism in his *Meditations*. Many more people been convinced by his skeptical doubts than his way out of them.

So it is here with the arguments given to Loschi in Poggio's *On Avarice*. Beyond offering a refreshing break from the predictable laments over greed, they are actually fairly convincing. A true commitment to avarice, says Loschi, requires many impressive qualities, such as vigor, endurance, and intelligence. Thus plenty of admired rulers have had a great appetite for wealth (*Avar.* 256–7). Such appetite is furthermore natural, at least if we agree with St Augustine that avarice is "the desire to have more than enough." By this standard, pretty well everyone is avaricious; who among us would not gladly have that second villa? Admittedly, one finds the occasional saintly exception, but such people are freaks of nature, like a newborn human with the head of a pig (258–9). Moreover, avarice does not undermine society, as its critics claim. As observed by another fictional character, Gordon Gecko, "greed is good." It motivates people to acquire the wealth used in charity, patronage, and the building of churches. "What are cities, states, provinces, and kingdoms," asks Loschi, "if not the workshops of avarice?" (260).

In fact, it seems that economic theory is particularly apt to produce philosophical own goals. We saw an example in late Byzantium, with Nicholas Kavasilas' treatise against usury giving a rather convincing devil's advocate case for allowing this practice (see Chapter 13). You might assume that in Renaissance Italy, the case for usury must even have won out against its critics. Otherwise, how could the Medici and others get so rich off banking? But not so. Even Cotrugli, for all his praise of the merchant's life, condemns usury, which he succinctly defines as "gain made on money loaned" (*Trade*, 95). Yet he also criticizes theologians who decry business practices that are perfectly acceptable, despite themselves having no expertise in the field: "like a blind man with colors," he scoffs (66–7). For Cotrugli the difference is made by risk. So long as an investor is taking a chance of losing his money, then he is morally in the clear when he profits from his investment (100). This would find agreement with none other than Bernardino, who deems it acceptable to take reward for one's own labor, and also from a willingness to risk one's wealth.[16]

So it looks like merchants are mostly going to be in the clear: it's fine to profit from an overseas trading expedition, given that the boat you've helped to finance might sink. Bankers too have some cover, insofar as they likewise invest money at risk. But what about the guaranteed interest they paid out on money invested in their banks? This looks patently usurious, but was often presented as a voluntary or "discretionary" gift generously given by the banker to the investor. A ludicrous suggestion of course, but if a fig leaf was good enough for Adam and Eve then it was good enough for the Medici. Interest on loans was also regularly concealed by changing money between the many currencies then circulating in Europe, and smuggling the interest into the exchange rate. The churchman Antoninus of Florence called foul here, saying that the deals did not involve enough risk and thus constituted usury. As one historian has remarked, this was "a rather strange attitude on the part of the archbishop of the leading banking center in Western Europe."[17]

Clearly, then, both the intellectuals and the financiers of the day were well aware that money itself has a value, and that this value can change. In fact, that was a way of defending the practice just described: a set agreement to exchange currencies at a future time was always risky, because of fluctuating rates. Even without comparing different denominations, there was the phenomenon of inflation, which began to be noticed in our period. A treatise about coinage written in 1588 by Bernardo Davanzati noted that an influx of precious metal from the recently "discovered" Americas was causing gold and silver to lose value.[18] If this went on, Davanzati observed, some other basis of currency would need to be found, or one would have to resort to trade by bartering.

Whether by barter or coinage, it was commonly accepted that there was a "just price" for each economic exchange. Bernardino followed scholastic precedent by defining this in terms of community practice at a given place and time.[19] The concept of just price is also discussed in Cotrugli's book of advice for merchants. He cites the Roman law, still in force in his day, that a sale is null and void if less than half of the "just" or "fair" price is offered (*Trade*, 32). Of course, that leaves a lot of margin to cheat, as Cotrugli recognizes. But as he says, not everything immoral is also illegal (*Trade*, 104). He wraps up many of the ideas we've just looked at in his definition of the "reasonable profit" a merchant should be aiming at. It is determined by "the real exchange, under the prevailing local conditions, taking into account the uncertainty of gain, a true and honest exchange between the parties, without interest, acting only with diligence and prudence in view of the risk and effort taken on" (*Trade*, 103).

For yet another philosophical own goal in a Renaissance treatise on economics, we may return to Francesco Guicciardini, whom we have met as a historian and critic of Machiavelli's political thought. This versatile author also composed a dialogue on what we now call progressive taxation; that is, taking a larger percentage of income from rich people than from poor people.[20] True to form as a defender of the more noble elements of his republican city, Guicciardini is totally against this. His spokesman in the dialogue says that taxation should *not* be used to ameliorate inequality between rich and poor. To the contrary, the government's aim should be to "conserve each in his rank." Equality should indeed be a goal, but only equality before the law, not full social or economic equality. Today's readers may be more persuaded by the dialogue's proponent of progressive tax. This character says that a flat taxation rate is unfair because the poor can afford to pay a smaller percentage of their income without it impacting on their lifestyle. Ideally, class distinctions should be eliminated altogether, a proposal reminiscent of the communist proposals in those treatises on utopia. But even leaving aside such ambitious objectives, the opponent says that a progressive tax is in fact "equal," because it causes an equal amount of "discomfort" to everyone (*tanto s'incomodi l'uno quanto l'altro*). Which is fairly persuasive, though Guicciardini's mouthpiece does offer an interesting response, namely that economic need is relative to one's status. It may be a real hardship for a rich man to be unable to afford fine clothes, since such clothes are expected in the circles he moves in.

A striking feature here is the tacit assumption that the total amount of wealth in a given community, or in the world as a whole, is fixed. The advocate of progressive tax in Guicciardini's dialogue offers a very Florentine image to illustrate: if you have a certain amount of cloth for a certain number of people, and use it to make elaborate robes for a few of these people, there won't be enough left to clothe everyone.[21] If the poor gain, the rich must lose, and vice versa. There is no hope here of a rising tide that might lift all boats. It's the economic equivalent of the zero-sum political world envisioned by Machiavelli, and by Guiccardini himself. Power and resources move from some hands to others, but they never increase overall. Indeed, this was assumed even in the fantasy context of the Renaissance utopias, which speak of wealth passing around freely from hand to hand but not of *everyone* getting rich. Perhaps to achieve this, everyone would have to become a philosopher. For, like Xenophon's Socrates, philosophers know that true wealth lies in knowing what you really need, and having no less than that.

44

TOWN AND GOWN ITALIAN UNIVERSITIES

You're probably aware that there are university league tables, which students can use to compare the places they might go to study. Believe it or not, there are also league tables for philosophy, which list philosophy departments (or at least, the ones in the English-speaking world) for overall quality and within a given discipline. The departments take this very seriously, looking to hire famous names that will bump them up the league table. It's comparable to the way people talk about summer transfers in soccer or other sports: just as that new striker may help Arsenal compete for the title against Liverpool, that new metaphysician will help Harvard gain ground on Princeton. If you find it vaguely unseemly for philosophers to be competing in this fashion, a sign of modern-day corruption in what should be a disinterested inquiry into truth, then you're at least half wrong. It may be unseemly, but there's nothing modern about it. Though they didn't literally have league tables, as far as I know, the scholars at universities in the Italian Renaissance would find the rivalry and one-upmanship of today's academia entirely familiar.[1]

A good example would be the contest over the services of Pietro Pomponazzi, a leading Aristotelian scholar around the turn of the sixteenth century.[2] He mostly taught at Padua, with brief stints at Ferrara, but was then enticed to join the university of Bologna in 1511 or 1512. Bologna worked hard to keep him, pulling political strings in Florence to stop them from bringing Pomponazzi to Tuscany. He also enjoyed a generous salary, and he was not the only one: the best and the brightest were paid well at the leading Italian universities.[3] Like soccer teams, these institutions looked beyond their borders to find talent, as when Bologna tried to hire Justus Lipsius, a scholar of Stoicism from what is now Belgium. The German philosopher and master of the occult sciences, Heinrich Cornelius Agrippa, was persuaded to teach at Pavia and Turin.[4] To keep the scholars on their toes, universities also fostered competition within their own ranks. It was standard practice for lectures on the same topic to be scheduled at the same time, forcing students to vote with their feet as to who was the best instructor, which makes today's teaching evaluations seem pretty gentle. Pomponazzi was, at various times, put up against "concurrent" lectures by Alessandro Achillini, Nicoletto Vernia, and Agostino Nifo, with students presumably agonizing over the choice between these stars of early sixteenth-century Aristotelian philosophy.

The university officials kept a close eye on their teaching staff, visiting classes to make sure that lectures were not ended too early, and levying fines for absenteeism. Padua even imposed fines on professors who read from a prepared text, since students then, like students today, preferred the spontaneity of an improvised delivery. Of course, the professors chafed under such measures. Later in the sixteenth century at Bologna, the botanist and zoologist Ulisse Aldrovandi wrote up a list of measures for reforming his university, complaining that his colleagues were reluctant to allow concurrent lectures despite their beneficial effect. Aldrovandi was in favor of this system and the competition it fostered, though he did make an exception for his own lectures: all students should be able to hear these, because they were so important![5] Even dress code became a bone of contention. When Galileo Galilei, who taught at Padua, was fined for not wearing his professor's gown, he responded with a satirical poem arguing that this long garment was unnatural, since it inhibited urination and the visiting of brothels.

Now *that* is the voice of a modern academic. But the universities of this era also maintained a significant degree of continuity with their medieval forebears.[6] Bologna had been the first university in all of Europe, with the founding date traditionally put in 1088, but in fact probably carrying out the expected activities of a university only in the 1180s or so. In the fifteenth and sixteenth centuries it had the largest faculty of Italy's sixteen universities.[7] Bologna set the tone for the rest of Italy. Founded by a collective union or "university" of students, it had a bottom-up organization that may be contrasted to the top-down structure used at Paris, Oxford, and their many imitators. In practice this meant not so much that students called the shots in Italy, as that there was a constant jockeying for power between students, instructors, and civic administrators. If he noticed this, Machiavelli no doubt approved, since it was the educational equivalent of the productive class tensions he so admired in the Roman republic.

Italy's universities were also distinctive in focusing on law and medicine, the traditional strengths of Bologna. Theology, so important at Paris and Oxford, was mostly taught outside the universities in Italy, at separate schools run by religious orders. So for example Savonarola initially studied at the university of Ferrara intending to learn medicine, but left the university system once he became a friar, and taught scripture and the scholastic curriculum in Dominican convents. One shouldn't exaggerate the gulf between the scholastic and religious worlds, since university students in a given city might attend lectures put on by the orders.[8] Still, the result was that there was a rather "secular" thematic focus at the universities. In fact one might tentatively suggest that the minor role played by theology at the universities was one reason sixteenth-century Italy was able to anticipate the scientific developments of the Enlightenment. With logic, medicine, and natural philosophy having a dominant position at these institutions, they were able to produce such scholars as Pomponazzi, Zabarella, Vesalius, and Galileo.

Another striking and unusual feature of the Italian university scene was what we might call "second city syndrome," in which a major civic power ran a university in a smaller nearby city. The template was set by the Duke of Milan in 1361, when he founded a university in the subject town of Pavia rather than Milan itself. He and his advisors handpicked the members of the faculty there. Likewise the Medici moved the school (*studio*) of Florence to Pisa in the 1470s. The university of Siena was also beholden to the power of Florence, with the grand duke of Tuscany approving its professorial roster. In 1581 a mendicant friar was stopped from teaching philosophy, since Florence deemed this inappropriate.[9] Rome also came to exert considerable control over Bologna, with the pope meddling in professorial appointments. Padua, which has already been mentioned several times and will be important in the story to come, was overseen from Venice. The city even tried to force all Venetian citizens who wanted to obtain a degree to do so in Padua, and made it a condition of state employment that one's degree be from this "home" university.[10]

University cities are never completely free of conflict between "town" and "gown," and the Italian Renaissance certainly had its share of unruly students and disputes between civic and academic authorities. But for the most part city authorities thought that higher learning was a good investment. It brought honor and renown, as recognized by Guicciardini in his *History of Florence* when he praised Lorenzo de' Medici for his university policy, through which he "sought glory and excellence more than anyone else."[11] At a more pragmatic level, professors of law often helped as advisors for city regimes, while teachers of medicine pursued private practice or attended on aristocratic clients. Students complained about this, because these literally extracurricular activities were a distraction for their teachers.

With the coming of the Protestant Reformation, another kind of political issue arose at the universities. Many students were visitors from other countries, with Germans often making up one of the largest factions or "nations" apart from the Italians. Foreigners were attracted by the excellence of the teaching and also the distinctive Italian curriculum, with its focus on science and law. For a time, Protestant students were welcome, something that was not reciprocated in Protestant lands, where Catholics were generally barred from studying. But eventually, in 1564, a decree by the pope demanded that all candidates for degree explicitly profess the Catholic faith. While this was sometimes ignored, in 1570 German students at Siena were arrested for heresy, showing that the threat to Protestants was a real one.[12] The Catholic response to the Reformation also left its mark on intellectual activities at the university. For instance a logic professor at Padua named Bernardino Tomitano translated a work on the Bible by the northern humanist Erasmus, and saw it placed on the index of proscribed books. He escaped further censure, but only after being made to declare his opposition to Erasmus' teachings.[13]

Tomitano's speciality, logic, gives us another point of continuity with medieval teaching practices. As had been the case in previous centuries, indeed as far back as late antiquity, logic was a young student's first encounter with philosophy. Logic was also standard preparation for studies in non-philosophical fields like law and medicine. This suggests that it was considered a fairly introductory discipline, and for many students that was no doubt the case. But under the heading of logic, challenging problems like the status of universals were also debated. A nice example is provided by Alessandro Achillini, who taught at Padua around the turn of the sixteenth century and was one of the aforementioned "concurrents" who competed with Pomponazzi. We have detailed records of the disputations he held at the university: of 238 such events, 75 were on natural philosophy and another 53 on logic. Confirming the lack of activity in theology, only six disputations fell under this heading.[14] A similar story is told by faculty numbers at Ferrara in the latter half of the sixteenth century, when the thirty professors in the arts and medical faculty included six logicians and only two theologians.[15]

It was part of Padua's excellence in Aristotelian philosophy that they had a long-standing strength in logic. This went back at least as far as Paul of Venice, who taught at Padua, Siena, and Perugia in the 1420s and wrote influential textbooks on the subject. For his so-called *Small Logic* (*Logica parva*) we have no fewer than eighty surviving manuscripts, and it was already printed in 1472.[16] A statute from Padua in 1496 makes Paul's writings set texts in the curriculum, alongside contributions by various medieval logicians. Particularly striking is the presence here of works by the so-called "Oxford Calculators," like William Heytesbury and Roger Swineshead.[17] Their habit of applying logical and mathematical analysis to problems of natural philosophy, like the dynamics of motion, was a natural fit for the combination of disciplines taught in the arts faculty at Padua. Thus we see Pomponazzi writing a treatise on a problem discussed by the Calculators back in the fourteenth century, the "intension and remission of forms," which concerns rates of change in motion and other physical alterations.[18]

One of the Aristotelian professors of Padua, Agostino Nifo, shows us how Renaissance logicians continued to draw on medieval sources. E. Jennifer Ashworth, writing in the 1970s, pointed out the surprising extent to which Nifo was aware of medieval terminist logic.[19] But she also pointed out that Nifo was not really in sympathy with the older approaches, in part because he preferred the even older approach of Aristotle himself. Determined to reduce the entire discipline of logic to the theory of the syllogism, as laid out by Aristotle, Nifo wound up presenting a stripped down version of medieval theories which, as Ashworth put it, "diminished their value and hence made them easier to abandon." Building on this study, Lisa Jardine has observed that Nifo was also aware of discussions of logic within the humanist tradition, in particular by Lorenzo Valla.[20] As we saw (Chapter 25), Valla was a bitter critic of scholasticism, and accordingly directed withering criticism and disdain at university logic. Jardine used this as context for understanding Nifo's minimalist approach, suggesting that he wanted logic to focus on its goal of "syllogistic perfection" by outsourcing all other aspects of argumentation to rhetoric, the speciality subject of Valla and other humanists.

As the case of Nifo illustrates, the denizens of the universities were far from unaware of what the humanists were doing. Conversely, the humanists were deeply engaged with university culture. True, leading heroes of the movement like Petrarch, Salutati, Bruni, Alberti, and Manetti were independent scholars, but Bruni for one studied law and dialectic in a scholastic setting.[21] He knew enough about law to declare, with customary wit, that it should be called "the yawning science." Alberti too studied law and found it boring because it involved too much memorization. A number of prominent humanists held university positions, even the aforementioned scourge of scholastic thought, Lorenzo Valla. He taught at the university of Pavia, but predictably enough caused uproar when he complained about the poor Latin skills of a degree candidate and impugned the intellectual credentials of the law faculty.[22]

The Renaissance scholar David Lines has nicely captured the way that humanism was co-opted by university culture, writing that "professors and university officials were well aware of the significance of the humanist challenge. Jointly, they paid it the ultimate compliment of stealing its ideas and hiring its proponents."[23] Beginning in the middle of the fifteenth century, the humanist study of rhetoric entered the teaching curriculum. Professors did philological work, edited and translated works of ancient literature, and taught a wide range of texts to their students, with the curriculum in humanism being far more open and flexible than that of fields like logic, law, and medicine. We've already met Angelo Poliziano, who at Florence in the 1490s offered courses on authors like Virgil and Homer before moving into the teaching of Aristotelian logic (Chapter 31). The backlash against this infringement of scholastic territory provoked him to defend his right to deal with such topics as a true "philologist." As that episode shows, the specialists in philosophy were happy to have humanist colleagues around, so long as they stayed in their lane. The Aristotelians could not deny that the humanist movement had done great good for their own studies, by establishing better editions of Greek texts including those of Aristotle, and also by bringing back into circulation the ancient commentaries on his works.[24] (Or rather, bringing them into circulation in the Latin West, since as we know these commentaries had been studied in Byzantium for centuries.)

The humanists' expertise put them in a good position to contribute to the philosophy of language, which as in the medieval period was still considered to fall into the domain of logic. Valla wanted to sweep away the Aristotelian approach and replace it with a more philological enterprise inspired by ancient rhetoricians like Quintilian. Other humanists adopted a less radical attitude, seeking to improve Aristotelianism rather than discard it. Giovanni Pontano, for one, agreed with Valla that careful attention to real Latin usage was vital.[25] But he presented a broadly Aristotelian account of language and its origins, seeing linguistic signs as conventional in nature. Words do not "fall from heaven," but are invented by humans to describe things in their immediate environment. This explained the relatively limited vocabulary that Pontano assumed to be in use among the newly discovered peoples of Americas. With the advance of civilization, words come to be used for more abstract meanings, so that for example the Latin verb *serere*, "to sow" seeds in agriculture, supposedly became the root for words like *sermo*, meaning "speech."

It seems then that neither institutional nor disciplinary boundaries neatly separate the humanists from the scholastics in our period. If we want to contrast them nonetheless, a better basis would be the fetishizing of Latin. The value placed on eloquent Latin was very high, which is why female humanists were able to break into the circle of respected intellectuals by mastering this language, despite being excluded from the universities. Authors felt the need to justify writing in their native tongues rather than in Latin, something that goes back as far as Dante, and that we just encountered with Benedetto Cotrugli, who elected to write his work on the art of the merchant in Italian despite the fact that it might be "judged less worthy of consideration."[26] But if vernacular languages were generally considered inferior to classical ones, committed Aristotelians were increasingly deciding that they didn't care. They adopted the view of the "barbarian" from Pico's letter to Barbaro, in which Pico ironically used elegant Latin to defend the use of inelegant language: what matters is the truth of the ideas expressed, not the way they are expressed. The Aristotelians made the same point, but without the same irony.

One of them was Sperone Speroni, a student of Pomponazzi.[27] Pomponazzi was no linguist: his Latin and Greek skills were so rudimentary that Speroni said he "knew no language outside of Mantuan," and Pomponazzi himself insisted that truth needs no adornment by eloquence. Speroni made him a character in a *Dialogue on Language* which promoted the use of vernacular languages. For Speroni, it was not the scholastics with their clunky Latin who were the barbarians, but rather the humanists, who "barbarously call non-Latin philosophy barbaric." He considered humanists as "scholars of the most inept sophistry ever to exist in the sciences."[28] Philosophy would flourish not through the cultivation of fine writing, but the use of straightforward vernacular language, so that intellectuals could concentrate on rigorous thinking rather than wasting years of their life mastering Latin grammar and Ciceronian style.

Not coincidentally, around this same time scholars did indeed seek to capture Aristotelian philosophy in Italian, as when Antonio Tridapale published the first logical textbook in this language in 1547. Speroni and Tridapale were both connected to the Accademia degli Infiammati, founded in 1540 as an organization committed to the use of vernacular language in scholarly activity. It ran into the problem that scholars visiting from other countries could not participate in its activities. Ciceronian eloquence might not be necessary, but it turned out to be quite useful to have Latin as the universal European language of scholarship. Still, the Aristotelians thought the language was accidental to the scholarship. The aforementioned logician Bernardino Tomitano, who was a friend of Speroni, stated that the words of different languages are merely "shells (*scorza*)" for ideas that are the same for everyone. This itself was a genuinely Aristotelian idea, since Aristotle had said in a much-discussed passage of his logical writings that spoken words are only outward "symbols of affections in the soul" (*en tei psuche pathematon sumbola,* at *On Interpretation,* 16a).

So specialists in scholastic Aristotelianism like Tomitano, Speroni, Pomponazzi, and Nifo can after all be contrasted to the humanists. They owed at least grudging appreciation to these philologists for helping to establish better editions of Aristotle's works. But for the Renaissance schoolmen, the right way to do philosophy was not to become expert in rhetoric or the languages of antiquity. It was to pursue the perfect knowledge envisioned by Aristotle himself, which would take the form of syllogistically structured arguments that come together to constitute demonstrative science. Philosophers should focus on thinking thoughts like that, and not care so much about the words they use to express those thoughts.

45

I'D LIKE TO THANK THE LYCEUM
ARISTOTLE IN RENAISSANCE ITALY

If the German language were a person, it would be an army drill sergeant: demanding, strict about rules, and devoted to questionable notions of masculinity. (According to German, tables, chairs, the sky, record players, and capitalism are all boys.) But like all languages, it does offer many pleasures. My favorite German word is *glimpflich*, in part because it is so fun to say. *Glimpflich*! It doesn't so much roll off the tongue as do a little dance on the tongue, and then hop out through the mouth and into the world, making it a better place. I also like it because it is so hard to translate. Usually you'll hear it in a context where someone has been fortunate in a bad situation, like if someone escapes from a car accident unharmed: *er ist glimpflich davongekommen*. Here you'd be hard pressed to render it with just one word. It's a phenomenon that will be familiar to anyone who has tried to render philosophical texts from one language into another. It can be tempting simply to leave tricky words in the original language. So tempting that, in an ancient Greek reading group I used to attend, we introduced a rule against having more than one untranslated word per session.

Leonardo Bruni might have rejected even that rule as being too permissive. When he translated Aristotle's *Nicomachean Ethics* into Latin, he added a preface in which he explained why it was necessary to replace the medieval version by Robert Grosseteste. This older translation was full of transliterated Greek words that would be incomprehensible to Greekless readers, which was entirely unnecessary, since Latin too is a rich language, amply equipped to express anything found in Aristotle's Greek. As Bruni sarcastically comments after quoting a passage full of untranslated terms, "surely all this could have been said in Latin? Does the fault lie with the tongue or with the translator?" That was only one of Grosseteste's shortcomings, whose translation displayed little philosophical understanding and less eloquence: "he is, so to speak, a mongrel, half Greek and half Latin; deficient in both languages, competent in neither."[1]

If you've read some Aristotle yourself, you might be wondering why anyone would expect to find eloquence in an accurate version of his writings. The answer, as usual with Bruni, has to do with Cicero. That Roman master of Latin eloquence had commented that Aristotle's writings were distinguished for their elegant style. When he said this, Cicero had in mind not the rather technical school treatises that survive today, but now lost works that were aimed at a wider audience. Not realizing this, Bruni managed to convince himself that Aristotle's treatises are beautifully written, especially the *Politics* which, Bruni said, contains "almost no passage without its rhetorical glitter and flourish."[2] He duly exerted himself to render Aristotle into fine, Ciceronian Latin. I already mentioned that Alonzo of Burgos was unimpressed by the resulting version, which he found inexact (Chapter 24), and there were other critics, like the Spanish bishop Alfonso of Cartagena. Alfonso didn't know Greek himself, but didn't let that stop him from censuring Bruni on the rather strange grounds that his Latin translation made Aristotle say things that were not true. This is a hint that philological accuracy as the standard of good translation was only just emerging in the fifteenth century, thanks to Bruni and the other humanists. Bruni embraced that standard, leaping to his own defense with the remark, "a translation is wholly correct if it corresponds to the Greek . . . Alteration is the translator's sin."[3]

The spread of this approach to translation is shown also by Giannozzo Manetti, who studied with Bruni. We met him already as the author of the *other* treatise called *On the Dignity of Man*, the one that wasn't written by Pico della Mirandola (Chapter 36). Manetti was no one-book wonder, but a polymath who learned Hebrew so that he could dispute with Jewish intellectuals and translate the Bible. If Bruni had to justify his choice to improve on Grosseteste, Manetti most definitely had to explain why he was giving the world another Latin Old Testament even though the sainted Jerome had produced one in antiquity. He wrote a whole treatise in defense of the project, which listed many errors in Jerome's version and also defined good translation practice more generally. Under the influence of Bruni, he complained about clumsy and misleading translations that replace individual words in the original text with Latin equivalents, rather than seeking to capture the meaning with elegance and accuracy. The translator must follow a middle path, "neither wandering too far from the work taken for translation nor clinging entirely and completely word for word to the original authors, but hewing to a middle and safe way."[4]

This policy went back further than Manetti's teacher Bruni, to Bruni's own teacher Chrysoloras. As he imported knowledge of Greek from Byzantium, Chrysoloras encouraged an *ad sensum* rather than *ad verbum* method; that is, trying to capture the meaning and not the words. But as Manetti himself implies by endorsing a happy medium between free and exact translation, the *ad sensum* technique could also be taken to extremes. Reacting to the output of another Greek émigré humanist, John Argyropoulos, the sixteenth-century Aristotle translator Francesco Vimercato commented that if the medieval versions were too literal, the humanist ones were too free. For Vimercato, a "middle" approach could retain technical terms from scholasticism, some of which are indeed so useful that they remain in use by English-speaking philosophers. We still speak of "substance (*substantia*)" and "alteration (*alteratio*)," which he endorsed as translations of the Greek words *ousia* and *alloiosis*. Another convincing point made by Vimercato is that a good translation should capture for the reader what it is like to read the original text, and not, for instance, make Aristotle's treatises into works of elegant rhetoric, as Bruni sought to do. Instead, Vimercato sought to mimic Aristotle's dense and compressed style, so that he might "appear the same to those speaking Latin as to those speaking Greek."[5]

We usually think of Italian humanism as a movement away from the Aristotelian interests of medieval scholasticism, and towards Plato and Hellenistic authors like Lucretius. But as we can see with the case of Bruni, the humanists felt that Aristotle too had to be "recovered," saved from his medieval translators and hidebound scholastic interpreters. After learning Greek, Poggio Bracciolini was thrilled to discover the real Aristotle hidden beneath the Latin Aristotle. He wrote, "I am becoming acquainted, in his own language, with an author who is practically speechless and ridiculous in translation," and said he wanted "to drink in the Greek greedily so as to escape those horrid translations."[6] Soon enough, it would become much easier to imbibe Aristotle in the original vintage. In the time of Bruni and Poggio, reading Aristotle in Greek (or Latin for that matter) meant reading a manuscript, just as it had in Byzantium. But by the end of the fifteenth century, there would be printed editions of his works.

This was thanks above all to Aldo Manuzio, usually called by the Latin version of his name, Aldus Manutius.[7] Manutius was a member of the circle gathered around the precocious, and let's not forget rich, Pico della Mirandola. He also associated with Ermolao Barbaro. You might remember Barbaro as the recipient of Pico's irony-laced defense of "barbaric" scholastic Latin, but more relevant here are the informal lectures he gave on Aristotle in Venice. By 1500, Venice was already a major center of Latin printed editions. Now, inspired by the philosophical interests of Pico and Barbaro, Manutius undertook to print Aristotle's works in the original Greek: a project of great scholarly significance, which would hopefully make him a nice pile of money in the process. The "Aldine" edition of Aristotle included work by his student Theophrastus, as well, and the project went on to print Aristotle's late ancient exegetes in the original Greek. Commentaries by Ammonius, Philoponus, and Alexander appeared before Manutius died in 1515. He also printed a Greek grammar written by Theodore of Gaza and works by Latin authors, notably the collected works of Poliziano, as well as Italian literature like Dante and Petrarch.

As that last choice suggests, Manutius was very much a representative of the humanist movement. He collaborated with no less a humanist than Erasmus, who stayed with Manutius and saw his translation of Euripides put out by the Aldine press. Manutius also consulted with humanist philologists to establish correct Greek texts. The printed versions still wound up containing many errors. Still, this was a pioneering attempt to usher Greek into the world of printed editions, much as the humanists sought to spread knowledge of Greek through the world of Italian scholarship. To give you a sense of just how innovative the project was, I need only mention that Manutius had to commission a special typeface for Greek, which was handmade for him by a goldsmith. The font, which imitated a cursive italic script, would make the Aldine texts distinctive and recognizable even once other printers started printing in Greek. Or at least, it should have. In 1503 Manutius had to issue a warning to buyers not to be fooled by knockoff editions using an imitation of his typeface.

As exciting a breakthrough as it was to have Aristotle printed in Greek, we should not imagine that Latin translations of his works became irrelevant in the sixteenth century. Though Greek was sometimes taught at the universities, only a handful of committed humanists achieved true mastery of the language. As the scholar Paul Grendler has commented, "Greek failed to find a secure place in the curriculum, because it only served the needs of Latin culture."[8] So the vast majority of readers still had to consult Latin translations. Charles Schmitt, the leading expert on the reception of Aristotle in this period, calculates that less than 10 percent of sixteenth-century works about Aristotle quote him in the original Greek.[9] In this respect, then, the Aristotle of the Italian Renaissance was not so different from the Aristotle of medieval scholasticism: mostly, he still spoke Latin.

In other respects, though, Aristotle was a changed man. Changed in part by the company he kept. The printing of the late ancient commentators, and their increased availability in Latin translations,[10] meant that Renaissance interpreters were closer to being in the enviable position earlier enjoyed by the circle of Anna Komnene. They could survey the whole history of Aristotelianism, and build upon the earlier commentaries written in late antiquity and Byzantium. Much like the circle of Anna Komnene, they explored areas of Aristotelian science that had been largely ignored in the medieval Latin tradition. Theophrastus' works on plants added botany to the menu, and Aristotle's zoological works were consulted as never before.[11] A central aspect of Aristotle's original project, his empirical investigation of the natural world, had been relatively unimportant to the medievals, with occasional exceptions like Albert the Great. Now, Aristotle reappeared as an acute observer and recorder of his physical environment, putting the "nature" back in Aristotelian natural philosophy.

An excellent example of this is meteorology.[12] This is a topic I have barely if ever mentioned in this whole book series, so you might be forgiven for being surprised that Aristotle wrote about it. Especially since he lived in Athens: what was he going to say, that the forecast was for plenty of sun, with a chance of Macedonian invasion? But as it turns out, Aristotelian meteorology was not mostly about weather prediction. It was a wide-ranging science dealing with all manner of phenomena observable in the sky, including "meteorological" events in our sense, like lightning storms, but also such things as comets and rainbows. Aristotle thought that many such phenomena could be explained by appealing to "exhalations," vapors that build up under the earth and are then released with more or less violence. From the point of view of the Renaissance commentators, meteorology was thus a fairly rudimentary discipline, in the sense that it dealt with non-living, brute material forces: the interaction of things like wind, water, and earth. This means that some of the standard conceptual tools in Aristotelian science were all but irrelevant. Where animals, plants, and humans have substantial forms, something like a rainbow or storm might simply result when air and vapor are pushed around in the atmosphere because of changes in heating, cooling, and the like. As Pietro Pomponazzi said, these things are "closer to matter than form."

In part for this reason, and in part because of the difficulty of discerning the causes of meteorological phenomena, the commentators were modest in their claims about what this science could achieve. Agostino Nifo, for instance, stated that Aristotle's proposals for the underlying causes in meteorology were purely "conjectural." Of particular interest was the question whether meteorological events have *final* causes, that is, whether they happen for the sake of some goal. Perhaps they are just random events, with all that pushing around and moving of vapor happening by sheer accident. An example would be Nifo's explanation of thunder, which happens when a mass of dense air collides with a mass of rarefied air in the sky. On the other hand, could a Renaissance Christian really believe that anything happens by sheer accident? Even if hailstorms and comets have no natural purpose, surely they play some role in God's providential design for our world? For all his empiricism and commitment to natural explanation, Pomponazzi was eager to concede this point. Even damaging storms and earthquakes are intended by God: they "seem bad to us," but are in fact for the best. It's just that "we are ignorant of their purpose."[13]

Earthquakes were a topic that received extensive discussion inspired by Aristotle's *Meteorology*, which explains (in book 2, chapter 8) that they are caused by eruptions of wind below the earth. In the 1570s, a series of earthquakes all but leveled the city of Ferrara, leaving observers to debate the scientific and theological meaning of this disaster. One scholar at Bologna lamented that the earthquakes could not possibly be part of God's benevolent natural order, since "they disrupt everything, strip away beauty, and demolish."[14] In keeping with this, naturalistic accounts inspired by Aristotle proposed that Ferrara had been struck because of its geological situation. Caves nearby were apt to trap exhalations that would then be released with sudden violence. At the other extreme, the pope chipped in with the suggestion that Ferrara was chosen for destruction because it hosted such a large Jewish population.

As we've seen before, Renaissance authors often reflected on such diversity of opinions by writing dialogues, with different characters adopting different points of view on the topic at hand. So it was here: several authors staged literary discussions about the causes of earthquakes. A representative example is Giacomo Buoni, whose dialogue features a series of speakers addressing the topic from different points of view: philosophical, historical, and theological. His philosophical spokesman affirms the "accidentality" of earthquakes, which are clearly foreign to the nature of earth, which tends towards stillness and being at rest, gathered as it is around the midpoint of the cosmos. But the final word is given to a theologian, who states that while earthquakes are "partly natural," they are also partly divine, "sent by God when He wants, how He wants, where, and how much He wants, and more often for sins, moving with His will the secondary causes, and nature, which He commands at His pleasure."[15]

Aristotle stood for the more empirical approach, which helps to explain why a figure like Galileo could say, as late as 1640, "I am sure that, if Aristotle returned to the world, he would receive me among his followers."[16] Such hard-nosed scientific interests seem a far cry from the philological concerns of the humanists, even if the textual productions of the humanists made it possible for Aristotelianism to achieve new breadth and diffusion in Renaissance culture. The aforementioned Charles Schmitt has proposed that we should speak not of "Renaissance Aristotelianism" but "Renaissance Aristotelianisms." That would more fittingly capture the different, and often innovative, approaches that were taken to this long-studied body of texts in the fifteenth and sixteenth centuries, a time that Schmitt boldly calls "the high-point of Western Aristotelianism."[17] "Like religious and biblical knowledge," he comments, "Aristotelian doctrine was available in many different forms, from the most learned annotated editions of the Greek text to the sketchiest of compendia in Latin or a number of different vernaculars."[18]

It's worth dwelling on that point. We've seen that for every humanist who could read Aristotle in Greek, there were ten scholars who read him in Latin. To which we can add that there would have been many more reading Aristotle, or reading about Aristotle, in Italian.[19] The history of Aristotle in European vernacular languages goes all the way back to the eleventh century, when Notker of St Gallen translated a couple of the logical works into that most unforgiving of tongues, German. Subsequently Nicole Oresme rendered Aristotle's *On the Heavens* into French, in 1377. But it was only in the Renaissance that we see a real blossoming of Aristotle outside of Latin, with figures like Antonio Brucioli producing Italian translations in the mid-sixteenth century. Not long after, in 1565, Lodovico Dolce wrote an Italian *Summary of Aristotle's Philosophy*, which integrates Platonist arguments for the immortality of the soul and ideas taken from Christian authorities into an overview of Peripatetic thought.[20]

Even such peripheral texts as the *Mechanics*, not really by Aristotle but ascribed to him as its author, got the treatment. The audience for Aristotelian texts was getting wider. Alessandro Piccolomini said explicitly that his version of the *Mechanics* was intended "principally for engineers." Later on, in the early seventeenth century, the beautifully monikered Panfilo Persico produced a vernacular compendium of the *Ethics* and *Politics*, and said it was aimed at "princes, men of the republic, and of the court." Women were also occasionally named as beneficiaries of Italian versions or summaries of Aristotle, since for the most part they could not read Latin, which is why the achievements of female humanists like Fedele and Cereta were so exceptional. As Piccolomini said, while stressing the usefulness of his philosophical textbooks on Aristotelian ethics, women "remain deprived, through no fault of their own, of those habits which could make them happy."[21] On the other hand, we also find vernacular works being aimed at more expert readers, including readers who were assumed to have the ability to go back and check the original Greek of Aristotle, or at least the Latin version, if they had a mind to. Luca Bianchi, a scholar who has explored the rise of vernacular philosophy, thus observes that by the sixteenth century, languages like Italian were emerging for the first time as an "instrument of scientific communication."[22]

Still, it would not be wrong to see vernacularization as a trend towards the popularization of philosophy, and Aristotle in particular. The vast majority of vernacular works devoted to him were not in fact translations, but summaries, paraphrases, and original treatises or dialogues like the ones about meteorology. Elite scholars were not necessarily thrilled by this development. Bernardo Segni, who translated the *Rhetoric* into Italian, said that he was criticized by some who blamed him for making it possible for "uneducated" people to learn what others had "acquired over many years with great effort from Greek and Latin books."[23] But there was not only Greek and Latin to contend with: there was also Arabic. The emergence of new forms of Aristotelianism in the Italian Renaissance goes hand in hand with a resurgence of his greatest medieval commentator, Ibn Rushd, known in

Latin as Averroes. His works caused a stir back in the thirteenth century, when his doctrines led to debate and condemnation in Paris. In the fifteenth and sixteenth centuries, these ideas returned with a vengeance.

It's a development inextricably entwined with the diffusion of Aristotelian literature,[24] most literally so in the case of the famous Giunta edition of Aristotle which appeared from 1550 to 1552.[25] It included Latin translations of Averroes' commentaries, so that every reader of Aristotle could turn to this Muslim guide to understand his works. Amazingly, out of the thirty-eight surviving exegetical works by Averroes on Aristotle, no fewer than thirty-six were printed in the sixteenth century. This can be understood as a blow for scholasticism against the antiquarian interests of the humanists. As Tommaso Giunta said in his preface to the edition, the humanists prized only classical languages and ignored contributions from the Islamic world: "our age accepts nothing and admires nothing coming from the despised and contemptible teaching of the Arabs, unless it knows it to have been transmitted to us from the Greek treasurehouse." But we're not going to make the same mistake. In the next chapter, we'll look at one particular type of Renaissance Aristotelianism, the one that carried on most directly from medieval scholasticism and dared to entertain the notorious teachings that went under the name of Averroism.

46

OF TWO MINDS
POMPONAZZI AND NIFO ON THE INTELLECT

Some people just don't like being told what to do, or what to think. And a lot of these people are named Peter. The tradition began with St Peter himself, who was not only martyred for his faith but even, according to legend, made the Romans crucify him upside down to avoid being tacitly compared with Christ. The Russian emperor Peter the Great, ruler of a land where men usually wore beards, decided that they should all go clean-shaven. Peter Pan refused even to grow up. The guitarist of the Who, Pete Townshend was, well, Pete Townshend, while the Reggae singer Peter Tosh was so annoyed at being forbidden to smoke marijuana that he wrote a song called "Legalize It." I myself contributed to this grand tradition of rebellious Peters as a lad, by occasionally refusing to eat my vegetables. Though to be honest, this hardly counted as rebellion in my family, given that my father likes to say, "I have a rule against eating anything green, but I make an exception for carrots: I don't eat those either."

In any case, it was entirely predictable that when, in 1513, the pope declared that the human soul is immortal and that this can be proven by rational argument, some philosopher named Peter would refuse to play along. Three years later, Pietro Pomponazzi published his work *On the Immortality of the Soul*. The pope would no doubt have approved of the title, but not the rest of it. It argues that philosophical arguments point rather towards the soul's mortality, its essential dependence upon the body. Pomponazzi concluded by acknowledging the truth of the Christian teaching that the human soul does live on after death, but he denied that this can be established philosophically. Unsurprisingly, this provoked a hostile reaction. The treatise was burned at Venice, and Pomponazzi was accused of heresy. Fortunately for him, his patron was named Peter too. This was the bishop Pietro Bembo, whom we met as the author of a dialogue on love called *Gli Asolani* (see Chapter 33). Despite being himself a Platonist philosopher, Bembo gave Pomponazzi political protection. Meanwhile, Pomponazzi got busy mounting his own defense. He wrote two works responding to critics, the most significant one being Agostino Nifo.

The two had clashed before, having been rivals since the 1490s, when both lectured at the university of Padua. As we've seen, Padua was a center of Peripatetic philosophy in the Italian Renaissance. Aristotle's treatises were assiduously taught and studied there, alongside commentaries on his works. But this does not imply that all the Paduans were in agreement about how to interpret Aristotle.[1] Actually the theory of soul most strongly associated with Padua is one that Pomponazzi would harshly criticize. It's a theory we can trace to Aristotle's greatest medieval commentator, the Muslim thinker Averroes.[2] One visitor to Padua at the end of the fifteenth century said that at the university there, "all agreed to the positions of this author and took them as a kind of oracle. Most famous with all was his position on the unity of the possible intellect, so that he who thought otherwise was considered worthy of the name neither of peripatetic nor philosopher."[3]

To which you may well say, "Latin Averroism? Is that still around?" The phrase is most commonly associated with thirteenth-century arts masters at Paris who flirted with the dangerous ideas of "the Commentator," in particular his belief in the eternity of the world and in the unity of the intellect.[4] This provoked condemnation from the bishop of Paris, and refutations by colleagues including Thomas Aquinas. But unlike the soul according to Pomponazzi, Averroism managed to live on. It flourished above all in Italy, where at the end of the fourteenth century Blasius of Parma was already reprimanded for accepting Averroes' view on the intellect. A hundred years later the same teaching was receiving support from Nicoletta Vernia, who taught both Nifo and Pomponazzi. Again, this provoked an official rebuke. In 1489 the bishop of Padua threatened that Averroism would be punished by excommunication. Vernia's first name was not Peter, so he obediently recanted, writing a treatise in 1492 against what he now called the "perverse opinion" of Averroes. This was presumably because of the pressure that had been brought to bear on him, though he claimed to have changed his mind upon reading more carefully and widely in the Aristotelian commentary tradition. And even here, he smuggled in the caveat that in terms of its operation, the human intellect is universal and not individual.[5]

It was precisely this premise that led Averroes himself to his notorious teaching on the intellect. He wrestled with the nature of the mind throughout his career, eventually reaching the conclusion that there is only one capacity for abstract, truly intellectual thought, which is shared by all humankind. The intellect's operation is universal, because its knowledge consists in grasping general realities or "universals." By contrast, other forms of cognition, like sensation and imagination, grasp particulars and their properties. You can see, or imagine, an individual giraffe, but you must use your intellect to grasp the universal nature that belongs to all giraffes. Averroes did not see how this universal nature could be received in a physical organ like the brain.[6] You can collect sensory images in the brain, remember them, fabricate new images you haven't experienced, like a giraffe eating broccoli, and even think about particulars to make plans for the future: what might you do if your pet giraffe refuses to eat its vegetables? But your brain cannot be the seat of *universal* thoughts. This fits well with something Averroes could find stated clearly in Aristotle, namely that the intellect's activity is not realized in any bodily organ. If the intellect's work takes place outside my bodily organs, Averroes thought, then it must not belong to me, or any other individual embodied person. The intellect is universal, and belongs to everyone.

While this may seem an outlandish conclusion, Averroes' standing as the premiere medieval commentator on Aristotle was by itself a good reason to take his view seriously. Vernia called him "Aristotle's most famous interpreter," while Nifo referred to him as "Aristotle's priest."[7] Averroes' position had something else to recommend it, too. It at least made the human intellect immaterial and immortal. For Christian readers, this might well seem preferable to saying that the intellect *is* closely linked to embodied individuals, just a part of the human soul that Aristotle had famously defined as the "form of the organic body potentially having life." The form of a table doesn't survive when you destroy the body of the table. So if the human's soul is the form of the human's body, why should it survive when the body is killed? Renaissance readers could find this line of thought being followed through by another great commentator on Aristotle, namely Alexander of Aphrodisias, who lived in the second century AD. In the fifteenth century, he was still valued as the most competent guide to Aristotle alongside Averroes, and was standardly interpreted as having held that the soul is indeed mortal, since it is only the form of a mortal body.

So devotees of Aristotelianism were caught between a rock and a hard place: the materialist theory of Alexander on the one hand, Averroes' hard-to-believe theory of the unity of the immaterial intellect on the other. Marsilio Ficino thus complained, "Almost the entire world is occupied and divided between two sects of Peripatetics, the Alexandrians and the Averroists. The one sect think our intellect is mortal, the other contend that it is one. Both schools alike are wholly destructive of religion... and in both cases they seem to have been failed by their Aristotle."[8] Ficino responded to the challenge with his massive work *The Platonic Theology*, which devoted hundreds upon hundreds of pages to proving the immortality of individual human souls. Surely at least one of those arguments must be right? The pope evidently thought so, and as we saw Ficino's work has been credited with helping inspire the church's declaration that immortality can be rationally proven.

But then Ficino was a Platonist, often arguing from different premises than would be accepted by the Aristotelians of Padua. It was an open question whether personal immortality was compatible with Aristotle's writings on the soul. Already around 1460 the Byzantine émigré John Argyropoulos, lecturing on Aristotle at Florence, decided that Averroism was the correct interpretation of Aristotle, though good Christians should still deem it to be false as an account of the soul.[9] It would be nice if you could use Aristotle and rational argumentation to prove the Christian doctrine of the afterlife, but sadly you can't. The same conclusion was reached by Alessandro Achillini and Luca Prasiccio, Averroists who taught at Bologna and Naples, respectively. Like Ficino, Achillini said that both Alexander and Averroes put forward false views on the soul, Alexander denying its immortality and Averroes accepting it as immortal but only one for all humans. Still Averroes was preferable in that he, not Alexander, had understood Aristotle correctly.[10] Similarly, Prasiccio said that "Aristotle was never more truly interpreted than by Averroes," and that he could "find nothing more certain and true on the immortality of the soul than what can be taken from Averroes." But Prasiccio too hastened to add that this apparently "certain and true" teaching is deemed false by Christian faith.

Against this backdrop, it becomes clear that Pomponazzi's treatise was a little less shocking than we might suppose. He differed from the Renaissance Averroists simply in his choice of which false theory of the soul should be ascribed to Aristotle: Alexander's reading was broadly correct, Averroes' completely wrong.[11] Like the Averroists, Pomponazzi offered detailed arguments for his preferred interpretation of Aristotle, and then piously distanced himself from the resulting theory with some final disclaimers.[12] But why was he so certain that Aristotle was committed to the mortality of the soul? He depended above all on passages where Aristotle closely associates intellectual thinking with imagination (*On the Soul*, 403a, 431a, cited by Pomponazzi at 287, 306).[13] Consider what happens when you think about giraffes, even at the most abstract, scientific level. Clearly you'll have a hard time doing that without having some sensory experiences of giraffes, and preserving representations of giraffes in your memory: the way they look, sound, and, yes, smell. You might remember seeing one graze on leaves, another walk past meat without showing the slightest interest, and arrive at the general truth that giraffes, unlike me as a boy, gladly restrict themselves to a plant-based diet.

Pomponazzi goes further than this. He certainly holds that universal thinking has its origins in sensory awareness, but this is just the standard empiricism of the Aristotelian scientific tradition. More controversial is his claim that for Aristotle, *every* act of universal thinking comes together with an act of imagination. You can't think about the fact that *all* giraffes are herbivores without remembering, or imagining, *particular* giraffes eating their vegetables. So even if, as Aristotle stated, universal thinking itself is not realized in the brain or any other bodily organ, that thinking is nonetheless "the act of a physical and organic body" (288). Intellect depends on powers that are realized in the body, so it cannot remain once your body dies. And since everyone agrees that the intellect is the part of the soul with the most plausible claim to immortality, this shows that the soul is not immortal at all.

In addition to setting out his own reading of Aristotle, Pomponazzi criticizes other views. Against Averroes he can make the obvious complaint that the single intellect of his theory may be immortal, but does not belong to each of us as individuals, so it would not secure *our* immortality.[14] Less obviously, Averroes depicted human thinking as being just like the pure, separate thinking that belongs to God and the celestial intellects of Aristotle's cosmology. The very fact that we need to use our imaginations to think is a clear sign that our intellects work quite differently than those exalted minds (317). In fact, Pomponazzi thinks that in comparison to them, we can claim to have only a "shadow of intellect" (322).

Pomponazzi also takes aim at Thomas Aquinas.[15] At this time Aquinas was already seen as a great Christian theologian, whose authority was more difficult to challenge than that of the Muslim Averroes. In fact, Pomponazzi was himself thoroughly schooled in Thomist philosophy as a student. Nonetheless, he dares to argue that Aquinas' theory cannot be sustained on rational grounds, or as an interpretation of Aristotle. Pomponazzi agrees with Thomas in rejecting Averroism: we all have our own single, individual souls. With the emphasis on *single*: we do not have two souls, a mortal one for sensation, and a second, immortal soul for intellection. On this view "soul and body would have no greater unity than oxen and plow" (298).[16] But if the single soul is immortal and immaterial, as Aquinas claims, then why would intellectual thought, the signature activity of the immaterial soul, depend on the body for its functioning, as we've seen that it does (305)? Aquinas' view might be true in the end, as testified by religion, but it cannot be established by reason (302–3).

Pomponazzi does acknowledge that the human soul has some share in immortality. He echoes the words of Pico della Mirandola, for whom the human being uniquely contains all creation, straddling the immortal and mortal, the immaterial and the material. Giraffes are pretty good at straddling, but they can't do this, nor can any other non-human animal. Yet the immortality unique to humans belongs to us only in respect of the universal truths we grasp when we use their minds (340). We are temporary creatures that grasp eternal verities, material beings that receive immaterial objects of thought, while using physical images to do so. Here Pomponazzi responds to a distinction introduced by Averroes, who contrasted the intellect's using the body as a "subject" to having body as its "object."[17] Our minds' needing images when we think shows that the intellect uses the body as an "object," drawing on memory and imagination as a kind of storehouse of information on the basis of which pure universals may be understood. Averroes and his followers agreed that the universal mind draws on such images, which are stored in individual human brains. But they claimed that the intellect performs its activity separately from the body as a "subject," because it has no specific organ. Pomponazzi disagrees. If the mind needs material images as objects, then it needs the body as its subject too (288).

So you can boil Pomponazzi's whole argument down to a claim that is apt to strike us as remarkably obvious: people think as individuals, and can't do so without their brains. In the early sixteenth century, though, this was far from obvious. Hadn't Pico and Ficino shown that we are part animal, part angel? Are we not made to partake even of divinity, in some small way? Didn't Aristotle himself say in his *Ethics* that we are capable of reaching beyond a merely human life, to reach ultimate felicity through theoretical contemplation? How then can intellect be inevitably linked to embodiment? Pomponazzi anticipates this line of objection, and responds that contemplation is indeed something quasi-divine, which is precisely why we shouldn't make it the purpose of human life. Look around: most people are peasants or artisans, and even among the elite very few men and hardly any women are concerned with philosophy (354). Which is perfectly fine, says Pomponazzi. Our aim as humans is to be morally upright, to make good use of what Aristotle called *practical* intellect. We do have a theoretical intellect too, which can be used to grasp universal truths, but this is just a kind of bonus that comes on top of the happiness already secured through a virtuous life (356). Indeed, to insist that human life loses its purpose if we are not immortal is to suggest that the only reason to be good is to gain reward and avoid punishment in the afterlife, whereas in fact virtue should be pursued here and now for its own sake (375).

When Pomponazzi published his treatise in 1516, it attracted the attention of his old rival Agostino Nifo.[18] Nifo had been thinking about these issues for decades. Around the turn of the century, he reprised the intellectual journey traveled by his teacher Nicoletto Vernia, at first presenting Averroes' theory of the single intellect sympathetically and then arguing against it. Having devoted great effort to grappling with the works of the Commentator, he turned against Averroes in 1503, writing a treatise *On the Intellect* which declares that the Averroist position is against both faith and Aristotle. It errs in supposing that the subject of thinking must be just as universal as its object, that if what we all grasp when learning about giraffes is a single, intelligible form of giraffe, then there can be only a single intellect that grasps it. Instead, we should say that each human intellect receives a unique form of its own, by means of which it understands the universal nature of giraffe. This is a major concession, since it gives up on an idea found in Aristotle and always stressed by Averroists like the younger Nifo, namely that the mind actually becomes *identical* to the form or nature that it grasps. Now Nifo replaces this with the idea that the mind has its own representation of that nature, sometimes called in scholastic jargon an "intelligible species." Or as Nifo puts it, the mind does not actually have within itself the "object of intellection (*intellectum*)," but "something through which it understands the object of intellection intellectually (*quo intellectum intelligitur*)."[19]

Having persuaded himself of this, Nifo is able to make the politically convenient move of embracing a position more like that of Aquinas. The human intellect is not so exalted as to be single and universal, but it is nonetheless immortal and independent from the body in its operation. As a result the philosophical study of the soul is itself like human nature according to Pico della Mirandola: it spans the material and immaterial realms, and is thus a science that belongs to both physics and metaphysics.[20] It is from this position that Nifo attacks Pomponazzi. He makes short shrift of Pomponazzi's main proof of the soul's mortality, namely that it cannot think without bodily images. It is true that images are needed *at first* so the intellect can learn about universal truths. But thereafter, it can dispense with the images and occupy itself with nothing but universals, when it is devoting abstract thought to things it originally learned via sensation.[21] So the mind can still be active after bodily death, continuing to enjoy the knowledge it acquired during earthly life.

Thus Nifo is able to say that humans are made for something else than practical virtue. We are also made to contemplate, as Aristotle said, and it is specifically the speculative intellect that differentiates us from other animals.[22] Of course, we are not born using this intellect, but need to work at it. As Nifo writes, "the rational soul develops... until it reaches the metaphysical intelligibles, when the speculative intellect is formed."[23] A problem with this is that, if the afterlife consists only in pure activity of the mind, it seems that very few people will be prepared for it. If you haven't acquired universal knowledge in this life, by becoming a philosopher or scientist, what will you think about after you die? And it's not just that, as Pomponazzi said, "almost an infinite number of people seem to have less intellect than many beasts" (323). It's also that many infants die before they even have the chance to start actualizing their capacity for intellectual thought, a problem that Pomponazzi pointed out in his response to Nifo.[24] To answer this kind of problem, Nifo too has to retreat into invocations of religion, assuring his readers that those humans who failed to join the intellectual elite in this life may nonetheless be granted beatitude through God's mercy.[25] But to be on the safe side, it's probably a good idea to realize your potential for philosophy. So you'd better read on.

47

THERE AND BACK AGAIN ZABARELLA ON SCIENTIFIC METHOD

Though many philosophers claim to prize clarity, in practice they are not always easy to follow. In the more difficult category, one thinks inevitably of Martin Heidegger. His most important work *Being and Time* is so hard to read that Edmund Husserl, himself not the most lucid of writers, had his wife ask for a face-to-face meeting with Heidegger. She wrote that Husserl had "occupied himself the whole vacation exclusively with its study and finds it necessary to let himself be instructed with you about much that does not want to become entirely clear to him."[1] Ancient and medieval commentators would have sympathized, except that they didn't have the luxury of sitting down with their own favorite author to ask him what in the world he was talking about.

That author was, of course, Aristotle. His works are sufficiently obscure that it became standard for commentators to offer excuses for their difficulty, saying for instance that this was intended to discourage non-expert readers. It may have seemed particularly galling that Aristotle did not write more clearly, given that Aristotle was renowned as a master of clear thinking. He had invented logic, for goodness' sake! In the treatise that was considered the culmination of his logical works, the *Posterior Analytics*, he laid out a theory of demonstration that seemed intended as the ideal method for setting out scientific truths. Why then did he not use this method when he wrote about other topics? There are plenty of philosophical arguments in Aristotle's works on natural philosophy, the soul, metaphysics, and ethics, but these arguments rarely, if ever, satisfy the stringent criteria for demonstrative proof laid down in the *Analytics*.[2]

Jacopo Zabarella, a professor at the university of Padua in the sixteenth century, proclaimed to be "second to no mortal in admiration of Aristotle" (*Meth.* §4.22.2).[3] Of course, Aristotle was "a man, not a god" and had not treated all topics in science so exhaustively as to render further efforts superfluous. Still, he had "planted the seed and made the basis from which even the things he did not write about can be known."[4] So Zabarella was at pains to show that Aristotle's works were, contrary to appearances, well designed for the student who would be reading them. For a thousand years and more, it had been common for commentators to uncover the demonstrative arguments lurking hidden within the apparently non-demonstrative writings of Aristotle. Zabarella knew this strategy well, having read Averroes and the Greek commentaries that were now circulating in printed versions. But he adopted a different approach to understanding Aristotle, by contrasting what he called the "method" of the sciences to the mere "order" of teaching that is to be used when writing for students (*Meth.* §1.3.2).

As Zabarella noted, this contrast could take inspiration from one drawn by Aristotle himself, between that which is "better known" or "primary" relative to us and that which is primary in itself (*Meth.* §3.1.4). Primary in themselves are the fundamental causes and principles in a science. In ancient physics this would have been, among other things, the four elements: fire, air, water, and earth. In a modern context it might be something like atomic particles, and the way their number and arrangements give rise to physical properties. But such foundations are not "primary relative to us." To the contrary, the atomic foundations of chemistry are so obscure to humankind that even Aristotle didn't figure them out. Now, Zabarella would say that when you are teaching, you shouldn't start with things like this. Instead, it is good policy to begin with things that are familiar or obvious to the student. In Aristotle's terms, these would be the things that are better known *to us*, not the things that are primary *in themselves*. Thus, if explaining chemistry, you might begin by showing your students a simple chemical reaction, and only then go on to say how this reaction can ultimately be explained through the interaction of atomic particles.

This basic contrast, between a discussion that works towards principles, and a discussion that begins from principles, was familiar in the commentary tradition. Averroes, in particular, had mentioned it in his commentary on Aristotle's *Physics*. He distinguished between the opening move in science, where we trace a "sign" or effect back to its cause, and a further step where, on the basis of that cause, we explain the effect from which we started (cf. *Meth.* §3.19.3).[5] As we'll be seeing, this was a core idea of Zabarella's scientific method too. But he claimed originality for his own contrast between "order" and "method," especially insofar as it provided a tool for analyzing much-debated texts from Aristotle's writings (*Regr.* §6.1). According to Zabarella, these writings are arranged in such a way that the order of presentation mirrors the order of discovery (*Meth.* §2.8.8). In other words, Aristotle teaches by taking us step by step along a path he has already traveled in the course of his scientific investigations, explaining everything in the order he came to understand them himself. Thus his exposition does not begin with the deepest insights and most fundamental principles, but goes gradually from the obvious to the obscure, from the posterior to the primary.

Zabarella offers several examples from Aristotle's texts. The most basic of the five senses is touch, and it is shared most widely by different kinds of animals. Yet in his treatment of sensation, Aristotle discusses vision first, because vision is the most striking and obvious kind of sense-perception: it is, in other words, primary to us, not in itself (*Meth.* §1.6.8). Aristotle also discusses humans in his natural philosophy before moving on to other animals, even though humans are only one kind of animal, so that animal nature is more fundamental than human nature (*Meth.* §1.6.11). Or, take a case Zabarella discusses in greater detail: Aristotle's demonstration that natural bodies are ultimately made of "prime matter." Prime matter is the featureless, pure potentiality that underlies concrete materials like the four elements, wood, or flesh and bone. Obviously prime matter is not "better known relative to us." To the contrary it is basically a theoretical postulate, like the subatomic particles of modern science which were initially posited without being directly observable. But, according to Zabarella, Aristotle proves that it exists by pointing to cases of change that we *can* observe, and noting that there must be something that underlies every change and survives through the change, like when one and the same human is at first uneducated, then becomes educated (*Physics*, 1.7, *Regr.* §4.4–5). Prime matter is what underlies *all* change, so it is the principle (*principium*) that explains why natural bodies are changeable.

As Averroes suggested, we can think about this discovery of principles as a discovery of *causes*. Usually what is obvious to us is the effect, not the cause. We feel heat every day but don't realize it is caused by the element of fire (or in modern physics, the agitation of particles in a body). We observe things changing, but don't realize that prime matter is an ultimate cause of change, in this case what Aristotelians would call a "material cause." In his writings Aristotle follows an order of teaching that makes it possible to "learn better and more easily" (*Meth.* §1.6.9). That means laying out the process of observation or argument that led to the discovery of the cause. But this part of scientific method only establishes what the cause is. In Zabarella's Latin scholastic terminology, it provides a proof *quod* or *quia* (this corresponds to *to hoti* in Aristotle's Greek). Once we know "what the cause is," we can use it to explain the effects from which we started. That will be a more perfect kind of proof, in fact a real "demonstration," precisely because it is explanatory. Zabarella, again following earlier scholastic terminology, calls it a demonstration *propter quid*, meaning "because of what" (corresponding to Greek *to dioti*). So to use the same example, we feel heat all the time, but have to do quite a bit of investigation to figure out what exactly causes it. Once we've done this, we'll be in a position to give a properly scientific explanation of heat, by saying that it is caused by agitated molecules.

Now there is an obvious potential problem here, one that worried Zabarella enough that he devoted a small treatise to it, entitled *On Regress*. The problem is that the whole procedure sounds circular. We first establish the cause on the basis of the effect, then go on to explain the effect by appealing to the cause (*Regr.* §1.2–3). Doesn't this involve arguing from A to B, and then from B back to A? Again, Zabarella was not the first to notice this difficulty. It had been a topic of discussion at Padua as far back as Paul of Venice.[6] But Zabarella provided the definitive solution, namely that there is no circularity involved because the two kinds of reasoning are different. Scientific "method," which is "demonstration" in the strict sense, comes only at the end, when we use the cause to explain the effect. The initial stage where we only determine "what the cause is" is not demonstrative in this strict sense. It doesn't have the ambition of *explaining* anything, because you don't "explain" a cause on the basis of the effect, but rather vice versa. Zabarella calls the first stage "progress," as we move towards the causal principles. Then we "regress" back to the effects. This is admittedly a case of retracing our steps, but with a different kind of understanding. Now, we are giving well-founded scientific explanations of the phenomena from which we began. Zabarella thinks this is what Aristotle meant in a passage that compares philosophical method to a U-shaped racetrack, where the competitors have to reach a bend at one end of the stadium and then return to the end where they started (*Nic. Ethics*, 1.4, *Meth.* §2.15.5).[7]

Zabarella makes a further point that may help us see why the method he describes is not circular. He borrows an idea from his fellow Paduan philosopher Agostino Nifo, by saying that upon establishing what the cause is, we should pause to think about its nature. This step of "examining" or "considering" the cause, which Zabarella, following Nifo, calls a "negotiation of the understanding (*negotatio intellectus*)" (*Regr.* §5.2), allows us really to understand the principles we'll be using in our scientific explanations.[8] Again, the example of prime matter is a useful one here. It's one thing to understand that something-or-other underlies all change in nature. It's another to understand what that underlying thing is. Upon reflection we may see that, if it underlies *all* change, it must be capable of taking on any natural property and cannot have any properties in its own right, like by being hot or dry, as fire is. Rather, prime matter is in itself only *potentially* all the things into which it can change (*Regr.* §5.7). By pondering the causal principle we have discovered and coming to an understanding of its nature, we'll also be in a position to have a deeper understanding of its effects. Thus Zabarella says that we initially have only a vague or "confused" grasp of the phenomenon we seek to explain, but once we have gone up to the principles and back, our grasp of this same phenomenon becomes "distinct" (*Meth.* §4.11.4, *Regr.* §3.4, §4.3).

Another contrast that Zabarella uses to account for all this, one he takes especially from the ancient doctor Galen, is that between "resolution" and "composition" (*Meth.* §2.1.2; the two procedures are defined at §2.16.1 and §2.17.1). The idea here is that, when presented with a complex phenomenon, you can "resolve" it into its components or principles. We can think about this as breaking something down to its basics. When you get down to these fundamental parts, you can then explain what you started with by showing how the parts are brought together: this is the stage of "composition." The most obvious illustration would be the analysis of something's physical constituents. You might be investigating an almond croissant, and realize it is sweet because it contains sugar, and fattening because it contains butter. But it should work with more abstract examples too: you can train your ear to hear how fusion jazz combines the musical techniques of classic jazz with sounds borrowed from rock music and funk.

These examples are a little bit misleading, though. Almond croissants and fusion jazz records are not phenomena we encounter in nature; they do not grow on trees (if they did I would have an almond croissant orchard). So in these cases someone, like a pastry chef or Miles Davis, had to *start* with the fundamental components and put them together to achieve the desired result. In other words, the process begins with composition, not with resolution. This is typical of the practical or productive arts and sciences, according to Zabarella (*Meth.* §2.6.4, 2.9.1). The producer has some purpose or "end" in mind, and thinks consciously about how to reach that end through composition. He refers here to house building, one of Aristotle's favorite examples. When building a house one begins with bricks and beams, and only then does one put them together according to the plan of the house. In the study of nature, by contrast, we are presented with already complete, complex things that need to be traced back to their causal principles, by "resolving" them into those principles. Only after doing that can we explain the natural phenomena on the basis of those causes, performing "composition" by seeing how the causes come together to produce the complex results we originally started from.

So the "there and back again" structure described by Zabarella is really only appropriate for "theoretical" sciences, especially the branches of natural philosophy like physics and zoology. His vaunted method is not applicable to practical contexts like the productive arts, or ethics and political philosophy (*Meth.* §3.20.4–5), where one begins from the desire to pursue some end rather than from observed phenomena that need explanation. Zabarella's focus on theoretical philosophy, and his treatment of natural philosophy as the paradigmatic kind of science, makes sense in biographical and institutional terms.[9] He began in Padua as a professor of logic, and later took up the chair of natural philosophy. His theory brings together these two parts of the university curriculum. As he says himself, "the sciences are nothing more than logic put to use,"[10] and his works on scientific methodology are in turn nothing more than an attempt to show how logic, especially the theory of demonstration, is used in natural philosophy. One might add that the prestige of natural philosophy at the university of Padua matches the central role natural philosophy occupies in his theory.

If this was only to be expected, it was no less predictable that within the competitive atmosphere of Italian scholasticism Zabarella's theory would be attacked by a rival. This was Alessandro Piccolomini, another philosopher at Padua who denied that the best order of teaching is the order of discovery.[11] To the contrary, one should often begin by explaining first principles to the students. So unlike Zabarella, Piccolomini would encourage a chemistry teacher to welcome students on their first day by presenting them with the theory of the atom, since it is fundamental for everything else they will learn. Piccolomini was also much more interested in metaphysics than Zabarella was, and stressed the dependence of natural philosophy on this higher science. Against this, Zabarella contended that the study of nature is independent of metaphysical considerations, which he leaves to the theologians.[12]

This is just one respect in which Zabarella and the Paduan thinkers leading up to him anticipated later ideas about science, ideas we associate more with the Enlightenment. We saw how Pomponazzi offered an account of soul and intellect that was deliberately independent from religious belief. He was not apologizing when he said that this account "agrees with reason and experience, it maintains nothing mythical, nothing depending on faith."[13] Likewise, Zabarella highlighted the empiricist side of Aristotle, writing that in the investigation of nature "all our knowledge takes its origin from sensation (*a sensu originem ducit*)."[14] Scholastics in this period also contrasted a priori and a posteriori knowledge, which is terminology that will become very familiar in later periods of philosophy. Whereas a posteriori knowledge is grounded in sensation, the kind of understanding Zabarella associates with natural philosophy, a priori knowledge is used in fields like mathematics that do not base themselves on empirical observation.

Still, before leaping to the conclusion that Zabarella was a forerunner of empiricists like David Hume and John Locke, we should pause over his comments about induction. He expects only modest gains from a strictly inductive investigation. This is not on the grounds famously mentioned by Hume, that induction can never rule out future counterexamples. Rather, it is because Zabarella thinks that induction is only a generalization of some obvious fact, and fails to reveal the essential natures of things (*Regr.* §4.7). So, for instance, you can use induction to notice that fire is hot, something that would need only "light confirmation," which would presumably involve checking out enough fires to satisfy yourself that they do indeed always give off heat. Mere induction would not, by contrast, allow you to realize that the heat is caused by the agitation of molecules, or that a triangle has internal angles whose sum is 180 degrees (*Meth.* §3.19.6). For that, one needs to do a proper scientific investigation.

Zabarella gives this latter example because it is mentioned by Aristotle, not because he's particularly interested in mathematics. He is mostly happy to stay within his remit of logic and the study of nature, and the union of the two that is his treatment of scientific method. Thus he has little to say about the a priori realm, and quite a bit about the various branches of natural philosophy. As we've seen, these are to be approached empirically, but also to be considered as "theoretical" sciences, which just means that they are undertaken purely for the sake of knowledge and not for pursuing some end or to make some product. For this reason, Zabarella insists that medicine does not really belong to natural philosophy: it pursues a practical end, namely the health of the patient. So he rigorously distinguishes the explanatory accounts that undergird medical treatment—the theory of the four humors, for instance, and in general whatever belongs to physiology and zoology—from medicine as an applied art.[15] This too can be seen as a way to pull rank within the university context. As an expert on Aristotelian natural philosophy, Zabarella was pleased to be able to tell his colleagues who taught medicine that the real science behind their activities was to be found in a work like Aristotle's *Parts of Animals*. But this was far from being the last word on science in the sixteenth century, at Padua and elsewhere. In the next couple of chapters we'll be exploring the two disciplines just mentioned, mathematics and medicine, and seeing that many scholars were, unlike Zabarella, more than happy to step outside the confines of Aristotelian science.

48

THE MEASURE OF ALL THINGS
MATHEMATICS AND ART

My grandfather on my father's side was a brilliant engineer who designed jet engines. His brother built his own plane by hand in his garage, and his sister had a Ph.D. in biochemistry. My grandmother and her sisters all had degrees in mathematics. Then there was my father, who has always loved numbers just as much as he hated vegetables. He worked in computing, having been a math prodigy who won statewide competitions as a high school student. Once my twin brother and I received phone calls from him on the same day, to congratulate us on being exactly 33 and 1/3 years old. I also have an aunt who is a wizard at business administration, and my non-existent sister is an expert on imaginary numbers. So it would be fair to say that mathematics runs in my family. But it ran right around me. My feeling about math is much like my feeling about using a motorcycle to jump over a row of burning cars: amazing, wondrous even, but something I'd just as soon leave to other people. Rather than reflect upon my failure to carry on a family tradition, I comfort myself by telling myself that I'm in good company. Many philosophers have admired mathematics while failing to work at it seriously themselves. Aristotle, for example, wrote no technical treatises on geometry, astronomy, or music. Yet his *Posterior Analytics*, which we just saw taking center stage in the methodological theories of Zabarella, is full of examples involving triangles.

The reason is not far to seek: mathematics seems to offer the ultimate example of certain, rigorous human knowledge. If you ask someone to name something they are most definitely sure about, they're likely to give an example like "2 + 2 = 4." And back in the Renaissance people felt the same way. The sixteenth-century mathematician Giambattista Benedetti wrote a treatise called *On Mathematical Philosophy* which called on Aristotle's authority in proclaiming the absolute certainty of this discipline.[1] And if mathematics is truly "philosophical," as suggested by Benedetti's title, then any philosopher worth their salt would have to get far beyond the level of 2 + 2 = 4. Nowadays, people tend to think of the "humanities" as, roughly, the academic disciplines that don't involve numbers, but the original humanists thought of mathematics as a central part of ancient philosophical wisdom.

Or at least, some of them did. Leonardo Bruni wasn't among them. Sounding not unlike me at the age of 15, he gave the excuse that "the subtleties of arithmetic and geometry are not worthy to absorb a cultivated mind."[2] But for the most part, humanists were eager to study manuscripts of Archimedes, Euclid, and other ancient mathematicians. Such works took pride of place in Renaissance libraries. Lorenzo de Medici, for instance, collected manuscripts of Euclid and Theon of Alexandria, and for the work on *Mechanics* ascribed falsely to Aristotle. Italy was a center of mathematical knowledge in the fifteenth century, as we can see from the fact that intellectuals from elsewhere in Europe came there to study and get access to texts that were unavailable elsewhere. Take the astronomer Regiomontanus, who came to Italy from Vienna and met a who's who of humanist scholars: Bessarion, Alberti, Theodore Gaza, Nicholas of Cusa, and George Trapezuntius. He even got into the spirit of humanism by joining in the petty feuds that so enlivened the era. As a devotee of Bessarion, Regiomontanus dutifully attacked the translation and commentary that Bessarion's rival Trapezentius had devoted to the central work of ancient astronomy, Ptolemy's *Almagest*.

Equally in the spirit of the age was the rhetoric of recovery and revival that surrounded the philological study of ancient mathematics. In the sixteenth century, by which time key works of mathematics were available in printed editions, scholars were still boasting that they had rescued this discipline from its formerly parlous state. Rafael Bombelli proclaimed, "I have restored the effectiveness of arithmetic, imitating the ancient writers."[3] As usual, such self-congratulation went together with denigration of the achievements of the medieval era. The scholastic "Calculators" who applied mathematical concepts to physics in the fourteenth century were, as I've mentioned, studied in the Italian universities. But the humanists were for the most part not impressed. In this case Bruni was more representative when he said that names like Heytesbury, Ockham, and Swineshead "filled him with horror."[4] As much as they could, the humanists sought to trace mathematical insight and innovation to the ancient Greeks. But they had to admit that progress had been made in the medieval period, especially in the Islamic world. There, al-Khwārizmī made breakthroughs in algebra, Ibn al-Haytham (Latinized as Alhazen) gave the most accurate account of optics to date, and astronomy was brought to new heights of sophistication. This was recognized in such works as *Lives of Mathematicians*, written by Bernardino Baldi in imitation of Diogenes Laertius' ancient *Lives of Philosophers*.

Baldi—whose name calls to mind another characteristic that runs in my family—was one of several interconnected mathematicians in the sixteenth century active in the city of Urbino. The founding figure was Federico Commandino, whom Baldi predictably enough credited with having returned ancient mathematics to "light, dignity, and splendor." A student of Commandino, Guidobaldo dal Monte, could not but agree, saying that his master had written "commentaries on Archimedes that smell of the mathematician's own lamp."[5] Commandino wrote on pure mathematics as well as "applied" topics like sundials and calculating a body's center of gravity. His successors followed suit. Guidobaldo anticipated Galileo's famous analysis of projectile motion as having the form of a parabola. He even proposed a nice experiment for establishing this: if you cover a ball with ink and roll it up a blank, inclined surface, you'll see that the track it makes is shaped like an arch. Guidobaldo and Baldi were also devoted to the study of mechanics. They thought that Archimedes had worked out the mathematical details of theories that could be found in more schematic form in the supposedly Aristotelian *Mechanics*. As Baldi put the point, "Archimedes followed completely in the footsteps of Aristotle as far as the principles were concerned, adding, however, the refinement of the proofs."

The study of mechanics showed how powerful it could be to combine mathematics with empirical observation. It was also useful in practical terms, as we can see with the example of clock-building, which transformed perceptions of time during the Renaissance. Imagine experiencing the transition from keeping time by the motions of the sun to having bells mark the time from church towers in your city. Excellent: it was now possible to be late to meetings! If you lived in Bologna, you'd have Bessarion to thank for this, since he collaborated on the construction of an astronomical clock there. The result was that, as never before, time was money. Already in 1353 Petrarch had spoken of the "price of time,"[6] and in his writings on household economics Leon Battista Alberti encouraged his readers to be thrifty with their days and hours. Time is a "most precious thing," and needs to be spent as efficiently as possible: "I avoid sleep and idleness, and I am always doing something."[7]

The name of Alberti brings us to another, more famous application of mathematics: the visual arts. Before you read this book, this would probably have been the first thing to come to your mind upon hearing the phrase "Italian Renaissance." Even if you have never set foot in a museum, you'll have seen images of the sculptures, paintings, and buildings of artists like Piero della Francesca, Michelangelo, da Vinci, Brunelleschi, Botticelli, Raphael, and so on, whether as dorm room posters or refrigerator magnets. And there is quite a lot of mathematics in the background of those images. Literally. Take da Vinci's *Last Supper*. You probably know what it looks like, more or less, but you may have to call it up on the internet to notice that the details on the walls and ceiling surrounding the apostles and Christ at the table provide a lovely example of single-point perspective. Notice that the lines of perspective converge on Christ's head, a use of geometry in art to make a theological point.[8] Perhaps less familiar is the painting called *Tribute Money* by Masaccio. It shows Christ surrounded by a circle of figures, again literally, in that he is the center of that circle. The arrangement of figures has both spiritual and aesthetic weight, with the apostles clustered tightly around the Savior in a beautifully orchestrated portrayal of physical space.

To learn how the effect was achieved, read Alberti. When painting a crowd, he advises, you should put the heads of the figures along the same horizontal line in the painting but their feet at different lines. This gives the impression that they are the same height, yet standing at various distances from the viewer.[9] It's only one of the many handy tips you can find in Alberti's writings on art, the most important of which are *On Painting* and *On the Art of Building*. It's pretty obvious that architecture involves a lot of mathematics, but perhaps less so with painting. Yet Alberti promises in the preface to *On Painting* that the first of its three books will be devoted entirely to mathematics, and so it is.[10] He says that the artist should be expert in all the liberal arts, but most especially in geometry (§53), because without an understanding of this discipline it is impossible to depict space convincingly.

In particular, one needs to understand the geometry used in the discipline of optics. Alberti looks back to Euclid, by way of Ptolemy and Ibn al-Haytham among others, as he explains that eyesight can be modeled as a "pyramid" whose apex is at the eye, and whose base is at the visible object. The pyramid is considered to be made up of lines, which stand either for visual rays extending from the eye to the object, or for rays bouncing off the object and reaching the eye.[11] For the purposes of art, says Alberti, there is no need to decide between these two theories (§5). The "extreme" rays, which are the outer bounds of the pyramid, allow eyesight to grasp the outline or shape of the object that is seen. (So this is why Alberti is speaking of a "pyramid" rather than a visual "cone," as was often done in treatises on optics: if you are looking at a square painting, the rays are arranged in a pyramid whose base is likewise square, not circular.) The reason things look smaller when they are further away is that the visual pyramid for a more distant object has a smaller base. Meanwhile, the rays inside the pyramid take on the color of what is seen, like a chameleon.

All this is just Alberti's account of normal vision. In the case of a painting, we have to imagine the surface of the picture as a meeting between the visual pyramid whose apex is at the eye, and a pyramid of rays coming from the virtual world of the painting, whose apex is the vanishing point of perspective. Without getting into further details, you can see how some fairly serious geometry is going to be involved in getting the painting right. Getting the correct representation involves working out what mathematicians call a "section" (like "conic sections" in the case of a cone), or what Alberti calls a "certain cut of the pyramid" (§12). In the case of a pavement or a wall with square panels, like the one in da Vinci's *Last Supper*, you can achieve the effect by using a straight edge. For more complex forms, Alberti gives another useful tip, which is to suspend a diaphanous veil between yourself and the scene to be painted, and mark on the veil where the objects appear on this vertical plane. This can then be used as a pattern for the painting itself (§31). Through such devices the artist quite literally takes the measure of the subject found in nature.

In fact, there's a sense in which the subject of every painting is proportion. This art renders the world in miniature, portrayed on a surface as it appears relative to the human viewer. This, speculates Alberti, may be what the ancient sophist Protagoras meant when he said that man is the "measure of all things": that everything we see is measured against our own stature and from our own point of view (§18). Another nice way that he makes the same point is to say that, if everything in the universe including us was suddenly halved in size, everything would still look the same to us (§18). We see here, yet again, the Renaissance fascination with the individual, contrasting the limited perspective of each individual and what we might call the God's eye view, which is from no particular vantage point and would see each thing as it truly is.[12]

Along the same lines, if you'll pardon the expression, what we see in the painted image is not pure, abstract mathematics but the use of an abstraction to capture a particular viewing situation. Alberti understood this. In another treatise on painting he remarked that the "points" considered by the artist are "a sort of mean between a mathematical point and a quantity capable of measurement, perhaps like atoms."[13] It's been observed that the "geometrically ordered space" of a perspective painting is "a staged imitation of what we might see if we were placed squarely before forms all lined up in parallel fashion."[14] Alberti was sufficiently conscious of this artificiality that he went to the trouble of inventing a "viewing box" that kept the observer at exactly the right distance from the image.

In the case of architecture, too, he realized that the task was to negotiate between the abstract and the concrete. As Anthony Grafton has written in his intellectual biography of Alberti, *On the Art of Building* seeks above all to strike a balance between "universal, mathematical proportion and local, site-specific adaptation." Alberti's ideal architect, says Grafton, is "a godlike figure who imposes a mathematical order on unruly matter."[15] This attitude was one that Alberti learned from his favorite source: classical antiquity. In particular, he took inspiration from the architectural work of Vitruvius, and even divided his own treatise into ten books in imitation of him. But there was another, more obviously philosophical, ancient influence at work, namely Platonism. Alberti frequented Ficino's circle of Platonists in the 1460s and was called a "Platonic mathematician" by Ficino himself. Coming from him, that was obviously a great compliment.[16]

Platonism gave architects a way to think about their application of abstract forms to concrete buildings, as when they designed churches as a half-sphere (that is, a dome) over a cube-shaped interior. This could be taken to represent heaven vaulting above the earth.[17] But it was also a way of giving two of the five geometrical solids, mentioned in Plato's *Timaeus*, a more literal kind of solidity. Even as Platonism was inspiring the architects, architecture was inspiring the Platonists. In his dialogue *On Love* Ficino explains the doctrine of Platonic Forms by comparing it to the way the plan of a building appears in the mind of the architect before it is realized in stone. To grasp the idea itself, you must simply imagine that you "subtract the matter mentally, but leave the design."[18] This sentiment echoes what we find in Alberti's treatise on architecture, when he writes about drafting the plan for a building as a "precise and correct outline, conceived in the mind, made up of lines and angles, and perfected in the learned intellect and imagination." Just to confirm the parallel between applied mathematics in the visual arts and in mechanics, it's worth quoting the aforementioned Bernardino Baldi, who wrote that not all "mathematical proofs apply to quantities separated from matter. Sometimes such proofs are adapted to sensible objects and demonstrate the marvellous effects which occur in them. Of such sort are the proofs in perspective and mechanics."[19]

When Renaissance men like Alberti, Ficino, and Baldi traced such ideas back to the classical world, they found that the trail did not end with Vitruvius, or Archimedes, or even Plato. It ended with Pythagoras. This shadowy, indeed nearly mythical, Presocratic philosopher was often held up as a moral exemplar, and was also the ultimate authority for the idea that the cosmos is fundamentally mathematical. Pythagoreanism ran deep in Renaissance humanism and Platonism. It manifested in everything from the circular design of those utopian cities (see Chapter 42 above), to Ficino's excitement over the fact that Plato died on his own birthday and at the age of 81 (which is 9^2), to Pico della Mirandola's choice to defend exactly 900 theses at Rome (the number, he said, of the "excited soul"). The mathematician Baldi went so far as to compose a lengthy biography of Pythagoras, whom he called the "prince of Italian philosophy" and "inferior to god but superior to all other humans."[20]

To think like a Pythagorean meant discerning mathematical structures everywhere in nature, and even beyond nature. For a Pythagorean portrayal of the natural world you can't beat *On the Harmony of the Cosmos*, written in 1525 by Francesco Giorgio, or Zorzi.[21] This work is influenced by Ficino's understanding of the history of philosophy, and looks back to themes of universal harmony found in both ancient Platonists and biblical sources. For a Pythagorean portrayal of the *super*-natural world, meanwhile, there is Luca Pacioli's 1509 work *On Divine Proportion*, published with illustrations by none other than Leonardo da Vinci. Pacioli was both an accomplished mathematician and a religious preacher, and wished to show that the divine Trinity can be understood in geometrical terms. Take, for instance, the "golden section," a line divided so that the ratio of its shorter segment to its longer segment is the same as the ratio of the longer segment to the whole line. Pacioli suggests that the two segments and whole line are a fitting image of the Trinity, especially since the ratio at work is an irrational number and thus undefinable, like God Himself.[22]

Pythagoras' influence also made itself felt, or rather seen, in the visual arts. Take the urban fantasyscape ascribed to Fra Carnevale, called *The Ideal City*. It's the ultimate distillation of the Renaissance fascination for classicism and mathematics into a single image. Or check out what may be the most familiar visual representation of philosophy ever created, Raphael's *School of Athens*. In the middle, famously, are Plato and Aristotle, Plato pointing to the heavens and Aristotle with his hand held flat, symbolizing that virtue is a mean. But ignore them for now, and notice instead two figures towards the front of the scene, dominating the left and right groups. They are Pythagoras and Euclid, the former writing in a book and representing arithmetic, the latter poised above a tablet with a compass and representing geometry. I think they really hold the whole thing together.

49

JUST WHAT THE DOCTOR ORDERED
RENAISSANCE MEDICINE

You've probably heard of the "placebo effect," in which patients respond positively to dummy medications like sugar pills. While there is controversy as to just how strong the placebo effect is and what causes it, some studies suggest that it can be astonishingly powerful. For instance, when it comes to pain relief, placebos may be half as effective as actual medication. This helps to explain the popularity of "alternative medicine." Crystals and homeopathic remedies presumably don't affect the body any differently than sugar pills, but they still "work" insofar as they are effective as placebos. The effect also explains a lot about the history of medicine. It seems at first perplexing that doctors were respected experts in pre-modern societies, from ancient Greece and India to the medieval Islamic world, given that these doctors largely had no idea what caused diseases or how they could be cured. Sometimes, to be sure, they could offer real treatment. Cataract eye surgery was performed successfully in the Islamic world, to give just one especially impressive example, and effective therapies were also identified by trial and error. Much of the benefit offered by these early doctors, though, would have derived from the placebo effect. Merely receiving attention from confident and renowned experts like Galen and Avicenna would itself have been an aid to recovery.

We congratulate ourselves with having come a long way since these bad old days, now having learned to compare drugs with placebos in blind trials. But it turns out that the placebo effect was not unknown to pre-modern medicine. In the sixteenth century Girolamo Cardano, who counted medicine as one of his main interests, noted that a magic charm may dull a toothache simply because the sufferer believes in its power.[1] And why not? When it came to matters of health, the people of this period needed all the help they could get. The Renaissance has been called a "golden age of disease," beginning with the Black Death in the mid-fourteenth century and featuring other bleak milestones like the outbreak of syphilis in Europe at the end of the fifteenth century.[2] Italian city-states responded with genuinely useful measures, like the founding of hospitals. At first they were little more than hospices for the poor and sick, but increasingly they acquired competent staff. Visiting Italy in 1511, Martin Luther, not an easy man to impress, marveled at hospitals "built like palaces; the best food and drink are given to everyone; the nurses are diligent, the doctors learned." The vectors of contagion were not yet well understood, though physicians did figure out that syphilis was sexually transmitted. Still the sheer *fact* of contagion was obvious.[3] This led governments to decree sanitary regulations, including the forty-day seclusion for newcomers to trading cities like Venice, Pisa, and Genoa, which gives us the word "quarantine." There was even a controversy in late sixteenth-century Rome about the safety of drinking water from the Tiber River.[4] This being the Renaissance, the arguments turned on evidence from antiquity, as doctor-historians debated whether aqueducts had been built to provide cleaner water and wrote treatises on the health benefits of the Roman baths.

Humanist expertise on ancient texts, including ancient medical literature, was one factor that gave Italy its Europe-leading reputation in medicine. Another was the university system. Bologna had always been associated with medical training, and the subject was also important at Padua, Ferrara, and elsewhere. The universities attracted aspiring physicians and scientists from all over Europe, who then returned home to spread medical learning in their home territories. To give just one example, the medical historian Nancy Siraisi has calculated that out of thirty-seven professors of medicine at the university of Erfurt in the fifteenth century, sixteen had studied in Italy.[5] This is comparable to the standing of Italy in legal scholarship. Indeed, nothing epitomizes Renaissance Italy's university culture better than the dispute over the relative superiority of these two disciplines, law and medicine. It was a question that attracted the attention of such sharp thinkers as the Averroist Nicoletto Vernia. He took the side of medicine, because of its close relationship to philosophy and its exemplary status as an application of proper scientific method. Another partisan of medicine, Bartolomeo Fazio, said that medicine is better than law because it involves an understanding of natural causes: "what could be more ingenious than to grasp through reason the composition, structure, order, and the very causes of the diseases, of our bodies?"[6]

Vernia was not wrong to emphasize the dependence of medicine on the philosophy of nature. Learned medicine in the Italian Renaissance drew extensively on the second-century AD doctor Galen and authors influenced by him, especially figures from the Islamic world like al-Rāzī, Ibn Sīnā, and Ibn Rushd, known respectively in Latin as Rhazes, Avicenna, and Averroes. Like them, Renaissance physicians were committed to the basic principles of Galenic medicine. Health and disease are determined in large part by the balance (and lack thereof) of the four humors, blood, phlegm, black bile, and yellow bile. This can be maintained and restored, in an emergency through interventions like drugs or bloodletting, but preferably through a healthful "regime" which ideally should be tailored to each patient by the doctor, given the wide variation in individual bodily constitution. Environment also plays a role, as already taught by Hippocrates in the treatise *Airs, Waters, and Places*. Thus doctors spoke of six factors that could be manipulated in order to preserve health: air, food and drink, exercise, sleep, evacuation, and emotional states.[7]

The points of contact with philosophy are many. The four humors have the properties associated with the four elements (e.g. yellow bile is hot and dry, like fire). Psychological and emotional health is related to ethics. The role of the environment connects medicine to meteorology, which is why the aforementioned debates over issues like contagion and clean drinking water invoked ideas from Aristotelian philosophy. It should be said, though, that the partnership between philosophy and medicine was not always an untroubled one. Back in the fourteenth century, Pietro d'Abano had written *Reconciler of the Differences between Philosophers and Physicians*, which itemizes and discusses the clashes between Aristotelian philosophy and Galenic medicine. One example was the different list of powers or faculties considered in medicine and in philosophical anthropology.[8] Galenic doctors spoke of the so-called "vital faculty" seated in the animal spirit, and of *pneuma* coursing through the body from its origin in the heart. It was not so clear how to fit such ideas into the psychological theory outlined in Aristotle's *On the Soul*.

Furthermore, it was not usually thought that medicine was actually a *part* of philosophy, like physics, meteorology, zoology, or botany. Medicine might take over principles from all of these disciplines, but, as we saw Zabarella arguing, it is an applied science. The true parts of natural philosophy are instead theoretical sciences, directed towards the pursuit of pure knowledge rather than practical action. One might compare the relation between architecture and mathematics, the former being concrete, the latter abstract. Zabarella captured the point as follows: "there cannot be a good physician who is not also a natural philosopher... But there is a difference between them: medicine is concerned only with accomplishing its purpose, while natural philosophy has no purpose to accomplish, but is only knowledge (*scientia*)."[9]

This contrast lay behind the frequent motto, "where the philosopher leaves off, the doctor begins (*ubi desinit philosophus ibi incipit medicus*)." In other words, the physician carries forward and applies what he has learned from physics. This idea was reflected in the teaching curriculum. A university-trained doctor would have studied physics or natural philosophy, and before that logic, before coming to their specialist subject. Pietro d'Abano explained why doctors needed to become acquainted with these fields: "logic, since it is the condiment of all the sciences, just as salt is of food; and natural philosophy, since it shows the principles of everything."[10] Doctors with this sort of training considered themselves to be far superior to mere practitioners like community surgeons and apothecaries, who simply applied the deliverances of past experience without any conception of an underlying causal theory. In this too, the university physicians were echoing Galen, who criticized the ancient "Empiricist" medical school for refusing to offer rational explanations for the efficacy of their treatments, and just blindly doing whatever seemed to work in the past.[11]

Here, we might think, is one reason that the bad old days were so bad, when it came to medicine. University doctors were trying to learn from old books, when they should have been abandoning the false theories in those books and learning from experience. But as usual, things are a bit more complicated. For starters, it was a matter of dispute which books the learned doctors should be reading. A pure humanist approach would encourage the exclusive study of Greek medicine, and some medical authors did take this approach.[12] Niccolò Leoniceno, at the beginning of the sixteenth century, wrote a treatise called *On the Formative Power* which rigorously adhered to Galen's account of embryology and mentioned authors who wrote in Arabic, like Averroes, mostly in order to disagree with them. Thus in his study of this work, Hiro Hirai has concluded that Leoniceno was motivated by "strong anti-Arabism and a steadfast love for the Greek sources."[13]

A particularly good illustration of the way Renaissance medical writers used ancient literature is supplied by the study of plants. Several cities saw the literal planting of botanical gardens, and at Padua there was a professorial chair just for *materia medica*, in other words, for the study of plants and other ingredients used in drugs. No effort was spared in the ambition to recreate classical drug recipes, a project that called for skill in philology as well as botany: what exactly were various obscure Greek words for plants referring to? Some authors looked back even further, writing about plants and stones mentioned in the Bible and discussing their healing properties. One of these was David de' Pomi, born in Spoleto in 1525 and educated in Perugia. He wrote a lexicon of biblical stones, including a lengthy discussion of hyacinth (the stone, not the flower) and its power to ward off the plague.[14] I highlight de' Pomi's contribution in part because he was Jewish, a reminder that in Renaissance Italy as in the Islamic world, Jews were strongly associated with the study and practice of medicine.

Speaking of the Islamic world, for all the classicism of this period, most authors found it impossible to escape medical literature written originally in Arabic. The curriculum in Bologna called for the study of al-Rāzī and Avicenna along with Galen, and both authors were cited abundantly in Renaissance tracts on medicine.

To cite again the historian Nancy Siraisi, she counts at least sixty Latin printings of Avicenna's *Canon* from 1500 to 1674, with a particularly impressive case being the 1523 five-volume edition of Avicenna together with later commentaries.[15] One medical author, Sebastiano Bresciani, went so far as to stipulate that any physician worth his salt should master Arabic, as well as Greek and Latin. That message didn't get through to a scholar named Andrea Grazioli, who offered a new "translation" of Avicenna without actually learning the original language. But that just goes to show the extent to which Arabic texts were absorbed into the world of Latin learning. This can also be seen from the frequent quotation of such authors. Take the anatomist Berengario da Carpi. He quotes Avicenna more than 1,000 times and considers al-Rāzī to be an authority second in importance only to Galen.[16]

But Berengario's field of anatomy demonstrates that authors of this period were interested in observation as well as books. It could hardly have been otherwise, since their reading of ancient and medieval sources emphasized the importance of empirical investigation in medicine. Galen prided himself on this. As just mentioned, he criticized the pure Empiricists for their lack of theory, but he was also critical of pure "Rationalists" who ignored the hard-won fruits of experience and tried to work out all their treatments from first principles. The same message could be found in Avicenna, whose subtle account of scientific experience (*tajriba*) encouraged the simultaneous use of observation and causal theory.[17] He even gave an example from pharmacology (namely the purging effect of a plant called scammony) to illustrate how this works.

Renaissance anatomists took this advice very much to heart, and to all the other organs as well. Human bodies had not been dissected for research purposes since ancient Alexandria, well before Galen himself. But now this practice began again, with an annual anatomical demonstration established in Bologna already in 1405 and in Padua by the middle of the fifteenth century. Dissection—and unfortunately, also vivisection—was also performed on pigs, which were thought to be anatomically close to humans, and other animals. Berengario da Carpi first cut his scalpel, though hopefully not his teeth, on the corpse of a pig under the instruction of none other than Aldus Manutius, the pioneer who printed the works of Aristotle in Greek (see Chapter 45). When he came to write on anatomy himself, Berengario emphasized the role of observation in this discipline, saying that it ultimately trumps the role of authority. While professing to be guided by "sensation, the authority of the divine Galen, and various reasonings," he would not accept an anatomical claim found in Galen if he found contrary evidence in actual dissected bodies.[18]

This critical attitude was taken further by the most famous anatomist of the Italian Renaissance, Andreas Vesalius (he was actually Flemish, but became professor of surgery in Venice after first learning his trade in Paris). His work *On the Fabric of the Body* is distinguished by its itemization of mistakes committed by Galen.[19] In keeping with the spirit of the age, Vesalius proclaimed that the study of anatomy was only just recovering from a long period of ignorance during the middle ages. It was an obvious step forward that anatomical treatises were now based on actual anatomical dissection. Berengario and Vesalius made a further breakthrough by including detailed anatomical illustrations in their works.[20] Vesalius offered the analogy of mathematical treatises, which are much easier to follow thanks to the diagrams they include. Indeed, the case of anatomy shows us that medicine and artistic production could go hand-in-hand, just like mathematics and art. Alberti's *On Painting* says that artists must become acquainted with the structure of the human body, since when we paint a person we should first think about where the bones would be, then the muscles, then "reclothe" these with skin and flesh.[21]

The woodcut images found in Renaissance anatomical works are remarkable for their artistic ingenuity and imagination. Berengario's treatises already include arresting depictions of people calmly spreading open the skin of their torsos so that we can look inside, while the skeletons and muscle-men of Vesalius strike dramatic poses as their flayed skin hangs from an elbow or hand. These illustrations are not just a substitute for the direct observation students could enjoy (if "enjoy" is the right word) during an anatomical display. They are idealizations, which make it artificially easy to see bodily structures that would be very difficult to make out in the messy gore of an actual autopsy, and which also convey the wondrous intricacy of the human body.

Specialists in anatomy never tired of emphasizing the perfect design of the body, a theme they could find in their ancient sources. Galen's treatise *On the Usefulness of the Parts* is a lengthy paean to the exquisite functionality of human bodies, and Aristotle's zoological writings are notorious for their commitment to the idea of final causality, or teleology: animal organs are shaped to pursue the purposes of the animal. Teleology was central to the project of Girolamo Fabrici d'Acquapendente, who was professor of anatomy at Padua beginning in 1565.[22] As a good Aristotelian, he was interested in the parts of animals, not just humans. He published studies of individual animal organs like the eye, larynx, and ear, which expressed his Aristotelian belief in the functionality of these body parts. Indeed he said himself that this distinguished his approach from that of Vesalius, who had been content to expose (literally) the structure of bodily organs without investigating their function. We can see Fabrici's approach as an application of the scientific method articulated at Padua by Zabarella. Anatomy is treated as a true empirical science, which begins with observation and works towards causal principles that explain what has been observed. In this case, this means determining the final cause—that is, the purpose or goal—of each organ, which will then explain the details of its physical structure. The result is a discipline that, in Fabrici's words, constitutes "the true and solid basis of the whole of medicine, and the ultimate perfection and consummation of natural philosophy."[23]

50

MAN OF DISCOVERIES GIROLAMO CARDANO

I don't have much in common with Georg Friedrich Wilhelm Hegel, one of the greatest philosophers of the nineteenth century. But I can at least say that, like him, I have spent a lot of time teaching German students about the history of philosophy. Hegel lectured on this subject many times, in Jena, in Heidelberg, and then in Berlin every year over the last decade of his life. His approach to the subject was rather different from mine, not least in his notorious dismissal of philosophy written in Arabic as involving "no proper principle and stage in the development of philosophy."[1] But I rather like the choice he makes when he comes to philosophy in the Renaissance. He starts off not with an obvious figure like Bruni, Ficino, or Machiavelli, but with several pages on Girolamo Cardano. Hegel's remarks are based especially on Cardano's autobiography, which he summarizes in part as follows: "in his habits, outer life, and conduct he went from one extreme to the other; at one moment he was calm, at another like a madman or lunatic, now industrious and studious, now dissolute and squandering all his goods. Naturally in these circumstances he brought up his children very badly."

I can readily understand why Hegel latched onto Cardano, who might be the philosopher from the Italian Renaissance whose personality comes down to us most vividly. He was a prolific writer, and scattered personal remarks throughout his many works. But it is his autobiography that gives the strongest sense of his personality.[2] It covers the main events of his life: born in Pavia in 1501, he studied in his home city and Padua and taught mathematics and medicine at several universities, including Bologna in the 1560s. This followed the execution of Cardano's son in 1560, on the grounds that the young man had poisoned his wife (to reiterate: "he brought up his children very badly"). As if this tragedy were not enough, ten years later Cardano himself was charged with heresy, imprisoned for a couple of months, and made to recant his supposedly unorthodox views.[3]

But it's not for these biographical milestones that one reads Cardano's account of his own life. It's for such details as a description of his favorite food (veal cooked in its own juice: §8), the strange dreams and portents that have followed him through life, his talent for name-dropping, with a whole chapter devoted to listing his friends (§15) and another to listing the various prominent men who have praised him (§48), to say nothing of Cardano's evident delight at his own genius, as when he tells us how many languages he was able to learn with no effort or study whatsoever (§39). Indeed, a keynote of the text is its self-aware boastfulness. He informs us (twice) that a friend dubbed him the "man of discoveries," and was right to do so. Cardano reckons that he has 40,000 significant discoveries to his name and about 200,000 minor ones (§44). He has no need to choose between the Aristotelian goal of contemplative fulfillment, and the Stoic ideal of withstanding all misfortune: he finds it possible to achieve both (§46). At one point Cardano even manages to brag about being average, when describing his own appearance: "so truly commonplace that several painters who have come from afar to make my portrait have found no feature by which they could so characterize me, that I might be distinguished" (§8).

Medicine, perhaps the most central of Cardano's many fields of expertise, is mentioned throughout the autobiography. No reader will soon forget the way he obsessively and frankly catalogues his physical and psychological ailments, which include fear of heights, insomnia, stuttering, excessive urination, and a decade of sexual impotence (§2, 6). Good thing then for his medical expertise, which has enabled him to devise the ideal exercise regime for preserving health. "I have," he winningly remarks, "reduced the whole to a system as is the fashion in matters of theology, with much profound meditation and brilliant reasoning" (§8). He wouldn't necessarily claim to be *better* at medicine than Galen and Avicenna, but it's only fair he should mention having lived longer than either of them managed (§40). Actually the talent for self-presentation is something else Cardano learned from Galen.[4] Cardano names him as a precedent for autobiographical writing, and many aspects of his life story ring Galenic bells. Like Galen, Cardano revels in telling stories where he humiliated rival scholars in debate or through superior medical diagnosis. He offers us a list of his own books, as Galen did, and is no less shy than Galen was when it comes to criticizing the books of others. In fact his targets include Galen himself, whom Cardano irreverently corrects on points of medical therapy (§45).

Cardano freely admits that writing has itself been a way for him to fend off grief and maintain his mental and physical health. This might be why he wrote so much. About half of his voluminous output is on medicine, and goes well beyond the kind of book-learning that he could have gleaned from reading Galen and Avicenna.[5] He was a practicing doctor, and (again like Galen) wrote up detailed case studies, most notably concerning his attendance on the archbishop of St Andrews, whom he traveled all the way to Scotland to treat in 1552 (§29, 40). He told the bishop to eat dry foods, since his body had been made overly moist by illness, and to chew gum (actually pistachio resin) to excite saliva, which would draw moisture out of the brain. Also, and more likely to be helpful, the bishop should get plenty of rest.[6] While confessing to lack of expertise in surgery (§39), Cardano encouraged the study of hands-on medical skills, complaining that contemporary medical education passes over such important disciplines as obstetrics, dentistry, surgery, and pediatrics—all the areas, as he wryly remarked, where the doctor's failure would be obvious.[7] He was a great believer in maintaining and restoring health through careful regimen. Alongside his aforementioned program of exercise, he recommended a largely vegetarian diet, while avoiding some fruits. He blamed a bout of dysentery in his own childhood on eating grapes (§4), and deemed melons so dangerous that they ought to be made illegal![8]

Despite the occasional point of correction, Cardano was largely an admirer of Galen, though in what seems to have been a rhetorical exercise he did compose a damning critique of his ancient role model as having had more luck than learning, and displayed more vice than virtue.[9] Of all medical authorities, the one he most admired was Hippocrates. Along with Ptolemy and Plotinus, Cardano named him as one of three figures who were "close to divinity" in their level of insight, literally incomparable to other scholars, which is why he deliberately excluded them from his list of the greats.[10] He excoriated the doctors of his own day for any departure from the advice given by Hippocrates—not least his ban on eating melons—and composed a series of commentaries on the Hippocratic corpus, on which he lectured during his years at Bologna. Cardano also lavished praise on Avicenna, even preferring him to Galen on the grounds of superior moral character and the better organization of his works.[11] Among his contemporaries, one figure he greatly esteemed was the anatomist Vesalius. In part this was because he thought the Vesalian theories were in harmony with the Hippocratic corpus, and helpful in correcting the errors of Galenic anatomy. Always wary of uncritically following anyone, though, Cardano assured his readers that his policy was to believe not Vesalius, but his own eyes.[12] Cardano thought far less, by the way, of Leonardo da Vinci. Having viewed the artist's anatomical drawings, he said they were "by all means beautiful and worthy of such a famous artist, but completely useless, being the work of one who did not know the number of intestines. The fact is that he was a mere painter, not a physician, nor a philosopher."[13]

Among the many things Cardano found to admire in Hippocrates was his teaching on the soul. This is, on the face of it, rather strange, because Cardano was a proponent of the soul's immateriality, whereas he ascribes to Hippocrates the view that the soul is nothing but heat. The reason Cardano likes this view is that it makes life and soul pervasive in the cosmos. Wherever you find heat, there would be some sort of soul present.[14] Departing from Aristotelian cosmology, he asserts that even the celestial bodies possess heat, since they are alive. Still, the Hippocratic idea of soul as heat does in a way establish the immortality of soul, because heat is never extinguished, but is a permanent feature of the universe. These ideas resonate with at least some of what Cardano himself says about the soul and the mind.[15] I say "some of" because he puts forward different ideas in different places and admits to difficulty in reaching a firm conclusion. Shortly before his death he admitted, "I know souls are immortal, but am not sure how."

One thing he was sure about is that Pomponazzi had been wrong to suggest that the human soul is tied to its body, needs the body as a basis for its operations, and dies along with it. To the contrary, Cardano argues, materiality impedes thought (this is why animals can't think: their bodies make it impossible) and the intellective soul can certainly survive independently of the body. He is confident that Aristotle would agree with this, and goes so far as to argue that for Aristotle it should be possible that individual souls are reincarnated, being associated now with one body, now with another. Of course, Cardano doesn't dare to endorse the transmigration of souls himself. But he does flirt with the notorious doctrine of Averroism, which envisions a single intellect shared by all humans as the sole guarantor of immortality. Cardano likewise makes the intellect alone to be immortal, while lower functions like imagination and memory die with the body. He also intimates that there is a kind of universal, active intellectual power in whose immortality we partake. As he nicely puts it, "the origin of all intellects seems to be the same for all, since human beings, from very early on, are endowed with the same principles, as in all swallows there is the same ability to build a nest."[16] Still, Cardano distances himself from the Averroist notion that there is only one universal mind. Instead, each of us gets a portion of intellect, which is why we each have our own acts of understanding that are not shared with others. As Cardano says, the active intellect is "within us (*in nobis*)" and a "part of us."[17]

Sadly, we can't enjoy the activities of this intellect non-stop. It's an effort to divert the mind from "the vexations of the body and the senses, such as pain, fear, pleasures and hope."[18] He knew whereof he spoke. If this was a man who got more than his share of intellect, he also experienced more than his portion of pain and grief. It seems he was trying to distract himself from these travails by making all those discoveries and writing so many books. By reading and writing about science, he could retreat temporarily from a troubled bodily existence. I find his remarks about this rather moving: "while I am actually writing this, my intellect is the things you grasp through what I have written: medicine while I discuss medical matters;

arithmetic at the time that I was writing about numbers, so much so that as must happen to everyone else who has been an author of various works, while I read over what I have written, I think myself different from the person I now am."[19] Elsewhere he speaks of the way that physical pain can be escaped by intense intellectual focus, though conversely the pain may make thinking impossible.

Fortunately, Cardano had a Plan B: have fun! His autobiography contains a whole chapter on things in which he takes pleasure (§18). To his credit, these include the joys of reading authors like Aristotle and Plotinus. But Cardano was also partial to a bit of gambling. Or more than a bit, actually. He makes it fairly clear that he is a gambling addict, even admitting that he once had to pawn his wife's jewelry and family furniture to pay off debts (§19, 24). No wonder that, as he cheerfully remarks, he has wound up "richer in the knowledge of nature's secrets than in money" (§23). The loss to his bank account turned out to be a gain to the storehouse of human knowledge, because his fascination with gambling led him to write a remarkable study of the mathematics of dice and card games.

This pioneering work has been called "the first text on the theory of probability."[20] It sets out observations that may now seem obvious, for instance that the probability of a favorable outcome is the number of good outcomes divided by the total number of outcomes (if you need to roll three on a six-sided die, your chance of doing so is one out of six). He also tries to work out the average result that should be expected over repeated trials, for instance, what the average roll will be if you roll three dice over and over. In addition to articulating genuine insights about probability, Cardano also inadvertently displays how easily our intuitions go astray when thinking about it. He assumes, wrongly, that the chance of success over a certain number of trials is the number of trials times the chance of succeeding in one trial. Thus, if you need to roll a three on one die, then your chance of doing so in two rolls should be double of what it is in one roll, namely two in six.[21] To see that this is wrong, consider that your chances of rolling a three after six rolls would be six out of six, so a guaranteed success; but of course that is not the case. Cardano also makes some comments connecting the topic of probability to standard philosophical issues. He speculates about the connection between destiny and luck, expressing doubt that the order of the universe would bother to affect a card game. But he also expresses a certain fatalism, suggesting that the outcome of a game of chance may be settled in advance so that it makes no difference what you do. He compares this to the way you are subject to the authority of the prince, whether you decide to stay at home or go out.

Cardano wrote a number of other mathematical works, of which the most famous is his *Great Art* (*Ars magna*), a study of algebra.[22] Alongside some nice mathematical observations that even I can appreciate—for instance, that the square root of a positive number can be negative—this book is revealing as concerns ideas of scientific originality and priority in the sixteenth century. Cardano characteristically boasts, at the outset, that the work "is so replete with new discoveries and demonstrations by the author—more than seventy of them—that its forerunners are of little account." Then there is his notorious inclusion of the method for solving cubic equations, which have the form $x^3 + ax = b$. Cardano does not claim this among his many novel discoveries. He credits it to Niccolò Tartaglia, and admits that Tartaglia would not want him to publish the secret. (In the event, Tartaglia was indeed furious.) But Cardano claims an excuse for his indiscretion, namely that another mathematician had discovered the same method a few decades ago, after which it was forgotten. This vignette demonstrates how ideas about originality were changing in the Renaissance. Increasingly, scholars wanted to claim new innovations for themselves, which is also why Cardano was so flattered to be called "man of discoveries." Yet the rules for scientific precedent remained unclear, and propriety was a matter of individual judgment, not commonly accepted practice.[23]

Perhaps Cardano was willing to risk annoying his colleague Tartaglia simply because he was so used to annoying people. His autobiography includes a long list of his critics and enemies, as if to balance out the lists of friends and admirers. Among those who Cardano accused of attacking him "for the sake of making a reputation for themselves" (§48), none was a more bitter opponent than fellow philosopher known as Julius Caesar Scaliger (his real name was Giulio Bordon).[24] Scaliger took issue with one of Cardano's most significant works, *On Subtlety*, a wide-ranging and enormous treatise dedicated to "the most obscure aspect in each branch of study," as Cardano puts it with typical immodesty.[25] Scaliger hated it. He wrote a treatise containing 365 chapters, presumably so the reader might spend every day of the year contemplating Cardano's shortcomings. Anthony Grafton has called it "the most savage book review in the bitter annals of literary invective."[26] It pours scorn on everything from Cardano's pitiful Latin skills to the aforementioned ideas about soul and intellect. Remember that moving passage about transforming one's mind into the object of one's contemplation? Well, it moves Scaliger only to sarcastic abuse: "well done, Cardano, you who say that when you think of a horse, your intellect is nothing other than a horse!"[27]

I wouldn't dream of taking a side in this dispute, but if I did, then Cardano would have just the book for me. It's a whole treatise on dreams, based to a large extent on an ancient guide to dream interpretation by an author named Synesius.[28] Cardano offers a whole theory as to how different kinds of dreams are caused. They may for instance result from bad digestion, or on the other hand from contact with the intelligible realm. In the latter case they can divulge visions of future events. This sounds pretty far from anything we now recognize as genuinely scientific, but for Cardano the topic of prophetic dreams is closely connected to medicine. We receive prophetic dreams when the "spirit" that flows through the body is well prepared and at rest, which is why the dreams come when we sleep. The skilled interpreter, like the skilled doctor approaching each patient, must take into account the dreamer's way of life and individual disposition.[29] Cardano himself enjoyed many prophetic dreams, and recounts them in his autobiography. He thinks that, at least in retrospect, he can understand the meaning of his visions. On one occasion, he was on the verge of administering what would have been a fatal therapy to a patient, but was held back by a dream warning. Still, he admits that interpretation, like medicine, will always remain an uncertain business. "Not only must the nature of dreams be infinite, the very analysis of them is infinite . . . the mind is infinite in its power and the number of things is infinite too."[30] No wonder he wrote so much.

51

SPIRITS IN THE MATERIAL WORLD TELESIO AND CAMPANELLA ON NATURE

If Aristotle, or any one of the legion of Aristotelian philosophers who worked in the 2,000 years after his death, were confronted with a textbook on modern physics, they would be stunned by many new and unfamiliar ideas, from gravity to magnetism to the structure of the atom. But they might be even more surprised at what was missing. Where, they would ask themselves, are all the references to the four elements? To the natural places towards which the elements tend, fire and air moving upward, water and earth downward? Where, above all, are the references to forms? For the Aristotelians, understanding nature was in large part about understanding forms, both accidental and substantial. Ultimate matter, in their worldview, was pure potentiality to receive form. So whenever scientific investigation revealed something about determinate properties, causal powers, or the natures of things, this was a matter of understanding the forms that reside in matter.

There was no one moment that European philosophy gave up on "hylomorphism"; that is, the theory that all things are constituted from matter and form (in Greek *hyle* and *morphe*). Science did not move from Aristotelian physics to modern physics in just one step. The change was instead, and as usual in the history of philosophy, incremental. This is nicely illustrated by the profound challenge posed to Aristotelianism in late sixteenth-century Italy by several thinkers, above all Bernardino Telesio and Tommaso Campanella. Their natural philosophy was explicitly presented as a rejection of Aristotle, and put forward with appeals to the value of "freedom in philosophizing (*libertas philosophandi*)." As Campanella said, such freedom led to the sort of innovations that Europe was seeing at this time, ranging from the telescope to the printing press and gunpowder weaponry.[1] "All the new doctrines," he observed, "please and render admirable both the state and religion, and they make it so that subjects turn more willingly to their duties; from foreigners they elicit admiration and obedience."[2] Yet the self-consciously original and innovative new science developed by Telesio, and eagerly adopted by Campanella, was itself a version of hylomorphism.

Telesio made this point himself. In his treatise *On the Nature of Things*, first published in 1565 and appearing later in revised editions, he argued that if Aristotle had been more consistent in following his own principles, he would have reached very different conclusions (§2.16).[3] In particular, he reminded readers that in the first book of Aristotle's *Physics*, we are told that all change requires three factors: something that undergoes the change, the feature that is acquired or lost as a result of the change, and the absence of that feature (§2.2). Abstractly speaking, we can say that what undergoes change is "matter," the positive feature is "form," and the lack of form is "privation." Yet Aristotle's own physical theory looks more complicated. Even his basic elements have more than one positive feature, since fire, air, earth, and water each have two primary qualities: fire is hot and dry, water is cold and wet, and so on (§2.20). Telesio wanted to keep things simpler, as suggested in the basic hylomorphic model of *Physics* book one. For him there were only three principles: matter, heat, which plays the role of form, and the absence of heat, also known as cold. With these three principles, he thought, he could explain the whole universe.

Though the Telesian universe is Aristotelian in general structure, it is profoundly un-Aristotelian in other respects. Neither Telesio nor Campanella after him adopted the new Copernican astronomy, so they still had the earth unmoving at the center of the universe, just as Aristotle had said. But whereas for Aristotle, the celestial realm was constituted from a "fifth element" that is neither hot nor cold, Telesio said that the luminous heavens are the body that is primarily hot, heat being closely associated with light. The earth by contrast is cold, and is thus opposed to the nature of the heavens. These two, earth and the heavens, are the "first bodies (*prima corpora*)" in our cosmos (§1.4). Other bodies are formed through their interaction, as heat and cold struggle against each other, producing ever more complex natures. Most basically, heat causes expansion and cold contraction, which is where moisture and dryness come from: these two properties are derived from hot and cold, not on a par with them as Aristotle believed. More complicated phenomena arise thanks to the stars, especially the sun. As they move over the earth, the increased heat in the affected parts of earth causes them to transform into vapors, fluid, metals, and stones (§1.15). More generally, variation in heat and cold due to heavenly motion can produce the bewildering multiplicity we see around us (§1.16, 1.18, 1.33).

According to Telesio, heat and cold are not bodies (§1.6). Instead, body is that which they act upon, and for him this is matter. What undergoes change, in other words, is not a mere seat of potentiality for the reception of form, as in

Aristotelianism; it is a "corporeal mass," a "stuff" whose total quantity never changes.[4] In another dramatic shift away from the Aristotelian tradition, Telesio recognizes bodily matter, heat, and cold as "substances," and thinks that all the more complex natures that arise in matter are accidental to it.[5] Though matter has its own, rudimentary nature insofar as it is corporeal, it is inert and passive, even "dead" as Telesio puts it, echoing a remark made by Plotinus, who called matter a "decorated corpse."[6] Matter and the earth made from it have a tendency to move towards the center of the cosmos, but this is not a natural downward motion like the one Aristotle ascribed to earth and water. Rather, it is just a matter of "falling," since matter has no active power at all (§1.44).

Cold and hot, by contrast, are "active" principles. Here Telesio has in mind not just the capacity to warm and chill, or, as we already saw, to cause expansion and contraction. Heat and cold also tend to pursue what is similar to them, as when fire comes together to make ever larger blazes, and to repel what is dissimilar to them, as when water is boiled away by fire. So the two fundamental principles are always working to preserve themselves and destroy what is contrary to them. This is an observation with far-reaching implications: it leads Telesio to claim that the two agent natures, heat and cold, must always be capable of sensation (§1.34). We lazily assume that sensation must involve sense-organs, but this is not the case, as such organs are needed only for more sophisticated forms of sensation (§1.35). The mere fact that cold and heat flee one another shows that they are in a very crude way able to respond to what is around them, while stones and plants have slightly less crude forms of sensation. As Campanella will later explain in his exposition of Telesio's views, sensation is really just the ability to respond to being affected. So we should consider warm, fluid air to be highly "sensitive," because it shapes itself so readily around other objects. In general, says Campanella, "heat and light are the most sentient things in the world, and the entire world senses in greater or lesser degrees."[7]

More advanced creatures like animals and humans have a higher form of "sensation," but this is still a fundamentally physical phenomenon. In humans, sensation occurs when the warm "spirit" that flows through the body is affected by things in the person's environment.[8] The spirit Telesio is talking about here is a borrowing from the Galenic medical tradition. Galen explained all manner of animal capacities by appealing to *pneuma*, a subtle, warm, and airy sort of "breath" that flows around the body. Yet again, Telesio is putting a traditional idea to untraditional ends: for him the spirit is not the "instrument" of the soul, as doctor-philosophers like Avicenna and Ficino had taught. The spirit just *is* the soul, so the composite of spirit and body is the same as the whole animal. Here we can see the extent to which Telesio has indeed departed from hylomorphism as the Aristotelians understood it.

The soul is no longer a "substantial form," but warm air or "spirit" circulating through the body. However, this (literally) breathtaking materialism comes with a major caveat in the case of humans. Telesio believes that, in addition to the "seed-like" soul that is spirit, humans alone among animals also have an immaterial "divine soul" which is created directly by God. So it turns out that his materialist revision of Aristotle is complemented by a borrowing from Platonism.

Yet Telesio's novel philosophical approach shows itself even here. He gives the "divine soul" little importance when it comes to our knowledge of the natural world, because it is dependent on the deliverances of sensation. This in fact is how Telesio begins his treatise *On the Nature of Things*: by saying that, where the ancients used abstract reasoning (*ratio*) to do science, he will base himself solely on sensation (§1.1). The Aristotelians insisted that true knowledge is universal in character and involves grasping the essences of things, but Telesio argues that universal thinking is inferior to sensation. It is really just a vague generalization of what we have experienced. To recall that all the giraffes one has encountered had long necks is wholly derivative of, and less informative than, the knowledge one has when inspecting a particular giraffe. Campanella gives the example of seeing something approach from a distance, first thinking it is some sort of animal or other, then realizing it is a human, and only then realizing which particular man is coming.[9] This illustrates the fact that grasping a particular through sensation is more informative than thinking abstractly about universal species and genera. Yet it was the latter that the Aristotelians supposed to be most appropriate for science.

Francis Bacon famously called Telesio the "first of the moderns," and you can see why: already in the 1560s, he was proposing a new, empirically based natural philosophy that resonates with those that will emerge in the seventeenth century. But I want to emphasize again the way that his ideas grew out of a close engagement with Aristotelianism. His appeal to heat and cold as fundamental explanatory principles has some basis in Aristotle's writings, in particular in the *Meteorology*, whose newfound importance during the Renaissance I've already mentioned (Chapter 45).[10] Even Telesio's irreverence towards the ancients could find support in the ancients themselves. While attacking Aristotle he quotes Aristotle's own justification for criticizing his teacher Plato, namely that we should value truth above even our friends (§2.1). Likewise, Telesio's adherent Antonio Persio, who wrote a *Treatise on the Nature of Fire and Heat* in defense of this new natural philosophy, observed that the ancients valued scientific innovation. Why shouldn't we do the same?[11]

One reason that followers like Persio appreciated Telesio was that he offered the chance to provide new answers to old questions. Telesio wrote a treatise on colors, for instance, in which he explained the spectrum between white and black in terms of light-giving heat and its absence.[12] In medicine too, many phenomena could be explained in terms of heat and the mechanistic processes derived from heat. We saw that already with Cardano, who appreciated Hippocrates' identification of soul with heat. A concrete application of the idea comes with Telesio's theory of the pulse, according to which it is caused by the compression and expansion of spirit in the vessels, which results when the heart dilates and contracts.[13] The phenomenon of sleep was another point in favor of Telesian theory. It is no coincidence that we are warmer when we are awake, engaging in sensation and other activities, and cool down when the bodily system shuts down at night.

With all due respect to Persio, the most famous thinker to be carried away with enthusiasm for this new theory was Tommaso Campanella. We already met him as author of the famous utopian work *City of the Sun* (Chapter 42). It is the most renowned of his many writings, but not particularly representative of his output. He composed systematic treatises on politics, theology, metaphysics, and natural philosophy, with the latter part of his output heavily influenced by Telesio. As a young scholar he even traveled to meet the great man, arriving just too late and getting to see only Telesio's corpse; Campanella dealt with the setback by writing a poem. He had encountered Telesio's ideas during a period of intense study which involved surveying ancient literature and more recent offerings, seeking to compare what he found with the "book of nature." This was a favorite metaphor of Campanella's: God has given us two "books," the revelation of the Bible and the world itself. In a typically provocative line, he observed that the universe is the better of the two books, for those who know how to read it, since it is "inscribed in living letters, not like Scripture in dead letters, which are only signs, not things."[14]

Campanella shared Telesio's delight in complaining about Aristotle's failures to read the book of nature correctly. He was thus at pains to distance his fellow Dominican, Thomas Aquinas, from the stain of Peripateticism. Surely Aquinas could have been no follower of Aristotle, he observed, given that he would hardly have defied the condemnations the Parisian authorities aimed at Aristotelian philosophy. If Aquinas nonetheless explored that philosophy, it was only to expose its weaknesses.[15] But Campanella was no more slavishly committed to the church's teachings than those of Aristotle. He spoke up in defense of Galileo, writing an *Apology* on his behalf in 1616. As he wrote to Galileo, his goal was to show that "the manner of philosophizing practiced by you is more compatible with divine Scripture than its opposite, or at least rather more than the Aristotelian manner of philosophizing."[16] This despite the fact that, as I mentioned, Campanella was not himself persuaded by the Copernican astronomy being expounded by Galileo. He simply bridled at the notion that scientific inquiry would be met with suppression and censorship.

No doubt he recognized something of himself in Galileo, having seen the works of his hero Telesio put on the list of proscribed texts by the Inquisition, and having himself been arrested for heresy. As we saw when discussing his *City of the Sun*, Campanella spent twenty-seven years in prison and wrote many of his works during that time, including the defense of Galileo (making it an even more impressive act of courage). Already before these travails, Campanella must have known he was flirting with danger by embracing Telesian philosophy. When he was still a young prodigy, a cardinal asked to assess him for the duke of Florence said of him that he was possessed of a "beautiful mind," but had "no hope of a good outcome, since his doctrine is Telesian, and full of chimeras, madness, and things that apparently can sound good at table to the ignorant, but that possess neither substance nor foundation."[17] To promote Telesio's natural philosophy was to court controversy. So it is apt that Campanella's first work was a rebuttal of a treatise entitled *Defense of Aristotle against Telesio*, by Giacomo Marta. Not content to argue for the cogency of Telesio's conception of nature, Campanella added invective aimed in Aristotle's direction, dismissing him as a non-Christian of poor character.

Far more important than Aristotle's personal failings, though, were his failings as a philosopher. We should look not to him for truth, but to our own experiences. Campanella was devoted to the Telesian principle that philosophy should be grounded in sensation. How sensation works, and its relation to our other psychological powers, is explained in the first treatise of his *Metaphysics*,[18] a work that he had to rewrite completely after an earlier version was confiscated. In this first part he presents a battery of skeptical arguments and responses to those arguments, sandwiched around a presentation of Campanella's own epistemology. His account of knowledge is explicitly, indeed relentlessly, anti-Aristotelian. He thinks that Peripatetic psychology is incoherent, since it presents the soul as nothing but a collection of powers or potentialities, but also defines soul as "form": but a form is not the same as pure potentialities (§1.5.2). Instead, the soul is a substantially, actually existing being (§1.4.6). Again, the Peripatetics are wrong to divide up soul into many powers, since in fact it is the same soul that senses, imagines, remembers, reasons, and engages in intellection (§1.6.5–7). Whereas Aristotle makes it sound as though perception is a matter of the soul's being affected or changed by whatever it perceives, Campanella thinks that we perceive when we notice a change in the body: in other words, what is affected when you see is your eye, and the soul then becomes aware of this affection.

He further contrasted perception of external objects to the constant awareness we have of our own selves, which he called "presential knowledge (*notitia praesentialitatis*)."[19] Here Campanella is finding a bit more for Telesio's "divine soul" to do, by making intellect or "mind (*mens*)" a self-directed power. Like Augustine before him and Descartes after him, he thinks that thoroughgoing skepticism can be defeated by appealing to the phenomenon of self-knowledge. Your grasp of yourself is one thing you can't be wrong about. The mind is also our way of grasping supernatural things, that is, God and the angels, and our possession of it allows us to outlive the death of the body. In the end, it will be through the mind that we achieve true happiness, by contemplating the divine.

As with Telesio, it looks like a healthy measure of Platonism has been mixed into Campanella's antidote to Aristotelianism. In keeping with this, another author Campanella admired and cited frequently was Marsilio Ficino. Ficino's revival of Neoplatonism may seem a strange bedfellow for the materialism of Telesian physics. But Campanella was able to find points of commonality, notably that the Platonists recognized a World Soul that vivifies the entire cosmos. Now, this is not exactly what Telesio had wished to say. He held that air and stones are sensitive, not that they are *ensouled*. His was a theory of universal perception, not one of universal animation.[20] But Campanella could find comments in Ficino that fit tolerably well with the Telesian picture, as with a passage from Ficino's commentary on Plotinus that spoke of a "hot spirit" nourishing the world, and breathed out by the World Soul.[21] He also found common ground with Platonism when it came to the ultimate destiny of humankind. High-flown speculations about an immortal life contemplating divinity sound pretty far removed from a physical theory grounded exclusively in sense-perception. But remember that Telesio's active principles, heat and cold, constantly pursue their own preservation. When we look towards immortality, we are just doing the same.

52

THE MEN WHO SAW TOMORROW RENAISSANCE MAGIC AND ASTROLOGY

When I was about 10 years old, I saw a documentary on television called *The Man Who Saw Tomorrow*, about the sixteenth-century astrologer and soothsayer Michel de Notredame, also known as Nostradamus. It credited him with accurately predicting many historical events, from the French Revolution to the Kennedy assassination, and went on to suggest that he had also predicted a nuclear apocalypse in the decade to come. I was absolutely terrified. Still today I can remember being unable to sleep, convinced that World War Three had already been foreseen in the Renaissance. So I can imagine pretty well how people back in the Renaissance felt in the 1420s, when a number of astrologers warned of a great flood, owing to a conjunction of Mars, Saturn, and Jupiter in the sign of Pisces. After the resulting panic proved to be unfounded, Martin Luther pointed out that whereas the flood hadn't happened, there was a huge peasant uprising instead: "of this no astrologer had breathed so much as a word."[1]

Nowadays, most people over the age of 10 chuckle at the idea that astrological predictions could be accurate, even if most of us also know our star signs and peek at the horoscopes in the newspaper now and again. But in the fifteenth and sixteenth centuries, as in antiquity and the middle ages, there was widespread, sincere belief in the efficacy of astrology and the closely related practice of magic. This conviction could be found at the highest echelons of society: you might recall that Christine de Pizan's father was a professor of astrology and went with his family to the court of Charles V, whom Christine called *roy astrologien*. Predictions based on this science could enhance political legitimacy or have the reverse effect, which is why it was possible to get in serious trouble for predicting the death of rulers and popes. In a study of the use of astrology in Milan, the scholar Monica Azzolini has shown how members of the powerful Sforza family retained astrologers to advise them.[2] When the sickly Gian Galeazzo Sforza died prematurely in 1494, his doctors explained their failure to keep him alive in astrological terms: his modest lifespan was foretold by the stars. Still, they did their best to ward off this fate, constantly consulting the stars, at one point delaying treatment until a conjunction of the moon with Mars had passed. But this noble patient's death was inevitable, due to the "terrible influence of the heavens." Besides which, Gian Galeazzo refused to stop eating dangerous fruits like pears, plums, and apples; had he also partaken of melon, the doctors would probably have considered it a suicide.

We can see from this example that astrology was closely connected to medicine. To cast the horoscope of one's patient was like taking a medical history, and observation of the stars could influence both diagnosis and prognosis. This is illustrated well by the controversial notion of "critical days," which goes all the way back to Hippocrates and Galen.[3] Both ancient doctors asserted that there are pivotal junctures in the development of an illness, which fall on day 7, 14, and 20, when the patient will either take a turn for the worse or begin to recover. Galen proposed that critical days are determined by the cycle of the moon, which is divided into periods of somewhat less than seven days, which is why the third critical day is 20 and not 21. Unfortunately his explanation of the astronomy governing this was not very convincing, in part because he failed to take account of variation in lunar cycles. So attempts were made to fix up the theory. Pietro d'Abano, an enthusiast for medical astrology, suggested a more elaborate theory that matched the four humors to different plants, and he also tried to improve the mathematical rationale underlying the sequence of critical days. Girolamo Cardano was unimpressed by the Galenic account, and said that when it comes to the study of the stars one should listen not to Galen, but to Ptolemy and Hippocrates.[4]

This is what we might expect Cardano to say, given his enthusiasm for both these ancient authors. He was deeply committed to the authoritative status of Ptolemy, who had written fundamental works in both astronomy and astrology. Cardano was deeply committed to astrology, too.[5] Curiously, he did not draw that much on astrology in his medical works, or often discuss medicine in his astrological writings. Yet he was confident that astrologers like himself could predict important events, or at least explain in retrospect why they had happened, as with the outbreak of syphilis in Italy, or the rise and fall of world religions. He foresaw a "renovation of all religions" owing to an astral conjunction, and looking back into history, explained such events as the rise of Islam and the fall of Byzantium with reference to the stars. The events of an individual person's life could be explained in the same way. Cardano tells of an amazing feat he himself performed, when he correctly divined that a certain person he had never met must have eye troubles and a scar made by an iron weapon, all based solely on a nativity.

A "nativity," I should explain, is a horoscope based on the position of the planets (including the sun and moon) at the moment of a person's birth. Cardano was not the first to produce and analyze nativities, of course, but he was the first to author a printed collection of them. He believed that such horoscopes foretold the eloquence of Petrarch, the learning of Trapezuntius, the theological acuity of Savonarola, and the brilliance and early death of Pico della Mirandola. Regarding Vesalius, he wrote that "Mercury in trine with Jupiter, and Venus in quadrature indicate wonderful genius and eloquence as related to his art."[6] Cardano courted controversy by also publishing the nativity of Jesus Christ. This appalled Cardano's many critics; one of them said it was "impious audacity" to suggest that the stars might rule over the Savior himself.[7] But Cardano denied that devotion to astrology equates to a belief in astral determinism. Rather, it tells us about the conditions that will prevail, which is useful precisely so that we may be prepared for them. He gives the example of knowing that there will be a heat wave and bringing a flock of sheep to a cool place so they will not die.[8]

As with medicine and other areas of the humanist movement, the Renaissance approach to astrology often involved an attempt to "purify" the discipline from medieval accretions, especially those from the Islamic world. Cardano wanted to make astrological practice authentically Ptolemaic, and free it from the influence of Abū Maʿshar, al-Qabīṣī (called in Latin Albumashar and Alchabitius), and other scientists of the Islamic world, whom he called a "crowd of idiots (*turba nebulonum*)."[9] Agostino Nifo took a similar view. For him, Abū Maʿshar was a "prince among the fabulists" who had distorted Ptolemy's original teachings. These Ptolemy purists rejected such practices as using astrology to make specific decisions, for instance when to marry or whether to make a journey. This technique of "interrogations," which played a significant role in Arabic astrology, was not even mentioned by Ptolemy. And for good reason, said Cardano, since they are "magical and unworthy, not only of a Christian, but also of a good man."[10] Another disputed point was planetary conjunctions, such as the one invoked in that prediction about the flood. Abū Maʿshar spoke extensively about their effects, and invoked them to explain religious and political upheaval; as already mentioned Cardano followed suit, but the idea was criticized by other authors.

Among these none was more critical than Pico della Mirandola. Dag Nikolaus Hasse has written that conjunction theory was a "main target" of Pico's *Disputations against Judicial Astrology*, published posthumously because he was still at work on it when he died.[11] Pico is relentless in his attacks on astrologers of the Islamic world, who made mistakes and also misread Ptolemy. Charging the eleventh-century astrologer Ibn Riḍwān with one such misinterpretation, he demands, "What do you hallucinate, barbarian?" Pico's formidable intelligence and historical knowledge is brought to bear to cast doubt on astrology as a science.[12] It was not, he points out, even discussed by such ancient authorities as Pythagoras, Plato, Aristotle, Seneca, Cicero, and the church fathers. Apparent counterexamples, like a work ascribed to Aristotle called *Secret of Secrets*, are (correctly) argued by Pico to be inauthentic. If astrologers get things right occasionally, this is simply a matter of chance, because the stars have no influence on particular people or events. Which is not to say that they are entirely without influence: that would be an untenable claim, given the obvious effect of the sun on climate and of the moon on the tides. But their effect is, says Pico, "general" and affects all equally, promoting the natural cycle of life and not, for instance, the progress of a disease in an individual patient.

Pico seems to have had several reasons for writing this polemic. The diatribe against the "Arabs" and their distortion of ancient science is of course a well-worn humanist trope. At a philosophical level, the thing that bothers him above all would seem to be the deterministic implications of astrology. As we just saw with the example of Cardano, some embraced the art of astral prediction without supposing that the stars determine everything. Pico, though, was convinced that astrology is incompatible with the Christian commitment to free will. In this he found an ally in Savonarola, another man who railed against astrology. Their attitude was shared by Guicciardini. Along the same lines as Pico, he noted that astrologers may seem to be more successful than they really are, because people only remember it when predictions come out true.[13] Of course, when astrologers did get it wrong their opponents were ready to pounce, as when the medical writer Giovanni Mainardi told the story of a doctor managing to heal someone whose death had been foretold by a stargazer.[14] In some cases the invective could get personal. One critic cruelly asked: if Cardano was such a brilliant astrologer, then "why didn't you keep the axe from your son's neck?"[15]

Yet Pico's *Disputations* also provoked numerous defenses of astrology, for example by Lucio Bellanti and Giovanni Pontano.[16] Often such defenses used the same tactic we found in Nifo and Cardano, of blaming all problematic aspects of astrology on the Arabic tradition, so as to preserve the authoritative status of the Greeks. Moderate views were also proposed, as by the Platonist cosmologist Francesco Patrizi. Like Cardano, he rejected determinism but retained such astrological ideas as the malicious nature of Mars and Saturn, and favorable nature of Jupiter and Venus.[17] In common with other learned defenders of astrology in the sixteenth century, he warned his readers not to confuse superstitious and irreligious practices with the properly scientific discipline that explores the causal influences of the stars on our world, especially the influences more subtle than what we can see in the obvious cases of the sun and moon.

Ironically another occult science, magic, was defended in very similar terms by none other than Pico della Mirandola. In the list of "conclusions" he intended to defend at Rome, he distinguished between "natural magic" and magic that invokes "powers of darkness." The latter is rightly condemned by the church, while the former is permitted and can be based upon "universal theoretical foundations." Indeed magic is the "noblest part of natural science."[18] For Pico, the correct approach lies in the study of the Jewish mystical tradition he calls Kabbalah, so that magical powers may be discovered in Hebrew words or Kabbalistic numerology. He also approves of the ancient Greek "Orphic hymns" as an important body of magical teachings, and draws a parallel between them and the Hebrew tradition: "just as the hymns of David miraculously serve a work of the Cabala, so the hymns of Orpheus serve a work of the true, permitted, and natural magic (*ita hymni Orphei operi uerae, licitae, et naturalis magiae*)."[19] In his list of propositions, Pico also draws connections between magic and astrology. This suggests that he may have at first looked favorably on astrological science, but changed his mind later, leading him to write his *Disputations* in order to debunk the pretensions of the astrologers.

But the great Renaissance proponent of the links between magic and astrology was Pico's older friend Marsilio Ficino. One of Ficino's most remarkable and controversial works, the *Three Books On Life*, has been called "a handbook for helping scholars and philosophers stay healthy, live long lives, and bask in the heavens' glow."[20] The first of the three books offers largely conventional medical advice, based on the principle that aging is caused by gradual loss of the body's moisture, and the vital heat that nourishes that moisture (§1.2). But as the work goes on, Ficino delves increasingly into astrology and magic. In book two, he describes two extreme ways of life, one associated with Saturn and characterized by relentless pursuit of contemplative knowledge, the other associated with Venus and involving the pleasures of the flesh (§2.15). Both have a pernicious effect on health, but the Saturnian lifestyle is preferable because, as Ficino wittily remarks, the wisdom attained through Saturn secures one an eternal life, whereas the sexual delights of Venus give life to someone else. Ficino saw himself as having a "Saturnian" personality, something he explained by the fact that Saturn was entering Aquarius when Ficino was born in October of 1433. Thus he is intellectually gifted but also moody, given to melancholy. He can at least comfort himself with the thought that "all the great men who have ever excelled in art have been melancholic."[21]

Like Cardano, Ficino holds that knowledge of astrology helps us to shape our futures, rather than telling us of an inescapable fate. So our actions can prolong our lifespan (§2.20), and Ficino tells us how, explaining that one may use knowledge of one's astral nature to choose beneficial diet and medical treatment. He mentions with approval the theory of critical days in the progress of a feverish illness, and explains that the vital spirit that courses through the body responds especially to the power of Mercury, since spirit is mostly air and Mercury is associated with this element (§3.6). Straightforwardly magical practices, like the wearing of talismans, are also discussed. Here Ficino is somewhat skeptical. While such instruments may do some good, this is probably more because of the innate powers of the stones and metal than the shapes into which they have been carved (§3.15). Standard medical treatment is more reliable than something like a magic ring (§3.8, 13, 19, 20).

The modern reader is apt to think that Ficino's moderate skepticism is not nearly skeptical enough. But he offers a well-considered theory to explain magical phenomena. To see why it is plausible, consider magnetism. All the way back in the time of the Presocratics, philosophers had already been interested in this phenomenon: Thales of Miletus said that the magnet must have a soul in it, presumably because it can move of its own accord towards metal. But of course, neither the Greeks nor the medievals had any understanding of magnetic force. For them it was an "occult" power, in the sense that its working is hidden. The same can be said of other puzzling natural phenomena, like the power of stingrays to stun their victims. Belief in magic can be seen as an extrapolation from these cases. An object like a talismanic stone may have an occult power of its own, which it acquired while forming in the earth thanks to the influence of the stars. If magic is simply the manipulation of such natural powers, then there is nothing wrong with it, any more than it would be wrong to use a magnet. As Cardano would later say, "magic is nothing unless you place it as part of either medicine or natural philosophy, and understood in this way magic is no more illicit than carpentry."[22]

Furthermore, Ficino has a way to explain how the hidden or occult forces work, namely that the whole universe is held together by bonds of "sympathy." He tells us that the third book of *On Life* developed out of his commentary on Plotinus, which explains his use of the sympathy theory. Plotinus too invoked this originally Stoic concept to explain a range of natural phenomena, including even human vision. For both Plotinus and Ficino, the idea has a pleasing affinity with Pythagoreanism, too. Ficino illustrates it with the case of two string instruments which vibrate "in sympathy" with one another (§3.17). Ficino also integrates his account of magic with his theory of love (see Chapter 33). The whole cosmos does have a unifying "love" or "sympathy" but there is a particular bond between things that have relevant similarity. Love is itself a magician, because "an act of magic is the attraction of one thing by another in accordance with a certain natural kinship."[23] This is why, according to Ficino, people of the same star sign are apt to fall in love with one another. It's also why planets are linked to certain bodily constitutions, material substances, colors, and so on, and why there can be a science for studying and exploiting such resonances.

Again, these are entirely natural powers and effects, like the magnet: if love is a magician, then nature herself is a sorceress (*maga*, §3.26). But Ficino knew that he was treading on dangerous ground, and wrote an *Apology* to explain why he had written so much about magic. He imagines critics complaining, "Marsilio is a priest, isn't he? Indeed he is. What business then do priests have with medicine or, again, with astrology? Another will say: What does a Christian have to do with magic or images?"[24] In his own defense he protests that he only ever practices "natural magic," as opposed to seeking concourse with daemons. Not that he doubts the existence of daemons. They are regularly invoked in the Platonist literature Ficino knows so well, with the most famous example being the divine voice of warning heard by Socrates, as mentioned in the Platonic dialogues.[25] A somewhat more recent source was Michael Psellos, whose work on daemons was translated by Ficino. Following Psellos, Ficino distinguished daemons into various types, classified in terms of their connection to different elements and planets.[26] These resonances explain why astral magic can summon daemons or induce them to influence our world.

But the fact that we *can* do this, doesn't mean that we *should*. Even enthusiasts for magic often disavowed daemonology, like Giambattista Della Porta, whose treatise *Natural Magic* appeared in several editions beginning in 1558. The title is carefully chosen. To engage in "natural" magic is precisely to avoid techniques that involve daemons, and instead to follow the lead of noble investigators of occult forces like Pythagoras and Plato.[27] If such reassurances were designed to keep Della Porta out of trouble with the authorities, they didn't work. His book was placed on the Index of proscribed books by the papal Inquisition, and unsurprisingly so given that it discussed such things as the "witches' salve," a potion that allows witches to teleport to black sabbaths.[28] To be fair, though, Della Porta discussed the witches' salve in order to provide a naturalist account of something that only *seemed* like magic or witchcraft: the potion affects the imaginations of those who imbibe it, and makes them think they have been elsewhere. Della Porta also took a naturalizing approach to the science of the stars, rejecting such astral divinations as could not be integrated with medical theories and physiognomics. This was a "science" about which he wrote extensively: the adept learns the correspondences between bodies of all kinds and more hidden properties, so as to be able to, say, judge character and fate on the basis of facial appearance or the lines on the palm of the hand.[29]

Della Porta's writings fit within our emerging picture of Renaissance attitudes towards the occult sciences, namely that a sober, scholarly approach would explain some magical phenomena while rejecting others in a display of sound, scientific skepticism. Hence Pico embraced magic but turned against astrology, Ficino thought talismans work but probably only because of the metal they are made of, and even Cardano admitted that astrology was a merely probable art. This is why his own predictions were sometimes wrong, in one case happily so: he forecast regular illnesses for his daughter, but she enjoyed good health.[30] Even the most skeptical thinkers had to allow some scope for the supernatural, as we can see from the case of Pietro Pomponazzi.[31] His work *On Incantations*, from 1556, is a splendid example of debunking, which shows how apparently magical effects can be explained without recourse to magic. For example, Pomponazzi offered various naturalistic explanations of a supposedly miraculous appearance of St Celestine, which put an end to torrential rainfalls. He was also unimpressed by the use of daemonology to heal illnesses: "do the daemons carry with them boxes, satchels, and bags full of plaster like surgeons and apothecaries?" But even Pomponazzi had to admit that genuine miracles sometimes occur: these are not brought about by human magicians, but by God, and they are beyond the power of human reason to explain.

From this we can see that the skeptically minded philosophers had to tread just as carefully as the believers in magic and astrology. The happy, and orthodox, medium was to accept that some things are beyond our ken, while steering clear of daemonology, astral determinism, or tracing the rise of religion or incarnation of Christ to the effects of the stars. The authoritative response was similarly ambiguous: papal bans were placed on only some forms of magic; Della Porta was put on trial but not convicted; and he managed to get his treatise on magic taken off the Index through some judicious revision for a further edition. Much depended on who was pope at any given time. When inquisitor general Michele Ghislieri took the post in 1565 that heralded a time of repression, but half a century later, Campanella found himself conducting a magical séance with Pope Urban VIII to ward off his death by astral influence, a story that embarrassed the pope once it got out. The key thing was to know which lines not to cross, a task at which the protagonist of the next chapter failed miserably, with tragic consequences.

53

BOUNDLESS ENTHUSIASM GIORDANO BRUNO

There seems to be a widespread assumption that it was humbling for humankind to abandon the old cosmology of Aristotle and Ptolemy, and accept the new astronomy of Copernicus. No longer do we find ourselves at the literal center of attention, on an earth which sits unmoving at the midpoint of a finite, spherical universe. Instead we are moving around the sun, which has usurped the earth's place. In fact, we now realize, our whole solar system takes up only a tiny part of a vast universe. There's no doubt that this shift of perspective did upset many people, and many preconceptions about humans and their role in the cosmos. But it's worth remembering that in the ancient and medieval worldview, the earth was never seen as the *best* part of the universe. The middle of everything was also the "bottom" of everything, with the celestial bodies above being seen as far superior, even divine in some sense. As we have just seen, these heavenly bodies were typically assumed to influence, if not completely determine, events down here on earth, while we cannot influence them at all. They are the instruments of God, steered by angels, free of decay, imperfection, and "the thousand natural shocks that our flesh is heir to," as people were saying at about the same time over in England.

In light of this, being moved away from the center of the cosmos could be seen as a promotion. But neither did the Copernican revolution simply reverse the older view, with the sun occupying the new "down" and the previously static earth catapulted into the heavens, now moving at the thrilling speeds previously reserved for planets and stars. His discoveries did not so much turn the universe upside down, as show that the universe has no up and down at all. That, at least, was the lesson drawn by Giordano Bruno. In several treatises beginning with *The Ash Wednesday Supper*, a dialogue published in 1584 in London, he presented a mind-boggling vision of the universe, infinite in extent and containing an infinity of worlds. As Copernicus had argued, our cosmos is just one of those worlds, and has the sun at its center with the earth revolving around it. Not everyone was impressed. The vice chancellor of Oxford University, where Bruno presented his ideas, mocked him as "that little Italian, with a name longer than his body," referring to the philosopher's full and rather splendid moniker, Philoteus Jordanus Brunus Nolanus. The chancellor summarized Bruno's performance like this: "he undertooke among very many other matters to set on foote the opinion of Copernicus, that the earth did goe round, and the heavens did stand still; whereas in truth it was his owne head which rather did run round."[1]

Then as now, Oxford was a unique place, but not by virtue of producing hostility towards Bruno. In his itinerant career, which brought him from Italy to cities including Paris, Toulouse, Geneva, Paris, London, and Wittenberg, he made plenty of enemies.[2] He has, as one scholar has noted, the "distinction of being the only known sixteenth-century philosopher to have been excommunicated from all three major confessions: Roman Catholic, Calvinist, and Lutheran."[3] During his wanderings he wrote prolifically, managing in one decade to produce a body of work that makes him one of the most important thinkers of the Renaissance. But he made the mistake of returning to Italy, and making one more, particularly decisive enemy: he came to Venice in 1591 to stay with Giovanni Mocenigo, who passed word of Bruno's unorthodox teachings to the Inquisition. In a further stroke of bad luck, the case came to the attention of the papal authorities in Rome, triggering a lengthy legal process that ended with Bruno's execution on February 17, 1600, by being burnt at the stake.[4]

As the length of the trial suggests, Bruno's persecution was highly bureaucratic, deliberate, and in the minds of its perpetrators, even fair-minded and cautious. He was given repeated chances to explain himself, and Bruno clearly believed, at least initially, that doing so would get him out of trouble. At his first interrogation he said that he had always perceived the threat of inquisition as a "joke" because he knew he could defend his teachings. Even when his ultimate fate became clear he said defiantly to his accusers, "you pass your sentence on me with greater fear than I feel in receiving it."[5] Evidently, he thought they would have misgivings even after their painstaking inquiry into his orthodoxy. This notwithstanding, the commission condemned his views on a variety of topics. These included aspects of his cosmology and also theological issues, like the Trinity and incarnation. On this score Bruno admitted to having private doubts, though not to having put forth his skepticism publicly. Besides, he was only ever speaking "as a philosopher." It was in this sense that he was unconvinced regarding, for instance, the applicability of the word "person" to the holy Trinity, while accepting on philosophical grounds a Trinitarian distinction between God the Father, His intellect, and His own love.[6] This suggests that Bruno was imagining that scholars like himself would be allowed the "freedom in philosophizing" also envisioned by Campanella. Like Campanella, he was wrong to think that such freedom was on offer around the turn of the seventeenth century.

One idea that the Inquisition deemed unacceptable was genuinely central to Bruno's thought. To put it in the terms of one of his favorite sayings: "there is nothing new under the sun." Or, to put it in more philosophical terms, there is in Bruno's universe no creation or destruction. Instead there is only alteration in the accidental properties of a single, infinite substance. Bruno was thus rejecting the concept of substantial forms, which we also saw being put under pressure by Telesio. In Aristotelian philosophy, substances are composites of matter and form, and they are the primary beings that populate the world: things like the four elements, plants, animals, and people. Bruno retains the form–matter analysis, but only at the level of the entire universe. This universe is a single great, indeed infinite, substance, which is constantly changing but only with respect to the superficial, accidental features that are the manifestations of its unbounded nature. And like an animal in Aristotelian metaphysics, the universe is an organism. It has a single soul, the "World Soul," which completely pervades the infinity of matter. As Bruno puts it in a treatise called *Cause, Principle and Unity*, the World Soul is "the act of everything and the potency of everything, and is present in its entirety in everything—whence it follows that (even if there exist innumerable individuals) all things are one" (*CPU* 81).[7]

While this is obviously a boldly original theory, it can also be seen as a fusion of ideas from Aristotelianism and Platonism: the World Soul is familiar from Plato's *Timaeus*, and as already mentioned the idea of substance as a composite of matter and form is Aristotelian. But for his conception of matter, Bruno also looks to other sources. He knows that his belief in the material basis of all things was anticipated by the medieval Jewish philosopher Ibn Gabirol, called in Latin "Avicebron" (*CPU* 55).[8] When he comes to explain the nature of matter, Bruno adopts a radically un-Aristotelian view. Just as there is a one-dimensional minimum, the point, and a two-dimensional minimum, the line, so there is a minimal three-dimensional body from which all other bodies are compounded. This atomic minimum has no parts, only "limits" at which it can contact other atoms.[9]

Obviously this is reminiscent of ancient atomism. Bruno is drawing on the Epicurean physical theories that had been made available through the rediscovery of Lucretius' poem, which he likes to quote, even as he anticipates the "corpuscularian" physics of the seventeenth century. But there are differences between his atomism and that of the ancients, starting with the shape of the atoms. Where the classical Greek theories postulated atoms of indefinitely various shapes and sizes, Bruno's atoms are regular spheres; any other shape would mean that the atom has "sides," and thus parts. But atoms are not supposed to have parts. Furthermore, in ancient atomism the atoms move in a void or vacuum, but Bruno agrees with

Aristotle that there is no actually empty space. Unlike Aristotle, he does have an abstract notion of space, which is in itself simply three-dimensional extension. Still, though, he thinks that this space is always full of bodies, and can be distinguished from bodies "not in fact, but only by reason (*non re sed ratione*)."[10] What fills the space not currently occupied by atoms is an unlimited, fluid medium, through which atoms and bodies composed from atoms can move. In that dialogue, the *Ash Wednesday Supper*, he describes this medium as "a single airy, ethereal, spiritual, and liquid body, a capacious place of motion and quiet which reaches out into the immensity of infinity" (*AWS* 117).[11] Bruno assumes that the infinite power of God must have an infinite expression; otherwise He would be like a musician who knows how to play an instrument, but sits idle without using it.[12] Therefore the universe is infinitely extended, and is full of an infinite number of worlds more or less like ours: "those other globes are earths, in no way different in species from this one except insofar as they are larger or smaller" (*AWS* 119).

Bruno breaks crucially with one final presupposition of the classical atomists, namely that atoms have "weight" or a tendency to move downwards. In Bruno's universe there is no "down," precisely because of the aforementioned "immensity of infinity." The Aristotelian cosmos is spherical, and so has a midpoint, which is where we find the center of the earth. Thus we can define "downward" motion as motion towards that point, "upward" motion as motion away from it. By contrast, as Bruno observes, an infinite universe has no central reference point and so there can be no motion towards or away from naturally defined places (*AWS* 115). Or as he elsewhere says, "nothing moves 'to' or 'around' the universe, but only within it" (*CPU* 91). Brief reflection will show that he cannot accept the Aristotelian idea of "natural place," for instance that earthy bodies try by nature to move towards the center of the cosmos. For there are an infinity of worlds, and clearly in those other worlds earth moves naturally towards the center of that world and not ours—otherwise rocks dropped by the people of other worlds would come hurtling through the infinite space and towards our earth, which sounds not only ridiculous, but extremely dangerous. Why then do we see bodies performing natural motions, as when rocks fall "down" in air (or what is "down" from our point of view), and air bubbles percolate "up" in water? His answer is that this can be explained only with reference to the animating power of the World Soul. It is present in the earth, in the stars, and in the sun, and since these bodies are all ensouled they perform voluntary motions just like animals do (*AWS* 121). In the case of the motions performed by the earth as a whole, this is providentially ordained. The earth's daily rotation about its own axis causes night and day, while its orbit around the sun gives us the cycle of seasons (*AWS* 153, 195).

Which brings us back to the contentious claim, taken from Copernicus, that the earth is in fact rotating and moving around the sun. When Bruno defended this proposition at Oxford he was greeted with incredulity and disdain. He took it hard, complaining that in England, "there reigns a constellation of pedantic and obstinate ignorance and arrogance, mixed with rustic incivility, which would try the patience of Job" (*AWS* 155). As far as he was concerned, the schoolmen had inherited all of Aristotle's ignorance and none of his wisdom. Not, by the way, a judgment he applied only to Englishmen, since he later said that the Dominican friars who trained him in Italy "were all asses and ignoramuses." In general, he thinks, "doctors come as cheaply as sardines, since they are made, found, and hooked with little trouble" (*CPU* 27). This invective is good fun, but we should not overlook the possibility that, as Renaissance scholar Charles Schmitt put it, "Bruno was a self-centred bigot who was obviously piqued because the men of Oxford did not consider him to be as brilliant as he considered himself to be."[13]

At any rate, Bruno got over his humiliation at Oxford by writing the *Ash Wednesday Supper* in defense of the Copernican theory. He rejects the comforting thought, which may have been put forward at Oxford before his appearance there by a scholar named Henry Savile, that Copernican heliocentrism is just a matter of mathematical convenience, a model for calculation rather than a description of the world's actual physical arrangement (*AWS* 89).[14] No, says Bruno, the earth really is moving at incredible speed. How is it then, that we don't notice this? For instance when we drop something, shouldn't it move laterally across the landscape, as it is no longer connected to the rotating earth? No, says Bruno again, giving the powerful analogy of a fast-moving ship. If someone drops a stone from the top of the mast of the ship, the stone will fall to the bottom of the mast, not further towards the back of the boat. This is because the stone retains a power impressed in it by the motion of the ship, so that it keeps a motion coordinated with that of the ship even as it is falling down (*AWS* 137).[15]

Bruno insists that he is not just following the authority of Copernicus here: he "sees through his own eyes." Still, he credits Copernicus with having unearthed an "ancient and true philosophy, buried for so many centuries in the dark caverns of a blind, malign, insolent, and envious ignorance" (*AWS* 27–31). Of course, by this point in the Renaissance, nothing is more familiar than claiming to overthrow familiar ideas by unearthing long-lost ancient wisdom. Bruno gives Aristotle a decidedly mixed review, sometimes calling him a "sophist" despite finding him far preferable to his later interpreters. But he is full of admiration for other figures of ancient thought, and claims agreement with them. His insight about the unity of matter was already put forward by Plotinus (*CPU* 76), while various Presocratics had taught the Brunian doctrine that natural things are brought forth by being separated from matter, which contains them all in its infinite power (*CPU* 83). Actually Bruno thinks he can find this idea in the Bible, too. He refers to the line "let the earth bring forth its animals, let the waters bring forth living creatures" (Genesis 1:2), even though in his view scripture does not "offer philosophical demonstrations or speculation concerning natural things" (*AWS* 139).

Broadly speaking, Bruno's intellectual heroes are the ones admired by Marsilio Ficino, who influenced him greatly. In fact, one accusation made against Bruno at Oxford was that his lectures there plagiarized from Ficino's book on magical therapies, *On Life*. Whatever the truth of this, Ficino's ideas about magic resonate powerfully in Bruno's own writings on the subject. Like Ficino, he distinguishes between "natural" magic and the invocation of wicked daemons (*CPU* 105–7). The latter is despicable, whereas natural magic is morally neutral, like a sword that can be used in either a just or unjust cause.[16] As for explaining how magic works, we've already seen how, for Bruno as for Ficino, the World Soul animates the entire universe. The result is that "everything has access to everything else" (*CPU* 130). The "bonds" between things can be manipulated by the magician, or rather the magician's own soul, whose powers are not limited to controlling his own body (*CPU* 113–14).

Ficino's *On Life* encouraged the use of magic specifically for medical purposes, and Bruno likewise thinks this is how it should be applied, alongside other, non-magical methods. The best healer should in fact be "not only physician, but also alchemist and astrologer" (*CPU* 63). This despite the fact that Bruno was rather skeptical about the claims of astrology, in part because he did not think that astral motions are as exact as the astronomical models we use to represent them. Like all natural phenomena, the heavens are mere shadows or images of the ideas conceived in the mind of the World Soul. But if this gives Bruno reason to doubt astrology, it encourages him to believe in magic. The symbols used by the magician are analogous to the images used by nature itself. The study of magic is thus "natural" in the most literal sense, namely that it teaches us how to produce effects in the same way the soul of the cosmos does. This is why Bruno says that "to obtain the absolute and perfect art, you should be coupled to the World Soul and act in connection to it."[17]

One of the most disputed questions concerning Bruno's philosophy has to do with the magical manipulation of images. His writing career began with the first of several works on the art of memory. Bruno explains a complicated method for inventing mnemonic devices, using several diagrams shaped like wheels, with letters from the Latin, Greek, and Hebrew alphabet inscribed on the wheels. The letters are associated with symbolic imagery, the idea being that you can call to mind a certain word by connecting it to the sequence of images dictated by the diagrams. All scholars agree that Bruno is here taking up the ideas of Ramon Llull, an unconventional medieval thinker whom I described in a previous volume as a forerunner of the Renaissance, in part because of his influence on Bruno.[18] But scholars emphatically do *not* agree about the significance of Bruno's mnemonic art.

A now classic, but controversial, study by Frances Yates posited that his writings on memory express ideas taken from a corpus of magical writings ascribed to the Greek divinity Hermes, alongside concepts from the Kabbalah, the Jewish mystical tradition whose influence also made itself felt in the works of Pico della Mirandola.[19] Yates was even convinced that Bruno's execution was in large part provoked by his interest in magic, though this does not seem to be borne out by the documentation of the trial. A diametrically opposed reading was proposed by Rita Sturlese, for whom the symbols of the wheels might *look* magical in character, but actually are simply convenient and memorable instruments.[20] For her Bruno's art of memory is no more magical than it would be if you, say, studied for a test on Renaissance Philosophy by associating various thinkers with characters from your favorite TV shows (Will Smith, the "fresh prince of Bel Air," would be a good choice for Pico della Mirandola, and for Bruno himself I'm thinking of Walter White from *Breaking Bad*).

Even on this purely pragmatic reading, there could still be a philosophical basis for the mnemonic theory. Bruno quotes Aristotle's claim that we cannot think without images to explain why this technique of "imaginative logic"[21] is so effective—a striking contrast with Pomponazzi, who quoted the same passage to show that the mind cannot operate without being linked to a body! And more recently, a kind of compromise view has been put forward by Manuel Mertens. As he observes, Bruno himself says that the memory writings are not works on magic, even though they are full of magical terminology and imagery. To resolve this contradiction, he suggests that the mnemonic technique is, apart from its own usefulness, an ideal preparation for the magician. Just as with my examples of television characters, images are not chosen randomly but have some kind of symbolic resonance with the target of memorization. As Mertens says, "the disciple in Bruno's art of memory, well instructed in the natural language of forms and figures, would be a good candidate for becoming a magical binder."[22] In other words, the two disciplines do call for similar skills and training, but they are not the same art.

Even though Bruno's mnemonic theory depends on the notion of thinking with imagery, he does not believe that the true philosopher should stop at the level of images. This is clear from one final, famous treatise, called *On the Heroic Frenzies*.[23] It again calls to mind themes familiar from Ficino, and other Renaissance authors who wrote about love (see Chapter 33 above), the "frenzies" of the title being a reference to the ecstatic transport that can befall the lover. Like several other explorations of love written in the Renaissance, the *Heroic Frenzies* is a dialogue. But in this case, as in a typical episode of *Breaking Bad*, there's a twist. Namely that the characters are commenting on poems written by Bruno himself, in what may be an echo of the poetic self-commentary of Dante. Bruno has some fun with this literary conceit, for instance by having the main spokesman admit that he is not entirely sure what Bruno the poet had in mind (267). But the main thrust of the dialogue is clear: true erotic "heroes" pursue a love more exalted than the concerns of physical pleasure, and "can no more sink to the level of common and natural loves than dolphins can been seen in the trees of the forest" (15). The highest love of contemplation takes the hero beyond this natural world of images and likenesses, in which we see divinity as if reflected in a mirror (79, 95). As we know from Bruno's other works, the universe is an infinite expression of God's limitless power, so it will inevitably outstrip the capacity of the human mind (99). But in a way this is good news, since it means the *potential* for new knowledge, and taking pleasure in the acquisition of that knowledge, is likewise infinite (193, 305). As is abundantly clear from Bruno's inventive, witty, and diverse writings, he himself took great delight in this endless philosophical exploration, until he met his own untimely end.

54

THE HARDER THEY FALL
GALILEO AND THE RENAISSANCE

In the last chapter, I suggested that we tend to overestimate or at least misjudge the psychological impact of Copernicus' removal of the earth from the center of the universe. By contrast, I believe that we tend to *underestimate* another feature of the new science of the heavens. Around this time it became increasingly clear that the celestial bodies are not, as Aristotle would have it, perfect and unchanging substances, made from a fundamentally different kind of matter from that found in our earthly sphere. The sixteenth and seventeenth centuries instead offered a single, unified physics, applicable to both the heavens and the things around us in our everyday experience. Things "up there" are made of more or less the same stuff as things "down here," and, as we now know, outer space is full of changing and unexpected phenomena, like comets, supernovas, and Sandra Bullock. The unification of physics was already propounded by Telesio and Campanella. On their theory, the whole universe is made from one kind of matter, with everything from stars to stones being governed by the simple principles of heat and cold. But what they offered was, indeed, only theory. It was at the beginning of the seventeenth century that another Italian scientist offered what he at least considered to be direct proof.

I refer, of course, to Galileo Galilei. He showed that the moon is not perfectly spherical but covered with irregularities and mountains, on the basis of shadows he could see on the moon's surface using the new technology of the telescope. With that same instrument, he discovered that there are spots moving across the surface of the sun itself; earlier, he had demonstrated that a nova that appeared in the night sky must lie beyond the moon, another example to show that things in the celestial world do change. Furthermore, his telescope delivered powerful confirmation of the Copernican theory, especially in the case of Venus. This planet could now be seen to have phases of illumination just like our moon, whose pattern would be different if Venus were orbiting the earth and not the sun. Galileo also found four of Jupiter's moons, which were clearly orbiting around it. This was not a direct proof of Copernicus' heliocentrism, but undermined a powerful argument for the ancient cosmology: given that the moon at least goes around the earth, surely everything else does too? Given the presence of bodies orbiting Jupiter, it was now easier to believe that the earth too might be circling the sun while having another heavenly body circling it.

Thanks to these and other discoveries, Galileo is rightly seen as a truly pivotal figure in the history of European science and philosophy. He literally saw things that no one had seen before, and as a result the universe as a whole came to be seen in a new light. If it takes one revolutionary thinker to appreciate another fully, then we might pay heed to the words of Immanuel Kant. In his *Critique of Pure Reason*, which famously presents itself as performing a "Copernican turn" of its own within philosophy, he claimed that Galileo introduced an innovative scientific method, according to which "reason has insight only into that which it produces after a plan of its own . . . It must itself show the way with principles of judgment based upon fixed laws, constraining nature to give answer to questions of reason's own determining."[1] Now, unlike Giordano Bruno, I would not insist that there is "nothing new under the sun." But it's a guiding principle of this book series that intellectual developments do not come out of nowhere, like the debris that caused all that trouble for Sandra Bullock in the movie *Gravity*. One reason it is worth our time to learn about supposedly "minor" authors is that it puts us in a better position to understand the achievement of more famous figures.

And so it is here. There is good reason to see Galileo's breakthroughs, which he mostly made in the early seventeenth century, as a continuation of trends we have learned about from the sixteenth century. We can see this already from his proposal about just what is causing the earth and the other planets to move along their orbits, namely a luminous, warm "fluid" emanating outwards from the sun. This so-called "caloric spirit" sounds quite a bit like what we found in Telesio and Campanella. And Galileo had other things in common with scientists of the Italian Renaissance. Like Campanella, Bruno, and Cardano he was a practicing astrologer, who was accused of believing in astral determinism and who cast nativities for patrons, friends, and even his own daughters.[2] When he discovered moons around Jupiter, he argued for their importance on the grounds that their fast motion should make their astral influence particularly intense. And by the way, he didn't call them "moons," but rather "Medicean planets," named in honor of a patron who was a member of the Medici, everyone's favorite family of Florence.[3] It doesn't get much more Renaissance Italian than that.

But as it turns out, the strongest links between Galileo's thought and what came before have to do with precisely the feature Kant picked out as most new, namely his scientific methodology. A number of scholars, especially William A. Wallace, have argued that in this area he was heavily indebted to the Aristotelian tradition, especially in the form represented at Padua by Jacopo Zabarella. After studying medicine in Pisa in the 1580s, Galileo lectured there until he moved to teach at Padua in 1592.[4] Studies of his early writings, which survive in Galileo's own handwriting, show that he was deeply schooled in the logic of the Paduan scholastics like Nifo and Zabarella. He seems to have been influenced especially by Jesuits at the Collegio Romano, rather than by reading the Paduans directly.[5] But he was widely read in scholastic literature, and made numerous references to Thomas Aquinas and other medieval scholastics, and also to Averroes.[6]

His studies convinced him that even though Aristotelian physics was shot through with errors, Aristotle himself remained a reliable guide to best practice in science. Indeed, a favorite theme of his was that fidelity to Aristotle's method required departures from Aristotle's conclusions. He scorned the Aristotelians of his own day: "few of them inquire whether what Aristotle said is true. For it suffices for them that they will be considered more learned, the more passages of Aristotle they have ready for use."[7] In contrast to these slavishly traditional schoolmen, Galileo thought that a true Aristotelian philosopher was one who "philosophizes according to Aristotelian teachings, proceeding from those methods and those true suppositions and principles on which scientific discourse is founded."[8] In keeping with this, he insisted that if Aristotle were presented with the sort of observations made possible by the telescope, he would be the first to change his views on the nature and arrangement of the heavens. Indeed, in his treatise on the newly discovered sunspots, Galileo said that denying change in the heavens would be *anti*-Aristotelian, because it would involve departing from Aristotle's empirical method for the sake of preserving an Aristotelian doctrine in natural philosophy, even though the method is more fundamental (100).[9]

On the basis of such remarks, John Herman Randall Jr. already said way back in 1940 that "in method and philosophy if not in physics [Galileo] remained a typical Paduan Aristotelian."[10] But much research has been done on this question since Randall wrote these words. It has shown that Galileo made flexible and innovative use of the scholastic methodology, without departing from it entirely. In particular, he fused the method with extensive use of mathematics. As we know, there was also precedent for applying mathematical analysis to physical phenomena, stretching back to the Oxford Calculators of the fourteenth century. Of more direct relevance was the humanist-driven study of Archimedes (see Chapter 48). Thus in an early work on the motion of bodies, Galileo said that he was adopting the methods of "my mathematicians" and praised the proofs of Archimedes as "rigorous, clear, and subtle."[11] Galileo was well aware that he was operating within the remit of the "mixed" or "middle" sciences, in which mathematics is applied to nature. Archimedes, with his attention to such phenomena as levers and floating bodies, was the chief ancient authority for these disciplines.

We can illustrate Galileo's method with his work on the problem of falling bodies. The first thing we need to understand is that this is really the same topic as the one just mentioned as an interest of Archimedes, namely floating bodies. After all, a falling body is just one that is *not* floating, and bodies can fall (slowly) in water just as much as they do (quickly) in air. For Galileo, floating is caused by balance, and falling is caused by imbalance. In a work called *On Motion*, written in 1590, he argues that bodies fall because of their relative "heaviness" or "gravity" (*gravitas*) compared to the medium in which they fall. By contrast, a body will float if it has the same gravity as the medium, or less, like Styrofoam floating in water. In a later work on floating bodies, Galileo sought to defend this account against an objection made by Aristotelians, namely that something heavier than water will still float in water if it is shaped the right way, like a broad, thin piece of ebony (93). This shows, they argued, that it is the resistance of water that causes bodies to float. Galileo retorted that the experiment involves a misleading appearance: in fact trapped air is holding up the ebony, as we can see from the fact that the ebony will sink if it is forced below the surface.

In further experiments using inclined planes, Galileo showed that a body falls with greatest force if it is moving straight down, with the force being reduced as the angle of fall is changed towards the horizontal by raising the surface along which the body is falling. (So, imagine a ball falling straight down, as opposed to rolling balls down a tilted piece of cardboard: the steeper the slope, the harder they fall.) These experiments allowed him to discover the law of free fall, showing that the distance covered increases in relation to the square of the time of the fall, with the body accelerating faster and faster the longer it has been falling. It was precisely these experiments with inclined planes that Kant mentioned when crediting Galileo with the modern "scientific method." But with all due respect to Kant, Galileo was not really using what has come to be known as the "scientific method," that is, formulating hypotheses and testing them empirically. Rather, he was using the scientific method of the Paduan school. This meant working from observed phenomena back to fundamental explanatory principles, and then showing that the principles would explain the observations. In other words, he was using the method of "regress" described by Zabarella, while integrating mathematics into the different steps of that method. Or at least, that's the interpretation put forward by the aforementioned William Wallace.

In favor of this reading we can first note Galileo's own description of his goal as a search for underlying "causes." Sometimes finding the cause is easy: you can infer it from just one observation. This is the case with the phases of illumination he saw in Venus, which immediately show that it orbits the sun.[12] Already this is a thoroughly Aristotelian point, since Aristotle says the same thing himself about a different astronomical phenomenon: if we were standing on the moon we could immediately see that the cause of the lunar eclipse is the earth blocking the light of the sun (*Posterior Analytics*, 2.2). More complicated is Galileo's way of arriving at causal explanations that are not obvious. In the case of floating and falling bodies the rule of heaviness was the right cause, in his view; experimentation was used simply to display the dependence of the observed effects on this cause. When he did things like testing how bodies float in water or changing the inclination of a plane on which balls are rolling, he was following a maxim he formulated as follows: "the cause is that which, when it is posited, the effect follows; and when removed, the effect is removed" (*causa è quella, la qual posta, seguita l'effetto; e rimossa, si rimuove l'effetto*).[13]

Though the earlier Paduan Aristotelians did not propose using experiments in this way, doing so fits neatly into the theory of regress, which as we saw involved a step that Nifo called "negotiation of the understanding."[14] Here we have identified the cause but are trying to understand exactly how it works, before going on to affirm that the effects really do proceed from this cause. Galileo even makes a point familiar from Zabarella, namely that this stage helps show why the whole procedure is not circular. We do arrive at a cause on the basis of its effects, then explain the effects on the basis of the cause. But the intermediate step of considering and testing the cause allows us to understand the effects differently than we did at first.[15] Galileo's use of the regressive method here helps to set his discoveries apart from what other mathematicians had done, like Guidobaldo del Monte, who as we saw also experimented with balls rolling on inclined planes. Unlike him, Galileo was able to identify what he called "principles of nature that are known and manifest," the sort of principles always invoked as the foundation of Aristotelian demonstrations.[16]

There's a further sign that Galileo did not use observations to test hypotheses, but to demonstrate the efficacy of his favored causal principles. This is the fact that he was surprisingly relaxed about whether experiment actually bears out his theory. In fact the inclined plane experiments never confirmed his laws perfectly, because of the effects of air resistance and friction. Galileo dismissed this as irrelevant, saying that we should simply imagine doing it with an "incorporeal" tilted surface, or a perfect sphere that contacts it at a single point so that there is no resistance. Such musings led him to the brilliant but untestable observation that in the absence of friction, even the slightest of pushes would suffice to move a body at rest in a horizontal direction, since its weight would have no effect on lateral movement.[17] On the other hand, experiment can disconfirm or refute causal explanations. This is why he proposed dropping objects off towers to show that the proportion of earth in a body would not make it fall faster, as the Aristotelians claimed.[18] And of course sightings of the phases of Venus and mountains on the moon directly refuted other Aristotelian doctrines.

For Galileo, then, empirical demonstration is often just a matter of ruling out alternative explanations of a given effect, leaving his own causal account as the only one available. As he has one of the characters say in his famous *Dialogues on the Two Chief World Systems*, "the primary and true cause of an effect is only one, and so I understand very well and am sure that at most one can be true, and I know that all the rest are fictitious and false" (251–2). When a physical test is not possible he finds other ways to reject rival theories, as when he (wrongly) argues that the tides are better explained by appealing to the motion of the earth rather than the effect of the moon pulling at the water. In this case the tides are, as Galileo says using scholastic terminology, a "sign" of the earth's motion, which is in turn the "cause" of the tides.[19] But this is a rather vulnerable position. If we are really proceeding by process of elimination, then we need to show not just that our causal explanation can account for the observed effects, but that there is *no other* causal explanation that could give rise to those same effects.

This is something that was well understood by Galileo's opponents, not least in the church hierarchy. The papacy wanted him to retreat from his Copernicanism at least to the extent of admitting that the new model was merely a possible, or mathematically useful, basis for astronomy, rather than insisting that it was the exclusive physical truth. But like Bruno, Galileo rejected this easy way out.[20] Of course, we now know that he was right about the facts, and admire him for his courage in standing up for what he knew to be true. But by the epistemological standards accepted on both sides at the time, it's actually not so clear that Galileo did "know" he was right, since this would mean achieving demonstrative understanding grounded in causal first principles. His style of proof by "regress" could discover a candidate cause for the observed effects, eliminate other proposed candidates, and then account for the effects in terms of his own preferred cause. But it could never show once and for all that no other explanation can ever be provided. Perhaps the true cause hasn't been suggested yet; perhaps it is even beyond the human capacity of discovery.[21]

This was not a merely technical point. As far as the churchmen were concerned, scripture was the most reliable guide to the nature of the world, since it was revealed by the God who made that world. They could point to biblical passages like one found in the Book of Joshua (10:12–13), in which the sun is miraculously commanded to stand still in the sky. What sense would this make if, as the Copernicans claimed, the sun is always standing still and it is the earth that moves around it? Of course, theologians were well aware that scripture was subject to allegorical and metaphorical readings; but why should they reject the clear meaning of scripture on the basis of scientific theories that fell short of absolute certainty, as codified in Aristotelian epistemology?[22] Galileo, himself thoroughly trained in the Aristotelian tradition, likewise associated true science with total certainty. So where a scientist of a later age might have contented himself with simply asserting his theory as the best hypothesis discovered so far, he had to insist that his theories were established beyond all doubt. In some cases human knowledge could, he claimed, reach a level of certainty matching even God's.[23]

Since he took such phenomena as the phases of Venus to have proved once and for all that the planets do go around the sun, Galileo demanded that interpretations of scripture be adapted to this empirical finding. He wrote that "physical conclusions which have been truly demonstrated should not be given a lower place than scriptural passages, but rather one should clarify how such passages do not contradict those conclusions; therefore, before condemning a physical proposition, one must show that it is not conclusively demonstrated" (126). In the case of the passage from the Book of Joshua, he cleverly noted that the miracle in question would make even less sense within the Aristotelian understanding of the cosmos, where all the visible stars and planets are seated upon spheres that move one another in a coordinated fashion. According to this worldview, God could not have made the sun stop without stopping "the whole system" (107–9).

In general, though, Galileo was rather unconcerned about possible clashes between the Bible and science, in part because they have different subject matters. The purpose of scripture is simply to tell us what we need to know for the sake of our salvation; he quotes a churchman who admitted that "the intention of the Holy Spirit is to teach us how one goes to heaven, not how heaven goes" (119). If scripture occasionally speaks as if the earth is unmoving, this is just to avoid confusing the common believer who assumes that the ground under his feet is at rest (131). And besides, all good Christians will readily agree that scripture is true. How then could it ever disagree with the demonstrated conclusions of science? Since these conclusions have been proven with certainty, they must surely be true, and it is impossible for one truth to conflict with another (105, 120). Galileo is here repeating, more or less verbatim, an idea about scriptural exegesis put forward by that great hero of Aristotelianism, the Muslim commentator Averroes. In his *Decisive Treatise* on the relation between reason and revelation, he had likewise argued that the scientist-philosopher is in a position to decide which interpretations of scripture are possible, since the philosopher knows the truth on the independent grounds of rational inquiry, and "truth does not contradict truth."[24]

That text was not translated into Latin, so Galileo would not have known that he was reiterating a point made already by Averroes. But perhaps he would have appreciated the parallel. As we've seen, he saw himself as upholding Aristotle's scientific method, while rejecting his scientific conclusions. Even towards the end of his life, Galileo was still insisting that he had always been an Aristotelian in matters of logic.[25] By that time, famously, he had paid the price for following scientific inquiry wherever it led. He was condemned by the Inquisition in 1633, made to reject his own teachings, and placed under house arrest. This is a story we will need to tell in more detail, by exploring the text that got him in trouble, the aforementioned *Dialogues on the Two Chief World Systems*, and the story of his trial. We'll be better placed to do that once we have learned more about the historical background across Europe in the fifteenth and sixteenth centuries. After all, plenty was happening outside Italy in this period, including the work of Copernicus and the small matter of the Protestant Reformation, which helped trigger the inquisitorial culture in Catholic countries that led indirectly to Galileo's downfall. So we will return to him once we have come to grips with the northern Renaissance, Reformation, and Counter-Reformation, in the next installment of the *History of Philosophy Without Any Gaps*.

NOTES

1. The Empire Strikes Back: Introduction to Byzantine Philosophy

1. For a more detailed but still fairly brisk overview see part 1, section 3 of E. Jeffreys et al. (eds), *The Oxford Handbook of Byzantine Studies* (Oxford: 2008). Other general works on Byzantine history include J. Haldon, *Byzantium: A History* (Stroud: 2000), C. Mango (ed.), *The Oxford History of Byzantium* (Oxford: 2002), W. Treadgold, *A History of the Byzantine State and Society* (Stanford, CA: 1997), and M. Whittow, *The Making of Orthodox Byzantium, 600–1025* (London: 1996).
2. See further L. Brubaker (ed.), *Byzantium in the Ninth Century: Dead or Alive?* (Aldershot: 1998).
3. J. Herrin, *Byzantium: The Surprising Life of Medieval Empire* (Princeton: 2007), 268.
4. N. G. Wilson, *Scholars of Byzantium* (London: 1996), 218.
5. D. M. Nicol, *The Last Centuries of Byzantium 1261–1453* (Cambridge: 1993).
6. For Maximus and the other Greek patristic thinkers see *A History of Philosophy Without Any Gaps: Philosophy in the Hellenistic and Roman Worlds.*
7. D. Gutas and N. Siniossoglou, "Philosophy and 'Byzantine Philosophy,'" in A. Kaldellis and N. Siniossoglou (eds), *The Cambridge Intellectual History of Byzantium* (Cambridge: 2017), 271–95. For other pieces on the status of philosophy in Byzantine culture see P. Golitsis, "Is Philosophy in Byzantium Anti-Byzantine?," *Deukalion* 28 (2011), 50–74; G. Kapriev, "Gibt es eine byzantinische Philosophie?," *Ostkirchliche Studien* 51 (2001), 3–28; M. Trizio, "Byzantine Philosophy as a Contemporary Historiographical Project," *Recherches de théologie et philosophie médiévales* 74 (2007), 247–94. Ample evidence that Byzantines engaged at least in "science" if not "philosophy" is provided in S. Lazaris, *A Companion to Byzantine Science* (Leiden: 2020).
8. All of them are covered in *A History of Philosophy Without Any Gaps: Philosophy in the Islamic World.* For a juxtaposition of scholarly approaches to the Islamic world and Byzantium, see M. Mavroudi, "The Modern Historiography of Byzantine and Islamic Philosophy: A Comparison," *Al-Masāq* 32 (2020), 1–18.

2. On the Eastern Front: Philosophy in Syriac and Armenian

1. B. E. Perry (ed.), *Secundus the Silent Philosopher* (Ithaca, NY: 1964), C. Sumner, *Ethiopian Philosophy*, 5 vols (Addis Ababa: 1974–82).
2. S. Brock, *Syrian Perspectives on Late Antiquity* (London: 1984), §II, 10.
3. On him see A. K. Sanjian, *David Anhaght', the "Invincible" Philosopher* (Atlanta: 1986).
4. For an overview of Eastern Christian confessions and their history see part I of A. Casiday (ed.), *The Orthodox Christian World* (London: 2012).

5. For background see S. Brock, "Greek and Syriac in Late Antique Syria," in *From Ephrem to Romanos* (Aldershot: 1999), §I.
6. On the reception of Aristotelian philosophy see S. Brock, "The Syriac Commentary Tradition," in C. Burnett (ed.), *Glosses and Commentaries on Aristotelian Logical Texts* (London: 1993), 3–18; H. Hugonnard-Roche, *La logique d'Aristote du grec au syriaque* (Paris: 2004). More generally see H. Takahashi, "Between Greek and Arabic: The Sciences in Syriac from Severus Sebokht to Barhebraeus," in H. Kobayashi and M. Kato (eds), *Transmission of Sciences: Greek, Syriac, Arabic and Latin* (Tokyo: 2010), 16–39; É. Villey (ed.), *Les sciences en syriaque* (Paris: 2014).
7. H. J. W. Drijvers, "The School of Edessa: Greek Learning and Local Culture," in J. W. Drijvers and A. A. MacDonald (eds), *Centres of Learning: Learning and Location in Pre-Modern Europe and the Near East* (Leiden: 1995), 49–59.
8. H. Hugonnard-Roche, "Aux origines de l'exégèse orientale de la logique d'Aristote: Sergius de Reš'ainā (d. 536), médecin et philosophe," *Journal asiatique* 277 (1989), 1–17, at 12.
9. For details on this group see H. Daiber, "The Syriac Tradition in the Early Islamic Era," in U. Rudolph, R. Hansberger, and P. Adamson (eds), *Philosophy in the Islamic World: 8th–10th Century* (Leiden: 2016), 74–94.
10. See *A History of Philosophy Without Any Gaps: Philosophy in the Islamic World*, ch. 3.
11. As noted by Brock, *Syrian Perspectives*, §II, 3. See also J. W. Watt, "Why Did Hunayn, the Master Translator into Arabic, Make Translations from Syriac?," in J. Scheiner and D. Janos (eds), *The Place to Go to: Circles of Learning in the Ninth and Tenth Centuries* (Princeton: 2014), 353–77.
12. See Brock, *Syrian Perspectives*, §V, 17–21 for the preceding quotes and anecdote. For the contrast between Ephrem and Philoxenus see also G. W. Bowersock, "The Syrian Tradition," ch. 3 of his *Hellenism in Late Antiquity* (Cambridge: 1990), 34. On Philoxenus see also A. De Halleux, *Philoxène de Mabbug, sa vie, ses écrits et sa théologie* (Louvain: 1963).
13. For studies on this tradition see R. W. Thomson, *Studies in Armenian Literature and Christianity* (Aldershot: 1994).
14. See R. W. Thomson, "The Formation of the Armenian Literary Tradition," in N. Garsoïan, T. Mathews, and R. W. Thomson (eds), *East of Byzantium: Syria and Armenia in the Formative Period* (Dumbarton Oaks, CA: 1982), 135–50.
15. For overviews see A. Terian, "The Hellenizing School: Its Time, Place and Scope of Activities Reconsidered," in Garsoïan et al., *East of Byzantium*, 175–86; C. Mercier, "L'école hellénistique dans la littérature arménienne," *Revue des études arméniennes* 8 (1978–9), 59–75; R. W. Thomson, "The Reception of Greek Literature in Armenia," in J. T. A. Koumoulides (ed.), *Greek Connections: Essays on Culture and Diplomacy* (Notre Dame, IN: 1987), 28–43.
16. I am grateful to Michael Papazian for the information that there are six extant medieval Armenian translations of Platonic dialogues, which some scholars think originated in the Hellenizing period of Armenian scholarship in the sixth to eighth centuries. Others argue for a later dating.

17. V. Calzolari and J. Barnes (ed.), *L'oeuvre de David l'Invincible* (Leiden: 2009), 13. Barnes doesn't say what the other best commentary on Porphyry is, but here's a clue: he did write one himself.
18. Calzolari and Barnes, *L'oeuvre*, 138.
19. A. Topchyan (trans.), *David the Invincible: Commentary on Aristotle's Prior Analytics* (Leiden: 2010), 41.
20. H. Hugonnard-Roche, "Le traité de logique de Paul le Perse: une intérpretation tardo-antique de la logique aristotélicienne en syriaque," *Documenti e studi sulla tradizione filosofica medievale* 11 (2000), 59–82.
21. Thomson, "The Reception," 36–7.
22. Thomson, "The Formation," 147.
23. For more on the reception of Plato see Y. Arzhanov, "Plato in Syriac Literature," *Le Muséon* 132 (2019), 1–36.
24. D. Miller, "George, Bishop of the Arab Tribes, on True Philosophy," *Festschrift in Honor of Sebastian Brock* (Oxford: 1996), 303–20.

3. Don't Picture This: Iconoclasm

1. L. Brubaker, *Inventing Byzantine Iconoclasm* (Bristol: 2012), 27–9.
2. L. Brubaker and J. F. Haldon, *Byzantium in the Iconoclast Era c.680–850: A History* (Cambridge: 2011), 115.
3. Quoted by L. Barnard, "The Theology of Images," in A. Bryer and J. Herrin (eds), *Iconoclasm: Papers Given at the Ninth Spring Symposium of Byzantine Studies* (Birmingham: 1977), 7–13, at 9.
4. Brubaker, *Inventing Byzantine Iconoclasm*, 13.
5. Quoted by C. Barber, *Figure and Likeness: On the Limits of Representation in Byzantine Iconoclasm* (Princeton: 2002), 18.
6. Cited from Barber, *Figure and Likeness*, 92.
7. For a more nuanced account to this general effect, see Brubaker and Haldon, *Byzantium in the Iconoclast Era*, at e.g. 642–50, 661: iconoclasm "certainly aroused passionate responses. But the people for whom this was the case were really very few in number."
8. *Life of Plotinus* ch. 1, in H. A. Armstrong (trans.), *Plotinus: Enneads*, 7 vols (Cambridge, MA: 1968–88), vol. 1.
9. Quoted by K. Parry, *Depicting the Word: Byzantine Iconophile Thought of the Eighth and Ninth Centuries* (Leiden: 1996), 35.
10. W.-M. Stock, "Theurgy and Aesthetics in Dionysios the Areopagite," in S. Mariev (ed.), *Aesthetics and Theurgy in Byzantium* (Boston: 2013), 13–30.
11. A. Louth (trans.), *John of Damascus: Three Treatises on the Divine Images* (Crestwood, NY: 2003); C. Roth (trans.), *St Theodor the Studite: On the Holy Icons* (Crestwood, NY: 1981); M.-J. Mondzain-Baudinet (trans.), *Nicéphore: discourse contre les iconoclasts* (Paris: 1989). For other sources including texts from the councils see D. Sahas, *Icon and Logos: Sources in Eighth-Century Iconoclasm* (Toronto: 1986).
12. Quoted at Barber, *Figure and Likeness*, 125.

13. See Parry, *Depicting the Word*, 52–7. For more on the use of logic in the debate, see T. Anagnostopoulos, "Aristotle and Byzantine Iconoclasm," *Greek, Roman, and Byzantine Studies* 53 (2013), 763–90.
14. For this treatise see S. H. Griffith, "Theodore Abū Qurrah's Arabic Tract on the Christian Practice of Venerating Images," *Journal of the American Oriental Society* 105 (1985), 53–73. For a similar point in Theodore the Studite see P. Henry, "What was the Iconoclast Controversy about?," *Church History* 45 (1976), 16–31, at 24.
15. Barber, *Figure and Likeness*, 128.
16. Parry, *Depicting the Word*, 73.
17. Brubaker, *Inventing Byzantine Iconoclasm*, 111.

4. Behind Enemy Lines: John of Damascus

1. On his life and works see the first study in V. Kontouma, *John of Damascus: New Studies on his Life and Works* (Farnham: 2015).
2. For an edition of John's writings see P. B. Kotter (ed.), *Die Schriften des Johannes von Damaskos*, 6 vols (Berlin: 1969–88), for translations F. H. Chase (trans.). *Saint John of Damascus: Writings* (Washington, DC: 1958). I quote from all works by chapter number in the main text.
3. On which see G. Richter, *Die Dialektik des Johannes von Damaskos: eine Untersuchung des Textes nach seinen Quellen und seiner Bedeutung* (Ettal: 1964). For a German translation of this part see G. Richter, *Johannes von Damaskos: Philosophische Kapitel* (Stuttgart: 1982).
4. On this see S. Markov, *Die metaphysische Synthese des Johannes von Damaskus: historische Zusammenhänge und Strukturtransformationen* (Leiden: 2015), 40–1.
5. A. Louth, *St. John Damascene: Tradition and Originality in Byzantine Theology* (Oxford: 2009), 159.
6. See Markov, *Die metaphysische Synthese*, 64.
7. See M. Frede, "John of Damascus on Human Action, the Will, and Human Freedom," in K. Ierodiakonou (ed.), *Byzantine Philosophy and its Ancient Sources* (Oxford: 2002), 63–95.
8. This is the judgment of Louth, *St. John Damascene*, 81.
9. I cite by page number from the Greek text of R. Glei and A. T. Khoury, *Johannes Damaskenos und Theodor Abū Qurra: Schriften zum Islam* (Würzburg: 1995). For the relation between Christianity and Islam in this period see H. Goddard, *A History of Christian–Muslim Relations* (Edinburgh: 2000); E. Grypeau et al. (eds), *The Encounter of Eastern Christianity with Early Islam* (Leiden: 2006); R. G. Hoyland, *Seeing Islam as Others Saw it: A Survey and Evaluation of Christian, Jewish and Zoroastrian Writings on Early Islam* (Princeton: 1997); J. C. Lamoreaux, "Early Eastern Christian Responses to Islam," in J. V. Tolan (ed.), *Medieval Christian Perceptions of Islam* (New York: 1996), 3–31; J. Meyendorff, "Byzantium Views of Islam," *Dumbarton Oaks Papers* 18 (1964), 115–32.
10. On him see N. G. Awad, *Orthodoxy in Arabic Terms: A Study of Theodore Abu Qurrah's Theology in its Islamic Context* (Boston: 2015), and for other texts in translation, S. H. Griffith, *Theodore Abū Qurra: A Treatise on the Veneration of the Holy Icons* (Louvain: 1997), J. C. Lamoreaux (trans.), *Theodore Abū Qurra* (Provo, UT: 2005).

11. Louth, *St. John Damascene*, 197.
12. A. Louth (trans.), *John of Damascus: Three Treatises on the Divine Images* (Crestwood, NY: 2003). In the following I cite the first of these treatises by section number.
13. See also Louth, *St. John Damascene*, 185, 211–12, and *On the Orthodox Faith* §4.16.
14. Markov, *Die metaphysische Synthese*, 195.

5. Collectors' Items: Photius and Byzantine Compilations

1. For his project see H. Baltussen, *Philosophy and Exegesis in Simplicius* (London: 2008).
2. M. Roueché, "Byzantine Philosophical Texts of the Seventh Century," *Jahrbuch der österreichischen Byzantinistik* 23 (1974), 61–76, at 67.
3. M. Roueché, "A Middle Byzantine Handbook of Logic Terminology," *Jahrbuch der österreichischen Byzantinistik* 29 (1980), 71–98, at 72.
4. N. G. Wilson, "Scholiasts and Commentators," *Greek, Roman, and Byzantine Studies* 47 (2007), 39–70, at 40. For the topic see further E. Dickey, *Ancient Greek Scholarship* (New York: 2007).
5. P. Lemerle, *Byzantine Humanism: The First Phase* (Canberra: 1986), 345. On "encyclopedism" in Byzantium see also P. Odorico, "La cultura della συλλογή: 1) Il cosiddetto enciclopedismo Bizantino. 2) Le tavole del sapere di Giovanni Damasceno," *Byzantinische Zeitschrift* 83 (1990), 1–21.
6. The Greek edition is A. Adler, *Suida lexicon*, 5 vols (Leipzig: 1928–38). For online texts and translations of the entries see <http://www.stoa.org/sol>.
7. My translation. For discussion see J. Duffy, "The Lonely Mission of Michael Psellos," in K. Ierodiakonou (ed.), *Byzantine Philosophy and its Ancient Sources* (Oxford: 2002), 139–56, at 142–3.
8. Figures taken from L. D. Reynolds and N. G. Wilson, *Scribes and Scholars: A Guide to the Transmission of Greek and Latin Literature* (Oxford: 1991), 64.
9. Quotation from J. Anton, "Neoplatonic Elements in Arethas' Scholia on Aristotle and Porphyry," in L. G. Benakis (ed.), *Néoplatonisme et philosophie médiévale* (Turnhout: 1995), 291–306, at 294.
10. J. Kraemer, *Humanism in the Renaissance of Islam* (Leiden: 1992); C. H. Haskins, *The Renaissance of the Twelfth Century* (Cambridge, MA: 1927).
11. Reynolds and Wilson, *Scribes and Scholars*, 62.
12. For his story in brief compass see J. M. Hussey, *The Orthodox Church in the Byzantine Empire* (Oxford: 1986), and for more detail F. Dvornik, *The Photian Schism: History and Legend* (Cambridge: 1948). See also the collection of articles in F. Dvornik, *Photian and Byzantine Ecclesiastical Studies* (Aldershot: 1974).
13. See A. E. Siecienski, *The Filioque: History of a Doctrinal Controversy* (Oxford: 2010).
14. For the following see G. Kapriev, *Philosophie in Byzanz* (Würzburg: 2005), 186–8.
15. For an English translation see N. G. Wilson, *Photius, The Bibliotheca: A Selection Translated with Notes* (London: 1994). The preface is also edited and translated in W. T. Treadgold, "The Preface of the *Bibliotheca* of Photius: Text, Translation, and Commentary," *Dumbarton Oaks Papers* 31 (1977), 343–9; the following quotation is from Treadgold's version, at 344.

16. W. T. Treadgold, *The Nature of the Bibliotheca of Photius* (Washington, DC: 1980), 34–6. See also F. Ronconi, "The Patriarch and the Assyrians: New Evidence for the Date of Photios' Library," *Segno e Testo* 11 (2013), 387–95, which casts doubt on Photius' account of the context of composition.
17. N. G. Wilson, "The Composition of Photius' *Bibliotheca*," *Greek, Roman, and Byzantine Studies* 9 (1968), 451–5, argues for the plausibility of Photius' claim.
18. For an overview of philosophy in the *Bibliotheca* see I. Christov, "Neoplatonic Elements in the Writings of Patriarch Photius," in M. Knežvić (ed.), *The Ways of Byzantine Philosophy* (Alhambra, CA: 2015), 289–309.
19. Treadgold, *The Nature of the Bibliotheca*, 13.
20. On this treatise, which is extant, see *A History of Philosophy Without Any Gaps: Philosophy in the Hellenistic and Roman Worlds*, ch. 19.
21. Though one might also mention his coverage of Damascius' *Life of Isidore*. Hierocles is mentioned briefly at *Philosophy in the Hellenistic and Roman Worlds*, 245–6, and discussed in P. Adamson, "Freedom, Providence and Fate," in P. Remes and S. Slaveva-Griffin (eds), *The Routledge Handbook of Neoplatonism* (London: 2014), 437–52.
22. Translation from H. S. Schibli, *Hierocles of Alexandria* (Oxford: 2002), 329.
23. Schibli, *Hierocles*, 334.
24. Whether Photius fully understands this is not so clear, since he also says that for Aenesidemus the Pyrrhonist attains happiness "through his conviction that he possesses no certain knowledge" (I have used Wilson's translation for this and the following quote in the main text). On the difference between these forms of skepticism see *Philosophy in the Hellenistic and Roman Worlds*, chs 16 and 18.

6. Consul of the Philosophers: Michael Psellos

1. This aspect is emphasized by A. Kaldellis, *The Argument of Psellos' Chronographia* (Leiden: 1999), 24.
2. M. Jeffrey, "Michael Psellos and the Monastery," in M. Jeffreys and M. D. Lauxtermann (eds), *The Letters of Psellos: Cultural Networks and Historical Realities* (Oxford: 2017), 42–58, at 45.
3. Surveyed in P. Moore, *Iter Psellianum: A Detailed Listing of Manuscript Sources for All Works Attributed to Michael Psellos* (Toronto: 2005).
4. D. Jenkins, "Psellos' Conceptual Precision," in C. Barber and D. Jenkins (eds), *Reading Michael Psellos* (Leiden: 2006), 131–51, at 149.
5. See N. G. Wilson, *Scholars of Byzantium* (London: 1996), 80, and on educational institutions P. Speck, *Die kaiserliche Universität von Konstantinopel* (Munich: 1974).
6. F. Bernard, "Educational Networks in the Letters of Michael Psellos," in Jeffreys and Lauxtermann, *The Letters of Psellos*, 13–41, at 16; the phrase "old boy network" I use below is suggested at 21.
7. For the quote and idea of Psellos as an isolated figure see J. Duffy, "Hellenic Philosophy in Byzantium and the Lonely Mission of Michael Psellos," in K. Ierodiakonou (ed.), *Byzantine Philosophy and its Ancient Sources* (Oxford: 2002), 139–56, 152, and for the point that he was

probably not quite so isolated K. Ierodiakonou, "Psellos' Paraphrasis on Aristotle's *De interpretatione*," in Ierodiakonou, *Byzantine Philosophy*, 157–81, at 158.

8. Translation from D. O'Meara, "Michael Psellos," in S. Gersh (ed.), *Interpreting Proclus from Antiquity to the Renaissance* (Cambridge: 2014), 165–81, at 166.
9. Bernard, "Educational Networks," 24.
10. F. Lauritzen, "Psellos and Plotinos," *Byzantinische Zeitschrift* 107 (2014), 711–24, at 720.
11. D. Walter, *Michael Psellos: Christliche Philosophie in Byzanz* (Berlin: 2017), 15.
12. For examples of particularly tendentious readings see Kaldellis, *The Argument*, 92, 119–20. The general interpretive approach is set out at 13–22.
13. Wilson, *Scholars of Byzantium*, 162.
14. Duffy, "Hellenic Philosophy," 150.
15. D. J. O'Meara, "Psellos' *Commentary on the Chaldean Oracles* and Proclus' Lost Commentary," in H. Seng (ed.), *Platonismus und Esoterik in byzantischem Mittelalter und italienischer Renaissance* (Heidelberg: 2013), 45–56.
16. O'Meara, "Michael Psellos," 173.
17. Duffy, "Hellenic Philosophy," 147, Walter, *Michael Psellos*, 79 (my trans. from the Greek given there).
18. Walter, *Michael Psellos*, 99–102.
19. Kaldellis, *The Argument*, 80–9; for the topic see also M. Jeffrey, "Michael Psellos and the Monastery," in Jeffreys and Lauxtermann, *The Letters of Psellos*, 42–58.
20. Both quotations from Jenkins, "Psellos' Conceptual Precision," 143–4.
21. D. O'Meara, "Political Philosophy in Michael Psellos: The *Chronographia* Read in Relation to his Philosphical Work," in B. Bydén and K. Ierodiakonou (eds), *The Many Faces of Byzantine Philosophy* (Athens: 2012), 153–70.
22. F. Lauritzen, "Psellos and Neo-Platonic Mysticism: The Secret Meaning of the Greek Alphabet (Opusc. phil. I. 36, 335–642)," in H. Seng (ed.), *Platonismus und Esoterik in byzantischem Mittelalter und italienischer Renaissance* (Heidelberg: 2013), 29–43, at 34.
23. G. Dennis, "Elias the Monk: Friend of Psellos," in J. W. Nesbitt (ed.), *Byzantine Authors: Literary Activities and Preoccupations* (Leiden: 2003), 43–62; Jenkins, "Psellos' Conceptual Precision," 144–5.

7. Hooked on Classics: Italos and the Debate over Pagan Learning

1. P. Joannou, *Die Illuminationslehre des Michael Psellos und Joannes Italos* (Freising: 1956), 50–1. For the School of Chartres see *A History of Philosophy Without Any Gaps: Medieval Philosophy*, ch. 14.
2. R. Browning "Enlightenment and Repression in Byzantium in the Eleventh and Twelfth Centuries," *Past and Present* 69 (1975), 3–23, at 5.
3. On whom see *A History of Philosophy Without Any Gaps: Philosophy in the Hellenistic and Roman Worlds*, ch. 42.
4. Quoted by P. A. Agapitos, "Teachers, Pupils and Imperial Power in Eleventh-Century Byzantium," in Y. L. Too and N. Livingstone (eds), *Pedagogy and Power: Rhetorics of Classical Learning* (Cambridge: 1998), 170–91, at 174.

5. My translation from the edition in N. G. Wilson, *Saint Basil on the Value of Greek Literature* (London: 1975), §3.
6. See further L. Elders, "The Greek Christian Authors and Aristotle," in L. P. Schrenk (ed.), *Aristotle in Late Antiquity* (Washington, DC: 1994), 111–42.
7. Quoted from B. Bydén, "'No Prince of Perfection': Byzantine Anti-Aristotelianism from the Patristic Period to Plethon," in D. Angelov and M. Saxby (eds), *Power and Subversion in Byzantium* (Farnham: 2013), 147–76, at 152.
8. As mentioned by F. Lauritzen, "The Debate on Faith and Reason," *Jahrbuch der österreichischen Byzantinistik* 57 (2007), 75–82, drawing on Cyril Mango.
9. Quoted from Agapitos, "Teachers, Pupils and Imperial Power," 187.
10. Quoted from A. Kaldellis, *Hellenism in Byzantium: The Transformations of Greek Identity and the Reception of the Classical Tradition* (Cambridge: 2007), 229.
11. See the discussion in L. Clucas, *The Trial of John Italos and the Crisis of Intellectual Values in Byzantium in the Eleventh Century* (Munich: 1981), 30–44; Clucas concludes that these accusations "tell us a good deal more about the mentality of his opponents" than about Italos' own doctrines.
12. P. Joannou, *Die Illuminationslehre des Michael Psellos und Joannes Italos* (Freising: 1956), 29.
13. Quotation from Agapitos, "Teachers, Pupils and Imperial Power," 184.
14. See Clucas, *The Trial of John Italos*, ch. 4; J. Gouillard, "Le procès officiel de Jean l'Italien: les actes et leurs sous-entendus," *Travaux et mémoires du Centre de Recherche d'Histoire et Civilisation de Byzance* 9 (1985), 133–74.
15. Suggested by, among others, R. Browning "Enlightenment and Repression in Byzantium in the Eleventh and Twelfth Centuries," *Past and Present* 69 (1975), 3–23, at 14. Clucas, *The Trial of John Italos*, 92 casts some doubt on this, since if suspicion of treason had been the motive Italos could simply have been tried on this basis.
16. M. Trizio, "Interpreting Proclus in 11th–12th c. Byzantium: John Italos, Eustratios of Nicaea, Nicholas of Methone," in S. Gersh (ed.), *Interpreting Proclus: From Antiquity to the Renaissance* (Cambridge: 2014), 182–215, at 183.
17. S. Kotzabassi, *Byzantinische Kommentatoren der aristotelischen Topik: Johannes Italos und Leon Magentinos* (Thessalonike: 1999).
18. For what follows see B. Bydén, "Photios and the Non-Synonymy of Substance: *Amphilochia* 138," in S. Ebbesen, J. Marenbon, and P. Thom (eds), *The Reception of Aristotle's Categories in the Byzantine, Latin and Arabic Traditions* (Copenhagen: 2013), 9–34; K. Ierodiakonou, "John Italos on Universals," *Documenti e studi sulla tradizione filosofica medievale* 18 (2007), 231–47.
19. Joannou, *Die Illuminationslehre*, 123, see also 48.
20. M. Trizio, "Escaping through the Homeric Gates: John Italos' Neoplatonic Exegesis of *Odyssey* 19.562–568 Between Synesius and Proclus," *Documenti e studi sulla tradizione filosofica medievale* 24 (2013), 69–83.
21. Summarized in Joannou, *Die Illuminationslehre*, 68–78 and 80–6; for the treatise on matter see also M. Trizio, "A Late Antique Debate on Matter-Evil Revisited in 11th-Century Byzantium: John Italos and His *Quaestio* 92," in P. d'Hoine and G. Van Riel (eds), *Fate, Providence, and Moral Responsibility in Ancient, Medieval, and Early Modern Thought* (Leuven: 2014), 383–94.

22. Joannou, *Die Illuminationslehre*, 63, and 64 for the following point.
23. Lauritzen, "The Debate," 76–7.

8. Purple Prose: Byzantine Political Philosophy

1. E. Barker, *Social and Political Thought in Byzantium from Justinian I to the Last Palaeologus* (Oxford: 1957), 1; P. Magdalino, "*Basileia*: The Idea of Monarchy in Byzantium, 600–1200," in E. Jeffreys et al. (eds), *The Oxford Handbook of Byzantine Studies* (Oxford: 2008), 575–609 at 575. Nonetheless Barker offers a useful collection of sources in translation, some of them discussed below, while Magdalino's article is a helpful overview of the topic.
2. D. Angelov, "Plato, Aristotle, and 'Byzantine Political Philosophy,'" *Mélanges de l'Université Saint-Joseph* 57 (2004), 499–523, at 503.
3. D. Nicol, "Byzantine Political Thought," in J. H. Burns (ed.), *Cambridge History of Medieval Political Thought, c.350–1450* (Cambridge: 1988), 51–82, at 53. For Eusebius' political ideas see also D. O'Meara, *Platonopolis: Platonic Political Philosophy in Late Antiquity* (Oxford: 2003), ch. 12.
4. For the anonymous text see O'Meara, *Platonopolis*, 171–84 and A. Fotiou, *A Sixth Century Greek Dialogue "On Political Science": Translation, with an Introduction* (Ph.D. University of Cincinnati, 1967); for Agapetus see P. Henry, "A Mirror for Justinian: The *Ekthesis* of Agapetus Diaconus," *Greek, Roman, and Byzantine Studies* 8 (1967), 281–308 and for his influence I. Ševčenko, "Agapetus East and West: The Fate of a Byzantine 'Mirror of Princes'," *State and Society in Europe from the Fifteenth to the Eighteenth Century* (Warsaw: 1985), 15–53. For the genre see also P. Odorico, "Les miroirs des princes à Byzance: une lecture horizontale," in Odorico, *Des textes et des contextes dans la littérature byzantine*, ed. R.-G. Curcă (Bucharest: 2013), 283–304.
5. Translation from O'Meara, *Platonopolis*, 173.
6. O'Meara, *Platonopolis*, 182.
7. On this see D. Angelov, *Imperial Ideology and Political Thought in Byzantium, 1204–1330* (Cambridge: 2007), 80.
8. J. Featherstone, "Emperor and Court," in *The Oxford Handbook of Byzantine Studies*, 505–17, at 505.
9. E. Limousin, "Les émotions de l'empereur byzantin," in P. Nagy and D. Boquet (eds), *La politique des émotions au moyen âge* (Florence: 2009), 33–48.
10. Angelov, *Imperial Ideology*, 192–3, and 78 for the point about virtues specific to the emperor.
11. A similar idea is expressed by the thirteenth-century archbishop Demetrios Chomatenos: in his imperial persona the emperor punishes justly much as God does, but if he kills for private reasons this is breaking the law. For the passage see P. Magdalino, "Aspects of Twelfth Century Byzantine *Kaiserkritik*," *Speculum* 58 (1983), 326–46, at 341.
12. Angelov, *Imperial Ideology*, 61.
13. M. Koutlouka, "La tyrannie dans la philosophie byzantine du XIe siècle," *Cahiers de philosophie politique et juridique* 6 (1984), 53–60.

14. Magdalino, "*Basileia*," 595.
15. Magdalino, "*Basileia*," 587.
16. J. García-Huidobro, "Michael of Ephesus and the Byzantine Reception of the Aristotelian Doctrine of Natural Justice," *Archiv für Geschichte der Philosophie* 94 (2012), 274–95.
17. See *A History of Philosophy Without Any Gaps: Medieval Philosophy*, ch. 55, and ch. 39 for the aforementioned topic of natural law.
18. Quoted from Nicol, "Byzantine Political Thought," 69.
19. G. Ostrogorsky, "Die byzantinische Staatenhierachie," *Seminarium Kondakovianum* 8 (1936), 41–61; D. Obolensky, *The Byzantine Commonwealth* (New York: 1971).
20. P. Wood, *"We Have No King but Christ": Christian Political Thought in Greater Syria on the Eve of the Arab Conquest (c.400–585)* (Oxford: 2010).
21. For this I have drawn on Angelov, *Imperial Ideology*; T. Shawcross, "'Do Thou Nothing without Counsel': Political Assemblies and the Ideal of Good Government in the Thought of Theodore Palaeologus and Theodore Metochites," *Al-Masāq* 20 (2008), 89–118; and T. Shawcross, "Mediterranean Encounters Before the Renaissance: Byzantine and Italian Political Thought Concerning the Rise of Cities," in M. S. Brownlee and D. H. Gondicas (eds), *Renaissance Encounters: Greek East and Latin West* (Leiden: 2013), 57–93. For another interesting later work, Makrembolites' *Dialogue Between Rich and Poor*, see below, Chapter 13.
22. In addition to Angelov, *Imperial Ideology*, ch. 7, see G. Richter, *Theodorus Dukas Laskaris: der natürliche Zusammenhang: ein Zeugnis vom Stand der byzantinischen Philosophie in der Mitte des 13. Jahrhunderts* (Amsterdam: 1989).

9. The Elements of Style: Rhetoric in Byzantium

1. V. Valiavitcharska, "Rhetoric in the Hands of the Byzantine Grammarian," *Rhetorica* 31 (2013), 237–60. For more on grammar see R. Webb, "A Slavish Art? Language and Grammar in Late Byzantine Education and Society," *Dialogos* 1 (1994), 81–103. For more on rhetoric see G. Kustas, *Studies in Byzantine Rhetoric* (Thessaloniki: 1973); H. Hunger, *Die hochsprachliche profane Literatur der Byzantiner*, vol. 1 (Munich: 1978), ch. 2; G. Kennedy, *Greek Rhetoric under Christian Emperors* (Princeton: 1983).
2. T. M. Conley, "Byzantine Teaching on Figures and Tropes: An Introduction," *Rhetorica* 4 (1986), 335–74.
3. Valiavitcharska, "Rhetoric in the Hands of the Byzantine Grammarian," 243.
4. T. M. Conley, "Aristotle's *Rhetoric* in Byzantium," *Rhetorica* 8 (1990), 29–44, at 32.
5. *A History of Philosophy Without Any Gaps: Classical Philosophy*, ch. 12, and ch. 17 for the critique in the *Gorgias*; for the Second Sophistic see *A History of Philosophy Without Any Gaps: Philosophy in the Hellenistic and Roman Worlds*, ch. 27.
6. The story is found in *Letter* 11 of Gregory of Nazianzus.
7. *Letter* 223, *Life of Macrina* 8.1.
8. S. Papaioannou, "Rhetoric and the Philosopher in Byzantium," in B. Bydén and K. Ierodiakonou (eds), *The Many Faces of Byzantine Philosophy* (Athens: 2012), 171–97, at 179.

9. The phrase has also been suggested for other phases of Greek literature, as in R. C. Fowler (ed.), *Plato in the Third Sophistic* (Berlin: 2014).
10. Papaioannou, "Rhetoric and the Philosopher," 192.
11. P. Magdalino, "From 'Encyclopaedism' to 'Humanism'," in M. D. Lauxtermann and M. Whittow (eds), *Byzantium in the Eleventh Century* (London: 2017), 3–18, at 12.
12. For works in translation see C. Barber and S. Papaioannou (eds), *Michael Psellos on Literature and Art: A Byzantine Perspective on Aesthetics* (Notre Dame, IN: 2017), cited in the main text in brackets.
13. S. Papaioannou, *Michael Psellos: Rhetoric and Authorship in Byzantium* (Cambridge: 2013), 46.
14. Papaioannou, *Michael Psellos*, 36; this concerns *Chronographia*, chs 44–6.
15. J. Walker, "Michael Psellos on Rhetoric: A Translation and Commentary on Psellos' Synopsis of Hermogenes," *Rhetoric Society Quarterly* 31 (2001), 5–40, at 11. The work is translated in B. Baldwin (trans.), *Timarion* (Detroit: 1984).
16. Papaioannou, *Michael Psellos*, 93.
17. Papaioannou, *Michael Psellos*, 117–18.
18. *Chronographia* 6.197, quoted from Walker, "Michael Psellos on Rhetoric," 13.
19. This is a central thesis of Papaioannou, *Michael Psellos*, see e.g. 125.
20. Conley, "Aristotle's *Rhetoric* in Byzantium," 30.
21. For these works I draw on M. Vogiatzi, *Byzantine Commentaries on Aristotle's Rhetoric: Anonymous and Stephanus* (Berlin: 2019).

10. Past Masters: Byzantine Historiography

1. For English translations see E. R. A. Sewter (trans.), *Fourteen Byzantine Rulers: The Chronographia of Michael Psellus* (Harmondsworth: 1966); E. R. A. Sewter (trans.), *Anna Komnene: The Alexiad* (Harmondsworth: 2009). For a comparison of the two works see S. Linnér, "Psellus' *Chronographia* and the *Alexias*: Some Textual Parallels," *Byzantinische Zeitschrift* 76 (1983), 1–9.
2. W. Treadgold, *The Middle Byzantine Historians* (New York: 2013), 388.
3. Translation in A. Kaldellis and D. Krallis (trans.), *Michael Attaleiates: History* (Washington, DC: 2012).
4. Applied to Attaleiates by A. Kazhdan and S. Franklin, *Studies on Byzantine Literature of the Eleventh and Twelfth Centuries* (Cambridge: 1984), 23.
5. Treadgold, *The Middle Byzantine Historians*, 361.
6. For classicizing tendencies see E. M. Jeffreys, "The Attitudes of Byzantine Chroniclers towards Ancient History," *Byzantion* 49 (1979), 199–238.

   R. Scott, "The Classical Tradition in Byzantine Historiography," in M. Mullet and R. Scott (eds), *Byzantium and the Classical Tradition* (Birmingham: 1981), 61–74; S. D. Syropoulos, "The Relation of Byzantine Historians to the Classical Tradition During the Mid-12th–15th Centuries AD," *Byzantinos Domos* 14 (2004–5), 65–72.
7. By Procopius and, much later in the fourteenth century, John Cantacuzenus: see J. Harris, "Distortion, Divine Providence and Genre in Nicetas Choniates's Account of the Collapse of Byzantium 1180–1204," *Journal of Medieval History* 26 (2000), 19–31, at 22.
8. Treadgold, *The Middle Byzantine Historians*, 379.

9. A. Kaldellis, "Historicism in Byzantine Thought and Literature," *Dumbarton Oaks Papers* 61 (2007), 1–24, from which I take the comparison to the historians. On the first text see M. Alexiou, "A Critical Reappraisal of Makrembolites' *Hysmine and Hysminias*," *Byzantine and Modern Greek Studies* 3 (1977), 23–43, and more generally R. Beaton, *The Medieval Greek Romance* (London: 1996).
10. A. Kaldellis, *The Byzantine Republic: People and Power in New Rome* (Cambridge, MA: 2015).
11. Quoted from L. C. Ruggini, "The Ecclesiastical Histories and the Pagan Historiography: Providence and Miracles," *Athenaeum* 55 (1977), 107–26, at 120.
12. As argued by D. Krallis, "'Democratic' Action in Eleventh-Century Byzantium: Michael Attaleiates's 'Republicanism' in Context," *Viator* 40 (2009), 35–53.
13. A. Kaldellis, "A Byzantine Argument for the Equivalence of All Religions: Michael Attaleiates on Ancient and Modern Romans," *International Journal of the Classical Tradition* 14 (2007), 1–22.
14. As noted by Ruggini, "The Ecclesiastical Histories," 108.
15. *Michael Attaleiates: History*, §15.2.
16. The resonance between the two works is noted by K. Perry, "Fate, Free Choice, and Divine Providence from the Neoplatonists to John of Damascus," in A. Kaldellis and N. Siniossoglou (eds), *The Cambridge Intellectual History of Byzantium* (Cambridge: 2017), 341–60, at 351. For a translation of the work see C. Garton and L. G. Westerink (ed. and trans.), *On Predestined Terms of Life* (New York: 1978).
17. For instance at *Michael Attaleiates: History*, §28.8 and 30.5.
18. Anna Komnene, *Alexiad*, §4.7.
19. Anna Komnene, *Alexiad*, §12.4.
20. English translation in H. J. Magoulias (trans.), *O City of Byzantium: Annals of Niketas Choniates* (Detroit: 1984). On him see J. Harris, "Distortion, Divine Providence and Genre in Nicetas Choniates's Account of the Collapse of Byzantium 1180–1204," *Journal of Medieval History* 26 (2000), 19–31; T. Urbainczyk, *Writing about Byzantium: The History of Niketas Choniates* (London: 2018).
21. Urbainczyk, *Writing about Byzantium*, 64.
22. As reported by R.-J. Lilie, "Reality and Invention: Reflections on Byzantine Historiography," *Dumbarton Oaks Papers* 68 (2014), 157–210, at 162.
23. Translation from Treadgold, *The Middle Byzantine Historians*, 455. The passage is also noted by P. Magdalino, "Aspects of Twelfth Century Byzantine *Kaiserkritik*," *Speculum* 58 (1983), 326–46, at 327; I draw on this latter article in what follows.
24. J. Wortley, *John Skylitzes: A Synopsis of Byzantine History, 811–1057* (Cambridge: 2010), 1–2.
25. *Alexiad*, §15.3, and §15.5 for the following quotation. Both passages are cited and discussed in E. Quandahl and S. C. Jarratt, "'To Recall Him . . . Will be a Subject of Lamentation': Anna Comnena as Rhetorical Historiographer," *Rhetorica* 26 (2008), 301–35. See further L. Neville, *Anna Komnene: The Life and Work of a Medieval Historian* (Oxford: 2016), 44.

11. Queen of the Sciences: Anna Komnene and Her Circle

1. For this oration see R. Browning, "An Unpublished Funeral Oration on Anna Comnena," in R. Sorabji (ed.), *Aristotle Transformed: The Ancient Commentators and their Influence* (London: 1990), 393–406.

2. P. Frankopian, "The Literary, Cultural and Political Context for the Twelfth-Century Commentary on the *Nicomachean Ethics*," in C. Barber and D. Jenkins (eds), *Medieval Greek Commentaries on the Nicomachean Ethics* (Leiden: 2009), 45–62, at 57–8.
3. See S. Takács, "Oracles and Science: Anna Comnena's Comments on Astrology," *Byzantinische Forschungen* 23 (1976), 35–44.
4. Quoted by L. Neville, *Anna Komnene: The Life and Work of a Medieval Historian* (Oxford: 2016), 93.
5. Frankopian, "The Literary, Cultural and Political Context," 60.
6. Neville, *Anna Komnene*, 118.
7. J. Howard-Johnson, "Anna Komnena and the *Alexiad*," in M. E. Mullett and D. C. Smythe (eds), *Alexios I Komnenos* (Belfast: 1996), vol. 1, 260–301.
8. As pointed out by R. Macrides, "The Pen and the Sword: Who Wrote the Alexiad?," in T. Gouma-Peterson (ed.), *Anna Komnene and Her Times* (New York: 2000), 63–81, at 67. The paper in the same volume by Reinsch also argues for Anna's primary authorship.
9. Neville, *Anna Komnena*, 8.
10. Neville, *Anna Komnena*, 73.
11. This is the approach of B. Hill, "Actions Speak Louder Than Words: Anna Komnene's Attempted Usurpation," in Gouma-Peterson, *Anna Komnene and Her Times*, 45–62.
12. H. P. F. Mercken, "The Greek Commentators on Aristotle's *Ethics*," in R. Sorabji (ed.), *Aristotle Transformed: The Ancient Commentators and their Influence* (London: 1990), 407–43, at 432.
13. For instance C. Steel, "Neoplatonic Sources in the Commentaries on the *Nicomachean Ethics* by Eustratios of Nicaea and Michael of Ephesus," *Bulletin de philosophie médiévale* 44 (2002), 51–7; M. Trizio, "Neoplatonic Source-Material in Eustratios of Nicaea's Commentary on Book VI of the *Nicomachean* Ethics," in Barber and Jenkins, *Medieval Greek Commentaries*, 71–109.
14. On this and the related issue of his views on universals, see K. Giocarinis, "Eustratios of Nicaea's Defense of the Doctrine of Ideas," *Franciscan Studies* 24 (1964), 159–204; A. C. Lloyd, "The Aristotelianism of Eustratios of Nicaea," in J. Wiesner (ed.), *Aristoteles, Werk und Werkung*, vol. 2 (Berlin: 1987), 341–51; K. Ierodiakonou, "Metaphysics in the Byzantine Tradition: Eustratios of Nicaea on Universals," *Quaestio* 5 (2005), 67–82; D. Jenkins, "Eustratios of Nicaea's 'Definition of Being' Revisited," in Barber and Jenkins, *Medieval Greek Commentaries*, 111–30. For Byzantine discussions of Platonic Forms see also more generally A. del Campo Echevarría, *La teoría platónica de las ideas en Bizancio: (siglos IX—XI)* (Madrid: 2012).
15. Lloyd, "The Aristotelianism of Eustratios," 347.
16. I am grateful to James Wilberding for making available to me a prepublication draft of a study on this subject.
17. On this see J. Wilberding, *Forms, Souls, and Embryos: Neoplatonists on Human Reproduction* (London: 2017), 111ff.
18. For an overview see M. Trizio, "Reading and Commenting on Aristotle," in A. Kaldellis and N. Siniossoglou (eds), *The Cambridge Intellectual History of Byzantium* (Cambridge: 2017), 397–412.

12. Wiser than Men: Gender in Byzantium

1. For example L. Garland, *Byzantine Empresses: Women and Power in Byzantium AD 527–1204* (London: 1999), J. Herrin, *Women in Purple: Rulers of Medieval Byzantium* (Princeton: 2001).
2. One rare exception is a passage in Eustathios that admiringly compares the women of Thessalonika to the Amazons for their role in resisting a Norman attack in 1185. See K. N. Ciggaar, *Western Travelers to Constantinople. The West and Byzantium, 962–1204: Cultural and Political Relations* (Leiden: 1996), 13.
3. A. Kaldellis, *Mothers and Sons, Fathers and Daughters: The Byzantine Family of Michael Psellos* (Notre Dame, IN: 2006), 25.
4. For her reign I follow the account in Garland, *Byzantine Empresses*. See 81 and 89 for the quotes from Theophanes just below.
5. See B. Hill, "Imperial Women and the Ideology of Womanhood in the Eleventh and Twelfth Centuries," in L. James (ed.), *Women, Men and Eunuchs: Gender in Byzantium* (London: 1977), 76–99, at 80, and F. Lauritzen, "A Courtier in the Women's Quarters: The Rise and Fall of Psellos," *Byzantion* 77 (2007), 251–66.
6. See further A. E. Laiou, "The Role of Women in Byzantine Society," *Jahrbuch der österreichischen Byzantinistik* 31 (1981), 233–60.
7. A.-M. Talbot, "Women and Mt Athos," in A. Bryer and M. Cunningham (eds), *Mount Athos and Byzantine Monasticism* (Aldershot: 1996), 67–79, at 69.
8. A. R. Brown, "Psalmody and Socrates: Female Literacy in the Byzantine Empire," in B. Neil and L. Garland (eds), *Questions of Gender in Byzantine Society* (London: 2016), 57–76. For a brief statement of literacy in the empire see A. E. Laiou and C. Morrisson, *The Byzantine Economy* (Cambridge: 2007), 19–20. They estimate a 30 percent literacy rate among male subjects of the empire; the rate for women would of course have been lower.
9. E. Jeffreys, "The Sevastokratorissa Irene as Literary Patroness: The Monk Iakovos," *Jahrbuch der österreichischen Byzantinistik* 32 (1982), 63–71.
10. I. Rochow, *Studien zu der Person, den Werken und dem Nachleben der Dichterin Kassia* (Berlin: 1967); E. Topping, "Women Hymnographers in Byzantium," *Diptycha* 3 (1982–3), 98–111.
11. Garland, *Byzantine Empresses*, 98.
12. C. Rapp, "Figures of Female Sanctity: Byzantine Edifying Manuscripts and Their Audience," *Dumbarton Oaks Papers* 50 (1996), 313–44.
13. Rapp, "Figures of Female Sanctity," 324.
14. On this work see J. W. Smith, "Macrina, Tamer of Horses and Healer of Souls: Grief and the Therapy of Hope in Gregory of Nyssa's *De anima et resurrectione*," *Journal of Theological Studies* 52 (2001), 37–60; P. Adamson, "Macrina's Method: Reason and Reasoning in Gregory of Nyssa's *On Soul and Resurrection*," forthcoming in J. Schultz and J. Wilberding (eds), *Women and the Female in Neoplatonism*. The dialogue is translated in A. M. Silvas, *Macrina the Younger, Philosopher of God* (Turnhout: 2008).
15. A. R. Littlewood, "The Byzantine Letter of Consolation in the Macedonian and Komnenian Periods," *Dumbarton Oaks Papers* 53 (1999), 19–41. On Byzantine epistolary culture see also M. E. Mullett, "The Classical Tradition in the Byzantine Letter," in M. E. Mullett and R. D. Scott (eds), *Byzantium and the Classical Tradition* (Birmingham: 1981), 75–93.

16. D. Casey, "The Spiritual Valency of Gender in Byzantine Society," in Neil and Garland, *Questions of Gender*, 167–81, at 175.
17. For the idea of "transcending gender" see V. E. Harrison, "Male and Female in Cappadocian Theology," *Journal of Theological Studies* NS 14 (1992), 441–71, at 467.
18. Translated in A. Kaldellis, *Mothers and Sons, Fathers and Daughters: The Byzantine Family of Michael Psellos* (Notre Dame, IN: 2006), cited by section number. See also J. Walker, "These Things I Have Not Betrayed: Michael Psellos' Encomium of his Mother as a Defense of Rhetoric," *Rhetorica* 22 (2004), 49–101.
19. S. Papaioannou, "Michael Psellos' Rhetorical Gender," *Byzantine and Modern Greek Studies* 24 (2000), 133–46, shows that Psellos is here repurposing a rhetorical flourish from Synesius of Cyrene.
20. For what follows I have drawn on K. M. Ringrose, *The Perfect Servant: Eunuchs and the Social Construction of Gender in Byzantium* (Chicago: 2003) and S. Tougher, *The Eunuch in Byzantine History and Society* (London: 2008).
21. Tougher, *The Eunuch in Byzantine History*, 103.
22. Ringrose, *The Perfect Servant*, 7.

13. Just Measures: Law, Money, and War in Byzantium

1. On this see *A History of Philosophy Without Any Gaps: Medieval Philosophy*, ch. 18.
2. As argued by D. Simon, "Legislation as Both a World Order and a Legal Order," in A. E. Laiou and D. Simon (eds), *Law and Society in Byzantium: Ninth–Twelfth Centuries* (Washington, DC: 1994), 1–25, and in the same volume J. H. A. Lokin, "The Significance of Law and Legislation in the Law Books of the Ninth to Eleventh Centuries," 71–91.
3. M. T. Fögen, "Legislation und Kodifikation des Kaisers Leon VI," *Subseciva Groningana* 3 (1989), 23–35.
4. For a balanced evaluation of this view see B. Stolte, "The Social Function of the Law," in J. Haldon, *A Social History of Byzantium* (Chichester: 2009), 76–91; two important earlier studies are D. Simon, *Rechtsfindung am byzantinischen Reichsgericht* (Frankfurt a.M.: 1973) and M. T. Fögen, "Gesetz und Gesetzgebung in Byzanz: Versuch einer Funktionsanalyse," *Jus commune* 14 (1987), 137–57.
5. A. E. Laiou, "Law, Justice, and the Byzantine Historians: Ninth to Eleventh Centuries," in Laiou and Simon, *Law and Society*, 151–85, at 176–7.
6. G. T. Dennis, "A Rhetorician Practices Law: Michael Psellos," in Laiou and Simon, *Law and Society*, 187–97, at 191–3.
7. For the development of Byzantine canon law see W. Hartmann and K. Pennington (eds), *The History of Byzantine and Eastern Canon Law to 1500* (Washington, DC: 2012).
8. See A. E. Laiou and C. Morrisson, *The Byzantine Economy* (Cambridge: 2007).
9. P. Magdalino, "Justice and Finance in the Byzantine State: Ninth to Twelfth Centuries," in Laiou and Simon, *Law and Society*, 93–115, at 94.
10. As stressed in V. Prigent, "The Mobilisation of Fiscal Resources in the Byzantine Empire (Eighth to Eleventh Centuries)," in J. Hudson and A. Rodriguez (eds), *Diverging Paths? The Shapes of Power and Institutions in Medieval Christendom and Islam* (Leiden: 2014), 182–229.

11. R. S. Lopez, "The Dollar of the Middle Ages," *Journal of Economic History* 11 (1951), 209–34.
12. Laiou and Morrisson, *The Byzantine Economy*, 61.
13. G. Ostrogorsky, *Pour l'histoire de la féodalité byzantine* (Brussels: 1954); J. Haldon, "The Feudalism Debate Once More: The Case of Byzantium," *Journal of Peasant Studies* 17 (1989), 4–40; A. Kazhdan, "State, Feudal, and Private Property in Byzantium," *Dumbarton Oaks Papers* 47 (1993), 83–100.
14. C. M. Brand, "Did Byzantium Have a Free Market?" *Byzantinische Forschungen* 26 (2000), 63–72.
15. Laiou and Morrisson, *The Byzantine Economy*, 162.
16. For usury in the medieval period see *A History of Philosophy Without Any Gaps: Medieval Philosophy*, ch. 67.
17. A. E. Laiou, "Economic Concerns and Attitudes of the Intellectuals of Thessalonike," *Dumbarton Oaks Papers* 57 (2003), 205–23, at 212, n. 30, and 214–16 for Kavasilas.
18. Translated in I. Sevcenko, "Alexius Makrembolites and his *Dialogue between the Rich and the Poor*," in his *Society and Intellectual Life in Late Byzantium* (London: 1981), §VII; for a summary see S. S. Harakas, "A Case Study in Eastern Orthodox Ethics on Rich and Poor: Alexius Makrembolites' '*Dialogue between the Rich and the Poor*'," *The Annual of the Society of Christian Ethics* 4 (1984), 315–40.
19. See *A History of Philosophy Without Any Gaps: Medieval Philosophy*, ch. 40. For the Byzantine side of the story see J. Haldon, *Warfare, State and Society in the Byzantine World 565–1204* (London: 1999), ch. 1; A. E. Laiou, "On Just War in Byzantium," in J. F. Haldon (ed.), *Byzantine Warfare* (Aldershot: 2007), 17–42.
20. W. Treadgold, "Byzantium, the Reluctant Warrior," in N. Christie and M. Yazigi (eds), *Noble Ideals and Bloody Realities: Warfare in the Middle Ages* (Leiden: 2006), 213–23. For a contrast of the Byzantines' approach to that of classical Rome, see E. N. Luttwak, *The Grand Strategy of the Byzantine Empire* (Cambridge, MA: 2011).
21. I here follow I. Stouraitis, "'Just War' and 'Holy War' in the Middle Ages: Rethinking Theory through the Byzantine Case-Study," *Jahrbuch der österreichischen Byzantinistik* 62 (2012), 227–64.

14. Made by Hand: Byzantine Manuscripts

1. For the material culture of ancient texts and their transmission I draw freely on H. Hunger et al., *Die Textüberlieferung der antiken Literatur und der Bibel* (Munich: 1988).
2. Diogenes Laertius, *Lives of the Philosophers*, §3.37.
3. C. N. Constantinides, *Higher Education in Byzantium in the Thirteenth and Early Fourteenth Centuries (1204–ca.1310)* (Nicosia: 1982), 75.
4. R. Chiaradonna, M. Rashed, and D. Sedley, "A Rediscovered *Categories* Commentary," *Oxford Studies in Ancient Philosophy* 44 (2012), 129–94. For another palimpsest copy of Aristotle's logic see B. Mondrain, "Le réutilisation de parchemin ancient dans les livres à Constantinople au XIVe et au XVe siècle," in *Libri palinsesti greci: conservazione, restauro digitale, studio* (Rome: 2008), 111–29.

5. Michele Trizio informs me that Psellos apparently did have at least one philosophical work in scroll form, Proclus' *Commentary on the Timaeus.*
6. Hunger et al., *Die Textüberlieferung*, 211.
7. N. Wilson, "The Libraries of the Byzantine World," *Greek, Roman and Byzantine Studies* 8 (1967), 53–80, at 63.
8. R. Goulet, "La conservation et la transmission des textes philosophiques grecques," in C. D'Ancona (ed.), *Libraries of the Neoplatonists* (Leiden: 2007), 29–61, at 34.
9. D. Harlfinger, *Die Textgeschichte der Pseudo-Aristotelischen Schrift Peri Atomon Grammon* (Amsterdam: 1971), 40–1. For a detailed description of one manuscript with logical material, see S. Kotzabassi, "Aristotle's *Organon* and its Byzantine Commentators," *Princeton University Library Chronicle* 65 (2002), 51–62.
10. A. Wartelle, *Inventaire des manuscrits grecs d'Aristote et de ses commentateurs* (Paris: 1963), 15.
11. For details see *A History of Philosophy Without Any Gaps: Philosophy in the Hellenistic and Roman Worlds*, ch. 25. An exception is Aristotle's record of the *Constitution of Athens*, which is preserved on ancient papyrus.
12. O. Primavesi (ed.) and K. Corcilius (trans.), *Aristoteles: De motu animalium. Über die Bewegung der Lebewesen* (Hamburg: 2018). His philological introduction is also a useful guide to the principles for editing Aristotelian texts more generally, and I am furthermore grateful to him for comments on a draft of this chapter.
13. Discussed in several papers collected in D'Ancona, *Libraries of the Neoplatonists.*
14. For this hypothesis see M. Rashed, "Nicolas d'Otrante, Guillaume de Moerbeke et la *Collection philosophique*," *Studi medievali* 43 (2002), 693–717.
15. See *A History of Philosophy Without Any Gaps: Medieval Philosophy*, ch. 20.

15. Georgia on My Mind: Petritsi and the Proclus Revival

1. *A History of Philosophy Without Any Gaps: Philosophy in the Islamic World*, ch. 50.
2. *A History of Philosophy Without Any Gaps: Philosophy in the Hellenistic and Roman Worlds*, ch. 35.
3. Cited from A. Gioffreda and M. Trizio, "Nicholas of Methone, Procopius of Gaza and Proclus of Lycia," in D. Calma (ed.), *Reading Proclus and the Book of Causes*, vol. 2 (Leiden: 2021), 94–135, at 109. For Psellos' use of Proclus see also above, Chapter 6, and J. Robinson, "'A Mixing Cup of Piety and Learnedness': Michael Psellos and Nicholas of Methone as Readers of Proclus' Elements of Theology," in Calma, *Reading Proclus*, 56–93. I am very grateful to Joshua Robinson and to Lela Alexidze for helpful comments on a draft of this chapter and for pointing me to resources on Nicholas of Methone and Petritsi.
4. On the medieval reception of Proclus more generally, see P. Adamson and F. Karfik, "Proclus' Legacy," in P. d'Hoine and M. Martijn (eds), *All from One: A Guide to Proclus* (Oxford: 2016), 290–321.
5. See M. Trizio, "Eleventh- to Twelfth-Century Byzantium," in S. Gersh (ed.), *Interpreting Proclus: From Antiquity to the Renaissance* (Cambridge: 2014), 182–215.
6. G. Podskalsky, "Nicholas von Methone und die Proklos-Renaissance in Byzanz," *Orientalia christiana periodica* 42 (1976), 509–23; F. Lauritzen, "The Renaissance of Proclus in the

Eleventh Century," in D. D. Butorac and D. A. Layne (eds), *Proclus and his Legacy* (Berlin: 2017), 233–40.

7. I have used the forthcoming edition and translation by Joshua Robinson, and also learned much from his doctoral thesis: "Nicholas of Methone's *Refutation* of Proclus: Theology and Neoplatonism in 12th-Century Byzantium," Ph.D. dissertation, University of Notre Dame, 2014. I refer to the text by the number of the proposition in the *Elements* Nicholas is criticizing. See also Gioffreda and Trizio, "Nicholas of Methone," for questions about authenticity (they defend Nicholas' authorship against interpretations which ascribe the work in whole or in part to the earlier Procopius).
8. For the neutral meaning of this term see J. M. Robinson, "Dionysius against Proclus: The Apophatic Critique of Nicholas of Methone's *Refutation of the Elements of Theology*," in Butorac and Layne, *Proclus and his Legacy*, 249–69, at 249.
9. On the Byzantine reception of this slogan see M. Mtchedlidzé, "Les interprétations d'un passage du *Discours* 29 de Grégoire de Nazianze par les auteurs byzantines et géorgiens des XIe–XIIe siècles," in V. Somers and P. Yannopoulos (eds), *Philokappadox* (Leuven: 2016), 247–68.
10. I here agree with Robinson, "Dionysius against Proclus."
11. On this see J. M. Robinson, "Proclus as Heresiarch: Theological Polemic and Philosophical Commentary in Nicholas of Methone's *Refutation* (*Anaptyxis*) of Proclus' *Elements of Theology*," in S. Mariev (ed.), *Byzantine Perspectives on Neoplatonism* (Berlin: 2017), 103–35.
12. For discussion see L. Gigineishvili, *The Platonic Theology of Ioane Petrisi* (Piscataway, NJ: 2007), 11–19.
13. For a German translation see L. Alexidze (trans.), *Ioane Petrizi: Kommentar zur Elementatio theologica des Proklos* (Amsterdam: 2009). Cited by proposition number. See also T. Iremadze, "Die *Elementatio theologica* des Proklos im Kontekt der kaukasischen Philosophie," in Calma, *Reading Proclus*, 139–53.
14. For the use of the word "divine" see L. Alexidze, "Zum Verhältnis zwischen Neuplatonischem und Christlichem im Prokloskommentar des Ioane Petrizi," in T. Kobusch and M. Erler (eds), *Metaphysik und Religion: Zur Signatur des spätantiken Denkens* (Munich: 2002), 429–52, at 436; for the status of the monads emanated from the One, see Gigineishvili, *The Platonic Theology*, 53, 86, 151.
15. L. Alexidze, "'One in the Beings' and 'One within Us': The Basis of the Union with the One in Ioane Petritsi's Interpretation of Proclus' *Elements of Theology*," in T. Nutsubidze et al. (eds), *Georgian Christian Thought and Its Cultural Context* (Leiden: 2014), 175–93, at 187.
16. Gigineishvili, *The Platonic Theology*, 91–2.
17. Mtchedlidzé, "Les interprétations," 263.
18. L. Alexidze, "*Dianoia* in Ioane Petritsi's *Commentary* on Proclus' *Elements of Theology*," in *Chôra: revue d'études anciennes et médievales* (Paris: 2016), 177–94; see 192 for the coining of artificial Georgian expressions to get at the right meaning.
19. Gigineishvili, *The Platonic Theology*, 203 n. 358 points out that this interpretation was already put forward by Origen.
20. Iremadze, "Die *Elementatio theologica* des Proklos," 146, which adds that we know of an Armenian commentary on Proclus from the seventeenth century, and two more written in Georgian in the eighteenth century.

16. People of the South: Byzantium and Islam

1. N. M. El Cheikh, *Byzantium Viewed by the Arabs* (Cambridge, MA: 2004), 64–5. On the military encounters see also W. E. Kaegi, *Byzantium and the Early Islamic Conquests* (Cambridge: 1992).
2. This is the argument of D. Olster, "Ideological Transformation and the Evolution of Imperial Presentation in the Wake of Islam's Victory," in E. Grypeou et al. (eds), *The Encounter of Eastern Christianity with Early Islam* (Leiden: 2006), 45–71.
3. See J. Meyendorff, "Byzantine Views of Islam," *Dumbarton Oaks Papers* 18 (1964), 113–32, at 125–6.
4. On this letter see E. Wakelnig, "Muḥammad ibn al-Layth's Letter to the Byzantine Emperor and its Arguments from Correct Language," *Journal of Eastern Christian Studies* 72 (2020), 217–39.
5. For a summary see H. Goddard, *A History of Christian–Muslim Relations* (Edinburgh: 2000), 57.
6. On this question see A. Argyriou, "Perception de l'Islam et traductions du Coran dans le monde byzantin grec," *Byzantion* 75 (2005), 25–69.
7. K.-P. Todt, *Kaiser Johannes VI Kantakuzenos und der Islam* (Würzburg: 1991).
8. M. Trizio, "A Neoplatonic Refutation of Islam from the Time of the Komneni," in A. Speer and P. Steinkrüger (eds), *Knotenpunkt Byzanz: Wissensformen und kulturelle Wechselbeziehungen* (Berlin: 2012), 145–66.
9. See *A History of Philosophy Without Any Gaps: Philosophy in the Islamic World*, ch. 3, and ch. 8 for the "Baghdad school" discussed below.
10. D. Gutas, *Greek Thought, Arabic Culture: The Graeco-Arabic Translation Movement in Baghdad and Early Society (2nd–4th/8th–10th Centuries)* (London, 1998), 61–9.
11. The most recent translation is M. Heimgartner (trans.), *Timotheos I., ostsyrischer Patriarch: Disputation mit dem Kalifen al-Mahdī* (Leuven: 2011), which I cite by page number; there is an older one in English by A. Mingana. See also V. Berti, *Vita e studi di Timoteo I, patriarca cristiano di Baghdad: ricerche sull'epistolario e sulle fonti contigue* (Paris: 2009), and for a briefer overview M. Heimgartner, "Die Disputatio des ostsyrischen Patriarchen Timotheus (780–823) mit dem Kalifen al-Mahdī," in M. Tamcke (ed.), *Christians and Muslims in Dialogue in the Islamic Orient of the Middle Ages* (Beirut: 2007), 41–56.
12. As pointed out by Heimgartner, "Die Disputatio," 45.
13. See M. Beaumont, "The Holy Spirit in Early Christian Dialogue with Muslims," in D. Pratt et al. (eds), *The Character of Christian–Muslim Encounter* (Leiden: 2015), 42–59, and D. Thomas, "Christian Theologians and New Questions," in Grypeou et al., *The Encounter of Eastern Christianity*, 257–76.
14. For this treatise, its connection to al-Kindī's more famous *On First Philosophy*, and the response by Ibn ʿAdī, see P. Adamson, "Yaḥyā Ibn ʿAdī against al-Kindī on the Trinity," *Journal of Eastern Christian Studies* 72 (2020), 241–71.
15. For an overview see S. H. Griffith, "Disputes with Muslims in Syriac Christian Texts: From Patriarch John (d. 648) to Bar Hebraeus (d. 1286)," in F. Niewohner (ed.), *Religionsgespräche im Mittelalter* (Wiesbaden: 1992), 251–73.
16. Cited by page number from the English translations in S. T. Keating, *Defending the "People of Truth" in the Early Islamic Period: The Christian Apologies of Abū Rā'iṭah* (Leiden: 2006).

17. See S. Noble and A. Trieger, "Christian Arabic Theology in Byzantine Antioch: ʿAbdallāh ibn al-Faḍl al-Anṭākī and his *Discourse on the Holy Trinity*," *Le muséon* 124 (2011), 371–417, and more generally A. Trieger, "Mutual Influences and Borrowings," in D. Thomas (ed.), *The Routledge Handbook on Christian–Muslim Relations* (London: 2018), 194–206, and A. Trieger, "Mutual Influences and Borrowings," in D. Thomas (ed.), *The Routledge Handbook on Christian-Muslim Relations* (London: 2018), 194–206.
18. Noble and Trieger, "Christian Arabic Theology," 383–4.
19. See H. Teule and C. F. Tauwinkl (eds), *The Syriac Renaissance* (Leuven: 2010).
20. See on him H. Teule, "Gregory Barhebraeus and his Time: The Syrian Renaissance," *Journal of the Canadian Society for Syriac Studies* 3 (2003), 21–43; H. Takahashi, "The Reception of Ibn Sīnā in Syriac: The Case of Gregory Barhebraeus," in D. C. Reisman (ed.), *Before and After Avicenna* (Leiden: 2003), 249–8; J. W. Watt, "Graeco-Syriac Tradition and Arabic Philosophy in Bar Hebraeus," in Teule and Tauwinkl, *The Syriac Renaissance*, 123–33. A good first orientation is H. Takahashi, "Barhebraeus," in A. Casiday (ed.), *The Orthodox Christian World* (London: 2012), 279–86.
21. For this section see N. P. Joosse, *A Syriac Encyclopedia of Aristotelian Philosophy: Barhebraeus (13th c.) Butyrum sapientiae. Books of Ethics, Economy, and Politics* (Leiden: 2004), and for its sources M. Zonta, "Structure and Sources of Bar-Hebraeus' 'Practical Philosophy' in *The Cream of Science*," in R. Lavenant (ed.), *Symposium Syriacum* 7 (Rome: 1998), 279–92; N. P. Joosse, "Expounding on a Theme: Structure and Sources of Bar Hebraeus' 'Practical Philosophy' in *The Cream of Wisdom*," in Teule and Tauwinkl, *The Syriac Renaissance*, 135–50.
22. Quoted from G. Schwarb, "Excursus III: The Coptic and Syriac Receptions of Neo-Ashʿarite Theology," in S. Schmitdke (ed.), *The Oxford Handbook of Islamic Theology* (Oxford: 2016), 550.
23. Quoted from El Cheikh, *Byzantium Viewed by the Arabs*, 104.
24. D. Gutas, A. Kaldellis, and B. Long, "Intellectual Exchanges with the Islamic World," in A. Kaldellis and N. Siniossoglou (eds), *The Cambridge Intellectual History of Byzantium* (Cambridge: 2017), 79–98, at 95.

17. Do the Math: Science in the Palaiologan Renaissance

1. See P. Magdalino, "The Road to Baghdad in the Thought World of Ninth-Century Byzantium," in L. Brubaker (ed.), *Bzyantium in the Ninth Century: Dead or Alive?* (Aldershot: 1998), 195–214.
2. P. Bouras-Vallianatos, "Galen's Reception in Byzantium: Symeon Seth and his Refutation of Galenic Theories on Human Physiology," *Greek, Roman, and Byzantine Studies* 55 (2015), 431–69. In what follows I draw on the contributions in part 3 of A. Kaldellis and N. Siniossoglou (eds), *The Cambridge Intellectual History of Byzantium* (Cambridge: 2017), which covers numerous scientific disciplines.
3. See on this period S. Runciman, *The Last Byzantine Renaissance* (Cambridge: 1970); C. N. Constantinides, *Higher Education in Byzantium in the Thirteenth and Early Fourteenth Centuries (1204–ca. 1310)* (Nicosia: 1982); I. Ševčenko, "The Palaeologan Renaissance," in W. Treadgold (ed.), *Renaissances Before the Renaissance: Cultural Revivals of Late Antiquity and*

the Middle Ages (Stanford, CA: 1984), 144–71; E. Fryde, *The Early Palaeologan Renaissance (1261–c.1360)* (Leiden 2000).

4. B. Bydén, *Theodore Metochites' Stoicheiosis astronomike and the Study of Natural Philosophy and Mathematics in Early Palaiologan Byzantium* (Göteborg: 2003), 239.
5. Constantinides, *Higher Education*, 20.
6. P. Golitsis, "Nicéphore Blemmyde lecteur du Commentaire de Simplicius à la *Physique* d'Aristote," in C. D'Ancona Costa (ed.), *The Libraries of the Neoplatonists* (Leiden: 2007), 243–56. Blemmydes' project may be compared to that discussed in M. Trizio, "Ancient Physics in the Mid-Byzantine Period: The Epitome of Theodore of Smyrna, Consul of the Philosopher under Alexios I Komnenos (1081–1118)," *Bulletin de philosophie médiévale* 53 (2012), 77–99.
7. Bydén, *Theodore Metochites' Stoicheiosis astronomike*, 40 n. 1, quoting George of Cyprus.
8. Constantinides, *Higher Education*, 44, 140. For her role in the transmission of Simplicius see D. Harlfinger, "Einige Aspekte der handschriftlichen Überlieferung des Physikkommentars des Simplikios," in I. Hadot (ed.), *Simplicius, sa vie, son œuvre, sa survie* (Berlin: 1987), 267–86.
9. S. Lazaris, *A Companion to Byzantine Science* (Leiden: 2020), 63.
10. B. Bydén, "'To Every Argument there is a Counter-Argument': Theodore Metochites' Defence of Scepticism (*Semeiosis* 61)," in K. Ierodiakonou (ed.), *Byzantine Philosophy and Its Ancient Sources* (Oxford: 2002), 183–208.
11. Fryde, *The Early Palaeologan Renaissance*, 185.
12. On the dispute see I. Ševčenko, *La vie intellectuelle et politique à Byzance sous les premieres Paléologues: études sur la polémique entre Théodore Métochite et Nicéphore Choumnos* (Brussels: 1962). On Choumnos see J. Verpeaux, *Nicéphore Choumnos, homme d'état et humaniste byzantin ca 1250/1255–1327* (Paris: 1959).
13. Fryde, *The Early Palaeologan Renaissance*, 325.
14. B. Bydén, "The Criticism of Aristotle in Nikephoros Gregoras' *Florentius*," in D. Searby et al. (eds), *ΔΩΡΟΝ ΡΟΔΟΠΟΙΚΙΛΟΝ: Studies in Honour of Jan Olof Rosenqvist* (Uppsala: 2012), 107–22.
15. For Theodore of Smyrna's earlier rejection of the need for pre-existing matter see Trizio, "Ancient Physics," 90–1.
16. On this dispute see Bydén, *Theodore Metochites' Stoicheiosis astronomike*, 133–41.
17. Bydén, *Theodore Metochites' Stoicheiosis astronomike*, 219–20.
18. P. Golitsis, "A Byzantine Philosopher's Devoutness Toward God: George Pachymeres' Poetic Epilogue to his Commentary on Aristotle's *Physics*," in K. Ierodiakonou and B. Bydén (eds), *The Many Faces of Byzantine Philosophy* (Athens: 2012), 109–27. See also on him P. Golitsis, "Georges Pachymère comme didascale: essai pour une reconstitution de sa carrière et de son enseignement philosophique," *Jahrbuch der österreichischen Byzantinistik* 58 (2008), 53–68.
19. D. Harlfinger, "Aristoteles aus dritter Hand: die Parekbolai aus der *Philosophia* des Georgios Pachymeres," *Parekbolai* 1 (2011), 171–86.

18. Through His Works You Shall Know Him: Palamas and Hesychasm

1. The chapter on Metochites in E. Fryde, *The Early Palaeologan Renaissance (1261–c. 1360)* (Leiden: 2000) includes reproductions of these images.
2. Or at least this is suggested by J. A. McGuckin, "Symeon the New Theologian (d. 1022) and Byzantine Monasticism," in A. Bryer and M. Cunningham (eds), *Mount Athos and Byzantine Monasticism* (Aldershot: 1996), 17–35, at 23. On him see also H. Alfeyev, *St. Symeon the New Theologian and Orthodox Tradition* (Oxford: 2000).
3. On this see Alfeyev, *St. Symeon the New Theologian*, 157–61.
4. Quoted at Alfeyev, *St. Symeon the New Theologian*, 40.
5. For texts associated with this community see R. P. H. Greenfield and A.-M. Talbot (eds and trans.), *Holy Men of Mt Athos* (Cambridge, MA: 2016).
6. For a detailed historical treatment of the debate see J. Meyendorff, *A Study of Gregory Palamas*, trans. G. Lawrence (Leighton Buzzard: 1974). For the early phase see Meyendorff's "Les débuts de la controverse Hésychaste" which is the first article collected in J. Meyendorff, *Byzantine Hesychasm: Historical, Theological, and Social Problems* (London: 1974); for the phase involving Akindynos see J. Nadal Cañellas, *La résistance d'Akindynos à Grégoire Palamas*, 2 vols (Leuven: 2002). A brief overview can be found in N. Russell, "The Hesychast Controversy," in A. Kaldellis and N. Siniossoglou (eds), *The Cambridge Intellectual History of Byzantium* (Cambridge: 2017), 494–508.
7. For this aspect of the debate see K. Ierodiakonou, "The Anti-Logical Movement in the Fourteenth Century," in K. Ierodiakonou (ed.), *Byzantine Philosophy and Its Ancient Sources* (Oxford: 2002), 219–36.
8. For the background see N. Russell, *The Doctrine of Deification in the Greek Patristic Tradition* (Oxford: 2004) and T. T. Tollefson, *Activity and Participation in Late Antique and Early Christian Thought* (Oxford: 2012).
9. See further *A History of Philosophy Without Any Gaps: Philosophy in the Hellenistic and Roman Worlds*, ch. 43.
10. For the relevance of Plotinus to the Cappadocians and Palamas see Tollefson, *Activity and Participation*, 48–9, 193.
11. In what follows I quote from two works of Palamas by section number: J. Meyendorff (trans.), *Gregory Palamas: The Triads* (Malwah, NJ: 1983); R. E. Sinkewicz (ed. and trans.), *Saint Gregory Palamas: The One Hundred and Fifty Chapters* (Toronto: 1988). Referred to respectively as *Triads* and *Chapters*.
12. Quoted from B. Bydén, *Theodore Metochites' Stoicheiosis astronomike and the Study of Natural Philosophy and Mathematics in Early Palaiologan Byzantium* (Göteborg: 2003), 5.
13. As pointed out by Meyendorff, *A Study of Gregory Palamas*, 128.
14. On this accusation see Tollefson, *Activity and Participation*, 194.
15. For this debate see A. N. Williams, *The Ground of Union: Deification in Aquinas and Palamas* (Cambridge: 1999), 39.
16. Meyendorff, *A Study of Gregory Palamas*, 224.
17. For the centrality of grace in the theory see Williams, *The Ground of Union*, 122.
18. D. Bradshaw, *Aristotle East and West: Metaphysics and the Division of Christendom* (Cambridge: 2004), 233.

19. As pointed out by R. E. Sinkewicz, "A New Interpretation for the First Episode in the Controversy," *Journal of Theological Studies* NS 31 (1980), 489–500.

19. United We Fall: Latin Philosophy in Byzantium

1. For the topic in general see K. M. Setton, "The Byzantine Background to the Italian Renaissance," *Proceedings of the American Philosophical Society* 100 (1965), 1–76; D. J. Geanakoplos, *Byzantine East and Latin West: Two Worlds of Christendom in Middle Ages and Renaissance* (New York: 1966); J. D. Howard-Johnston (ed.), *Byzantium and the West: c.850–c.1200* (Amsterdam: 1988); K. N. Ciggaar, *Western Travelers to Constantinople. The West and Byzantium, 962–1204: Cultural and Political Relations* (Leiden: 1996); T. Kolbaba, *The Byzantine Lists: Errors of the Latins* (Urbana, IL: 2000); D. Searby (ed.), *Never the Twain Shall Meet? Latins and Greeks Learning from Each Other* (Berlin: 2017).
2. For the wider history of the split see H. Chadwick, *East and West: The Making of a Rift in the Church* (Oxford: 2003).
3. A. Bucossi, "The *Sacred Arsenal* by Andronikos Kammateros, a Forgotten Treasure," in A. Rigo and P. Ermilov (eds), *Byzantine Theologians: The Systematization of Their Own Doctrine and Their Perception of Foreign Doctrines* (Rome: 2009), 33–50.
4. T. Kolbaba, "Theological Debates with the West, 1054–1300," in A. Kaldellis and N. Siniossoglou (eds), *The Cambridge Intellectual History of Byzantium* (Cambridge: 2017), 479–93, at 493.
5. For a list of the translations see Appendix B.6, compiled by J. A. Demetracopolous, in R. Pasnau (ed.), *The Cambridge History of Medieval Philosophy*, 2 vols (Cambridge: 2010), vol. 2, 822–6.
6. W. O. Schmitt, "Lateinische Literatur in Byzanz: die Übersetzungen des Maximos Planudes und die moderne Forschung," *Jahrbuch der österreichischen byzantinischen Gesellschaft* (1968), 127–48; E. Fisher, "Planoudes, Holobolos, and the Motivation for Translation," *Greek, Roman, and Byzantine Studies* 43 (2002), 77–104.
7. R. Flogaus, "Inspiration—Exploitation—Distortion: The Use of St Augustine in the Hesychast Controversy," in G. H. Demacopoulos (ed.), *Orthodox Readings of Augustine* (New York: 2008), 63–80.
8. L. P. Schrenk, "Augustine's *De Trinitate* in Byzantine Skepticism," *Greek, Roman, and Byzantine Studies* 30 (1989), 451–6. I quote from the Greek text at 453; my translation. For doubts about the connection drawn by Schrenk and more on the reception of Augustine see M. Trizio, "Alcune osservazione sulla ricezione bizantina del De trinitate di Agostino," in Rigo and Ermilov, Byzantine Theologians, 143–68.
9. See M. Plested, *Orthodox Readings of Aquinas* (Oxford: 2012).
10. On them see N. Russell, "Palamism and the Circle of Demetrios Cydones" and A. Glycofrydi-Leontsini, "Demetrios Cydones as a Translator of Greek Texts," both in C. Dendrinos et al. (eds), *Porphyrogenita: Essays on the History and Literature of Byzantium and the Latin East in Honour of Julian Chrysostomides* (Aldershot: 2003), 153–74 and 175–85.
11. Plested, *Orthodox Readings of Aquinas*, 73.
12. Setton, "The Byzantine Background," 33–4.

13. Glycofrydi-Leontsini, "Demetrios Cydones as a Translator," 183–4.
14. See *A History of Philosophy Without Any Gaps: Medieval Philosophy*, ch. 48. For Demetrius' use of the idea see Russell, "Palamism and the Circle of Demetrios Cydones," 162.
15. Setton, "The Byzantine Background," 43.
16. I. Ševčenko, "The Decline of Byzantium Seen Through the Eyes of Its Intellectuals," *Dumbarton Oaks Papers* 15 (1961), 169–86, at 176.
17. As argued at length in Plested, *Orthodox Readings of Aquinas*, e.g. concerning John VI Kantakuzene, Theophanes of Nicaea, and Neilos Kabasilas (at 87, 91, 98).
18. A quotation from Joseph Bryennios, cited at Plested, *Orthodox Readings of Aquinas*, 121.
19. Plested, *Orthodox Readings of Aquinas*, 112–13.
20. For earlier background see K. Parry, "Fate, Free Choice, and Divine Providence from the Neoplatonists to John of Damascus," in A. Kaldellis and N. Siniossoglou (eds), *The Cambridge Intellectual History of Byzantium* (Cambridge: 2017), 341–60. For Blemmydes see W. Lackner, *Nikephoros Blemmydes: gegen die Vorherbestimmung der Todesstunde* (Athens: 1985) and, for the proposal that Latin scholasticism influenced him, J. A. Munitiz, "The Predetermination of Death: The Contribution of Anastasios of Sinai and Nikephoros Blemmydes to a Perennial Byzantine Problem," *Dumbarton Oaks Papers* 55 (2001), 9–20.
21. Ševčenko, "The Decline of Byzantium," 184.
22. M. C. Briel, "Freedom, Necessity, and the Laws of Nature in the Thought of Gennadios Scholarios," in A. Torrance and S. Paschalidis (eds), *Personhood in the Byzantine Christian Tradition: Early, Medieval, and Modern Perspectives* (London: 2018), 128–33.

20. Platonic Love: Gemistos Plethon

1. For these figures see *A History of Philosophy Without Any Gaps: Medieval Philosophy*, chs 10, 28, and 53.
2. On Scholarios see C. J. G. Turner, "The Career of George Gennadios Scholarios," *Byzantion* 39 (1969), 420–55; C. Livanos, *Greek Tradition and Latin Influence in the Work of George Scholarios: "Alone Against All of Europe"* (Piscataway, NJ: 2006); M.-H. Blanchet, *Georges-Gennadios Scholarios (vers 1400–vers 1472): un intellectuel orthodoxe face à la disparition de l'Empire byzantin* (Paris: 2008).
3. J. Monfasani, "Pletho's Date of Death and the Burning of his *Laws*," *Byzantinische Zeitschrift* 98 (2005), 459–63.
4. V. Hladký, *The Philosophy of Gemistos Plethon: Platonism in Late Byzantium, between Hellenism and Orthodoxy* (Aldershot: 2014), 252.
5. For a summary of the *Laws* and translations or summaries of other works by Plethon, see C. M. Woodhouse, *George Gemistos Plethon: The Last of the Hellenes* (Oxford: 1986). Other general studies include F. Masai, *Pléthon et le Platonisme de Mistra* (Paris: 1956); W. Blum and W. Seitter (eds), *Georgios Gemistos Plethon (1355–1452): Reformpolitiker, Philosoph, Verehrer der alten Götter* (Zurich: 2005); B. Tambrun, *Pléthon: le retour de Platon* (Paris: 2006); N. Siniossoglou, *Radical Platonism in Byzantium: Illumination and Utopia in Gemistos Plethon* (Cambridge: 2011); and Hladký, *The Philosophy of Gemistos Plethon*.

6. On Plethon's use of Proclus see S. Gersh, "George Gemistos Plethon," in S. Gersh (ed.), *Interpreting Proclus: From Antiquity to the Renaissance* (Cambridge: 2014), 216–25.
7. Cited from Woodhouse, *George Gemistos Plethon*, 168; see Siniossoglou, *Radical Platonism*, 128. The reliability of this report is dismissed by Hladký, *The Philosophy of Gemistos Plethon*, 230.
8. See J. Monfasani, "Pletho and the West: Greek Émigrés, Latin Scholasticism and Renaissance Humanism," in his *Greek Scholars between East and West in the Fifteenth Century* (Farnham: 2016), 1–16.
9. On his political thought see, in addition to the general works mentioned above, N. P. Peritore, "The Political Thought of Gemistos Plethon: A Renaissance Byzantine Reformer," *Polity* 10 (1977), 168–91; P. Garnsey, "Gemistus Plethon and Platonic Political Philosophy," in P. Rousseau and E. Papoutsakis (eds), *Transformations of Late Antiquity* (Aldershot: 2009), 327–40.
10. Peritore, "The Political Thought," 180. Peritore also argues for the "nationalist" reading of Plethon I discuss in what follows, as does Siniossoglou, *Radical Platonism*, 334. For doubts about this reading see Hladký, *The Philosophy of Gemistos Plethon*, 13.
11. See the summary at Woodhouse, *George Gemistos Plethon*, 332–4.
12. Translated in Woodhouse, *George Gemistos Plethon*, 192–214. For a new edition and annotated translation of the first sections see B. Bydén, "George Gemistos (Plethon), *On Aristotle's Departures from Plato* 0–19," in B. Bydén and C. T. Thörnqvist (eds), *The Aristotelian Tradition: Aristotle's Works on Logic and Metaphysics and Their Reception in the Middle Ages* (Toronto: 2017), 267–344. On this work and Scholarios' reply see also G. Karamanolis, "Plethon and Scholarios on Aristotle," in K. Ierodiakonou (ed.), *Byzantine Philosophy and Its Ancient Sources* (Oxford: 2002), 253–82.
13. As reported by Simplicius; the relevant text is translated in R. Sorabji, *The Philosophy of the Commentators, 200–600 AD: A Sourcebook*, 3 vols (Ithaca, NY: 2005), vol. 2, §8c.
14. G. Steiris, "Pletho, Scholarios and Arabic Philosophy," in D. Searby (ed.), *Never the Twain Shall Meet? Latins and Greeks Learning from Each Other* (Berlin: 2017), 309–34.
15. Karamanolis, "Plethon and Scholarios," 268.
16. Translated in Woodhouse, *George Gemistos Plethon*, 24–5.
17. Siniossoglou, *Radical Platonism*; Hladký, *The Philosophy of Gemistos Plethon*.
18. As suggested by Woodhouse, *George Gemistos Plethon*, 362.

21. Istanbul (Not Constantinople): The Later Orthodox Tradition

1. D. R. Reinsch, "Kritobulos of Imbros: Learned Historian, Ottoman *Raya* and Byzantine Patriot," *Recueil des travaux de l'Institut d'études byzantines* 40 (2003), 297–308.
2. See on him J. Monfasani, *George Amiroutzes: The Philosopher and his Tractates* (Leuven: 2011).
3. Quoted in P. Guran, "Genesis and Function of the 'Last Emperor' Myth in Byzantine Eschatology," *Bizantinistica* 8 (2006), 273–303, at 280. See further P. J. Alexander, *The Byzantine Apocalyptic Tradition* (Berkeley: 1985), P. Magdalino, "The End of Time in Byzantium," in W. Brandes and F. Schmieder (eds), *Endzeiten: Eschatologie in den monotheistischen Weltreligionen* (Berlin: 2008), 119–33.

4. G. Podskalsky, *Griechische Theologie in der Zeit der Türkenherrschaft* (Munich: 1988), 47. For the period in question see also S. Runciman, *The Great Church in Captivity* (Cambridge: 1968); A. E. Vacalopoulos, *The Greek Nation, 1453–1669* (New Brunswick, NJ: 1976).
5. Podskalsky, *Griechische Theologie*, 106–16.
6. Podskalsky, *Griechische Theologie*, 172.
7. For the figures named in this paragraph see Podskalsky, *Griechische Theologie*, 213, 219, 183, 312–16.
8. For them see Podskalsky, *Griechische Theologie*, 49, 191ff, and for Athanasius also D. J. O'Meara, "The Philosophical Writings, Sources, and Thought of Athanasius Rhetor (ca.1571–1663)," *Proceedings of the American Philosophical Society* 121 (1977), 483–99.
9. R. Demos, "The Neo-Hellenic Enlightenment (1750–1821)," *Journal of the History of Ideas* 19 (1958), 523–41, at 531.
10. O'Meara, "The Philosophical Writings," 496.
11. A. S. Horton, "Jefferson and Korais: The American Revolution and the Greek Constitution," *Comparative Literature Studies* 13 (1976), 323–29; P. Kitromelides, *Adamantios Korais and the European Enlightenment* (Oxford: 2010).
12. Demos, "The Neo-Hellenic Enlightenment," 536–9.
13. For what follows see Podskalsky, *Griechische Theologie*, 89–96, 41, and 259–61.
14. For Nil Sorksii and Neagoe Basarab see the relevant chapters of A. Casiday (ed.), *The Orthodox Christian World* (London: 2012). For Sorskii's works see G. A. Maloney, *Nil Sorsky: The Authentic Writings* (Kalamazoo, MI: 2008).
15. For the Western debate see *A History of Philosophy Without Any Gaps: Medieval Philosophy*, ch. 31.
16. Podskalsky, *Griechische Theologie*, 64–5.
17. The importance of this work is emphasized in A. Louth, *Modern Orthodox Thinkers: From the Philokalia to the Present* (Downers Grove, IL: 2015), which provides a good introduction to the figures discussed in the remainder of this chapter. See further G. E. H. Palmer et al. (eds and trans.), *The Philokalia: The Complete Text* (London: 1979–95); K. Ware, "St Nikodemos and the *Philokalia*," in D. Conomos and G. Speake (eds), *Mount Athos the Sacred Bridge: The Spirituality of the Holy Mountain* (Bern: 2005), 69–121; B. Bingaman and B. Nassif (eds), *The Philokalia: A Classic Text of Orthodox Spirituality* (Oxford: 2012).
18. Louth, *Modern Orthodox Thinkers*, 36–8.
19. Louth, *Modern Orthodox Thinkers*, 39–40 and E. Freeman, "Flesh and Spirit: Divergent Orthodox Readings of the Iconic Body in Byzantium and the Twentieth Century," in A. Torrance and S. Paschalidis (eds), *Personhood in the Byzantine Christian Tradition: Early, Medieval, and Modern Perspectives* (London: 2018), 137–60, at 145–6.
20. Quoted in A. Louth, "The Patristic Revival and its Protagonists," in M. B. Cunningham and E. Theokritoff (eds), *The Cambridge Guide to Orthodox Christian Theology* (Cambridge: 2008), 188–202, at 196.
21. Quoted from D. P. Payne, *The Revival of Political Hesychasm in Contemporary Orthodox Thought: The Political Hesychasm of John S. Romanides and Christos Yannaras* (Lanham, MD: 2011), 175.
22. For him I have drawn especially on Payne, *The Revival of Political Hesychasm* and A. Andreopoulos (ed.), *Christos Yannaras: Philosophy, Theology, Culture* (London: 2019). Works by Yannaras in English translation include *The Freedom of Morality* (Crestwood,

NY: 1984), *On the Absence and Unknowability of God* (London: 2005), *On the Absence and Unknowability of God* (London: 2005), *Orthodoxy and the West* (Brookline, MA: 2006), and *Person and Eros* (Brookline, MA: 2007).

23. Quoted from S. Mitralexis, "On the Early Development of Christos Yannaras's Political Theology," in Andreopoulos, *Christos Yannaras*, 105–24, at 116.
24. See *A History of Philosophy Without Any Gaps: Philosophy in the Islamic World*, ch. 62.

22. Old News: The Italian Renaissance

1. For translation from both Arabic and Greek into Latin see *A History of Philosophy Without Any Gaps: Medieval Philosophy*, ch. 20.
2. For this topic see P. F. Grendler, *Schooling in Renaissance Italy: Literacy and Learning, 1300–1600* (Baltimore: 1989).
3. Quoted at Grendler, *Schooling in Renaissance Italy*, 118, and 76 for the following information about Machiavelli's early schooling.
4. As pointed out at J. M. Najemy, *Italy in the Age of the Renaissance* (Oxford: 2004), 10. On the *popolo* see the contribution of Andrea Zorzi to the same volume.
5. For details see Grendler, *Schooling in Renaissance Italy*, 69.
6. For a survey broken down by ancient author, see J. Hankins and A. Palmer, *The Recovery of Ancient Philosophy in the Renaissance: A Brief Guide* (Florence: 2008).
7. The line appears in his *On Ignorance*; translation taken from J. Haskins (ed.), *Cambridge Companion to Renaissance Philosophy* (Cambridge: 2007), 41.
8. Hankins and Palmer, *The Recovery of Ancient Philosophy*, 20.
9. See J. Kraye (ed.), *Cambridge Companion to Renaissance Humanism* (Cambridge: 1996), 149.

23. Greeks Bearing Gifts: Byzantine Scholars in Italy

1. For the story see J. Monfasani, *George of Trebizond: A Biography and a Study of his Rhetoric and Logic* (Leiden: 1976), 109–11. For more material on him see also J. Monfasani, *Collectantea Trapezuntiana: Texts, Documents, and Bibliographies of George of Trebizond* (Binghamton, NY: 1984).
2. For Bessarion's role in Byzantine politics see S. Ronchey, "L'ultimo bizantino: Bessarione e gli ultimi regnanti di Bisanzio," in G. Benzoni (ed.), *L'eredità greca e l'ellenismo veneziano* (Florence: 2002), 75–92.
3. See J. Monfasani, *Greeks and Latins in Renaissance Italy: Studies on Humanism and Philosophy in the 15th Century* (Aldershot: 2004), §1, and for the wider context F. Ciccolella, *Donati graeci: Learning Greek in the Renaissance* (Leiden: 2008); D. J. Geanaloplos, *Greek Scholars in Venice: Studies in the Dissemination of Greek Learning from Byzantium to Western Europe* (Cambridge, MA: 1962), M. S. Brownlee and D. H. Gondicas (eds), *Renaissance Encounters: Greek East and Latin West* (Leiden: 2013); H. Lamers, *Greece Reinvented: Transformations of Byzantine Hellenism in Renaissance Italy* (Leiden: 2015).
4. Quoted in J. Hankins, *Plato in the Italian Renaissance*, 2 vols (Leiden: 1990), vol. 1, 29.

5. Angelo Decembrio, quoted at C. S. Celenza, *The Intellectual World of the Italian Renaissance: Language, Philosophy, and the Search for Meaning* (Cambridge: 2017), 235–6.
6. J. Monfasani, "Bessarion Latinus," *Rinascimento* 21 (1981), 165–209, comments that poor Bessarion "found himself forced into the role of the public man with grand literary pretensions, who needed . . . a ghost writer to revise the style of his speeches" (181). In this piece Monfasani also queries the accuracy of the tag given to Bessarion by Valla, finding that the latter actually called him "most Greek of the Greeks and most Latin of the Latins."
7. Monfasani, *George of Trebizond*, 13; H. S. Wilson, "George of Trebizond and Early Humanist Rhetoric," *Studies in Philology* 40 (1943), 367–79, at 372 n. 23.
8. Monfasani, *George of Trebizond*, 19, 258.
9. Monfasani, *George of Trebizond*, 158–9.
10. J. Hankins, "George of Trebizond, Renaissance Libertarian?," in A. Frazier and P. Nold (eds), *Essays in Renaissance Thought and Letters in Honor of John Monfasani* (Leiden: 2015), 87–106.
11. Quoted from Hankins, "George of Trebizond," 103.
12. On whom see L. Mohler, *Kardinal Bessarion als Theologe, Humanist und Staatsmann*, 3 vols (Paderborn: 1923), G. Fiaccadori (ed.), *Bessarione e l'Umanesimo* (Naples: 1994), C. Bianca, *Da Bisanzio a Roma: studi sul cardinale Bessarione* (Rome: 1999), G. L. Coluccia, *Basilio Bessarione: lo spirito greco e l'occidente* (Florence: 2009), C. Märtl, C. Kaiser, and T. Ricklin (eds), *Inter graecos latinissimus, inter latinos graecissimus: Bessarion zwischen den Kulturen* (Berlin: 2013).
13. On this aspect of the controversy see C. Kaiser, "Leben und Lieben des 'göttlichen Platon' zwischen Byzanz und Italien im Quattrocento," in Märtl et al., *Inter graecos latinissimus*, 391–437.
14. On his early years see B. Tambrun-Krasker, "Bessarion, de Trébizonde à Mistra, un parcours intellectuel," in Märtl et al., *Inter graecos latinissimus*, 1–35.
15. C. L. Joost-Gaugier, *Pythagoras and Renaissance Europe: Finding Heaven* (Cambridge: 2009), 69.
16. For this see S. Mariev et al. (ed. and trans.), *Bessarion: über Natur und Kunst* (Hamburg: 2015), with discussions of the treatise in E. Del Soldato, "Platone, Aristotele e il cardinale: il *De natura et arte* di Bessarione," *Rinascimento* 2nd ser. 48 (2009), 61–9, S. Mariev, "Der Traktat *De nature et arte* des Kardinals Bessarion," in Märtl et al., *Inter graecos latinissimus*, 368–89.
17. Monfasani, *Greeks and Latins*, §IV, 281; see §VI for Theodore's translations.
18. J. W. Taylor (ed. and trans.), *Theodore Gaza's De fato* (Toronto: 1925).
19. P. F. Grendler, *The Universities of the Italian Renaissance* (Baltimore: 2002), 220.
20. For references on Argyropoulos see A. Field, *The Origins of the Platonic Academy of Florence* (Princeton: 1988), 56 n. 5.
21. Monfasani, *Greeks and Latins*, §V.
22. My thanks to Okihito Utamura for his advice on this chapter.

24. Republic of Letters: Italian Humanism

1. On him see R. G. Witt, *Hercules at the Crossroads: The Life, Works, and Thought of Coluccio Salutati* (Durham, NC: 1983).

2. As pointed out by R. G. Witt, *"In the Footsteps of the Ancients": The Origins of Humanism from Lovato to Bruni* (Leiden: 2001), 303.
3. See *A History of Philosophy Without Any Gaps: Medieval Philosophy*, ch. 78.
4. See A. Mazzocco, "Petrarch: Founder of Renaissance Humanism?," in A. Mazzocco (ed.), *Interpretations of Renaissance Humanism* (Leiden: 2006), 215–42.
5. Translated in G. Griffiths et al. (trans.), *The Humanism of Leonardo Bruni* (Binghamton, NY: 1987), cited by page number. For the genre in this period see D. Marsh, *The Quattrocento Dialogue: Classical Tradition and Humanist Innovation* (Cambridge, MA: 1980).
6. For the importance of Malpaghini see Witt, *"In the Footsteps of the Ancients"*, 340–44.
7. For a classic reading emphasizing the political context, see H. Baron, *The Crisis of the Early Italian Renaissance* (Princeton: 1966). Baron's interpretation turned on the idea that the two parts of the dialogue might have been written separately, but this is now widely rejected. See further D. Quint, "Humanism and Modernity: A Reconsideration of Bruni's Dialogues," *Renaissance Quarterly* 38 (1985), 423–45; L. B. Mortensen, "Leonardo Bruni's *Dialogus*: A Ciceronian Debate on the Literary Culture of Florence," *Classica et mediaevalia* 37 (1986), 259–302; C. Quillen, "The Uses of the Past in Quattrocento Florence: A Reading of Leonardo Bruni's Dialogues," *Journal of the History of Ideas* 71 (2010), 363–85.
8. See *A History of Philosophy Without Any Gaps: Medieval Philosophy*, ch. 55.
9. C. S. Celenza, *The Intellectual World of the Italian Renaissance: Language, Philosophy, and the Search for Meaning* (Cambridge: 2017), 62–4.
10. *The Humanism of Leonardo Bruni*, 116–17.
11. M. King, *Venetian Humanism in an Age of Patrician Dominance* (Princeton: 1986).
12. J. M. Najemy, *Italy in the Age of the Renaissance* (Oxford: 2004), 173.
13. Not "who."
14. Quoted by J. E. Siegel, *Rhetoric and Philosophy in Renaissance Humanism: The Union of Eloquence and Wisdom, Petrarch to Valla* (Princeton: 1968), 79.
15. *The Humanism of Leonardo Bruni*, 240–51.
16. Quoted by R. Fubini, *Humanism and Secularization from Petrarch to Valla*, trans. M. King (Durham, NC: 2003), 24 and 34. See further A. Rizzi and E. del Soldato, "Latin and Vernacular in Quattrocento Florence and Beyond: An Introduction," *I Tatti Studies in the Italian Renaissance* 16 (2013), 231–42.
17. See Celenza, *The Intellectual World of the Italian Renaissance*, chs 5–6.
18. Fubini, *Humanism and Secularization*, 27.
19. Celenza, *The Intellectual World of the Italian Renaissance*, 179.
20. Quoted by Siegel, *Rhetoric and Philosophy in Renaissance Humanism*, 108.
21. Witt, *"In the Footsteps of the Ancients"*, 400.
22. Celenza, *The Intellectual World of the Italian Renaissance*, 72.
23. Siegel, *Rhetoric and Philosophy in Renaissance Humanism*, 128. For Bruni's take on the issue see *The Humanism of Leonardo Bruni*, 216.
24. Mortensen, "Leonardo Bruni's *Dialogus*," 297; Quillen, "The Uses of the Past," 369.
25. Quoted by Fubini, *Humanism and Secularization*, 109.
26. Quoted by Siegel, *Rhetoric and Philosophy in Renaissance Humanism*, 74.

25. Literary Criticism: Lorenzo Valla

1. For this and other details on his biography see P. Mack, *Renaissance Argument: Valla and Agricola in the Traditions of Rhetoric and Dialectic* (Leiden: 1993), 23–4.
2. On which see D. Marsh, "Grammar, Method, and Polemic in L. Valla's *Elegantiae*," *Rinascimento* 19 (1979), 91–116.
3. C. S. Celenza, "Lorenzo Valla's Radical Philology: The 'Preface' to the Annotations to the New Testament in Context," *Journal of Medieval and Early Modern Studies* 42 (2012), 365–94.
4. Cited by page from G. W. Bowersock (ed. and trans.), *Valla: On the Donation of Constantine* (Cambridge, MA: 2007).
5. S. I. Camporeale, *Christianity, Latinity, and Culture: Two Studies on Lorenzo Valla*, ed. and trans. P. Baker and C. S. Celenza (Leiden: 2014), 52.
6. As pointed out by R. Fubini, "Humanism and Truth: Valla Writes against the Donation of Constantine," *Journal of the History of Ideas* 57 (1996), 79–86.
7. For a translation of his encomium by P. Baker and further discussion see Camporeale, *Christianity, Latinity, and Culture*. For the reception of Aquinas in this period see also J. W. O'Malley, "Some Renaissance Panegyrics of Aquinas," *Renaissance Quarterly* 27 (1974), 174–92.
8. Translation in E. Cassirer, P. O. Kristeller, and J. H. Randall (eds), *Renaissance Philosophy of Man* (Chicago: 1948), 155–82.
9. C. S. Celenza, *The Intellectual World of the Italian Renaissance: Language, Philosophy, and the Search for Meaning* (Cambridge: 2017), 183.
10. Cited by book and chapter number from B. P. Copenhaver and L. Nauta (eds and trans.), *Lorenzo Valla: Dialectical Disputations*, 2 vols (Cambridge, MA: 2012), whose translation I also quote. For the aforementioned passages see §I.2 and §I.17. For studies see E. Kessler, "Die Transformation des aristotelischen Organon durch Lorenzo Valla," in E. Kessler (ed.), *Aristotelismus und Renaissance* (Wiesbaden: 1988), 53–74; P. Mack, *Renaissance Argument: Valla and Agricola in the Traditions of Rhetoric and Dialectic* (Leiden: 1993); M. Laffranchi, *Dialettica e filosofia in Lorenzo Valla* (Milan: 1999); L. Nauta, *In Defense of Common Sense: Lorenzo Valla's Humanist Critique of Scholastic Philosophy* (Cambridge, MA: 2009).
11. As argued by Nauta, *In Defense of Common Sense*, e.g. at 16–17, 93. For Ockham's view see *A History of Philosophy Without Any Gaps: Medieval Philosophy*, ch. 58, and ch. 25 for the following topic of transcendentals.
12. See Camporeale, *Christianity, Latinity, and Culture*, 192.
13. M. Roick, "Aristotelismus, Humanismus und die Kritik am habitus: Anmerkungen zu einer Geschichte der Haltung in der frühen Neuzeit," in F. A. Kurbacher and P. Wüschner (eds), *Was ist Haltung? Begriffsbestimmung, Positionen, Anschlüsse* (Würzburg: 2016), 25–39.
14. L. Nauta, "Lorenzo Valla's Critique of Aristotelian Psychology," *Vivarium* 41 (2003), 120–43.
15. For this see *A History of Philosophy Without Any Gaps: Medieval Philosophy*, ch. 61.
16. Mack, *Renaissance Argument*, 45.

26. Difficult to be Good: Humanist Ethics

1. Quoted by R. Fubini, *Humanism and Secularization from Petrarch to Valla*, trans. M. King (Durham, NC: 2003), 101.
2. Cited by page number from G. Griffiths et al. (trans.), *The Humanism of Leonardo Bruni* (Binghamton, NY: 1987); the remark about the superiority of moral philosophy is at 268.
3. See D. A. Lines, "The Commentary Literature on Aristotle's *Nicomachean Ethics* in Early Renaissance Italy: Preliminary Considerations," *Traditio* 54 (1999), 245–82, at 259 and 264.
4. L. Bianchi, "Renaissance Readings of the *Nicomachean Ethics*," in D. A. Lines and S. Ebbersmeyer (eds), *Rethinking Virtue, Reforming Society: New Directions in Renaissance Ethics, c.1350–c.1650* (Turnhout: 2013), 131–67.
5. See the dates given by D. A. Lines, "The Importance of Being Good: Moral Philosophy in the Italian Universities, 1300–1600," *Rinascimento* 36 (1996), 139–91, at 142. See more generally D. Lines, "Aristotle's Ethics in the Renaissance," in J. Miller (ed.), *The Reception of Aristotle's Ethics* (Cambridge: 2012), 171–93.
6. D. A. Lines, "Rethinking Renaissance Aristotelianism: Bernardo Segni's *Ethica*, the Florentine Academy, and the Vernacular in Sixteenth-Century Italy," *Renaissance Quarterly* 66 (2013), 824–65, at 833–4.
7. J. Kraye, "Eclectic Aristotelianism in the Moral Philosophy of Francesco Piccolomini," in G. Piaia (ed.), *La presenza dell'aristotelismo padovano nella filosofia della prima modernità* (Padua: 2002), 57–82; D. A. Lines, "Latin and Vernacular in Francesco Piccolomini's Moral Philosophy," in D. A. Lines and E. Refini (eds), *Aristotele fatto volgare: tradizione aristotelica e cultura volgare nel Rinascimento* (Pisa: 2014), 169–99.
8. Lines, "Bernardo Segni's *Ethica*," 833 and Lines, "Latin and Vernacular," 187.
9. L. Nauta, *In Defense of Common Sense: Lorenzo Valla's Humanist Critique of Scholastic Philosophy* (Cambridge, MA: 2009), ch. 5.
10. A. K. Hiett and M. Lorch (ed. and trans.), *Lorenzo Valla, On Pleasure: De voluptate (Of the True and the False Good)* (New York: 1977). See also M. P. Lorch, *A Defense of Life: Lorenzo Valla's Theory of Pleasure* (Munich: 1985).
11. As proposed by Lorch, *A Defense of Life*, 53.
12. On this see Lorch, *A Defense of Life*, 128, Fubini, *Humanism and Secularization*, 63.
13. B. Vickers, "Valla's Ambivalent Praise of Pleasure: Rhetoric in the Service of Christianity," *Viator* 17 (1986), 271–319.
14. Translation by L. Deitz in J. Kraye (ed.), *Cambridge Translations of Renaissance Philosophical Texts*, vol. 1: *Moral Philosophy* (Cambridge: 1997), 234–6.
15. For a useful summary see T. Kircher, *Living Well in Renaissance Italy: The Virtues of Humanism and the Irony of Leon Battista Alberti* (Tempe, AZ: 2012), 118–33.
16. See I. Kajanto, "Poggio Bracciolini's *De Infelicitate Principum* and its Classical Sources," *International Journal of the Classical Tradition* 1 (1994), 23–35.
17. German translation and Latin edition in K. Scheiner and E. Wenzel, *Hofkritik im Licht humanistischer Lebens- und Bildungsideale* (Leiden: 2012), cited by page from Latin.
18. For his life and ethical works see M. Roick, *Pontano's Virtues: Aristotelian Moral and Political Thought in the Renaissance* (London: 2017).

19. Quoted from G. Bull (trans.), *Baldesar Castiglione: Book of the Courtier* (London: 1976). For discussion see J. R. Woodhouse, *Baldesar Castiglione: A Reassessment of the Courtier* (Edinburgh: 1978), W. R. Albury, *Castiglione's Allegory: Veiled Policy in The Book of the Courtier (1528)* (Farnham: 2014).
20. For this point see Albury, *Castiglione's Allegory*, 149–52.

27. Chance Encounters: Reviving Hellenistic Philosophy

1. The story is told with much engaging detail in S. Greenblatt, *The Swerve: How the World Became Modern* (New York: 2012).
2. References to Poggio's letters are from P. W. G. Gordon (trans.), *Two Renaissance Book Hunters: The Letters of Poggius Bracciolini to Nicolaus de Niccolis* (New York: 1991).
3. A. Palmer, *Reading Lucretius in the Renaissance* (Cambridge, MA: 2014).
4. Palmer, *Reading Lucretius*, 43, and see 75 for more on Leto's annotations.
5. J. Kraye, "The Revival of Hellenistic Philosophies," in J. Haskins (ed.), *Cambridge Companion to Renaissance Philosophy* (Cambridge: 2007), 97–112, at 105.
6. Translated by M. Davies in J. Kraye (ed.), *Cambridge Translations of Renaissance Philosophical Texts*, vol. 1: *Moral Philosophy* (Cambridge: 1997), 238–44.
7. See *A History of Philosophy Without Any Gaps: Medieval Philosophy*, ch. 64.
8. Palmer, *Reading Lucretius*, 199.
9. For Ficino and Scala see A. Brown, *The Return of Lucretius to Renaissance Florence* (Cambridge, MA: 2010), ch. 2; on Ficino see further S. G. Passanante, *The Lucretian Renaissance: Philology and the Afterlife of Tradition* (Chicago: 2011), 69.
10. Brown, *The Return of Lucretius*, 62, and 52–3 for *Nil admirare*.
11. Palmer, *Reading Lucretius*, 82.
12. Quoted from Brown, *The Return of Lucretius*, 73.
13. T. Kircher, *Living Well in Renaissance Italy: The Virtues of Humanism and the Irony of Leon Battista Alberti* (Tempe, AZ: 2012), 161; see Brown, *The Return of Lucretius*, 8, for the provenance of the image.
14. M. Roick, *Pontano's Virtues: Aristotelian Moral and Political Thought in the Renaissance* (London: 2017), 144–5.
15. Cited by page number from D. Marsh (trans.), *Leon Battista Alberti: Dinner Pieces* (Binghamton, NY: 1987). See further Kircher, *Living Well in Renaissance Italy*, 168.
16. Kraye, "The Revival of Hellenistic Philosophies," 100.
17. N. Bignotto, "Skeptical Aspects of Francesco Guicciardini's Thought," in J. R. M. Neto et al. (eds), *Skepticism in the Modern Age* (Leiden: 2009), 107–21.
18. C. B. Schmitt, "The Rediscovery of Ancient Skepticism in Modern Times," in C. B. Schmitt, *Reappraisals in Renaissance Thought* (London: 1989), §XIII, at 230.
19. C. B. Schmitt, *Cicero Scepticus: A Study of the Influence of the Academica in the Renaissance* (The Hague: 1972).
20. G. M. Cao, "The Prehistory of Modern Skepticism: Sextus Empiricus in Fifteenth-Century Italy," *Journal of the Warburg and Courtauld Institutes* 64 (2000), 229–79, at 263.
21. As noted by Passanante, *The Lucretian Renaissance*, 61.

22. Quoted from G. M. Cao, *Scepticism and Orthodoxy: Gianfrancesco Pico as a Reader of Sextus Empiricus* (Pisa: 2007), 283.

28. We Built This City: Christine de Pizan

1. For overviews of her writings and biography see C. Cannon Willard, *Christine de Pizan: Her Life and Works* (New York: 1984) and N. Margolis, *An Introduction to Christine de Pizan* (Gainesville, FL: 2011). For her attack on the misogyny of the *Romance of the Rose* see *A History of Philosophy Without Any Gaps: Medieval Philosophy*, ch. 75.
2. For the latter see K. Green, C. J. Mews, and J. Pinder, *The Book of Peace by Christine de Pizan* (University Park, PA: 2008), cited by section in what follows. On her political thought see K. Langdon Forhan, *The Political Theory of Christine de Pizan* (Aldershot: 2002).
3. K. Langdon Forhan, *Christine de Pizan: Book of the Body Politic* (Cambridge: 1994), 54. See further K. Langdon Forhan, "Reflecting Heroes: Christine de Pizan and the Mirror Tradition," in M. Zimmermann and D. De Rentiis (eds), *The City of Scholars: New Approaches to Christine de Pizan* (Berlin: 1994), 189–96.
4. *Book of Peace*, §III.40, and §III.10 for the comparison to different breeds of animal.
5. See *A History of Philosophy Without Any Gaps: Medieval Philosophy*, ch. 40.
6. This is called a "stunning departure" from the previous just war tradition by Langdon Forhan, *The Political Theory*, 152.
7. *Book of the Body Politic*, 11.
8. *Book of Peace*, §III.48.
9. As pointed out by Langdon Forhan, *The Political Theory*, 108.
10. D. F. Hult (trans.), *Christine of Pizan et al.: Debate of the Romance of the Rose* (Chicago: 2010), 50.
11. This translation is taken from Langdon Forhan, *The Political Theory*, 13, but in general I cite from G. McLeod (trans.), *Christine de Pizan: Christine's Vision* (New York: 1993).
12. E. J. Richards (trans.), *Christine de Pizan: The Book of the City of Ladies* (New York: 1998). Cited by section number.

29. More Rare Than the Phoenix: Italian Women Humanists

1. On this genre see G. McClure, *Sorrow and Consolation in Italian Humanism* (Princeton: 1991).
2. For the social position of women, and the work of female authors, in this period see e.g. C. Jordan, *Renaissance Feminism: Literary Texts and Political Models* (Ithaca, NY: 1990); M. L. King, *Women of the Renaissance* (Chicago: 1991); M. Migiel and J. Schiesari (eds), *Refiguring Woman: Perspectives on Gender and the Italian Renaissance* (Ithaca, NY: 1991); P. J. Benson, *The Invention of Renaissance Woman: The Challenge of Female Independence in the Literature and Thought of Italy and England* (University Park, PA: 1992); R. Russell (ed.), *Italian Women Writers: A Bio-Bibliographical Sourcebook* (Westport, CT: 1994); V. Cox, "The Single

Self: Feminist Thought and the Marriage Market in Early Modern Venice," *Renaissance Quarterly* 48 (1995), 513–81; L. Panizza and S. Wood (eds), *A History of Women's Writing in Italy* (Cambridge: 2000).

3. I will cite in the main text from M. L. King and D. Robin (trans.), *Isotta Nogarola: Complete Writings. Letterbook, Dialogue on Adam and Eve, Orations* (Chicago: 2004); D. Robin (trans.), *Laura Cereta: Collected Letters of a Renaissance Feminist* (Chicago: 1997); and D. Robin (trans.), *Cassandra Fedele: Letters and Orations* (Chicago: 2000), referring to these volumes respectively as *Nogarola, Cereta,* and *Fedele.*
4. M. L. King, "Thwarted Ambitions: Six Learned Women of the Italian Renaissance," §VIII in M. L. King, *Humanism, Venice and Women: Essays on the Italian Renaissance* (Aldershot: 2005), at 296.
5. Quoted at King, "Thwarted Ambitions," 285.
6. As discussed by M. L. King, "The Religious Retreat of Isotta Nogarola (1418–1466): Sexism and Its Consequences in the Fifteenth Century," §IX in King, *Humanism.* For the problem in general see M. L. King, "Book-Lined Cells: Women and Humanism in the Early Italian Renaissance," which is §XI in the same volume.
7. As noted in Robin, *Cassandra Fedele,* 6.
8. The point has also been noted by Robin, *Laura Cereta,* 30, albeit without noting the change that comes in subsequent letters.

30. All About Eve: The Defense of Women

1. W. L. Gundersheimer, "Bartolommeo Goggio: A Feminist in Renaissance Ferrara," *Renaissance Quarterly* 33 (1980), 175–200.
2. A favorite of women authors, she is mentioned e.g. by Christine de Pizan, Isotta Nogarola, and Laura Cereta.
3. For this I have consulted P. Gothein (trans.), *Francesco Barbaro: Das Buch der Ehe (De re uxoria)* (Berlin: 1933), cited by section number. On him see also P. Gothein, *Francesco Barbaro: Früh-humanismus und Staatskunst in Venedig* (Berlin: 1932). For a second, related work by Barbaro, see M. L. King (trans.), *Francesco Barbaro: The Wealth of Wives. A Fifteenth-Century Marriage Manual* (Toronto: 2015).
4. Quoted by M. L. King, *Women of the Renaissance* (Chicago: 1991), 37.
5. M. L. King, *Humanism, Venice and Women: Essays on the Italian Renaissance* (Aldershot: 2005), §VIII, at 289–90.
6. For Aristotle's and Plato's views on women see *A History of Philosophy Without Any Gaps: Classical Philosophy,* chs 21, 40, 42.
7. Again cited by page number from G. Bull (trans.), *Baldesar Castiglione: Book of the Courtier* (London: 1976).
8. It should be mentioned that other male authors also defended the female sex, e.g. Mario Equicola, Galeazzo Flavio Capra, and, most famous, Henricus Cornelius Agrippa, whose *The Nobility and Preeminence of the Female Sex,* trans. A. Rabil Jr. (Chicago: 1996), was known in Italy in the middle of the sixteenth century.

9. Cited by page from M. L. King and D. Robin (trans.), *Isotta Nogarola: Complete Writings. Letterbook, Dialogue on Adam and Eve, Orations* (Chicago: 2004).
10. Cited by page from V. Cox (trans.), *Moderata Fonte: The Worth of Women* (Chicago: 1997); Adam and Eve are discussed at 94. On Fonte see B. Collina, "Moderata Fonte e *Il merito delle donne*," *Annali d'Italianistica* 7 (1989), 142–64; P. Malpezzi Price, "A Woman's Discourse in the Italian Renaissance: Moderata Fonte's *Il merito delle donne*," *Annali d'italianistica* 7 (1989), 165–81.
11. Cited by page from A. Dunhill (trans.), *Lucrezia Marinella: The Nobility and the Excellence of Women and the Defects of Men* (Chicago: 1999). See further A. Chemello, "La donna, il modello, l'immaginario: Moderata Fonte e Lucrezia Marinella," in M. Zancan (ed.), *Nel cerchio della luna: figure di donna in alcuni testi del XVI secolo* (Venice: 1983), 59–170; S. D. Kolsky, "Moderata Fonte, Lucrezia Marinella, Giuseppe Passi: An Early Seventeenth-Century Feminist Controversy," *Modern Language Review* 96 (2001), 973–89.
12. On this see M. Deslauriers, "Marinella and Her Interlocutors: Hot Blood, Hot Words, Hot Deeds," *Philosophical Studies* 174 (2017), 2525–37.

31. I'd Like to Thank the Academy: Florentine Platonism

1. For a lively account of these events see C. Hibbert, *The House of Medici: Its Rise and Fall* (New York: 1980), ch. 10.
2. A. M. Brown, "Platonism in Fifteenth-Century Florence and Its Contribution to Early Modern Political Thought," *Journal of Modern History* 58 (1986), 383–413. For the patronage issue see also J. Hankins, "Lorenzo de' Medici as Patron of Philosophy," *Rinascimento* 34 (1994) 15–53, and J. Kraye, "Lorenzo and the Philosophers," in M. Mallett and N. Mann (eds), *Lorenzo the Magnificent* (London: 1996), 151–66.
3. J. Hankins, *Plato in the Italian Renaissance*, 2 vols (Leiden: 1990), 75; Brown, "Platonism in Fifteenth-Century Florence," 393 and 395.
4. Hankins, *Plato in the Italian Renaissance*, 105–9.
5. On this institution see J. Davies, *Florence and Its University During the Early Renaissance* (Leiden: 1998).
6. For this debate see E. Garin, *La cultura filosofica del Rinascimento italiano* (Florence: 1961) and the response by A. Field, *The Origins of the Platonic Academy of Florence* (Princeton: 1988).
7. Field, *The Origins of the Platonic Academy*, 231.
8. Field, *The Origins of the Platonic Academy*, 242.
9. References to *Lamia* are by section number from C. S. Celenza, *Angelo Poliziano's Lamia: Text, Translation, and Introductory Studies* (Leiden: 2010).
10. See A. Scaglione, "The Humanist as Scholar and Politian's Conception of the Grammaticus," *Studies in the Renaissance* 8 (1961), 49–70.
11. Celenza, *Angelo Poliziano's Lamia*, 41.
12. For a list of the texts he lectured on, moving from literary works like Virgil, Juvenal, and Homer to Aristotle, see P. F. Grendler, *The Universities of the Italian Renaissance* (Baltimore: 2002), 238.
13. I apologize to Poliziano for the previous note.

14. P. Godman, *From Poliziano to Machiavelli: Florentine Humanism in the High Renaissance* (Princeton: 1998), 125–8. On Scala see further A. M. Brown, *Bartolomeo Scala, 1430–1497, Chancellor of Florence: The Humanist as Bureaucrat* (Princeton: 1979).
15. Godman, *From Poliziano to Machiavelli, 113.*
16. A. Grafton, "On the Scholarship of Politian and Its Context," *Journal of the Warburg and Courtauld Institutes* 40 (1977), 150–88, at 155.
17. Godman, *From Poliziano to Machiavelli*, 61.
18. Grafton, "On the Scholarship of Politian," 164.
19. Field, *The Origins of the Platonic Academy*, 129.
20. See the remarks of Denis Robichaud in Celenza, *Angelo Poliziano's Lamia*, 152, 164.
21. Hankins, *Plato in the Italian Renaissance*, 339. For Ficino's approach to the characters in the dialogues see D. J. Robichaud, *Plato's Persona: Marsilio Ficino, Renaissance Humanism, and Platonic Traditions* (Philadelphia: 2018).
22. J. Hankins, "Cosimo de' Medici and the 'Platonic Academy,'" *Journal of the Warburg and Courtauld Institutes* 53 (1990), 144–62, and "The Myth of the Platonic Academy of Florence," *Renaissance Quarterly* 44 (1991), 429–75.
23. For an example from Poliziano see Godman, *From Poliziano to Machiavelli*, 18.
24. Godman, *From Poliziano to Machiavelli*, 12.

32. Footnotes to Plato: Marsilio Ficino

1. Quoted in D. Benesch, *Marsilio Ficino's De triplici vita* (Frankfurt a.M.: 1977), 8.
2. For the role of Christian theology in his works see several of the papers collected in M. J. B. Allen and V. Rees (eds), *Marsilio Ficino: His Theology, His Philosophy, His Legacy* (Leiden: 2002), and M. J. B. Allen, *Plato's Third Eye: Studies in Marsilio Ficino's Metaphysics and its Sources* (Aldershot: 1995), §IX.
3. M. J. B. Allen, *Studies in the Neoplatonism of Marsilio Ficino and Giovanni Pico* (Abington: 2017), 212.
4. See P. O. Kristeller, *The Philosophy of Marsilio Ficino*, trans. V. Conant (Gloucester, MA: 1964), 108, and for Allen's critique see *Plato's Third Eye*, §VIII. For more on Ficino's use of Plotinus see S. Gersh, "Marsilio Ficino as Commentator on Plotinus: Some Case Studies," in S. Gersh (ed.), *Plotinus' Legacy: The Transformation of Plotinus from the Renaissance to the Modern Era* (Cambridge: 2019), 19–43.
5. M. J. B. Allen (trans.) and J. Hankins (ed.), *Marsilio Ficino: Platonic Theology*, 6 vols (Cambridge, MA: 2001–6), quoted by book and chapter number in the main text of this chapter. The quotation just above is at §3.2.
6. As pointed out by Jörg Lauster in *Marsilio Ficino: His Theology*, 50.
7. For the following see Allen, *Plato's Third Eye*, §I.
8. On medieval ideas about angels see *A History of Philosophy Without Any Gaps: Medieval Philosophy*, ch. 70.
9. Studied by M. J. B. Allen, *The Platonism of Marsilio Ficino: A Study of his Phaedrus Commentary, its Sources and Genesis* (Berkeley: 1984); see also his *Marsilio Ficino and the Phaedran Charioteer: Introduction, Texts, Translations* (Berkeley: 1981).

10. Allen, *The Platonism of Marsilio Ficino*, 80.
11. See *A History of Philosophy Without Any Gaps: Medieval Philosophy*, ch. 42.
12. See Monfasani's piece in *Marsilio Ficino: His Theology*.
13. The same point had already been made by Plethon, giving a grudging compliment to Aristotle in order to highlight Averroes' even worse inadequacies. See C. M. Woodhouse, *George Gemistos Plethon: The Last of the Hellenes* (Oxford: 1986), 192.
14. See P. Blum, *Philosophy of Religion in the Renaissance* (Farnham: 2010), 116.
15. Allen, *The Platonism of Marsilio Ficino*, 131–2. See 116 for a chart of the equivalences.

33. True Romance: Theories of Love

1. T. W. Reeser, *Setting Plato Straight: Translating Ancient Sexuality in the Renaissance* (Chicago: 2016), 102–3.
2. Cited by book and chapter number from S. Jayne (trans.), *Marsilio Ficino's Commentary on Plato's Symposium* (Columbia, MO: 1944). On the commentary see S. Ebbersmeyer, *Sinnlichkeit und Vernunft: Studien zur Rezeption und Transformation der Liebestheorie Platons in der Renaissance* (Munich: 2002), ch. II.2; S. Glanzmann, *Der einsame Eros: eine Untersuchung des Symposion-Kommentars "De amore" von Marsilio Ficino* (Tübingen: 2006); and M. J. B. Allen, "Cosmogony and Love: The Role of Phaedrus in Ficino's *Symposium* Commentary," in M. J. B. Allen, *Plato's Third Eye: Studies in Marsilio Ficino's Metaphysics and Its Sources* (Aldershot: 1995).
3. See further D. A. Beecher and M. Ciavolella (eds), *Eros and Anteros: The Medical Traditions of Love in the Renaissance* (Ottawa: 1992), and on this aspect of Ficino's commentary, Glanzmann, *Der einsame Eros*, 52.
4. M. J. B. Allen, *The Platonism of Marsilio Ficino: A Study of his Phaedrus Commentary, Its Sources and Genesis* (Berkeley: 1984), 49.
5. See L. Westra, "Love and Beauty in Ficino and Plotinus," in K. Eisenbichler and O. Z. Pugliese (eds), *Ficino and Renaissance Neoplatonism* (Ottawa: 1986), 175–87, at 179.
6. Cited by section number from S. Jayne (trans.), *Pico della Mirandola: Commentary on a Canzone of Benivieni* (New York: 1984). On the treatise see M. J. B. Allen, "The Birth Day of Venus: Pico as Platonic Exegete in the *Commento* and the *Heptaplus*," in M. V. Dougherty, *Pico della Mirandola: New Essays* (Cambridge: 2008), 81–113.
7. On whom see S. Fellina, *Alla scuola di Marsilio Ficino: il pensiero filosofico di Francesco Cattani da Diacceto* (Pisa: 2017).
8. Cited by page number from R. B. Gottfried (trans.), *Pietro Bembo: Gli Asolani* (Bloomington, IN: 1954).
9. Cited from G. Bull (trans.), *Baldesar Castiglione: Book of the Courtier* (London: 1976). For Bembo and Castiglione see also Ebbersmeyer, *Sinnlichkeit und Vernunft*, ch. III.1.
10. W. R. Albury, *Castiglione's Allegory: Veiled Policy in The Book of the Courtier (1528)* (Farnham: 2014), 80.
11. Cited from R. Russell (trans.), *Tullia d'Aragona: Dialogue on the Infinity of Love* (Chicago: 1997).
12. See *A History of Philosophy Without Any Gaps: Medieval Philosophy*, ch. 44.

34. As Far as East from West: Jewish Philosophy in Renaissance Italy

1. Cited by page number from D. Bacich and R. Pescatori (trans.), *Leone Ebreo: Dialogues of Love* (Toronto: 2009).
2. This aspect of the text is explored by T. A. Perry, "Dialogue and Doctrine in Leone Ebreo's *Dialoghi d'amore*," *Modern Language Association* 88 (1973), 1173–9.
3. G. Veltri, *Renaissance Philosophy in Jewish Garb: Foundations and Challenges in Judaism on the Eve of Modernity* (Leiden: 2008), 7.
4. *A History of Philosophy Without Any Gaps: Philosophy in the Islamic World*, ch. 40.
5. R. Bonfil, *Jewish Life in Renaissance Italy* (Berkeley: 1994), 50. Other general studies include C. Roth, *The Jews in the Renaissance* (Philadelphia: 1959); M. A. Shulvass, *The Jews in the World of the Renaissance* (Leiden: 1973).
6. Bonfil, *Jewish Life*, 67.
7. I cite page numbers from D. Harrán, *Jewish Poet and Intellectual in Seventeenth-Century Venice: The Works of Sarra Copia Sulam in Verse and Prose* (Chicago: 2009). On Sulam see also U. Fortis, *La "bella ebrea": Sara Copio Sullam, poetessa nel ghetto di Venezia del '600* (Turin: 2003); G. Veltri, "Body of Conversion and Immortality of the Soul: Sara Copio Sullam, the 'Beautiful Jewess,'" in Veltri, *Renaissance Philosophy in Jewish Garb*, 226–47; L. L. Westwater, *Sarra Copia Sulam: A Jewish Salonnière and the Press in Counter-Reformation Venice* (Toronto: 2020).
8. On this question see B. Garvin, "The Language of Leone Ebreo's *Dialoghi d'Amore*," *Italia* 13–14 (2001), 181–201, and for the wider context A. M. Lesley, "The Place of the *Dialoghi d'amore* in Contemporaneous Jewish Thought," in K. Eisenbichler and O. Z. Pugliese (eds), *Ficino and Renaissance Neoplatonism* (Ottawa: 1986), 69–86.
9. D. Almagor et al., "A Complaint Against the Time," *Jewish Quarterly* (1992–3), 59.
10. Bonfil, *Jewish Life*, 149–51.
11. See *A History of Philosophy Without Any Gaps: Philosophy in the Islamic World*, ch. 36.
12. D. Geffen, "Insights into the Life and Thought of Elijah Medigo Based on his Published and Unpublished Works," *Proceedings of the American Academy for Jewish Research* 41–2 (1973–4), 69–86; S. Di Donato, "Traduttori di Averroè e traduzioni ebraico-latine nel dibattito filosofico del XV e XVI secolo," in G. Licata (ed.), *L'averroismo in età moderna* (Macerata: 2013), 25–49; M. Engel, *Elijah Del Medigo and Paduan Aristotelianism* (London: 2016).
13. Quoted by Michael Engel, "Elijah Del Medigo's Critique of the Paduan Thomists," *Medioevo* 38 (2013), 295–318, at 303.
14. C. Fraenkel, "Considering the Case of Elijah Delmedigo's Averroism and its Impact on Spinoza", in A. Akasoy and G. Giglioni (eds), *Renaissance Averroism and Its Aftermath: Arabic Philosophy in Early Modern Europe* (Dordrecht: 2013), 213–36.
15. Quoted by K. Bland, "Elijah Del Medigo: Unicity of the Intellect and Immortality of Soul," *Proceedings of the American Academy for Jewish Research* 61 (1995), 1–22, at 17.
16. K. Bland, "Elijah del Medigo's Averroist Response to the Kabbalas of Fifteenth Century Jewry," *Journal of Jewish Thought and Philosophy* 1 (1991), 23–53.
17. Bonfil, *Jewish Life*, 183.

18. E. Lawee, "Abravanel in Italy: The Critique of the Kabbalist Elijah Hayyim Genazzano," *Jewish History* 23 (2009), 223–53.
19. B. Ogren, *Renaissance and Rebirth: Reincarnation in Early Modern Italian Kabbalah* (Leiden: 2009), 164.
20. M. Idel, *Kabbalah in Italy, 1280–1510: A Survey* (New Haven: 2011).
21. Idel, *Kabbalah in Italy*, 132; Lesley, "The Place of the *Dialoghi*," 74.
22. A. Melamed, "The Myth of the Jewish Origins of Philosophy in the Renaissance: From Aristotle to Plato," *Jewish History* 26 (2012), 41–59.
23. For what follows see B. C. Novak, "Giovanni Pico della Mirandola and Jochanan Alemanno," *Journal of the Warburg and Courtauld Institutes* 45 (1982), 125–47; C. Wirszubski, *Pico della Mirandola's Encounter with Jewish Mysticism* (Cambridge, MA: 1989); F. Lelli, "Un collaboratore ebreo di Giovanni Pico della Mirandola: Yohanan Alemanno," *Vivens Homo* 5 (1994), 401–30.
24. D. B. Ruderman, "The Italian Renaissance and Jewish Thought," in A. Rabil Jr. (ed.), *Renaissance Humanism* (Philadelphia: 1988), vol. 1, 382–433, at 386.
25. Lawee, "Abravanel in Italy," 234.
26. Ogren, *Renaissance and Rebirth*, 203.

35. The Count of Concord: Pico della Mirandola

1. Translated in C. Wallis, P. Miller, and D. Carmichael, *Pico della Mirandola: On the Dignity of Man, On Being and the One, Heptaplus* (Indianapolis: 1965), cited by page number. See further G. Di Napoli, "L'essere e l'uno in Pico della Mirandola," in G. Tarugi (ed.), *Il pensiero italiano del Rinascimento e il tempo nostro* (Florence: 1970), 117–29; M. J. B. Allen, "The Second Ficino–Pico Controversy: Parmenidean Poetry, Eristic, and the One," §X in his *Plato's Third Eye: Studies in Marsilio Ficino's Metaphysics and its Sources* (Aldershot: 1995).
2. *A History of Philosophy Without Any Gaps: Medieval Philosophy*, ch. 48.
3. M. J. B. Allen, *Icastes: Marsilio Ficino's Interpretation of Plato's Sophist* (Berkeley: 1989).
4. Cited from S. A. Farmer, *Syncretism in the West: Pico's 900 Theses (1486)* (Tempe, AZ: 1998).
5. Farmer, *Syncretism in the West*, 48.
6. For the scholastic precedents of Pico's project see M. V. Dougherty, "Three Precursors to Pico della Mirandola's Roman Disputation and the Question of Human Nature in the *Oratio*," in M. V. Dougherty (ed.), *Pico della Mirandola: New Essays* (Cambridge: 2008), 114–51.
7. On the inquisition and its aftermath see A. Biond, "La doppia inchiesta sulle *Conclusiones* e le traversie romane di Pico nel 1487," in G. C. Garfagnini (ed.), *Giovanni Pico della Mirandola: convegno internazionale di studi nel cinquecentesimo anniversario della morte (1494–1994)* (Florence: 1997), 197–212.
8. As noted by P. R. Blum, "Pico, Theology, and the Church," in Dougherty, *Pico della Mirandola: New Essays*, 37–60, at 41.
9. The *Oration* and *Heptaplus* are cited in this and the next chapter by page number from Wallis et al., *Pico della Mirandola*.
10. *A History of Philosophy Without Any Gaps: Philosophy in the Islamic World*, ch. 39.

11. C. Wirszubski, *Pico della Mirandola's Encounter with Jewish Mysticism* (Cambridge, MA: 1989), 55.
12. For this and comparable material in Jewish authors see B. Ogren, *The Beginning of the World in Renaissance Jewish Thought* (Leiden: 2016).
13. See further Wirszubski, *Pico della Mirandola's Encounter*, 107.
14. For the Kabbalistic background see B. C. Novak, "Giovanni Pico della Mirandola and Jochanan Alemanno," *Journal of the Warburg and Courtauld Institutes* 45 (1982), 125–47, at 133.
15. For both see Wirszubski, *Pico della Mirandola's Encounter*, 3–4.
16. Cited by page from Q. Breen, "Giovanni Pico della Mirandola on the Conflict of Philosophy and Rhetoric," *Journal of the History of Ideas* 13 (1952), 384–426. For studies see F. Bausi, *Nec rhetor neque philosophus: fonti, lingua e stile nelle prime opere latine di Giovanni Pico della Mirandola (1484–87)* (Florence: 1996) and J. Kraye, "Pico on the Relationship of Rhetoric and Philosophy," in Dougherty, *Pico della Mirandola: New Essays*, 13–36, with further bibliography at 13 n. 2.
17. Cited by Kraye, "Pico on the Relationship," 30.

36. What a Piece of Work is Man: Manetti and Pico on Human Nature

1. P. Singer, "All Animals are Equal," *Philosophic Exchange* 5 (1974), 103–16, at 112–13.
2. Four layers of revision are postulated by C. Wallis, P. Miller, and D. Carmichael, *Pico della Mirandola: On the Dignity of Man, On Being and the One, Heptaplus* (Indianapolis: 1965), 33.
3. Cited by section number from B. P. Copenhaver (trans.), *Giannozzo Manetti: On Human Worth and Excellence* (Cambridge, MA: 2018). For a summary with commentary see O. Glaap, *Untersuchungen zu Giannozzo Manetti, "De dignitate et excellentia hominis": ein Renaissance-Humanist und sein Menschenbild* (Stuttgart: 1994), and for Manetti's eventful biography see D. Marsh, *Giannozzo Manetti: The Life of a Florentine Humanist* (Cambridge, MA: 2019).
4. A comparison drawn at Copenhaver, *Giannozzo Manetti: On Human Worth*, xxxvi, who suggests that this could have encouraged Manetti's "smaller risk" in writing against papal authority.
5. I cite and (with modifications) quote from Wallis et al., *Pico della Mirandola: On the Dignity of Man, On Being and the One, Heptaplus*. For a newer translation with the Latin text, see F. Borghesi, M. Papio, and M. Riva (eds and trans.), *Pico della Mirandola: On the Dignity of Man. A New Translation and Commentary* (Cambridge: 2012).
6. A. Buck, "Giovanni Pico della Mirandola e l'antropologia dell'umanesmo italiano," in G. C. Garfagnini (ed.), *Giovanni Pico della Mirandola: convegno internazionale di studi nel cinquecentesimo anniverario della morte (1494–1994)* (Florence: 1997), 1–12, at 5. For medieval genres of writing as a relevant comparison see also M. V. Dougherty, "Three Precursors to Pico Della Mirandola's Roman Disputation and the Question of Human Nature," in M. V. Dougherty, *Pico della Mirandola: New Essays* (Cambridge: 2008), 114–51.

7. This case is made by M. Idel, "The Anthropology of Yohanan Alemanno: Sources and Influences," *Topoi* 7 (1988), 201–10. See also B. P. Copenhaver, "The Secret of Pico's Oratio: Cabala and Renaissance Philosophy," *Midwest Studies in Philosophy* 26 (2002), 56–81.
8. I am here in agreement with M. J. B. Allen, "*Cultura hominis*: Giovanni Pico, Marsilio Ficino and the Idea of Man," in Garfagnini (ed.), *Giovanni Pico della Mirandola*, 173–96, which was my source for the following quote from Ficino (at 184). See also L. Valcke, "Entre raison et foi: le néoplatonisme de Pic de la Mirandole," *Recherches de théologie ancienne et médiévale* 54 (1987), 186–237.
9. See M. Klaes, "Zur Schau und Deutung des Kosmos bei Hildegard von Bingen," in A. Führkötter (ed.), *Kosmos und Mensch aus der Sicht Hidegards von Bingen* (Mainz: 1987), 37–115; the Brethren of Purity wrote a treatise called *That the World is a Great Human*, which is translated in P. E. Walker, et al. (eds and trans.), *Sciences of the Soul and Intellect Part I: An Arabic Critical Edition and English Translation of Epistles 32–36* (Oxford: 2015).
10. A similar idea appears in Jewish and Christian authors, e.g. Philo of Alexandria and Nemesius of Emesa.
11. For a commentary on it bringing out this theme see G. Aubry, *Plotin: Traité 53 (I,1)* (Paris: 2004): "we" are a "puissance d'orientation vers un devenir-animal ou un devenir-humain" (308).
12. S. Jayne (trans.), *Pico della Mirandola: Commentary on a Canzone of Benivieni* (New York: 1984), §3.2.
13. R. B. Gottfried (trans.), *Pietro Bembo: Gli Asolani* (Bloomington, IN: 1954), 177; R. Russell (trans.), *Tullia d'Aragona: Dialogue on the Infinity of Love* (Chicago: 1997), 90.
14. M. J. B. Allen (trans.) and J. Hankins (ed.), *Marsilio Ficino: Platonic Theology*, 6 vols (Cambridge, MA: 2001–2006), §9.3.
15. R. B. Gottfried (trans.), *Pietro Bembo: Gli Asolani* (Bloomington, IN: 1954), 146.
16. For the following I draw on C. Muratori, *Renaissance Vegetarianism: The Philosophical Afterlives of Porphyry's On Abstinence* (Cambridge: 2020), 166–81. I am grateful to Cecilia Muratori for allowing me to consult a pre-publication copy.
17. M. Sgarbi, *The Italian Mind: Vernacular Logic in Renaissance Italy (1540–1551)* (Leiden: 2014), 45.
18. Quoted by R. Lo Presti, "(Dis)embodied Thinking and the Scale of Beings: Pietro Pomponazzi and Agostino Nifo on the 'Psychic' Processes in Men and Animals," in S. Buchenau and R. Lo Presti (eds), *Human and Animal Cognition in Early Modern Philosophy and Medicine* (Pittsburgh: 2017), 37–54, at 52.

37. Bonfire of the Vanities: Savonarola

1. See T. Herzig, *Savonarola's Women: Visions and Reform in Renaissance Italy* (Chicago: 2008).
2. Citations in the main text are to A. Borelli and M. Pastore Passaro (eds and trans.), *Selected Writings of Girolamo Savonarola: Religion and Politics, 1490–1498* (New Haven: 2006).
3. L. Martines, *Fire in the City: Savonarola and the Struggle for the Soul of Renaissance Florence* (Oxford: 2006), points out that Savonarola makes an "easy target" for critique from a

modern-day perspective and that demonizing him is a "flawed historical proceeding." Maybe so, but that doesn't mean I have to like him.

4. G. C. Garfagnini, "Pico e Savonarola," in P. Viti (ed.), *Pico, Poliziano e l'Umanesimo di fine Quattrocento* (Florence: 1994), 149–57.
5. The many studies of his career and its context include R. Ridolfi, *Vita di Girolamo Savonarola*, 2 vols (Rome: 1952); D. Weinstein, *Savonarola and Florence: Prophecy and Patriotism in the Renaissance* (Princeton: 1970); D. Weinstein and V. R. Hotchkiss (eds), *Girolamo Savonarola: Piety, Prophecy, and Politics in Renaissance Florence* (Dallas: 1994); S. Fletcher and C. Shaw (eds), *The World of Savonarola: Italian Elites and Perceptions of Crisis* (Aldershot: 2000); M. Mayer, *Die politische Theologie Girolamo Savonarolas* (Tübingen: 2001); Martines, *Fire in the City*; P. Antonetti, *Savonarola: die Biographie* (Düsseldorf: 2007); S. Dall'Aglio, *Savonarola and Savonarolism*, trans. J. Gagné (Toronto: 2010); D. Weinstein, *Savonarola: The Rise and Fall of a Renaissance Prophet* (New Haven: 2011).
6. *A History of Philosophy Without Any Gaps: Medieval Philosophy*, ch. 31.
7. Quoted in Weinstein, *Savonarola: The Rise and Fall*, 88.
8. For a list of points made in his forced confession see Martines, *Fire in the City*, 260–1. Both Martines and Weinstein (in *Savonarola: The Rise and Fall*, 282) offer nuanced discussions of the reliability of the trial documents.
9. See J. H. Whitfield, "Savonarola and the Purpose of *The Prince*," *Modern Language Review* 44 (1949), 44–59; D. Weinstein, "Machiavelli and Savonarola," in M. P. Gilmore (ed.), *Studies on Machiavelli* (Florence: 1972), 253–64; A. Fuhr, *Machiavelli und Savonarola: politische Rationalität und politische Prophetie* (Frankfurt a.M.: 1985).
10. An ambitious attempt to answer this question is A. Edelheit, *Ficino, Pico and Savonarola: The Evolution of Humanist Theology, 1461/2–1498* (Leiden: 2008).
11. These examples are taken from A. M. Brown, "Platonism in Fifteenth-Century Florence and its Contribution to Early Modern Political Thought," *Journal of Modern History* 58 (1986), 383–413, at 396 and 404. She argues for the following interpretation, that Platonism was for Savonarola linked to Medici power.
12. Martines, *Fire in the City*, 104.
13. For this and what follows see M. Jurdjevic, "Prophets and Politicians: Marsilio Ficino, Savonarola and the Valori Family," *Past and Present Society* 183 (2004), 41–77.
14. Partial translation, with summary of the rest, in *Selected Works*. Complete text in M. M. Mulchahey (ed. and trans.), *Savonarola: Apologetic Writings* (Cambridge, MA: 2015). For the following point that sense faculties are unerring, but only regarding their special objects, see §2.4.
15. *Dialogue on Prophetic Truth*, §2.19.
16. *Dialogue on Prophetic Truth*, §6.6–7.
17. Quoted at Edelheit, *Ficino, Pico and Savonarola*, 455.

38. The Sweet Restraints of Liberty: Republicanism and Civic Humanism

1. The most important publication is H. Baron, *The Crisis of the Early Italian Renaissance: Civic Humanism and Republican Liberty in an Age of Classicism and Tyranny* (Princeton: 1966); see also

H. Baron, *In Search of Florentine Civic Humanism*, 2 vols (Princeton: 2014). For assessments of Baron and his legacy see R. Fubini, "Renaissance Historian: The Career of Hans Baron," *Journal of Modern History* 64 (1992), 541–74; A. Brown, "Hans Baron's Renaissance," *Historical Journal* 33 (1990), 441–8; J. Hankins, "The 'Baron Thesis' after Forty Years and Some Recent Studies of Leonardo Bruni," *Journal of the History of Ideas* 56 (1995), 309–38; R. G. Witt, "The Crisis after Forty Years," *American Historical Review* 101 (1996), 110–18.

2. For these passages see Baron, *In Search of Florentine Civic Humanism*, vol. 1, 136 and 146.
3. As in his *Die Kultur der Renaissance in Italien*, published in 1860; English version in J. Burckhardt, *The Civilization of the Renaissance in Italy*, trans. S. G. C. Middlemore (London: 1950).
4. Translated in B. G. Kohl and R. G. Witt (eds), *The Earthly Republic: Italian Humanists on Government and Society* (Manchester: 1978), 135–75. Cited by section number. For the date and occasion see J. Hankins, "Rhetoric, History, and Ideology: The Civic Panegyrics of Leonardo Bruni," in J. Hankins (ed.), *Renaissance Civic Humanism: Reappraisals and Reflections* (Cambridge: 2000), 143–78, at 144.
5. On this see S. Daub, *Leonardo Brunis Rede auf Nanni Strozzi: Einleitung, Edition und Kommentar* (Stuttgart: 1996). Translation in G. Griffiths et al. (trans.), *The Humanism of Leonardo Bruni* (Binghamton, NY: 1987).
6. *Humanism of Leonardo Bruni*, 125.
7. Trans. in R. N. Watkins (trans.), *Humanism and Liberty: Writings on Freedom in Fifteenth-Century Florence* (Columbia, SC: 1978).
8. Citing Rinuccini's *Risponsiva* from M. Hörnqvist, *Machiavelli and Empire* (Cambridge: 2004), 55.
9. Q. Skinner, *The Foundations of Modern Political Thought*, vol. 1: *The Renaissance* (Cambridge: 1976), 172. See also J. G. A. Pocock, *The Machiavellian Moment: Florentine Political Thought and the Atlantic Republican Tradition* (Princeton: 1975), ch. 5.
10. Cited from M. Cesa, *Debating Foreign Policy in the Renaissance: Speeches on War and Peace by Francesco Guicciardini* (Oxford: 2017), 9.
11. Quoted from Pocock, *The Machiavellian Moment*, 130.
12. N. Rubinstein, "Oligarchy and Democracy in Fifteenth-Century Florence," in S. Bertelli et al. (eds), *Florence and Venice: Comparisons and Relations*, 2 vols (Florence: 1979–80), at vol. 1, 107.
13. J. M. Najemy, *Corporatism and Consensus in Florentine Politics, 1280–1300* (Chapel Hill, NC: 1982).
14. J. M. Najemy, "Civic Humanism and Florentine Politics," in Hankins, *Renaissance Civic Humanism*, 75–104, at 85.
15. R. Dees, "Bruni, Aristotle, and the Mixed Regime in *On the Constitution of the Florentines*," *Medievalia et humanistica* NS 15 (1987), 1–23.
16. On Patrizi see Skinner, *Foundations*, 117 and 153; F. Ricciardelli, *The Myth of Republicanism in Renaissance Italy* (Turnhout: 2015), 64–5.
17. Skinner, *Foundations*, 141.
18. J. M. Blythe, "Civic Humanism and Medieval Political Thought," in Hankins, *Renaissance Civic Humanism*, 30–74, at 67.
19. Quoted by M. Hörnqvist, "The Two Myths of Civic Humanism," in Hankins, *Renaissance Civic Humanism*, 105–42, at 116.
20. For the contrast see Skinner, *Foundations*, 6.

21. Baron, *In Search of Florentine Civic Humanism*, vol. 1, 281.
22. For this critique see M. Jurdjevic, "Civic Humanism and the Rise of the Medici," *Renaissance Quarterly* 52 (1999), 994–1020.
23. This point is stressed in C. J. Nederman's article on "Civic Humanism" in the online *Stanford Encyclopedia of Philosophy*.
24. Mentioned by A. Brown, "De-Masking Renaissance Republicanism," in Hankins, *Renaissance Civic Humanism*, 179–99, at 191. See further A. Brown, *The Medici in Florence: The Exercise and Language of Power* (Florence: 1992).
25. J. Hankins, "The 'Baron Thesis' after Forty Years and Some Recent Studies of Leonardo Bruni," *Journal of the History of Ideas* 56 (1995), 309–38, at 327.
26. Hobbes, *Leviathan*, ch. 21, cited by Ricciardelli, *The Myth of Republicanism*, 53, and see 39 for Lucca's earlier institutions.
27. J. Hankins, "Leonardo Bruni on the Legitimacy of Constitutions (Oratio *in funere Johannis Strozze* 19–23)," in C. T. Callisen (ed.), *Reading and Writing History from Bruni to Windschuttle* (Farnham: 2014), 73–86.
28. H. Yoran, "Florentine Civic Humanism and the Emergence of Modern Ideology," *History and Theory* 46 (2007), 326–44.
29. See Skinner, *Foundations*, especially ch. 2; I summarize his findings in what follows.

39. No More Mr Nice Guy: Machiavelli

1. For an English translation see Q. Skinner and R. Price (eds), *Niccolò Machiavelli: The Prince* (Cambridge: 1988). For a collection of his works including *The Prince* and the *Discourses* see A. H. Gilbert (trans.), *Niccolò Machiavelli: Chief Works and Others*, 3 vols (Durham: 1965).
2. *King Henry the Sixth Part 3*, act 3, scene 2.
3. Q. Skinner, *The Foundations of Modern Political Thought*, vol. 1: *The Renaissance* (Cambridge: 1976), 118.
4. I take the translation and story from the introduction to J. M. Najemy, *The Cambridge Companion to Machiavelli* (Cambridge: 2010), 1–3.
5. As stressed by J. G. A. Pocock, *The Machiavellian Moment: Florentine Political Thought and the Atlantic Republican Tradition* (Princeton: 1975), 158.
6. Pocock, *The Machiavellian Moment*, 166.
7. Quoted from E. Nelson, "The Problem of the Prince," in J. Hankins (ed.), *Cambridge Companion to Renaissance Philosophy* (Cambridge: 2007), 319–27, at 320; my contrast between Petrarch and Machiavelli is inspired by Nelson's discussion.
8. For the theme in Machiavelli see C. J. Nederman, "Amazing Grace: Fortune, Thought, and Free Will in Machiavelli's Thought," *Journal of the History of Ideas* 60 (1999), 617–38.
9. For his views on religion see A. Tenenti, "La religione di Machiavelli," *Studi storici* 10 (1969), 709–48; J. S. Preus, "Machiavelli's Functional Analysis of Religion: Content and Object," *Journal of the History of Ideas* 40 (1979), 171–90; T. J. Lukes, "To Bamboozle with Goodness: The Political Advantage of Christianity in the Thought of Machiavelli," *Renaissance and Reformation* NS 8 (1984), 266–71; V. A. Santi, "Religion and Politics in Machiavelli," *Machiavelli Studies* 1 (1987), 17–24; M. L. Colish, "Republicanism, Religion,

and Machiavelli's Savonarolan Moment," *Journal of the History of Ideas* 60 (1999), 597–616; M. Viroli, *Machiavelli's God* (Princeton: 2010).

10. *History of Florence*, §1.9, in *Chief Works*, vol. 3.
11. On this chapter see M. Martelli, "La logica provvidenzialistica e il capitolo 26 del Principe," *Interpres* 4 (1982), 262–384; M. Vatter, "Machiavelli and the Republican Conception of Providence," *Review of Politics* 75 (2013), 605–23.

40. Sense of Humors: Machiavelli on Republicanism

1. This is my own translation, but I will generally quote from the version in vol. 1 of A. H. Gilbert (trans.), *Niccolò Machiavelli: Chief Works and Others*, 3 vols (Durham: 1965). Cited by book and chapter number.
2. Cited from Q. Skinner, *The Foundations of Modern Political Thought*, vol. 1: *The Renaissance* (Cambridge: 1976), 182.
3. *Chief Works*, vol. 2, 572.
4. On this metaphor see A. J. Parel, *The Machiavellian Cosmos* (New Haven: 1992), 101–12; S. Kalff, *Politische Medizin der Frühen Neuzeit: die Figur des Arztes in Italien und England im frühen 17. Jahrhundert* (Berlin: 2014), 50–3.
5. *History of Florence*, 4.1, in *Chief Works*, vol. 3.
6. See further Q. Skinner, "Machiavelli on the Maintenance of Liberty," *Politics* 18 (1983), 3–15.
7. J. McCormick, *Machiavellian Democracy* (Chicago: 2011). McCormick's analysis of Guicciardini as an elitist is, however, rejected by N. Regent, "Guicciardini and Economic (In)equality," *European Journal of the History of Economic Thought* 27 (2020), 49–65. Regent argues that, while Guicciardini does have a fairly low opinion of the *popolo*, his aim is to maximize civic virtue and not oligarchy or rule by the rich as such; he would welcome the rise of a lower born man to a position of power if the man were of sufficiently excellent character.
8. For this theme I draw on M. Hörnqvist, *Machiavelli and Empire* (Cambridge: 2004).
9. Cited from Hörnqvist, *Machiavelli and Empire*, 116.
10. *Chief Works*, vol. 2, 578.
11. M. Jurdjevic, "Machiavelli's Hybrid Republicanism," *English Historical Review* 122, no. 499 (2007), 1228–57.

41. The Teacher of Our Actions: Renaissance Historiography

1. *Discourses*, §3.43, in A. H. Gilbert (trans.), *Niccolò Machiavelli: Chief Works and Others*, 3 vols (Durham: 1965), vol. 1. For an introduction to history in Machiavelli see C. S. Celenza, *Machiavelli: A Portrait* (Cambridge, MA: 2015), ch. 5.
2. *On the Art of War*, in *Chief Works*, vol. 2, 571.
3. *History of Florence*, §5.1, in *Chief Works*, vol. 3.

4. M. L. King and D. Robin (trans.), *Isotta Nogarola: Complete Writings. Letterbook, Dialogue on Adam and Eve, Orations* (Chicago: 2004), 77.
5. G. Griffiths et al. (trans.), *The Humanism of Leonardo Bruni* (Binghamton, NY: 1987), 195.
6. J. Hankins, "Rhetoric, History, and Ideology: The Civic Panegyrics of Leonardo Bruni," in J. Hankins (ed.), *Renaissance Civic Humanism: Reappraisals and Reflections* (Cambridge: 2000), 143–78, at 161 and 167.
7. F. Gilbert, *Machiavelli and Guicciardini: Politics and History in Sixteenth Century Florence* (Princeton: 1965), 205–6.
8. G. Ianziti, *Writing History in Renaissance Italy: Leonardo Bruni and the Uses of the Past* (Cambridge, MA: 2012), 21. On his historical work see D. Hay, "Flavio Biondo and the Middle Ages," *Proceedings of the British Academy* 45 (1960), 97–125.
9. Q. Skinner, *The Foundations of Modern Political Thought*, vol. 1: *The Renaissance* (Cambridge: 1976), 90.
10. N. Struever, *The Language of History in the Renaissance: Rhetorical Consciousness in Florentine Humanism* (Princeton: 1970), 77.
11. Gilbert, *Machiavelli and Guicciardini*, 216.
12. *Humanism of Leonardo Bruni*, 196.
13. Ianziti, *Writing History in Renaissance Italy*, 48–50, and 96 for the following quote. On Plutarch see *A History of Philosophy Without Any Gaps: Philosophy in the Hellenistic and Roman Worlds*, ch. 24.
14. D. J. Wilcox, *The Development of Florentine Humanist Historiography in the Fifteenth Century* (Cambridge, MA: 1969), 8.
15. On the history of ideas about the founding see S. U. Baldassarri, "Like Fathers Like Sons: Theories on the Origins of the City in Late Medieval Florence," *MLN* 124 (2009), 23–44.
16. H. Baron, *In Search of Florentine Civic Humanism*, vol. 1: *Essays on the Transition from Medieval to Modern Thought* (Princeton: 2014), chs 3 and 4.
17. See *A History of Philosophy Without Any Gaps: Medieval Philosophy*, ch. 55.
18. G. Ianziti, "Leonardo Bruni, the Medici, and the *Florentine Histories*," *Journal of the History of Ideas* 69 (2008), 1–22, at 10. The article is reprinted as ch. 8 of Ianziti, *Writing History in Renaissance Italy*.
19. Quoted at Wilcox, *The Development*, 88–9.
20. See F. Krantz "Between Bruni and Machiavelli: History, Law and Historicism in Poggio," in P. Mack and M. C. Jacob (eds), *Politics and Culture in Early Modern Europe* (Cambridge: 1987), 119–52, at 134.
21. Quoted at Krantz "Between Bruni and Machiavelli," 133.
22. Wilcox, *The Development*, 140, 151.
23. *Discourses*, §1.37, §1.44, *History of Florence*, §3.10.
24. *Discourses*, §2.19.
25. *History of Florence*, §3.1.
26. *History of Florence*, §3.13.
27. *Discourses*, §1.39.
28. See Ianziti, *Writing History in Renaissance Italy*, 130, and for more on this term in Bruni Wilcox, *The Development*, 211–12.
29. Quoted at Gilbert, *Machiavelli and Guicciardini*, 215.

30. *On the Art of War*, 639. On this work and its deliberately ironic choice of spokesman see M. Colish, "Machiavelli's *Art of War*: A Reconsideration," *Renaissance Quarterly* 51 (1998), 1151–68.
31. *History of Florence*, §6.1.
32. Translations in M. Cesa, *Debating Foreign Policy in the Renaissance: Speeches on War and Peace by Francesco Guicciardini* (Oxford: 2017). On him see further M. Phillips, *Francesco Guicciardini: The Historian's Craft* (Toronto: 1977); G. Sasso, *Per Francesco Guicciardini: quattro studi* (Rome: 1984); C. Varotti, *Francesco Guicciardini* (Naples: 2009), and on his ideas concerning warfare, A. Bonadeo, "Guicciardini on War and Conquest," *Il pensiero politico* 14 (1981), 214–42.
33. *Speeches on War and Peace*, 43–4; 74; 8.
34. R. Fubini, *Humanism and Secularization from Petrarch to Valla*, trans. M. King (Durham, NC: 2003), 117.
35. *On the Art of War*, 718.
36. *History of Florence*, §7.5.
37. *History of Florence*, §3.5, and for the Romans mastering fortune, *Discourses*, §2.1.
38. *Discourses*, §5.1; on this passage see S. de Maria, "Machiavelli's Ironic View of History: The *Istorie fiorentine*," *Renaissance Quarterly* 65 (1992), 248–70, at 251.
39. *Speeches on War and Peace*, 15; 55.
40. *Speeches on War and Peace*, 43–4; 76.
41. N. G. Siriasi, *History, Medicine, and the Traditions of Renaissance Learning* (Ann Arbor: 2007), 157.
42. Gilbert, *Machiavelli and Guicciardini*, 249 n. 20, my translation.

42. The Good Place: Utopias in the Italian Renaissance

1. See L. Firpo, "Thomas More e la sua fortuna in Italia," *Il pensiero politico* 9 (1976), 209–36; T. Wheeler, "Thomas More in Italy: 1535–1700," *Moreana* 7 (1970), 15–23; S. Seidel Menchi, *Erasmo in Italia* (Turin: 1987), E. Nelson, "Utopia Through Italian Eyes: Thomas More and the Critics of Civic Humanism," *Renaissance Quarterly* 59 (2006), 1029–57.
2. Quoted at Nelson, "Utopia Through Italian Eyes," 1042.
3. This appears as part of his larger collection of writings, *The Worlds* (*I Mondi*). English version in A. Donato (trans.), *Italian Renaissance Utopias: Doni, Patrizi, and Zuccolo* (New York: 2019); this volume is cited by page number in the main text of this chapter.
4. On him see C. Vasoli, *Francesco Patrizi da Cherso* (Rome: 1989); P. Castelli (ed.), *Francesco Patrizi filosofo platonico nel crepuscolo del Rinascimento* (Florence: 2002); J. Prins, *Echoes of an Invisible World: Marsilio Ficino and Francesco Patrizi on Cosmic Order and Music Theory* (Leiden: 2015).
5. *The Prince*, ch. 15, in vol. 1 of A. H. Gilbert (trans.), *Niccolò Machiavelli: Chief Works and Others*, 3 vols (Durham: 1965).
6. Donato, *Italian Renaissance Utopias*, 187.
7. As argued in detail by F. E. Manuel and F. P. Manuel, *Utopian Thought in the Western World* (Cambridge: 1979), ch. 5.

8. For a drawing by Fabio Calvo that imagines ancient Rome as a radial city, see C. L. Joost-Gaugier, *Pythagoras and Renaissance Europe: Finding Heaven* (Cambridge: 2009), 214.
9. D. J. Donno (trans.), *Tommaso Campanella: The City of the Sun* (Berkeley: 1981).
10. For the Platonic and Telesian background see further M. Subialka, "Transforming Plato: *La Città del sole*, the *Republic*, and Socrates as Natural Philosopher," *Bruniana & Campanelliana* 17 (2011), 417–33.
11. For this problem see J. M. Headley, *Tommaso Campanella and the Transformation of the World* (Princeton: 1997), 204; G. Ernst, *Tommaso Campanella: The Book and the Body of Nature*, trans. D. L. Marshall (Dordrecht: 2010), 57.
12. L. Perini, "Tommaso Campanella tra monarchie e imperi," *Bruniana & Campanelliana* 13 (2007), 191–207, 195.
13. Headley, *Tommaso Campanella*, 234.
14. A. Pagden, *Spanish Imperialism and the Political Imagination* (New Haven: 1990), 47. See further J. M. Headley, *Tommaso Campanella and the Transformation of the World* (Princeton: 1997), ch. 5.
15. Cited at Pagden, *Spanish Imperialism*, 50.
16. For this problem see Manuel and Manuel, *Utopian Thought*, 177; P. Castelli, "Le fonti de *La Città Felice*," in Castelli, *Francesco Patrizi filosofo platonico*, 3–30, at 8.
17. This is the argument of T. Renna, "Campanella's *City of the Sun* and Late Renaissance Italy," *Utopian Studies* 10 (1999), 13–25.
18. J.-P. De Lucca, "Prophetic Representation and Political Allegorisation: The Hospitaller in Campanella's *The City of the Sun*," *Bruniana & Campanelliana* 15 (2009), 387–504.
19. Manuel and Manuel, *Utopian Thought*, 165. For a similar comparison between a human body and a church see Anthony Grafton, *Leon Battista Alberti: Master Builder of the Italian Renaissance* (Cambridge, MA: 2002), 281.
20. J. Rykwert, N. Leach, and R. Tavenor (trans.), *Leon Battista Alberti: On the Art of Building in Ten Books* (Cambridge: 1995), §6.2 and 9.7.
21. On the gender theme in Campanella see L. Bolzoni, "Tommaso Campanella e le donne: fascino e negazione della differenza," *Annali d'Italianistica* 7 (1989), 193–216, with this idea discussed at 197.
22. P. F. Grendler, "Utopia in Renaissance Italy: Doni's *New World*," *Journal of the History of Ideas* 26 (1965), 479–94, at 482.
23. Grendler, "Utopia in Renaissance Italy," 475.
24. P. R. Blum, "The Economy of Slavery in Campanella's Political Thought," *Bruniana & Campanelliana* 23 (2017), 563–72.
25. Blum, "The Economy of Slavery," 567 and 571 for the following quote.

43. Greed is Good: Economics in the Italian Renaissance

1. On this genre of antique works see *A History of Philosophy Without Any Gaps: Philosophy in the Hellenistic and Roman Worlds*, ch. 35.
2. Xenophon, *Oeconomicus*, §2.4, in E. C. Marchant and O. J. Todd (trans.), *Memorabilia, Oeconomicus, Symposium, Apology* (Cambridge, MA: 1923).

3. Cited by page number from the translation in R. N. Watkins, *Leon Battista Alberti: The Family in Renaissance Florence, Book Three* (Long Grove, IL: 1994), abbreviated in this chapter as *Fam.*
4. On this passage see M. L. King, *Women of the Renaissance* (Chicago: 1991), 63.
5. See M. L. King "Personal, Domestic, and Republican Values in the Moral Philosophy of Giovanni Caldiera," *Renaissance Quarterly* 28 (1975), 535 74.
6. Cited by page number from J. F. Phillimore (trans.), *Benedetto Cotrugli: The Book of the Art of Trade* (Venice: 2017); abbreviated in this chapter as *Trade.*
7. A. Sangster, "The Source of Pacioli's Bookkeeping Treatise," *The Accounting Historians Journal* 39 (2012), 97–110, at 100. Pacioli's discussion of double bookkeeping was historically more influential since it appeared in 1494, several decades after Cotrugli wrote but almost a century before his *On the Art of Trade* was printed, in 1573.
8. H. Baron, *In Search of Florentine Civic Humanism*, vol. 1: *Essays on the Transition from Medieval to Modern Thought* (Princeton: 2014), 232. For Baron's views on the active life as including the pursuit of wealth, see also his "Franciscan Poverty and Civic Wealth as Factors in the Rise of Humanistic Thought," *Speculum* 12 (1938), 1–37.
9. Cited by J. F. McGovern, "The Rise of New Economic Attitudes—Economic Humanism, Economic Nationalism—During the Later Middle Ages and the Renaissance, A.D. 1200–1500," *Traditio* 26 (1970), 217–53, at 236–7.
10. O. Nuccio, *La storia del pensiero economico italiano: come storia della genesi dello spirito capitalistico* (Roma: 2008), 534–7.
11. K. Langdon Forhan, *Christine de Pizan: Book of the Body Politic* (Cambridge: 1994), 103–4. For de Pizan as a precursor of Italian Renaissance ideas about wealth see C. J. Nederman, "Avarice as a Princely Virtue? The Later Medieval Backdrop to Poggio Bracciolini and Machiavelli," in C. J. Nederman (ed.), *Mind Matters: Studies of Medieval and Early Modern Intellectual History in Honour of Marcia Colish* (Turnhout: 2009), 255–74.
12. On whom see I. Origo, *The World of San Bernardino* (New York: 1962); R. De Roover, *San Bernardino of Siena and Sant'Antonio of Florence: The Two Great Economic Thinkers of the Middle Ages* (Boston: 1967).
13. For earlier scholastic discussions see *A History of Philosophy Without Any Gaps: Medieval Philosophy*, ch. 67.
14. Cited by page number from the translation in B. G. Kohl and R. G. Witt (eds), *The Earthly Republic: Italian Humanists on Government and Society* (Manchester: 1978), abbreviated as *Avar.*
15. See e.g. J. Oppel, "Poggio, San Bernardino of Siena, and the Dialogue *On Avarice*," *Renaissance Quarterly* 30 (1977), 564–87.
16. De Roover, *San Bernardino of Siena*, 13.
17. De Roover, *San Bernardino of Siena*, 35.
18. Nuccio, *La storia*, 624.
19. De Roover, *San Bernardino of Siena*, 20.
20. N. Regent, "Guicciardini's *La Decima scalata*: The First Treatise on Progressive Taxation," *History of Political Economy* 46 (2014), 307–31; N. Regent, "Guicciardini and Economic (In) equality," *European Journal of the History of Economic Thought* 27 (2020), 49–65.
21. Regent, "Guicciardini's *La Decima scalata*," 316.

44. Town and Gown: Italian Universities

1. Making this same point, P. Denley, "Career, Springboard, or Sinecure? University Teaching in Fifteenth-Century Italy," *Medieval Prosopography* 12 (1991), 95–114 even suggests the analogy to sports league tables.
2. P. F. Grendler, *The Universities of the Italian Renaissance* (Baltimore: 2002), 15–16.
3. For salary figures see J. Davies, *Culture and Power: Tuscany and its Universities 1537–1609* (Leiden: 2009), ch. 3. A good example would be Alessandro Piccolomini, who in 1589 was "almost certainly the best-paid philosopher in the world," with an annual salary of one thousand florins, as reported by N. Jardine "Keeping Order in the School of Padua: Jacopo Zabarella and Francesco Piccolomini on the Offices of Philosophy," in D. DiLiscia et al. (eds), *Method and Order in Renaissance Philosophy of Nature: The Aristotle Commentary Tradition* (Aldershot: 1997), 183–209, at 197.
4. Grendler, *The Universities*, 230, 297.
5. D. A. Lines, "Reorganizing the Curriculum: Teaching and Learning in the University of Bologna, c.1560–c.1590," in M. Feingold (ed.), *History of Universities* (Oxford: 2012), 1–59, at 10.
6. For what follows see P. Denley, "'Medieval', 'Renaissance', 'Modern': Issues of Periodization in Italian University History," *Renaissance Studies* 27 (2013), 487–503. For medieval universities see also P. Renzi (ed.), *L'università e la sua storia: origini, spazi istituzionali e pratiche didattiche dello Studium cittadino* (Siena: 1998), and *A History of Philosophy Without Any Gaps: Medieval Philosophy*, chs 21 and 77.
7. Grendler, *The Universities*, 5.
8. Lines, "Reorganizing the Curriculum," 3.
9. Davies, *Culture and Power*, 91.
10. Grendler, *The Universities*, 22, 28.
11. B. Dooley, "Social Control and the Italian Universities: From Renaissance to *Illuminismo*," *The Journal of Modern History* 61 (1989), 205–39, 214.
12. Davies, *Culture and Power*, 135.
13. Grendler, *The Universities*, 187. On Tomitano see M. R. Davi, *Bernardino Tomitano filosofo, medico e letterato (1517–1576): profilo biografico e critico* (Trieste: 1995).
14. H. S. Matsen, "Students' 'Arts' Disputations at Bologna around 1500," *Renaissance Quarterly* 47 (1994), 533–55, at 535. See also N. Gilbert, "The Early Italian Humanists and Disputation," in A. Molho and J. A. Tedeschi (eds), *Renaissance Studies in Honor of Hans Baron* (Dekalb, IL: 1971), 201–26.
15. Grendler, *The Universities*, 102.
16. E. J. Ashworth, "Developments in the Fifteenth and Sixteenth Centuries," in D. Gabbay and J. Woods (eds), *Handbook of the History of Logic*, vol. 2: *Mediaeval and Renaissance Logic* (Amsterdam: 2008), 609–43, at 619.
17. On the Calculators see *A History of Philosophy Without Any Gaps: Medieval Philosophy*, ch. 63.
18. C. B. Schmitt, *The Aristotelian Tradition and Renaissance Universities* (London: 1984), §V, 64.
19. E. J. Ashworth, "Agostino Nifo's Reinterpretation of Medieval Logic," *Rivista critica di storia della filosofia* 31 (1976), 355–74.

20. L. Jardine, "Dialectic or Dialectical Rhetoric? Agostino Nifo's Criticism of Lorenzo Valla," *Rivista critica di storia della filosofia* 36 (1981), 253–70.
21. D. A. Lines, "Humanism and the Italian Universities," in C. S. Celenza and K. Gouwens (eds), *Humanism and Creativity in the Renaissance* (Leiden: 2006), 327–46, at 328–9.
22. Grendler, *The Universities*, 210–11.
23. Lines, "Humanism and the Italian Universities," 342.
24. Schmitt, *The Aristotelian Tradition*, §XV, 304.
25. L. Nauta, "Philology as Philosophy: Giovanni Pontano on Language, Meaning, and Grammar," *Journal of the History of Ideas* 72 (2011), 481–502.
26. J. F. Phillimore (trans.), *Benedetto Cotrugli: The Book of the Art of Trade* (Venice: 2017), 26.
27. For what follows see M. Sgarbi, *The Italian Mind: Vernacular Logic in Renaissance Italy (1540–1551)* (Leiden: 2014), ch. 2. On Speroni see also A. Cotugno, *La scienza della parola: retorica e linguistica in Sperone Speroni* (Bologna: 2018).
28. Sgarbi, *The Italian Mind*, 48. On Speroni see further H. Mikkeli, "The Cultural Programmes of Alessandro Piccolomini and Sperone Speroni at the Paduan Accademia degli Infiammati in the 1540s," in C. Blackwell and S. Kusukawa (eds), *Philosophy in the Sixteenth and Seventeenth Century: Conversations with Aristotle* (Aldershot: 1999), 76–85.

45. I'd Like to Thank the Lyceum: Aristotle in Renaissance Italy

1. G. Griffiths et al. (trans.), *The Humanism of Leonardo Bruni* (Binghamton, NY: 1987), 213–14. For the topic more generally see P. Botley, *Latin Translation in the Italian Renaissance* (Cambridge: 2004).
2. *The Humanism of Leonardo Bruni*, 223.
3. *The Humanism of Leonardo Bruni*, 207.
4. M. McShane (ed.) and M. Young (trans.), *Giannozzo Manetti: A Translator's Defense* (Cambridge, MA: 2016), §5.77.
5. C. B. Schmitt, *Aristotle and the Renaissance* (Cambridge, MA: 1983), 80.
6. P. W. G. Gordon (trans.), *Two Renaissance Book Hunters: The Letters of Poggius Bracciolini to Nicolaus de Niccolis* (New York: 1991), 43 and 69.
7. On whom see M. Lowry, *The World of Aldus Manutius: Business and Scholarship in Renaissance Venice* (Oxford: 1979); M. Davies, *Aldus Manutius: Printer and Publisher of Renaissance Venice* (Tempe, AZ: 1999).
8. P. F. Grendler, *Schooling in Renaissance Italy: Literacy and Learning, 1300–1600* (Baltimore: 1989).
9. Schmitt, *Aristotle and the Renaissance*, 44.
10. C. H. Lohr, "Renaissance Latin Translations of the Greek Commentators on Aristotle," in J. Kraye and M. W. F. Stone (eds), *Humanism and Early Modern Philosophy* (London: 2000), 24–40.
11. S. Perfetti, *Aristotle's Zoology and Its Renaissance Commentators* (Leuven: 2000).
12. For what follows see C. Martin, *Renaissance Meteorology: Pomponazzi to Descartes* (Baltimore: 2011). Compare also P. Lettinck, *Aristotelian Meteorology and Its Reception in the Arab World*

(Leiden: 1999). For Byzantine engagements see I. Telelis, "Meteorology and Physics in Byzantium," in S. Lazaris (ed.), *A Companion to Byzantine Science* (Leiden: 2020), 177–201.

13. Martin, *Renaissance Meteorology*, 46.
14. Martin, *Renaissance Meteorology*, 50.
15. Martin, *Renaissance Meteorology*, 70.
16. Schmitt, *Aristotle and the Renaissance*, 28.
17. C. B. Schmitt, *The Aristotelian Tradition and Renaissance Universities* (London: 1984), §VI, 43.
18. Schmitt, *Aristotle and the Renaissance*, 61.
19. For what follows see L. Bianchi, "Per una storia dell'aristotelismo 'volgare' nel renascimento: problemi e prospettive di ricerca," *Bruniana & Campanelliana* 15 (2009), 367–85; L. Bianchi, "Volgarizzare Aristotele: per chi?," *Freiburger Zeitschrift für Philosophie und Theologie* 59 (2012), 480–95; M. Sgarbi, "Aristotle and the People: Vernacular Philosophy in Renaissance Italy," *Renaissance and Reformation* (2016), 59–109.
20. Bianchi, "Per una storia," 382–4.
21. Sgarbi, "Aristotle and the People," 72.
22. Bianchi, "Volgarizzare Aristotele," 493.
23. Sgarbi, "Aristotle and the People," 103.
24. See Schmitt, *The Aristotelian Tradition*, §VIII.
25. On which see C. Burnett, "Revisiting the 1550–1552 and 1562 Aristotle–Averroes Edition," in A. Akasoy and G. Giglioni (eds), *Renaissance Averroism and its Aftermath: Arabic Philosophy in Early Modern Europe* (Dordrecht: 2013), 55–64.

46. Of Two Minds: Pomponazzi and Nifo on the Intellect

1. As emphasized by C. B. Schmitt, "Aristotelianism in the Veneto and the Origins of Modern Science: Some Considerations on the Problem of Continuity," in L. Olivieri (ed.), *Atti del convegno internazionale su aristotelismo Veneto e scienza moderna* (Padua: 1983), 104–23, at 109; C. B. Schmitt, *The Aristotelian Tradition and Renaissance Universities* (London: 1984), §XV, 301. See also J. H. Randall, "Paduan Aristotelianism Reconsidered," in E. P. Mahoney (ed.), *Philosophy and Humanism* (New York: 1976), 275–82.
2. On his theory of the mind see *A History of Philosophy Without Any Gaps: Philosophy in the Islamic World*, ch. 26. On his reception in the Renaissance see D. N. Hasse, "The Attraction of Averroism in the Renaissance: Vernia, Achillini, Prassicio," *Bulletin of the Institute of Classical Studies Supplement* 83, vol. 2 (2004), 131–47; C. Martin, "Rethinking Renaissance Averroism," *Intellectual History Review* 17 (2007), 3–28; A. Akasoy and G. Giglioni (eds), *Renaissance Averroism and Its Aftermath: Arabic Philosophy in Early Modern Europe* (Dordrecht: 2010); D. N. Hasse, *Success and Suppression: Arabic Sciences and Philosophy in the Renaissance* (Cambridge, MA: 2016), ch. 5.
3. Quoted by J. H. Randall, *The School of Padua and the Emergence of Modern Science* (Padua: 1961), 82–3.
4. See *A History of Philosophy Without Any Gaps: Medieval Philosophy*, ch. 42.
5. As pointed out by Hasse, "The Attraction of Averroism," 137.

6. For this argument see P. Adamson, "From Known to Knower: Affinity Arguments for the Mind's Incorporeality in the Islamic World," *Oxford Studies in the Philosophy of Mind* 1 (2021), 373-96.
7. Hasse, *Success and Suppression*, 181.
8. Quoted at J. Hankins, *Plato in the Italian Renaissance*, 2 vols (Leiden: 1990), vol. 1, 274.
9. J. Monfasani, "The Averroism of John Argyropoulos," *I Tatti Studies: Essays in the Renaissance* 5 (Florence: 1993), 157–208, at 180.
10. Hasse, "The Attraction of Averroism," 138, and 142 for Prasiccio.
11. I say "broadly" correct because Pomponazzi does not signal his allegiance to Alexander and in fact rejects some aspects of Alexander's view. Still, his reading is certainly closer to Alexander's than Averroes'. On this see T. Gontier, "Matérialisme alexandriste et matérialisme pomponazzien," in J. Biard and T. Gontier (eds), *Pietro Pomponazzi entre traditions et innovations* (Amsterdam: 2009), 99–119.
12. On this problem see M. Pine, "Pomponazzi and the Problem of 'Double Truth,'" *Journal of the History of Ideas* 29 (1968), 163–76.
13. Citations in the main text are by page number from W. H. Hay and J. H. Randall (trans.), *Pietro Pomponazzi: On the Immortality of the Soul*, in E. Cassirer et al. (eds), *The Renaissance Philosophy of Man* (Chicago: 1956).
14. J. Sellars, "Pomponazzi Contra Averroes on the Intellect," *British Journal for the History of Philosophy* 24 (2016), 45–66.
15. A. Petagine, "Come una donna di rara saggezza: il *De immortalitate animae* di Pietro Pomponazzi e la psicologia di Tommaso d'Aquino," in M. Sgarbi (ed.), *Pietro Pomponazzi: Tradizione e dissenso* (Florence: 2010), 41–74.
16. This part of the refutation probably aims at followers of Scotus who affirm the presence of multiple forms in the human. See on this L. Casini, "The Renaissance Debate on the Immortality of the Soul: Pietro Pomponazzi and the Plurality of Substantial Forms," in P. J. J. M. Bakker and J. M. M. H. Thijssen (eds), *Mind, Cognition, and Representation: The Tradition of Commentaries on Aristotle's De Anima* (London: 2007), 127–50.
17. On this see J.-B. Brenet, "Corps-sujet, corps-objet: notes sur Averroès et Thomas d'Aquin dans le *De immortalitate animae* de Pomponazzi," in Biard and Gontier, *Pietro Pomponazzi entre traditions*, 11–28.
18. On whom see E. P. Mahoney, *Two Aristotelians of the Italian Renaissance: Nicoletto Vernia and Agostino Nifo* (Aldershot: 2000).
19. M. Engel, "Elijah del Medigo and Agostino Nifo on Intelligible Species," *Documenti e studi sulla tradizione filosofica medievale* 26 (2015), 495–516, at 513.
20. P. J. J. M. Bakker, "Natural Philosophy, Metaphysics, or Something in Between? Agostino Nifo, Pietro Pomponazzi, and Marcantonio Genua on the Nature and Place of the Science of the Soul," in Bakker and Thijssen, *Mind, Cognition, and Representation*, 151–77.
21. M. L. Pine, *Pietro Pomponazzi: Radical Philosopher of the Renaissance* (Padua: 1986), 156.
22. R. Lo Presti, "(Dis)embodied Thinking and the Scale of Beings: Pietro Pomponazzi and Agostino Nifo on the 'Psychic' Processes in Men and Animals," in S. Buchenau and R. Lo Presti (eds), *Human and Animal Cognition in Early Modern Philosophy and Medicine* (Pittsburgh: 2017), 37–54, at 49.

23. Quoted by L. Spruit, "Intellectual Beatitude in the Averroist Tradition: The Case of Agostino Nifo," in A. Akasoy and G. Giglioni (eds), *Renaissance Averroism and its Aftermath: Arabic Philosophy in Early Modern Europe* (Dordrecht: 2010), 125–44, at 141.
24. L. Spruit, "The Pomponazzi Affair: The Controversy over the Immortality of the Soul," in H. Lagerlund and B. Hill (eds), *Routledge Companion to Sixteenth-Century Philosophy* (New York: 2017), 225–46, at 236.
25. Spruit, "Intellectual Beatitude," 142.

47. There and Back Again: Zabarella on Scientific Method

1. Letter to Heidegger dated Dec. 30, 1927, cited by D. Welton, *The Other Husserl: The Horizons of Transcendental Phenomenology* (Bloomington, IN: 2000), 122.
2. For an influential modern-day discussion of this problem see J. Barnes, "Aristotle's Theory of Demonstration," *Phronesis* 14 (1969), 123–52.
3. Citations in this chapter are to J. P. McCaskey (ed. and trans.), *Jacopo Zabarella: On Methods, On Regressus*, 2 vols (Cambridge, MA: 2013), by section number (*Meth.* stands for *On Methods* and *Regr.* for *On Regressus*).
4. Cited by H. Mikkeli, *An Aristotelian Response to Renaissance Humanism: Jacopo Zabarella on the Nature of Arts and Sciences* (Helsinki: 1992), 44.
5. For the importance of Averroes as background to Zabarella see N. W. Gilbert, *Renaissance Concepts of Method* (New York: 1960), 166. For Averroes' scientific methodology see C. Cerami, "Signe physique, signe métaphysique: Avicenne et Averroès sur la démonstration des causes premières," in C. Cerami (ed.), *Nature et Sagesse: les rapports entre physique et métaphysique dans la tradition aristotélicienne* (Louvain: 2014), 429–74.
6. J. H. Randall, *The School of Padua and the Emergence of Modern Science* (Padua: 1961), 40; see also G. Papuli, "La teoria del *regressus* come metodo scientifico negli autori della Scuola di Padova," in L. Olivieri (ed.), *Aristotelismo Veneto e Scienza Moderna*, 2 vols (Padua: 1983), vol. 1, 221–77.
7. On this passage see D. Scott, *Levels of Argument: A Comparative Study of Plato's Republic and Aristotle's Nicomachean Ethics* (Oxford: 2015), ch. 9.
8. For the background in Nifo see Randall, *The School of Padua*, 42.
9. As argued by N. Jardine, "Keeping Order in the School of Padua: Jacopo Zabarella and Francesco Piccolomini on the Offices of Philosophy," in D. DiLiscia, E. Kessler and C. Methuen (eds), *Method and Order in Renaissance Philosophy of Nature: The Aristotle Commentary Tradition* (Aldershot: 1997), 183–209.
10. Cited by Randall, *The School of Padua*, 50.
11. For their conflict see Randall, *The School of Padua*, 62; Gilbert, *Renaissance Concepts of Method*, 174.
12. Jardine, "Keeping Order in the School of Padua," 195. See further H. Mikkeli, "The Foundations of an Autonomous Natural Philosophy: Zabarella on the Classification of Arts and Sciences," in D. DiLiscia et al., *Method and Order*, 211–28.
13. W. H. Hay and J. H. Randall (trans.), *Pietro Pomponazzi: On the Immortality of the Soul*, in E. Cassirer et al. (eds), *The Renaissance Philosophy of Man* (Chicago: 1956), 323.

14. Cited by Randall, *The School of Padua*, 54, and 47 for a priori vs a posteriori.
15. Mikkeli, "The Foundations of an Autonomous Natural Philosophy," 224.

48. The Measure of All Things: Mathematics and Art

1. P. L. Rose, *The Italian Renaissance of Mathematics: Studies on Humanists and Mathematicians from Petrarch to Galileo* (Geneva: 1975), 155. Many of the details in what follows are drawn from this book.
2. P. L. Rose, "Humanist Culture and Renaissance Mathematics: The Italian Libraries of the Quattrocento," *Studies in the Renaissance* 20 (1973), 46–105, at 52.
3. Rose, *The Italian Renaissance of Mathematics*, 146.
4. Rose, *The Italian Renaissance of Mathematics*, 13.
5. Both quotes cited from Rose, *The Italian Renaissance of Mathematics*, 185. See further 185 for the inked ball experiment and 268 for the quote on Archimedes as a follower of Aristotle.
6. O. Nuccio, *La storia del pensiero economico italiano: come storia della genesi dello spirito capitalistico* (Rome: 2008), 587.
7. R. N. Watkins (trans.), *Leon Battista Alberti: The Family in Renaissance Florence, Book Three* (Long Grove, IL: 1994), 36, 41–2.
8. As pointed out by C. H. Carman, *Leon Battista Alberti and Nicholas Cusanus: Towards an Epistemology of Vision for Italian Renaissance Art and Culture* (Farnham: 2014), 18.
9. Anthony Grafton, *Leon Battista Alberti: Master Builder of the Italian Renaissance* (Cambridge, MA: 2002), 90. For more on Alberti see J. Gadol, *Leon Battista Alberti: Universal Man of the Early Renaissance* (Chicago: 1969); F. Furlan (ed.), *Leon Battista Alberti: actes du congrès international de Paris 10–15 avril 1995*, 2 vols (Paris: 2000).
10. Cited by section number from R. Sinisgalli (ed. and trans.), *Leon Battista Alberti: On Painting* (Cambridge: 2011).
11. For the history of this debate see P. Adamson, *A History of Philosophy Without Any Gaps: Philosophy in the Islamic World*, ch. 11.
12. Carman, *Leon Battista Alberti*, 6.
13. Cited from Grafton, *Leon Battista Alberti*, 121, and 88 for the viewing box.
14. Carman, *Leon Battista Alberti*, 52.
15. Grafton, *Leon Battista Alberti*, 270–1; 263. For more on architecture in this period see C. Smith, *Architecture in the Culture of Early Humanism: Ethics, Aesthetics and Eloquence 1400–1470* (Oxford: 1992); A. Payne, *The Architectural Treatise in the Italian Renaissance: Architectural Invention, Ornament, and Literary Culture* (Cambridge: 1993).
16. K. B. Moore, "Ficino's Idea of Architecture: The 'Mind's-Eye View' in Quattrocento Architectural Drawings," *Renaissance Studies* 24 (2010), 332–52, 351.
17. C. L. Joost-Gaugier, *Pythagoras and Renaissance Europe: Finding Heaven* (Cambridge: 2009), 180.
18. S. Jayne (trans.), *Marsilio Ficino's Commentary on Plato's Symposium* (Columbia, MO: 1944), 92–3, cited at Moore, "Ficino's Idea of Architecture," 337, and 347 for the following quote from Alberti.
19. Rose, *The Italian Renaissance of Mathematics*, 247.

20. Joost-Gaugier, *Pythagoras and Renaissance Europe*, 52; 57.
21. S. Campanini, *Francesco Zorzi: l'armonia del mondo* (Florence: 2010). See further C. Moreschini, "Francesco Zorzi e la 'pia philosophie': richerche sulle fonti," *Bruniana e Campanelliana* 20 (2014), 97–113; L. Spruit, "Francesco Giorgio on the Harmony of the Creation and the Catholic Censorship of his Views," in J. Prins and M. Vanhaelen (eds), *Sing Aloud Harmonious Spheres: Renaissance Conceptions of Cosmic Harmony* (London: 2017), 123–38.
22. M. A. Peterson, *Galileo's Muse: Renaissance Mathematics and the Arts* (Cambridge, MA: 2011), 140. On Pacioli and his influence see also I. D. Rowland, *The Culture of the High Renaissance: Ancients and Moderns in Sixteenth-Century Rome* (Cambridge: 1998), ch. 5.

49. Just What the Doctor Ordered: Renaissance Medicine

1. N. Siriasi, *The Clock and the Mirror: Girolamo Cardano and Renaissance Medicine* (Princeton: 1997), 165.
2. D. O. Hughes, "Bodies, Disease, and Society," in J. M. Najemy (ed.), *Italy in the Age of the Renaissance* (Oxford: 2004), 103–22, at 105; the following quote from Luther is taken from 107–8. For hospitals see also J. Henderson, *The Renaissance Hospital: Healing the Body and Healing the Soul* (New Haven: 2006).
3. Notable for his idea that contagion occurs by the dispersing of tiny particles is Girolamo Fracastoro (d. 1553). See V. Nutton, "The Reception of Fracastoro's Theory of Contagion: The Seed That Fell among Thorns?" *Osiris* 6 (1990), 196–234.
4. N. G. Siraisi, *History, Medicine, and the Traditions of Renaissance Learning* (Ann Arbor: 2007), 178–87.
5. N. G. Siraisi, *Medieval and Early Renaissance Medicine: An Introduction to Knowledge and Practice* (Chicago: 1990), 63. See also N. G. Siraisi (ed.), *Medicine and the Italian Universities 1250–1600* (Leiden: 2001).
6. Quoted by Siraisi, *Medieval and Early Renaissance Medicine*, 78.
7. For a more detailed overview see G. Giglioni, "Health in the Renaissance," in P. Adamson (ed.), *Health: A History* (Oxford: 2019), 141–73.
8. For discussion see G. Giglioni, "Medical Approaches to the Mind in the late Middle Ages and the Renaissance," in S. Schmid (ed.), *Philosophy of Mind in the Late Middle Ages and Renaissance* (London: 2019), 41–62.
9. C. B. Schmitt, "Aristotle among the Physicians," in A. Wear et al. (eds), *The Medical Renaissance of the Sixteenth Century* (Cambridge: 1985), 1–15, at 8. See 15 for texts citing the following motto *ubi desinit philosophus* . . .
10. Siraisi, *Medieval and Early Renaissance Medicine*, 67. Pietro adds as a third ancillary art astrology, "since it is directive of judgments"; for more on the links between astrology and medicine see below, Chapter 52.
11. See *A History of Philosophy Without Any Gaps: Philosophy in the Hellenistic and Roman Worlds*, chs 19–20.

12. For more on humanism and Renaissance medicine see e.g. R. Schmitz and G. Keil (eds), *Humanismus und Medizin* (Weinheim: 1984); Vivian Nutton, "The Rise of Medical Humanism: Ferrara, 1464–1555," *Renaissance Studies* 11 (1997), 2–19.
13. H. Hirai, *Medical Humanism and Natural Philosophy: Renaissance Debates on Matter, Life and the Soul* (Leiden: 2011), 44.
14. A. D. Berns, *The Bible and Natural Philosophy in Renaissance Italy* (Cambridge: 2015), 112–41.
15. N. G. Siraisi, "The Changing Fortunes of a Traditional Text: Goals and Strategies in Sixteenth-Century Latin Editions of the *Canon* of Avicenna," in Wear, *The Medical Renaissance*, 16–41, at 17. See further N. G. Siraisi, *Avicenna in Renaissance Italy: The Canon and Medical Teaching in Italian Universities After 1500* (Princeton: 1987).
16. R. K. French, "Berengario da Carpi and the Use of Commentary in Anatomical Teaching," in Wear, *The Medical Renaissance*, 42–74, at 67–9.
17. See J. McGinnis, "Scientific Methodologies in Medieval Islam: Induction and Experimentation in the Philosophy of Ibn Sīnā," *Journal of the History of Philosophy* 41 (2003), 307–27; J. Janssens "'Experience (*tajriba*)' in Classical Arabic Philosophy (al-Fārābī-Avicenna)," *Quaestio* 4 (2004), 45–62; D. Gutas, "The Empiricism of Avicenna," *Oriens* 40 (2012), 391–436.
18. French, "Berengario da Carpi," 57–9. For early anatomy see also L. R. Lind, *Pre-Vesalian Anatomy, Biography, Translations, Documents* (Philadelphia: 1975).
19. W. F. Richardson and J. B. Carman (trans.), *Andreas Vesalius: On the Fabric of the Human Body* (San Francisco: 1998). On him see L. Edelstein, "Andreas Vesalius, the Humanist," *Bulletin of the History of Medicine* 14 (1943), 547–61; C. D. O'Malley, *Andreas Vesalius of Brussels* (Los Angeles: 1965); A. Cunningham, *The Anatomical Renaissance* (Aldershot: 1997); R. Cuir, *The Development of the Study of Anatomy from the Renaissance to Cartesianism: Da Carpi, Vesalius, Estienne, Bidloo* (Lewiston, ME: 2009). On the extent to which anatomists in this period were willing to challenge authority, see A. Carlino, *Books of the Body, Anatomical Ritual and Renaissance Learning*, trans. J. Tedeschi and A. C. Tedeschi (Chicago: 1999).
20. On which see J. Sawday, *The Body Emblazoned: Dissection and the Human Body in Renaissance Culture* (London: 1995); M. Kemp, *Visualisations: The Nature Book of Art and Science* (Berkeley: 2000).
21. R. Sinisgalli (ed. and trans.), *Leon Battista Alberti: On Painting* (Cambridge: 2011), §§41–2.
22. For what follows see A. Cunningham, "Fabricius and the 'Aristotle Project' in Anatomical Teaching and Research at Padua," in Wear, *The Medical Renaissance*, 195–222.
23. Cunningham, "Fabricius," 202.

50. Man of Discoveries: Girolamo Cardano

1. R. F. Brown and J. M. Stewart (trans.), *G.W.F. Hegel: Lectures on the History of Philosophy*, vol. 3 (Berkeley: 1990), 36, and 74 for the following quote on Cardano.
2. Cited by chapter from J. Stoner (trans.), *Girolamo Cardano: The Book of My Life* (New York: 2002).
3. On this episode see I. Maclean, "Girolamo Cardano: The Last Years of a Polymath," *Renaissance Studies* 21 (2007), 587–607.

4. For Cardano as imitating Galen's persona see G. Giglioni, "Autobiography as Self-Mastery: Writing, Madness, and Method in Girolamo Cardano," *Bruniana e Campanelliana* 7 (2001), 331–62, at 334.
5. On his medical writings see N. Siraisi, *The Clock and the Mirror: Girolamo Cardano and Renaissance Medicine* (Princeton: 1997).
6. M. Fierz, *Girolamo Cardano, 1501–1576: Physician, Natural Philosopher, Mathematician, Astrologer, and Interpreter of Dreams* (Boston: 1983), 43.
7. Siraisi, *The Clock and the Mirror*, 28.
8. Siraisi, *The Clock and the Mirror*, 74.
9. N. G. Siraisi, *History, Medicine, and the Traditions of Renaissance Learning* (Ann Arbor: 2007), 162.
10. J. M. Forrester (trans.), *The De subtilitate of Girolamo Cardano*, 2 vols (Tempe, AZ: 2013), vol. 2, 820.
11. G. Giglioni, "Girolamo Cardano: University Student and Professor," *Renaissance Studies* 27 (2013), 517–32, at 520.
12. Siraisi, *The Clock and the Mirror*, 142, 58.
13. Cited at Giglioni, "University Student and Professor," 526.
14. H. Hirai, *Medical Humanism and Natural Philosophy: Renaissance Debates on Matter, Life and the Soul* (Leiden: 2011), 111.
15. On this topic see G. Giglioni, "The Eternal Return of the Same Intellects: A New Edition of Girolamo Cardano's *De immortalitate animorum*," *Bruniana e Campanelliana* 13 (2007), 177–83; J. M. G. Valverde, "The Arguments Against the Immortality of the Soul in *De immortalitate animorum* of Girolamo Cardano," *Bruniana e Campanelliana* 13 (2007), 55–77; I. Maclean, "Cardano's Eclectic Psychology and its Critique by Julius Caesar Scaliger," *Vivarium* 46 (2008), 392–417; J. M. G. Valverde, "Averroistic Themes in Girolamo Cardano's *De immortalitate animorum*," in A. Akasoy and G. Giglioni (eds), *Renaissance Averroism and Its Aftermath: Philosophy in Early Modern Europe* (Dordrecht: 2013), 145–71.
16. Cited by Valverde, "Averroistic Themes," 165.
17. Giglioni, "The Eternal Return," 178.
18. Cited by G. Giglioni, "Girolamo Cardano on the Passions and their Treatment," *Bruniana & Campanelliana* 12 (2006), 25–40, at 26.
19. Forrester, *The De subtilitate*, vol. 2, 751.
20. O. Ore, *Cardano: The Gambling Scholar* (Princeton: 1953), 143; this book also contains a translation of the work.
21. Ore, *Gambling Scholar*.
22. T. R. Witmer (trans.), *Girolamo Cardano: Ars magna or The Rules of Algebra* (New York: 1968).
23. The Byzantine tradition, incidentally, also sees authors playing fast and loose with intellectual priority. It has been noted that in mathematical treatises, Byzantine scholars regularly provide the same solution to the problem of extracting square roots, but each author "pretends that it was his own original elaboration": S. Lazaris (ed.), *A Companion to Byzantine Science* (Leiden: 2020), 107.
24. On this clash see I. Maclean, "The Interpretation of Natural Signs: Cardano's *De subtilitate* versus Scaliger's *Exercitationes*," in B. Vickers (ed.), *Occult and Scientific Mentalities in the Renaissance* (Cambridge: 1984), 231–52; Maclean, "Cardano's Eclectic Psychology";

G. Giglioni, "Scaliger versus Cardano versus Scaliger," in D. A. Lines et al. (eds), *Forms of Conflict and Rivalries in Renaissance Europe* (Bonn: 2015), 109–30.

25. Forrester, *De subtilitate*, vol. 1, 15.
26. A. Grafton, *Cardano's Cosmos: The Worlds and Works of a Renaissance Astrologer* (Cambridge, MA: 1999), 4.
27. Cited at Giglioni, "Scaliger versus Cardano," 118.
28. See G. Giglioni, "Synesian Dreams: Girolamo Cardano on Dreams as Means of Prophetic Communication," *Bruniana & Campanelliana* 16 (2010), 575–84.
29. Fierz, *Girolamo Cardano*, 128.
30. Cited at Giglioni, "Synesian Dreams," 582.

51. Spirits in the Material World: Telesio and Campanella on Nature

1. J. M. Headley, *Tommaso Campanella and the Transformation of the World* (Princeton: 1997), 160.
2. Cited from G. Ernst, *Tommaso Campanella: The Book and the Body of Nature* (Dordrecht: 2010), 171.
3. I cite by section number from the 1570 edition, which is provided (with a facing-page Italian translation) in R. Bondì (ed. and trans.), *Bernardino Telesio: la natura secondo i suoi principi, con testo originale a fronte secondo l'edizione del 1570* (Milan: 2009). For general studies of Telesio see N. van Deusen, *Telesio: The First of the Moderns* (New York: 1932); R. Bondì, *Introduzione a Telesio* (Rome: 1997); P. Ponzio, *Tommaso Campanella: filosofia della natura e teoria della scienza* (Bari: 2002); G. Mocchi, *Bernardino Telesio tra filosofia naturale e scienza moderna* (Pisa: 2012); R. Bondì, *Il primo dei moderni: filosofia e scienza in Bernardino Telesio* (Rome: 2018).
4. K. Schuhmann, "Telesio's Concept of Matter", in K. Schuhmann, *Selected Papers on Renaissance Philosophy and on Thomas Hobbes* (Dordrecht: 2004), 99–116.
5. H. Hattab, "The Metaphysics of Substantial Forms," in H. Lagerlund (ed.), *Routledge Companion to Sixteenth Century Philosophy* (New York: 2017), 436–57, at 443.
6. Plotinus, *Enneads*, 2.4.5.
7. Cited from Ernst, *Tommaso Campanella*, 120.
8. L. Spruit, "Telesio's Reform of the Philosophy of Mind", *Bruniana & Campanelliana* 3 (1997), 124–43; G. Giglioni, "The First of the Moderns or the Last of the Ancients? Bernardino Telesio on Nature and Sentience," *Bruniana & Campanelliana* 16 (2010), 69–87.
9. B. M. Bonansea, *Tommaso Campanella: Renaissance Pioneer of Modern Thought* (Washington, DC: 1969), 88.
10. As pointed out by M. Mulsow, *Frühneuzeitliche Selbsterhaltung: Telesio und die Naturphilosophie der Renaissance* (Tübingen: 1998), 98.
11. Bondì, *Il primo dei moderni, 36.*
12. Mulsow, *Frühneuzeitliche Selbsterhaltung*, 111.
13. Mulsow, *Frühneuzeitliche Selbsterhaltung*, 269, and 253 for the following point about sleep. See further J. Bylebyl, "Disputation and Description in the Renaissance Pulse Controversy," in A. Wear, R. K. French and I. M. Lonie (eds), *The Medical Renaissance of the Sixteenth Century* (New York: 1985), 223–45.

14. Cited from Headley, *Tommaso Campanella*, 169.
15. Headley, *Tommaso Campanella*, 157.
16. Ernst, *Tommaso Campanella*, 160.
17. Ernst, *Tommaso Campanella*, 21.
18. I cite by section number from the edition in P. Ponzio (ed. and trans.), *Tommaso Campanella: Metafisica* (Bari: 1994). This reproduces the Latin text of the final of several versions of the work, which was printed in 1638.
19. Bonansea, *Tommaso Campanella*, 59.
20. As pointed out by Bondì, *Il primo dei moderni*, 13.
21. Ernst, *Tommaso Campanella*, 12–13.

52. The Men Who Saw Tomorrow: Renaissance Magic and Astrology

1. I take the story from W. Eamon, "Astrology and Society," in B. Dooley (ed.), *A Companion to Astrology in the Renaissance* (Leiden: 2014), 141–91, at 141–3.
2. M. Azzolini, *The Duke and the Stars: Astrology and Politics in Renaissance Milan* (Cambridge, MA: 2013), with the following case discussed in ch. 4.
3. On this see C. Pennuto, "The Debate on Critical Days in Renaissance Italy," in A. Akasoy et al. (eds), *Astro Medicine: Astrology and Medicine, East and West* (Florence: 2008), 75–98; G. M. Cooper, "Approaches to the Critical Days in Late Medieval and Renaissance Thinkers," *Early Science and Medicine* 18 (2013), 536–65.
4. A. Grafton and N. Siraisi, "Between the Election and My Hopes: Girolamo Cardano and Medical Astrology," in W. R. Newman and A. Grafton (eds), *Secrets of Nature: Astrology and Alchemy in Early Modern Europe* (Cambridge, MA: 2001), 69–131, at 90.
5. In what follows I draw on A. Grafton, *Cardano's Cosmos: The Worlds and Works of a Renaissance Astrologer* (Cambridge, MA: 1999).
6. Eamon, "Astrology and Society," 147.
7. G. Ernst, "*Veritatis amor dulcissimus*: Aspects of Cardano's Astrology," in Newman and Grafton, *Secrets of Nature*, 39–68, at 52.
8. Grafton, *Cardano's Cosmos*, 143.
9. D. N. Hasse, *Success and Suppression: Arabic Sciences and Philosophy in the Renaissance* (Cambridge, MA: 2016), 283, and 252 for the quote from Nifo.
10. Grafton and Siraisi, "Between the Election and My Hopes," 106.
11. Hasse, *Success and Suppression*, 272, and 263 for the quote about Ibn Riḍwān.
12. See S. J. Rabin, "Pico on Magic and Astrology," in M. V. Dougherty (ed.), *Pico della Mirandola: New Essays* (Cambridge: 2008), 152–78.
13. Grafton, *Cardano's Cosmos*, 10–11.
14. Cooper, "Approaches to the Critical Days," 557.
15. Ernst, "*Veritatis amor dulcissimus*," 60.
16. O. P. Faracovi, "In difesa dell'astrologia: risposte a Pico in Bellanti e Pontano," in M. Bertozzi (ed.), *Nello Specchio del cielo, Giovanni Pico della Mirandola contro l'astrologia divinatoria* (Florence: 2008), 47–65.

17. J. Prins, *Echoes of an Invisible World: Marsilio Ficino and Francesco Patrizi on Cosmic Order and Music Theory* (Leiden: 2014), 231–2.
18. S. A. Farmer, *Syncretism in the West: Pico's 900 Theses (1486)* (Tempe, AZ: 1998), §9.1–4.
19. Farmer, *Syncretism in the West*, §10.4.
20. D. J.-J. Robichaud, "Ficino on Force, Magic, and Prayers: Neoplatonic and Hermetic Influences in Ficino's Three Books on Life," *Renaissance Quarterly* 70 (2017), 44–87, at 44. For a facing page Latin text and English translation see C. V. Kaske and J. R. Clark, *Marsilio Ficino: Three Books on Life* (Binghamton: 1989); I quote from this in what follows, by section number.
21. Quoted at I. P. Couliano, *Eros and Magic in the Renaissance*, trans. M. Cook (Chicago: 1987), 48. See further R. Klibansky et al., *Saturn and Melancholy: Studies in the History of Natural Philosophy, Religion, and Art* (New York: 1963).
22. Quoted at N. Siraisi, *The Clock and the Mirror: Girolamo Cardano and Renaissance Medicine* (Princeton: 1997), 166.
23. B. P. Copenhaver, *Magic in Western Culture: From Antiquity to the Enlightenment* (Cambridge: 2015), 97. For the topic see also Couliano, *Eros and Magic*.
24. Kaske and Clark, *Marsilio Ficino: Three Books on Life*, 396.
25. See C. Addey, "The Daimonion of Socrates: Daimones and Divination in Neoplatonism," in D. A. Layne and H. Tarrant (eds), *The Neoplatonic Socrates* (Philadelphia: 2014), 51–72; L. Brisson et al., *Neoplatonic Demons and Angels* (Leiden: 2018).
26. M. J. B. Allen, *Studies in the Neoplatonism of Marsilio Ficino and Giovanni Pico* (Abington: 2017), 218–19. See also D. P. Walker, *Spiritual and Demonic Magic: From Ficino to Campanella* (London: 1958).
27. P. Zambelli, *White Magic, Black Magic in the European Renaissance* (Leiden: 2007), 29.
28. N. Tarrant, "Giambattista Della Porta and the Roman Inquisition: Censorship and the Definition of Nature's Limits in Sixteenth-Century Italy," *British Journal for the History of Science* 46 (2013), 601–25, at 616.
29. C. Caputo, "Un manuale di semiotica del Cinquecento: il *De humana physiognomonia* di Giovan Battista della Porta," in M. Torrini (ed.), *Giovan Battista della Porta nell' Europa del suo tempo* (Naples: 1990), 69–91.
30. Grafton, *Cardano's Cosmos*, 146.
31. See M. L. Pine, *Pietro Pomponazzi: Radical Philosopher of the Renaissance* (Padua: 1986), ch. 3.

53. Boundless Enthusiasm: Giordano Bruno

1. Quoted at H. Gatti, *Essays on Giordano Bruno* (Princeton: 2011), 18 and 23.
2. For introductions to Bruno's life and career see I. D. Rowland, *Giordano Bruno: Philosopher/Heretic* (Chicago: 2008); P. R. Blum, *Giordano Bruno: An Introduction*, trans. P. Henneveld (Amsterdam: 2012); H. Gatti, *Giordano Bruno* (Florence: 2017).
3. D. Knox, "Giordano Bruno," in the online *Stanford Encyclopedia of Philosophy*.
4. For the trial and documents it produced see L. Firpo, *Il processo di Giordano Bruno* (Rome: 1993), French trans. by A.-P. Segonds, *Le procès de Giordano Bruno* (Paris: 2000).

5. M. A. Finocchiaro, "Philosophy versus Religion and Science versus Religion: The Trials of Bruno and Galileo," in H. Gatti (ed.), *Giordano Bruno and Renaissance Science* (Ithaca, NY: 2002), 51–96, at 73–4.
6. Blum, *Giordano Bruno*, 5.
7. I cite by page from R. J. Blackwell and R. de Lucca (trans.), *Giordano Bruno: Cause, Principle and Unity and Essays on Magic* (Cambridge: 2004), abbreviated *CPU*. See also S. T. Greenburg, *The Infinite in Giordano Bruno* (New York: 1978).
8. On Ibn Gabirol's "universal hylomorphism" see *A History of Philosophy Without Any Gaps: Philosophy in the Islamic World*, ch. 29.
9. Gatti, *Essays*, 81. See further E. Schettino, "The Necessity of the Minima in the Nolan Philosophy," in Gatti, *Giordano Bruno and Renaissance Science*, 299–325; W. Neuser, "Atom, Matter, and Monade," in H. Hufnagel and A. Eusterschulte (eds), *Turning Traditions Upside Down: Rethinking Giordano Bruno's Enlightenment* (Budapest: 2013), 107–19.
10. My translation of the text cited by P. R. Blum, *Giordano Bruno Teaches Aristotle* (Nordhausen: 2016).
11. I cite by page from H. Gatti (trans.), *Giordano Bruno: The Ash Wednesday Supper* (Toronto: 2018), abbreviated as *AWS*.
12. Blum, *Giordano Bruno*, 48.
13. C. B. Schmitt, *John Case and Aristotelianism in Renaissance England* (Montreal: 1983), 58. My thanks to James Hannam for the reference.
14. For the contrast to Savile see Gatti, *Essays*, 22.
15. See also D. Massa, "Giordano Bruno and the Top-Sail Experiment," *Annals of Science* 30 (1973), 201–11.
16. Finocchiaro, "Philosophy versus Religion," 79.
17. Quoted at M. Mertens, *Magic and Memory in Giordano Bruno: The Art of a Heroic Spirit* (Leiden: 2018), 141.
18. On Llull see *A History of Philosophy Without Any Gaps: Medieval Philosophy*, ch. 78.
19. F. A. Yates, *Giordano Bruno and the Hermetic Tradition* (London: 1964). See also K. S. De Léon-Jones, *Giordano Bruno and the Kabbalah: Prophets, Magicians, and Rabbis* (New Haven: 1997).
20. For example in her introduction to her edition of Bruno's *De umbris idearum* (Florence: 1991). For a discussion of this controversy see S. Clucas, "Simulacra et Signacula: Memory, Magic and Metaphysics in Brunian Mnemonics," in Gatti, *Giordano Bruno and Renaissance Science*, 251–72. Yates' stress on the Hermetic sources of Renaissance thought has also been criticized by Brian Copenhaver, e.g. in his "Natural Magic, Hermetism, and Occultism in Early Modern Science," in D. C. Lindberg and R. S. Westman (eds), *Reappraisals of the Scientific Revolution* (Cambridge: 1990), 261–301.
21. For this phrase and the use of Aristotle see Clucas, "Simulacra et Signacula," 267.
22. Mertens, *Magic and Memory in Giordano Bruno*, 126.
23. Cited by page from I. D. Rowland (trans.) and E. Canone (ed.), *Giordano Bruno: On the Heroic Frenzies* (Toronto: 2013). On the work see J. C. Nelson, *Renaissance Theory of Love: The Context of Giordano Bruno's Eroici furori* (New York: 1958).

54. The Harder They Fall: Galileo and the Renaissance

1. Quoted from E. McMullin, "The Conception of Science in Galileo's Work," in R. E. Butts and J. C. Pitt (eds), *New Perspectives on Galileo* (Dordrecht: 1978), 209–57, at 209–10. The passage is in the preface to the second edition of the *Critique*.
2. See H. D. Rutkin, "Galileo Astrologer: Astrology and Mathematical Practice in the Late Sixteenth and Early Seventeenth Centuries," *Galilaeana* 2 (2005), 107–43.
3. Apart from Savanarola.
4. For an overview of his career and its connection to the scholastic tradition see W. A. Wallace, "Galileo's Pisan Studies in Science and Philosophy," in P. Machamer (ed.), *The Cambridge Companion to Galileo* (Cambridge: 1998), 27–52.
5. This is the central contention of W. A. Wallace, *Galileo and His Sources: The Heritage of the Collegio Romano in Galileo's Science* (Princeton: 1984).
6. W. A. Wallace, *Prelude to Galileo: Essays on Medieval and Sixteenth-Century Sources of Galileo's Thought* (Dordrecht: 1981), 136.
7. Cited by C. B. Schmitt, "Experience and Experiment: A Comparison of Zabarella's View with Galileo's *De motu*," *Studies in the Renaissance* 16 (1969), 80–138, at 113.
8. Cited by W. A. Wallace, *Galileo's Logic of Discovery and Proof: The Background, Content, and Use of His Appropriated Treatises on Aristotle's Posterior Analytics* (Dordrecht: 1992), 295.
9. Citations throughout the chapter are to M. A. Finocchiaro (trans.), *The Essential Galileo* (Indianapolis: 2008).
10. J. H. Randall Jr., "The Development of Scientific Method in the School of Padua," *Journal of the History of Ideas* 1 (1940), 177–206, at 183.
11. Cited by P. L. Rose, *The Italian Renaissance of Mathematics: Studies on Humanists and Mathematicians from Petrarch to Galileo* (Geneva: 1975), 281 and 283. For more on Galileo and the mixed sciences see J. G. Lennox, "Aristotle, Galileo, and 'Mixed Sciences'," in W. A. Wallace (ed.), *Reinterpreting Galileo* (Washington, DC: 1986), 29–51; W. R. Laird, "Galileo and the Mixed Sciences," in D. DiLiscia et al. (eds), *Method and Order in Renaissance Philosophy of Nature: The Aristotle Commentary Tradition* (Aldershot: 1997), 253–70, and P. Machamer, "Galileo's Machines, His Mathematics, and His Experiments," in Machamer, *Cambridge Companion*, 53–79. Relevant texts are translated in I. E. Drabkin and S. Drake (trans.), *Galileo Galilei, On Motion and On Mechanics* (Madison: 1960).
12. W. L. Wisan, "Galileo's Scientific Method," in Butts and Pitt, *New Perspectives on Galileo*, 2–57, at 22.
13. Cited by S. Ducheyne, "Galileo's Interventionist Notion of 'Cause,'" *Journal of the History of Ideas* 67 (2006), 443–64, at 450. On the topic see also P. Machamer, "Galileo and the Causes," in Butts and Pitt, *New Perspectives on Galileo*, 161–80.
14. For experiment as Galileo's version of *negotatio* see W. A. Wallace, "Circularity and the Paduan *Regressus*: From Pietro d'Abano to Galileo Galilei," *Vivarium* 33 (1995), 76–97, at 95.
15. Wallace, *Galileo's Logic of Discovery and Proof*, 185–6.
16. Wallace, *Galileo's Logic of Discovery and Proof*, 251.
17. Wisan, "Galileo's Scientific Method," 8; McMullin, "The Conception of Science," 230; Wallace, *Galileo's Logic of Discovery and Proof*, 252, 261.
18. Schmitt, "Experience and Experiment," 117–19.

19. Wallace, "Circularity and the Paduan Regressus," 97; see also P. Palmieri, "Re-examining Galileo's Theory of the Tides," *Archives for the History of the Exact Sciences* 53 (1998), 223–375.
20. R. J. Blackwell, *Galileo, Bellarmine, and the Bible* (Notre Dame, IL: 1991), 73. For a comparison of the two thinkers see H. Gatti, "Giordano Bruno's *Ash Wednesday Supper* and Galileo's *Dialogue of the Two Major Systems,*" *Bruniana e Campanelliana* 3 (1997), 283–300.
21. Wallace, *Galileo's Logic of Discovery and Proof*, 233.
22. Wisan, "Galileo's Scientific Method," 4.
23. McMullin, "The Conception of Science," 222.
24. See *A History of Philosophy Without Any Gaps: Philosophy in the Islamic World*, ch. 25.
25. Wallace, "Galileo's Pisan Studies," 51.

FURTHER READING

Further reading is suggested here for the two main sections of the book, followed by recommendations for the topics of specific chapters. References on more specific topics and for primary literature in translation can be found in notes to the chapters of this volume.

In addition to the suggestions below, the online *Stanford Encyclopedia of Philosophy* has many pages on individual Renaissance thinkers and a good entry on Byzantine philosophy.

Byzantine Philosophy: General Overviews

L. G. Benakis, *Byzantine Philosophy: An Introductory Approach* (Saarbrücken: 2017).

B. Bydén and K. Ierodiakonou, "Greek philosophy", in J. Marenbon (ed.), *The Oxford Handbook of Medieval Philosophy* (Oxford: 2012), 29–57.

B. Bydén and K. Ierodiakonou (eds), *The Many Faces of Byzantine Philosophy* (Athens: 2012).

M. Cacouros and M.-H. Congourdeau (eds), *Philosophies et Sciences à Byzance de 1204 à 1453* (Leuven: 2006).

K. Ierodiakonou (ed.), *Byzantine Philosophy and Its Ancient Sources* (Oxford: 2002).

A. Kaldellis and N. Siniossoglou (eds), *The Cambridge Intellectual History of Byzantium* (Cambridge: 2017).

G. Kapriev, "The Modern Study of Byzantine Philosophy," *Bulletin de philosophie médiévale* 48 (2006), 1–13.

G. Kapriev, *Philosophie in Byzanz* (Würzburg: 2005).

M. Knežvić (ed.), *The Ways of Byzantine Philosophy* (Alhambra, CA: 2015).

S. Lazaris, *A Companion to Byzantine Science* (Leiden: 2020).

B. Tatakis, *Byzantine Philosophy*, trans. N. J. Moutafakis (Indianapolis: 2003).

M. Trizio, "Byzantine Philosophy as a Contemporary Historiographical Project," *Recherches de théologie et philosophie médiévales* 74 (2007), 247–94.

Renaissance Italian Philosophy: General Overviews

P. R. Blum, *Philosophers of the Renaissance* (Washington, DC: 2010).

C. S. Celenza, *The Italian Renaissance and the Origins of the Modern Humanities: An Intellectual History, 1400–1800* (Cambridge: 2021).

B. Copenhaver and C. B. Schmitt, *Renaissance Philosophy* (Oxford: 1992).

E. Garin, *Storia della filosofia italiana*, 3 vols (Turin: 1966).

É. Gilson, *Humanisme et Renaissance* (Paris: 1983).

J. Haskins (ed.), *Cambridge Companion to Renaissance Philosophy* (Cambridge: 2007).

J. Kraye (ed.), *Cambridge Translations of Renaissance Philosophical Texts*, 2 vols (Cambridge: 1997).

P. O. Kristeller, *Eight Philosophers of the Italian Renaissance* (Stanford, CA: 1964).

H. Lagerlund and B. Hill (eds), *Routledge Companion to Sixteenth-Century Philosophy* (New York: 2017), 225–46.

C. B. Schmitt and Q. Skinner (eds), *Cambridge History of Renaissance Philosophy* (Cambridge: 1988).

Philosophy in Syriac and Armenian

S. Brock, *Syrian Perspectives on Late Antiquity* (London: 1984).

V. Calzolari and J. Barnes (eds), *L'oeuvre de David l'Invincible* (Leiden: 2009).

H. Hugonnard-Roche, *La logique d'Aristote du grec au syriaque* (Paris: 2004).

H. Takahashi, "Between Greek and Arabic: The Sciences in Syriac from Severus Sebokht to Barhebraeus," in H. Kobayashi and M. Kato (eds), *Transmission of Sciences: Greek, Syriac, Arabic and Latin* (Tokyo: 2010), 16–39.

É. Villey (ed.), *Les sciences en syriaque* (Paris: 2014).

J. W. Watt, *Rhetoric and Philosophy from Greek into Syriac* (Farnham: 2010).

Iconoclasm

T. Anagnostopoulos, "Aristotle and Byzantine Iconoclasm," *Greek, Roman, and Byzantine Studies* 53 (2013), 763–90.

C. Barber, *Figure and Likeness: On the Limits of Representation in Byzantine Iconoclasm* (Princeton: 2002).

L. Brubaker, *Inventing Byzantine Iconoclasm* (Bristol: 2012).

A. Bryer and J. Herrin (eds), *Iconoclasm: Papers Given at the Ninth Spring Symposium of Byzantine Studies* (Birmingham: 1977).

K. Parry, *Depicting the Word: Byzantine Iconophile Thought of the Eighth and Ninth Centuries* (Leiden: 1996).

D. Sahas, *Icon and Logos: Sources in Eighth-Century Iconoclasm* (Toronto: 1986).

John of Damascus

V. Kontouma, *John of Damascus: New Studies on his Life and Works* (Farnham: 2015).

A. Louth, *St. John Damascene: Tradition and Originality in Byzantine Theology* (Oxford: 2009).

S. Markov, *Die metaphysische Synthese des Johannes von Damaskus: historische Zusammenhänge und Strukturtransformationen* (Leiden: 2015).

P. Schadler, *John of Damascus and Islam: Christian Heresiology and the Intellectual Background to Earliest Christian–Muslim Relations* (Leiden: 2018).

Photius and Byzantine Compilations

J. Anton, "The Aristotelianism of Photius", in L. R. Schrenk (ed.), *Aristotle in Late Antiquity* (Washington, DC: 1994), 158–83.

P. Lemerle, *Byzantine Humanism: The First Phase* (Canberra: 1986).

M. Roueché, "Byzantine Philosophical Texts of the Seventh Century," *Jahrbuch der österreichischen Byzantinistik* 23 (1974), 61–76.

J. Schamp, *Photios historien des lettres: la Bibliothèque et ses notices biographiques* (Paris: 1987).

W. T. Treadgold, *The Nature of the Bibliotheca of Photius* (Washington, DC: 1980).

Michael Psellos and John Italos

C. Barber and D. Jenkins (eds), *Reading Michael Psellos* (Leiden: 2006).
L. Clucas, *The Trial of John Italos and the Crisis of Intellectual Values in Byzantium in the Eleventh Century* (Munich: 1981).
P. Joannou, *Die Illuminationslehre des Michael Psellos und Joannes Italos* (Freising: 1956).
A. Kaldellis, *The Argument of Psellos' Chronographia* (Leiden: 1999).
A. Kaldellis, *Hellenism in Byzantium: The Transformations of Greek Identity and the Reception of the Classical Tradition* (Cambridge: 2007).
D. J. O'Meara, "Michael Psellos," in S. Gersh (ed.), *Interpreting Proclus from Antiquity to the Renaissance* (Cambridge: 2014), 165–81.
D. Walter, *Michael Psellos: Christliche Philosophie in Byzanz* (Berlin: 2017).

Political Philosophy and Rhetoric in Byzantium

D. Angelov, *Imperial Ideology and Political Thought in Byzantium, 1204–1330* (Cambridge: 2007).
E. Barker, *Social and Political Thought in Byzantium from Justinian I to the Last Palaeologus* (Oxford: 1957).
E. Jeffreys (ed.), *Rhetoric in Byzantium* (Aldershot: 2003).
S. Papaioannou, *Michael Psellos: Rhetoric and Authorship in Byzantium* (Cambridge: 2013).
M. Vogiatzi, *Byzantine Commentaries on Aristotle's Rhetoric: Anonymous and Stephanus* (Berlin: 2019).

Byzantine Historiography

D. Krallis, *Michael Attaleiates and the Politics of Imperial Decline in Eleventh Century Byzantium* (Tempe, AZ: 2012).
P. Magdalino, "Aspects of Twelfth Century Byzantine *Kaiserkritik*," *Speculum* 58 (1983), 326–46.
W. Treadgold, *The Middle Byzantine Historians* (New York: 2013).
T. Urbainczyk, *Writing about Byzantium: The History of Niketas Choniates* (London: 2018).

Anna Komnene and her Circle

C. Barber and D. Jenkins (eds), *Medieval Greek Commentaries on the Nicomachean Ethics* (Leiden: 2009).
T. Gouma-Peterson (ed.), *Anna Komnene and Her Times* (New York: 2000).
A. C. Lloyd, "The Aristotelianism of Eustratius of Nicaea", in J. Wiesner (ed.), *Aristoteles, Werk und Werkung*, vol. 2 (Berlin: 1987), 341–51.
L. Neville, *Anna Komnene: The Life and Work of a Medieval Historian* (Oxford: 2016).
M. Trizio, *Il neoplatonismo di Eustrazio di Nicea* (Bari: 2016).

Gender in Byzantium

L. James (ed.), *Women, Men and Eunuchs: Gender in Byzantium* (London: 1977).
B. Neil and L. Garland (eds), *Questions of Gender in Byzantine Society* (London: 2016).
K. M. Ringrose, *The Perfect Servant: Eunuchs and the Social Construction of Gender in Byzantium* (Chicago: 2003).
S. Tougher, *The Eunuch in Byzantine History and Society* (London: 2008).

Law, Money, and War in Byzantium

J. Haldon, *Warfare, State and Society in the Byzantine World 565–1204* (London: 1999).
W. Hartmann and K. Pennington (eds), *The History of Byzantine and Eastern Canon Law to 1500* (Washington, DC: 2012).
A. E. Laiou, "On Just War in Byzantium," in J. F. Haldon (ed.), *Byzantine Warfare* (Aldershot: 2007), 17–42.
A. E. Laiou and C. Morrisson, *The Byzantine Economy* (Cambridge: 2007).
A. E. Laiou and D. Simon (eds), *Law and Society in Byzantium: Ninth–Twelfth Centuries* (Washington, DC: 1994).

Byzantine Manuscripts

C. Holmes and J. Waring (eds), *Literacy, Education and Manuscript Transmission in Byzantium and Beyond* (Leiden: 2002).
H. Hunger et al., *Die Textüberlieferung der antiken Literatur und der Bibel* (Munich: 1988).
L. D. Reynolds and N. G. Wilson, *Scribes and Scholars: A Guide to the Transmission of Greek and Latin Literature* (Oxford: 1991).
N. Wilson, *Scholars of Byzantium* (London: 1983).

Petritsi and the Proclus Revival

P. Adamson and F. Karfik, "Proclus' Legacy," in *All From One: A Guide to Proclus*, ed. P. d'Hoine and M. Martijn (Oxford: 2016), 290–321.
L. Alexidze, "The Supreme One: Its Transcendence and its 'Kataphatic' Characteristics in Ioane Petritsi's Philosophy," *Bochumer philosophisches Jahrbuch für Antike und Mittelalter* 20 (2017), 63–86.
D. Calma (ed.), *Reading Proclus and the Book of Causes*, vol. 2 (Leiden: 2021).
S. Gersh (ed.), *Interpreting Proclus: From Antiquity to the Renaissance* (Cambridge: 2014).
L. Gigineishvili, *The Platonic Theology of Ioane Petrisi* (Piscataway, NJ: 2007).
G. Podskalsky, "Nicholas von Methone und die Proklos-Renaissance in Byzanz," *Orientalia christiana periodica* 42 (1976), 509–23.
J. M. Robinson, "Dionysius against Proclus: The Apophatic Critique of Nicholas of Methone's *Refutation of the Elements of Theology*," in D. D. Butorac and D. A. Layne (eds), *Proclus and his Legacy* (Berlin: 2017), 249–69.

Byzantium and Islam

N. M. El Cheikh, *Byzantium Viewed by the Arabs* (Cambridge, MA: 2004).
H. Goddard, *A History of Christian–Muslim Relations* (Edinburgh: 2000).
S. H. Griffith, "Disputes with Muslims in Syriac Christian Texts: From Patriarch John (d. 648) to Bar Hebraeus (d. 1286)," in F. Niewohner (ed.), *Religionsgespräche im Mittelalter* (Wiesbaden: 1992), 251–73.
A. T. Khoury, *Polémique byzantine contre l'Islam (VIIIe–XIIIe s.)* (Leiden: 1972).
J. Meyendorff, "Byzantine Views of Islam," *Dumbarton Oaks Papers* 18 (1964), 113–32.
D. Pratt et al. (eds), *The Character of Christian–Muslim Encounter* (Leiden: 2015).
H. Teule and C. F. Tauwinkl (eds), *The Syriac Renaissance* (Leuven: 2010).

Science in the Palaiologan Renaissance

B. Bydén, *Theodore Metochites' Stoicheiosis astronomike and the Study of Natural Philosophy and Mathematics in Early Palaiologan Byzantium* (Göteborg: 2003).

C. N. Constantinides, *Higher Education in Byzantium in the Thirteenth and Early Fourteenth Centuries (1204–ca.1310)* (Nicosia: 1982).

E. Fryde, *The Early Palaeologan Renaissance (1261–c. 1360)* (Leiden: 2000).

I. Ševčenko, *La vie intellectuelle et politique à Byzance sous les premiers Paléologues: études sur la polémique entre Théodore Métochite et Nicéphore Choumnos* (Brussels: 1962).

Gregory Palamas and Hesychasm

D. Bradshaw, *Aristotle East and West: Metaphysics and the Division of Christendom* (Cambridge: 2004).

J. Meyendorff, *A Study of Gregory Palamas*, trans. G. Lawrence (Leighton Buzzard: 1974).

J. Meyendorff, *Byzantine Hesychasm: Historical, Theological, and Social Problems* (London: 1974).

J. Nadal Cañellas, *La résistance d'Akindynos à Grégoire Palamas*, 2 vols (Leuven: 2002).

T. T. Tollefson, *Activity and Participation in Late Antique and Early Christian Thought* (Oxford: 2012).

Latin Philosophy in Byzantium

M. Plested, *Orthodox Readings of Aquinas* (Oxford: 2012).

N. Russell, "Palamism and the Circle of Demetrios Cydones," in C. Dendrinos et al. (eds), *Porphyrogenita: Essays on the History and Literature of Byzantium and the Latin East in Honour of Julian Chrysostomides* (Aldershot: 2003), 153–74.

D. Searby (ed.), *Never the Twain Shall Meet? Latins and Greeks Learning from Each Other* (Berlin: 2017).

K. M. Setton, "The Byzantine Background to the Italian Renaissance," *Proceedings of the American Philosophical Society* 100 (1965), 1–76.

I. Ševčenko, "The Decline of Byzantium Seen Through the Eyes of Its Intellectuals," *Dumbarton Oaks Papers* 15 (1961), 169–86.

M. Trizio, "Alcune osservazione sulla ricezione bizantina del *De trinitate* di Agostino," in A. Rigo and P. Ermilov (eds), *Byzantine Theologians: The Systematization of their own Doctrine and their Perception of Foreign Doctrines* (Rome: 2009), 143–68.

George Gemistos Plethon

W. Blum and W. Seitter (eds), *Georgios Gemistos Plethon (1355–1452): Reformpolitiker, Philosoph, Verehrer der alten Götter* (Zurich: 2005).

V. Hladký, *The Philosophy of Gemistos Plethon: Platonism in Late Byzantium, between Hellenism and Orthodoxy* (Aldershot: 2014).

F. Masai, *Pléthon et le Platonisme de Mistra* (Paris: 1956).

N. Siniossoglou, *Radical Platonism in Byzantium: Illumination and Utopia in Gemistos Plethon* (Cambridge: 2011).

B. Tambrun, *Pléthon: le retour de Platon* (Paris: 2006).

C. M. Woodhouse, *George Gemistos Plethon: The Last of the Hellenes* (Oxford: 1986).

The Later Orthodox Tradition

A. Casiday (ed.), *The Orthodox Christian World* (London: 2012).
M. B. Cunningham and E. Theokritoff (eds), *The Cambridge Guide to Orthodox Christian Theology* (Cambridge: 2008).
R. Demos, "The Neo-Hellenic Enlightenment (1750–1821)," *Journal of the History of Ideas* 19 (1958), 523–41.
A. Louth, *Modern Orthodox Thinkers: From the Philokalia to the Present* (Downers Grove, IL: 2015).
G. Podskalsky, *Griechische Theologie in der Zeit der Türkenherrschaft* (Munich: 1988).
I. Ševčenko, "The Decline of Byzantium Seen Through the Eyes of Its Intellectuals," *Dumbarton Oaks Papers* 15 (1961), 169–86.
A. Torrance and S. Paschalidis (eds), *Personhood in the Byzantine Christian Tradition: Early, Medieval, and Modern Perspectives* (London: 2018).

Byzantine Scholars in Italy

D. J. Geanakoplos, *Greek Scholars in Venice: Studies in the Dissemination of Greek Learning from Byzantium to Western Europe* (Cambridge, MA: 1962).
H. Lamers, *Greece Reinvented: Transformations of Byzantine Hellenism in Renaissance Italy* (Leiden: 2015).
C. Märtl, C. Kaiser, and T. Ricklin (eds), *Inter graecos latinissimus, inter latinos graecissimus: Bessarion zwischen den Kulturen* (Berlin: 2013).
L. Mohler, *Kardinal Bessarion als Theologe, Humanist und Staatsmann*, 3 vols (Paderborn: 1923).
J. Monfasani, *George of Trebizond: A Biography and a Study of his Rhetoric and Logic* (Leiden: 1976).
J. Monfasani, *Byzantine Scholars in Renaissance Italy: Cardinal Bessarion and Other Émigrés* (Aldershot: 1995).
J. Monfasani, *Greeks and Latins in Renaissance Italy: Studies on Humanism and Philosophy in the 15th Century* (Aldershot: 2004).
J. Monfasani, *Greek Scholars Between East and West in the Fifteenth Century* (Farnham: 2016).

Lorenzo Valla

S. I. Camporeale, *Lorenzo Valla, umanesmo e teologia* (Florence: 1972).
S. I. Camporeale, *Christianity, Latinity, and Culture: Two Studies on Lorenzo Valla*, ed. and trans. P. Baker and C. S. Celenza (Leiden: 2014).
M. Laffranchi, *Dialettica e filosofia in Lorenzo Valla* (Milan: 1999).
P. Mack, *Renaissance Argument: Valla and Agricola in the Traditions of Rhetoric and Dialectic* (Leiden: 1993).
L. Nauta, *In Defense of Common Sense: Lorenzo Valla's Humanist Critique of Scholastic Philosophy* (Cambridge, MA: 2009).

Humanist Ethics

T. Kircher, *Living Well in Renaissance Italy: The Virtues of Humanism and the Irony of Leon Battista Alberti* (Tempe, AZ: 2012).
D. Lines, "Aristotle's Ethics in the Renaissance," in J. Miller (ed.), *The Reception of Aristotle's Ethics* (Cambridge: 2012), 171–93.

D. A. Lines and S. Ebbersmeyer (eds), *Rethinking Virtue, Reforming Society: New Directions in Renaissance Ethics, c.1350–c.1650* (Turnhout: 2013).
M. P. Lorch, *A Defense of Life: Lorenzo Valla's Theory of Pleasure* (Munich: 1985).
M. Roick, *Pontano's Virtues: Aristotelian Moral and Political Thought in the Renaissance* (London: 2017).

Reviving Hellenistic Philosophy

A. Brown, *The Return of Lucretius to Renaissance Florence* (Cambridge, MA: 2010).
G. M. Cao, *Scepticism and Orthodoxy: Gianfresco Pico as a Reader of Sextus Empiricus* (Pisa: 2007).
S. Greenblatt, *The Swerve: How the World Became Modern* (New York: 2012).
A. Palmer, *Reading Lucretius in the Renaissance* (Cambridge, MA: 2014).
C. B. Schmitt, *Cicero Scepticus: A Study of the Influence of the Academica in the Renaissance* (The Hague: 1972).

Christine de Pizan

B. K. Altmann and D. L. McGrady (eds), *Christine de Pizan: A Casebook* (New York: 2003).
R. Brown-Grant, *Christine de Pizan and the Moral Defence of Women: Reading Beyond Gender* (Cambridge: 1999).
C. Cannon Willard, *Christine de Pizan: Her Life and Works* (New York: 1984).
K. Langdon Forhan, *The Political Theory of Christine de Pizan* (Aldershot: 2002).
N. Margolis, *An Introduction to Christine de Pizan* (Gainesville, FL: 2011).
M. Zimmermann and D. De Rentiis (eds), *The City of Scholars: New Approaches to Christine de Pizan* (Berlin: 1994).

Italian Women Humanists

M. Deslauriers, "Marinella and her Interlocutors: Hot Blood, Hot Words, Hot Deeds," *Philosophical Studies* 174 (2017), 2525–37.
C. Jordan, *Renaissance Feminism: Literary Texts and Political Models* (Ithaca, NY: 1990).
M. L. King, *Women of the Renaissance* (Chicago: 1991).
M. L. King, *Humanism, Venice and Women: Essays on the Italian Renaissance* (Aldershot: 2005).
L. Panizza (ed.), *Women in Italian Renaissance Culture and Society* (Oxford: 2000).
L. Panizza and S. Wood (eds), *A History of Women's Writing in Italy* (Cambridge: 2000).

Florentine Platonism

A. M. Brown, "Platonism in Fifteenth-Century Florence and its Contribution to Early Modern Political Thought," *Journal of Modern History* 58 (1986), 383–413.
A. Field, *The Origins of the Platonic Academy of Florence* (Princeton: 1988).
P. Godman, *From Poliziano to Machiavelli: Florentine Humanism in the High Renaissance* (Princeton: 1998).
A. Grafton, "On the Scholarship of Politian and its Context," *Journal of the Warburg and Courtauld Institutes* 40 (1977), 150–88.
J. Hankins, *Plato in the Italian Renaissance*, 2 vols (Leiden: 1990).
J. Hankins, "The Myth of the Platonic Academy of Florence," *Renaissance Quarterly* 44 (1991), 429–75.

Marsilio Ficino

M. J. B. Allen, *Plato's Third Eye: Studies in Marsilio Ficino's Metaphysics and Its Sources* (Aldershot: 1995).

M. J. B. Allen, *Studies in the Neoplatonism of Marsilio Ficino and Giovanni Pico* (Abington: 2017).

M. J. B. Allen and V. Rees (eds), *Marsilio Ficino: His Theology, His Philosophy, His Legacy* (Leiden: 2002).

K. Eisenbichler and O. Z. Pugliese (eds), *Ficino and Renaissance Neoplatonism* (Ottawa: 1986).

G. C. Garfagnini (ed.), *Marsilio Ficino e il ritorno di Platone: studi e documenti*, 2 vols (Florence: 1986).

S. Howlett, *Ficino and His World* (New York: 2016).

P. O. Kristeller, *The Philosophy of Marsilio Ficino*, trans. V. Conant (Gloucester, MA: 1964).

D. Robichaud, *Plato's Persona: Marsilio Ficino, Renaissance Humanism, and Platonic Traditions* (Philadelphia: 2018).

Theories of Love

S. Ebbersmeyer, *Sinnlichkeit und Vernunft: Studien zur Rezeption und Transformation der Liebestheorie Platons in der Renaissance* (Munich: 2002).

K. Eisenbichler and O. Z. Pugliese (eds), *Ficino and Renaissance Neoplatonism* (Ottawa: 1986).

S. Glanzmann, *Der einsame Eros: eine Untersuchung des Symposion-Kommentars "De amore" von Marsilio Ficino* (Tübingen: 2006).

T. W. Reeser, *Setting Plato Straight: Translating Ancient Sexuality in the Renaissance* (Chicago: 2016).

Jewish Philosophy in Renaissance Italy

B. D. Cooperman (ed.), *Jewish Thought in the Sixteenth Century* (Cambridge, MA: 1983).

M. Engel, *Elijah Del Medigo and Paduan Aristotelianism* (London: 2016).

D. B. Ruderman, "The Italian Renaissance and Jewish Thought," in A. Rabil Jr. (ed.), *Renaissance Humanism* (Philadelphia: 1988), vol. 1, 382–433.

G. Veltri, *Renaissance Philosophy in Jewish Garb: Foundations and Challenges in Judaism on the Eve of Modernity* (Leiden: 2008).

C. Wirszubski, *Pico della Mirandola's Encounter with Jewish Mysticism* (Cambridge, MA: 1989).

Pico della Mirandola

W. G. Craven, *Giovanni Pico della Mirandola, Symbol of His Age: Modern Interpretations of a Renaissance Philosopher* (Geneva: 1981).

M. V. Dougherty (ed.), *Pico della Mirandola: New Essays* (Cambridge: 2008).

E. Garin, *Giovanni Pico della Mirandola: vita e dottrina* (Florence: 1937).

G. C. Garfagnini (ed.), *Giovanni Pico della Mirandola: convegno internazionale di studi nel cinquecentesimo anniverario della morte (1494–1994)* (Florence: 1997).

Human Nature

S. U. Baldassarri (ed.), *Dignitas et excellentia hominis: atti del Convegno internazionale di studi su Giannozzo Manetti* (Florence: 2008).

O. Glaap, *Untersuchungen zu Giannozzo Manetti, "De dignitate et excellentia hominis": ein Renaissance-Humanist und sein Menschenbild* (Stuttgart: 1994).
D. Marsh, *Giannozzo Manetti: The Life of a Florentine Humanist* (Cambridge, MA: 2019).
C. Muratori, "Animals in the Renaissance: You Eat What You Are," in P. Adamson and G. F. Edwards (eds), *Animals: A History* (Oxford: 2018), 163–86.
C. Muratori, *Renaissance Vegetarianism: The Philosophical Afterlives of Porphyry's On Abstinence* (Cambridge: 2020).
C. M. Trinkaus, *In Our Image and Likeness: Humanity and Divinity in Italian Humanist Thought*, 2 vols (London: 1970).

Girolamo Savonarola

S. Dall'Aglio, *Savonarola and Savonarolism*, trans. J. Gagné (Toronto: 2010).
A. Edelheit, *Ficino, Pico and Savonarola: The Evolution of Humanist Theology, 1461/2–1498* (Leiden: 2008).
L. Martines, *Fire in the City: Savonarola and the Struggle for the Soul of Renaissance Florence* (Oxford: 2006).
M. Mayer, *Die politische Theologie Girolamo Savonarolas* (Tübingen: 2001).
D. Weinstein, *Savonarola: The Rise and Fall of a Renaissance Prophet* (New Haven: 2011).
D. Weinstein and V. R. Hotchkiss (eds), *Girolamo Savonarola: Piety, Prophecy, and Politics in Renaissance Florence* (Dallas: 1994).

Republicanism and Civic Humanism

H. Baron, *The Crisis of the Early Italian Renaissance: Civic Humanism and Republican Liberty in an Age of Classicism and Tyranny* (Princeton: 1966).
H. Baron, *In Search of Florentine Civic Humanism*, vol. 1: *Essays on the Transition from Medieval to Modern Thought* (Princeton: 2014).
J. Hankins (ed.), *Renaissance Civic Humanism: Reappraisals and Reflections* (Cambridge: 2000).
J. Hankins, *Virtue Politics: Soulcraft and Statecraft in Renaissance Italy* (Cambridge, MA: 2019).
M. Jurdjevic, "Civic Humanism and the Rise of the Medici," *Renaissance Quarterly* 52 (1999), 994–1020.
F. Ricciardelli, *The Myth of Republicanism in Renaissance Italy* (Turnhout: 2015).
Q. Skinner, *The Foundations of Modern Political Thought*, vol. 1: *The Renaissance* (Cambridge: 1976).

Niccolò Machiavelli

E. Benner, *Machiavelli's Prince: A New Reading* (Oxford: 2013).
N. Capponi, *An Unlikely Prince: The Life and Times of Machiavelli* (Cambridge: 2010).
C.S. Celenza, *Machiavelli: A Portrait* (Cambridge: 2015).
F. Chabod, *Scritti su Machiavelli* (Turin: 1964).
M. Coyle (ed.), *Niccolò Machiavelli's The Prince: New Interdisciplinary Essays* (Manchester: 1995).
C. Holman, *Machiavelli and the Politics of Democratic Innovation* (Toronto: 2018).
M. Hörnqvist, *Machiavelli and Empire* (Cambridge: 2004).
M. Hulliung, *Citizen Machiavelli* (Princeton: 1983).
H. Mansfield, *Machiavelli's New Modes and Orders: A Study of the Discourses on Livy* (Ithaca, NY: 1979).

J. M. Najemy, *The Cambridge Companion to Machiavelli* (Cambridge: 2010).
C. J. Nederman, *Machiavelli* (Oxford: 2009).
J. G. A. Pocock, *The Machiavellian Moment: Florentine Political Thought and the Atlantic Republican Tradition* (Princeton: 1975).
Q. Skinner, *Machiavelli* (Oxford: 1981).
C. Vivanti, *Niccolò Machiavelli: An Intellectual Biography* (Princeton: 2013).
C. H. Zuckert, *Machiavelli's Politics* (Chicago: 2017).

Renaissance Historiography

F. Gilbert, *Machiavelli and Guicciardini: Politics and History in Sixteenth Century Florence* (Princeton: 1965).
G. Ianziti, *Writing History in Renaissance Italy: Leonardo Bruni and the Uses of the Past* (Cambridge, MA: 2012).
M. Phillips, *Francesco Guicciardini: The Historian's Craft* (Toronto: 1977).
N. Struever, *The Language of History in the Renaissance: Rhetorical Consciousness in Florentine Humanism* (Princeton: 1970).
D. J. Wilcox, *The Development of Florentine Humanist Historiography in the Fifteenth Century* (Cambridge, MA: 1969).

Renaissance Utopias

A. Cameron, "Doni's Satirical Utopia," *Renaissance Studies* 10 (1996), 462–73.
A. Donato (trans.), *Italian Renaissance Utopias: Doni, Patrizi, and Zuccolo* (New York: 2019).
M. Eliav-Feldon, *Realistic Utopias: The Ideal Imaginary Societies of the Renaissance 1516–1630* (Oxford: 1982).
L. Firpo, "Political Philosophy: Renaissance Utopianism," in E. Cochrane (ed.), *The Late Italian Renaissance: 1525–1630* (London: 1970), 149–67.
F. E. Manuel and F. P. Manuel, *Utopian Thought in the Western World* (Cambridge: 1979), ch. 5.

Renaissance Economics

R. De Roover, *San Bernardino of Siena and Sant'Antonio of Florence: The Two Great Economic Thinkers of the Middle Ages* (Boston: 1967).
R. Faucci, *A History of Italian Economic Thought* (Abingdon: 2014), ch. 2.
O. Nuccio, *La storia del pensiero economico italiano: come storia della genesi dello spirito capitalistico* (Rome: 2008).
J. Oppel, "Poggio, San Bernardino of Siena, and the Dialogue *On Avarice*," *Renaissance Quarterly* 30 (1977), 564–87.
N. Regent, "Guicciardini and Economic (In)equality," *European Journal of the History of Economic Thought* 27 (2020), 49–65.

Italian Universities

P. Denley, "'Medieval,' 'Renaissance,' 'Modern': Issues of Periodization in Italian University History," *Renaissance Studies* 27 (2013), 487–503.
P. F. Grendler, *The Universities of the Italian Renaissance* (Baltimore: 2002).

D. A. Lines, "Humanism and the Italian Universities," in C. S. Celenza and K. Gouwens (eds), *Humanism and Creativity in the Renaissance* (Leiden: 2006), 327–46.
C. B. Schmitt, *The Aristotelian Tradition and Renaissance Universities* (London: 1984).
M. Sgarbi, *The Italian Mind: Vernacular Logic in Renaissance Italy (1540–1551)* (Leiden: 2014).

Aristotle in Renaissance Italy

L. Bianchi, "Per una storia dell'aristotelismo 'volgare' nel renascimento: problemi e prospettive di ricerca," *Bruniana & Campanelliana* 15 (2009), 367–85.
M. Davies, *Aldus Manutius: Printer and Publisher of Renaissance Venice* (Tempe, AZ: 1999).
E. Del Soldato, *Early Modern Aristotle: On the Making and Unmaking of Authority* (Philadelphia: 2020).
E. Kessler et al. (eds), *Aristotelismus und Renaissance* (Wiesbaden: 1988).
M. Lowry, *The World of Aldus Manutius: Business and Scholarship in Renaissance Venice* (Oxford: 1979).
C. B. Schmitt, *Aristotle and the Renaissance* (Cambridge, MA: 1983).
M. Sgarbi, "Aristotle and the People: Vernacular Philosophy in Renaissance Italy," *Renaissance and Reformation* 39 (2016), 59–109.

Pietro Pomponazzi and Agostino Nifo

A. Akasoy and G. Giglioni (eds), *Renaissance Averroism and its Aftermath: Arabic Philosophy in Early Modern Europe* (Dordrecht: 2010).
J. Biard and T. Gontier (eds), *Pietro Pomponazzi entre traditions et innovations* (Amsterdam: 2009).
E. P. Mahoney, *Two Aristotelians of the Italian Renaissance: Nicoletto Vernia and Agostino Nifo* (Aldershot: 2000).
C. Martin, "Rethinking Renaissance Averroism," *Intellectual History Review* 17 (2007), 3–28.
B. Nardi, *Studi su Pietro Pomponazzi* (Florence: 1965).
M. L. Pine, *Pietro Pomponazzi: Radical Philosopher of the Renaissance* (Padua: 1986).
J. Sellars, "Pomponazzi *contra* Averroes on the Intellect," *British Journal for the History of Philosophy* 24 (2016), 45–66.
M. Sgarbi (ed.), *Pietro Pomponazzi: tradizione e dissenso* (Florence: 2010).

Jacopo Zabarella

D. DiLiscia et al. (eds), *Method and Order in Renaissance Philosophy of Nature: The Aristotle Commentary Tradition* (Aldershot: 1997).
N. W. Gilbert, *Renaissance Concepts of Method* (New York: 1960).
H. Mikkeli, *An Aristotelian Response to Renaissance Humanism: Jacopo Zabarella on the Nature of Arts and Sciences* (Helsinki: 1992).
A. Poppi, *La dottrina della scienza in Giacomo Zabarella* (Padua: 1972).
J. H. Randall, *The School of Padua and the Emergence of Modern Science* (Padua: 1961).

Mathematics and Art

C. L. Joost-Gaugier, *Pythagoras and Renaissance Europe: Finding Heaven* (Cambridge: 2009).
Anthony Grafton, *Leon Battista Alberti: Master Builder of the Italian Renaissance* (Cambridge, MA: 2002).

J. Prins and M. Vanhaelen (eds), *Sing Aloud Harmonious Spheres: Renaissance Conceptions of Cosmic Harmony* (London: 2017).

P. L. Rose, *The Italian Renaissance of Mathematics: Studies on Humanists and Mathematicians from Petrarch to Galileo* (Geneva: 1975).

C. Smith, *Architecture in the Culture of Early Humanism: Ethics, Aesthetics and Eloquence 1400–1470* (Oxford: 1992).

Renaissance Medicine

J. Bylebyl, "The School of Padua: Humanistic Medicine in the Sixteenth Century," in C. Webster (ed.), *Health, Medicine, and Mortality in the Sixteenth Century* (New York: 1979), 335–70.

A. Cunningham, *The Anatomical Renaissance* (Aldershot: 1997).

G. Giglioni, "Health in the Renaissance," in P. Adamson (ed.), *Health: A History* (Oxford: 2019), 141–73.

H. Hirai, *Medical Humanism and Natural Philosophy: Renaissance Debates on Matter, Life and the Soul* (Leiden: 2011).

I. Maclean, *Logic, Signs and Nature in the Renaissance: The Case of Learned Medicine* (Cambridge: 2002).

K. Park, *Doctors and Medicine in Early Renaissance Florence* (Princeton: 1985).

J. Sawday, *The Body Emblazoned: Dissection and the Human Body in Renaissance Culture* (London: 1995).

N. G. Siriasi, *Medieval and Early Renaissance Medicine: An Introduction to Knowledge and Practice* (Chicago: 1990).

A. Wear et al. (eds), *The Medical Renaissance of the Sixteenth Century* (Cambridge: 1985).

Girolamo Cardano

M. Baldi and G. Canziani (eds), *Girolamo Cardano: le opere, le fonti, la vita* (Milan: 1999).

M. Fierz, *Girolamo Cardano, 1501–1576: Physician, Natural Philosopher, Mathematician, Astrologer, and Interpreter of Dreams* (Boston: 1983).

G. Giglioni, "Girolamo Cardano: University Student and Professor," *Renaissance Studies* 27 (2013), 517–32.

A. Ingegno, *Saggio sulla filosofia di Cardano* (Florence: 1980).

E. Keßler (ed.), *Girolamo Cardano: Philosoph, Naturforscher, Arzt* (Wiesbaden: 1994).

N. Siriasi, *The Clock and the Mirror: Girolamo Cardano and Renaissance Medicine* (Princeton: 1997).

Bernardino Telesio and Tommaso Campanella

B. M. Bonansea, *Tommaso Campanella: Renaissance Pioneer of Modern Thought* (Washington, DC: 1969).

R. Bondí, *Il primo dei moderni: filosofia e scienza in Bernardino Telesio* (Rome: 2018).

G. Ernst, *Tommaso Campanella: The Book and the Body of Nature* (Dordrecht: 2010).

J. M. Headley, *Tommaso Campanella and the Transformation of the World* (Princeton: 1997).

G. Giglioni, "The First of the Moderns or the Last of the Ancients? Bernardino Telesio on Nature and Sentience," *Bruniana e Campanelliana* 16 (2010), 69–87.

G. Mocchi et al. (eds), *Bernardino Telesio tra filosofia naturale e scienza moderna* (Pisa: 2012).

M. Mulsow, *Frühneuzeitliche Selbsterhaltung: Telesio und die Naturphilosophie der Renaissance* (Tübingen: 1998).

Renaissance Magic and Astrology

B. P. Copenhaver, *Magic in Western Culture: From Antiquity to the Enlightenment* (Cambridge: 2015).
B. Dooley (ed.), *A Companion to Astrology in the Renaissance* (Leiden: 2014).
E. Garin, *Astrology in the Renaissance: The Zodiac of Life*, trans. C. Jackson and J. Allen (London: 1983).
A. Grafton, *Cardano's Cosmos: The Worlds and Works of a Renaissance Astrologer* (Cambridge, MA: 1999).
C. Vasoli, *Magia e scienza nella civiltà umanistica* (Bologna: 1976).
D. P. Walker, *Spiritual and Demonic Magic: From Ficino to Campanella* (London: 1958).

Giordano Bruno

P. R. Blum, *Giordano Bruno: An Introduction*, trans. P. Henneveld (Amsterdam: 2012).
H. Gatti (ed.), *Giordano Bruno and Renaissance Science* (Ithaca, NY: 2002).
H. Gatti, *Essays on Giordano Bruno* (Princeton: 2011).
H. Gatti, *Giordano Bruno* (Florence: 2017).
I. D. Rowland, *Giordano Bruno: Philosopher/Heretic* (Chicago: 2008).
L. Spruit, *Il problema della conoscenza in Giordano Bruno* (Naples: 1988).
F. A. Yates, *Giordano Bruno and the Hermetic Tradition* (London: 1964).

Galileo and the Renaissance

R. E. Butts and J. C. Pitt (eds), *New Perspectives on Galileo* (Dordrecht: 1978).
S. Drake, *Galileo at Work: His Scientific Biography* (Chicago: 1978).
N. Jardine, "Galileo's Road to Truth and the Demonstrative Regress," *Studies in the History and Philosophy of Science* 7 (1976), 277–318.
P. Machamer (ed.), *The Cambridge Companion to Galileo* (Cambridge: 1998).
C. B. Schmitt, "Experience and Experiment: A Comparison of Zabarella's View with Galileo's *De motu*," *Studies in the Renaissance* 16 (1969), 80–138.
W. A. Wallace, *Prelude to Galileo: Essays on Medieval and Sixteenth-Century Sources of Galileo's Thought* (Dordrecht: 1981).
W. A. Wallace (ed.), *Reinterpreting Galileo* (Washington, DC: 1986).

INDEX

Note: page ranges marked in bold indicates that the topic is the subject of the chapter.